1994

STUDIES IN
EARLY
CHRISTIANITY

A Collection of Scholarly Essays

edited by
Everett Ferguson
ABILENE CHRISTIAN UNIVERSITY

with
David M. Scholer
NORTH PARK COLLEGE AND THEOLOGICAL SEMINARY

and
Paul Corby Finney
CENTER OF THEOLOGICAL INQUIRY

A Garland Series

CONTENTS OF SERIES

VOLUME XVIII

Art, Archaeology, and Architecture of Early Christianity

edited with an introduction by

Paul Corby Finney

Garland Publishing, Inc.
New York & London
1993

Library of Congress Cataloging-in-Publication Data

Art, archaeology, and architecture of early Christianity / edited by Paul
Corby Finney.
    p.   cm. — (Studies in early Christianity ; v. 18)
  ISBN 0–8153–1078–1 (alk. paper)
  1.Art, Early Christian. 2. Church history—Primitive and early
church, ca. 30–600. I. Finney, Paul Corby. II. Series.
N7832.A716 1993
709'.01'5—dc20   92–40135
                                      CIP

Printed on acid-free, 250-year-life paper
Manufactured in the United States of America

Contents

Series Introduction

Christianity has been the formative influence on Western civilization and has maintained a significant presence as well in the Near East and, through its missions, in Africa and Asia. No one can understand Western civilization and the world today, much less religious history, without an understanding of the early history of Christianity.

The first six hundred years after the birth of Jesus were the formative period of Christian history. The theology, liturgy, and organization of the church assumed their definitive shape during this period. Since biblical studies form a separate, distinctive discipline, this series confines itself to sources outside the biblical canon, except as these sources were concerned with the interpretation and use of the biblical books. During the period covered in this series the distinctive characteristics of the Roman Catholic and Eastern Orthodox Churches emerged.

The study of early Christian literature, traditionally known as Patristics (for the church fathers), has experienced a resurgence in the late twentieth century. Evidences of this are the flourishing of a new professional society, the North American Patristics Society, a little over twenty years old; the growing number of teachers and course offerings at major universities and seminaries; the number of graduate students studying and choosing to write their dissertations in this area; the volume of books published in the field; and attendance at the quadrennial International Conferences on Patristic Studies at Oxford as well as at many smaller specialized conferences. This collection of articles reflects this recent growing interest and is intended to encourage further study. The papers at the International Conferences on Patristic Studies from the first conference in 1951 to the present have been published in the series *Studia Patristica,* and interested readers are referred to these volumes for more extensive treatment of the topics considered in this series of reprints and many other matters as well.

The volumes in this series are arranged topically to cover biography, literature, doctrines, practices, institutions, worship, missions, and daily life. Archaeology and art as well as writings are drawn on in order to give reality to the Christian movement in its early centuries. Ample attention is also given to the relation of Christianity to pagan thought and life, to the Roman state, to Judaism, and to doctrines and practices that came to be judged as heretical or schismatic. Introductions to each volume will attempt to tie the articles together so that an integrated understanding of the history will result.

The aim of the collection is to give balanced and comprehensive coverage. Early on I had to give up the idealism and admit the arrogance of attempting to select the "best" article on each topic. Criteria applied in the selection included the following: original and excellent research and writing, subject matter of use to teachers and students, groundbreaking importance for the history of research, foundational information for introducing issues and options. Preference was given to articles in English where available. Occasional French and German titles are included as a reminder of the international nature of scholarship.

The *Encyclopedia of Early Christianity* (New York: Garland, 1990) provides a comprehensive survey of the field written in a manner accessible to the average reader, yet containing information useful to the specialist. This series of reprints of Studies in Early Christianity is designed to supplement the encyclopedia and to be used with it.

The articles were chosen with the needs of teachers and students of early church history in mind with the hope that teachers will send students to these volumes to acquaint them with issues and scholarship in early Christian history. The volumes will fill the need of many libraries that do not have all the journals in the field or do not have complete holdings of those to which they subscribe. The series will provide an overview of the issues in the study of early Christianity and the resources for that study.

Understanding the development of early Christianity and its impact on Western history and thought provides indispensable insight into the modern world and the present situation of Christianity. It also provides perspective on comparable developments in other periods of history and insight into human nature in its religious dimension. Christians of all denominations may continue to learn from the preaching, writing, thinking, and working of the early church.

Introduction

Art and archaeology (esp. the latter) tend to be neglected subjects in many academic settings where early Christian subjects are taught. Curricular commitments in such places (colleges, universities, seminaries) tend to be weighted in favor of text-related disciplines, i.e., Bible, Patristics, and other literatures from the period of later antiquity. In the study of early Christianity, archaeology and epigraphy are often simply ignored, and art-historical study, even of major monuments, fares only slightly better. Within early Christian studies overall, it is no exaggeration to speak of a tyranny of logos: the field has been held in its grip for generations.

The twenty-two essays that follow here give a glimpse (but, alas, not much more) of what is being missed when one sidesteps art and archaeology in the study of early Christianity. There is a wealth of information here, and this is only a very small sampling from a field of study that is growing by leaps and bounds. As to the traditional material categories by which the discipline is defined, including architecture, painting, sculpture, mosaics, and small finds, the following are represented in the articles presented here: architecture (1, 11, 18, 19), painting (4, 8, 14, 15, 21, 22), sculpture (2, 4, 5, 7), mosaic (6, 17), and under the hybrid "small finds/minor arts/decorative arts" rubric, we find discussions of early Christian relief sculpture in wood (2) and ivory (5), of stone and other intaglios (8), of engraved glass (9), of recently discovered silver vessels (13), of textiles (18) and of illustrated manuscripts (21, 22). Under the "small finds" rubric, the major material category that this volume lacks is ceramics, consisting of early Christian ampullae, bread stamps, lamps, terra sigillata bowls, plates and vessels, plaques, and clay architectural tiles, all of them marked with figural or non-figural subjects suggesting Christian influence. For a very brief overview of secondary literature on these and related ceramic subjects, the interested reader may consult my "Early Christian Art and Archaeology I & II (A.D. 200-500): A Selected Bibliography," *The Second Century* 6.1 & 4 (1987/88): 21-42, 203-38, esp. 221-22.

The study of iconography (pictorial subject matter) is a discipline which cuts across nearly all the articles reprinted here, with the important qualification that the essays by Armstrong (1), McVey (11), and Ward-Perkins (19, 20) should be identified as treating architectural rather than pictorial iconography. On architectural iconography (and on all other subjects relating to early Christian architecture) readers now have available a splendid survey of selected secondary literature in W.E. Kleinbauer, *Early Christian and Byzantine Architecture: An Annotated Bibliography and Historiography* (Boston, 1992), passim, esp. 1555-93.

Iconography is rooted in literature, and in most of early Christian art and archaeology (the present articles included) one of the most conspicuous threads of disciplinary continuity is the inevitable reliance on literary evidence as a first and sometimes last court of appeal. Dinkler's essay (3), written from the perspective of a Protestant "Neutestamentler," exemplifies this generalization: his subject is at once epigraphic, paleographic, and iconographic (i.e., the formation of the so-called staurogram ⨸). Murray's article (12) is also literary in character: she evokes and challenges a long tradition of scholarship that bases itself primarily on literary evidence and that seeks to portray early Christianity as a form of religiosity (along with Judaism and Islam) hostile to pictures. So is McVey's essay (11) also subsumed under the literary rubric: here we encounter a fresh, new translation of a Syriac text that reflects a literary/theological tradition of architectural "theoria" as practiced in the east Mediterranean during the period of later antiquity.

The three examples mentioned above (Dinkler, Murray, McVey) exhibit an intimate relationship between early Christian literature and early Christian art and archaeology. But the truth is that, overall, the study of early Christian art and archaeology is closely intertwined with literature and epigraphy. Indeed, of all the disparate archaeologies that have sprung forth from Mediterranean cultures in antiquity (from the Bronze Age in the Near East to late Roman culture east and west), none exhibits a closer relationship between literary and material culture than early Christianity. This is both a strength and a liability. It means that levels of certitude and verification which are unthinkable elsewhere are in fact within reach in the study of early Christian monuments, but it also means that there is a conspicuous tendency within early Christian art and archaeology to let literary (and epigraphic) evidence constrict the discussion of material evidence. The most dramatic example of this latter tendency within the articles reprinted here is Lietzmann's essay (10) which concerns the now perennial (and mostly futile) effort to reconcile the archaeology of a subterranean basilica on the Via Appia (San Sebastiano) with a famous inscription (E. Diehl, *ILCV* I.951) by Pope

Damasus, suggesting that the bodies of Peter and Paul were interred not on the Vatican (Peter) and on the Via Ostiensis (Paul), but instead beneath San Sebastiano. The reader who wishes to pursue this difficult subject should consult J.M.C. Toynbee & J. Ward Perkins, *The Shrine of St. Peter and the Vatican Excavations* (London, N.Y., Toronto, 1956), 167-82.

Those who want to read further on early Christian reliefs in wood (2) and ivory (5), on early Christian engraved glass (9), mosaics (6, 17), and metals (13) are referred to the appropriate sections in my bibliography, mentioned above. On Vikan's subject, namely the Hebrew Bible's story of Joseph on early Christian textiles, the reader will find an interesting recent discussion in H. Maguire's "Garments pleasing to God . . ." *Dumbarton Oaks Papers* 44 (1990): 215ff. Early Christian intaglios, which Klauser (8) mentions briefly, are now summarized in P. Zazoff, *Die antiken Gemmen* (Munich, 1983 = *HbArchäologie*), 374-86. Weitzmann (21 and 22) has reasserted his position on book illustration in K. Weitzmann and H. Kessler, *The Frescoes of the Dura Synagogue and Christian Art* (Wash., D.C., 1990). To my knowledge, no one has superseded Reekmans' two splendid *Forschungsberichte* (15 and 16).

Other articles dealing with art and archaeology will be found in this series: in Volume VI, Gutmann on the influence of Jewish art on Christian art; in Volume XI, deBruyne on Christian initiation depicted in art; in Volume XII, Toynbee on Britain, and Judge and Pickering on the papyri from Egypt; and in Volume XV, Mathew on the eucharist in art.

Constantine's Churches: Symbol and Structure

GREGORY T. ARMSTRONG   Department of Religion, Sweet Briar College

. . . It is ever my first, and indeed my only object, that . . . our souls may all become more zealous, with all sobriety and earnest unanimity, for the honor of the Divine law. I desire, therefore, especially, that you should be persuaded . . . that I have no greater care than how I may best adorn with a splendid structure that sacred spot, which, under Divine direction, I have disencumbered as it were of the heavy weight of foul idol worship; a spot which has been accounted holy from the beginning in God's judgment, but which now appears holier still, since it has brought to light a clear assurance of our Saviour's passion. It will be well, therefore, for your sagacity to make such arrangements and provision of all things needful for the work, that not only the church itself as a whole may surpass all others whatsoever in beauty, but that the details of the building may be of such a kind that the fairest structures in any city of the empire may be excelled by this. . . . For it is fitting that the most marvelous place in the world should be worthily decorated.[1]

WITH THESE WORDS the Emperor Constantine directed the bishop of Jerusalem, Macarius, to build the Church of the Holy Sepulchre at the newly discovered tomb of Jesus. This church was to be a monument without parallel, excelling all others in the empire, a witness to the central event of the Christian faith, the death and resurrection of Jesus Christ. The Church of the Holy Sepulchre may also be interpreted as the center of the world, for it quickly became such for Christian pilgrims and for Constantine's religious policy in the empire.[2] A suggestion of this policy, and therefore of the symbolic value of this church and others, is already given in the letter to Macarius. Zeal, sobriety, unanimity, and honor for the divine law are civic virtues to be inculcated in the subjects of the empire with the help of Christianity, the new religion to which the emperor declared himself publicly by this church and a score of others.

The Constantinian churches have always exerted a strong attraction for historians of architecture. In 1693, for example, Joannes Ciampini published a catalogue of *The Sacred Edifices Constructed by Constantine the Great*, listing fifty-eight churches and baptisteries and two monasteries.[3] Even before that, a number of ecclesiastical historians beginning with Eusebius of Caesarea recorded the building program of Constantine and in fact added to it over the years. Of special importance for current research into Constantine's church buildings are the publications of Richard Krautheimer of New York University.[4]

Among the churches of Constantine, one encounters five major types of structure, often in combination with one

This essay was first delivered as a lecture for the School of Architecture at the University of Tennessee, 12 Jan. 1972. I am grateful for that occasion to summarize several years of research carried on with support from the American Council of Learned Societies, Vanderbilt University, Sweet Briar College, and the National Endowment for the Humanities, to each of whom I express my sincere thanks. The text has since been revised and read before the American Society of Church History, meeting in New Orleans, 28 Dec. 1972. The article of Suzanne Spain Alexander, "Studies in Constantinian Church Architecture," *Rivista di Archeologia Cristiana*, XLVII (1971), 281–330 (to be continued), appeared after the original preparation of this material and may now supplement it although it does not incorporate the most recent findings at the Church of the Holy Sepulchre.

1. Eusebius, *Vita Constantini*, 3.30, 31; translated in *The Nicene and Post-Nicene Fathers*, Series Two, I (reprinted, Grand Rapids, 1961), 528.

2. Cf. William Telfer, "Constantine's Holy Land Plan," *Studia Patristica*, I, Part 1 (Berlin, 1957), 696–700.

3. *De sacris aedificiis a Constantino magno constructis: Synopsis historica* (Rome, 1693); this catalog was updated and provided with a bibliography by the writer in "Constantine's Churches," *Gesta*, VI (Jan. 1967), 1–9.

4. *Early Christian and Byzantine Architecture* (Harmondsworth, Middlesex, and Baltimore, 1965); "The Constantinian Basilica," *Dumbarton Oaks Papers*, XXI (1967), 117–140; "Constantine's Church Foundations," *Akten des VII. Internationalen Kongresses für christliche Archäologie*, Trier, 5–11 Sept. 1965, Text volume (Vatican City and Berlin, 1969), pp. 237–255.

5

1

6

another but each with its own particular symbolic value. This analysis will examine these five types in approximately chronological order. As it happens, chronological order corresponds rather closely with geographical order because Constantine established his rule first over the western half of the Roman Empire in the decade between 306 and 316; he then extended it to the East in the next decade with the defeat of his co-emperor and brother-in-law, Licinius, in 324; and he consolidated it in the third decade with the founding of New Rome at Byzantium on the Bosporus.[5] He never visited old Rome after 326. In addition, one must keep in mind the influence of regional traditions in architecture and of regional and even local materials and craftsmanship. One further refinement in the analysis, which has not yet been adequately developed, is the assessing of regional and local variations in the liturgy which was still in the process of development.[6]

I

The first building associated with the emperor is the Lateran or Constantinian basilica in Rome, begun about 313[7] (Fig. 1.) This edifice falls into the category of the cathedral, the seat of the bishop of Rome for many centuries and the site of several mediaeval councils. The basic plan, revealed by the excavations of Josi, Krautheimer, and Corbett, was rectangular with longitudinal axis, nave, and side aisles. The length exceeded 300′, and the height in the nave approached 100′. This monumental structure publicly declared the newly acquired importance of the bishop of Rome. In fact Constantine gave all the bishops a recognized

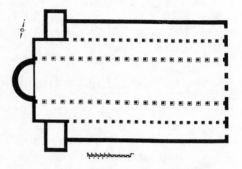

Fig. 1. Rome, Lateran or Constantinian Basilica, begun ca. 313 (drawing by Constance D. Goodrich after Krautheimer and Corbett).

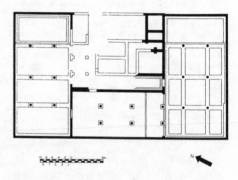

Fig. 2. Aquileia, Double Basilica, ca. 313-319 (drawing by Constance D. Goodrich after Krautheimer and Lampl).

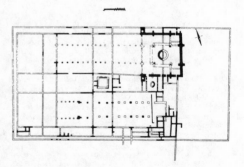

Fig. 3. Trier, Double Basilica, after 325 (drawing by Nancy W. Blackwell after Krautheimer and Wightman).

5. Ramsay MacMullen, *Constantine* (New York, 1969), and John Holland Smith, *Constantine the Great* (New York, 1971). Of special interest because of the author's competence in Christian archaeology is Ludwig Voelkl, *Der Kaiser Konstantin: Annalen einer Zeitenwende: 306-337* (Munich, 1957).

6. See a new translation of the *Peregrinatio Aetheriae, Egeria's Travels* by John Wilkinson with supporting documents, introduction, and notes (London, 1971); Thomas F. Mathews, *The Early Churches of Constantinople: Architecture and Liturgy* (University Park, Pa., and London, 1971); Massey H. Shepherd, Jr., "Liturgical Expressions of the Constantinian Triumph," *Dumbarton Oaks Papers*, XXI (1967), 59-78; Gregory Dix, *The Shape of the Liturgy* (London, 1945), esp. chaps. VII-XII.

7. For this and subsequent buildings: Carl Andresen, *Einführung in die Christliche Archäologie* (Göttingen, 1971), with extensive bibliographies; Armstrong, "Constantine's Churches," with references to ancient and mediaeval writings as well as modern; Krautheimer, *Architecture*; Krautheimer, Wolfgang Frankl, and Spencer Corbett, *Corpus basilicarum christianarum Romae: The Early Christian Basilicas of Rome (IV-IX Cent.)*, 4 vols. (Vatican City, 1937-1970). On the Lateran church specifically: Krautheimer and Spencer Corbett, "The Constantinian Basilica of the Lateran," *Antiquity*, XXXIV (1960), 201-206, and "La Basilica Constantiniana al Laterano: Un tentativo di ricostruzione," *Rivista di Archeologia Cristiana*, XLIII (1967), 125-154.

Fig. 4 Trier, Palace Aula or Basilica, ca. 305-312 (from H. Kähler, *The Art of Rome and Her Empire* [1965]; used by permission of Holle Bildarchiv).

civil and judicial role,[8] and church buildings became official buildings possessing a legal status and function. They were also, like many "secular" basilicas of the same period and earlier, meetings halls for the congregation on the one hand, and audience halls for the Lord on the other, except that for Christians it was the Lord Christ, the King of Heaven. Such a basilica was highly functional in terms of the Christian community's needs as a worshiping congregation and in terms of its new official status in the empire.

At Aquileia in northern Italy, where Constantine visited in 315 and 318, a double basilica served as the cathedral[9] (Fig. 2). The role of the emperor in this instance has been much debated. There is no doubt, however, about the association of the double basilica at Trier with Constantine. This large cathedral was built on imperial property some fifteen years after the Lateran basilica, or about 328[10] (Fig. 3). Although the original buildings do not survive, one can still see portions of the original brickwork from the Con-

stantinian building preserved in the existing cathedral. The palace aula or basilica, which was a judicial building erected by Constantine between 305 and 312 while Trier was his headquarters, does stand in restored form (Fig. 4). It gives a sense of the proportions of the Lateran and other Constantinian basilicas, being about the same height—100 Roman feet—although somewhat shorter and wider than the Lateran. The cathedral was to be on the same imperial scale as this hall and actually exceeded it in both length and width, namely 240′ × 125′ and 100′ for the north and south halls, respectively. Large atriums stood before the basilicas proper.

In the East the important imperial residence of Nicomedia in Bithynia, which had experienced a great building boom during the reign of Diocletian (284-305), later received a basilica, called the Victoria, but it is thus far lost to direct knowledge.[11] Likewise, very little is known of the Church of Hagia Eirene in Constantinople, although it is attributed to Constantine by the fifth-century historian Socrates and may have been the first cathedral for the bishop of the new capital. The title "Holy Peace" parallels that of Hagia Sophia or "Holy Wisdom," located adjacent to it and to the palace but probably later in date. The first

8. Armstrong, "Church and State Relations: The Changes Wrought by Constantine," *The Journal of Bible and Religion*, XXXII (1964), 1–7, and "Imperial Church Building and Church-State Relations, A.D. 313–363," *Church History*, XXXVI (1967), 5–10, with references to other literature.

9. Krautheimer, *Architecture*, pp. 23, 24; Andresen, *Einführung*, pp. 79–82.

10. Edith Mary Wightman, *Roman Trier and The Treveri* (New York and Washington, 1971), pp. 103–113; Krautheimer, *Architecture*, p. 27; Andresen, *Einführung*, pp. 79, 80.

11. Eusebius, *Vita Constantini*, 3.50. There are as yet no archaeological studies. On the dedication or title of this basilica, see Voelkl, *Die Kirchenstiftungen des Kaisers Konstantin im Lichte des römischen Sakralrechts* (Cologne and Opladen, 1964), pp. 28, 32, 39.

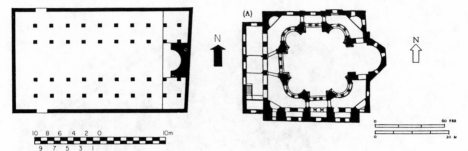

Fig. 5. Orléansville, Basilica of St. Reparatus, dedicated 324 (drawing by Constance D. Goodrich after Krautheimer).

Fig. 6. Constantinople, Hagioi Sergios and Bakchos, ca. 525 (from R. Krautheimer, *Early Christian and Byzantine Architecture* [1965]; used by permission).

Church of Hagia Sophia seems to have been begun by Constantine but was only completed under his son, Constantius II, and dedicated 15 February 360 by Patriarch Eudoxius. Krautheimer conjectures that its structure was basilican in plan with double side aisles and galleries above them as in the Church of the Holy Sepulchre.[12] The Victoria church at Nicomedia and the Concordia church at Antioch are the others, all in the East, to be dedicated, like Hagia Eirene and Hagia Sophia, in Greek metaphysical fashion to divine virtues and blessings. One may speculate that the central city locations desirable for cathedrals and palaces lacked the tombs of martyr saints as patrons, and that more abstract dedications were used instead. However, all churches in this period were dedicated to Christ and only secondarily to a patron saint.[13] One last cathedral in the East, attributed to Constantine but known only from a literary reference, is the Great Church of Heliopolis in Phoenicia.[14]

There are three smaller churches in the West which also fall in the episcopal category. Two are at Cirta in North

Africa and are known only from correspondence.[15] The first church, built with an imperial subsidy in the early 320s, was seized by a schismatic Christian group called the Donatists. Preferring not to employ force in this instance to recapture the building, the emperor ordered a new piece of land and new church to be provided in 330. It and the first one may well have resembled the basilica at Orléansville in the same region (Fig. 5). This small, yet double-aisled basilica with apse is securely dated to 324 and presumably enjoyed an imperial subsidy.[16]

Two other churches whose primary function was other than episcopal but which did serve the resident bishop were the Church of the Holy Sepulchre in Jerusalem and the Great Church or Octagon in Antioch. The former was used by the bishop in the fourth century prior to the rebuilding of the St. Sion Church. The Octagon at Antioch, also called the Concordia Church and the Domus Aurea or Golden House, was basically a palace church but seems to have been the cathedral as well.[17] It would be the only one of the group not to have a basilican plan. It is described by ancient writers as large and magnificently decorated and may have inspired copies.

The common plan of all these basilicas is significant. It is

12. Krautheimer, "The Constantinian Basilica," p. 133; "Constantine's Church Foundations," pp. 243, 251, 253. On Hagia Eirene see Raymond Janin, *La Géographie ecclésiastique de l'empire byzantin*, 1e Partie: *Le siège de Constantinople et patriarcat oecuménique*, Tome III: *Les églises et les monastères* (Paris, 1953), 107–111. On Hagia Sophia see Janin, pp. 471–485; Mathews, *The Early Churches of Constantinople*, pp. 11–19; and Krautheimer, *Architecture*, p. 46.

13. Voelkl, *Die Kirchenstiftungen*, pp. 31–33; André Grabar, *Martyrium: Recherches sur le culte des reliques et l'art chrétien antique*, 1: *Architecture* (Paris, 1946), 210: "C'est la *puissance de Dieu* que Constantin célèbre dans les sanctuaires qu'il fixe sur des lieux saints." The same observation applies to St. Peter's and other churches. The inscription on the triumphal arch of the original St. Peter's confirms this fact. "Quod duce te mundus surrexit in astra triumphans, hanc Constantinus victor tibi condidit aulam." Ernestus Diehl, *Inscriptiones Latinae Christianae Veteres*, 3 vols. (Berlin, 1961), inscription no. 1752.

14. Eusebius, *Vita Constantini*, 3.58.

15. Optatus of Milevis, *Libri VII*, ed. Carolus Ziwsa, *Corpus Scriptorum Ecclesiasticorum Latinorum*, XXVI (Vienna, 1893), Appendix 10: *Epistula Constantini*, pp. 213–216. Cf. Stephane Gsell, *Les monuments antiques de l'Algérie*, II (Paris, 1901), 191–194.

16. Krautheimer, *Architecture*, pp. 23, 24; Gsell, *Les monuments*, II, 236–241.

17. Krautheimer, *Architecture*, pp. 52–54; Grabar, *Martyrium*, I, 212–227; Voelkl, *Die Kirchenstiftungen*, pp. 21, 24, 28, 31, 32, 39; Glanville Downey, *A History of Antioch in Syria from Seleucus to the Arab Conquest* (Princeton, 1961), pp. 342–349, 358, 434, 522, 552, 657; Wayne Dynes, "The First Christian Palace-Church Type," *Marsyas*, XI (1962–1964), 1–9, who suggests that Hagioi Sergios and Bakchos in Constantinople and San Vitale in Ravenna are modelled after the octagonal Great Church in Antioch (Fig. 6).

the plan among the existing forms of Roman imperial public architecture best suited to the needs of the Christian congregations—a large and well-lighted hall, with a sense of movement along a longitudinal axis toward the apse where the bishop and other clergy sat and before which the altar stood, capable of being enlarged by extension or by a second aisle, and suitable for liturgical processions. The well-known distinction between classical temple and Christian church is worth repeating. The temple is a house for the god; the church is a gathering place for communal worship. Symbol *and* structure are fundamentally different.

II

The second type of Constantine's churches is less numerous and is confined entirely to Rome. It is the cemetery basilica, or better, the covered cemetery. Again Krautheimer has done the most to clarify this type.[18] The earliest building in this group may even predate Constantine's benefactions although subsequent modifications and a monogram at the entrance to the complex are attributable to Constantine or his family (Fig. 7). It is the Church of San Sebastiano, or more correctly the Church of the Apostles, on the Via Appia.[19] The distinguishing characteristics of this type of basilica are: the side aisle continuing as an ambulatory around the west end or apse, the circular west end itself, the adjacent mausolea, the presence of a catacomb, and—two features not shown in most drawings—the graves literally paving the floor of the nave and aisles and the site outside the city ramparts (*extra moenia*).

This church and the others like it were favored burial places for Roman Christians in the fourth and fifth centuries because they were at the place of the martyrs, the catacombs. The Church of the Apostles had a claim to the relics of both Peter and Paul, deposited there according to one tradition during the persecutions of the third century but later returned to their original burial places.[20] It was

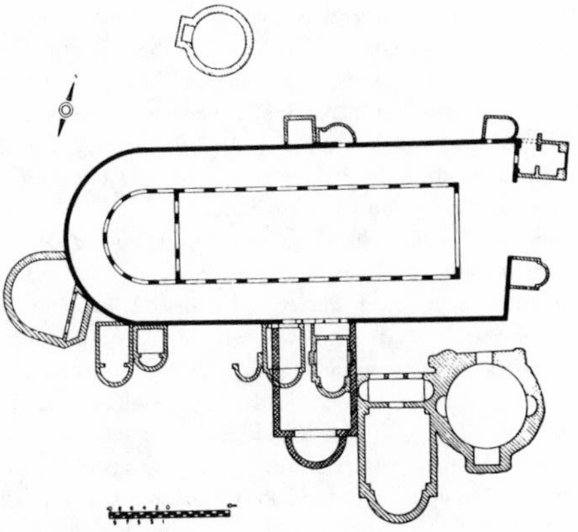

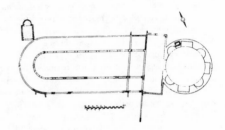

Fig. 7. Rome, Church of the Apostles (S. Sebastiano), ca. 312–313 or 340 (drawing by Constance D. Goodrich after Deichmann and Tschira).

Fig. 8. Rome, Saints Marcellinus and Peter, ca. 320, with the Mausoleum of Helena (drawing by Constance D. Goodrich after Deichmann and Tschira).

also the custom then to celebrate the anniversary of martyrdom with a vigil and feast that have been compared to an Irish wake, and even the anniversary of death of ordinary Christians was commemorated with a banquet.[21] These buildings functioned then as a sort of banquet hall as well as cemetery—at least until the bishops Ambrose and Augustine undertook an attack on these customs. The covered cemeteries seem to have had no resident clergy, although clergy from parish churches were assigned to celebrate Mass at the graves of the martyrs on their anniversaries. The Church of the Apostles is slightly different from the three other basilicas of this category in that the grave and shrine of Saint Sebastian, who became the primary martyr here

18. "Mensa-Coemeterium-Martyrium," *Cahiers Archéologiques*, XI (1960) 15–40; cf. also Andresen, *Einführung*, p. 25, who rejects the designation "basilica" for these "hall" churches.

19. Krautheimer, Frankl, and Corbett, *Corpus basilicarum*, IV (1970), 99–147; Krautheimer, *Architecture*, pp. 31, 32, and "Constantine's Church Foundations," p. 250, on the date; Andresen, *Einführung*, p. 94, who adopts a date soon after 312–313; Friedrich Wilhelm Deichmann and Arnold Tschira, "Das Mausoleum der Kaiserin Helena und die Basilika der Heiligen Marcellinus und Petrus an der Via Labicana vor Rom," *Jahrbuch des deutschen archäologischen Instituts*, LXXII (1957), 81–87, 92–98.

20. Engelbert Kirschbaum, *The Tombs of St. Peter and St. Paul*, trans. John Murray (New York, 1959), pp. 142, 143, 153, 154, 195–200; Jocelyn Toynbee and John Ward Perkins, *The Shrine of St. Peter and the Vatican Excavations* (New York, 1957), pp. 167–182; Daniel William O'Connor, *Peter in Rome: The Literary, Liturgical, and Archeological Evidence* (New York and London, 1969), pp. 93–158, 209.

21. F. van der Meer, *Augustine the Bishop: Religion and Society at the Dawn of the Middle Ages*, trans. Brian Battershaw and G. R. Lamb (New York, 1965), pp. 498–526; Krautheimer, "Mensa," pp. 31–34.

after Peter and Paul received their own churches, were directly beneath the nave, not adjacent to the building. The basilica is 241' long and 100' wide and had a clerestory.

Next in date is the Basilica of Saints Marcellinus and Peter on the Via Labicana[22] (Fig. 8). The site was a former imperial estate, and a catacomb is adjacent to the church. The basilica was not quite so long, 213', but almost as wide, 95', as the Church of the Apostles. Piers carried arches to support the nave walls, clerestory, and roof and to separate the aisle from the nave. The desirability of being buried near the martyrs is nowhere more evident than here. The great mausoleum directly connected with the basilica is known as that of Helena, the mother of Constantine, but she may in fact never have been buried there. Indeed here is every indication that Constantine planned this complex for himself. His decision to leave Rome in 326 and establish a new capital changed that intent, but a magnificent porphyry sarcophagus in the Vatican Museum testifies by its battle scenes to the funeral preparations of the emperor, not his mother.[23] Curiously this sarcophagus was used for Pope Anastasius IV in the twelfth century. One may note on the drawing a tomb chapel at the northwest corner of the basilica as well as the outlines of catacomb passages. Some of the finest catacomb paintings are from this site.

The Mausoleum of Helena represents a third type of Constantinian building, all of which eventually became churches analogous to the shrines of the martyrs. Helena, his mother, became Sant'Elena, and the daughter of the emperor, Constantina, became Santa Costanza. The church bearing her name was her mausoleum and is one of the best-preserved fourth-century buildings in Rome[24] (Fig. 9). The natural focus of this centralized structure was on the sarcophagus. The cylindrical form is of long standing in Roman funerary architecture. The centralized form could serve other categories of sacred architecture as in the case of the Pantheon which became a Christian church in the seventh century and now contains a Christian altar to Mary and all the saints and martyrs. Santa Costanza also preserves some of the most important fourth-century mosaics, probably dating like the building before 354.

What really matters for our analysis, however, is the surprising discovery only within our generation that Santa

Fig. 9. Rome, Sta. Costanza (the Mausoleum of Constantina), before 354 (photo: Hirmer Fotoarchiv, München).

Contanza like the Mausoleum of Helena is located next to a fourth-century covered cemetery (Fig. 10). This is the Basilica of Saint Agnes, an early fourth-century Roman martyr. It was almost as large as the Lateran basilica, 318' long and about 131' wide. Its date is later than the other Constantinian foundations in Rome, namely 338 or after the death of Constantine, but it was undoubtedly imperial.[25] Again there is a catacomb nearby where the seventh-century Church of Sant'Agnese was built in accord with the custom by that time of the *basilica ad corpus*. It is due to this custom as well as the eventual covering of the entire basilica floor with graves, even with a second layer in some cases, and to the abandonment of the banqueting on the anniversary of death that these monumental basilicas were lost to memory from the eighth or ninth century until this generation, with the exception of San Sebastiano which had a martyr's shrine within and beneath it.

22. Deichmann and Tschira, "Das Mausoleum," pp. 44–110; Krautheimer, *Architecture*, pp. 31, 32; Krautheimer, Frankl, and Corbett, *Corpus basilicarum*, II (1959), 191–204.

23. MacMullen, *Constantine*, p. 142; Wolfgang Fritz Volbach and Max Hirmer, *Early Christian Art*, pls. 22 and 23 with notes on p. 317; Deichmann and Tschira, "Das Mausoleum," p. 64.

24. Krautheimer, *Architecture*, pp. 42, 43; Andresen, *Einführung*, p. 94; Volbach and Hirmer, *Early Christian Art*, pls. 29–35 with notes on p. 319 and figs. 12 and 13 on p. 318.

25. Krautheimer, *Architecture*, pp. 31, 32; Deichmann and Tschira, "Das Mausoleum," pp. 83–87, 92–98, 100; Deichmann, "Die Lage der constantinischen Basilika der heiligen Agnes an der via Nomentana," *Rivista di Archeologia Cristiana*, XXII (1946), 213–234.

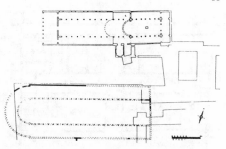

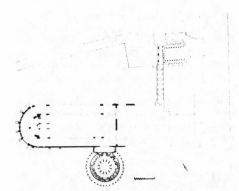

Fig. 10. Rome, St. Agnes, ca. 338–353, with the Mausoleum of Constantina and the Church of S. Agnese (seventh century) upper right (drawing by Constance D. Goodrich after Deichmann and Tschira).

Fig. 11. Rome, St. Lawrence, ca. 326–330, with the later double Church of S. Lorenzo f. l. M. above (drawing by Constance D. Goodrich after Deichmann and Tschira).

These last observations are confirmed by the fourth covered cemetery, the Basilica of Saint Lawrence on the Via Tiburtina[26] (Fig. 11). It was discovered almost by chance in 1950 after it was established a few years before that the sixth-century Church of San Lorenzo fuori le Mura was erected over catacombs in a hillside. A gallery of the catacombs extended beneath the Constantinian basilica which seems to have fallen into disuse after the later church was built *ad corpus* and the earlier one was filled with graves. The site today is that of a major public cemetery. This basilica was the longest of the group, 328', and was 105' wide. Closely placed columns supported the nave walls, roof, and clerestory and marked off the aisle. A reconstruction gives a good indication of the appearance of the covered cemetery type in general (Fig. 12).

All the basilicas in this category are clearly the same in form and function. Although they were not even full-fledged churches, that is, were not intended for regular Sunday worship, they can be said to represent the imperial seal of approval on the Christian cult of the dead—a cult which involved the martyrs, funeral banquets in old Roman tradition, and the Christian Eucharist. They also suggest Constantine's hope in the Christian life after death. The recent discovery of a similar basilica and mausoleum in the Villa dei Gordiana on the Via Prenestina, still not fully excavated and published, poses the intriguing problem

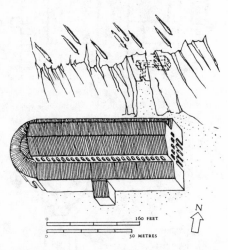

Fig. 12. Rome, St. Lawrence, isometric reconstruction showing underground memoria, ca. 330 (from R. Krautheimer, *Early Christian and Byzantine Architecture*; used by permission).

of a predecessor or continuator of the type, one for which there is no literary record.[27]

III

The third category, that of imperial mausolea, may be resumed with two examples contemporary with Constantine, one built by Diocletian, in whose court he grew up,

26. Krautheimer, Frankl, and Corbett, *Corpus basilicarum*, II, 1–144; Deichmann and Tschira, "Das Mausoleum," pp. 84–87, 92–98.

27. Andresen, *Einführung*, p. 95; G. Bovini, "Coemeteria-Basilicae d'età costantiniana a Roma," *Corsi Ravenna*, XV (1969), 91–97; Guglielmo Gatti, "Una Basilica di età costantiniana recentemente riconosciuta presso la via Prenestina," *Capitolium*, XXXV, n. 6 (June 1960), 3–8.

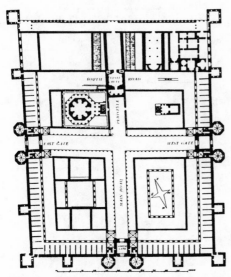

Fig. 13. Spalato, Palace of Diocletian with octagonal mausoleum, ca. 300 (from Kähler, *The Art of Rome*).

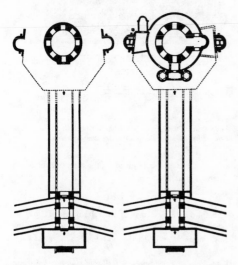

Fig. 14. Thessalonica, Mausoleum of Galerius with triumphal arch, ca. 300, left, and Hagios Georgios, ca. 390, right (from E. Dyggve, "Recherches sur le palais impérial de Thessalonique," *Studia Orientalia Ioanni Pedersen* [Copenhagen, 1953]).

and the other by Galerius, a rival for the imperial throne. Each built a centralized tomb in connection with the palace complex in his city of primary residence. Diocletian's was at Spalato and octagonal; Galerius's grandiose round tomb was at Thessalonica[28] (Figs. 13–14). In the last quarter of the fourth century the latter was converted by Theodosius I to a church dedicated to Saint George. Although Galerius had been a persecutor of Christians, the building itself was considered appropriate for a church. A centralized structure on imperial property is the mark of this category and is repeated with the Church of the Holy Apostles in Constantinople where Constantine was buried. This church was probably cruciform, focussing on the sarcophagus of the emperor surrounded by cenotaphs symbolizing the twelve apostles.[29] Constantine seems to have wanted to be remembered as the thirteenth apostle. Although this aspiration proved too much for later churchmen who brought in relics of real saints from the Holy Land and moved Constantine into an adjacent mausoleum, itself circular, the church was an influential monument for subsequent Byzantine architecture.

Also related to the mausolea category is the Anastasis Rotunda of the Church of the Holy Sepulchre (Fig. 15). Charles Coüasnon's rendering suggests the sort of imperial monument called for in those directions to Bishop Macarius. In addition Constantine displayed a clear preference for elaborate decoration—marble revetment, fine columns, gilded coffered ceilings, precious liturgical vessels.[30] Although the reconstruction of this church in the original Constantinian form constitutes an exceedingly complex problem, this view of the rotunda may fairly represent the fulfillment of the emperor's directions "that the most marvelous place in the world should be worthily decorated."

IV

Another category of building, the palace church, has been noted already in passing. It could take almost any form—an

28. Krautheimer, *Architecture*, pp. 41, 53–55; Volbach and Hirmer, *Early Christian Art*, pls. 122–127 with notes on p. 335 and figs. 14 and 15; Ejnar Dyggve, "Recherches sur le palais imperial de Thessalonique," *Studia Orientalia Ioanni Pedersen* (Copenhagen, 1953), pp. 59–70; D. S. Robertson, *A Handbook of Greek and Roman Architecture*, 2nd ed. (Cambridge, 1964), pp. 316–321; Heinz Kähler, *The Art of Rome and her Empire*, trans. J. R. Foster (New York, 1965), pp. 192, 202–206.

29. Andresen, *Einführung*, pp. 69, 70; Krautheimer, "Constantine's Church Foundations," pp. 242–255; Joseph Vogt, "Der Erbauer der Apostelkirche in Konstantinopel," *Hermes*, LXXXI (1953), 111–117; Downey, "The Builder of the Original Church of the Apostles," *Dumbarton Oaks Papers*, VI (1951), 53–80, with many additional references.

30. Krautheimer, "The Constantinian Basilica," pp. 129, 130, 135–138.

octagon at Antioch in Syria, of which we know so little, or a basilica with double side aisles and galleries above them as Krautheimer proposes for Constantine's Hagia Sophia, or a simple rectangular hall with apse but no side aisles in the Sessorian Palace at Rome, the residence of the dowager Empress Helena. This palace church is known as Santa Croce in Gerusalemme[31] (Fig. 16). Its structure is explained as the conversion of an existing reception hall or the equivalent to a chapel in the 320s by the addition of an apse and of cross arches. The others were new buildings.

V

The fifth and final type of Constantinian church is very closely related to, yet distinguishable from, the imperial mausoleum category and is found both in Rome and in the

---

31. Krautheimer, Frankl, and Corbett, *Corpus basilicarum*, I (1956), 165–195; Krautheimer, "The Constantinian Basilica," p. 130, which dates the entire remodelling to the later 320s.

Fig. 15. Jerusalem, Anastasis Rotunda of the Church of the Holy Sepulchre, after 333 (drawing by Charles Coüasnon; used by permission).

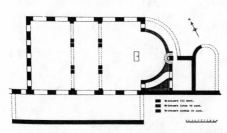

Fig. 16. Rome, Sta. Croce in Gerusalemme, modified into a palace church before 330 (drawing by Bonnie B. Moe after Krautheimer, Frankl, and Corbett).

Holy Land. It is the *martyrium*.[32] Although one may rightly observe that the covered cemetery halls are all connected to martyrs' shrines, in no case did Constantine erect the building which housed the shrine proper—as far as we know. Indeed the actual structures at the martyrs' tombs were quite small, and even at the Church of the Apostles the shrine of St. Sebastian was in a separate chamber beneath the basilica. At the shrine of St. Peter on the Vatican hill, however, this changes[33] (Fig. 17). Here one encounters the largest of all early Christian churches. The nave length alone was 295', and the total inner length was 390'. The width was 210', and there was a large atrium of comparable size. The nave and side aisles were a covered cemetery, "carpeted," as Krautheimer puts it, with graves. Mausolea were built around the walls in the course of the fourth century, including an imperial tomb in 400. Thus much is the same.

New and distinctive, however, is the transept, a great cross hall as tall as the nave with a large apse that is the focus of the entire building. In front of the apse was, and

---

32. Grabar is fundamental. See fn. 13 and "Christian Architecture, East & West," *Archaeology*, II (1949), 95–104; also J. B. Ward-Perkins, "Memoria, Martyr's Tomb and Martyr's Church," *Akten des VII. Internationalen Kongresses für christliche Archäologie*, Text volume, pp. 3–27; Krautheimer, "Mensa"; Deichmann, "Früh-christliche Kirchen in antiken Heiligtümern," *Jahrbuch des deutschen archäologischen Instituts*, LIV (1939), 105–136.

33. Kirschbaum, *The Tombs*; Toynbee and Ward Perkins, *The Shrine*; O'Connor, *Peter in Rome*; Angelus A. De Marco, *The Tomb of Saint Peter: A Representative and Annotated Bibliography of the Excavations*, Supplements to *Novum Testamentum*, VIII (Leiden, 1964); Jürgen Christern, "Der Aufriss von Alt-St.-Peter," *Römische Quartalschrift für christliche Altertumskunde und Kirchengeschichte*, LXII (1967), 133–183; Andresen, *Einführung*, pp. 68, 69; Krautheimer, *Architecture*, pp. 32–36, 41, 44; on the later influence of old St. Peter's see Krautheimer, "The Carolingian Revival of Early Christian Architecture," *The Art Bulletin*, XXIV (1942), 1–38.

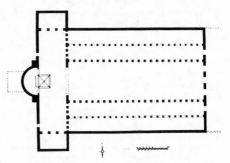

Fig. 17. Rome, St. Peter's, after 326 (drawing by Constance D. Goodrich after Krautheimer and Fraser).

14

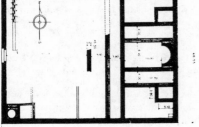

Fig. 19. Mamre, Basilica and enclosure, proposed reconstruction (from E. Mader, *Mambre* [1957]; used by permission).

Fig. 18. Mamre, Basilica and enclosure, ca. 333 (drawing by Thomas E. Fortner after Mader).

still is in the new St. Peter's, the shrine of the Prince of the Apostles. The transept is the martyrium proper, the hall in which pilgrims gathered and dispersed. It sheltered also the tables on which oblations were received, the altar (presumably movable), and the clergy seats. We take the form for granted now because it has been copied so often with or without modifications, but in Constantine's day it was a new and even experimental solution to a church building problem.

A similar but much smaller church seems to have been built at about the same time, around the year 326, for the shrine of St. Paul on the Via Ostiensis.[34] It was replaced in the 380s by a very large basilica copied after St. Peter's which also enjoyed imperial patronage. The present church is a rebuilding after a fire in 1823 and bears a general resemblance to the second.

It is only guessing to propose any plans for the Church of St. Acacius in Heptascalon and the Church of the Archangel Michael at Anaplus (Hestiae) in Constantinople.[35] Literary attributions to Constantine and the probability that there were some churches commemorating local saints justify mentioning these two, but we really know nothing about them.

In Palestine there are four churches, either extant or excavated, which were built to commemorate the places associated with Jesus or with a theophany in Old Testament

times. All were begun after 324 when Constantine defeated Licinius and assumed sole rule in the East, and all were essentially completed before the Emperor's death in 337. The category is still that of the *martyrium*, for these are places of witness to God for the Christian worshiper and pilgrim. They symbolize the divine activity and presence, and although each includes a basilica for the congregation of pilgrims to worship, the focus is on a particular holy place. One also sees great variation in arrangement and size, somewhat proportional to the importance of the site and the anticipated crowds. Several of them are associated with Helena as well as Constantine, for on her pilgrimage to the Holy Land she was distressed that these sacred sites lacked appropriate monuments. In fact some of them had been the sites of pagan shrines, as may have been the case for some of the churches in Constantinople and elsewhere. Such is not, however, mere happenstance. It is rather an illustration of the power of the holy. Once a place was marked as sacred by some special religious phenomenon, it was almost never desacralized although it could be reconsecrated to another deity or power.

The smallest of these memorial basilicas is the basilica at the Oak and Spring of Mamre, near Hebron south of Bethlehem[36] (Fig. 18). Here the sacred objects, the oak and well, were in one corner of the enclosure. The basilica was tiny and wider than long. The larger complex incorporated walls and materials from a Roman temple of the time of Hadrian and had a great altar in the center. A reconstruction shows that it could have been quite impressive (Fig. 19).

Another small basilica is the Eleona Church on the Mount of Olives in Jerusalem (Fig. 20). It was erected over

34. Kirschbaum, *The Tombs*, pp. 153, 154, 176–184; Krautheimer, *Architecture*, pp. 36, 63, 64. This church and St. Peter's are not included in the four volumes of the *Corpus basilicarum* but are to be treated in a supplementary volume.
35. Andresen, *Einführung*, pp. 36, 37; Janin, *La Géographie*, 1e Partie, III, 17–19, 349, 351, 352.

36. Evaristus Mader, *Mambre: Die Ergebnisse der Ausgrabungen im heiligen Bezirk Ramet El-Halil in Südpalästina*, 1926–28, 2 vols. (Freiburg im Breisgau, 1957), I, 95–115; Armstrong, "Imperial Church Building in the Holy Land in the Fourth Century," *The Biblical Archaeologist*, XXX (1967), 95–96.

10

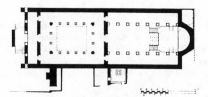

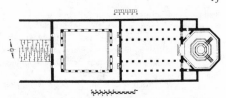

Fig. 20. Jerusalem, Eleona Church, Mount of Olives, ca. 333 (drawing by Thomas E. Fortner after Vincent).

Fig. 21. Bethlehem, Church of the Nativity, ca. 333 (drawing by Constance D. Goodrich after Richmond).

the cave where Jesus was believed to have taught the disciples about the "last things" (Matt. 24) and where by the fourth and fifth centuries some even believed that the Last Supper had been held. By the Middle Ages the tradition had shifted to the teaching of the Lord's Prayer; hence the Pater Noster Church came to be located very close to the site of the Eleona. Père Vincent in reconstructing the plan of the basilica on the basis of excavations early in this century suggested a raised chancel area extending into the nave above the cave-crypt and possibly an inscribed apse.[37] Thereby the sacred place was fully incorporated within the basilica, an arrangement which was to be more characteristic of the West than the East. Its length was 98', and the width, 60'. Equally significant is the colonnaded atrium with a monumental portico. Its area was as great as the basilica and reflects the importance for the pilgrim of the place of rest, gathering, and preparation before entering the sanctuary proper.

37. L.-H. Vincent, "L'Éléona: Sanctuaire primitif de l'Ascension," *Revue Biblique,* LXIV (1957), 48–71; Vincent and F.-M. Abel, *Jérusalem: Recherches de topographie, d'archéologie et d'histoire,* Tome 2: *Jérusalem nouvelle* (Paris, 1914–1926), 301–395; Armstrong, "Imperial Church Building in the Holy Land," pp. 94–95.

The original Church of the Nativity at Bethlehem incorporated a basilica not much larger than the Eleona Church (Fig. 21). It was nearly square, 95'×93'; then there was an equally large atrium surrounded by colonnades on all four sides, and in front of that a large forecourt.[38] The distinctive part of the structure was the octagon over the cave in which Jesus was believed to have been born. It is again a centralized structure; the octagon is the *martyrium,* integrally related to the basilica where the congregation worshiped and where presumably the altar stood. Over the cave itself at the center of the octagon was an oculus which gave the pilgrims a direct view into the sacred place. The whole was a harmonious structure with the double side aisles characteristic of the major imperial basilicas.

Closely related to the Church of the Nativity are the buildings which complete this study of Constantine's churches and their interrelationships. The original, fourth-century Church of the Holy Sepulchre embodied a similar harmonious alternation of open and enclosed areas in a sophisticated articulation of space (Figs. 22–23). From the

38. Andresen, *Einführung,* p. 70; Krautheimer, *Architecture,* pp. 36–43; J. W. Crowfoot, *Early Churches in Palestine* (London, 1941), pp. 22–30; R. W. Hamilton, *The Church of the Nativity, Bethlehem* (Jerusalem, 1947); Armstrong, "Imperial Church Building in the Holy Land," pp. 92–94.

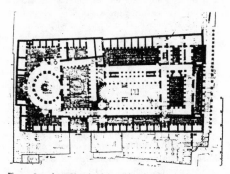

Fig. 22. Jerusalem, Church of the Holy Sepulchre, 328–336 (completion of the Rotunda probably later) (drawing by Charles Coüasnon; used by permission).

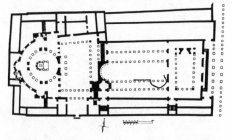

Fig. 23. Jerusalem, Church of the Holy Sepulchre (drawing by Bonnie B. Moe after Corbo and Coüasnon, with modifications by the author).

standpoint of both symbol and structure, it is the most interesting and important of early Christian churches. According to the historian Eusebius, notwithstanding his penchant for hyperbole and his personal involvement with this church, it was the most important for Constantine. Eusebius calls it a "conspicuous monument of the Saviour's resurrection, . . . embellished . . . throughout on an imperial scale of magnificence." Its length from the entrance of the basilica to the westernmost end of the rotunda is 384´, compared to the 390´ of the basilica and transept of St. Peter's. Only in the last decade could we be sure of the plan of the rotunda with its three apsidoles and façade. Earlier reconstructions posited a perfectly circular west end, originally open to the sky, with the tomb enclosed in an aedicula at the center.[39] Although the rotunda may not have been completed within the lifetime of Constantine, the overall plan was intended from the beginning.

The Church of the Holy Sepulchre is the classic type of the holy place where God has been made manifest.[40] It was a place to be set apart, to be enclosed—or more precisely, one that set itself apart. There was a monumental entrance, a gate of heaven in the sense that in this holy place earth meets heaven and one may pass between. The atrium was a place of preparation for the worshiper, of separation from the world. In the Christian pattern one next moved into the house of prayer which afforded an opportunity for further preparation and a place for congregational worship. Then he came to the place of the theophany proper. At the Holy Sepulchre there was an inner atrium enclosing an-other inseparable holy place, the rock of Calvary. Finally, the tomb, the site of the resurrection, was roofed over with a dome—the dome of heaven or of the cosmos—which had an oculus at the apex like the Pantheon in Rome. This oculus gave direct access to heaven from the holy place, and the rotunda was the focal point of the whole, structurally and symbolically.

At the same time many Jewish traditions of Jerusalem as the Holy City were transferred by Christians from the Temple to the Holy Sepulchre. The *omphalos* or navel of the world was fixed at Golgotha and is still marked there. The twelve columns in the hemisphere of the apse symbolized the twelve disciples and the twelve tribes of Israel, and perhaps the columns and pillars of the Holy Sepulchre were echoes of the sacred forest of religious mythology, just as the inner atrium was in fact understood as a sacred garden or paradise. The centralized structure may also be conceived as a *heroon*, a tomb temple to a founder or patron of a city or land, for Jesus Christ was considered both the founder of Christianity and the founder of the New Jerusalem, a term applied by Eusebius specifically to the Church of the Holy Sepulchre. One characteristic of the *heroon* is that it was often placed at the geographical center of the city, and so it was with the Church of the Holy Sepulchre in respect to Roman Jerusalem and with the Church of the Holy Apostles, Constantine's *heroon* in Constantinople.

The Church of the Holy Sepulchre was, moreover, to be a center for the spiritual unity of the empire, a focus for the ideological basis chosen by Constantine and developed by his successors to stem the crisis of the empire. The way of pilgrimage which was launched for Christianity in the empire was to be a way of salvation for all, both individuals and the society. Politically it was advantageous that Jerusalem was not prominent as a metropolis or even a provincial capital. It had never been an imperial residence like most of the other cities where Constantine built churches. It could serve him solely for religious purposes without arousing old rivalries such as that between Alexandria and Antioch. Indeed Jerusalem's importance to subsequent rulers—the sons of Constantine, Justinian, Heraclius, Charlemagne, Pope Urban II, Louis IX—remained religious and symbolic, not political or strategic. With this significance it appeared frequently at the center of mediaeval maps of the world, often indicated by the buildings of the Holy Sepulchre. Constantine's Church of the Holy Sepulchre may stand as the epitome of his building program, both as symbol and as structure, and as the ultimate achievement among the five categories here delineated—cathedral, covered cemetery, mausoleum, palace church, and *martyrium*.

---

39. Vincent and Abel, *Jérusalem*, II, 89–217, whose plan has been most frequently reproduced, and Krautheimer, *Architecture*, pp. 36–43, 50, whose plan based on Wistrand must also be modified in light of the following: Virgilio Corbo, "La basilica del S. Sepolcro a Gerusalemme," *Studii Biblici Franciscani, Liber Annus*, XIX (1969), 65–144, which summarizes his reports in the same publication, volumes XII, XIV, and XV; P. Testini, "L'Anastasis alla luce della recenti indagini," *Oriens Antiquus*, III (1964), 263–292; Charles Coüasnon, "Analyse des éléments du IVe siècle conservés dans la basilique du S. Sépulcre à Jérusalem," *Akten des VII. International Kongresses für christliche Archäologie*, text volume, pp. 447–463, with accompanying illustrations in the plates volume (in addition he has provided drawings and responses to several inquiries by mail); Wilkinson, *Egeria's Travels*, pp. 36–46; my own anticipated article, "The Original Church of the Holy Sepulchre." The best of the earlier studies is Kenneth John Conant and Glanville Downey, "The Original Buildings of the Holy Sepulchre in Jerusalem," *Speculum*, XXXI (1956), 1–48.

40. Mircea Eliade, *The Sacred and the Profane*, trans. Willard R. Trask (New York, 1961), pp. 20–65. The writer dealt with this theme in a paper, "Jerusalem and the Holy Sepulchre: The Center of the World," for the American Society of Church History, meeting in Boston, 28 Dec. 1970.

NOTE

NOTES ON THE WOODEN DOORS
OF SANTA SABINA*

RICHARD DELBRUECK

The church of S. Sabina on the Aventine was consecrated under Pope Sixtus III shortly after the year 432 (w 7).[1] The wooden doors (see text fig.) are hung in an older marble doorway, presumably of the Flavian era; they measure 3.22 by 5.41 meters (w 8) which is approximately, though not quite exactly, 11 by 18 Roman feet. They are divided vertically so as to allow the inner halves alone to open. The antique parts of the doors are made of cypress wood. Of the very narrow outer frames which hold them in place nothing is antique. However, the original ones cannot have differed much from the ones now there, except for possible ornamentation.

Each half-door bore seven panels provided with borders; of these panels three were large and four small. Out of a total of twenty-eight panels for the whole work, four of the large and six of the small ones are missing, while the fronts of eighteen panels have been preserved. Their original arrangement cannot be determined, for which reason no mention is made here of their present position. There is no central mullion; there would not be room for one. On the outside, the top and bottom borders nearly touch the lintel and threshold of the marble portal, although one might expect to find a wide outer frame. These unique abnormalities lead us to assume that the wooden doors were too large for the marble portal and had therefore to be cut down to size. No other explanation of this extraordinary arrangement seems plausible.

Some of the reliefs on the panels show a "plain" style, of medium quality, whose variations need not be mentioned here; some, a "brilliant" style based on classic forms, of a unified and highly artistic quality.

Structure and Ornamentation. On both inside and out, the panels have broadly beveled borders all around. On the outside, their moldings have rich profiles (Fig. 2), showing: (1) a thick roll ornamented with undulating vines carrying large leaves and grapes on alternating sides. The roll has been largely restored, but the work was very accurately done after preserved

remnants (w 10.12), though the antique ornament may have varied in places; (2) an astragal of barrel-shaped beads which is almost entirely new (w 12)

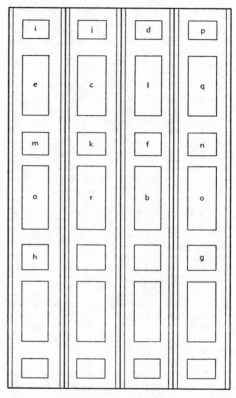

Schematic drawing of the doors

and therefore does not allow any definite conclusions to be drawn from its shape, unusual for the late period; (3) an undecorated band with an elevated ridge on its inner edge; (4) a vegetabilized Lesbian cyma, modern only in part (w 12). The "hearts" in it are

* Translated by Mrs. Ursula Stechow.
  1. W = J. Wiegand, *Das altchristliche Hauptportal an der Kirche der hl. Sabina auf dem aventinischen Hügel in Rom*, Trier, 1900. Excellent description and the best reproductions; contains the older literature most of which is antiquated.
  Eastern: D. Ainalov, "The Hellenistic Bases of Byzantine Art," *Zapiski* of the Russian Archaeological Society, XII, pp. 2ff.; *Trudy* of the Classical . . . Section, no. 5, pp. 121-126 (in Russian); incomplete report by O. Wulff, *Repertorium für Kunstwissenschaft*, XVI, 1903, pp. 35ff. Idem, *Altchristliche und byzantinische Kunst (Handbuch der Kunstwissenschaft)*, I, p. 137, and *Nachtrag* . . , pp. 16, 22; O. M. Dalton, *Byzantine Art and Archaeology*, Oxford, 1911, p. 145 (references).
  Italo-Gallic or *North Italian*: E. Baldwin Smith, *Early*

Christian Iconography, Princeton, 1918, pp. 102ff.; M. Lawrence, ART BULLETIN, XIV, 1932, p. 165; E. Weigand, *Byzantinische Zeitschrift*, XXX, 1930, pp. 587ff. (on monogram nimbus); A. C. Soper, ART BULLETIN, XX, 1938, pp. 163, 168ff. (careful motivation of this view); K. Wessel, *Jahrbuch des deutschen archäologischen Instituts*, LXIII-LXIV, 1948-49, pp. 111ff.; C. R. Morey, *Early Christian Art*, Princeton, 1942, pp. 137ff.
  Roman: G. Rodenwaldt, *Römische Mitteilungen*, XXXV-XXXVI, 1921-22, pp. 103ff. (shoulder cloak); A. Heisenberg, *Sitzungsberichte der bayerischen Akademie der Wissenschaften*, phil.-hist. Kl., no. 4, p. 65 (Denial of Peter); H. Schrade, *Vorträge der Bibliothek Warburg*, 1928-29, pp. 66ff. (Ascension).

replaced by open blossoms, the "darts" by vine leaves and curled-up shoots, while the ends of the "tongues" are connected by rings. There is no second astragal, though one might expect one running along on the inside of the cyma.

On the inside of the door (w pl. 3 and p. 14, ill. 2; here Fig. 1), the moldings around the panels consist merely of an ovolo turned partly inward, partly out. The large panels show a continuous geometric pattern in five spirited variations, while the small panels show arrangements of naturalistic twigs of ivy and olive and, in one instance, a scale-like pattern of oak leaves and acorns.

Closely related to the moldings on the outside are fragments of niche framings built into the terrace of the Bel temple of Palmyra which was consecrated in A.D. 32 and belongs therefore to the first century B.C. at the latest (Figs. 3-5).[2] At that time, Palmyra still gravitated toward the Hellenistic cities of Mesopotamia rather than toward Syria, which was more receptive to classic influence. Seyrig's suggestion that this sumptuously decorative art is Graeco-Mesopotamian seems therefore well founded. From what time on and how far it spread westward is not yet sufficiently clear. But the unparalleled fact remains that so flourishing and so refined a decorative art lived through half a millennium without developing further. Concerning the ornamentation of the insides of the doors, we can state merely that similar flat geometric designs occur in the late period, and often earlier, on floor mosaics and silver ware.[3] The mosaics follow the designs found on rugs—perhaps, or even probably, Oriental ones. The outward-turned ovolo occurs around 400 in the Western Empire;[4] it can hardly be assumed, what with the lack of comparative material, that it was unknown in the East. On the whole, the assumption seems justified that the ornamentation of the door is Graeco-Mesopotamian.

Features of Clothing. The clothing on the panel figures is of the normal type with but one exception. Pilate and his boy servant (h, w pl. 8; here Fig. 6) as well as the two servants at the *Feast of Manna* (c, w pl. 10; here Fig. 7) are wearing long-sleeved, unpleated tunics of heavy cloth, indicated as being fleecy by close dotting or semicircular carving marks; similar patterns occur on the doors as indication of scalp hair. Furthermore, the figures wear medium-high boots apparently woven of broad leather strips. Both panels in question belong to the "plain" style. Considering the exactness with which the artists of the late period executed all official attire, it would be unheard-of for Pilate to appear in a furry robe and wear provincial boots instead of the prescribed *campagi*. His attire here is de-

cidedly provincial but cannot be determined as to definite locality. At least, I myself have found no analogies, and inquiries among my better informed colleagues have brought no different results. The warm tunic suggests colder regions such as the Balkan or Alpine countries, Northern Gallia, Belgica, Germania, Britannia, or even Northern Spain. One may also consider a region where the civic and religious life still followed the Roman pattern, but the official Roman attire was no longer adhered to. Such might have been the case in the outlying, politically abandoned provinces of the Empire. Many a landowner of the Romania may have been clad in the same manner as Pilate. The diadem may have been added by the artist to indicate its owner's high rank (the diadem on the panel is antique, though the face itself is new).

The shepherd boy in the scene depicting the abduction of Habakkuk (n, w pl. 19) is wearing a small shoulder cloak such as can frequently be found in the West. However, Rodenwaldt's assumption that this is an apparel characteristic of the West goes too far. For such a cloak is worn also by the hunter's knave on the sapphire of Constantine II whose Eastern provenance is assured by the accompanying inscription naming the reclining local goddess: ΚΕϹΑΡΙΑ ΚΑΠΠΑΔΟΚΙΑϹ.[5]

Iconographical Remarks. The work done in the "plain" style corresponds primarily with the canonical reports, and there are no specific connections with localizable cycles.

(a) Moses receiving the Tablets of the Law (w pl. 7).

(b) Exodus from Egypt (w pl. 16): The Drowning of Pharaoh; Aaron with two Serpents (Exodus 7:10 mentions only one serpent, but that is unimportant here).

(c) The Journey through the Desert (w pl. 10): The Feast of the Quail; The Feast of Manna; the Miracle of the Rock.

(d) The Adoration of the Magi (w pl. 13): Mary's chair raised on six steps is unique, as far as I know; the Child already seated on his mother's lap is in accordance with the proto-evangelium of St. James, ch. 21, and with Pseudo-Matthew, ch. 16, in which the Child is two years old.

(e) Three Miracles of Christ (w pl. 5): The Healing of the Blind; The Miracle of the Loaves and Fishes; the Wedding of Cana.

(f) Prediction of the Denial of Christ (w pl. 15). Compare Heisenberg's footnote 1.[1]

(g) The Trial of Christ (w pl. 21). The seated figure is attired in a *chlamys*, which would not be suitable for the High Priest Caiaphas. The head of the figure

---

2. H. Seyrig, *Syria,* XXI, 1940, pp. 276ff.; for the ornament: pl. 29, 1, 2, 5, 8; pl. 33, 20. For connections with Seleucia ad Tigrim: pp. 328ff., also on the extent of the spreading of this style. The interpretation of Seyrig has been discussed with reservations by F. W. von Bissing, *Abhandlungen der bayerischen Akademie der Wissenschaften,* phil.-hist. Kl., new series, LII, 1951, pp. 32f.

3. Mosaics: H. Peirce and R. Tyler, *L'art byzantin,* Paris,

1932, I, pp. 65, 68f.; II, pp. 120f., 194, 115. Silver: *ibid.,* I, p. 61; some material also in T. Dohrn, *Mitteilungen des deutschen archaeologischen Instituts,* II, 1949, p. 106f.

4. Soper, *op.cit.,* pp. 158, 169f.

5. Rodenwaldt, *op.cit.*—On the sapphire of Constantine II: R. Delbrueck, *Spätantike Kaiserporträts,* Berlin, 1933, p. 152, pl. 74, 1.

is new. With some hesitation, one might consider this to be Jesus before Herod (Luke 25:6); but in this scene Jesus should remain silent, while here he is raising his hand in a gesture of speech.

(h) Pilate washing his Hands; Jesus going to Calvary (w pl. 8).

(i) The Crucifixion (w pl. 1).

(j) The Two Women and the Angel at the Tomb (w pl. 9).

(k) The Resurrected Christ appearing to two Women (w pl. 11).

(l) The Ascension (w pl. 12).

(m) The Resurrected Christ appearing to three Disciples (w pl. 6). The background shows a wall which presumably indicates the interior of a room. The foremost disciple may be Simon Peter as far as the damaged face permits identification. The second disciple has an individual head, beardless, with a strongly curved nose. He shows a resemblance to the apostle to the left of Christ on the lid of the silver box at San Nazario.[6] The third disciple is youthful, with no special characterization. The source for this panel is Luke 24:36 or possibly a related version.[7] Behind the head of Christ is suspended the Constantinian Monogram of Christ with Alpha and Omega, though decidedly without nimbus. The furrows of the background pattern touch the letters; thus, the nimbus could not have been painted there either. This representation is, as far as I know, unique, and it hardly allows any conclusions as to a definite localization of this type. The Constantinian Monogram was, of course, known throughout the Empire. It appears characteristically on the shield carried by the first Protector of the Emperor,[8] and also on the silver dish of Constantius II and on the imperial mosaics of San Vitale, though in this instance without the Alpha and Omega. Weigand[1] concluded from the monogram that this type was developed in Northern Italy, where it actually does occur rather frequently, though invariably with the nimbus. But the material for comparison with other regions is not ample enough to fully justify such a conclusion.

Of the reliefs of the "brilliant" style, only the first one follows the Biblical text to the letter:

(n) The Abduction of Habakkuk by the Angel (w pl. 19). Compare Daniel 14:32.

(o) The Ascension of Elijah (w pl. 20; here Fig. 8*). Compare II Kings 2. In accordance with the Biblical text are Elijah's chariot, his slipping robe, and the storm cloud, indicated by a flashing abstract shape. The hovering angel could be considered plausible, but this is hardly true of his gesture: he touches Elijah's shoulder with a long wand as if to convey celestial powers upon him. This may well be the only example of a magic wand in action. The accessories certainly go beyond the Biblical report. Elisha, the brother of Elijah,

stands upon a set of small stairs. There is a rocky mountain sloping down to the left with a fountain house at its foot from which pours a strong jet of water. At the lower right is a strip of tilled land, correctly identified as such by Wiegand. Two tillers with hoes are jumping aside in fright. Several of these additions to the Biblical text correspond with the local legend told the Christian pilgrims in Jericho.[9] Though not related in full, it is mentioned in itineraries, especially in the Breviarium de Hierosolyma and in Antonius Martyr. The legend drew the far-distant Mount Hebron (I Kings 19:8) closer, near the place of the Ascension at the Jordan. It mentioned the spring which Elisha blessed after Elijah's Ascension (II Kings 2:19) and also the Ager Domini upon which Jesus cast the seed. The small stairs are perhaps meant to indicate the path down to the Jordan, and the tillers to show the field being tended, though the Bible speaks only of the youths watching the prophets of Jericho. Without stating his reasons, Ainalov[1] presumed a Palestinian model to have influenced this representation. This is not certain, for the local legends of the Holy Land became known everywhere through the pilgrims. Ainalov's further suggestion that the subsequent miracle of Elisha, in which he drew back to the surface an axe that had fallen into a well, was depicted simultaneously here, is not reconcilable with the representation (II Kings 6:5; Prudentius, Dittochaeum XXII).

(p) Christ between two Apostles (w pl. 17 and p. 77; here Figs. 2 and 9). To the left of Christ stands Paul, bald-headed and short-bearded, gesticulating excitedly with both hands. To his right stands Peter(?), not definitely characterized as such, holding his pallium forward and thus forming a pouch in which to receive an object which Christ is holding against his chest with great care between thumb and the first two fingers of his left hand, while he raises his right in a gesture of impressive speech. All three figures have nimbi. They are separated by date palms which may indicate the location as Paradise. The object held by Jesus has the size and the shape of a goose egg. As far as I know, no acceptable interpretation for it has been suggested as yet. Wiegand believed it to be a small loaf of bread; but the antique loaves were never of that shape. It could only be a real egg or a pearl. An egg, however, is an unlikely interpretation because in the entire Christian area it occurs with symbolical meaning only among the Mandaeans. For a pearl, the object is exceedingly large. But it would, after all, be a Heavenly pearl and might well be rendered larger because of its very significance. Nor would it be altogether impossible that a pearl of approximately that size should exist. The baroque pearl which the angel on the Pala d'Oro holds in his hand is not much smaller, if I remember correctly; the pearls of Theodora on the imperial mosaics of San Vitale

6. Antike Denkmäler, IV, no. 1 (1927), pl. 2.

7. E.g., E. Hennecke, Neutestamentliche Apokryphen, 2nd ed., Tübingen, 1924, p. 532, 3.

8. Delbrueck, op.cit., pl. 37. Dohrn, op.cit., p. 123, does not accept this identification.

* Acknowledgment is made to Fratelli Alinari, Florence, for use of a photograph for Fig. 8.

9. T. Tobler and A. Molinier, Itinera Hierosolymitana et descriptiones terrae sanctae, Geneva, 1879, I and II, pp. 68, 96, 99; Guide Bleu: Syrie et Palestine, pp. 201ff.; on the iconography of the Ascension of Elijah: Schrade, op.cit., pp. 82ff., and the index of Cabrol s.v. Elias and Elisa.

would in reality be about five centimeters high; and the pearl on the headband of the Empress on the ivory in the Bargello would even be six centimeters in height. Thus the assumption that the object is a pearl seems permissible, if not the only one possible.

The detour we would have to take for a complete understanding of the scene in question leads through territory with which I am not entirely familiar. But I hope that experts will complement and correct my statements. I am grateful to P. Odilo Heiming, O.S.B., for valuable leads to literature on the subject, though some of it, even the more important, was not accessible to me. I cannot give here an exposition on pearl symbolism. Suffice it to enumerate and document the most important of the meanings attached to the pearl. The sources are listed in the appendix, together with a number of pertinent quotations.

Christian pearl symbolism originates in two parables of Christ as told by St. Matthew. They correspond with well known rabbinic pronouncements. The first parable (Matthew 7:6) sets up the pearl as a symbol of divine teachings not to be cast before the swine. In the second (Matthew 13:46), the pearl stands for the Heavenly Kingdom: in exchange for this precious pearl the wise pearl merchant gave all his riches. The text does not say that he gave, as might be assumed, several smaller pearls for it. Since the teaching, the Logos, stands for Christ, the pearl of the first parable came to be interpreted as a symbol of Christ, and the identification of Christ with the pearl has led to a proof, by analogy, of the inviolate conception and birth of Christ, derived from Hellenistic nature fables. The pearl oysters live, so it was said, in colonies, much like the bees. They even have kings. Pearls are formed when dewdrops or rain fall into the open shell while celestial light, from sun, moon, or stars, shines into them; hence the moist sheen of the pearl. According to another version, pearls are created by lightning as it flashes across the shell—though yet another tradition has it that lightning frightens the shell into miscarrying an immature pearl. The analogy was developed first in the Alexandrian School; according to Clement (ca. 200), Mary is the shell, the Holy Ghost the lightning, and Christ the pearl. Within the same tradition, this analogy is reiterated, in an amplified form, by Athanasius. Origen too relates it, though in a somewhat modified fashion. The three versions of the Greek Physiologus may be assumed to be an Alexandrian heritage. The more critical school of Antioch, however, seems not to have seen any special significance in the analogy, and it does not occur in Johannes Chrysostomus. In Constantinople, too, Proklos and Theophylactus of Achrida mention it only in terms of a feeble comparison. However, in Eastern Syria and Mesopotamia—countries where the pearl had always been not only a valuable but also a much admired and coveted jewel—such an analogy, and pearl symbolism on the whole, exerted an exciting and convincing influence upon the theologians. Ephrem keeps emphasizing it in ever new versions before his followers; as a proof of the restitution of virginity after

birth, he points to the fact that the oyster closes its shell after the expulsion of the pearl; its perforation is paralleled with the nailing of Christ to the cross; the apostles are the divers who find the pearl, which is Christ, in the Sea of Genezareth; and so forth. Especially in his versified homilies, Ephrem is often a real poet. This is perhaps even more true of Jacob of Sarug, the monophysite bishop of Batna near Edessa. He pays homage to the pearl in a hymnic letter to the abbot of the monastery of Mar Bassus near Apamea who had expressed doubt as to the orthodoxy of his faith. To Jacob of Sarug, the pearl stands not only for Christ, but also for the human soul lost in worldliness but redeemed by the Saviour and returned to its Heavenly Homeland. This belief originates in the Babylonian Gnosis, e.g., of the Manichaeans and Mandaeans, but the East Syrian and Mesopotamian church leaders took no exception to it; it returns, for instance, with Ephrem and constitutes the core of the Hymn of the Soul which, though non-Christian in origin, was included in the Acts of Thomas. Furthermore, pearls can stand for believers such as apostles, prophets, monks, and catechumens. All these various meanings—and still more on which we cannot elaborate here—connect and weave into each other beyond separation.

In the Mediterranean countries west of Alexandria and Constantinople, we find but mere traces of pearl symbolism; it seems to have made no impression upon the *nüchterne Katholiker* (Gressmann's expression). The analogy is never used. Among the forty-two *epikleses* of Christ in an epigram by Damascus, the pearl is lacking, or at best only hinted at by the word *gemma*. Wherever the pearl is mentioned as a symbol of the teachings or of the Heavenly Kingdom of Christ, an Eastern source may safely be assumed.

Because of the manifold meanings possible for the pearl symbol, no unequivocal interpretation can be given for the scene in question here. The pearl may stand for the Word of God, thus rendering the *Traditio Legis*; or for the Host, as pledge of the Heavenly Kingdom; or for the soul redeemed, the Christian purified through baptism, and so on. We are safer in assuming that the prototype of this scene stems from Eastern Syria or Mesopotamia where alone the pearl was an object of the deepest devotion at the approximate time when the door was made. The artist, too, who was familiar with the subject of the Giving of the Pearl, can be assumed to have come from the same region—as did the ornamentalist (see above p. 140). Perhaps it is no self-delusion if one feels that an inner kinship exists between the "brilliant" style and the religious poetry of the Christians and the Heretics of the pearl region. Art-historically, however, nothing definite can be said concerning this question because, of the sculptural art of Eastern Syria and Mesopotamia dating back to that period, virtually nothing has been preserved. The coastal cities of Phoenicia showed, toward the end of the fourth century, a classicism which might be considered comparable, at least in its basic forms, though not in temperament.[10]

10. On Classicism at Sidon: E. Will, *Syria*, XXVII, 1950, pp. 261ff.

1. Section of the inside of the doors of S. Sabina

2. Christ with two Apostles, doors of S. Sabina

5. Ornament from Palmyra (*Syria*, 1940, pl. 33, 26)

3. Ornament from Palmyra (*Syria*, 1940, pl. 29, 8)

4. Ornament from Palmyra (*Syria*, 1940, pl. 31, 6)

17

6. Pilate and boy servant, doors of S. Sabina

7. Servant from *Feast of Manna*, doors of S. Sabina

8. Ascension of Elijah, doors of S. Sabina

9. Christ with pearl (detail of Fig. 2)

The only point in favor of the interpretation of the object held by Christ as an egg is that the Mandaeans had their Uthras—a kind of angel—store away their banners inside of eggs which lay at the Gate of Heaven. Against this interpretation, however, stands the fact that the egg—as stated before—does not, to my knowledge, occur anywhere else in Christian symbolism of that era.

(q) The *Parusia* (w pl. 16). Its interpretation has been firmly established by Kantorowicz.[11] The scriptural source for it may have been the Apocalypse of Peter or some similar writing. The titular inscription indicating Christ by the initials upon his *codicilli*—IXOYCK—might perhaps be decoded thus: I HSOYC —X PICTOC—Θ EOY—Y IOC—C ΩTHP (or C TAYPOC)—K YPIOC, possibly in the vocative, as upon the imperial *codicilli*.

For the one panel in the "plain" style not yet discussed, a Biblical interpretation seems to be out of the question.

(r) Homage paid to a *Chlamydatus* (w pl. 12). As I see it, the interpretation suggested by Kantorowicz, that this panel represents the *Advent of the Kyrios*, is precluded by the attire indicating a worldly rank, and especially by the riding boots worn by the *chlamydatus*.[12] The difficulties may seem negligible if one recognizes in the *chlamydatus* the emperor Theodosius II with whose portrait the head on the panel coincides fairly well. But the diadem is lacking and that makes this explanation difficult to accept, though not entirely impossible. In any case, the scene seems to be an historical one. There was room enough for a small series of non-Biblical subjects. Ten of the panels are missing, of which only four or six were definitely Biblical in nature: Daniel in the Lions' Den, ascertained by the Habakkuk scene; the Annunciation; the Birth of Christ; and perhaps one or another episode from the Childhood gospels.

Summary. The wooden doors were hardly made for their present location; apparently they had to be cut down to size so as to fit into the marble portal. They may well have been made for an earlier building in Rome or even for use in a different locality. In this latter case, transportation difficulties would have been less severe than for the roof beams of S. Sabina. The date of the foundation of the church therefore does not provide a *terminus post quem* for the doors, which may however be furnished by the portrait head of the *chlamydatus* in the homage scene (s), which represents either the emperor Theodosius II or a personality likened to and therefore contemporary with him. The emperor's beard has the same shape on the scepter bust of the Consul Aspar, dated 434.[13]

Several different artistic trends can be distinguished on the wooden doors. The ornamental framework around the panels on the outside of the doors belongs to the Graeco-Mesopotamian style, the time and extent of whose westward expansion have not yet been suf-

ficiently established; at any event, I have found nothing comparable in the Western Empire at that time. The geometric designs on the inside do not stem from any classical tradition and are probably also of Oriental origin. The conclusion that a Graeco-Mesopotamian artist was employed on these parts of the work seems therefore inevitable.

The panel reliefs of the "brilliant" style stand alone in the material preserved. The picture of Christ who seems to be holding a pearl (q) also leads us—provided the interpretation of this attribute is correct—to Eastern Syria and Mesopotamia, where alone at that time the pearl was a highly significant symbol. The other panels of the "brilliant" style furnish nothing to establish the locality of the pictorial type, and thereby of the origin of its artist. That the shoulder cloak in the Habakkuk scene (o) is a garment occurring only in the West is an erroneous assumption.

The reliefs of the "plain" style have no stylistic or iconographic analogies with localizable contemporary work beyond those which can be attributed to the fact that they treat the same subjects and use the same formal elements. A hint as to the origin of the models and of the executing artists lies in the provincial costumes worn by Pilate and by the servants at the *Feast of Manna*. The heavy woolen tunic points to a country of cooler climate, and the circumstance that Pilate is not attired in the official robe suggests a politically abandoned, outlying territory of the Empire. The Constantinian Monogram behind the head of Christ in the scene in which the Resurrected meets three disciples (n) permits no conclusions, since it occurs without nimbus only on the door, and since the monogram as such was familiar everywhere.

Thus, the artisan in charge of executing the doors may have called upon two groups of artists, one Oriental and one "Nordic," with both groups using in the main their own customary patterns. Only for the *Homage to the Chlamydatus* (s), if it actually was meant to depict a contemporary scene, may special instructions have been given. There is nothing improbable in the thought that around the year 430 artists from various outlying provinces, where life was precarious and commissions were scarce, should have met in one of the secure cities of the interior Empire. This could have happened in Rome, too. The recovery following the Gothic terror of 410 must have held its attractions for artistic talent from abroad.

BONN, GERMANY

APPENDIX

Some Sources on Pearl Symbolism

I. *Selected Literature on Pearl Symbolism*
  Pauly-Wissowa, *Real-Encyclopaedie*, s.v. margaritai; *Thesaurus linguae latinae* and *Stephani thesaurus lin-*

---

11. E. Kantorowicz, ART BULLETIN, XXVI, 1944, pp. 207ff.; R. Delbrueck, *ibid.*, XXXI, 1949, pp. 217ff.
12. On the acclamation scene: Delbrueck, ART BULLETIN,

XXXI, 1949, pp. 215ff., with reference to Kantarowicz, *op.cit.*
13. R. Delbrueck, *Die Consulardiptychen*, Berlin, 1929, no. 35.

guae graecae, s.vv. (insufficient for the late period); H. Usener, "Die Perle," in *Vorträge und Aufsätze*, Leipzig, 1907, pp. 219ff., with verbatim excerpts from Christian authors; C. M. Edsman, "Le baptême du feu," *Acta seminarii neotestamentici Upsaliensis*, IX, Upsala-Leipzig, 1940, pp. 190ff., particularly on Manichaean and Mandaean material; F. Sbordone, *Physiologus*, Milan, 1936, pp. 133ff.; E. Hennecke, *Neutestamentliche Apokryphen*, 2nd ed., Tübingen, 1924; Migne, *Patrologia graeca* (PG) and *Patrologia latina* (PL); Ephrem = S. *Ephraem Syri opera omnia . . . in sex tomos distributa*, ed. J. S. Assemani, Rome, 1732-46; Lamy (Ephrem) = T. J. Lamy, *Ephraim Syrus, hymni et sermones*, 4 vols., Malines, 1883-1902; M. Lidzbarski, *Mandaeische Liturgien*, Berlin, 1920; C. R. C. Allberry, *A Manichaean Psalmbook*, II, Stuttgart, 1938.

For classical authors, reference is usually made to Pauly-Wissowa, *Real-Encyclopaedie*; for Christian authors, to B. Altaner, *Patrologie*, 2nd ed., Freiburg, 1950.

II. *Some References to Different Meanings of the Pearl*

(Asterisks refer to section III.)

Rabbinical: The Jewish Encyclopaedia, s.v. "pearl"; Strack-Billerbeck, on St. Matthew 7:6; 13:46.

Pearl = Word of God: *Ps. Gregorius Thaumaturgus (Caesarea Pal., 4th-5th century): J. B. Pitra, *Analecta sacra*, IV, p. 390; Syrian *Passio Quirici et Julittae*: H. Gressmann, *Berliner Sitzungsberichte*, 1887, pp. 339ff.

Pearl = Heavenly Kingdom: *Cyprianus, *De opere et eleemosynis*, ch. VII, p. 378 (ed. Hartel); Ps. Makarios (Mesopotamian, 5th century?), PG XXXIV, 666 CD; Ephrem, VI, 154 D, 162 CD.

Pearl = Christ: Acta Johannis (Asia minor, 2nd century), c. 113. Version of the doxology for the Communion: *Acta Apostolorum apocrypha*, ed. Lipsius-Bonnet, 2, 1, p. 213, 12; Clemens Alexandrinus, *Stromateis*, c. 16, 3; Gregory of Nazianzus, ed. Maurina, Paris, 1778, 1, *Homilia*, 39, 16 1, p. 658 B; Euagrius (Southern Gaul, ca. 430), PL XX, 1181; Origen (†202), *In Mattheum*, x, 8, PG XIII, 654 B.

Pearl = Host: C. Brockelmann, *Lexicon Syriacum*, 2nd ed., Halle, 1928; Payne-Smith, *Thesaurus syriacus*, s.v. margarita; Lamy (Ephrem) 1, 314; Johannes Chrysostomus, *Homilia*, 47, ed. Montfaucon, Paris, 1735, XII, p. 771 C = PG LXIII, 868 above; *Liturgia S. Johannis Chrysostomi, ibid.*, 798 DE = PG LXIII, 922 middle (on particles of the host).

Hellenistic nature fables: Pauly-Wissowa; Sbordone, *op.cit.*, pp. 133ff.

Proof by analogy: *Clemens Alexandrinus, *Paedagogus*, 1, ch. 12; *Catene* of Nicetas of Heraclea from Clemens, ed. Staehlin, 1, 328, and Usener, 231; Athanasius (†373): PG XXVIII, 790 CD, 791 AB; Origen: PG XIII, 849; *Physiologus*: Sbordone, *op.cit.*; Proklos (patriarch in Constantinople, 434-440): PG LXV, 720 C; Theophylactus of Achrida (ca. 1100): PG CXXIII, 290; *Ephrem Syrus (ca. 306-373), Nisibis, later

Edessa), II, 259-279, particularly 263 C, 267, 268 ABD, 269 D. Quoted, partly verbatim, by Usener, *op.cit.*, pp. 261f.; VI, 150-164: *Homiliae in Margaritam*, partly translated by H. Burgess, *Select Metrical Hymns and Homilies by Ephrem Syrus*, London, 1853, LXVIIff.; *Jacob of Sarug (Batna near Edessa, †521): P. Martin, *Zeitschrift der deutschen morgenländischen Gesellschaft*, XXX, 1876, pp. 217ff., 252f., 255.

Pearl = Soul: Manichaean: Edsman, *op.cit.*, pp. 190, 195; Mandaean: *ibid.*, p. 195; *Lidzbarski, *op.cit.*, p. 102; Christian: Ephrem, II, 279; Jacob of Sarug, *op.cit.*, p. 253; Soul Hymn in the *Acts of Thomas*: Hennecke, *op.cit.*, pp. 277ff.; Edsman, p. 193 (references).

Pearls = Men: Apostles: Edsman, p. 196; Allberry, I, p. 23; II, p. 199; Lamy (Ephrem), I, p. 69 (Thomas). Prophets: *Origen, PG XIII, 654 B. Catechumens: Ephrem, VI, 164 D; Lamy (Ephrem), I, pp. 70, 18. Monks: Lamy (Ephrem), IV, pp. 181, 701.

Pearl = Talisman: *Ephrem VI, 5th homily (see above); F. Haase, *Texte und Untersuchungen*, XXXIV, 4, pp. 51f.

Pearl Symbolism in the West (completeness of references has been aimed at in this case): *Cyprianus († at Carthage in 258), ed. Hartel, p. 278 (vita aeterna); Phoebadius of Agen († after 392), PL XX, 42 C (*epiklesis* of the Logos); *Euagrius (Southern Gaul, ca. 430): PL XX, 1181 at the end; Eucherius (Lyon, ca. 440), in J. B. Pitra, *Spicilegium Solesmense*, Paris, 1855, III, p. 403, n. 195 (doctrina evangelica); Ps-Ambrosius, *Sermo* 54, 2 (VI, 513, Mediolanum, not in PL) (Christ); Venantius Fortunatus (Tours, † ca. 500), *Carmen* III: PL LXXXVIII, 144 with commentary (Host); Damasus, *Carmen* VI: PL XIII, 578 (42 *cognomena* of Christ, without mention of the pearl).

Eggs at the *Mandaeans*: M. Lidzbarski, *Mandaeische Liturgien*, pp. 236, 273f.

III. *Some selected texts*

(The references are marked with asterisks in section II).

Clemens Alexandrinus, Stromateis, I, ch. 16, 3: "[Christ is] among the many small pearls the one (great one), in the great number of fishes the fish of splendor (καλλιχθύς)."

Idem, Paedagogus, I, ch. 12: "[The wretched women adorn themselves with pearls] and yet they would have the privilege of adorning themselves with the stone [in an extended sense, the jewel], the *Logos* of God, which the Scriptures once called a pearl (St. Matthew 7:6), the transparent and pure Jesus, the eye which became ἐπόπτης in the flesh, the transparent *Logos* through whom the flesh became worthy in the water [of baptism]; for likewise that shell which is created in the water surrounds the flesh, and out of it, the pearl is born."

Idem, from a *catene* of Nicetas of Heraclea, ed. Stählin, I, 328: "From Clement: A pearl is likewise the transparent and wholly pure Jesus whom the Virgin bore out of the divine lightning. For even as the pearl which originates in the flesh [of the oyster], in the shell, and in moisture, is logically a moist-shimmering and transparent body, so the divine *Logos*, after becoming flesh, is spiritual light out of the light and his body radiates with a shimmer."

Origen, In Mattheum, 10, 8: PG XIII, 654 B: "[The pearls can be likened to the prophets] but the leading pearl of them all, after the finding of which all others are found likewise, the highly esteemed pearl, the Christ of God, the *Logos* who stands above the venerable writings and thoughts of the law. . . ."

Gregory of Nazianzus, I, *Homilia* 39, 16, p. 658 B: "He [Christ] is addressed (προσαγορεύεται) as lamb, as pearl, and as drop [jewel in form of a drop?]."

Ephrem Syrus, ed. Assemani, II (in Greek): 263 CD: "The pearl is a stone born out of flesh, because from the shells emerges the pearl. Who then should not believe that even a god was born out of a [human] body? The former is created not through intercourse of the shells but through fusion of lightning and water. In the same way, Christ was conceived in the Virgin without sensuous desire; the Holy Ghost adding, out of her dough, that which was necessary to complete God."

Ibid., 268 AB: "Neither did He who was born crowd the seal of the Virgin nor did the virginity suffer damage; true, the virginity was expanded by the bulk of the Child at the hour of birth, but it returned to its seal even as the shells of the oyster, after having cast out the pearl, are reunited to form the identical inseparable junction and seal."

Homiliae in Margaritam, Syrian, VI, metric translation by Burgess, LXVIIf.: Beginning of the first homily: "Once upon a time/ I took up, my brethren/ a precious pearl./ I saw in it mysteries,/ relating to the kingdom/ images and types of the high majesty. . . ."

End of the second homily: "In thy beauty is depicted/ the beauty of the son./ Who put on suffering as a garment/ when the nails passed through him. The boring tools passed through thee,/ as they did through his hands. / And because of his sufferings he/ reigned,/ even as by thy suffering / thy beauty is increased."

Fifth homily: "Men who had put off their clothing/ dived and drew thee forth a precious pearl./ . . . natives of Galilee. They buried their bodies in the sea / and descended to thy side / and thou didst receive them kindly. . . . These poor men opened / their bosoms and

drew forth and displayed / their new riches / among the merchants. / They placed them as bracelets upon the wrists of men / as a life-saving amulet."

Lamy (Ephrem), I, *Hymni in festum Epiphaniae*, 70 n. 18: [Speaking of baptism] "immergit se qui vult e mare educere margaritas. Immergite vos, educite ex aquis absconditam munditiei margaritam, qua divina exornatur corona."—*Sermo de peccatrice* . . . 314 n. 1: ". . . nobis autem [Christus] margaritas dedit, sanctum scilicet suum corpus et sanguinem."

Jacob of Sarug (*Zeitschrift der deutschen morgenländischen Gesellschaft*, XXX, 1876, p. 252): "Voilà une véritable image du Christ . . . ; p. 253 [to the pearl] "Tu surpasses les mystères de la lumière et c'est pourquoi sa splendeur te sert de manteau. La fille du roi est gravée en toi et c'est pour cela que l'éclat t'environne. Il y a en toi quelque chose de mystérieux et de là vient que la vue de ta beauté subjugue ceux qui te contemplent. . . . [The pearl says:] Je suis la fille de la lumière et en moi il y a son image. Partie des hauteurs célestes je suis descendue jusqu'aux profondeurs des abîmes. . . . j'ai quitté la maison de mon père pour descendre aux abîmes. . . . je me suis lavée dans les eaux et ma beauté n'a pas été voilée; je me suis incarnée là et je suis montée ensuite à la lumière. . . . j'ai été conçue sans commixtion et je suis née sans copule antérieure."

Ps. Gregorius Thaumaturgus (Pitra, *Analecta sacra*, IV, p. 390): "Judaei legis tabulas tulerunt, Christiani adorandam margaritam possederunt."

Passio Quirici et Julittae, ed. Gressmann, pp. 339ff.: [The boy Quiricus says:] "When I prayed, my mother made a dress for me and adorned it with pearls. My mother is the church, and the pearls are the teachings of the Holy Ghost."

Cyprianus, De opere et eleemosynis, ch. 7, p. 378, ed. Hartel: "Margaritam, hoc est vitam aeternam, Christi cruore pretiosam."

Euagrius, PL XX, 1181: [In the final prayer of the converted Jew] "Tu es ipse vita et margarita, cristallum et jugum argenteum."

M. Lidzbarski, *Mandaeische Liturgien*, pp. 102f.: [The creator of the body speaks to the departed soul:] "Go in peace, thou noble one / who has been called a servant in the dwelling of the evil one / go in peace, thou pure pearl / who has been fetched out of the treasure of life . . . . the soul flies away and wanders on / until it arrives at the house of life."

Älteste Christliche Denkmäler*

Bestand und Chronologie

Vor fünfzehn Jahren schrieb A. M. Schneider im Blick auf die stadt-
römische Kirche: „Weder Archäologie noch Epigraphik haben bis heute
— trotz ausgedehnter Forschungsarbeit — auch nur ein christliches Denkmal zutage gefördert, das mit Sicherheit vor 200 angesetzt werden
könnte."[1] Schneiders Aufsatz diente dem Nachweis dieser These und
mußte sich notwendig primär mit den römischen Denkmälern befassen,
die man stellenweise noch heute in das 1. Jh. zurückdatieren möchte.
Schneider sah an dem Sarkophag des Prosenes, datierbar auf 217, die
älteste christliche Inschrift Roms[2]; er machte ferner wahrscheinlich, daß
als erste Katakombe die unter dem Namen des Calixtus laufende „um
200", unter Bischof Zephyrinus (199—217), angelegt wurde[3], womit erst
die Voraussetzungen für die ab ca 220 greifbare Katakombenmalerei geschaffen wurden[4]. Auf eine Einzeldiskussion der hier und dort als christlich behaupteten Denkmäler aus dem 1. oder 2. Jh. ging Schneider nicht

---

* unveröffentlicht.
[1] A. M. SCHNEIDER, Die ältesten Denkmäler der Römischen Kirche, in: Festschr. z.
Feier des zweihundertjähr. Bestehens der Akad. d. Wiss. in Göttingen, II Phil.-Hist.
Kl. (1951), 166.
[2] Ebd S. 168. — Beschreibung bei MATZ-v. DUHN, Antike Bildwerke in Rom II
(1881), 120 Nr. 2453. Inschrift bei CIL VI, 8598; DIEHL, ILCV II, 3332. — Zum Sarkophag bes. G. RODENWALDT, Ein Typus römischer Sarkophage, in: Bonner Jbb 147
(1942), 217—227, bes. 220 ff; Taf. 15, 2. — Neuerdings H. U. INSTINSKY, Marcus Aurelius Prosenes — Freigelassener und Christ am Kaiserhof (in: AAMZ [1964], Nr. 3, 113
bis 129); dazu Besprechung durch H. BRANDENBURG, in: JbAC 7 (1964), 155 ff.
[3] A. M. SCHNEIDER, aaO 177. — Weiterführend und die spätere Datierung im Ganzen bestätigend jetzt L. REEKMANS, La tombe du Pape Corneille et sa région cémétériale (Roma Sotterranea Cristiana IV) Città del Vaticano 1964.
[4] Zum Stande der Forschung vgl. RGG³ IV, 630—639 (Malerei und Plastik); in
Bälde: J. KOLLWITZ, Die Malerei der konstantin. Zeit, in: Akten des VII. Internat.
Kongresses für Christl. Archäologie in Trier 1965.

ein; auch klammerte er bewußt die Funde unter der Confessio von S. Peter zu Rom aus — „bis zum Erscheinen der Grabungspublikation"[5].

Unsere Frage ist nun darauf gerichtet, die von Schneider ausgeklammerten oder als außer-römisch bewußt übergangenen Denkmäler der frühesten Zeit daraufhin zu betrachten, ob oder wieweit sie von Christen stammen oder für Christen gemacht wurden. Wir wollen dabei versuchen, den Wahrscheinlichkeitsgrad möglicher Feststellungen anzugeben.

Bei einer Sichtung der Materialien wird man sich zunächst über grundlegende methodische Regeln Rechenschaft geben müssen. Der Einblick in die Literatur zeigt, daß häufig bei der Untersuchung „christlicher" Denkmäler andere methodische Kriterien angewandt werden als bei paganen; handelt es sich doch, so heißt es, um „Zeugnisse des Glaubens", bei deren Deutung auch der Glaube hermeneutisch in Ansatz gebracht werden muß. So richtig das ist, so selbstverständlich sollte doch anderseits sein, daß Chronologie und religionsgeschichtliche Bestimmung eines Denkmals nicht Glaubensfragen sind, vielmehr glaubensindifferente und profane Methoden fordern. Als methodische Regel muß gelten: bei einem Denkmal, das *nicht* durch eindeutige Merkmale — neutestamentliche Thematik, Inschrift u. ä. — sich als christlich ausweist, darf eine Zuweisung zur christlichen Kunst nur mit größter Vorsicht geschehen. Alttestamentliche Bilder und Symbole besagen in der Frühzeit — insbesondere der vorkonstantinischen Zeit — noch nichts für den christlichen Glauben des Bestellers oder Künstlers, da jüdische Herkunft möglich ist. Der Fundort kann gewisse Rückschlüsse erlauben, ist aber nicht eindeutiges Indiz, wie der Befund der Praetextat-Katakombe zu Rom illustrieren kann[6]. — Da wir in diesem Aufsatz nach den ältesten christlichen Denkmälern fragen, spielt es keine Rolle, ob ein Denkmal „häretisch" oder „großkirchlich" ist, ob es sich um ein Werk von künstlerischer Qualität, des Handwerks, um eine Inschrift oder auch eine fehlerhafte Kritzelei handelt. Auch eine Mauer oder eingestürzte Aedicula könnte dann als christliches Denkmal gelten, wenn sie nachweisbar einst für Christen errichtet wurden.

---

[5] A. M. SCHNEIDER äußerte sich zum offiziellen Grabungsbericht in: ThLZ 77 (1952), 321—326.

[6] Vgl. M. GUETSCHOW, Das Museum der Praetextat-Katakombe (Città del Vaticano 1938, MemPontAcc IV, 2), 35 ff. — Die verdienstvolle Verf. vermag gegen P. STYGER, Die Röm. Katakomben (1933), 35, 76, 159 f aufzuzeigen, daß in den Gängen der christlichen Katakomben eindeutig heidnische Sarkophage und Deckel, zT als Fragmente, gefunden wurden.

Vorsicht ist geboten bei Verwendung der Kategorie „kryptochristlich",
da hiermit leicht jede pagane Darstellung als „getauft" ausgegeben werden kann. Gelegentlich wird man freilich von religiös „neutraler" Thematik sprechen dürfen, etwa wenn sich Christen oder auch Juden der
paganen Jahreszeiten-Symbolik bedienen, oder auch der Komposition
der „dextrarum iunctio". Um allerdings bei einer religiös neutralen Thematik ein christliches Denkmal zu behaupten, bedarf es wenigstens *eines*
eindeutigen Kriteriums.

I

Wir setzen ein im *Westen,* weil hier für die chronologische Bestimmung der Denkmäler bessere Voraussetzungen gegeben sind. Daß seit
Mitte des 1. Jh.s im Westen des Imperium Romanum Christen lebten,
und zwar als Gemeinde, als ἐκκλησία, wird eindeutig durch die Existenz
des paulinischen Römerbriefes bezeugt[7]. Er erlaubt zwar keine detaillier-
ten Rückschlüsse auf Stärke und genauere Zusammensetzung der Gemeinde in Rom, macht aber deutlich, daß es sich um eine griechisch sprechende Gemeinde handelt. Vermutlich weist auch das, was in Röm 9—11
ausgeführt wird, auf einen Dialog mit der Synagoge hin. Man wird auch
im Westen an den vielerorts wahrscheinlichen Weg der Ausbreitung des
Christentums über die Synagoge zu denken haben. Ist nun aber ab Mitte
des 1. Jh.s in Rom eine griechisch sprechende christliche Gemeinde gesichert, so spricht grundsätzlich nichts dagegen, daß auch in Ostia und
Puteoli, den Hafenstädten, wie auch in Pompeji und Herculaneum schon
früh Gemeinden bestanden haben können. Freilich wird man gerade bei
den letzten beiden, die i. J. 79 zerstört wurden, dies erst evident zu machen haben.

a) Wie ein vaticinium ex eventu liest sich die seit 1885 durch A. Mau
bekannt gewordene Kritzelei in einem *pompejanischen* Hause, die nur
aus den beiden untereinander geschriebenen Worten *„Sodom"* und *„Gomorrha"* besteht und durch keinen Kontext interpretiert wird (Fig. 4)[8].

---

[7] Der aus Korinth von Paulus zw. 56 und 58 geschriebene Brief setzt eindeutig eine
gemischte, dh aus Juden- und Heidenchristen zusammengesetzte Gemeinde voraus;
vgl. SANDAY-HEADLAM, The Epistle to the Romans (ICC 7 Edinburgh 1955), XIII ff; O.
MICHEL, Der Brief an die Römer (Meyerk[11] 1957), 1; M. DIBELIUS, Rom und die
Christen im 1. Jh., in: Botschaft und Geschichte II (1956), 177 ff.

[8] Regio IX, Insula I, Haus 26; vgl. die Notiz in Bull. Inst. di Corrisp. Archeol.
(1885), 97 f; E. DIEHL, ILCV II, 4935; M. DELLA CORTE, Pompei e i Cristiani, in:
Archivio Storico della Prov. di Salerno 6 (1927), 178; J.-B. FREY, Les juifs à Pompei,
in: Rev. Bibl. 42 (1933), 369 f; A. BALDI, La Pompei Giudaico-Cristiana (Cava dei Tir-
reni 1964), 21.

Fig. 4: Pompeji, Graffito: Sodom Gomorrha

Mau schreibt 1909 zu dem Graffito: „Aut ab Judaeo aut ab Christiano scriptam esse apparet."[9] Man hat immer wieder versucht — ausgehend von Röm 9,29 oder auch in Heranziehung von Mt 10,15 (vgl. Mk 6,11, textus receptus) — in diesen Worten ein christliches Bekenntnis in letzter Stunde bei Ausbruch des Vesuvs im Jahre 79 zu erkennen. Besser noch als die angegebenen Stellen ließe sich 2Petr 2,6 mit dem Schicksal Pompejis und dem fragmentarischen Graffito verbinden: „So hat Er auch die Städte Sodom und Gomorrha zum Untergang durchs Feuer verdammt, als warnendes Beispiel für die künftigen Frevler"; oder auch Jud 7. Jedoch ist die alttestamentliche Geschichte von Sodom und Gomorrha, neben der von Adma und Zeboim, derart stark verbreitet — teils auch mit der letzteren verbunden[10] —, daß sich schon durch jüdische Tradition allein[11] die Aufnahme der beiden Worte als Unheilsbezeichnung erklären und sogar ihre Verbreitung in nichtjüdischen und nichtchristlichen Sprachräumen verstehen lassen würde. Besonders auch die Verbindung von „Sodom und Gomorrha" mit dem „Rest"-Gedanken in Jes 1,9 ist von nachweisbarer geschichtlicher Wirkung gewesen. Der Hinweis auf die Leiden des sodomitischen Landes zwar, der am Ende des VI. Buches der Oracula Sibyllina — unmittelbar vor den Versen über das dereinst am Himmel erscheinende „glückselige Holz"[12] — steht, gehört in eine spätere Zeit und bezieht sich auf die Parusie Christi als endzeitlicher Richter. Ob man nun die Sodom-Gomorrha-Kritzelei von jüdi-

---

[9] CIL IV, Suppl. 2 (1909), 568 Nr. 4976.

[10] Vgl. O. Eissfeldt, in: RGG³ VI, 114 f. — Ein Echo von Mt 10,15 sah in der Sodom-Inschrift Eb. Nestle, in: ZNW 5 (1904), 167 f: er nimmt an, sie stamme von einem Christen, „der in Pompeji schlechte Aufnahme fand". Dort weitere Lit.

[11] H. L. Strack-P. Billerbeck, Komm. zum NT aus Talmud und Midrasch I³ (1961), 571 ff, mit reichem rabbinischem Material.

[12] Or. Sib. VI, 21—25 und 26—28 (GCS 8, 131 f; Geffcken).

scher — was wahrscheinlicher ist — oder von heidnischer Hand angebracht sein läßt, ob auf das Erdbeben d. J. 62 nChr bezogen oder auf die
ersten Aschenregen d. J. 79, jedenfalls läßt sich von hier aus kein Beweis
für Christen in Pompeji führen[13].

b) Anders wäre die Lage mit der *Christianus-Inschrift* in Pompeji —
von M. Guarducci kürzlich als „la più antica iscrizione col nome dei Cristiani" bezeichnet[14] —, wenn diese noch erhalten und eindeutig interpre-
tierbar, bzw. wenn die Lesart „christianos", die ja hier in Pompeji in lateinischer Form ca drei Jahrzehnte vor der griechischen Form χριστιανοί[15]
aufträte, eindeutig bezeugt wäre. Jedoch ist seit der Erstveröffentlichung
1862 durch A. Kiessling[16] (Fig. 5a) die Kohle-Kritzelei verschwunden,
nachweislich seit 1864. Da außer durch Kiessling eine von diesem unabhängige Kopie durch G. Minervini angefertigt wurde (Fig. 5b), ferner
ein schriftliches Zeugnis des Grabungsleiters G. Fiorelli besteht, so liegen
drei, und zwar entscheidend voneinander abweichende Lesarten vor[17]:

CHRISTIANOS (Minervini) — HRISTIANI (Kiessling) — HRISTIA-
NUS (Fiorelli).

C. Zangemeister endlich bietet in CIL IV, 679 (1871): CIIRISTIR.ĄII
(Fig. 5c). Aufgrund des nur noch aus zweiter Hand feststellbaren Tatbe-
standes und wegen der nicht mehr überprüfbaren Differenzen wird man
sagen müssen, daß Kiesslings Urteil, hier „das erste der in Pompeji gefundenen Denkmäler zu haben, das sich auf Christen bezieht"[18], nicht

---

[13] Für Juden in Pompeji wird vielfach als Beleg herangezogen ein semitischer Graffito, gefunden 1931 an einem pompejanischen Kryptoporticus; J.-B. FREY, in: Rev.
Bibl. 42 (1933), 382 f; Pl. XXIII, 2, 3, sowie M. DELLA CORTE und A. BALDI, aaO 21 ff.
— Der Text ist schwer zu lesen u. die Schrift — ob hebräisch, palmyrenisch oder gar
griechische Worte in hebr. Buchstaben — ist schwer eindeutig zu machen. Bis jetzt ist
es wohl richtiger auf eine Verwertung zu verzichten, da die Anwesenheit von Juden in
Pompeji ohnehin größte Wahrscheinlichkeit für sich hat.

[14] RQ 57 (1962), 116—125.

[15] Erstmalig für Antiochien in Apg 11,26 bezeugt. Es ist im Griechischen „entweder
ganz ein lateinisches Lehnwort . . . oder es besitzt eine entlehnte lateinische Endung"
(KARPP, in: RAC II, 1132). Vgl. H. CONZELMANN, Die Apostelgeschichte (HNT 7, 1963),
68; zum Christennamen bereits A. v. HARNACK, in: SAB 43 (1915), 762.

[16] Bull. Inst. di Corrisp. Archeol. (1862), 92 f. — KIESSLINGS Apographon ist in CIL
IV, Tab. XVI, 2 wiedergegeben; die Inschrift wird unter Nr. 679 besprochen; biblio-
graph. Nachträge in CIL IV, Suppl. 2, 461. — Vgl. auch DACL VI, 1482 ff.

[17] Minervinis Apograph: CIL IV, Tab. XVI, 3. G. FIORELLI bei G. B. DE ROSSI, in:
Bull. di Arch. Christ. 2 (1864), 70 f.

[18] Bull. Inst. (1862), 92: „Per quanto sappia io, è questo il primo fra' monumenti
trovati a Pompei, il quale si referisca ai Cristiani . . ." Er schlägt als Lesart vor: „igni
gaude Christiane" — in bezug auf die Neronische Christenverfolgung. Zur Kritik vgl.
V. SCHULTZE, in: ZKG 5 (1881), 125 ff. — A. BALDI, aaO 25 f, nimmt — wie meist — M.

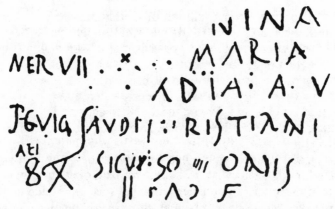

Fig. 5a: Pompeji, „Christianos“-Graffito (Kiessling)

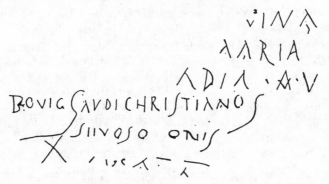

Fig. 5b: Pompeji, „Christianos“-Graffito (Minervini)

VINΛ

N E R V I I . . . . . ΛARIA

Λ DIA · AV

℞G · VIG SAVDI CIIRISTIRΛII

AET

8 X SICVI · SO . . ONIS

. . . . . . F

Fig. 5c: Pompeji, „Christianos“-Graffito (Zangemeister)

haltbar ist. Welche neuen Argumente bringt nun aber M. Guarducci vor? Sie greift auf die ältesten Apographa zurück und möchte, da Minervini und Kiessling in Zeile 4 der Inschrift weitgehend übereinstimmten, lesen:

Bovios audi(t) Christianos
sevos o(s)ores

„Bovios hört auf die Christen, die grausamen Hasser". Hierbei würde die den Christen beigelegte Apposition „sevos" die später bei Tacitus den Juden und Christen gegebene Charakteristik des „odium humani generis" (Annales XV, 44, 4; Hist. V, 5. 1) der Sache nach vorwegnehmen[19]. M. Guarducci nimmt an, auf der Kritzelei habe ein Heide einen Mitbürger mit dem öfter belegten Namen Bovios verhöhnen wollen; es handele sich hier also nicht um einen christlichen, sondern um einen *anti*christlichen Graffito, der aber die Existenz von Christen in Pompeji beweise[20]. Das vermutlich nach dem Erdbeben d. J. 62 erbaute und in ärmlicher Umgebung stehende Haus ein „albergo dei Cristiani" zu nennen, nur weil sich hier die soeben besprochene Kritzelei befand, möchte man schon wegen der mindestens vier obszönen Kritzeleien der Umgebung ablehnen[21].

Der neue Vorstoß von M. Guarducci, eine bereits durch A. v. Harnack verworfene Inschrift[22] aufzuwerten und als historische Quelle für die Anwesenheit von Christen in Pompeji zu sichern, läßt sich methodisch

---

DELLA CORTE unkritisch auf und verteidigt die christliche Lesart; weitere Lit. zur Frage RQ 57, 118 f. Erwähnenswert ist nur noch der Vorschlag von W. R. NEUBOLD, in: AJA 30, 1926, 291 ff, es handele sich um eine aramäische Kritzelei, bei der das Wort ‚Christianos‘ untranskribiert blieb. Der übersetzte Text verweise auf eine pagane Inschrift über Christen und laute: „A strange mind has driven A. and he has pressed in among the Christians who make a man a prisoner as a laughing—stock (to the people of Pompeji)". — Die sachlichste Stellungnahme stammt von D. MALLARDO, in: Riv. di Studi Pompeiani 1934/35, 136 ff: Aramäische Lesart scheidet aus, das Wort ‚Christianos‘ ist nicht sicher genug bezeugt; die Inschrift läßt sich weder pro noch contra verwenden.

[19] Vgl. RQ 57 (1962), 121 ff. Für das den Juden zugesprochene odium humani generis verweist schon H. FUCHS, Tacitus über die Christen, in: VigChr 4 (1950), 86 f auf Diodor XXXIV, 1, 1–2, der den Haß der Juden gegen die Menschheit als παραδόσιμος seit der Austreibung aus Ägypten bezeichnet, von Moses so gewollt.

[20] M. GUARDUCCI, in: RQ 57 (1962), 124.

[21] Vgl. CIL IV, Nr. 2010, 2013, 2016, 2021. Die Bezeichnung „Albergo dei Cristiani" bei M. DELLA CORTE, I Cristiani a Pompei, in: RendAcc Napoli, NS 19 (1938/39), 7. — M. GUARDUCCI geht noch weiter und meint, DE ROSSIS Deutung dieses Hauses als eines „luogo di convegno degli antichi Cristiani", sei „molto discutibile".

[22] Vgl. A. v. HARNACK, Mission und Ausbreitung des Christentums, (1924), 624 Anm. 8.

nicht bejahen. Gewiß sagt die Verfasserin, man könne nur mit größter Vorsicht Hypothesen aufstellen, erhofft aber von der vorgetragenen schließlich, daß sie „ins Schwarze getroffen habe"[23]. Jedoch: Die Lesart der vermutlich durch Witterungseinflüsse verwischten Kritzelei war von Anfang an vom Wunschdenken geprägt, wodurch allein sich die Verschiedenheit der Apographa erklären läßt. Wenn M. Guarducci davon ausgeht, daß man De Rossi-Fiorelli vertrauen dürfe — so ist das kein Argument; auch daß hinsichtlich Zeile 4 weitgehend Übereinstimmung bestehe, kann nicht überzeugen. Zu fragen ist vielmehr: Wie kommt Zangemeister 1871 dazu zu lesen: PG. VIG SAUDI CIIRISTIRAII? Weiter müßte man fragen, ob Kiesslings Apographon beim Vergleich mit dem von Minervini sich nicht nur als wesentlich vollständiger, sondern auch als in den Einzelzügen zuverlässiger erweist. Ist dem aber so, dann ist — angesichts vorliegender Divergenzen und der Unmöglichkeit nachzuprüfen — die „Christianus"-Lesart als nicht gesichert zu verwerfen und muß M. Guarduccis Hypothese ausscheiden.

c) In den Notizie degli Scavi della Accademia Nazionale dei Lincei hatte 1958 der inzwischen verstorbene verdiente Ausgräber von Pompeji M. Della Corte die zwischen 1951 und 1956 in Pompeji gefundenen Inschriften veröffentlicht, darunter eine nicht unbeträchtliche Anzahl von neuen „christlichen Denkmälern". Wir diskutieren hier nur die für das Gesamtbild weiterführenden, zunächst das auf einer Amphore säuberlich aufgetragene *Monogramm* ✳[24]. Es ist bekannt, daß man in diesem Zeichen die Verbindung von Chi und Rho sieht, daß man vom konstantinischen Monogramm oder Christogramm spricht, weil seine christliche Verwendung ab Konstantin gesichert ist. Die erste durch Datum gesicherte Verwendung des christlichen ✳ begegnet auf einem Inschriftenfragment unter S. Lorenzo f. l. m. zu Rom, auf 323 datierbar[25]. Die entscheidende Frage ist, ob schon vor dem 4. Jh. die Buchstabenverbindung als Christogramm angenommen werden darf. Auffallend ist, daß besonders auf Amphoren das Zeichen häufig erscheint; so auch in Pompeji. Bereits 1868 war auf drei Amphoren das Zeichen im Zusammenhang mit dem Namen Diokles festgestellt[26] und zwar jeweils verbunden mit zwei vorangehenden Buchstaben: λ̄ Γ ✳; vermutlich handelt es sich

---

[23] RQ 57 (1962), 125: „. . . ha colto nel segno . . .“

[24] Vgl. Notizie degli Scavi (1958), 180 Nr. 645 (mit Abb.).

[25] DIEHL, ILCV II, Nr. 3257 — und dazu G. B. DE ROSSI in: Bull. Arch. Crist. I (1863), 22 f.

[26] CIL IV, Nr. 2878—2880 und dazu Tab. XLVII, 6—8.

um ein Warenzeichen und soll mit Chi und Rho die Qualität des Inhaltes der Amphore als χρηστός bezeichnet werden. Die Buchstabenverbindung ist auch in Form von ⳨ auf einer weiteren Amphore belegt und durch die Aufschrift Σέραπις δῶρα als nichtchristlichen Ursprungs geklärt[27]. Daß ⳨ in den Oxyrhynchos- und anderen ägyptischen Papyri Abkürzung für χρηματίζειν, χρῆσθαι, χρίω, χειρόγραφον, aber auch sonst einfach für χρόνος, χρυσός, χρηστός sein kann, darauf ist öfters hingewiesen worden[28]. Beispiele des auf nichtchristlichen Münzprägungen vorkommenden Chi-Rho gibt bereits H. Leclercq[29]. Hat man sich einmal mit der Reichhaltigkeit des Vorkommens von Monogrammen allgemein und der Chi-Rho-Verbindung speziell in der Antike vertraut gemacht, so kann man nicht umhin, eindeutige Kriterien für ein Christogramm zu fordern. Denn das Monogramm als solches bleibt ja konstant und wird von den Christen nur in neuer Sinngebung — eben als Hinweis auf Christus — gebraucht, kann also nur durch den Kontext und die Eindeutigkeit des Fundmilieus in seiner Bedeutung bestimmt werden. Da bei den Vorkommen in Pompeji kein derartiger Kontext vorliegt und das Fundmilieu eher gegen als für Christen spricht[30], wird man einen Bezug auf Christus in das Monogramm nicht einlesen dürfen. Es wird sich vielmehr um Besitzer-, Hersteller-, oder auch Prüfer-Zeichen handeln[31].

Anhangsweise mag noch gesagt sein, daß die Möglichkeit einer Verwendung des Christogramms in vorkonstantinischer Zeit nicht auszuschließen ist, daß aber bis jetzt ein klarer Beweis nicht erbracht werden konnte. Die von F. J. Dölger in Band I seines IXΘYC-Werkes verzeichneten vorkonstantinischen Vorkommen basieren auf der zu seiner Zeit üblichen Frühdatierung aller christlichen Denkmäler, deren Anfänge man in das 1. Jh. zu setzen trachtete[32]. So nahm man auch keinen Anstoß an einer von L. Ross 1845 edierten und in die Antoninen-Zeit datierten christlichen Inschrift aus Melos, die auf einer kleinen, in einer Katakombe gefundenen Stele unter dem ⳨ in schönen Lettern den Namen ΑΛΕΞΑΝΔΡΟΥ zeigt[33]. Man datierte aufgrund der Schrifttypen,

---

[27] CIL IV Suppl. 3 Nr. 9812 — vgl. auch IV, 2777.

[28] Vgl. zB F. J. Dölger, Ichthys I, 369 ff; M. Sulzberger, Le symbole de la croix, in: Byzantion 2 (1925), 397 f; J. Sauer, in: LThK² II (1958), 1177.

[29] DACL III, 1, 1481 ff.

[30] Vgl. E. Renan, in: Journal des Savants (1876), 703 f.

[31] Dies gilt für CIL IV, Nr. 2878—2880, sowie ebenso für die nicht monogrammatisch verbundenen XPE-Buchstaben in CIL IV, 6344—6346 und XV, 4760.

[32] Dölger, aaO 364 f.

[33] L. Ross, IG III 246b; Kirchhoff, CIG IV, Nr. 9290; H. Grégoire, Recueil des inscriptions grecques chrétiennes d'Asie Mineure I (Paris 1922), Nr. 208.

stellte jedoch nicht in Rechnung, was später H. Grégoire nachweisen konnte, daß in dem unweit gelegenen Delos, im Umkreis der vielen alten Vorbilder, sich eine Tendenz zur archaisierenden Schrift nachweisen läßt[34], sodaß Gleiches auch auf Melos der Fall sein könnte. Grégoires Datierung in das 4. Jh. dürfte sachgemäßer sein. Ebensowenig dürfen das Chi-Rho auf einem Ossuar der Dominus-flevit-Grabung in Jerusalem, das dem 1. Jh. anzugehören scheint[35], christlich interpretiert und von hier aus andere Kreuze oder kreuzähnliche Zeichen der Nekropole als judenchristlicher Symbolismus verstanden werden[36]. Endlich ist noch der Versuch von M. Burzachechi zu erwähnen[37], etwa 20 Beispiele als vorkonstantinische Christogramme zu diskutieren, wobei sein Beweis für das Alter entweder allgemein von der Schrifttypik ausgeht oder er sich der Datierung von De Rossi anschließt. Noch einen Schritt weiter ging jüngst P. Ciprotti, der in den mit ☧ versehenen Amphoren unter Berufung auf Della Corte und A. Maiuri Gefäße sieht, möglicherweise „usate dai cristiani per l'aqua ed il vino, necessari per le celebrazioni liturgiche"[38]. Das dürfte reichlich gesucht sein und wäre für eine so frühe Zeit erst zu beweisen. Ebenso wie man in Dura-Europos nicht auf Christus zu beziehende Chi-Rho-Monogramme aus der Mitte des 3. Jh.s gefunden hat[39], so wird man wegen fehlender Evidenz für Pompeji — und für die vorkonstantinische Zeit überhaupt bis zum Beweis des Gegenteils — auf eine interpretatio christiana des Zeichens ☧ verzichten müssen[40].

---

[34] Ebd. Nr. 214 und dazu M. SULZBERGER, aaO 398.

[35] B. BAGATTI — J. T. MILIK, Gli scavi del „Dominus Flevit" (Pubblicazioni dello Studium Biblicum Franciscanum 13 Jerusalem 1958), 178 u. Falttaf. vor dem Titelblatt. Zur Kritik vgl. M. NOTH, in: ZDPV 67 (1960), 184.

[36] Vgl. E. TESTA, Il Simbolismo dei Giudeo-Cristiani (Jerusalem 1962); zur Kritik vgl. meinen Aufsatz: Kreuzzeichen u. Kreuz in: JbAC 5 (1962), 96 und Anm. 16—18 [in diesem Band S. 30 f].

[37] M. BURZACHECHI, Sull'uso pre-costantiniano del monogramma greco di Cristo, in: RendPontAcc Ser. III 28, 3 (1955/56), 197—211.

[38] P. CIPROTTI, Postille sui Cristiani di Pompei e di Ercolano, in: Miscellanea Antonio Piolanti II (Rom 1964), 1—17, bes. S. 9 unter Bezug auf Zeitungsaufsätze von DELLA CORTE, in: „Roma" vom 18. 1. 1953 und A. MAIURI, in: „Corriere della Sera" vom 22. 1. 1953.

[39] Vgl. C. B. WELLES, in: Yale Classical Studies 14 (1955), 123—209, Inschr. Nr. 206, 210 und 216.

[40] Vgl. J. CARCOPINO, Études d'histoire chrétienne² (1963), 307; beachtlich ist, daß für Pompeji selbst M. GUARDUCCI, I graffiti sotto la Confessione di S. Pietro in Vaticano I (1958), 258 Anm. 1, die Lösung als Christogramm ablehnt; zuletzt auch P. BRUUN, in: Acta Instituti Romani Finlandiae I, 2 (Helsinki 1963), 97 ff. — Mit Recht hat jüngst auch W. KELLNER die 319 auf Münzen Konstantins auftretenden T-Zeichen — in einer Münz-Emission sogar vom Kranz umgeben — als lateinische Ordinalzahlen erweisen können und die Deutung auf Tau-Kreuz verworfen: „T — ein

d) In einem Hause der Insula XIII der I. Region von Pompeji fand Della Corte 1955 die Kritzelei (Höhe 20 cm, Breite 11 cm):

Fig. 6: Pompeji, sog. „Vivat Crux"-Akklamation

Della Corte erblickt hierin eine neue Bestätigung für die Anwesenheit von Christen in Pompeji und liest: *viv(at) crux, v(ivat)*[41]. Die entscheidende Schwierigkeit dieser Deutung liegt darin, daß vor 79 nChr die theologischen Voraussetzungen dafür fehlen, im Kreuz nicht nur ein Symbol für Kreuzigung und Auferstehung, sondern ein „Siegeszeichen" zu sehen, das man „hochleben" lassen kann. Eine solche Kreuzes-Akklamation setzt eine Weiterentfaltung der paulinischen und johanneischen Theologie voraus, wie sie in den ersten Jahrhunderten der Kirche nur selten faßbar ist. Man spricht zwar im Blick auf Kreuzesvorkommen des 1. Jh.s nicht von Kreuzes*theologie*, sondern von Kreuzes*kult*[42], läßt also der Reflexion den Brauch vorangehen, was nicht a limine abzuweisen ist; fragwürdig aber wird es, wenn man als Beleg für einen christlichen Kreuzeskult im 1. Jh. das „Kreuz" in der Casa del Bicentenario zu Herculaneum heranzieht[43] und mit der christlichen Interpretation dieses „Kreuzes" den „vivat-crux-vivat"-Graffito von Pompeji stützt (Abb. 30).

christliches Symbol auf Münzen Constantins des Großen?" in: Tortulae (30. Suppl. Heft zur RQ), 1966, 187 ff. — Zur Frage, ob das „Christogramm" auf ein ursprünglicheres „Staurogramm" zurückgeht, vgl. unten S. 177 f.

[41] Siehe Notizie degli Scavi (1958), 113 Nr. 181 und Tav. V; A. Baldi, La Pompei Giudaico-Cristiana (1964), 67 u. fig. 13; P. Ciprotti, aaO 14 f.

[42] F. di Capua, Il „Mysterium Crucis" di Ercolano, in: RendAcc Napoli NS 23 (1946—1948), 159—189.

[43] So P. Ciprotti, aaO 15; vgl. auch M. Guarducci, Osservazioni sulla Croce di Ercolano, in: RM 60/61 (1953/54), 224—233, in dem die Verf. in Herculaneum das christliche Kreuz-Symbol bejaht, freilich nicht mit Maiuri soweit gehen will, in dem mitgefundenen Schränkchen (mit den Spielwürfeln) einen Altar und im kleinen

Zwei häufig begegnende Zirkelschlüsse wird man erkennen und meiden müssen: einerseits arbeitet man oftmals mehrere Hypothesen heraus und läßt sie in der Neben- und Zuordnung dann als These, schließlich als Evidenz erscheinen; anderseits geht man vom Dogma einer Spätdatierung aus und stempelt deshalb bereits die Diskussion eines frühen Auftretens als „unwissenschaftlich" ab. Beispiel für den ersten Zirkel: Da Christogramme auf Amphoren in Pompeji möglich sind und das „Kreuz" in Herculaneum die Anwesenheit von Christen am Fuße des Vesuv vor d. J. 79 wahrscheinlich macht, darf das Graffito „vivat-crux-vivat" für einen christlichen Kreuzeskult sprechen. Beispiel für den zweiten Zirkel: Da wir erst ab 350 Gewißheit für ein Vorkommen des Kreuzes als christliches Symbol haben, kann es weder in Talpioth noch in Herculaneum christliche Kreuze geben.

Die Bemerkung war notwendig, weil der Fund in Herculaneum immer erneut als feststehendes Zeugnis des Christentums aus der 2. Hälfte des 1. Jh.s angesehen und zur Erhellung anderer Funde verwendet wird[44]. Dies gilt auch für eine 1954 in Pompeji gefundene Inschrift[45]:

REX ES
XI DO

Unter der Voraussetzung, daß mit lateinisch sprechenden Christen in Pompeji und Herculaneum zu rechnen ist, haben Della Corte und Ciprotti die zweite Zeile aufgelöst in: „Christus Jesus Dominus" und in dem Gesamttext eine Anspielung auf die Worte des Pilatusverhörs vermutet[46]. Indes kann Zeile 2 auch als eine bei Wandkritzeleien oft begegnende Datums-Angabe gelesen werden: X ID(us) O(ctobres). Zeile 1 hätte dann nur eine der üblichen Spottbezeichnungen enthalten.

Zimmer des Oberstocks ein Haus-Oratorium zu erkennen (op. cit. 229). — Vgl. auch meine Ausführungen in diesem Bande S. 11.

[44] Gegen die christliche Interpretation des Herculaneum-„Kreuzes" sprachen sich von katholischer Seite aus: G. DE JERPHANION, La croix d'Herculaneum?, in: OrChrP 7 (1941), 5—35; C. ALBIZZATI, Tre casi insigni, in: Athenaeum, Studi Periodici di Letteratura e Storia dell'Antichità NS 19 (1941), 59—71; L. DE BRUYNE, La „crux interpretum" di Ercolano, in: RivAC 21 (1944/45), 281—309; vgl. auch E. LUCCHESI-PALLI, LThK² VI (1961), 610: „Das Kreuz . . . von Herculaneum . . . wird . . . nicht einstimmig als christlich gedeutet."

[45] M. DELLA CORTE, Notizie degli Scavi (1958), 136 u. Tav. V.

[46] M. DELLA CORTE, ibid. und P. CIPROTTI, aaO 14: Lk 23,3 oder 37 — nicht Joh 18,37, da die Entstehung des Vierten Evangeliums zu nahe an 79 nChr herankomme! Wenn aber Psalm 43,5 aufgenommen würde, so wäre eher ein Jude als ein Christ Verfasser der Kritzelei.

---

e) Zu den pompejanischen Neufunden gehört ferner ein von Della Corte christlich interpretiertes schönes Fresko am Eingang zu einer Schenke (mit Bacchus- und Priapus-Bildern), das einen *Phönix* mit zwei flankierenden Pfauen darstellt[47] und die Beischrift trägt: PHOENIX FELIX ET TU (Taf. XII Abb. 31). Della Corte hat hierin ein christliches Sinnbild gesehen. Dagegen spricht, abgesehen von dem gesamten Kontext der Räumlichkeit, die Tatsache, daß die erste literarische Aufnahme der Phönixlegende im Christentum erst um 95 nChr, in 1Clem 25, als Sinnbild der Auferstehung, begegnet und weitere Verbreitung auch in der Kunst wohl erst nach Entstehung des Physiologus im 4. Jh. möglich wurde. Wir bezweifeln sehr, daß das als ältestes christliches Vorkommen geltende Phönix-Fresko in der Cappella Greca der Priscilla-Katakombe zu Rom[49] wirklich schon in das 3. Jh. gehört. Man bedenke, daß F. Wirth von stil- und baugeschichtlicher Analyse ausgehend die Zeit 320—350 zur Erwägung stellte, freilich ohne Sicherheit[50]. Es kann zwar nicht ausgeschlossen werden, daß der Phönix — im paganen Bereich Symbol des aurum saeculum und der renovatio[51] — im Christentum schon vor den ersten literarischen Zeugnissen Ende 1. Jh. eine Deutung auf die Unsterblichkeit, also im eschatologischen Sinne, erfuhr; eine derartige christliche Übernahme müßte jedoch eindeutig nachgewiesen werden; in Pompeji spricht nichts dafür.

f) Vor einigen Jahren wurde von H. L. Hempel ein Neufund mitgeteilt, den er 1957 zusammen mit F. Gerke in *Cimitile* bei *Nola* machte: bisher „so gut wie unbeachtete" *Fresken* in der sog. Basilica dei SS. Martiri, die bei Grabungen südlich der Felixbasilika des Paulinus von Nola zutage kamen und deren Datierung „in das zweite Jahrhundert . . . als sicher gelten" könne[52]. Die Datierung wurde, übereinstimmend mit dem Ausgräber Chierici, mit den „Ziegelmaßen und der Mauertechnik" be-

---

[47] M. Della Corte, aaO 83 Nr. 25 (mit Abb auf S. 84). Vgl. auch P. Ciprotti, aaO 16; A. Baldi, aaO 150 f.

[48] Ed. Funk-Bihlmeyer, Die Apostol. Väter (1924), 49 f.

[49] A. Ferrua, Tre note d'iconografia paleocristiana, in: Miscellanea Giulio Belvederi (Città del Vaticano 1954), 273 ff.

[50] F. Wirth, Die römische Wandmalerei vom Untergang Pompejis bis ans Ende des 3. Jh.s (1934), 213 ff; zustimmend A. M. Schneider, aaO (vgl. oben Anm. 1), 190. Neuerdings hat auch J. Kollwitz (vgl. oben Anm. 4) sich für eine Datierung der Cappella Greca ins 4. Jh. ausgesprochen.

[51] Zum Thema E. Dinkler-v. Schubert, in: RGG³ V, 358 ff (Lit.); dies., Der Schrein der Hl. Elisabeth zu Marburg, Studien zur Schrein-Ikonographie (1964), 127; vgl. auch H. Castritius, Der Phoenix auf den Aurei Hadrians und Tacitus' Annalen VI, 28, in: Jb. f. Numismatik u. Geldgesch. XIV (1964), 89—96.

[52] H. L. Hempel, in: ZAW 73 (1961), 300 ff. Vgl. auch die Berichte von G. Chierici,

gründet, sowie dem Stil, der in spätantoninische Zeit weise. Es handelt sich um alttestamentliche Szenen, für die Hempel Abhängigkeit von illustrierten Handschriften, und zwar jüdischen Quellen, vermutet. An der Frühdatierung hat bereits H. Belting Kritik geübt und sich – ausgehend vom Stil – für „die Zeit um 300“ ausgesprochen[53]. Um christliche Fresken des 2. Jh.s, und „damit die ältesten, die wir bis heute überhaupt kennen“[54], zu konstatieren, fehlen eindeutige Kriterien. Die angekündigte Publikation des Fundes steht leider noch aus.

g) Bevor wir uns Rom zuwenden, ist noch ein Blick auf die Denkmäler von *Ostia* erforderlich. Es ist überraschend angesichts der großen Zahl jüdischer Inschriften aus dem nahen Porto[55], sowie der in Ostia 1960 entdeckten Synagoge – deren älteste Mauerreste, vielleicht etwas zu kühn, bereits in das 1. Jh. nChr datiert werden[56], deren Existenz im 3. Jh. aber gesichert zu sein scheint –, daß zuverlässig christliche Denkmäler aus vorkonstantinischer Zeit in Ostia bislang fehlen. Eine Baugruppe, die man als Basilika deutete und in konstantinische Zeit datierte, wurde 1939 freigelegt. Neben ihr glaubte man ein Baptisterium erkennen zu können, vor allem aufgrund der Inschrift am Architrav:

IN ☧ GEON FISON TIGRIS EUFRATA
IANORUM SUMITE FONTES[57].

Hier ist sowohl die Lesart der Inschrift unsicher (Taf. XIII Abb. 32) als auch, und vor allem die Deutung des Baues. Nach v. Gerkan, der die Baureste und die Rekonstruktion einer Analyse unterzogen hat[58], kann es sich nicht um eine Basilika mit Baptisterium handeln, auch nicht um einen

in: RivAC 33 (1957), 99–125; DERS., in: RendPontAcc Ser. III, 29 (1956/57), 139 bis 149; ferner den Hinweis von L. VOELKL, in: RQ 54 (1959), 94 ff.

53 H. BELTING, Die Basilica dei SS. Martiri in Cimitile und ihr frühmittelalterl. Freskenzyklus, Forschungen z. Kunstgesch. u. Christl. Archäol., hrsg. v. F. GERKE, V (1962), 12.

54 HEMPEL, aaO 302.

55 H. J. LEON, The Jewish Community of Ancient Porto, in: HThR 45 (1952), 165 bis 175 verweist mit Recht auf J. B. FREY, CIJ I, 535–551e.

56 Vgl. M. F. SQUARCIAPINO, in: Boll. d'Arte 46 (1961), 326 ff; DIES., RendPontAcc 34 (1962), 119–132; ferner Archeologia II Nr. 19 (1964), 174. Zu den ersten Fundberichten H. L. HEMPEL, in ZAW 74 (1962), 72 f; J. SCHMITZ VAN VORST, in: FAZ vom 30. 10. 62.

57 Erster Fundbericht von G. CALZA, Una Basilica di età costantiniana scoperta ad Ostia, in: RendPontAcc 16 (1940), 63–88; zur Inschrift M. BURZACHECHI, in: Rend PontAcc Ser. III 30–31 (1957/58, 1958/59), 177–187; R. EGGER, in: RQ 55 (1960), 226 ff und wieder M. BURZACHECHI, in: RQ 59 (1964), 103 ff.

58 A. v. GERKAN, Die christliche Anlage von Ostia, in: RQ 47 (1937, erschienen 1942),

konstantinischen Bau; vielmehr vermutet er eine Katechumenenschule mit einem Nutzraum für Trink- und Waschwasser, der früher ein Nymphäum war, und datiert den Umbau, ebenso wie die Inschrift mit Christogramm, in die 2. H. des 4. Jh.s. Die Ausgräber haben für ihre These auf Spuren frühen Christentums in Ostia hingewiesen[59]: War nicht durch Cyprian bereits in der Mitte des 3. Jh.s der Christen in Ostia Erwähnung getan[60]? Hatte Ostia nicht auch eine beträchtliche Anzahl eigener Märtyrer[61]? Bezeugten nicht einige Sarkophage Christen auch gehobenen Standes[62]? War Ostia nicht schon 311 Sitz eines Bischofs[63]? Gewiß, es gab offenbar bereits in vorkonstantinischer Zeit Christen in Ostia und Porto; doch sind bisher — jedenfalls für diese Periode — keine eindeutig christlichen Denkmäler gefunden worden. Der Fund eines Schaf-

---

22 ff; abgedruckt in: v. GERKAN, Von antiker Architektur und Topographie (1959), 335—338. Ebenfalls gegen eine Deutung auf Basilika: H. FUHRMANN, in: AA (1941), 471 und TH. KLAUSER, in: RQ 47 (1952), 29 ff.

[59] G. CALZA, Nuove testimonianze del cristianesimo a Ostia, RendPontAcc Ser. III 25/26 (1949/50, 1950/51), 123—138. G. BECATTI, Scavi di Ostia IV, Mosaici e pavimenti marmorei (1962), 52—59, behandelt das Fußbodenmosaik des Raumes E der Neptuns-Thermen mit seinen verschiedenen Kreuz-, Hakenkreuz- und anderen Zeichen und Monogrammen; vgl. ebd fig. 16, 17; u. vol. V Taf. CXCVI—CXCVIII. Das Mosaik wird auf Ende 3./Anfang 4. Jh. datiert. Die Zeichen werden alle in der Linie von M. GUARDUCCI, I graffiti sotto la Confessione di S. Pietro in Vaticano I—III (1958), als kryptographisch und symbolisch interpretiert, so daß hier als Mosaizist des Thermen-Fußbodens ein Christ postuliert wird, der mit dieser zu seiner Zeit verbreiteten Methode sein Bekenntnis ablege. Das X wird damit zum Chi und als Monogramm des Namens Christi gedeutet (S. 54). Ja, sogar ein Vogel, vor dem, reichlich beziehungslos, ein R in den Tesselli erkennbar ist, wird als Phönix ausgelegt, dessen Symbolwert mit R = resurrectio angedeutet sei.

[60] CYPRIANUS, Epist. 21, 4 (CSEL III, 2, 532; HARTEL).

[61] Hierzu: R. MEIGGS, Roman Ostia (Oxford 1960), 518—531.

[62] Vgl. G. CALZA, in RendPontAcc Ser. III, 25—26 (1949/50, 1950/51), 123 ff. Unter diesen ist der Orpheus-Sarkophag (ebd Fig. 1) heidnisch, Ende 3. Jh.; die Inschrift „Hic Quiriacus dormit in pace" kann dem 4./5. Jh. angehören und ist jedenfalls nicht mit dem Märtyrer Cyriacus zu verbinden; vgl. P. A. FÉVRIER, Ostie et Porto à la fin de l'antiquité, in: MélArchHist 70 (1958), 295 ff. Das eindeutig Christliche ist späteren Datums. — Soeben, Sommer 1966, erscheint zu unserem Thema ein längerer Aufsatz mit teilweise guten Abb. von R. CALZA, Le sculture e la probabile zona cristiana di Ostia e di Porto, RendPontAcc Ser. III, 37 (1964/65), 155—257. Die Verf. hat in verdienstvoller Weise die Neufunde und auch die aus dem Episcopium von Porto abgegebenen Fragmente zusammengestellt und damit die letzten Arbeiten ihres verstorbenen Mannes, die 1950 in den Rendiconti (vgl. Anm. 59) erschienen, fortgeführt. Sie behandelt insgesamt 52 Stücke, die sie als „christlich" versteht. M. E. ist diese Zahl durch Ausfall der bukolischen Darstellungen wesentlich kleiner. Vgl. auch unten Anm. 66.

[63] DUCHESNE, Histoire ancienne de l'église, II⁴ (1910), 110 f. — Spuren der konstantinischen Petrus-Paulus-Johannes-Basilika, von der im Lib. Pont. ed. DUCHESNE I, 183 f die Rede ist, wurden bisher nicht gefunden. Ist sie ein Teil der Silvester-Legende?

trägers, aus einem Säulenschaft herausgearbeitet[64], kann nicht als christliches Zeugnis gelten. Ebenso gilt das für weitere Schaftträger-Fragmente in Ostia und Porto und vor allem für ein als Verleugungsansage an Petrus[65] oder, mit Stommel, als Beauftragung Petri, in Anlehnung an Joh 21,15—17, interpretiertes zweiteiliges Fragment[66]. Stilistisch weist dieses letzte, 1937 unweit der Nekropole der Isola Sacra gefundene Stück in die Zeit um 300, also in tetrarchische Zeit. Es würde sich um die älteste Petrusdarstellung handeln, die uns erhalten ist. Obgleich es für unseren Zeitraum unerheblich ist, ob in Ostia vorkonstantinische christliche Sarkophag-Plastik bezeugt ist oder nicht, muß für die Interpretation des diskutierten Reliefs methodisch gefordert werden, bei einer im ganzen religiös neutralen Darstellung für die interpretatio christiana einer Einzelszene zumindest im ikonographischen Kontext oder auch in einer Inschrift ein einziges eindeutig christliches Merkmal aufzuzeigen. Es genügt nicht, auf die Überwindung der Idyllik im Bukolischen durch „überraschend konkrete Züge" (Stommel) hinzuweisen. Gerade in der Frühzeit sind stärkere Evidenzen erforderlich.

Man wird R. Calza zustimmen, wenn sie vermutet, daß die Christen am Stadtrand siedelten — wie auch die Juden —, daß also mit neuen Funden außerhalb der bisherigen Scavi gerechnet werden darf.

h) Gehen wir über zu *Rom* selbst und lassen wir die von A. M. Schneider behandelten Katakomben und deren Inschriften beiseite, so wäre eingangs nur kurz der unter der *domus Flavia* auf dem *Palatin* im Herbst 1952 ‚gefundene' Graffito zu erwähnen:

PANIS ACCEP· IN LUCE CHRESTOS
SUSCEPTUS PR·K·MAI·COM· PRIS· COSS
gelesen als:

Panis accep(tus) in luce Chr(i)st(i)
Susceptus pr(idie) k(alendas) mai(as) Com(modo)
Pris(co) co(n)s(ulibu)s

„Brot empfangen im Lichte Christi, erhalten am 30. April unter dem

---

[64] Notizie degli Scavi (1916), 143 und 410 f; G. Calza, in: RendPontAcc Ser. III, 25—26 (1949/50, 1950/51), 130 u. Fig. 5.

[65] Vgl. G. Calza, ebd und Fig. 6.

[66] E. Stommel, Beiträge zur Ikonographie der konstant. Sarkophagplastik (Theophaneia 10) 1954, 98 ff. — Zwar nehmen Calza, ebd, wie auch Meiggs, aaO 396 noch an, daß es sich um christliche Skulpturen handele; indes hat Th. Klauser, in: JbAC I (1958), 36 u. 50 Nr. 88 den heidnischen Charakter dieser Stücke deutlich machen können.

Konsulat von Commodus und Priscus" (= 78 nChr). Der Graffito wurde am 16. 11. 1952 im Osservatore Romano durch A. Bartoli veröffentlicht als früheste christliche Inschrift Roms und der Christenheit überhaupt und als Zeugnis einer am 30. April d. J. 78 gefeierten Eucharistie[67]. Das der ersten Zeile vorangehende Symbol des Ankers würde sich damit als christlich eindeutig in die 2. Hälfte des 1. Jh.s zurückführen lassen. Die Richtigkeit wurde rasch bezweifelt. J. Carcopino war der erste, der die Schwierigkeiten, die sich einer epigraphischen und philologischen Analyse in den Weg stellen, betonte und die Integrität des Fundes bezweifelte. Es dauerte nicht lange, bis der Finder des Graffito seine Fälschung eingestand[68].

i) Auf sicherem geschichtlichen Boden stehen wir mit dem wenig entfernt am Südwesthange des Palatin in Raum III des Pädagogiums bereits 1856 entdeckten und heute im Antiquarium des Palatin befindlichen „*Spott-Kruzifix*" (Taf. XIII Abb. 33)[69]. So sicher hier die Integrität des Fundes ist, so unsicher sind adäquate Deutung und exakte Datierung. Mit einem scharfen Gegenstand ist auf der Fläche, von rückwärts gesehen, ein Mensch mit Eselskopf eingeritzt, mit kurzer ärmelloser Tunika bekleidet, an einem Kreuz. Dieses, durch Ritz-Linien angedeutet, ist T-förmig. Die Figur steht auf einem suppedaneum. Der Eselskopf wendet sich nach links, wo ein Adorant steht, die Linke erhoben, die Rechte leicht abgespreizt; der Kopf ist im Profil gegeben dem Gekreuzigten zugewandt. Die recht grobe Ritzzeichnung ist begleitet von dem Graffito: Ἀλεξάμενος σέβετε (= σέβεται) ϑεόν (Alexamenos betet zu Gott). Eingeritzt ist ferner, in bemerkenswert klarer Schreibweise, der Einzelbuchstabe Y oberhalb des rechten Kreuz-Armes; er unterscheidet sich vom Duktus der übrigen Kritzelei, so daß man fragen muß, ob dieses Y überhaupt integrierender Bestandteil des Ganzen ist[70]. Entgegen M. Guar-

---

[67] Vgl. A. W. van Buren, News Letters from Rome, in: AJA 57 (1953), 211.

[68] Vgl. M. Guarducci, in: AJA 58 (1954), 53 f. Über mögliche Inschriften-Fälschungen vgl. Stevenson, in: Nuovo Bull. di Arch. Crist. 3 (1897), 313 f. Zur modernen Prüfung von Inschriften-Authentie vgl. L. Borelli Vlad, in: Bollettino dell'Ist. Centrale del Restauro 13 (1953), 47 ff, hier fig. 11 der von stud. med. E. C. verfaßte und „entdeckte" Graffito. − Zur Fälschung vgl. auch J. Carcopino, Études d'histoire chrétienne (Paris 1953), 284 f und (Paris 1963²) 305 f.

[69] Das abgelöste Stuck-Rechteck, ursprünglich im Museo Kircheriano, dann im Thermenmuseum, ist jetzt im Antiquarium auf dem Palatin. Vgl. H. Riemann, in: PW XVIII, 2, 2211 ff (Paedagogium Palatini); K. Parlasca, in: Helbig, Führer durch die Sammlungen klass. Altertümer in Rom II⁴ (1966), Nr. 2077, mit neuerer Lit.; zum Paedagogium E. Nash, Bildlexikon zur Topographie des antiken Rom I, 316.

[70] So richtig Riemann, aaO; neuerdings K. Parlasca, aaO.

ducci, die das Y als Abkürzung für ὑγιεία im Sinne von „croce-salute"[71] liest, wird man in diesem Buchstaben aufgrund des Schriftcharakters ein nachträglich angefügtes Zeichen sehen müssen.

Die hundertjährige Auslegungsgeschichte dieses Fundes ging zunächst aus von den Bemerkungen Tertullians über eine Verspottung der Christen und Juden als Eselsanbeter[72]. Von hier aus ergibt sich, daß die Verspottung eines Christen und seines Glaubensgegenstandes als Gekreuzigter mit Eselskopf gemeint sein kann. Es würde unter diesem Aspekt die Bezeichnung „Spottkruzifix" auch in dem Sinne berechtigt sein, daß in der Zeichnung das Befremdliche eines als Gott verehrten Gekreuzigten zum Ausdruck kommt. — Eine andere Forschungsrichtung sah in dem Graffito ein *positives* Zeugnis der Eselsverehrung, der Onolatrie[73]. Nach dem Vorstoß von J. Haupt, der in dem „Spottkruzifix" ein Votiv zu erkennen glaubte, und eine Darstellung des ägyptischen Gottes Typhon-Seth in dem Gekreuzigten mehr postulierte als bewies[74], hatte R. Wünsch bei Behandlung der sethianischen Verfluchungstafeln aus Rom auf die Verehrung eines eselsköpfigen Gottes bei einer gnostischen Sekte hingewiesen und den Graffito als Darstellung, entstanden aus der Gleichsetzung von Christus mit Seth-Typhon erklärt[75]; dabei gewinnt der Buchstabe Y als pythagoräisches Symbol der Lebenswege eine hermeneutische Schlüsselstellung. Doch fehlen für die Gleichsetzung Christus—Seth—Typhon die Parallelen. Das selbständig zu beurteilende Y kann „pythagoräisch", aber auch „christlich", als Zeichen für „Zwei-Wege"-Entscheidungen angebracht und aufzufassen sein. Während manche Forscher — zB F. Cu-

---

[71] M. Guarducci, I graffiti sotto la Confessione di S. Pietro I (1958), 353 ff.

[72] Die Quellen sind vor allem: Tertullianus, Ad nat. I 14, 1 (CC Ser.Lat. I 32 f); Apol. 16, 12 (CC Ser.Lat. I 116); Minucius Felix, Oct. 9, 3 (CSEL 2, 13; C. Halm). — Ferner: Origenes, Contra Celsum 8, 49 (GCS Orig. II, 263—265; P. Koetschau). Unbeachtet blieb bisher in diesem Zusammenhang, daß der Ausdruck „Eseltöten" im Mari-Text II, 37 als terminus technicus für „Bundschließen" erscheint (vgl. M. Noth, in: Ges. Studien zum AT² 1960, 142 ff und den dort gegebenen Verweis auf G. Dossin, Les archives épistolaires du palais de Mari, in: Syria 19 [1938], 108). Wenn das sakrale Tieropfer mit dem Bundschließen im AT auch zusammengehört, so doch nicht das Töten eines Esels. Aus AT Traditionen gibt es keinen Zugang zur „Eselskreuzigung". — Zur Thematik zuletzt: L. Vischer, Le prétendu „culte de l'âne" das l'Église primitive, in: RHR 139 (1951), 14—35; Ilona Opelt, Esel, in: RAC VI, 592 ff (hier weitere Lit.).

[73] Vgl. die Literaturübersicht bei Riemann, aaO 2215 f; E. Grube, in: Zs. f. Kunstgesch. 20 (1957), 268 ff.

[74] J. Haupt, Das Spottkruzifix im Kaiserl. Palaste zu Rom, in: Mitteilungen der K.u.K. Central-Kommission Wien, XIII (1868), 150—168.

[75] R. Wünsch, Sethianische Verfluchungstafeln aus Rom, (1898), 110 ff; M. Sulzberger, in: Byzantion 2 (1925), 388—391; R. Verdière, Le dieu qui braît, in: La nouvelle Clio 6 (1954), 324 ff.

mont — sofort bei Y Pythagoräismus oder seine Auswirkung im Topos von Herkules am Scheidewege sehen, sind andere höchst skeptisch — zB A. D. Nock — und vermuten einen nur scheinbar tiefsinnigen „commonplace"[75a]. Literarisch faßbar wird die Auslegung des Buchstabens Y als bivium zwischen Tugend und Laster, Weg des Lichts und Weg der Finsternis, im 4. Jh. bei Ausonius (De litteris monosyllabis 9), Martianus Capella (De nuptiis philologiae et Mercurii 2,102), Hieronymus (Epist. 107, 6,3 = CSEL 55,297) u. a.

Ebensowenig überzeugend war der Versuch, mittels einer zweiten Inschrift in einer der Nachbarkammern des Paedagogiums Klarheit zu gewinnen: in Raum II hatte sich ein Graffito: „Alexamenos fidelis" gefunden, dessen Schriftform als identisch mit der des „Spottkruzifix" beurteilt wurde[76]. Dies läßt sich indes nicht beweisen, und ebensowenig kann „fidelis" als ausschließlich christliche Qualifikation in Anspruch genommen werden. Die Frage, ob die palatinische Ritzzeichnung auch ohne eine christliche Tradition erklärbar wäre, ist u. E. verneinend zu beantworten. Das aber heißt, daß wir in bekennender oder diffamierender Weise, direkt oder indirekt, einen Reflex des Glaubens an Christus als Gekreuzigten hier noch vor uns haben. Entweder ist Alexamenos ein gnostischer Bekenner und Verfasser von Zeichnung und Graffito im positiven Sinne, oder er ist Gegenstand einer Lächerlichmachung und wird sein Christusglaube verspottet. Die letzte Alternative ist u. E. am einleuchtendsten, zumal sie unabhängig bleibt von dem in ursprünglicher Zugehörigkeit und in der Deutung fraglichen Buchstaben Y. Die Kritzelei mag um 200 oder — vorsichtiger — in die 1. H. des 3. Jh.s anzusetzen sein[77]. In jedem Falle zeigt sie die erste Darstellung einer Kreuzigung, und zwar aus einer Zeit, in der diese Strafe noch nicht abgeschafft war. Folgerungen auf eine in Rom beheimatete „theologia crucis" oder auf das Vorhandensein einer kirchlichen Darstellung des Crucifixus, die hier

---

[75a] F. Cumont, Recherches sur le symbolisme funéraire des Romains (Paris 1942), 429 ff; A. D. Nock, in: AJA 50 (1946), 145 f Anm. 25 und 153 Anm. 54. Für Spätantike und Mittelalter vgl. Th. E. Mommsen, Petrarch and the Story of the Choice of Hercules, in: Journal of the Warburg and Courtauld Institutes 16 (1953), 178—192, hier weitere Lit. — Zum Buchstaben Y bereits A. Dieterich, Nekyia (1893), 192.

[76] Vgl. schon C. L. Visconti, Di un nuovo graffito Palatino relativo al cristiano Alessameno, in: Giornale arcadico (Rom 1870), Nr. 62, 139—141; der Vergleich der beiden Inschriften ist auf den Apographa bei C. M. Kaufmann, Handbuch der altchristlichen Epigraphik (1917), 302 und 303 leicht möglich. Er bestätigt nicht die Annahme einer gleichen Hand.

[77] Vgl. die Bemerkungen bei C. Cecchelli, Il Trionfo della Croce (Roma 1954), 200; jetzt Parlasca in: Helbig II⁴, Nr. 2077.

verspottet bzw. karikiert werden solle, dürfen natürlich nicht gezogen werden. Wohl aber wird man es nicht für ausgeschlossen ansehen können, daß die ersten Darstellungen eines Crucifixus von Nichtchristen stammen. Auch wäre einmal mehr bestätigt, was auch die von Ph. Derchain kürzlich veröffentlichte magische Gemme zeigte (Abb. 33 b)[78], daß historisch gesehen das T-Kreuz, die crux commissa, eine größere Wahrscheinlichkeit hat, Instrument der Kreuzigung gewesen zu sein, als das lateinische Kreuz[79].

Im Blick auf unsere leitende Frage nach den ältesten Denkmälern der christlichen Kirche wird man das palatinische Spottkruzifix mit hoher Wahrscheinlichkeit als ein indirektes Zeugnis des Christentums in Rom ansprechen dürfen. Aus einer Zeit, als die Christen selbst die Kreuzigung noch nicht als Bildthema gelten ließen, ist hier, im außerchristlichen Bereich, ein Hinweis auf den Gekreuzigten als Glaubensgegenstand, ja als „Gott" erhalten. Zeitlich geht dieses Zeugnis zusammen mit dem Einsetzen der Katakombenmalerei, die allerdings — soweit wir wissen — das Thema der Kreuzigung Christi nie aufgenommen hat.

k) Das eindeutig älteste christliche Denkmal würde Rom dann bergen, wenn die unter der Confessio von St. Peter in der Vatikanstadt ausgegrabene *Aedicula an der Roten Mauer* nachweisbar mit dem τϱόπαιον identisch wäre, das der römische Presbyter Gajus nennt[80]. Die römischen Ausgräber sind der Überzeugung, daß diese Identität bestehe; auch Kritiker der Grabungen unter St. Peter wie J. Carcopino und Th. Klauser meinen, daß die Frage bejaht werden dürfe[81]. Die entscheidende Stelle — aufgenommen bei Euseb — lautet: „Unter ihm (sc. Nero) wurde, wie berichtet wird, Paulus in Rom selbst enthauptet und Petrus ebenso gekreuzigt. Dieser Bericht wird bestätigt durch die bis heute an den dortigen Zömeterien haftende Bezeichnung mit den Namen Petrus und Paulus. Aber nicht weniger auch durch einen Kirchenmann namens Gaius,

---

[78] Vgl. Ph. Derchain, Die älteste Darstellung des Gekreuzigten auf einer magischen Gemme des 3. (?) Jahrhunderts, in: Christentum am Nil, hg. von K. Wessel (1964), 109 ff. Zur Frage der Datierung der Gemme s. in diesem Band, Seite 75 f. — Hinzuweisen ist noch auf einen Crucifixus mit Lamm-Kopf auf einem englischen Grabstein der Zeit um 1000 nChr, zuletzt besprochen in: Antiquity 39, Nr. 153 (1965), 55 f.

[79] Vgl. E. Dinkler, in: JbAC 5 (1962), 100 Anm. 27; siehe oben S. 36.

[80] Vgl. den kritischen Bericht von Th. Klauser, Die römische Petrustradition (1956), und dazu ferner A. v. Gerkan, in: JbAC 7 (1964), 62; E. Dinkler, in: ThR 27 (1961), 33 f und 31 (1966), 232 ff.

[81] J. Carcopino, Études d'histoire chrétienne² (Paris 1963), 175 ff; Th. Klauser, aaO 48 ff.

der unter dem römischen Bischof Zephyrinus (sc. 199—217) lebte. Dieser setzte sich mit Proklus, welcher einer phrygischen Sekte vorstand, in einer Schrift auseinander. Über die Plätze, wo die heiligen Leiber der besagten Apostel beigesetzt sind, sagt er folgendes: ‚Ich aber bin imstande, die τρόπαια der Apostel zu zeigen. Denn wenn du zum Vatikan gehen willst oder auf die Straße nach Ostia, wirst du die τρόπαια derer finden, die diese Kirche (sc. die römische) gegründet haben'.“[82] Euseb läßt zwar im Kontext nicht daran zweifeln, daß die Verbindung τρόπαιον = Grab dem Leser nahegelegt werden soll, daß er sie aber auch nicht als von selbst sich ergebend voraussetzen kann. Doch ist für uns nicht entscheidend, was Euseb meint, sondern was Gaius sagen wollte, als er mit dem Montanistenführer Proklus über die rechtmäßige Tradition argumentierte. Auf diese Argumentation geht Euseb hier nicht ein; vielmehr zeichnet er die Anfänge der Kirche, besonders die neronische Zeit, und spricht vom Martyrium der Apostel in Rom. Hierbei fällt auch die rätselhafte Bemerkung, daß bis heute die Namen Petrus und Paulus in den römischen Zömeterien erhalten seien, und daß man ihre „tropaia“ noch zeigen könne[83]. Erst 380, als Damasus in catacumbas — und zwar vermutlich zur Zeit der Titeländerung von Basilica Apostolorum in Basilica S. Sebastiani — seine bekannte Inschrift anbringen ließ, heißt es, die Gebeine der cives Romae, die „nomina Petri pariter Paulique“, seien nicht mehr an der Via Appia zu suchen[84].

Es wäre freilich die ganze Erörterung über die Identität von freigelegter Aedicula unter St. Peter und dem von Gaius apostrophierten Tropaion unnötig, falls ein an der Roten Mauer gefundener Graffito auf Πέτρος ἔνεστι ergänzt und für das 2. Jh. angenommen werden dürfte[85]. Jedoch ist diese Ergänzung völlig ungesichert und die von M. Guarducci vorgeschlagene Lesart ἔνι als Kontraktion von ἔνεστιν durch A. Coppo[86]

---

[82] EUSEBIUS, HE II, 25, 7 (GCS 9, 1 ed. SCHWARTZ 178): Ἐγὼ δὲ τὰ τρόπαια τῶν ἀποστόλων ἔχω δεῖξαι. ἐὰν γὰρ θελήσῃς ἀπελθεῖν ἐπὶ τὸν Βασικανὸν ἢ ἐπὶ τὴν ὁδὸν τὴν Ὠστίαν, εὑρήσεις τὰ τρόπαια τῶν ταύτην ἱδρυσαμένων τὴν ἐκκλησίαν. Vgl. auch E. DINKLER, in: ThR NF 27 (1961), 41 ff.

[83] EUSEBIUS, HE II, 25, 5 (ed. SCHWARTZ 176): καὶ πιστοῦνταί γε τὴν ἱστορίαν ἡ Πέτρου καὶ Παύλου εἰς δεῦρο κρατήσασα ἐπὶ τῶν αὐτόθι κοιμητηρίων πρόσρησις.

[84] DIEHL, ILCV I, 951; vgl. H. LIETZMANN, Petrus und Paulus in Rom² (1927), 145 f. Interessant, daß es auch im Lib.Pont. (ed. DUCHESNE I, 84 c. 39) in der Damasus-Vita heißt: „hic dedicavit platomum in Catacumbas, ubi corpora Petri et Pauli apostolorum iacuerunt . . .“

[85] So M. GUARDUCCI, La tomba di S. Pietro, (Rom 1959), 124 ff; E. KIRSCHBAUM, Die Gräber der Apostelfürsten² (1959), 140. — Neuerdings datiert M. GUARDUCCI, Le reliquie di Pietro (Lib. Ed. Vaticana, 1965), 37 f auf Anfang 4. Jh.

[86] A. COPPO, Contributo alla lettura dei graffiti Vaticani del muro Rosso, in: RivAC

und J. Carcopino[87] als philologisch und epigraphisch unhaltbar erwiesen; das Alter ist paläographisch nicht auszumachen. Da aber auch archäologisch kein einziges Denkmal unter der Confessio in das 1. Jh. zurückführt[88] und erst Ende des 3. oder gar Anfang des 4. Jh.s eindeutig christliche Graffiti auftreten[89], so gewinnt die Bedeutung des Wortes τρόπαιον im Gaius-Zitat bei Euseb entscheidendes Gewicht. Seine Wortgeschichte darf dabei nicht von der späteren „latinité chrétienne" aus erschlossen werden[90], sondern ist vom Profangriechischen und der ersten Aufnahme bei den Apologeten her zu untersuchen. Daß infolge von begrifflichen und ikonographischen Wandlungen unter Trajan und Hadrian das Tropaion zum virtus-Symbol wurde, haben besonders die Untersuchungen von G. Ch. Picard gezeigt[91]. In der Sprache christlicher Schriftsteller begegnet der Ausdruck erstmalig bei Justinus Martyr, einmal als Vergleich mit dem Mast und Segel des Schiffes (Apologia I,55,3), sodann wird das Kreuz Christi den σύμβολα der Macht, eben den τρόπαια, verglichen, wobei Justin auf die Kreuzform als tertium comparationis verweist, da die auf T-förmigem Kreuz aufgehängte Waffenrüstung des Feindes eben das Zeichen des Triumphes ist[92]. Hier wird erstmalig der metaphorische Gebrauch von Tropaion greifbar. Es ist nicht ohne Gewicht, daß bald Hippolyt von Rom in seiner Bildersprache in der Linie Justins fortfährt und die Welt mit dem Meere vergleicht, ἐν ᾧ ἡ ἐκκλησία ὡς ναῦς ἐν πελάγει χειμάζεται μὲν ἀλλ᾽ οὐκ ἀπόλλυται. Und

---

38 (1962), 97—118 (erschienen Dez. 1964). Vgl. auch E. DINKLER, in: ThR NF 27 (1961), 47 f (sowie dort besprochene Lit.) und 31 (1966), 232 ff.

[87] J. CARCOPINO, Études d'histoire chrétienne ²(1963), 299 ff; DERS., Études d'histoire chrétienne II (1965), 33 ff. Vgl. ferner R. EGGER, in RQ 57 (1962), 74 ff und dagegen M. GUARDUCCI, in: RQ 59 (1964), 247 ff, mit Wiederholung ihrer alten Thesen, bes. 251 ff.

[88] Zur Diskussion über die Datierung gefundener Gräber vgl. E. DINKLER, in: ThR NF 25 (1959), 317 ff; 27 (1961), 52; 31 (1966), 236 ff. Die Gesamtlänge der Nekropole wird auf ca. 500 m geschätzt; Sondagen stellten eine ursprüngliche Ausdehnung bis östlich vom Obelisken fest. Die Grabung unter St. Peter umfaßte den Bereich von 50 x 20 m.

[89] Zum neuesten Stand der Forschung J. CARCOPINO, Études d'hist. chrét. II (Paris 1965).

[90] So, methodisch anfechtbar, bei CH. MOHRMANN, in: VigChr 8 (1954), 154 ff; dagegen bereits TH. KLAUSER, Die römische Petrustradition (1956), 20 u. Anm. 20.

[91] G. CH. PICARD, Les Trophées Romains (Paris 1957).

[92] JUSTINUS, Apologia I, 55, 6 (KRÜGER 47 f): καὶ τὰ παρ᾽ὑμῖν δὲ σύμβολα τὴν τοῦ σχήματος τούτου δύναμιν δηλοῖ, λέγω δὲ τὰ τῶν οὐηξίλλων καὶ τῶν τροπαίων, δι᾽ὧν αἵ τε πρόοδοι ὑμῶν πανταχοῦ γίνονται, τῆς ἀρχῆς καὶ δυνάμεως τὰ σημεῖα ἐν τούτοις δεικνύντες, εἰ καὶ μὴ νοοῦντες τοῦτο πράττετε. Zum Ganzen vgl. auch H. RAHNER, Symbole der Kirche (1964), 377 ff.

der erfahrene Steuermann ist Christus, der, so fährt Hippolyt fort: φέρει δὲ ἐν μέσῳ καὶ τὸ τρόπαιον τὸ κατὰ τοῦ θανάτου, ὡς τὸν σταυρὸν τοῦ κυρίου μεθ' ἑαυτῆς βαστάζουσα[93]. Beide Autoren dürfen für Rom herangezogen werden. Justin fand der Überlieferung nach 165 in Rom den Märtyrertod, zusammen mit 6 anderen Bekennern[94]. Hippolyt starb 235 in der Verbannung, wurde aber in Rom an der Via Tiburtina beigesetzt und als Märtyrer verehrt[95]. Beide Autoren heben ab auf die Form des Kreuzes und seine δύναμις, seine Macht κατὰ τοῦ θανάτου. Wenn, zeitlich zwischen beiden stehend, Gaius von Rom den Begriff τρόπαιον verwendet, so darf man zwar keine gefestigte Metaphorik postulieren, wird aber trotz des vom Gegner — laut Euseb — benutzten Begriffes τάφος nicht einfach aus der Rede von τὰ τρόπαια τῶν ἀποστόλων auf etwas anderes als auf Siegeszeichen, d. h. Ort und Zeichen des Martyriums schließen dürfen. Die Verwendung des Begriffes Tropaion für Märtyrergrab oder gar -gebeine ist erstmalig bei Euseb, dann bei Ambrosius von Mailand nachweisbar[96]. Angesichts dieser Gegebenheit läßt sich keinesfalls für Gaius die Identität von τρόπαιον und τάφος als selbstverständlich voraussetzen.

Fällt diese Ausgangsbasis fort, so heißt das, daß die älteste eindeutige Evidenz für einen Petrus- und Paulus-Kult *in catacumbas* zu erkennen ist, inschriftlich ab 260 bezeugt und ab 29. Juni 258 mittels des Filocalus-Kalenders erschließbar[97]. Der Märtyrerkult für Petrus am Vatikan dagegen ist erst in der 1. Hälfte des 4. Jh.s gesichert. Man wird gewiß auf Grund der unbezweifelbar in das 2. Jh. nChr zurückreichenden Nekropole unter St. Peter geneigt sein, dort auch der christlichen Lokaltradition ein ähnliches Alter zuzusprechen, zumal es feststeht, daß Konstantin d. Gr. an eine solche anknüpfte und — relativ spät — durch die Aedicula die Orientierung der nach ca 324/326 errichteten Petrus-Basilika bestimmen ließ. Gerade angesichts dieser Tatsache ist es wichtig, daran zu erinnern, daß bis heute für den gesamten Westen die *Graffiti in der Triclia* unter S. Sebastiano das *älteste gesicherte Zeugnis* eines *Märtyrerkultes* darstellen.

---

[93] HIPPOLYT, Περὶ τοῦ ἀντιχρίστου, cap. 59; (GCS HIPPOLYT I, 2, 39; ACHELIS).

[94] Zu Justinus Martyr vgl. A. M. SCHNEIDER, in: JdI (1934), 416 ff. Text bei G. KRÜGER, Ausgew. Märtyrerakten (1929), 15 ff.

[95] Zu Hippolyt vgl. P. STYGER, Die römischen Märtyrergrüfte I (1935), 185 ff.

[96] EUSEBIUS: vgl. unsere Anm. 82; AMBROSIUS v. Mailand, Epist 22, 12 (MPL 17, 1066).

[97] Zu den Einzelheiten vgl. meinen Bericht in ThR NF 25 (1959), 326 ff und 31 (1966), 252; für das Liturgiegeschichtliche bes. L. C. MOHLBERG, Historisch-kritische

l) Wenden wir uns nach dem *Osten*, und zwar nach *Palästina*, so ist es nicht notwendig, in unserem Zusammenhang noch einmal die Problematik des Διάταγμα Καίσαρος von Nazareth zu besprechen, das sich gegen Grabfrevel richtet, wohl an den Anfang des 1. Jh. nChr zu datieren und auf keinen Fall zu den christlichen Denkmälern zu zählen ist[98]. Weiter scheint es mir nicht möglich, ohne Autopsie in eingehende Überprüfung der Grabungsergebnisse von P. B. Bagatti und J. T. Milik hinsichtlich der *Nekropole „Dominus flevit"* am Ölberg einzutreten[99]. Auf Grund der Veröffentlichung ist nur deutlich, daß sich eine jüdische Periode, die bis zum Barkochba-Aufstand 132—135 nChr reicht, von einer christlich-byzantinischen Periode abhebt, daß erstere durch Loculusgräber, letztere durch Arcosolgräber gekennzeichnet ist. Die christliche Periode setzt Ende 4. Jh. mit einem Kloster ein, dessen Veröffentlichung noch aussteht. Die Frage ist, ob am Ende der jüdischen Periode zum Christentum übergetretene Juden in der Nekropole „Dominus flevit" (nach Lk 19,41) bestattet wurden, und ob man mit Bagatti die Grabkammer 79 auf Grund von Kreuz-Vorkommen und Namen, die alttestamentlich sind, aber auch im NT vorkommen, als „judenchristlich" bezeichnen darf[100]. Mit M. Avi-Yonah und M. Noth meine ich, die Frage verneinen zu müssen, da keine eindeutigen Zeugnisse für Christusglauben vorliegen, sondern alle Symbole und Namen im Kontext des jüdischen Brauches leicht erklärbar sind[101].

Ähnlich ist die Lage bei dem *Ossuar des „Alexander, Sohn des Simon"*, das von E. L. Sukenik bereits 1941 in einem Grab des Kidron-Tals entdeckt, aber erst 1962 von Avigad ediert wurde[102]. Auf der 50 cm langen Vorderseite steht in zwei Zeilen:

Bemerkungen zum Ursprung der sog. „Memoria Apostolorum" an der Appischen Straße, in: Colligere Fragmenta, Festschr. f. A. Dold (1952), 52 ff.

[98] M. GUARDUCCI, L'iscrizione di Nazareth sulla violazione dei sepolcri, in: Rend PontAcc 18 (1941/42), 85—98, sieht in der Inschrift ein Echo der Botschaft vom Leeren Grabe Christi; sie schlägt eine Datierung in die Zeit des Claudius vor. — Kritisch gegen einen Bezug auf Jesus Christus: J. IRMSCHER, Zum Διάταγμα Καίσαρος von Nazareth, ZNW 42 (1949), 172—184. Neueste Behandlung m. W. durch L. CERFAUX, L'inscription funéraire de Nazareth . . ., Rev. intern. des droits de l'antiquité 3. Série 5 (1958), 347 bis 363.

[99] Vgl. P. B. BAGATTI-J. T. MILIK, Gli scavi del „Dominus Flevit" I, La necropoli del periodo Romano (Jerusalem 1958), bes. 166 ff; s. auch unsere Anm. 35.

[100] E. DINKLER, in: JbAC 5 (1962), 99; siehe oben Seite 34 f.

[101] Vgl. M. AVI-YONAH, in: IEJ 11 (1961), 91 ff; M. NOTH, in: ZDPV 76 (1960), 181 ff.

[102] N. AVIGAD, A Depository of Inscribed Ossuaries in the Kidron Valley, in: IEJ 12 (1962), 1—12.

ΑΛΕΞΑΝΔΡΟC   Alexander
CIMΩN   (Sohn des) Simon

Auf der Rückseite, in drei Zeilen:
CIMΩN ΑΛΕ   (offenbar irrtümlicher Anfang
                                     des Schreibers)

ΑΛΕΞΑΝΔΡΟC   Alexander

CIMΩNOC   (Sohn) des Simon

Das eigentliche Problem aber ist durch die Inschrift des Deckels gegeben, die zweisprachig ist:

ΑΛΕΞΑΝΔΡΟΥ   des Alexander
אלכסנדרום קרנית   Alexander QRNYT

Das hebräische Wort קרנית (Qornīt) ist als Bezeichnung einer aroma-
tischen Pflanze identifizierbar und müßte dann, als hebräischer Rufna-
me gebraucht, zur hebräischen Schreibweise Anlaß gegeben haben. Nun
hat J. T. Milik den Vorschlag gemacht, das Schluß-Tav als Schreibfeh-
ler anzusehen und קרניה zu lesen, also: Alexander *von Cyrene*. Damit
würde „Simon" als Vater, zusammen mit „Alexander von Cyrene" an
Mk 15,21 erinnern und die Möglichkeit gegeben sein, hier das Grab
der Familie zu erkennen, aus der Simon von Cyrene stammte[103]. Da
aber epigraphisch eindeutig ת und nicht ה gegeben ist, da ferner sonst
keinerlei Kriterien für die Identität dieses Simon mit dem biblischen
Kreuzträger sprechen und endlich der Name Simon sehr häufig unter
den Juden der hellenistischen Zeit begegnet[104], läßt sich keinerlei Wahrscheinlichkeit für die urchristliche Familie des Simon von Cyrene be-
gründen.

m) Als christlich wird im allgemeinen mit gewissem Wahrscheinlichkeitsgrad die Aberkios-Inschrift (Taf. XIII Abb. 34) beurteilt, die aus Hieropolis am Glaukos in Phrygien stammt und zuletzt im Lateran-Mu-
seum zu Rom war. Es handelt sich um eine in zwei Bruchstücken erhal-
tene, vor 216 nChr anzusetzende Grabinschrift, die 1883 von W. M.

---

[103] Vgl. Milik, aaO 81: „Senza voler insistere troppo, non si può pertanto scartare
la possibilità, che la tomba in questione appartenesse alla famiglia di colui che aiutò
Gesù a portare la croce." Zur Kritik schon N. Avigad, aaO 11 f.

[104] Vgl. die Literaturangabe für das Vorkommen auf Ossuarinschriften bei Milik
aaO 76 f. — Es fand sich in den gleichen Grabräumen noch das Ossuar einer CΑΠΑ
CIMΩNOC ΠΤΥΛΕΜΑΙΚΗ, „Sara (Tochter) des Simon, aus Ptolemais" — wobei es
ein Ptolemais in der Cyrenaica gibt und damit Sara als Schwester des Alexander angesehen werden könnte, vorausgesetzt, man würde mit Milik konjizieren.

Ramsay gefunden wurde[105]. Der Text war teilweise schon durch die auf Ende des 4. Jh.s zurückgehende, von Symeon Metaphrastes im 10. Jh. überarbeitete legendarische Vita des Bischofs Aberkios von Hierapolis am Lykos bekannt, die zur Ergänzung des Fragmentes diente[106]. Sieht man die Inschrift auf ihr christliches Credo hin genauer an, so muß man zunächst das Enigmatische der Sprache konstatieren. Aber seitdem W. H. Calder die umstrittene Epigraphie in Zeile 7/8: ΒΑΣΙΛ als βασιλείαν erweisen konnte[107], und überhaupt für die frühe Zeit Kleinasiens die verhüllende Sprache bei christlichen Inschriften mit Beispielen zu belegen vermochte[108], hatte die Annahme christlicher Autorschaft weitgehend Boden gewonnen. Jedoch, weitaus schwerwiegender als Unstimmigkeiten im Text (so spricht die Inschrift von Aberkios als μαθητὴς ποιμένος ἁγνοῦ, die Vita von einem ἐπίσκοπος) oder in der Örtlichkeit (der Stein ist aus Hieropolis, die Vita ist in Hierapolis verankert), dünkt mich, daß der rechteckige Cippus auf der einen Breitseite noch deutlich die Reste eines eingemeißelten Blätterkranzes aufweist.

In der Monographie über den „Kranz in Antike und Christentum" von K. Baus wird zwar der Aberkios-Stein nicht behandelt, wohl aber das literarische Material über die eindeutige Ablehnung der Toten- und Grabmal-Bekränzung bei Christen in der Zeit um 200 und im ganzen 3. Jh. vorgelegt[109a]. Minucius Felix gibt in dem Dialog Octavius (38,3 f) als christliche Sitte wieder: „nec mortuos coronamus . . . nec adnectimus arescentem coronam, sed a deo aeternis floribus vividam sustinemus" (wir bekränzen auch die Toten nicht . . . wir setzen keinen verwelkenden Kranz auf, sondern erwarten von Gott einen solchen, der lebend ist durch ewige Blumen). Tertullian sieht in der Anbringung eines Kranzes im

---

[105] W. M. RAMSAY, in Journ. of Hellenic Studies 4 (1883), 424. — Die zeitliche Ansetzung war möglich durch die 1881 von RAMSAY gefundene Grabinschrift eines Alexandros (DERS., Bull. de corresp. hellen. 6 (1882), 518 f, die auf 216 nChr datiert ist und für deren Text die Aberkiosinschrift Voraussetzung bildet. Vgl. ferner DERS., The Cities and Bishoprics of Phrygia I, 2, 721; F. J. DÖLGER, Ichthys II, 454 ff.

[106] MPG 115, 1245; TH. NISSEN, S. Abercii Vita (1912), 53 f, 81 f, 121 f. Text, Übersetzung und Kommentar der A.-Inschrift in RAC I, 12—17 (H. STRATHMANN-TH. KLAUSER). Zur älteren Lit: AnBoll (1896), 332 ff; DACL I, 1 (1907), 85 ff. Zur Inschrift wichtig: G. FICKER, Der heidn. Charakter der A.-Inschrift, in: SAB 1894, 87 ff und dagegen V. SCHULTZE, in: ThBl 1894, 209 ff, 217 ff; ferner C. ROBERT, Archeol. Nachlese, in: Hermes 29 (1894), 421 ff; A. HARNACK, Zur A.-Inschrift TU 12,4b (1895); A. DIETERICH, Die Grabschrift des A. (1896); A. JÜLICHER, in: PW 2, 2393 f; F. J. DÖLGER, aaO.   [107] Vgl. W. H. CALDER, in: JRomS 29 (1939), 1f.

[108] W. H. CALDER, The Epigraphy of the Anatolian Heresies, in: Anatolian Studies, presented to W. M. RAMSAY, Manchester (1923), 59—91. Verf. greift zurück auf F. CUMONT, Les inscriptions chrét. de l'Asie mineure, in: MélArchHist 15 (1895), 245—299 (277 und 290 zur Aberkiosinschrift).   [109a] K. BAUS, aaO (1940), 113 f und 132 ff.

Totenkult eine secunda idolatria (De cor. 10), Clemens Alexandrinus (Paidagogos II, 8 [73,1 f]) folgt der gleichen Linie. Daß auch am Grabmal ein Kranz vor dem 4. Jh. bei Christen kaum denkbar ist, geht aus Bemerkungen bei Justinus Martyr (Apol. I, 24; Krüger[3] [1904], 20) und Minucius Felix (Octavius 12,6) deutlich hervor. Die Bekränzung bedeutet für sie eine Apotheose, sie steht dem Menschen nicht zu. So wird es auch verständlich, daß der Kranz erstmalig auf den Passionssarkophagen Mitte des 4. Jh.s und zwar für das Christogramm als Rahmung auftritt.

Auch wenn Aberkios kein Bischof gewesen sein sollte, so wäre die Wahl eines Grabsteines mit dem heidnischen Kranz zu Lebzeiten — und von diesen spricht die Inschrift — bei einem Christen kaum denkbar. War der Stein vorfabriziert, so hätte der Kranz sich unschwer fortmeißeln lassen. Der Historiker muß auf Grund des Kranzes die vom Text her mögliche interpretatio christiana in Frage stellen und kann das Aberkios-Denkmal nicht als eindeutig christlich verzeichnen[109b].

II

Der kurze Überblick, bei dem wir bewußt manches übergangen, manches aber gewiß auch übersehen haben, hat bisher ein Dokument ausgeklammert: das *Rotas-Quadrat*, das auf Grund von Funden in Pompeji, Aquincum und Dura-Europos in unseren Zeitraum zurückreicht. Wenn Calder von dem Wörtchen ΒΑΣΙΛ sagte: „No disputed reading in the whole range of ancient epigraphy has aroused keener controversy"[109c], so wird man heute ohne Zweifel das *Rotas-* oder *Sator-Quadrat* noch darüber stellen dürfen. Da ein christlicher Ursprung noch immer diskutiert wird, läßt sich die Einbeziehung dieses rätselhaften und wohl weitest verbreiteten Palindroms nicht vermeiden. Wir beginnen mit einem Katalog der ältesten Vorkommen:

1. *Pompeji*, Regio II, campus ad amphitheatrum, West-Porticus der Palaestra, Graffito auf einer Säule mit vollständigem Quadrat.

[109b] Die genaue Anordnung der A.-Inschrift im Verhältnis zum Kranz auf dem Cippus ist ungesichert: vgl. C. ROBERT, in: Hermes 29 (1894), 424 ff; J. WILPERT, Fractio Panis (1896), 123 ff; A. DIETERICH, aaO, 11 f. — Da seit 1962 Sarkophage und Inschriften des Lateranmuseums verpackt sind und auf neue Aufstellung warten, war mir eine Untersuchung des Kranzes nicht möglich. Eine brauchbare Abbildung bringt C. M. KAUFMANN, Handbuch der altchristl. Epigraphik (1917), 170, Abb. 143. TH. KLAUSER-Bonn danke ich für Hinweise.

[109c] JRomS 29 (1939), 1.

ROTAS
OPERA
TENET
AREPO
SATOR

Der Text ist in lateinischen Buchstaben geritzt, wobei der Schreiber in Zeile 3 offenbar zunächst versehentlich mit AREPO angesetzt und dann verbessert hat. Oberhalb des Quadrates ist ein übergroßes S, darunter ein Δ zu erkennen, unterhalb des Quadrates ANO sowie ober- und unterhalb SAUTRAN(e) VALE. Jedoch ist wegen des verschiedenen Duktus anzuzweifeln, ob diese Kritzeleien von der gleichen Hand stammen[110]. Zeit: 79 (62?) nChr[111].

2. *Pompeji*, Regio I, Insula VII, Nr. 1; Peristyl[112]. Fragment mit den Resten:

ENET
REPO
ATOR

Ein gleichfalls mit ROTAS einsetzendes Quadrat in lateinischen Buchstaben ist damit gesichert. Zeit: vor 79 nChr.

3. *Aquincum* (Alt-Ofen, Ungarn), Palast des Statthalters: Ziegel mit Stempel, der auf Anfang des 2. Jh. verweist (Taf. XIV Abb. 35a und b)[113],

---

[110] CIL IV, Suppl. 3, 86 23 — DELLA CORTE liest: S(alus tibi sit per) trinitatem, indem er Δ als Zeichen der Trinität versteht und deutet ANO als A und O, N als „Mitte" (mittlerer Buchstaben des Alphabets). Zur Kritik schon J. SUNDWALL, L'enigmatica iscrizione „Rotas" in Pompei, in: Acta Acad. Aboensis, Humaniora 15, 5 (Åbo 1945). Vgl. ferner H. WEHLING-SCHÜCKING, Zum Deuteproblem der Sator-Inschrift, in: Album philologicum voor TH. BAADER (Tilburg 1939), 197 ff (N als Abkürzung für Nazarenus). Zum Dreieck: RAC IV, 310 ff (STUIBER).

[111] Zur Inschrift DELLA CORTE, in: RendPontAcc 12 (1936), 398; Ders., in: RendPontAcc Nap 15 (1937), 99 ff; G. DE JERPHANION, in: La voix des monuments, NS (1938), 77 ff. Daß die Palaestra-Graffiti vor dem Erdbeben d. J. 62 nChr angebracht wurden, nimmt an MAIURI, Notizie degli Scavi (1939), 177. Vgl. auch DERS., Sulla datazione del „quadrato magico" in: RendAcc Napoli NS 28 (1954), 101—111. — Die von J. CARCOPINO, in: Museum Helveticum 5 (1948), 44 ff. erwogene Möglichkeit, daß die Rotas-Graffiti von späteren Antiquitäten-Räubern angebracht wurden, ist nach den bes. von D. ATKINSON, in: Journal Eccl. Hist. 2 (1951), 1 ff. vorgebrachten Gegengründen in der Forschung aufgegeben worden.

[112] DELLA CORTE, in: RendPontAcc 12 (1936), 399, und vorher in: Notizie degli Scavi (1929), 449 Nr. 112; A. BALDI, La Pompei Giudaico-Cristiana (1964), 41 ff.

[113] Da Aquincum i. J. 107 Provinzhauptstadt wurde und der Palastflügel, dem der Ziegel entstammt, gleich 107/108 erbaut wurde, datiert der Erstbearbeiter des Fundes, J. SZILÁGYI, Ein Ziegelstein mit Zauberformel aus dem Palast des Statthalters in Aquincum, in: Acta Antiqua Academicae Scientiarum Hungaricae II (Budapest 1954),

11 Dinkler, Signum Crucis

und das mit ROTAS beginnende Quadrat in lateinischen Lettern vollständig enthält, eingeleitet durch die darüber gesetzten Worte:

ROMA   TIBI SUB
ITA
ROTAS
OPERA
etc.

Mit Recht weist J. Szilágyi darauf hin, daß die erste Zeile mit Sidonius Apollinaris[114] zum versus recurrens zu ergänzen ist: Roma tibi sub
(-ito motibus ibit amor), und daß es sich vielleicht um einen Wettstreit
zweier Schreiber handelt, wobei der Leistung des ersten der zweite die
seinige mit „ita" anfügt. Zeit: 107/108 nChr.

4.—6. *Dura-Europos*, Raum W 14 des Azzanathkona-Tempels, der
vermutlich eine militärische Dienststelle beherbergte; das Quadrat erscheint dreimal, davon eines (Nr. 481a) in nur zwei Zeilen:

ROTAS
OPERI

also fehlerhaftes I statt A beim zweiten Wort. Die beiden anderen Vorkommen des gleichen Raumes bestätigen die mit Rotas einsetzende
Wortfolge[115]. Zeit: um 250 nChr.

7. *Dura-Europos*. Im gleichen Raum wurde nachträglich ein Rotas-
Quadrat in griechischen Buchstaben erkannt; darunter liest man die Inschrift (Nr. 477):

ΓΓΓ
ΕΕΕ
ΑΑ
ΖΖ
ΠΙCΤΑΥΤΑ ΑΠΟ ΤΡΙΩΝ

305—310, auf 107/108. Bedenken gegen diese Datierung erhebt J. Carcopino, Études
d'hist. chrét. ²(1963), 94 ff.
[114] Sidonius Apollinaris, Epist. IX, 14, 4 (MGH, Auct. Ant. 8, 167). Vgl. F. J. Dölger, Ichthys V, 61, Anm. 19b. Zu diesem jüngsten Fund auch J. Carcopino, Encore le
carré magique, in: CRAInscr. (1955), 500—507; K. Karner, Die Sator-Inschrift von
Aquincum, in: ThLZ 82 (1957), 391—394.
[115] M. I. Rostovtzeff, The Excavations at Dura-Europos, Preliminary Report V
(New Haven 1934), 158—161 und Taf. XXVII, 2; auch Nr. 481 c hat in der 2. Zeile
fehlerhaft „operi". — H. v. Kaltenborn-Stachau, Die älteste bisher bekannte christl.
Originalurkunde, in: Pastoralblätter 79 (1937), 561 ff geht leider von der irrigen Annahme aus, die Rotas-Quadrate seien im Baptisterium bzw. dem christl. Haus bei
Turm 17 gefunden und deshalb durch den Fundort als „christlich" interpretiert.

C. Hopkins, der Herausgeber des vorläufigen Berichtes, liest die letzte Zeile als: πιστὰ (α)ὐτὰ ἀπὸ τριῶν (γραμμάτων) und fügt hinzu: „The meaning may be of a mantic character: divination by means of letters is declared reliable."[116] Einen mittelbaren Zusammenhang mit dem hier erstmalig in griechischen Buchstaben sich präsentierenden ROTAS-Quadrat haben die fünf Abschluß-Zeilen natürlich durch die für jeden Zauber wesentlichen Konsonanten- und Vokalreihen. Unmittelbar aber ergibt sich nichts Positives für das Verständnis. Zeit: um 250.

8. *Cirencester* (Westengland), römisches Haus. Wandkritzelei mit ROTAS-Quadrat in lateinischen Lettern[117]. Die Datierung in das 4. Jh. ist üblich geworden, aber nur paläographisch annähernd bestimmbar. Die alte Formgebung liegt in dem Beginn mit ROTAS vor.

9. *Berlin*, Staatl. Museen, Amulett aus Kleinasien (Taf. XIV Abb. 36). Auf der Vorderseite zwei einander zugekehrte Fische, darüber und darunter unerklärte Buchstaben. Auf der Rückseite das Quadrat, in griechischen Lettern, schachbrettartig verteilt, einsetzend mit SATOR. Darüber die Buchstaben IC ✝ XC also I(ησου)C X(ριστο)C, beiderseits eines Kreuzzeichens; unterhalb: Θ(εο)υ. An beiden Seiten je fünf nicht deutbare Buchstaben[118]. Zeit: 6. (?) Jh.

10. *Faras* (Nubien), Grabkapelle des 8. Jh.s mit verschiedenen wichtigen Inschriften. Das SATOR-Quadrat in koptischer Schrift[119].

11.—18. *Wien*, Papyrus-Sammlung Erzherzog Rainer, Koptische Zaubertexte des 6.—11. Jh.s, alle mit SATOR einsetzend (die lateinischen Worte opera, bzw. arepo mit T statt P)[120].

---

[116] Zur Inschrift Nr. 477 vgl. Report V, 158; die Rotas-Inschrift: Report VI (1936), 486, Nr. 809.

[117] Vgl. Ephemeris Epigraphica IX (1910), Nr. 1001; F. J. HAVERFIELD, in: The Archeological Journal 56 (1899), 319—323.

[118] Vgl. F. J. DÖLGER, Ichthys V (1943), 57 ff und Tafelband III, 98.

[119] Vgl. DACL I, 2, 1813 f; S. SELIGMANN, (s. unten Anm. 121) bes. 157; JERPHANION, La voix des monuments (1938), 49 ff. Die erste Veröffentlichung von A. H. SAYCE, Gleanings from the Land of Egypt, in: Recueil de travaux relatifs à la philologie et à l'archéologie égyptiennes et assyriennes 20 (1897), 174 war mir nicht zugänglich; u. a. soll auch der apokryphe Abgarbrief Jesu als Wandinschrift hier überliefert gewesen sein.

[120] V. STEGEMANN, Die koptischen Zaubertexte der Sammlung Papyrus Erzherzog Rainer in Wien, in: SAH 1933/34, Heft 1 der Phil.-Hist.Kl.Nr. XIX, XXIV, XXVIII, XXXVI, XLV, XLVII, XLVIII, XLIX. Fast alle scheinen apotropäischen Sinn oder Zweck als Heilungszauber gehabt zu haben. Wir geben in Übersetzung durch V. STEGEMANN (aaO S. 38 f) den Text eines Amuletts (Nr. XIX) zum Schutze gegen Schmerzen und Krankheit: „Sator Areto Tenet Otera Rotas. Alpha Leon Phone Aner Akrammata Periton Surithion Paramerao Ochamen Orophaeon Robiel Thriechs Apabathuel Mamarioth: ich bitte und rufe (παρακαλεῖν) euch an, und ich beschwöre euch bei dem,

11*

19. *Insel Thasos*, Ortschaft Panaghia, Altertumssammlung. Amulett mit griechischen Lettern, schachbrettähnlich wie 9, ebenfalls mit SATOR einsetzend. Schreibweise zwischen Majuskel und Minuskel wechselnd[121]. Die Formel ist umgeben von Lettern und Zeichen: Kreuz mit Beischrift I ƆXS N K (= Ιησοῦς Χριστὸς νικᾷ), ferner das Wort ζοα, Pentagramm, Hexagramm u. a. Das Exemplar gehört zu einer Gruppe von Amuletten, die Deonna auf Grund von Verwendung arabischer Ziffern in eine Zeit nach dem 15. Jh. datiert.

Eine beträchtliche Anzahl weiterer Belege ließe sich aus dem koptischen und byzantinischen Raume beibringen, die aber für das Bild der Frühzeit nichts besagen. Für die ersten Jahrhunderte nChr zeigen die oben aufgeführten Denkmäler erstaunliche Übereinstimmung in folgenden Zügen:

a) Die älteste Form des Rebus begann offensichtlich mit ROTAS.

b) Die Schreibweise war lateinisch, nur gelegentlich und sekundär in griechische Buchstaben transskribiert.

c) Die Verbreitung spricht dafür, daß römische Soldaten das Rebus in die Provinzen exportierten.

d) Ein ursprünglicher Bezug auf das Christentum läßt sich weder aus Kontext noch aus Fundort erkennen, ebensowenig Bezug auf jüdische oder hellenistische Religiosität. Solche Bezüge lassen sich freilich auch nicht a limine ausschließen.

e) Die ersten christlichen Fassungen oder Interpretationen treten ab 6. (?) Jh. auf, in unserm Katalog mit Nr. 9. Randzeichen und beigegebene Buchstaben erweisen hier eine christliche Hand. Es erscheint nicht zufällig, daß von jetzt ab das Quadrat mit SATOR einsetzt.

Auffallend ist die relativ späte Verwendung durch Christen. Ebenso aber ist auch die gleichzeitig einsetzende, d. h. seit dem 6. Jh. nachweisbare apotropäisch-magische Verwendung neu.

Was zunächst das literarische Genus des Rotas-Quadrats angeht, so handelt es sich um einen versus recurrens[122], bzw. ein Palindrom[123]

---

den man am Kreuz (σταυρός) gekreuzigt hat (σταυροῦν), daß ihr entfernt das Leid und den Schmerz aus der Herrin (κυρία) Hew, der Tochter der Maria, und daß ihr ihr die Heilung gebt durch die Kraft der Herrschaft des Jao Sabaoth Alpha. Alpha Leon (?) Phone Aner. Thebna Ator Archechon. Sator Areto Tenet Otera Rotas. Amen (?). Schnell, Schnell (ταχύ ταχύ)." Der Text wird in das 11 Jh. datiert.

[121] W. Deonna, Talismans magiques trouvés dans l'île de Thasos, in: Revue des Études Grecques XX (1907), 365, Nr. 2. Vgl. auch S. Seligmann, Die Sator-Formel, in: Hess. Blätter f. Volkskunde 13 (1914), 160, Fig. 3.

[122] Diese Bezeichnung bereits bei Sidonius Apollinaris (vgl. Anm. 114).

[123] Vgl. K. Preisendanz, Palindrom, in: PW 36, 2, 133 ff.

(auch Boustrophedon oder Karkinos = Krebsvers). Das Roma-Amor-Zitat, das auf dem Ziegel von Aquincum aufgenommen war, bietet ebenfalls ein derartiges Palindrom, ohne jedoch Quadrat zu sein. Es gab freilich auch, wie jetzt ein Neufund in Ostia in der Nähe der „Caserma dei vigili" bestätigt, der zugleich einen von M. Della Corte im Supplementband von CIL IV veröffentlichten pompejanischen Graffito in Erinnerung ruft[123a], ein Roma-Amor-Quadrat:

R O M A
O L I M
M I L O
A M O R

Es wird paläographisch ins 2. Jh., vielleicht sogar in die Zeit Hadrians datiert. Die technische Ausgewogenheit hat zur Seite eine inhaltliche Banalität. OLIM ist Adverb: einst, seinerzeit. MILO könnte sich auf zwei historische Personen beziehen: einerseits auf den Krotoniaten und Athleten, andererseits auf den Volkstribun Milo, Gegner und Mörder des P. Clodius, den Cicero verteidigte (Cic. Or. 165). Doch müßte man einen verbindenden Text zwischen den vier Worten selbst herstellen, um einen Sinn herauszuholen. Insofern ist dieses 16-Buchstaben-Quadrat ein Beispiel dafür, daß von den vier äußeren Buchstaben-Reihen ausgegangen worden ist, die inneren Ausfüllungen mit LI und IL dann von selbst sich ergaben, daß also eine technische Bedingtheit bei der Komposition anzunehmen ist[123b]. Daß man auch in christlichen Kreisen das Buchstaben-Spiel liebte, zeigt die auf dem koptischen Amulett (vgl. Anm. 120) zitierte, aus Ez 1,10 entwickelte Alpha-Formel, die schon im 7. Jh. auf einem Ostrakon im koptischen Museum zu Kairo[124] als Vier-Zeilen-Quadrat neben das SATOR-Quadrat gestellt ist:

Α Λ Φ Α
Λ Ε Ω Ν
Φ Ω Ν Η
Α Ν Η Ρ

Gewiß handelt es sich hier nicht um einen versus recurrens, sondern zunächst um ein — biblisch ableitbares, auf Gottes Thronträger oder so-

---

[123a] Vgl. CIL IV, 8297. Zum Ostia-Graffito siehe M. Guarducci, Il Misterioso „Quadrato Magico", in: Archeologia Classica 17 (1965), 264 ff.

[123b] Richtig M. Guarducci, ebd 266.

[124] Vgl. DACL I, 2, 1812 und W. E. Crum, Coptic Monuments, in: Catalogue Général des Antiquitées Égyptiennes (Cairo 1902), 42, Nr. 8147.

gar die vier Evangelien (Apk 4,6—8; Irenäus, Adv. Haereses III,11,8) zu beziehendes — Wortspiel, das, von links nach rechts und von oben nach unten gelesen, die gleichen vier Worte je zweimal ergibt. Dies genügt offenbar, um in der Namen-Harmonie geheimnisvolle Kräfte zu glauben und die vier Worte als magisches Mittel, als Beschwörungsformel zu nutzen[125]. Das aber heißt zugleich, daß nicht noch ein weiteres Geheimnis durch Neuordnung der hier vorliegenden 16 Buchstaben erhoben werden *muß*, daß natürlich aber auch ein Anagramm nicht ausgeschlossen werden kann.

Ein Geheimnis innerhalb des ROTAS-Rebus meinte man freilich entdeckt zu haben, als zwischen 1924 und 1927 unabhängig von einander drei Forscher die gleiche Lösung publizierten, Kurat Chr. Frank aus Kaufbeuren[126], Pfarrer F. Grosser aus Chemnitz[127] und S. Agrell aus Lund[128]. Ihre These ging dahin, daß ein Anagramm vorliege, also durch Umstellung der Buchstaben (ἀναγραμματίζειν) der eigentliche Sinn zutage käme und zwar ein Pater-Noster-Kreuz mit zweimaligem A und O:

```
                          P
                          A
  S A T O R        A  T   O            R O T A S
  A R E P O           E                O P E R A
  T E N E T           R                T E N E T
  O P E R A    P A T E R N O S T E R    A R E P O
  R O T A S           O                S A T O R
                      S
                   A  T   O
                      E
                      R
  Fig. 7a           Fig. 7b               Fig. 7c
```

Dieser Lösungsversuch (Fig. 7b) wurde insbesondere von kritischen Gelehrten wie M. Rostovtzeff, F. Cumont, H. Lietzmann[129] als durchschla-

---

[125] Zu verweisen ist bes. auf das reichhaltige Werk von M. KROPP, Ausgewählte koptische Zaubertexte, 3 Bde. (Brüssel 1930); speziell Bd. III, 129 (§ 221).

[126] Vgl. CHR. FRANK, in: Deutsche Gaue 25 (1924), 76 — zitiert nach F. FOCKE, in: Würzburger Jbb f. d. Altertumswiss. 3 (1948), 371 — freilich ohne nähere Begründung.

[127] Vgl. F. GROSSER, Ein neuer Vorschlag zur Deutung der Sator-Formel, in: ARW 24 (1926), 165-169 — eingehend begründet.

[128] Vgl. S. AGRELL, Runornas talmystik och dess antika förebild, Lund (1927), 31 f — im Zusammenhang mit der Runen-Magie und ihren antiken Wurzeln kurz besprochen.

[129] Vgl. M. ROSTOVTZEFF, in: The Excavations at Dura-Europos, Preliminary Report V, (1934), 158 ff; VI, (1936), 486; F. CUMONT, in: RendPontAcc 13 (1937), 7 f; H. LIETZMANN, in: AA 1937, 477 f (jetzt in: Kleine Schriften 1 [1958], 484 ff).

gend und richtig angesehen, sowie von den Ausgräbern Pompejis, Della Corte und Maiuri, als Bestätigung ihrer Annahme von Christen am Fuße des Vesuv *vor* d. J. 79 begrüßt und verteidigt[130]; kritische Stimmen ließen sich anfangs nur vereinzelt vernehmen[131]. War zunächst auch, solange das Zeugnis des ROTAS-Quadrats bis Dura Europos und damit bis zur Mitte des 3. Jh.s zurückreichte, möglicher christlicher Charakter kein eigentliches Problem, so änderte sich dies mit dem Funde in Pompeji und Aquincum. Denn jetzt mußte man — die Auflösungsthese vorausgesetzt — entweder annehmen, daß eine von dem Herrngebet unabhängige Gottes-Anrufung hier zugrunde liege, oder aber man war genötigt, die Übersetzung des Herrngebets ins Lateinische in eine Zeit zu setzen, die bei dem jetzigen Stand der Synoptikerforschung etwa ein Jahrzehnt vor der literarischen Gestaltwerdung des Matthäus-Evangeliums läge. Das wäre zwar nicht unmöglich, da das Herrngebet natürlich zur ältesten mündlichen Tradition der Gemeinde gehörte. Aber es wäre doch überraschend, besonders angesichts der bis Mitte des 3. Jh.s weitgehend griechisch sprechenden Christengemeinde Roms und der Hafenstädte, bereits so früh eine Übersetzung ins Lateinische zu finden, zugleich auch die uns erst durch die Johannes-Apokalypse bekannte Gottes- und Christus-Symbolik des A und Ω (Apk 22,13) in der Transskription von A und O[132]. Sodann müßte man wohl doch — diese Hypothese vorausgesetzt — mit einer Kenntnis der besonderen Symbolik des Kreuzes rechnen, sei es als + oder auch als ×, wie sich die im Buchstaben N schneidenden Linien ebenfalls anordnen lassen. Erstaunlich wäre endlich, daß das im Quadrat als Kreuz stehende TENET an

---

[130] M. DELLA CORTE, in: RendPontAcc 12 (1936), 397 ff; A. MAIURI, in: RendAcc Napoli 27 (1953),101; zur Diskussion vgl. ferner das leidenschaftlich für christliche Herkunft sich einsetzende Referat bei A. BALDI, aaO 41 ff.

[131] Vgl. jedoch: G. DE JERPHANION, in: La voix des monuments, NS (1938), 90 ff; C. WATZINGER, in: ThBl 17 (1938), 118 f; STUHLFAUTH, in: Pfälz. Pfarrerblatt 38 (1938), 113 ff; DERS. in: ThBl 18 (1939), 210 f; J. SUNDWALL, in: Acta Acad. Aboensis Humaniora 15, 5 (1945), 3 ff; F. J. DÖLGER, Ichthys V (1943), 254 ff; F. FOCKE, Sator Arepo: Abenteuer eines magischen Quadrats, in: Würzburger Jbb f. d. Altertumsw. 3 (1948), 366 ff; S. EITREM, in: Eranos 48 (1950), 73 f. Siehe auch RGG³ V (1961), 1373 f (dort auch Lit.).

[132] F. DORNSEIFF, Martialis IX, 95 und Rotas-Opera-Quadrat, in: Rhein.Mus.f.Philologie, NF 96 (1953), 373 ff setzt freilich christlichen Charakter des Rebus als Pater-Noster-Kreuz mit A und O bei seiner Martialis-Interpretation voraus, wobei er aus dem Wechsel von *Alf*ius zu *Olf*ius in dem Epigramm eine Anspielung auf den ersten und letzten Buchstaben des griechischen Alphabets heraushört. — H. LIETZMANN, aaO 480 (485) hält die Voraussetzung, daß A und O im Diaspora-Judentum aus Jes 41,4 entwickelt wurde, für möglich.

den vier Enden jeweils ein von A und O gerahmtes T zeigt (vgl. Fig. 7c), das mit Barn 9,8 als Tau-Kreuz verstanden werden könnte. Allerdings dürfte man nicht von chronologischen Konsequenzen her eine Deutung ausschließen, wenn sie im übrigen hohe Wahrscheinlichkeit beinhalten würde; es wäre ja zB möglich, daß das Tenet-Kreuz und seine Flankierung durch A und O technisch bedingt waren und keineswegs eine Kreuz-Symbolik voraussetzten.

Um den religionsgeschichtlichen Boden des Rebus zu bestimmen, bedarf es zunächst der Erklärung der fünf Worte, wobei die älteste, mit ROTAS einsetzende Fassung zugrunde zu legen ist. Man könnte dann übersetzen: *Die Räder und ihr Werk hält Arepo, der Sämann.* Wir lassen hierbei AREPO bewußt unübersetzt, da die Herleitung von dem keltischen Wort „arepennis" (= französisch arpent) und eine auf diese Etymologie aufbauende gallische Herkunft des Quadrates[133] nicht einleuchten. Wir meinen, daß bei Aufnahme des Wortes OPERA die Umkehrung in AREPO kompositionstechnisch unvermeidlich war, und daß AREPO als Eigenname unübersetzt bleiben sollte[134].

Eine weitere Frage ist, ob man dem Hinweis von Cumont folgen darf, der eine Aufnahme des lateinischen Textes von Ez 1,16 vermutet[135]. Hier heißt es unter Bezug auf den Thronwagen, die Merkaba:

Vg: Et aspectus *ro-tarum* et *opus* earum quasi visio maris; et

LXX: καὶ τὸ εἶδος τῶν τροχῶν ὡς εἶδος θάρσις, καὶ ὁμοίωμα

Die *Räder* und ihre Arbeit waren anzusehen wie das Blin-

---

[133] Vgl. zuletzt J. Carcopino, Études d'histoire chrétienne² (Paris 1963), 33 ff; zum Problem bes. H. Fuchs, Die Herkunft der Satorformel, in: Schweizerisches Archiv f. Volkskunde 47 (1951), 28 ff.

[134] Die vorgeschlagene Lösung von F. Dornseiff, in: ZNW 36 (1937), 222 ff, bes. 231 f in arepo das Wort rapere zu erkennen, halte ich für nicht begründet. Sie ist freilich besser als die von L. Crozet, Credo secret antique dans un carré magique, in: Bull.Assoc. G. Budé, Suppl.Lettres d'Humanité 19 (1960), 572 ff, der für AREPO als Auflösung vorschlägt: A REP(ARATIONE) O(PTIMA) und mit Sator beginnend übersetzt: „Le créateur, depuis qu'a eu lieu une restauration parfaite, retient l'action du destin." — Jüngst hat sich M. Guarducci in dem oben, Anm. 123ᵃ, zit. Aufsatz gegen J. Carcopinos Ableitung des Wortes AREPO vom gallischen *arepennis* erneut und mit Recht gewendet, bes. 224 f u. 227 f. Sie kommt, 267, zu der gleichen Lösung wie wir (vgl. schon in RGG³ V, 1373 f), daß nämlich *arepo* nichts anderes ist als die Umkehrung von *opera*. — Auch in der Gesamtbeurteilung kommt Verf. zu weitgehend ähnlichen Ergebnissen, wie die hier vorgetragenen: 1. Es unterliegt keine Paternoster-Formel. 2. Die Auflösung von Grosser u. a. ist Zufall. 3. Der Sinn des Quadrates liegt im Geheimnisvollen des Buchstabenspiels.

[135] F. Cumont, in: RendPontAcc 13 (1937), 7 f, der das Werk eines getauften Juden annimmt.

una similitudo ipsarum quatuor; et aspectus earum et *opera* quasi sit *rota* in medio rotae.

ἐν τοῖς τέσσαρσιν, καὶ τὸ ἔργον αὐτῶν ἦ καθὼς ἂν εἴη τροχὸς ἐν τροχῷ.

ken von Chrysolith und die Vier hatten einerlei Aussehen. Und ihr Aussehen und ihre *Arbeit* waren, als wenn ein *Rad* in dem andern wäre.

Es handelt sich um eine Epiphanieschilderung, die nur Anknüpfungspunkt für die Komposition des Rotas-Quadrates sein könnte, das dann von einem lateinisch sprechenden Juden oder auch Judenchristen stammen würde, jedenfalls schon bei Ableitung von der LXX auf Schwierigkeiten stößt. Auch wäre bei solcher Annahme hier das früheste Zeugnis für eine Vetus latina des AT zu postulieren, was ebenfalls nicht auszuschließen, aber doch eine zusätzliche Schwierigkeit ist. Cumonts These, daß ein lateinischer Jude im Westen das Rebus komponierte, verliert also doch bei näherem Zusehen an Wahrscheinlichkeit. Gleiches läßt sich bei Analyse der anderen Thesen kritisch sagen, etwa gegen A. Omodeo, der in Sator Mithras erkennen wollte[136], oder gegen J. Sundwall, dessen Arbeit auf eine orphisch-eleusinische Deutung hinausliefe[137], und endlich gegen H. Hommel, der die Stoa als geistige Welt der Sator-Idee wie der Auflösung in Pater-Noster-A/O erkennen will[138].

Läßt die Untersuchung der fünf Worte keine geistes- oder religionsgeschichtliche Eingrenzung zu, so könnte gerade dies für eine *hinter* den Worten liegende und erst durch Buchstabenumstellung zu gewinnende Sinnhaftigkeit sprechen, also für ein *Anagramm*. G. de Jerphanion hat eine ganze Reihe von Auflösungsmöglichkeiten verzeichnet, von denen wir nur einige als Illustration bringen[139]. Zugrunde liegt solchen Neubildungen der Bestand an 25 Buchstaben, die in dem ROTAS-Quadrat enthalten sind:

A A A A
E E E E
O O O O
R R R R
T T T T
P P
S S
N

---

[136] A. OMODEO, La croce d'Ercolano e il culto precostantiniano della croce, in: La Critica 38 (1940), 45—61.

[137] J. SUNDWALL, aaO bes. 15 ff.

[138] H. HOMMEL, Schöpfer und Erhalter (1956), 32—79.

[139] G. DE JERPHANION, in La voix des monuments (1938), 72 f.

Beispiele von Neubildungen aus diesem Buchstaben-Reservoir wären:

a) Petro et reo patet rosa Sarona (Auch Petrus, ob er gleich schuldig war, steht die Rose von Saron offen; vgl. Apg 9,35)[140].

b) Retro Satana toto opere asper[141].

c) Oro te Pater, oro te Pater, sanas.

d) Sat or/are po/ten(ter) et/Opera(re) r(ati)o t(u)a s(it).-(Variante statt ratio: r[eligi]o).

e) Ora, operare, ostenta te Pastor.

f) O Pater ores pro aetate nostra.

Diese Möglichkeiten der Buchstaben-Neuordnung, deren es noch mehr gibt, stellen die Frage: Geht die Komposition eines Palindroms in Quadratform aus von der Suche nach geeigneten Worten, die sich zusammenfügen lassen, oder von einer Aussage wie in den Beispielen a)—f), um von hier aus durch Umstellung der Buchstaben zum Kryptogramm zu gelangen? Der einzige, der bisher auf die Frage der technischen Erstellung des SATOR-Quadrates einging, ist D. Atkinson[142]. Er nimmt als *Ausgangspunkt* die Worte Pater-Noster an, als gleicharmiges Kreuz gestaltet, von A und O flankiert, d. h. er setzt voraus, daß das Quadrat aus einem Kreuz heraus entwickelt sei. Er vermutet, daß direkt als Aufgabe gestellt wurde, das Kreuz in ein „mystisches Quadrat" zu verwandeln — „perhaps in a period of actual or expected persecution"[143], und daß man hierfür von einer Synopse der zu verwertenden Buchstaben ausging (s. oben). Als Phasen der Komposition läßt er (Fig. 8a) das Kreuz mit vier T-Enden, sodann (Fig. 8b) das Kreuz mit jeweils flankierenden A und O folgen.

Die restlichen Buchstaben: E E E E / R R R R / P P / S S werden in einer 3. Phase sinnvoll verteilt, wobei schon die Einsetzung der vier E zwischen T und N obligatorisch ist und damit kein Spielraum mehr für Variationen besteht. So einleuchtend die Arbeitsphasen dargestellt sind,

---

[140] Die Lösung stammt nach G. DE JERPHANION aaO 73 Anm. 2 von K. v. HARDENBERG, in: Darmstädter Tageblatt (1925), Nr. 69.

[141] Die Lösungen b, c, e, u. f ebenfalls bei JERPHANION S. 73, zitiert nach G. FRITSCH, in: Zeitschr. f. Ethnologie 15 (1883), 535 ff, der sie der 1764 in Nürnberg erschienenen „Onomatologia curiosa artificia et magica" entnahm. d) stellt eine monastische Regel dar und wird von Dekan DR. KOLBERG in: Verhandlungen der Berliner Gesellsch. f. Anthropologie (1887), 72 als Lösung vorgeschlagen und begründet — in einer Zeit also, in der noch nicht die Zeugnisse der ersten drei Jhh. bekannt waren. — Zum Thema auch J. CARCOPINO, Études d'histoire chrétienne² (1963), 36 ff.

[142] D. ATKINSON, The Origin and Date of the „Sator" Word-Square, in: Journal of Ecclesiastical History 2 (1951), 1 ff.

[143] Ebd S. 6.

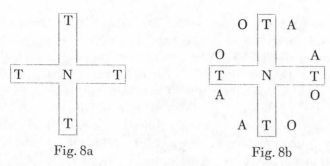

Fig. 8a   Fig. 8b

so muß doch die petitio principii gesehen und in Frage gestellt werden:
1. Die interpretatio christiana des Rebus ist vorausgesetzt. 2. Kreuz-Symbolik und lateinische Sprache bei Christen sind für die Jahre zwischen 63—79 nChr angenommen.

Demgegenüber erscheint mir, gerade angesichts der Vielfalt von Neuordnungsmöglichkeiten, die nächstliegende Erklärung zu sein, daß sowohl Pater-Noster mit A/O, als auch die Möglichkeiten a)—f) *Zufallslösungen* sind[144]. Ja, solange kein einziges Beispiel eines Buchstaben-Quadrats in der Antike nachgewiesen werden kann, das eine sinnenthüllende Auflösung *verlangt*, wird man auch für das ROTAS-Quadrat ein Anagramm auszuschließen haben und sich mit der Erklärung als Wortspiel, wie banal auch immer der Sinngehalt ist, begnügen müssen[145].

Wie sich im Wortspiel, an der Oberfläche der zusammengestellten vier Worte alles erschöpft, zeigte bereits das Alpha-Leon-Quadrat. Das gleiche gilt für die *Satan- und Ruach-Quadrate*[146], die anhangsweise hier genannt seien:

S A T A N	R U A C H
A D A M A	V A C H C
T A B A T	A C H C A
A M A D A	C H C A V
N A T A S	H C A V R

---

[144] Gegen Hugh Last (JThS NS 3, [1953], 92 ff) und H. Lietzmann op. cit.; anderseits mit A. Dieterich, ABC-Denkmäler (in: Kl. Schriften, 1911, 216) u. F. J. Dölger (Ichthys 5, [1943], 60).

[145] Vgl. J. Carcopino, aaO 35: „ . . . une trivial banalité avec une navrante platitude. Mais, justement, c'est cela qui doit alerter notre sens critique, attirer notre attention . . . En d'autres termes, notre „carré" est, exterieurement, trop insignificant par rapport à sa fortune, pour qu'il n'ait pas, intérieurement, recélé, à la manière d'une cryptogramme, une signification profonde dont il est à la fois légitime et nécessaire de tenter le déchiffrement."

[146] Vgl. S. Seligmann, aaO 177 ff.

Der Bau dieser beiden Quadrate ist zwar anders als bei Alpha-Leon etc, insofern hier nur die vier Außenseiten, vom S bzw. R ausgehend, das Schlüsselwort wiederholen. Wenn Seligmann daneben noch auf je ein inneres durch DAM und ACH gebildetes Quadrat hinweist und in ersterem ADAM, in letzterem: אך (= Trauer) erkennt, so stellt er doch beide Beobachtungen selbst als „Zufall" hin[147]. Beide Formeln sind als Texte auf einem Amulett und in einem Zaubertext belegt[148] und nicht etwa als Anagramm aufzulösen; vielmehr ist die Magie der Worte RUACH (= Geist) und SATAN das allein Entscheidende.

Auch die magischen Zahlenquadrate — bis hin zum Hexeneinmaleins in Goethes Faust — haben nur in der gleichbleibenden Quersumme ihr Kompositionsgesetz, bergen aber nicht darüber hinaus Geheimnisse[149].

Zum ROTAS-Quadrat zurückkehrend wäre als Letztes die Frage nach dem Grund der *Verchristlichung* zu erörtern. Wenn in den christlichen Formeln die Wortfolge mit SATOR beginnt, so ist hier ein Hinweis noch erkennbar: SATOR wurde früh anstelle von creator gebraucht und dann im frühmittelalterlichen Latein mit dem spätgebildeten Worte salvator ausgewechselt[150]. So nimmt Prudentius, Liber Cathemerinon, mehrfach den Begriff auf (CSEL 61, 21 und 71).

> fons vitae liquida fluens ab arce,
>
> infusor fidei, sator pudoris,
>
> mortis perdomitor, salutis auctor (IV, 10 ff).
>
> . . . .
>
> Hunc et profetis testibus
>
> hisdemque signatoribus
>
> testator et sator iubet
>
> adire regnum et cernere (XII, 85 ff)

Im gleichen Sinne Boethius[151]:

---

[147] Ebd 178.

[148] Ebd 177 Anm. 2 und 179 Anm. 1.

[149] Zu magischen Zahlenquadraten vgl. W. DEONNA, in: Rev. Ét. Grecques 20 (1907), 369 f. Zur Umrechnung des Rotas-Quadrates S. AGRELL, aaO 31 f; G. DE JERPHANION, aaO 64 f; kritisch H. FUCHS, aaO 37 Anm. 15. — Vgl. auch das „Hexen-Einmaleins" in Goethes Faust, I. Teil, 2540—2593.

[150] Zu „sator" in der Profanlatinität vgl. die bei FORCELLINI (F. Corrandini-I. Perin), Lexicon totius latinitatis IV (1940), 232 angegebenen Stellen. — Zum philologischen „Salvator"-Problem vgl. W. MATZKOW, De Vocabulis quibusdam Italae et Vulgatae Christianis. Questiones Lexicographae (Phil. Diss. Berlin, 1933), 18 ff; CH. MOHRMANN, Les emprunts grecs dans la latinité chrétienne, in: VigChr 4 (1950), 193 ff und DIES., Quelques traits caractéristiques du Latin des Chrétiens, in: Miscell. G. Mercati I (1956), 937 ff (=Études sur le Latin des Chrétiens I [Rom 1958], 21 ff).

[151] CC Ser. Lat. 94, 1 (1957, ed. L. BIELER) und die Übertragung von K. BÜCHNER,

O qui perpetua mundum ratione gubernas
terrarum caelique sator, qui tempus ab aevo
ire iubes stabilisque manens das cuncta moveri
(Philos. Consolatio III, 9, M. IX, 1–3)

Bei Walafrid Strabo heißt es sodann in den Carmina de singulis festivi-
tatibus anni:

Natus enim est hodie sator atque redemptor
Christus de Maria Virgine factus homo . . .[152].

Wenn also SATOR sowohl Gottes- bzw. Schöpferbezeichnung als auch
Christus-Titel sein kann, so ist der Wechsel vom ROTAS- zum SATOR-
Quadrat verständlich, zumal damit der Zaubercharakter getarnt wurde.

Neben der meist magischen Verwendung einher geht im christlichen
Bereich eine vielfältige fromme *Interpretation* der fünf Worte: sie sollen die Namen der Nägel am Kreuze Christi bezeichnen[153], die Namen
von fünf Hirten aus der lukanischen Geburtsgeschichte[154], der fünf Wun-
den Christi[155]. Ja, im 20. Jh. kam eine Deutung auf die Hl. Drei Könige
und Nazareth hinzu[156]. Historisch-kritisch beurteilt sind dies alles a
posteriori gegebene Legitimationen eines sekundär mit Christus in Verbindung gebrachten Textes.

Was ist nun das *Ergebnis* für unsere leitende Frage? Die ältesten Vorkommen des ROTAS-Quadrates weisen auf keinerlei christlichen Ursprung hin. Die Auflösung des Rebus in ein Pater-Noster-Kreuz mit A/O
ist eine Zufallslösung des 20. Jh.s, allerdings in Form und Inhalt beste-
chend. Die Verchristlichung des ROTAS-Quadrats wird historisch greifbar mit dem Aufkommen des SATOR-Quadrats gegen 500. Aus den
ROTAS-Zeugnissen der Frühzeit ist deshalb kein Rückschluß auf eine
entsprechende Verbreitung des Christentums im Imperium Romanum
möglich.

Boethius Trost der Philosophie, m. Einführung v. F. KLINGNER, Sammlung Dieterich
33 (1964), S. 74: „Du, der das Weltall in ewiger Satzung beherrschest, des Himmels
und der Erden Schöpfer, der du von Ewigkeit wandeln hießest die Zeit und in Ruh
selbst, gibst, daß sich alles bewege . . .“

[152] MPL 114, col. 1083/C. – Für Hrabanus Maurus vgl. E. STEINMANN, Die Tituli
und die kirchliche Wandmalerei im Abendlande (1892), 138.

[153] Vgl. W. C. CRUM, in: Report of the Egypt. Expl. Fund (1897/98), 63; G. DE JER-
PHANION, aaO 50 f.

[154] Vgl. W. DEONNA, in: Revue des Études Grecques 20 (1907), 364 ff.

[155] Vgl. G. DE JERPHANION, aaO 64 unter Verweis auf den Mailänder Arzt Hieronymus CARDANUS, De rerum varietate Libri XVII, (Basileae 1557), 327.

[156] F. SAUERHERING, in: Tägliche Rundschau vom 25. 10. 1925.

III

Bei der kritischen Sichtung der Materialien haben wir die um 200 zu datierende und in der Regel als christlich beurteilte Aber-kios-Inschrift als ältestes Denkmal des Ostens in Frage stellen müs-sen. Für den Westen zitierten wir eingangs A. M. Schneider, der die ältest datierbare christliche Inschrift auf dem *Prosenes-Sarkophag* zu Rom sieht, welcher außerzömetrial an der Via Labicana vor den Toren der Stadt gefunden wurde (Taf. XV Abb. 37 und 38). Ebenso hat sich der jüngste Bearbeiter, H. U. Instinsky, der von De Rossi über Wilpert bis Schneider gehenden Ansicht angeschlossen, die an der Schmalseite des Sarkophags angebrachte Inschrift böte „einen unbezweifelbaren Hinweis darauf, daß der Verstorbene ein Christ gewesen ist"[157]. Die Inschrift lau-tet: Prosenes receptus ad deum V non (......)s Sa (...........)nia Prae-sente et Extricato II regrediens in urbe (!) ab expeditionibus (!). Scripsit Ampelius lib(ertus). Was den Bildschmuck des großen Sarkophags an-geht, der heute nahe dem Eingang zum Park der Villa Borghese bei der Piazza Flaminia steht, so enthält dieser ebensowenig Hinweise auf den christlichen Glauben des Prosenes, wie die Inschrift auf der Frontseite: M. Aurelio Augg(ustorum) lib(erto) Proseneti a cubiculo Aug(usti), proc (uratori) thesaurorum, proc(uratori) patrimoni, proc(uratori) munerum, proc(uratori) vinorum, ordinate a divo Commodo in kastrense, patrono piissimo liberti bene merenti sarcophagum de suo adornaverunt (CIL VI 8498). Die Inschrift steht auf einer tabula, die seitlich von Delphinen ge-rahmt und von schreitenden Eroten gehalten wird, denen Bögen, Köcher und Fackeln beigegeben sind, während unter der tabula zwei gekreuzte Füllhörner mit Früchten und Kornähren dargestellt sind. Die flacher gearbeiteten Schmalseiten zeigen Greifen, die G. Rodenwaldt apotro-päisch verstanden wissen will[158]. Die Seiten-Inschrift scheint von anderer Hand angebracht als die der tabula auf der Frontseite; wenn Wilpert sie als „Postskriptum" bezeichnet, so wird man dem insofern zustimmen,

---

[157] Vgl. H. U. Instinsky, aaO (s. oben Anm. 2), 114; A. M. Schneider, s. oben Anm. 1; G. B. de Rossi, Inscr. Christ. urbis Romae I, 5 und Suppl. fasc. 1, 1378; J. Wilpert, in: Die Papstgräber und die Cäciliengruft in der Katakombe des Hl. Kallistus (1909), 62 ff. – Sehr viel vorsichtiger urteilt, wie in der Regel, A. Stuiber, Refrigerium Inte-rim (Theophaneia 11, 1957), 113 Anm. 19: „Fraglich bleibt, ob sich bereits die Prose-nes-Inschrift vom Jahre 217 . . . mit Prosenes receptus ad deum paganen Formulie-rungen nähert."
[158] In: Bonner Jahrbücher 147 (1942), 220 f; s. oben Anm. 2; vgl. auch E. Weigand, Die spätantike Sarkophagskulptur im Lichte neuerer Forschung, in: ByZ 41 (1941), 416.

als hier das Todesdatum nachgetragen ist — ohne daß man einen größeren zeitlichen Abstand postulieren muß[159]. Die für uns entscheidende
Frage ist nun: Wird mit den Worten „receptus ad deum" = aufgenommen zu Gott, eine eindeutig christliche Formel benutzt, die das im übrigen Pagane des Bildschmuckes zu christianisieren vermag? Sowohl Instinsky als auch zuletzt H. Brandenburg betonen gegen Wilpert[160], daß
es sich hier nicht um eine besonders häufig in christlichen Inschriften
aufgenommene Formel handele. Es kann sogar eine eindeutig vorchrist-
liche Sepulkralinschrift aus Spanien vom Jahre 19 vChr nachgewiesen
werden: C. Sentio Sat(urnino) c(on)s(ule) k(alendis) Sextilib(us) dei Ma-
nes receperunt Abulliam N(umerii) l(ibertam) Nigellam[161]. Anderseits
lassen im 3. Jh. nChr bezeugte christliche Formeln wie receptus in pace
o. ä. auch für receptus ad deum die Möglichkeit christlichen Charakters
offen. Man wird daher gut tun, gerade bei der Prosenes-Inschrift beide
Möglichkeiten in Rechnung zu stellen, d. h. mit einem *non liquet* zu urteilen.

Muß aber der Prosenes-Sarkophag zumindest als sicherer Einsatz
christlicher Denkmäler des Westens zurückgestellt werden, so sind die
ältesten Regionen der Calixt-Katakombe, bald nach 200 nChr, als frü-
hest gesicherte Zeugnisse zu werten. Es folgen christliche Denkmäler in
großer Dichte, wenn auch die Entwicklung einer christlichen „Kunst"
zunächst langsam vor sich geht und diese erst seit konstantinischer Zeit
zur Entfaltung kommt.

Fragt man nach den Gründen für das späte Einsetzen, so bedarf A. M.
Schneiders Antwort für Rom, es habe dort „wenig historischen Sinn" gegeben und „mit dem sprachlichen Umbruch — seit der Mitte des 3. Jh.s
wird die Amtssprache der Bischöfe lateinisch — (sei) die Erinnerung an
die griechische Frühgeschichte verloren" gegangen[162], wohl doch der Ergänzung. Für das Fehlen frühester Denkmäler sind verschiedene Gründe
in Rechnung zu stellen:

Zunächst ist zu bedenken, daß die vom Judentum übernommene und
durch den Dekalog vorgeschriebene Bilderlosigkeit lange kirchlich unter-
strichenes Theologumenon blieb[163]. Hinzu kommt der Wille, sich gegen

---

[159] J. Wilpert, aaO 63; Instinsky aaO, 118.
[160] Instinsky aaO 120; H. Brandenburg, in: JbAC 7 (1964), 155 f.
[161] CIL II Nr. 2255.
[162] A. M. Schneider aaO 166 ff.
[163] Siehe H. v. Campenhausen, Die Bilderfrage als theol. Problem der alten Kirche,
in: Das Gottesbild im Abendland² (1959), 77 ff. Th. Klauser, Erwägungen zur Entstehung der altchristlichen Kunst, in: ZKG 76 (1965), 1—11.

das Heidentum abzusetzen; er steht der Aufnahme des antiken, auch in das Judentum eingedrungenen Heroenkultes und des Totenkultes überhaupt zunächst entgegen. Sodann spielt gewiß in der Anfangszeit die eschatologische Naherwartung eine Rolle. Doch wird man schon für Ende des 1. Jh.s damit zu rechnen haben, daß sich die Christen stärker in der Welt und in ihrer Geschichte einrichteten. Soviel wir noch zu erkennen vermögen, haben sie in den ersten zwei Jahrhunderten keine eigene Architektur für ihre Versammlungsräume entwickelt, also keine eigenen Kirchengebäude errichtet. Wenn heute Grundmauern freigelegt werden, so ist es nur bei Bauten jüngeren Datums möglich, vom Grundriß her christliche Erstellung abzulesen, während gerade die ältesten der vorkonstantinischen Zeit oft ihren möglicherweise christlichen Charakter verheimlichen[164]. Ebenso steht es mit den ältesten christlichen Gräbern. Natürlich ist anzunehmen, daß es unter den heute freigelegten Gräbern in Rom und Ostia, wie auch in Jerusalem und Kleinasien, solche gibt, in denen Christen der ersten zwei Jahrhunderte bestattet worden sind, aber man vermag dies keinem Zeichen mehr abzulesen. Bis etwa 200 nChr wird man grundsätzlich mit gemischten Beisetzungen zu rechnen haben, in Familien-Zömeterien und Privat-Mausoleen, weil erst mit der Calixtus-Katakombe eine kirchliche Organisation des Begräbnisses einsetzte. Der private Ursprung der christlichen Zömeterien und die erst spätere Überführung in kirchliches Eigentum, ja das Nebeneinander von privaten und kirchlichen Begräbnisstätten bis in das ausgehende 4. Jh. wird heute immer deutlicher[165]. Damit aber entfällt einerseits ein weites und entscheidendes Feld möglicher Bewahrung christlicher Denkmäler, erklärt sich anderseits die große Zahl außerzömeterial gefundener Sarkophage[166]. Alle diese Faktoren sprechen dafür, daß wahrscheinlich im 1. und 2. Jh. nChr als „christlich" zu bezeichnende Denkmäler zwar bestanden, aber sich von den paganen der Umwelt nicht abhoben.

Doch übersieht man in der Regel, daß schon mit dem 1. Viertel des 2. Jh.s nChr eine andere Gattung von Zeugnissen einsetzt, die in einem

[164] Vgl. R. KRAUTHEIMER, Early Christian and Byzantine Architecture (1965), 1 ff.

[165] Vgl. einerseits GERDA KRÜGER, Die Rechtsstellung der vorkonstantinischen Kirche (1935), die noch damit rechnet, daß Kirche u. kirchl. Zömeterien vor Konstantin öffentlich-rechtliche Größen waren. Anderseits ist F. DE VISSCHER, in: Analecta Boll 69 (1951), 39 ff zuzustimmen, daß die Familiengruft und das Familienzömeterium als Privatbesitz in der Verfolgungszeit bei Christen toleriert wurden. Siehe auch A. M. SCHNEIDER, aaO S. 191 ff. Eine Katakombe für christliche *und* heidnische Glieder einer Familie liegt zweifellos in der von A. FERRUA herausgegebenen und bearbeiteten Via Latina Katakombe (Roma 1960) vor.

[166] Vgl. die Liste bei A. M. SCHNEIDER, aaO 194 f.

weiteren Sinn als „christliche Denkmäler" zu werten sind: die *ältesten Papyri mit neutestamentlichen Texten*. Gewiß gehören sie zu den literarischen Quellen, aber als Papyrus-*Funde* sind auch sie „archäologische" Denkmäler, die durch ihre Texte als von Christen bearbeitet sich ausweisen. Beurteilt man sie in ihrem Charakter als datierbare Funde, so sind sie — nach dem augenblicklichen Stand der Forschung — die absolut ältesten erhaltenen „Denkmäler" der Christenheit. Wenn heute P[52] der John Rylands Library, Manchester, der als Fragment den Text Joh 18, 31—34.37—38 enthält, an den Anfang des 2. Jh.s datiert wird[167], so ist dies überlieferungsgeschichtlich ein außerordentlicher Fall; ist doch diese Abschrift nur etwa 30 bis 50 Jahre jünger als das johanneische Autographon selbst. Solche Verhältnisse sind literargeschichtliche Ausnahmen, wenn auch keine Garantie für besondere Texttreue[168].

Die christliche Archäologie hat bisher nicht ausreichend beachtet, was die Textgeschichte und -kritik des Neuen Testamentes dargelegt haben: Die neuen Papyri der Bibliotheca Bodmeriana bezeugen für die Zeit um 200 für σταυροῦν und σταυρός eine Kontraktionsform, in der das älteste Zeichen für das Kreuz als Christi Marterinstrument bezeugt wird und damit neben das Kreuzzeichen als Tauf-Sphragis tritt. Es wurde von K. Aland richtig beobachtet und erstmals herausgestellt, daß in der Handschriftenüberlieferung biblischer Texte die neutestamentlichen Papyri P[66] und P[75] die Kontraktion ⳨, aus T und P gebildet, erstmalig für uns faßbar und häufig benutzen. Es erscheint fast als Regel, mit diesem Zeichen die Buchstaben ταυρ verkürzt zu geben: σ ⳨ ος. Da das historische Kreuz auf Golgatha mit größter Wahrscheinlichkeit T-Form hatte und auch theologisch der griechische Buchstabe τ auf das Kreuz bezogen wurde — wie der Barnabasbrief (9,8) bezeugt[169] —, so ist unsere Kontraktion ⳨ unter die frühbelegbaren „Heiligen Worte" zu zählen, wie vorher schon Θ͞C und K͞C und auch I͞H[170]. Mit Recht macht Aland darauf

---

[167] Vgl. K. Aland, Kurzgefaßte Liste der griechischen Handschriften des NT I (1963), 32.

[168] Vgl. zum hier berührten Problem H. Useners berühmte Abhandlung: Unser Platontext. Nachr. d. königl. Ges. d. Wiss. zu Göttingen (1892), Nr. 2, 25—50 u. 6, 181 ff (= Kleine Schriften III [1914], 104—162). Ferner H. Lietzmann, in: Kleine Schriften II (1958), 160—169.

[169] Siehe oben S. 168 und dazu jetzt H. Rahner, Symbole der Kirche (Salzburg 1964), 406—431.

[170] Vgl. K. Aland, Neutestamentl. Papyri II, in: NTS 10 (1963/64), 75 ff und 11 (1964/65), 1 f. Der Papyrus Bodmer 2 = P[66] enthält das nahezu vollständige Johannesevangelium und wird oft kurz nach 200 datiert. Papyrus Bodmer 14.15 = P[75] ist Anfang des 3. Jh.s anzusetzen. Zur Datierung der ntl Papyri vgl. noch K. Aland, in: ZNW

---

aufmerksam, daß somit das Staurogramm älter ist als das Christogramm ✻. Dessen „Sitz im Leben" wird man dann wohl auch zuerst in den Skriptorien biblischer Handschriften zu suchen haben. Entscheidend ist nun freilich für unsere Themastellung, daß älter als jedes „christliche" Bild, älter als die christianisierte oder auch schöpferisch-christliche Ikonographie, das Zeichen der Christen für *das* Heilsereignis, für das Kreuz Christi ist.

Der Befund unserer Untersuchungen ist nur scheinbar negativ. Mit Nachdruck ist zu sagen, daß damit nicht etwa der Beginn der christlichen Tradition erst auf Anfang des 3. Jh.s gesetzt wird; vielmehr darf man unter Beachtung der ältesten literarischen Fragmente von einer nahezu ungebrochen durchlaufenden Überlieferung sprechen. Diese ältesten Papyrus-Fragmente stammen sogar aus einer Zeit, in der es noch keinen Kanon des Neuen Testaments neben der „Schrift", dem Alten Testament, gab. Das „Wort" in schriftlich fixierter Form reicht also weiter in die Vergangenheit zurück als das „Ding" oder „Kunstwerk" als Reflex des Glaubens an Christus.

Angesichts aller kritischen Ausklammerungen ist zu bedenken, daß hiermit nur einer romantischen Frühdatierung entgegengetreten wird, die mit einer Vordatierung archäologischer Denkmäler eine an sich unbezweifelbare innere Kontinuität sichern will. Daß es in Palästina seit dem Ereignis von Kreuzigung und Erhöhung Jesu Christi Kirche gibt, daß bald christliche Gemeinden in Kleinasien und Griechenland und ebenso am Golf von Neapel und in Rom sich bildeten — das ist durch die neutestamentlichen Schriften bezeugt. Die innere Kontinuität der Kirchengeschichte ist derart, daß man bei einer kritischen Sichtung der facta archaeologica theologisch und historisch beurteilt gar nichts verlieren kann. Es stünde schlecht um den christlichen Glauben, wenn er sich archäologisch sichern müßte.

---

48 (1957), 148 ff und zusammenfassend die oben Anm. 167 zitierte „Kurzgefaßte Liste". Zu den ältesten Kontraktionen weiteres Material bei: L. TRAUBE, Nomina Sacra (1907); G. RUDBERG, Neutestamentl. Text und Nomina Sacra, Uppsala-Leipzig (1915), bes. 47 ff; neuerdings A. H. R. E. PAAP, Nomina Sacra in the Greek Papyri of the First Five Centuries A. D. (Leiden, 1959), Papyrologica Lugduno-Batava VIII, freilich ohne Berücksichtigung der das Staurogramm betreffenden Beobachtungen von ALAND. — Über den Forschungsstand hinsichtlich der Nomina Sacra informiert gut H. GERSTINGER, in: Gnomon 32 (1960), 371—374.

DID GNOSTICS MAKE PICTURES?

BY

PAUL CORBY FINNEY

IRENAEUS says that Carpocratian Gnostics had images and venerated them (*Haer.* 1.24.6 [Harvey 1. 210]). He does not specify their subject matter, but writes only that they worshipped these images together with those of Pythagoras, Plato, Aristotle, and others. This account implies that Carpocratian Gnostics had their own distinct form of iconography. Elsewhere Irenaeus mentions images in connection with Basilidians and magic (*Haer.* 1.24.5 [Harvey 1. 201]), but this account is not useful for history.[1]

If some Gnostics did make images, as Irenaeus claims for the Carpocratians, what kind of images were they, what was their subject matter, in what media were they executed and on what scale? Do any examples survive? The latter is a reasonable expectation, if we consider that a parade of Gnostics is said to have marched through Rome during the years of the early Principate, and that our archaeological knowledge of the city is good: Rome ought to be a good place to hunt down material traces left by Gnostics. But what should we be looking for? Discontinuity in the material record is surely the key, but what kind of discontinuity makes us suspect the presence of Gnostics? And where are we likely to find this discontinuity? If we should use behavior as a guide, we might be able to find the Gnostics: did they

---

For bibliography and useful advice I am very grateful to Hugo Brandenburg. Nikolaus Himmelmann, Bentley Layton, George MacRae, Kathleen McVey. Birger Pearson, Patrick Skehan, and Morton Smith. Because of technical reasons the photo documentation could not be included here.

[1] Cf. my "Gnosticism and the Origins of Early Christian Art." *Atti del IX Congresso Internazionale di Archeologia Cristiana* (Rome 21-27.ix.75), in press. Justin, 1 *Apol.* 26, 56 (ed. Otto I/1. 78, 79, 154) confuses a sculptural dedication to the Sabine Semo/Sancus (*CIL* VI i 567, 568; in the Vatican's Galleria Lapidaria) with one to Simon. Irenaeus repeats the error, *Haer.* 1.23.1 (Harvey 1. 190, 191); also Eusebius. *H.E.* 2.13.3 (ed. Schwartz, GCS 9/1, 134) and Tertullian, *Apol.* 13.9.38 ff. (ed. Dekkers. CCL 1, 112). Among these authors none says anything about a specifically Gnostic form of iconography; cf. *Haer.* 1.23.4 (Harvey 1. 194): Simonians worship a statue of the master as Jupiter, one of Helen as Minerva. i.e., old bottles filled with new wine. *CIL* VI i 567, 568: R. P. Garrucci, *Relazione generale degli scavi e scoperte fatte lungo la Via Latina* ... (Rome, 1859) 80 ff.

behave as groups in special ways that set them off from their neigh-
bors? For example, did Gnostics have special cults[2] that required unusual furnishings or spaces? Did they dispose of their dead in unusual
ways, perhaps using grave goods marked with Gnostic subjects? Unfortunately the premise of distinct Gnostic group behavior cannot be
demonstrated from the sources, and hence the archaeological search
is in vain.

We can be sure that Gnostics were different and distinct only in
one culture trait: thought. The literature that they produced proves
the point. The material and social context which accompanied the
production of this literature is lost, but the distinctness of the literary
product cannot be gainsaid. Gnostic answers to questions of cosmogony, cosmology, ethics, anthropology, and history are attested abundantly. Although they borrowed freely from the store of Greco-Roman
and Near Eastern wisdom, Gnostics combined traditional themes in
new unusual ways.

Did Gnostics translate any of their unusual myths and beliefs into
pictures? Irenaeus hints that the Carpocratians did, but in Origen we
have a clear-cut, positive answer. In *Cels.* 6.24-38 (ed. Koetschau,
GCS 3, 94-107), he discusses an Ophite ideograph which he claims
to know at first hand. Unfortunately he does not reproduce the
diagram, but modern scholars have attempted reconstructions, some
of them plausible.[3] Apparently the ideograph of the Ophite cosmos
was inhabited by images of archontic demons who made up the Ophite

---

[2] Marcosian cult (the locus classicus): *Haer.* 1.13.2, 3; 1.21.3-5 (Harvey 1. 115;
183 ff.) = Epiphanius, *Haer.* 34.2.1; 34.20.1 (ed. Holl, GCS 31, 6 ff., 36 ff.). *Haer.* 1.21.5
creates a cultic context for the recitation of a Marcosian creed, fragments of which
appear in a noncultic setting, Codex V,3 from Nag Hammadi (A. Böhlig and P. Labib,
Koptisch-gnostische Apokalypsen aus Codex V von Nag Hammadi [Halle/Saale, 1963]):

Irenaeus, *Haer.* 1.21.5	*IApocJas* 33 : 16-24
ἐγώ	16 ⲀⲚⲀⲔ
υἱὸς ἀπὸ	17 ⲞⲨϢⲎⲢⲈ ⲀⲨⲰ ⲀⲚⲞⲔ ⲞⲨⲈⲂⲞⲖ ⲀⲘ
πατρὸς	18 ⲠⲒⲰⲦ . . .
πατρὸς προόντος	22 ⲠⲒⲰⲦ ⲈⲦⲢ ϢⲞⲢⲠ [ⲚϢⲞⲞⲠ]
υἱὸς δὲ ἐν τῷ	23 ⲞⲨϢⲎⲢⲈ ⲀⲈ ⲈϤ2Ⲙ ⲠⲈⲦ[Ⲣ]
παρόντι	24 ϢⲞⲢⲠ ⲚϢⲞⲞⲠ

Which is the correct setting? Naassene cult: Hippolytus, *Haer.* 5.8.6 ff. (ed. Wendland,
GCS 26, 90). Phibionite cult: Epiphanius, *Haer.* 26.4 ff. (GCS 25, 280 ff.). Mandaean
cult: E. S. Drower, *The Canonical Prayerbook of the Mandaeans* (Leiden, 1959); there
the older literature. Theodotian Valentinianism: R. P. Casey, *The Excerpta of Clement
of Alexandria* (SD 1; London, 1934) 36 ff., 91 ff. *Gospel of Philip:* H. G. Gaffron,
Studien zum koptischen Philippusevangelium ... (Bonn, 1969) 71-99.

[3] H. Chadwick, *Contra Celsum* (Cambridge, 1953) 358, 359.

hebdomad. Origen says he had seen pictures of these demons and that their details accorded with the description of them transmitted by Celsus: monsters with composite attributes, both zoomorphic and anthropomorphic. Although lost, these pictures surely constituted Gnostic iconography.

Beyond the evidence of Irenaeus and Origen there is the Bruce Codex, the only extant Gnostic document containing pictorial marginalia. The Sahidic codex is late and fragmentary and the product of several hands, but these are not reasons to doubt that the pictures were in the Greek prototype(s). The first forty leaves, to which Schmidt assigned the title *First and Second Books of Jeu*, contain a total of sixty-nine pictorial schemata, some simple, others rather complex. Basically these pictures fall into two classes. The first are linear ideographs schematizing the *typos* of the true god, Jeu, his emanations, and seals marking the identity of emanations. The second class of pictures consists in seals apart from a linear matrix: there are eight examples at the end of the so-called *First Book of Jeu* (chapters 33-38, 40) and twenty-three further examples in the so-called *Second Book of Jeu*. The former group of eight have names and numerical equivalents, whereas the twenty-three have names only. Eight of the twenty-three seals (*Second Book of Jeu*, chapters 45-48) appear in a very interesting narrative framework where Jesus performs a magical initiation of his disciples, as in these two examples:

> Jesus stood near the sacrifice and spread out linen garments. On them he placed a wine beaker and enough bread for his disciples. He laid olive branches on the place of sacrifice and crowned the disciples with olive

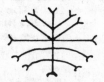

Fig. 1.   Bruce Codex. Gnostic seal. (Drawing by J. Steczynski.)

> branches. And Jesus sealed his disciples with this seal [see fig. 1]. Its explanation is this: thezozaz. And its name: sazapharas (after the trans. of Schmidt, GCS 45 [13] 308).

> Now thereafter it happened that Jesus spoke to his disciples: "Look, you have received the baptism of the holy spirit." He laid out the censer of baptism in the holy spirit, and placed on it grape sprays, juniper berries, casdalanthos, remains of saffron, the resin of a mastich tree, cinnamon, myrrh, balsam, honey. And he laid out two vessels of wine, one to

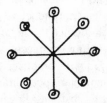

Fig. 2. Bruce Codex. Gnostic seal. (Drawing by J. Steczynski.)

the right of the censer and the other to the left. And he laid out enough bread for the disciples. And Jesus sealed the disciples with this seal [fig. 2]. This is the name of the seal: zakzoza. And this its explanation: thozonoz. (GCS 45 [13], 311)

Many of the seals in the Bruce Codex excluding those that mark emanations sent forth by Jeu) consists in some combination of the following three elements:

Fig. 2a.   Hastae common in late Roman monogrammatic ligatures.
(Drawing by Carol Sneed.)

Although we cannot pursue this detail here, it is probably worth looking into: these three linear elements appear with great frequency in late Roman and Byzantine ligatures, especially monogrammatic ligatures. This could point to an interesting connection between Gnostics and non-Gnostics in the conventions by which both sealed. Gnostic sphragistics could borrow from late Roman sigillography.

The pictures in the Bruce Codex have nothing to do with the world as we know it. They are conceptual images, abstracted from nature and nonrepresentational. This is just as we might expect, since the pictures follow a text that is itself several times removed from ordinary experience. The only exception in the text falls in chapters 45-48 where Jesus is made to perform a rite of magical initiation which has parallels in ancient cult and literature, notably in the magical papyri.[5] Anthro-

---

[4] Cf. my article "A Monogrammed Byzantine Garnet from Carthage," *Carthage Excavations 1975, Punic Project, First Interim Report* (ed. L. E. Stager; Chicago, 1978), in press (there the literature).

[5] *PGM* 7. 222ff.; 8. 65ff.; F. J. Dölger, *Sphragis* (Paderborn, 1911), and by the same author: *AC* 1 (1929) 66-78, 88-91, 197-201; 2 (1930) 100-41, 297-300; 3 (1932) 204-9; O. Lassaly, *ARW* 29 (1931), 130ff.; H. Lietzmann, *An die Galater* (Tübingen, [3]1932): cf. Gal 6:17.

pology and ethnography also provide parallels, as does a broad spectrum of Greco-Roman religious practice. The literary scenario, depicting a leader initiating an inner circle of disciples in a rite that culminated in a magical sealing, connects at least a section of the codex with common non-Gnostic practice, but there is no pictorial illustration of Jesus the magician performing the rite. Instead the pictures remain consistently abstract, linear schematizations of an imaginary world inhabited by concepts, not people.

The Ophite monsters reported by Celsus are also abstractions, Goyaesque creatures of fantasy, removed from ordinary experience. But they are not so far removed as are the pictures in the Bruce Codex. In the first place, the Ophite creatures have anthropomorphic and zoomorphic attributes. True, these attributes are combined in unnatural and fantastic combinations; however, the details are immediately recognizable. But more importantly, the joining of diverse attributes in one subject is a practice that has ancient roots, as we know from Homer and Hesiod and, even earlier, from Iron and Bronze Age iconographies. The parallels from the Greco-Egyptian environment contemporary with Gnosticism number in the dozens. In other words, just as the shaman marking and sealing his inner circle is a familiar figure in antiquity and in prehistory, so also is the composite demon, part man, part animal, a familiar creation in ancient (and modern) iconography. Naturally, the crucial question is whether the Gnostics ever invented their own special pictorial equivalents of composite demons. A well-known example in a nonliterary setting seems to suggest that they did.

In the Brummer Collection, an oval pendant of green jasper clouded with red and fashioned like a cabochon shows on its reverse six of the seven names in the Ophite hebdomad described by Irenaeus, *Haer.* 1.30.5; 1.30.11 (Harvey 1. 230, 237). On its obverse the exergual letters show Aariel and Ialdabaoth, the latter being the seventh member of the Gnostic sphere. Also on the obverse is the image of a lion-headed man, in three-quarter view, dressed in a brief Egyptian apron, with a staff in the right hand and a situla in the other (fig. 3). This figure is probably the visual counterpart of Ialdabaoth, described in *Cels.* 6.31 (GCS 2, 100ff.) and *Pistis Sophia* 31 (tr. Schmidt and Till, GCS 45, 28ff.). We do not know when or where this stone was cut, or for whom. Nor do we know who conceived the idea of translating the literary description into its visual equivalent. The owner of the stone could have belonged to any one of several religions, or to none. But

Fig. 3. Lion-headed demon on a gemstone in the Brummer Collection. C Bonner, *SMA*, Plate IX. 188. (Drawing by J. Steczynski.)

surely the most likely explanation is that he or she was a Gnostic and that the iconographic conception was Gnostic from the start. The demonic image on this gemstone is probably not an isolated example. No doubt there are others like it, and within the corpus of magical iconography there may be different examples of iconographic equivalences which point to Gnostic inspiration.

But before we turn to that subject, we need to look briefly at the other areas within ancient iconography where Gnostics are said to have left their mark. Due to the limitations of the present format, I can do little more than name the sources and comment in highly abbreviated form without pictorial documentation.

Five kinds of figured artifacts are sometimes labelled Gnostic: (1) inscriptions; (2) papyri; (3) sculptures; (4) paintings; (5) gemstones and related small finds (lamellae, lead defixiones, small bronze and terracotta plaques). The first and second groups do not concern us here. Though the inscription of Flavia Sophe and the intriguing metrical fragment in the Capitoline Museum (Inv. No. 2276) were surely inspired by Valentinian ideology and possibly executed for Roman Gnostics, neither is accompanied by pictures that have any claim to Gnostic inspiration.[6] And as noted, excepting the Bruce

---

[6] Flavia Sophe (*CIG* 4. 959a, ed. Curtius and Kirchoff): R. P. Garrucci, *Via Latina*, 43 (circumstances of discovery); A. Ferrua, *RivAC* 21 (1944) 176-93; G. Quispel, *Mélanges Ghellinck* 1 (Gembloux, 1951) 201-14; M. Guarducci, *MDAIR* (1973) 182-86. On the fragment in the Capitoline: M. Guarducci, *MDAIR* 59, 169ff.; also *MDAIR* 81 (1974) 341-43. Marcionite inscription of Deir-Ali: A. von Harnack, *Marcion: Das Evangelium vom fremden Gott* (Leipzig, 1924; reprinted, Darmstadt, 1960) 341. The Gnosticism of Julia Evaresta's epitaph is doubtful: I. B. de Rossi, *ICUR* 2/1. XXVIII; A. Ferrua, *RivAC* 21, 165-76 (there the literature); also M. Guarducci, *MDAIR* 80 (1973) 186, 187 (author notes the proximity of the find spot to that of the dedication

Codex, the Gnostic papyri are devoid of pictures. As we would expect, throughout the Gnostic corpus the copyists joined uncials in ligatures, but none of the hands reflects any distinctness which might lead us to suspect that their combinations were intended to be pictorial or were inspired by Gnostic concepts. Besides, paleographic ligatures are only one possible step (though surely an important one: witness the cross) in the evolution of thought from words to pictures. Again the exception is the Bruce Codex, which contains important ideographic and sphragistic inventions (or are they borrowed conventions?): a subject worthy of full-scale investigation, but not here. Thus, eliminating epigraphy and papyri from the present discussion, we are left with three possible candidates for inclusion within the category "Gnostic" art: sculpture, painting, and gemstones. The first two promise little for our understanding of Gnosticism.

1. "GNOSTIC" SCULPTURE

The Khirbet Qilqis collection and the alabaster phiale formerly in the collection of Jacob Hirsch are the artifacts contemplated within this grouping. In 1960-61, the Franciscans of the Monastery of the Flagellation in Jerusalem acquired (under conditions that strain the limits of credibility) a collection of limestone artifacts, some resembling miniature stelae with occasional cruciform and anthropoid projections, some statuettes, and some crosses.[7] Many pieces are marked with linear incisions said to be an esoteric Semitic script, and some of the symbols etched onto these stones are believed to carry cosmic meaning. The find spot, Khirbet Qilqis (coordinates 159.100 on the 1:100,000 British Survey Map of Palestine, 1942 edition), is tied to the Gnostic secretarians whom Epiphanius calls Archontics (*Haer.* 40.1.1-40.8.2 [ed. Holl, GCS 31, 80-90]). The sculptures are said to

to Flavia Sophe and concludes, "L'epigrafe di Giulia Euaresta è dunque, un misto di orthodossia e di gnosticismo ..."). The epitaph to Julia Evaresta has a pictorial accompaniment, namely, a bird with a twig in its beak, certainly not a "Gnostic" motif; cf. P. Bruun, *AIRF* 1/2 (1963) 86ff., and H. Instinsky, *CIL* VIII Suppl. 5.2 (Berlin, 1865) 240ff. ("Anaglypha cristiana").

[7] E. Testa, *Il simbolismo dei giudei cristiani* (Jerusalem, 1962). Testa's work was popularized and made to support a "new" chapter in the history of doctrine: J. Daniélou, *Les symboles chrétiens primitifs* (Paris, 1961). Also B. Bagatti, *La Terra Santa* 40 (1964) 264-69. Archontics: H.-Ch. Puech, *RAC* 1. 633-43. Criticism: R. le Déaut, *Biblica* 47 (1966) 283-89; J. Starcky, *RB* 75 (1968) 278-80; R. North, *CBQ* 24 (1962) 441-43. Also useful is J. T. Milik's review, *Biblica* 48 (1967) 450, 451, of E. Testa, *L'Huile de la foi* (tr. O. Englebert; Jerusalem, 1967). On Khirbet Qilqis (Caphar Baricha): M. Avi-Yonah, *Qedem* 5 (1976) 46.

exhibit Archontic ideology. But the authenticity of the entire Khirbet Qilqis assemblage is seriously in question, and until that issue is clarified, discussion of the Archontic hypothesis is superfluous.

The alabaster phiale, by contrast, is probably ancient, though its date and provenience are unknown.[8] The interior of the bowl shows a cult scene in which naked devotees of both sexes, the males infibulated, worship a reptilian sun deity wound about an egg-shaped omphalos[9] at the bowl's center. The exterior of the bowl shows an arcade of columns and unidentified male figures, perhaps erotes, heralds of the snake god, or winds. On the exterior lower base rim is a metric inscription in raised uncials. Three of the inscription's four lines derive from an Orphic poem that first circulated in Cornelius Labeo's lost *De Oraculo Apollinis Clarii*,[10] preserved in fragments by Macrobius. The fourth line gives a fragment from Euripides' monologue of Melanippe the Wise who recites the Orphic cosmogony from a world egg. In short, the phiale's iconography and epigraphy point unmistakeably to Orphism. Leisegang[11] wanted to go beyong Orphism: he saw on the vessel's interior Epiphanius's Ophite eucharist (*Haer.* 37.56 ff. [GCS 31, 57]), and called the bowl Gnostic. But the Orphic connection is the right one.

If there are further pieces of sculpture that scholars want to call Gnostic, they are unknown to me. Doresse mentioned the well-known bronze statuette wrapped in snakes and laid on the ground with seven chicken eggs beneath the altar of the third temple to Jupiter Heliopolitanus, presently on the Sciarra-Wurts property in Rome.[12] Ap-

---

[8] The bowl appears in *Bedeutende Kunstwerke aus dem Nachlass Dr. Jacob Hirsch* (auction catalogue, 5.xii.57, Hotel Schweizerhof, Lucerne) no. 105: "Orphische Schale. Alabaster. D. oben 22 cm., unten 19 cm., H. 7 cm." (Tafel 49). Published by R. Delbrueck and W. Vollgraf, *JHS* 54 (1934) 120-39.

[9] Navel stones and φιάλαι: A. A. Barb, *JWarb* 16 (1953) 200; H. Luschey, *PWSup* 7 (Stuttgart, 1940) 1026-30; also N. Himmelmann, *Marburger Winckelmann-Programm*, 1960, 13-40. A black steatite amulet (formerly?) in the Collection de Clercq (A. de Ridder, *Catalogue méthodique et raisonné* 7/3 [Paris, 1885] no. 3514) shows a snake coiled about an omphalos. The amulet bears an inscription which may read: שֹׂפֿרֿפּפֿחֿנֿעֿרֿפֿלֿרֿבֿרֿרֿהֿשֿרֿוֹד] (פֿרֿשֹׂ = πρᾶξις?). E. Goodenough, *GRBS* 1 (1958) 71-80 (adds nothing but more bad photos and unnecessary speculation).

[10] Macrobius, *Sat.* 1.18.21 (ed. J. Willis [Leipzig, 1963] 106): "... huius oraculi vim, numinis, nominisque interpretationem, qua Liber Pater et sol 'Ιαώ significatur, executus est Cornelius Labeo in Libro cui titulus est *De oraculo Apollinis Clarii* ..." The phiale's metrical fragments paralleled in Macrobius, *Sat.* 1.18.12; 1.23.21 (Willis, 104, 127); A. Nauck, *TGF* fr. 484.

[11] H. Leisegang, *ErJB* 7 (1939) 151 ff.

[12] J. Doresse, *Les livres secrets des Gnostiques d'Égypte* (Paris, 1958) 96-102; also *Bulletin de l'Institut d'Égypte* 32 (1949) 364, 365. Iuppiter Optimus Maximus Helio-

parently Doresse saw some (unexplained) connection between this Syrian solar deity and Gnosticism.

2. "GNOSTIC" PAINTING

In modern history the idea of a Gnostic iconography dates to the seventeenth-century works by Chiflet and l'Heureux.[13] In the present century, the notion gained a lot of ground after the important discovery (November, 1919) of the Tomb of the Aureli in Rome's Viale Manzoni. The seventeenth-, eighteenth-, and nineteenth-century studies of Gnostic iconography focused correctly on small finds and papyrological evidence. By contrast, the literature since 1919 turns to wall and ceiling paintings.

Mainly a study of Roman funerary painting, Cecchelli's book[14] popularizes this unlikely shift of focus and confirms the notion which had apparently become historical orthodoxy between the two world wars: Gnostics coined new pictorial currencies, especially in the realm of painting, and the decoration in the Tomb of the Aureli is the Gnostic pièce de résistence. While we can thank Cecchelli for bringing this monument to a larger audience, the manner of presentation, namely by subsuming it under the rubric Gnostic, advances neither our understanding of the hypogaeum's complicated iconography nor our understanding of Gnosticism.

Burial activity in the tomb spans the second and third centuries down to 270-272. The funerary complex consists in an upper chamber, mostly destroyed, and two lower chambers joined by a gallery of

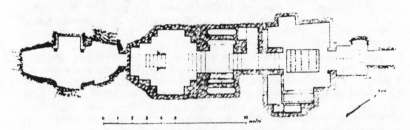

Fig. 4. Rome. Tomb of the Aureli. Plan. (From G. Bendinelli, *MonAnt* 28 [1922].)

politanus (*CIL* VI 422): N. Goodhue, *The Lucus Furrinae and the Syrian Sanctuary on the Janiculum* (Amsterdam, 1975); also V. von Graeve, *AA* 87 (1972) 314-47.

[13] J. Chiflet and J. L'Heureux (= Macarius), *Abraxas seu Apistopistus* (Antwerp, 1657).

[14] C. Cecchelli, *Monumenti Cristiano-Eretici di Roma* (Rome, 1944); cf. A. Ferrua, *CivCatt* 95 (1944) 388-92.

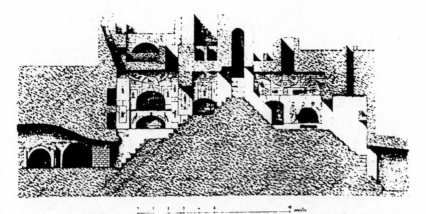

Fig. 5. Rome. Tomb of the Aureli. Elevation (looking west.)

stairs and platforms (figs. 4 and 5). Arcosolia, formae, and loculi indicate that the Aureli inhumed their dead, but recessed niches painted with showers of rose petals and resembling the urn emplacements in Roman columbaria suggests that a few of the Aureli cremated.[15] The dedicatory inscription and two other epigraphic fragments do not advance our understanding of the occupants' religion.[16]

The west wall of the upper chamber contains a loculus burial flanked by two fragmentary paintings that are thought to connect with Gnosticism. The one to the left shows a fragmentary standing male figure and small fragments of a second figure (fig. 6). There is also a snake that rises from the ground. The iconographic components suggest Adam and Eve. Jason and Medea have been contemplated, as has Hercules,[17] but the details, insofar as we can make them out,

[15] G. Bendinelli, *MonAnt* 28 (1922), 371-73 and fig. 34: "... decorazione pittorica delle nicchiette di testata. Questa consiste di semplici macchie di colore rosso e verde, sparse irregolarmente sull' intonaco, a rappresentare una caduta di foglie e di petali di rosa. ..." Parallels in the Vatican necropolis (Tombs E, I, O, T): B. M. Apollonj Ghetti et al., *Esplorazioni sotto la confessione di San Pietro in Vaticano* (Vatican City, 1961) passim. Symbolism of the rose petals: P.-A. Février, "Le culte des morts dans les communautés chrétiennes durant le IIIᵉ siècle," *IX.CIAC* (Rome, 21-28.ix.75), in press. My thanks to Paul Février for a galley proof copy of his useful study. J. Carcopino, *De Pythagore aux Apôtres* (Paris, 1953) 86: "Il n'y a nulle part traces de tombes à incineration" (*sic!*); cf. J. M. C. Toynbee, *Gnomon* 29 (1957) 261 ff.

[16] Dedicatory inscription: G. Bendinelli, *MonAnt* 28, 320, fig. 15; Aurelia Myrsina: ibid., 426, 427, and G. Wilpert, *AttiPARA* (Serie 3, Memorie I/II; Rome, 1924) 5, fig. 2; dipinto di R(em)meus Celerinus who apparently celebrated a refrigerium in the lower north chamber: G. Bendinelli, *MonAnt* 28, 369.

[17] N. Himmelmann, "Das Hypogäum der Aurelier am Viale Manzoni," *AbhAkMainz* (1975) 1-27.

Fig. 6. Rome. Tomb of the Aureli. Upper chamber West wall. Reconstruction of the panel to the left of the loculus burial. (Drawing by C. Sneed.)

suggests neither the Argonaut nor the Hercules cycles. Archaeological and iconographic context are no help. The Gnostic theory builds on the panel's irregularities and departures from the iconographic "convention": there is no tree separating the figures, the snake is in the wrong place, and the male figure does not cover his genitals. From these details it is argued that the scene must be heterodox, representing, according to Wilpert,[18] an Ophite revelation discourse. The snake seduces Eve with its "lingua bifida" rather than with the apple. Wilpert could find no documentary prototype of this scene, but more important, the fundamental premise (iconographic irregularity = heterodoxy) is anachronistic. There existed no pictorial canon at this early date. The translation of biblical subjects into pictures was still at the stage of experimentation.[19]

The panel to the right of this same loculus shows a seated male figure and the head and shoulders of a second male (fig. 7). The setting is an orchard or garden. Wilpert identified this scene as the pictorial equivalent of Irenaeus, Haer. 1.30.6 (Harvey 1. 232), in which Ialdabaoth and six other members of the Ophite hebdomad create "hominem immensum latitudine et longitudine." On the model of Prometheus,[20] we would expect a creator to touch his creation, a detail for which the pictorial evidence is wanting. The other members of the hebdomad are missing also. And the diminutive figure which could well be a common garden-variety herm, hardly evokes the presence of the Ophite giant.

In the lower south room of the Tomb, philosophy and magic[21] clearly have the upper hand. Which philosophy and what kind of magic we cannot specify, but the generic themes are clear. The symbolism in the north room is more difficult. Philosophy and magic are present, but it is not clear that they are intended as the unifying themes. The shepherd-criophoros appears four times. There is also a seated philosopher-shepherd,[22] an unusual adventus

---

[18] G. Wilpert, AttiPARA 3, I/II, 10; J. Carcopino, Pythagore, 112 (follows Wilpert).

[19] I will treat this subject in my forthcoming book. My Ph.D. thesis (Harvard University, 1973) contains the full bibliography. Chronology of early Christian painting (very uncertain): L. Reekmans, RivAC 49 (1973) 271ff.

[20] G. Bendinelli, MonAnt 28, 311, 312 (does not mention any material connection between the two figures); J. Carcopino, Pythagore, 110 (misreads Bendinelli). Prometheus: K. Bapp, in Ausführliches Lexikon der griechischen und römischen Mythologie (ed. W. H. Roscher; Leipzig, 1884ff.) 2. 3032ff., especially 3103-10.

[21] The main clue is the kerykeion-virgula: G. Bendinelli, MonAnt 28, 472, 473 (denies the magical connection); N. Himmelmann, "Hypogäum," 16 (unnecessarily circumspect); H. Achelis, KuK 2 (1926) 69 (sees the magical connection). Cf. F. J. M. de Waele, The Magic Staff or Rod in Graeco-Italian Antiquity (The Hague, 1927) (there the literature).

[22] Shepherd-criophoros: G. Bendinelli, MonAnt 28, 335-43, fig. 20-23; G. Wilpert, AttiPARA 3, I/II, 34ff., tav. 19, fig. 8; J. Carcopino, Pythagore, 133-37 (Gnostic interpretation). Cf. Th. Klauser, JAC 1 (1958) 20ff.; 3 (1960) 112ff.; 5 (1962) 113ff.; 7 (1964) 67ff.; 8/9 (1965) 126ff.; 10 (1967) 82ff. Criticism: V. Buchheit, RQ 69

Fig. 7. Rome. Tomb of the Aureli. Upper chamber. West wall. Panel to the right of the loculus burial. (Drawing by C. Sneed.)

narrative,[23] a scene apparently from Odysseus's homecoming,[24] a meal sequence, and a lunette showing an enclosed garden connected to a courtyard crowded with people, including a seated magician. Eleven standing philosophers dressed in tunica laticlava and bearing scrolls adorn the room's lower registers. And finally, on the east wall of the gallery that connects the two lower rooms is the famous green Latin cross, Wilpert's Valentinian *horos*, but in truth the surviving fragment of a decorative garland.[25] In short, the iconography at the lower level of the hypogaeum bears no relationship to Gnosticism.

The second funerary complex containing iconography said to exhibit

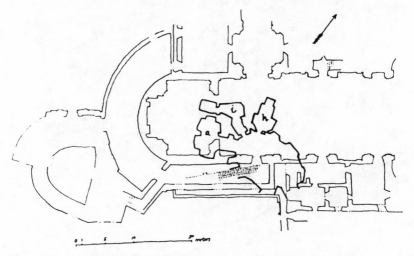

Fig. 8. Rome. San Sebastiano. Plan of the west end of the church showing (in dark outli. :) the position of the Piazzuola. (Drawing by J. Steczynski.)

(1974) 133 f. and my thesis, 306 ff.; also A. Provoost, *Iconologisch onderzoek van den laatantieke herdervoorstellingen* (Proefschrift, Katholieke Universiteit te Leuven, 1976). My thanks to Arnold Provoost for a copy of his monumental work, otherwise inaccessible to me. Philosophy and shepherding: N. Himmelmann, *RhM* 115 (1972) 342-56.

[23] E. Kantorowicz, *ArtB* 26 (1944) 207 ff. (important numismatic parallels); J. Carcopino, *Pythagore* 167-75 (Gnostic adventus).

[24] Ch. Picard, *CRAIBL*, 1945, 26 ff.

[25] G. Bendinelli, *MonAnt* 28, 380, 381; G. Wilpert, *AttiPARA* 3, I/II, 24, tav. X.1; J. Carcopino, *Pythagore*, 113 (follows Wilpert; the scene = Hippolytus, *Haer.* 6.31.1 ff. [GCS 26, 158 ff.]); N. Himmelmann, "Hypogäum," 23.

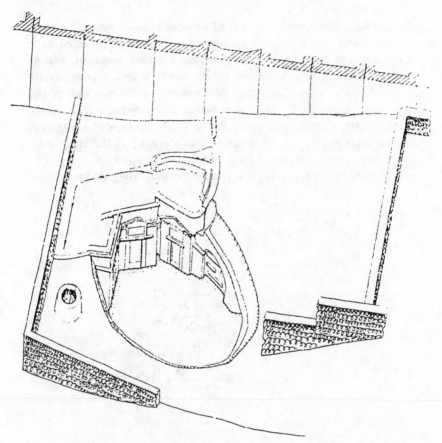

Fig. 9. Rome. San Sebastiano. Axionometric reconstruction showing the facades of Tombs h, i, and a in the Piazzuola. (From F. Tolotti, *Memorie degli Apostoli in Catacumbas* [Vatican City, 1953] fig. 31.)

Gnostic inspiration is the so-called Piazzuola,[26] representing the second phase of occupancy beneath the church of San Sebastiano on the Via Appia Antica (figs. 8 and 9). Burial activity in the Piazzuola continued for approximately a century and a half, ca. 100/125-250 A.D.

---

[26] Excavation of the Piazzuola: G. Mancini, *Accademia nazionale dei Lincei, Notizie degli scavi di antichità* 20 (1923) 3-79. Interpretation: F. Tolotti, *Memorie degli Apostoli in Catacumbas* ... (Vatican City 1953) 66ff. (Tolotti argues diachronic continuity of Christian occupancy at the site; the thesis is wrong, but the book is good). Gnostics: H. Lietzmann (with A. von Gerkan), *Petrus und Paulus in Rom* (Leipzig and Berlin, [2]1927) 160ff. (Cecchelli and Carcopino follow this dead end). Literature: *CBCR* 4 (Vatican City 1970) 99; J. Ward Perkins and J. M. C. Toynbee, *The Shrine of St. Peter* ... (London, 1956) 167ff.

The most important funerary installations introduced during this second phase are the three mausolea on the Piazzuola's north/northwest perimeter, from east to west, Tombs h, i, and a. Loculi were also dug outside of the mausolea in adjacent galleries and in the Piazzuola's vertical tufa which opened to the sky.

Iconography on the attic of Tomb h, consisting in shepherd-criophoroi, meals, and pastoral scenes, could connect with Christianity, if we knew that the tomb's occupants were Christians. The paintings on the interior of Tomb h include a Medusa-Gorgo's head, a prothesis, a seated figure with bystanders, a standing figure, perhaps Hermes Psychopompos, and numerous birds, garlands, flowers, and fruits. Tomb i is distinguished by a nicely stuccoed representation of a conch and a peacock with its tail coverts erect. Noteworthy in Tomb a is the image of the fossor's axe[27] on the tympanum over the doorway. Pictorial motifs associated with inhumations outside of the mausolea are equally neutral in character, with the exception of the curious iconography (unexplained) accompanying the burial of the eight-year-old Atimetus.[28] Excepting the evidence in Tomb i, the epigraphy in the Piazzuola is equally indistinct: Tomb i's accumulation of theophoric and philanthropic epithets, its possibly distinctive (?) onomastic usages, and the fish acrostic[29] point to Christian occupancy. But where are the Gnostics?

The assumptions which underlie the Gnostic interpretation of this iconography (and occasionally other pieces, for example, the Tomb of Trebius Justus)[30] are four: (1) like other religions in the ancient world, Gnosticism created a distinct religious iconography (possibly true, possibly false); (2) Gnostic iconography was painted onto walls and ceilings (probably false); (3) Gnostic iconography was of a narrative sort: pictures illustrating stories (probably false); (4) Genesis 1-3

---

[27] A disputed subject. For Carcopino, *Pythagore*, 366-73 (and in numerous other publications; cf. *RivAC* 31 [1955] 298), ascia = Irenaeus's *crux dissimulata*, [*Haer.* 5.17.4 (Harvey 2. 371). Carcopino's thesis is mostly indefensible; cf. P.-L. Couchond and A. Audin, *RHR* 142 (1952) 36-66; H. J.-J. Hatt, *La tombe gallo romaine* (Paris, 1951) 85-107.

[28] *ICUR* 5. 12892.

[29] P. Styger, *Die römischen Katakomben* (Berlin, 1933) 339; *Romische Märtyrergrüfte* 1 (Berlin, 1935) 41: "Selbst das Graffito ITXΘYC ist nicht als christlich anzusprechen." In the annals of early Christian archaeology, this is a classic counsel of despair, matched only by Th. Klauser's treatment of Jesus the shepherd-criophoros in the Dura baptistery, *JAC* 10 (1967) 105-7. ITXΘYC paralleled in IX†ΘYC at Qanawât: F. J. Dölger, *IXΘYC* 1 (Münster, ²1928) no. 89 (also nos. 3 and 12).

[30] Trebius Justus: C. Cecchelli, *Monumenti* 135-46 (there the literature).

was the probable point of departure (a reasonable guess, if no. 3 were true, but lacking evidence).

The first point remains just as unresolved today as it was yesterday. As for the second point, the bits of evidence that we can assemble favor an iconography executed on small artifacts or papyri. With the third point, the improbabilities obtrude. True, Gnostics had their stories and told them (at least to one another), but the contents were quite unlike other ancient myths and narrations, in setting, in dramatis personae, in plots, themes, time sequence, unfolding of events and resolutions. Christian (or Jewish) illustrations of the biblical text are not an appropriate analogue in the search for a Gnostic iconography. There exists no iconographic equivalent of a Gnostic Genesis.[31] If Gnostics made pictures, they were probably esoteric and fantastic, laconic signs and symbols devoid of narrative context, and no doubt executed on an intimate scale.

Goodenough called Gnosticism "that limbo of lost causes."[32] The phrase fits well the study of "Gnostic" painting since 1919. Gnosticism has become a kind of iconographic dumping ground, a place to discard miscellaneous *ignota*, the pieces that cannot be harmonized with the archaeological typologies established for the religions of the Empire: toss them into the Gnostic wastebasket and forget them. Since we do not know what Gnostic iconography is, or if one ever existed, this method of labelling artifacts by their relationship to Gnosticism amounts to explaining one unknown by another. The results are unedifying. A more sensible approach, one consistent with real possibilities in the sources, is long overdue.

3. "Gnostic" Iconography on Gemstones and Related Small Finds

In an important article published in 1929 Arthur Darby Nock called for a corpus of magical drawings on papyri and a corpus of the so-called Abrasax (Latin Abraxas) gems.[33] In the intervening half-century no one has taken up Nock's challenge, which remains the basic point of departure for the study of "Gnostic" iconography. Why, in looking for a Gnostic iconography, should one compile a corpus of magical

---

[31] Gnostic Genesis exegesis: B. Pearson, *Ex Orbe Religionum: Studia Geo Widengren* 1 (Leiden, 1972) 457-70 (there the literature).

[32] E. R. Goodenough, *Jewish Symbols in the Greco-Roman Period* 2 (New York, 1953) 154.

[33] *JEA* 15 (1929) 219ff.

images?[34] Because the task ahead is to separate magical images from those possibly conceived and executed in other environments, such as Gnosticism. Naturally it is possible that Gnostics invented no new pictorial clichés. The search for a Gnostic iconography could be illusory, based altogether on false premises. But we will not know until the magical images have been sorted out and ordered according to traditional critical categories. The place to begin is magical drawings on dated papyri. Once this corpus is compiled, the evidence which dated magical images afford may help us to move ahead with some sense of bearings into the unknown territory, namely the *materia magica* in small finds. The latter survive almost entirely apart from their original context: without context, especially chronology, small finds together with the images executed on them are virtually lost for history.

All images that accompany magical texts (including the "aggressive magic"[35] of the curse tablets) appear in a context that requires us to classify them under the rubric magical iconography. But this does not tell the whole story. As with Gnosticism, so also with magic, we must distinguish carefully between primary and secondary impulses. The well-known fourth century Oslo Papyrus,[36] for example, shows a snake-footed, cock-headed Seth, a rendering certainly derived from an earlier prototype (fig. 10). It is very unlikely that the original was

Fig. 10. Oslo Papyrus. Cock-headed, snake-footed Seth. (Drawing by J. Steczynski.)

---

[34] The scholarly presupposition seems to be that magic and Gnosticism are radically different: A. D. Nock, *JEA* 15, 232; H. Lietzmann, *Forschungen und Fortschritte* 9 (1933) 154ff. (= *Kleine Schriften* 1 [ed. K. Aland; TU 67; Berlin, 1958] 84ff.).

[35] C. Bonner, *Studies in Magical Amulets* (Ann Arbor, Michigan, 1950) 103ff.; Tacitus, *Ann.* 2.69: Black magic used against Germanicus; C. Bonner, *TAPA* 63 (1932) 34ff.: black magic against Libanius (a mutilated chameleon hidden in his classroom); curse tablets: A. Audollent, *Defixionum Tabellae* (Paris, 1904); R. Wünsch, *Sethianische Verfluchungstafeln aus Rom* (Leipzig, 1898); cf. Bonner, *Studies* 110ff., and B. Pearson, *SBLSP 1977* 28, 29; R. Mouterde, *MUSJ* 15 (1930) 106ff. (no. 34).

[36] S. Eitrem, *Papyri Osloënses* 1 (Oslo, 1925) = *PGM* 36.

not conceived as the pictorial equivalent of Seth: the prototype could have been executed in some environment other than a magical one. But where and when was this image first executed and what was intended? For the moment the answers to these questions are beyond our reach: all critical queries attendant upon the conception and execution of this image are shrouded in uncertainty.

The cock-headed, snake-footed monster is more than just an example chosen at random. Before Campbell Bonner's magisterial study, students of late Roman glyptic asumed that Gnostics invented this pictorial convention. Bonner doubted the connection but did not prove the point conclusively. As an iconographic cliché the composite monster with cock's head, human torso, and snake feet is very common on small finds. I give here in line drawing an exceptionally well modelled example that survives on a gemstone in Kassel (fig. 11). Often (but

Fig. 11. Kassel (*Antike Gemmen in Deutsche Sammlungen* [Munich/Wiesbaden: 1968 seq.] 3. 127a). Cock-headed anguiped from a gemstone. (Drawing by J. Steczynski.)

not invariably) this composite creation appears together with the word Abrasax, a conjunction of image and word that has led scholars to infer the Gnostic origin of the pictorial type.

The key link connecting the word Abrasax with Gnosticism is the second-century heresiological literature. Irenaeus, *Haer.* 1.24.7 (Harvey l. 203), and Hippolytus, *Haer.* 7.26.6 (ed. Wendland, GCS 26, 204, 205), make Abrasax a Basilidian power, not just any power, but the strongest of 365 archons. Neither heresiologist tells us how Abrasax functions within the system, other than being on top, nor do we learn the form (if any were known) by which one might recognize Abrasax. According to Irenaeus, as chief of the 365 Basilidian heavens Abrasax subsumes all others. Hippolytus agrees: the Basilidians have a very large book, and in it is written that there are 365 heavens and that their ruler is Abrasax. Because the numerical equivalent of the word's letters is 365, there are that many days in the year: Hippolytus makes Abrasax the subject of a simple (if not simple-minded) aetiology. Both heresiologists clearly understand the word as the name of a heaven or archon, and both accept the isopsephic interpretation: Abrasax = 365. If these reports are reliable, we may conclude that the word Abrasax had become the personification of a cosmic power in the Basilidian system known to the heresiologists of the later second century A.D. It might even be possible to argue greater precision in situating Abrasax within the Basilidian cosmos. If analogies with Μειθρὰς and Νεῖλος (also isopsephisms) are relevant, Abrasax may point to solar associations. In any case, the word is unusual for the following three details: it is firmly attested in a second-century context; it is attributed to Gnostic usage, probably reliably so; and it appears often in a nonliterary setting together with a very popular iconographic commonplace.

Bonner argued that the word Abrasax was only a word of power, like IAO/IAHU.[37] The word should not be construed, he maintained, as the proper name of the cock-headed anguiped. To give only one of many examples, the Oslo Papyrus, Bonner's interpretation finds support. There the monster is identified, as we have seen, with Seth (more precisely with Typhon-Seth Ζαγουρη), and a string of magical names and names of power are appended to the papyrus's several ἀγωγαί. There are numerous other examples which complicate the equation cock-headed anguiped = Abrasax. In some the word appears alone with no accompanying image, or vice versa. The details of the image change in other instances: the image becomes, for example, simocephalic, onocephalic, cynocephalic or ithyphallic. And in still other examples the word appears with a completely different image.

While it is tempting to conclude with Bonner that Abrasax is simply another magical word of power, not a personal name, and not a word that bears any necessary relationship to the iconographic convention, this conclusion is premature. First the sources must be collected, published, classified, and dated, however provisionally. Why does the word appear so often in conjunction with the image, and why do the heresiologists make the word the personification of a Basilidian archon?

[37] Iao: Bonner, *Studies* 134ff.; W. Fauth, *Der kleine Pauly* 2 (ed. K. Ziegler and W. Sontheimer; Stuttgart, 1967) 1314-19. Abrasax: M. Nilsson, *HTR* 44 (1951) 61-64; M. Pieper, *MDAIK* 5 (1934) 119-43; A. A. Barb, *Hommages à Waldemar Deonna* (Brussels, 1957) 67ff.; Nag Hammadi library: *GEgypt* III 52:26, 53:9, 65:1; *ApocAd* 75:22; *Zost* 47:13.

Are they guilty of still another caprice (as surely they are in imputing image worship to Gnostics), or is there a kernel of history here? If it could be shown that the iconographic convention became a common currency in the second century, and if further its provenience could be fixed in Egypt (a likely setting), we would have to deal with the probability that Basilides, or Isidore, or some other members of the Basilidian circle, were more than just casual bystanders. If on the other hand, it could be shown that there are no pre-Constantinian attestations, we should probably rule out the direct involvement of Basilidians in the conception and execution of the image or in its common conjunction with the word Abrasax.

In dating images on small finds, the major pitfall is the absence of context and the concomitant necessity that we rely exclusively on internal criteria: style, iconography, epigraphic types. This kind of evidence is likely to promote circular reasoning. Whenever possible, the student of the subject should turn to external guides, the stratified sediments (sealed loci and not secondary fills) in which these small artifacts were deposited in antiquity. Of course it is impossible to rely on external evidence unless the field archaeologist considers gemstones and other small finds important enough to warrant proper excavation and recording. Even if we had only a few examples of magical gemstones in dated sediments, we would be better off then we are at present.

Finally, aprioristic reasoning must be laid to rest. The presumption that Gnostics could not have used figured and sphragistic talismans to achieve their goals, because Gnosticism's methods and objectives differed so widely from those of magic, is mistaken. Origen's report proves the point. So, apparently, does the pictorial evidence in the Bruce Codex.

Scenes from the Acts of the Apostles on Some Early Christian Ivories

HERBERT L. KESSLER
The Johns Hopkins University

For Kurt Weitzmann on his 75th birthday,
March 1979

Recent studies have begun to elucidate the history of illustrations based on the *Book of Acts*.[1] Whereas these studies have focused principally on works from the later Middle Ages, they strongly suggest that the *Acts* text had served as a popular source for artists already during the earliest Christian centuries. This is not surprising. Written by Luke himself, the *Acts of the Apostles* is a continuation of the Gospel story in which is recounted Christ's departure from earth and the establishment of his church in the world. It is a vivid tale of miracles, brutal persecution, and ultimate triumph.

Isolated scenes from the lives of Peter and Paul appeared on sarcophagi even before the conversion of Constantine;[2] but it was after the Peace of the Church, when interest in the apostolic legacy intensified, that illustrations derived from the *Book of Acts* attained significant popularity. The *Liber Pontificalis* reports, for example, that Constantine himself donated to the basilica of St. Peter "four brass candlesticks, ten feet in height, overlaid with silver, with figures in silver of the acts of the apostles (cum sigillis argenteis actus apostolorum)."[3] The appearance of these monumental candlesticks can no longer be reconstructed; it might be suggested, however, by several bronze lamps in Florence and Rome.[4] A century later, the left nave wall of San Paolo f.l.m., the brother church of St. Peter's, was decorated with forty-two pictures from *Acts*.[5] The San Paolo frescoes remained the most extensive *Acts* cycle produced during the Middle Ages, but unhappily they were repeatedly restored and in 1823 were destroyed by fire. The sequence of compositions is known only from a set of seventeenth-century drawings preserved in the Vatican (Cod. Barb. lat. 4406).[6]

Unique examples of Early Christian *Acts* illustrations survive in a group of ivories produced in Italy, probably in Rome, during the years around 400. The group includes several elegant carvings of the period: the Ascension plaque in Munich (Bayerisches Nationalmuseum; Fig. 1),[7] the Brescia lipsanotheca (Museo Civico Cristiano; Fig. 2),[8] three plaques from a casket (London, British Museum; Fig. 5),[9] and the Carrand Diptych in Florence (Museo Nazionale; Fig. 10).[10] These ivories, unusually sumptuous and refined, reflect aristocratic patronage of Christian art

FIGURE 1. *The Ascension and the Three Marys at the Tomb; ivory plaque in Munich, Bayerisches Nationalmuseum.*

during the century following Constantine's conversion. They are also rare witnesses of a fractured iconographic tradition; and, as such, they reveal the processes used by Early Christian artists to illustrate an important New Testament text.

Christ's Ascension, an opening episode of *Acts* (1, 9-11),[11] is depicted above a portrayal of the Three Marys at the

109

GESTA XVIII/1 © The International Center of Medieval Art 1979

Tomb in the upper right of the Munich plaque (Fig. 1). The presentation of the theme is perfectly consonant with the serene classicism of the carving. All reference to supernatural happenings is suppressed; the "men in white" are absent; the suggestion of a miraculous levitation is avoided; and the acclaiming crowd is missing. Instead, an apollonian Christ, assisted by the divine hand, earnestly climbs the mountain into heaven as two apostles witness the event from below.[12]

The very association on the Munich plaque of Christ's Ascension and the visit of the three women at the sepulcher reflects the artist's familiarity with extra-biblical traditions. *Acts* specifies that Christ ascended to heaven forty days after the Resurrection. In the apocryphal *Gospel of Peter*,[13] however, and in various patristic writings,[14] Christ is reported to have ascended directly from the tomb. Whether the ivory carver knew the apocryphal narrative or actually consulted exegetic texts cannot be ascertained. His emphatic departure from the canonical chronology, however, surely indicates his acquaintance with an established theological tradition. The isolation of two apostles on the ivory also derives from an extra-biblical account. According to the *Apocryphon Jacobi*, a second-century Egyptian text, Christ chose Peter and James from among the apostles to witness his Ascension.[15]

Borrowings from images account for other features of the Munich ivory. Citing the Moggio pyxis (Washington, Dumbarton Oaks), Gertrud Schiller argued that the figure of Christ striding up the mountain was patterned after a depiction of Moses receiving the law from the hand of God.[16] An analogous figure of Moses on a recently discovered fourth-century lipsanotheca in Thessalonica supports this thesis.[17] The connection between Moses's confrontation with God on Mt. Sinai and Christ's ascension had been made early by Christian liturgists; Exodus 19 was a pericope read in western churches on Ascension Day.[18] The adaptation of the Old Testament iconography for a scene from *Acts* may, therefore, have been intended to convey a precise, exegetic meaning.

The unusual postures assumed by Christ's companions on the Munich relief bring to mind the *Gospel of Nicodemus* which, as Tsuji has noted, reports that, at the Ascension, "the disciples lay on their faces."[19] This account recalls Matthew's description of another epiphany, the Transfiguration: "at the sound of the voice the disciples fell on their faces in terror" (17, 6). The carver of the Munich ivory seems also to have made the connection between the Ascension and the Transfiguration. Both the prostrate man who buries his face in his hands and the more accepting apostle who, crouching on one knee looks up with raised hands, find close parallels in such early Transfiguration pictures as the sixth-century mosaic on Mt. Sinai.[20] Both New Testament events were glorifications of Christ witnessed by apostles; both episodes prefigure the *parousia*.[21] What is more, on the Munich ivory, Peter and James, two apostolic witnesses at the Transfiguration, are featured.[22]

By fashioning his Ascension after other pictures, the

FIGURE 2. *Peter, Sapphira and Ananias; detail from an ivory lipsanotheca in Brescia, Museo Civico Cristiana.*

carver of the Munich ivory communicated several levels of meaning in a highly distilled image. Jesus, returning to heaven with the law, fulfills the mission of Moses; the Ascension, watched by awestruck apostles, is a glorification of Christ equal to the Transfiguration. No other portrayal of Christ's Ascension condenses so much meaning as effectively. Even the fragmentary Servanne sarcophagus in Arles, which preserves the portrayal most like that on the ivory,[23] is more narrative with Christ seen looking back toward three other companions. So alike are the iconographic cores of the two portrayals however, that there is little doubt the ivory and the sarcophagus are related to each other. The nature of the relationship is yet to be explained.

Of all Early Christian ivories with biblical subjects, only the Brescia lipsanotheca matches the Munich Ascension plaque in refinement and elegance.[24] It too includes a scene from the *Acts of the Apostles*. On the back of the casket, the story of Ananias and Sapphira is presented as an example of deceit and venality (Fig. 2). Two moments from Acts 5, 1-10 are depicted. At the left, with Ananias's money bag still at his feet, Peter confronts Sapphira; at the right, four young men carry away Ananias's corpse. In the text these two events are separated by three hours; otherwise, the portrayal is quite literal.

Classical models for the men carrying Ananias's body can easily be adduced: the figures of trophy bearers on the Arch of Titus, for instance, or youths attending Meleager on Roman sarcophagi. The similarities with classical compositions are, however, only general. The rendering on the Brescia casket seems to be a direct pictorialization of the *Acts* text in which classical forms were used but no significant allusion was attempted.

The Punishment of Ananias and Sapphira, portrayed in a manner quite similar to that on the lipsanotheca, appears on a number of Early Christian sarcophagi. Of the extant examples, a fragment in Avignon (Musée Calvet; Fig. 3) is most like the Brescia relief. In fact, the three men carrying the corpse on the sarcophagus are so like their counterparts

110

FIGURE 3. *Ananias' corpse; fragment of a sarcophagus in Avignon, Musée Calvet.*

FIGURE 4. *Peter, Sapphira and Ananias; rotulus in Vercelli, Biblioteca Capitolare.*

on the ivory that Wilpert used the Brescia casket to reconstruct the sarcophagus composition.[25]

The episode was rarely portrayed after the Early Christian period. A uniquely rich rendering of the Ananias story appears in the ninth-century *Sacra Parallela* of John of Damascus (Paris, Bibliothèque Nationale, Cod. gr. 923, fols. 314[r] and 114[v]).[26] The Rockefeller-McCormick New Testament (Chicago, University of Chicago, Cod. 965, fol. 111[r])[27] also includes a miniature of Peter Confronting Ananias but only a very general relationship to the ivory is evident. A thirteenth-century copy of the Romanesque frescoes that once adorned the walls of San Eusebio in Vercelli offers the most striking comparison to the Brescia relief (Vercelli, Biblioteca Capitolare, rotulus, Fig. 4).[28] The same two moments are juxtaposed to one another and both resemble the Early Christian representation in essential features. The Vercelli rotulus shows Peter, seated on a bench, gesturing toward Sapphira; and, to the right, it presents young men (here only three) bearing Ananias's body. The source of the eighteen scenes from Acts recorded on the Vercelli rotulus has yet to be identified. The S. Eusebio frescoes belonged to an Italian tradition of monumental depictions of events in the lives of Peter and Paul that goes back to San Paolo f.l.m. and includes the mosaics of Palermo and Monreale.[29] Like those of the other cycles, the scenes on the Vercelli rotulus are closely connected to manuscript illumination;[30] their ultimate source may well have been an illustrated text. Whatever its origin, the Vercelli cycle clearly establishes a context for the

depictions on the Brescia ivory and strongly suggests that carving, too, was copied from a narrative model.

A second ivory casket, produced about the same time as the Brescia lipsanotheca, presumably in the same place, also presents scenes from the lives of Peter and Paul. Only one of the four episodes portrayed on the British Museum ivories, however, is derived from the *Acts of the Apostles* (Fig. 5).

The sole canonical scene represents the Raising of Tabitha (Acts 9, 36-42). The composition focuses on the central action. Peter, grasping the young woman's hand, raises Tabitha in her bed. A man, nearly identical in appearance to Peter and presumably another apostle, watches the miracle from the far right; a woman genuflects at Peter's feet; and a second woman, raising her hands in fright, rushes off at the left. The women must be the widows who, according to *Acts*, "came and stood around (Peter) in tears." Stricken woman are included in other depictions of the Raising of Tabitha; a sarcophagus in Arles for instance, portrays two women kneeling before Peter and two others standing behind Tabitha's bed.[31] The wailing woman of the London casket suggests the ivory carver's familiarity with classical conventions. Similar women, hysterical with grief, appear in ancient depictions of death, for example, the Death of Dido in the

111

FIGURE 5. *Peter's Miracle of the Spring, the Raising of Tabitha, Paul and Thecla and the Stoning of Paul; ivory plaques from a casket in London, British Museum.*

FIGURE 6. *Christ healing Jairus' daughter; detail from an ivory lipsanotheca, Brescia, Museo Civico Cristiana.*

Vatican Virgil (Biblioteca, Cod. lat. 3225, fol. 41ʳ).[32] In fact, the entire composition has close parallels on ancient grave steles such as an Attic relief in the Louvre.[33]

The immediate source of the Raising of Tabitha was not a pagan image, however; rather it was a portrayal of an event from the Gospels. Like Luke when he wrote the text, the carver fashioned Peter's miracle after Christ's healing of Jairus's daughter (Matt. 9, 18-26, Mark 5, 23-43, and Luke 8, 41-56). Both the Tabitha story and the miraculous cure of Jairus's daughter involve the resurrection of a young woman, and the New Testament uses similar language to describe the two miracles. That the analogous action of the Gospel miracle and the reference to Talitha inspired the carver of the London ivory to pattern his Raising of Tabitha after a representation of Christ Healing Jairus's Daughter is evident from the depiction of the latter event on the left side of the Brescia casket (Fig. 6).[34] The lipsanotheca shows Christ grasping the wrist of Jairus's daughter and the young woman sitting upright in bed as her companions, still grief-stricken, look on. Even the dolphin-shaped bedposts recur in both reliefs. Because they

also include a woman genuflecting at Christ's feet, the representations of the Healing of Jairus's Daughter on fourth-century sarcophagi in Florence (Museo Archeologico) and Arles (Musée Lapidaire) are even closer to the London depiction and leave no doubt as to the ivory carver's model.[35]

In scenes of Christ's miraculous healings, Peter often looks on. By fashioning the Raising of Tabitha after the Healing of Jairus's Daughter, the carver of the London casket established in visual terms that Peter not only witnessed the miracles performed by Christ, he was the heir to Christ's power and ministry.

The Raising of Tabitha was illustrated in later art. Mourning women, but not the prostrate figure, are included in the Tabitha scenes of Palermo and Monreale which, like the London ivory, also include the apostle accompanying Peter. The Vercelli rotulus also portrays Peter's companion but depicts only one mourning woman. The Raising of Tabitha is preceded on the rotulus by a rare representation of the display of the "shirts and coats that Dorcas (Tabitha) used to make." (Acts 9, 39).

A second scene on the London casket, though also featuring Peter, does not illustrate the *Book of Acts*. It shows the apostle accompanied by another man, bringing water forth from a rock to slake the thirst of two soldiers. The first reference to this event in literature is found in the sixth-century *Passio Processi et Martiani*;[36] in art, the episode was popular from the third century. Peter's miracle of the spring is portrayed in much the same fashion, for instance, on the famous "Dogmatic" sarcophagus from c. 325 (Vatican, Museo Pio Cristiano; Fig. 7);[37] here, the representation follows a depiction of the antecedent episode, Peter's arrest by the two Roman soldiers who were later to be converted by the water miracle.

The reason Peter's legendary miracle of the spring appeared in art before it was cited in literature is clear. The event is a pictorial invention, created as a counterpart to the popular Old Testament picture of Moses in the wilderness causing a stream to issue forth to refresh the Israelites (Ex. 17, 2 and Num. 20, 2-6).[38] Moses's water miracle on a sarcophagus in Arles

112

FIGURE 7. *Peter's Miracle of the spring; detail of a sarcophagus in the Vatican, Museo Paolino.*

FIGURE 8. *Moses causing a stream to come forth; fragment of a sarcophagus in Arles, Musée Lapidaire.*

(Musée Lapidaire, Fig. 8),[39] for example, is nearly identical to the representations in London and the Vatican. Only the difference in costume distinguishes the two episodes and secures the proper identification of the compositions.[40]

Peter was Moses's Christian successor. He received the law from Christ's hand; he was a leader of his people.[41] By including a scene that alludes to Moses's miracle together with one that recalls Christ's supernatural healing powers, the carver of the London casket established, visually, Peter's special role as heir to both the Old and the New Testament missions.

The third scene on the London casket is also based on an apocryphal tale rather than on the *Acts* text. The ivory shows Paul reading to a young woman who listens attentively behind a city wall. It illustrates the central event in the *Acta Pauli et Theclae*, a fable incorporated during the second century into the *Acti Pauli*, 7.[42] In composition and poses, the representation recalls depictions of the philosopher and muse frequently found on Roman sarcophagi. The sarcophagus of Publius Peregrinus in the Museo Torlonia in Rome is a good example.[43] Christians had adopted the pagan motif for their own use by the end of the third century as on a sarcophagus in the Palazzo Sanseverino-Rondanini in Rome (Fig. 9).[44] The carver of the London ivory had simply to apply the formula to the specific narrative of his story.

To the right of Paul and Thecla, the plaque portrays the stoning of Paul. According to the *Acti Pauli*, when Thecla persisted in her Christian faith, the governor of Iconium "had Paul scourged and drove him out of the city, but Thecla he condemned to be burned" (chap. 21). This legend elaborates the report of *Acts* 14, 19, "the Jews from Antioch and Iconium came on the scene and won over the crowds. They

stoned Paul and dragged him out of the city, thinking him dead." The ivory shows Paul, fallen to the ground, trying to shield himself from the missile hurled by a man at the left.

The lively tale of Paul and Thecla failed to attract other Early Christian artists. The canonical episode of Paul's stoning was portrayed occasionally. It is depicted on a sarcophagus in Marseilles[45] in a manner unlike the London composition; it was also portrayed on the walls of San Paolo f.l.m., but unhappily the painting was badly damaged even before it was copied during the seventeenth century.[46] The central figure of the San Paolo panel is, in pose, so like the man assaulting Paul on the ivory that a connection between the two works seems plausible.

Paul is also featured on the Carrand diptych (Fig. 10), one of the most magnificent ivories that has come down from the Early Christian period. As a counterpart to the bucolic representation of Adam in Paradise on the left wing of the diptych, the right leaf presents three scenes from Paul's life. At the top, Paul is shown seated before a man who seems to be debating with him; another man, standing behind the apostle, is shown listening attentively to the discussion. The episode is impossible to identify with certainty. Throughout his journeys, Paul frequently delivered sermons and debated issues of faith; the depiction could refer to any of Paul's encounters. Paul Preaching at Athens (*Acts* 17, 15) has been proposed but in this context, Paul's defense before Festus or Agrippa (Acts 25-26) seems more likely.

The central episode of the Carrand leaf is the Miracle of the Viper. Following the text of *Acts* 28, 1-6, the relief shows a snake biting Paul's hand and three men of Malta, including the chief magistrate, Publius, reacting in amazement as Paul fails to "swell up or drop down dead."

Publius's two companions are recognizable in the scene

113

FIGURE 10. *Scenes from Paul's life; right wing of an ivory diptych in Florence, Museo Nazionale.*

below which portrays the miraculous healing of the sick men of Malta told in *Acts* 28, 7-9. One of the men conducts an emaciated companion, presumably Publius's father, who had been "suffering from recurrent bouts of fever and dysentery" and the other conducts a man with a paralyzed arm to Paul. The carver did not repeat the figure of the apostle in this episode; he simply merged the two compositions by having the man at the right point toward Paul in the scene above.

After they witnessed Paul's immunity to the snake, the inhabitants of Malta declared "he is a God" (*Acts* 28, 6) and brought their sick to him for revival. By representing the miracle at the fire and Paul healing the sick, the carver of the Carrand ivory emphasized the apostle's authority as one of Christ's successors. The artist reinforced the allusion to Christ by showing one of the "other sick people on the island" as a man with a paralyzed arm, recalling thereby the miraculous cure of a man with a withered hand effected by Christ (Matt. 12, 9-13, Mk. 3, 1-6, and Luke 6, 6-11.).[47]

Although Paul's adventure on Malta is among the most exciting stories in the New Testament, it rarely inspired

114

artists; the only other Early Christian rendering of the event was found on the walls of San Paolo. In the seventeenth-century copy, Paul stands at the right before a fire, a snake attached to his right hand; and three men of Malta, seated at the left, watch in awe.[48] By far the closest parallel to the Carrand composition is found in a thirteenth-century New Testament in Venice (Giustiniani Collection, New Testament, fol. 143ʳ, Fig. 11).[49] The illustration is included within the column of text describing the event. Like the San Paolo fresco, the composition is reversed; but it shares all the essential features of the Carrand depiction as well as such less important details as the grouping and gestures of the Maltese men. Despite its much later date, the Giustiniani New Testament provides important evidence for the narrative origin of the iconography.

One other ivory, also part of the Carrand bequest in the

FIGURE 11. *Miracle of the Viper; Venice, Giustiniani Collection, New Testament,* fol. 143ʳ.

FIGURE 12. *Peter preaching and baptizing; ivory plaque in Florence, Museo Nazionale.*

Museo Nazionale, is to be considered with the Italian group.[50] The ivory (Fig. 12) has been assigned to the late Carolingian Metz school by Adolph Goldschmidt and probably dates from around 900;[51] but like so many Carolingian ivories, it may copy an Early Christian model. The precise acanthus borders and bead-and-reel ornament have analogies on fourth- and fifth-century ivories, and the lively narrative scenes comprising large assemblies of figures arranged in depth recall works of the late antique period.

In two scenes, the ivory portrays Peter preaching to a gathering of men and then baptizing one member of the group. Goldschmidt believed that the scenes illustrate *Acts* 2, 40-41, Peter's sermon and the general baptism after Pentecost. More likely, they portray the Conversion and Baptism of Cornelius recounted in *Acts* 10. Whereas both compositions conform to established formulae, the man in the upper panel who bends forward toward Peter suggests the action of Cornelius approaching the apostle, "When Peter arrived, Cornelius came to meet him, and bowed to the ground in deep reverence."

(*Acts* 10, 25). Two compositions on the Vercelli rotulus (Fig. 13) verify this identification.[52] In the first, the gestures of Peter, Cornelius, and Cornelius's relatives are closely analogous to those on the Carolingian relief; in the second, as on the ivory, Peter himself baptizes Cornelius. The Vercelli rotulus allows a precise identification of the episodes depicted on the Florence plaque; it also establishes the existence of the ivory's iconography in Italy, albeit at a later date. With caution, then, the ivory may be considered additional, indirect evidence of *Acts* illustration in Early Christian Italy.

What models did the ivory carvers use? The especially close relationship to sarcophagi, on which isolated episodes from various texts are juxtaposed for symbolic reasons, suggests that the ivory depictions originated in the emblematic tradition of third- and fourth-century funereal art. Nevertheless, certain aspects of the ivory indicate that *Acts* illustrations were taken from a narrative source. The ivories display a remarkable homogeneity; taken together, they depict episodes from *Acts* 1, 5, 9, possibly 14 and 25 or 26, and 28, in itself, an extensive narrative sequence. Individual episodes also have a clear narrative character. Judging from the Servanne sarcophagus, for example, the original composi-

115

FIGURE 13. *The Conversion and Baptism of Cornelius; rotulus in Vercelli, Biblioteca Capitolare.*

tion of the Ascension, severely epitomized on the Munich ivory, included all of the apostles and perhaps even Mary. The ivories, in turn, contain details of the Punishment of Sapphira and Ananias and the Raising of Tabitha that were eliminated when the sculptors adapted the scenes for the sarcophagi.

The relationship of emblematic images to narrative art is still a subject of scholarly discussion. Erich Dinkler has recently argued persuasively that in certain instances, at least, narrative sequences were the source of abbreviated, symbolic compositions.[53] Illustrations of the *Book of Acts* must now be numbered among those instances.

Connections with the San Paolo frescoes and with such later cycles as the Sicilian mosaics, the Vercelli rotulus, and the Giustiniani New Testament support the conclusion that the depictions on the ivories originated in a narrative context. And whereas only one of these works is actually a manuscript, and is the latest of the group, considerable evidence points to an illuminated *Book of Acts* as the ultimate source of all the cycles. The ivories contain only excerpts from the lost manuscript cycle. They are, then, like the seventh-century Cyprus plates, early witnesses in a luxury medium of a narrative tradition known more fully only in works of a later time.[54]

Not every portrayal on the Early Christian ivories was copied from a text illustration. Peter's Miraculous Spring, for example, is a pictorial invention that entered literature only after the London ivory was created. The scene of Paul Instructing Thecla might have been derived from an illustrated *Acti Pauli;* its composition is so conventional, however, that no manuscript source for it need be assumed.

Several depictions on the ivories belong to a second generation of Christian imagery, that is, they were developed from other biblical illustrations and depend on the viewer's

116

recognition of these sources for their full effect. The presentation of Christ's Ascension alludes to Moses Receiving the law and to the Transfiguration. Peter Healing Tabitha and Paul Curing the Men of Malta suggest miracles effected by Christ. With great skill and sophistication, the ivory carvers selected and adjusted their models to extend the content of their illustrations.

The ivories cannot, of course, be treated exclusively as narrative works. The episodes depicted on them were, after all, chosen for a purpose related to the overall program or use of the object. The scene of Ananias and Sapphira on the Brescia lipsanotheca, for instance, is one of several examples on the casket of retribution for lack of faith.[55] The scenes on the London plaques focus on the apostles' accomplishments in converting Jews and pagans to Christianity. Conversion through teaching and miracles is also the theme of the Carrand diptych and Florence ivory.

Scenes of miraculous cures were appropriate particularly for reliquaries such as the Brescia and London caskets. By the end of the fourth century, belief in the curative power of relics was universal and numerous texts from the period proclaim the efficacy of sacred remains. Paulinus, for example, described how during his own lifetime "there came a certain blind man, who by touching the coffin in which the remains of the saints were being carried, that same day received sight" (*Life of St. Ambrose,* ch. 52).[56] And in *The City of God,* Augustine publicized various cures effected by relics, asserting that "the truth is that even today miracles are being wrought in the name of Christ, sometimes through His sacraments and sometimes through the intercession of His saints" (XXII, 8).[57] Depictions of miraculous cures worked by the apostles, on chests containing the apostles' remains or those of other saints, provided confirmation of the divine source of healing miracles attributed to the holy relics.[58]

The special interest in the activities of Peter and Paul on ivories produced in Rome around the turn of the fifth century also reflected entirely local concerns. For Christian commentators of the period, Peter and Paul were not merely the co-founders of the Roman church, of the *ecclesia ex circumcisione* and the *ecclesia ex gentibus;* they were civic heroes, the successors of Romulus and Remus who, by establishing a Christian Rome, had restored the glory of the empire and had ushered in a new golden age of peace and unity.[59] In their battle against the pagan aristocracy, the new Christian elite enlisted Peter and Paul. They set June 29, the anniversary of Rome's founding, as the day for the joint festival of Peter and Paul and they designated the apostles as the protectors of the city.[60] That a sequence of pictures portraying the lives of Peter and Paul was chosen for the nave wall of San Paolo f.l.m. is no mere coincidence; nor is it chance that all the early ivories with scenes from *Acts* originated in Rome around the year 400.

The *Acts of the Apostles* served the Christian propagandists of the period as both history and paradigm. Defending their faith against the persistent and sophisticated assault of the pagans, these apologists envisioned their own activities as a continuation of the apostolic mission and sought support for their work in the *Acts* text. Around 402, for instance, Prudentius prefaced his *Contra Symmachum* with an elaborate paraphrase of *Acts* 27-28. He compared Paul's encounter with the "rough" people of Malta to the contemporary confrontation with the pagans and he likened the crafty arguments of the pagan leader Symmachus to the viper that had attacked the shipwrecked Paul (Pref., 45-77). For Prudentius, the conversion of the gentiles begun by Paul and the other apostles was nearing completion only during his lifetime in a Rome "still sick with pagan terrors."

Prudentius's use of the *Acts* text to attack paganism offers a striking parallel to the Carrand ivory. Both the treatise and the carving emphasize Paul's ability to "subdue the wild hearts of the Gentiles with his holy pen and his peaceable teaching" as well as with supernatural deeds; and both adopt an overtly classical style to meet the challenge of the pagans on their own terms. That the ivory carver was actually inspired by Prudentius's tract cannot, of course, be proven; but both works do reflect the special significance attached to the *Acts of the Apostles* just before the final victory of Christianity in Rome. In this light the upper-most scene of the Carrand plaque may be interpreted. The debate between Paul and the unidentified man standing before him may not depict a specific episode reported in *Acts*. It may refer instead to the encounter between Christian theology and pagan philosophy initiated by Paul and still raging at the time the ivory was produced. As H.P. L'Orange has argued, the presentation of Paul on the diptych "in his pallium with a scroll in his left hand and his right raised in a rhetorical gesture, in his whole being and in expression conforms exactly to the traditional picture of the philosopher in antique art."[61] Paul's opponent, elevated and dignified may have been intended to represent the contending philosophy.

The ivories's refined classicism has been interpreted as a Christian response to the final pagan assault.[62] Now their subject matter, too, may be understood as a reaction to the conflict of religions at the end of the fourth century.

The carvings in Munich, Brescia, London, and Florence are only accidental survivors of a once extensive artistic production; hard conclusions are hazardous to draw from them. Nonetheless, a study of the scenes from the Acts of the Apostles on these ivories permits several observations. The fourth/fifth century reliefs were not created *de novo* but were copied from models used also by artists in other media. The basic source appears to have been a narrative cycle; individual scenes were selected from it to suit the special purpose of each work. The iconography of several scenes was refashioned after other images to extend the theological references of the episodes. And, finally, the concentration of *Acts* illustrations on Roman products of c. 400 reflects the special fascination with the apostolic mission, especially with the deeds of Peter and Paul, at the moment the goal of that mission was at last about to be realized.

NOTES

1. M. Sotomayor, *S. Pedro en la iconografia paleocristiana,* Granada, 1962; A. Weiss, "Ein Petruszyklus des 7. Jahrhunderts im Querschiff der Vaticanischen Basilika," *Römische Quartalschrift* 58 (1963): 230ff.; H. Buchthal, "Some Representations from the Life of St. Paul in Byzantine and Carolingian Art," *Tortulae: Studien zu altchristlichen und byzantinischen Monumenten,* Rome, 1966, 43ff.; P. Testini, "L'iconografia degli apostoli Pietro e Paolo nelle cossiddette 'arti minori,' " *Studi di Antichita Cristiana* 28 (1969): 241ff.; D. Glass, "The Archivolt Sculpture at Sessa Arunca," *Art Bulletin* 52 (1970): 119ff; L. Eleen, "The Illustration of the Pauline Epistles" (unpubl. Ph.D. dissertation, The University of Toronto, 1972); H. Kessler, "Paris 102: A Rare Illustrated Acts of the Apostles," *Dumbarton Oaks Papers* 27 (1973): 211ff.; K. Weitzmann, "The Study of Byzantine Book Illumination, Past, Present, and Future," *The Place of Book Illumination in Byzantine Art,* Princeton, 1975, 21; idem., "The Selection of Texts for Cyclic Illustration in Byzantine Manuscripts," *Byzantine Books and Bookmen,* Washington, 1975, 76f.; A. Weyl Carr, "The Byzantine Cycle of the Acts in Chicago 2400; *Byzantine Studies Conference, Abstracts of Papers,* Cleveland, 1975, 38f.; idem., "Chicago 2400 and the Byzantine Acts Cycle," *Byzantine Studies* 3 (1976): 1ff; H. Kessler, *The Illustrated Bibles from Tours,* Princeton, 1977, 111ff.; and L. Eleen,

"Acts Illustration in Italy and Byzantium," *Dumbarton Oaks Papers* 31 (1977): 255ff.

2. Testini, "L'iconografia," and L. de Bruyne, "L'iconographie des apôtres dans une lumière nouvelle," *Studi di Antichità Cristiana,* 28 (1969): 37ff.

3. *Monumenta Germaniae Historica. Gestorum Pontificum Romanorum,* Berlin, 1898, 1: 57; *The Book of the Popes,* trans. L.R. Loomis, New York, 1916, 49.

4. Testini, "L'iconografia," 264ff.

5. J. Garber, *Wirkungen der frühchristlichen Gemäldezyklen der alten Petrus und Pauls-Basiliken in Rome,* Berlin and Vienna, 1918.

6. S. Waetzoldt, *Die Kopien des 17. Jahrhunderts nach Mosaiken und Wandmalereien in Rom,* Vienna and Munich, 1964, 58ff. and *Age of Spirituality,* Cat. no. 439.

7. W.F. Volbach, *Elfenbeinskulpturen der Spätantike und des frühen Mittelalters,* 3rd ed., Mainz, 1976, 79f. Richard Lyman of the University of Chicago is preparing a Ph.D. dissertation on the Roman ivories.

8. Volbach, *Elfenbeinskulpturen,* J. Kollwitz, *Die Lipsanothek zu Brescia, Studien zur spätantiken Kunstgeschichte 7,* Berlin 1933

117

97

and R. Delbrueck, *Probleme der Lipsanothek in Brescia*, Bonn, 1952.

9. Volbach, *Elfenbeinskulpturen*, 83 and *Age of Spirituality*, Cat. no. 455.

10. Volbach, *Elfenbeinskulpturen*, 78 and *Age of Spirituality*, Cat. no. 454.

11. Abbreviated accounts are also given in Mark 16, 19 and Luke 24, 50.

12. Cf. E.T. Dewald, "The Iconography of the Ascension," *American Journal of Archaeology* 19 (1915): 279ff.; H. Schrade, "Zur Ikonographie der Himmelfahrt Christi," *Vorträge der Bibliothek Warburg* 8 (1929-30): 66ff.; and G. Schiller, *Ikonographie der Christlichen Kunst*, Gütersloh, 1966-76, 3: 444ff.

13. Sahoko Tsuji, "Les portes de Sainte-Sabine: Peculiarités de l'iconographie de l'Ascension," *Cahiers Archéologiques*, 1962, 13ff. and E. Hennecke, *New Testament Apocrypha*, Philadelphia, 1963, 1: 186.

14. C.P. Charalambidis, "Une interpretation theologique de l'ivoire du 'Bayerisches Museum' de Munich," *Byzantina* 7 (1975): 33ff. The prominent tree may refer to an old tradition that Christ ascended from Olivet; cf. Prudentius, *Tituli Historianum*, 44. *Tituli Historianum*, 44.

15. Hennecke, *New Testament Apocrypha*, 1: 336.

16. *Ikonographie*, 3: 145f.

17. M. Panayotidi and A. Grabar, "Un reliquaire paléochrétien recémment découvert près de Thessalonique," *Cahiers Archéologiques* 24 (1975): 33ff.

18. Schiller, *Ikonographie*, 3: 145f.

19. "Les portes de Sainte-Sabine," 21 and Hennecke, *New Testament Apocrypha*, 1: 468.

20. E. Dinkler, *Das Apsismosaik von S. Apollinare in Classe*, Cologne and Opladen, 1964, 25ff. and K. Weitzmann, "A Metamorphosis Icon or Miniature on Mt. Sinai," *Starinar* 20 (1969): 415ff. A close comparison in ivory is found on a tenth-century plaque in London discussed by J. Beckwith, *Ivory Carvings in Early Medieval England*, London, 1972, no. 21. As in the Munich ivory, the apostles on the Victoria and Albert plaque are beardless. The beardless St. Peter appears also in other Early Christian depictions (cf. C. Morey, *The Gold Glass Collection of the Vatican Library*, 1950, figs. 75 and 83). The date and form of the first Transfiguration pictures remain uncertain. The Ambrosian tituli indicate that the Transfiguration was depicted by the end of the fourth century, but the authorship and date of these verses are controversial. Cf. Dinkler, *Das Apsismosaik*, 34.

21. A. Grabar, *Martyrium*, Paris, 1946, 2: 193.

22. Schiller, *Ikonographie*, 3: fig. 456. A parallel between the Ascension and the Transfiguration had been established in early medieval art. See for example an eighth-century pectoral cross in Leningrad.

23. J. Wilpert, *I Sarcophagi cristiani antichi*, Rome, 1929, pl. XV; idem, "Una perla della scultura cristiana antica di Arles", *Rivista di Archeologia cristiana*, 1925, 35 ff.; and F. Benoit, *Sarcophages paleochrétiens d'Arles et de Marseille*, Paris, 1954, 48f.

24. Delbrueck, *Probleme der Lipsanothek*.

25. J. Wilpert, *Sarc. Crist.*, 1: pl. XXXVII, 5.

26. Weitzmann, "Place of Byzantine Book Illumination," 21 and fig. 16.

27. *Ibid.*, 21, Fig. 17; Carr, "Chicago 2400," *passim*.

28. C. Cipolla, "La Pergamena Rappresentate le Antiche Pitture della Basilica di S. Eusebio in Vercelli, *Miscellanea di Storia Italiana*, Ser. 3, Vol. 6 (1901): 3ff.

29. O. Demus, *The Mosaics of Norman Sicily*, London, 1948 and E. Kitzinger, *The Mosaics of Monreale*, Palermo, 1960.

30. Kessler; *Tours*, 119ff. and Eleen, "Acts Illustrations."

31. Wilpert, *Sarc. crist.*, 1: CXLV (6) and Benoit, *Sarcophages*, 39.

32. J. de Wit, *Die Miniaturen des Vergilius Vaticanus*, Amsterdam, 1959.

33. F. Johansen, *Attic Grave Reliefs*, Copenhagen, 1951, Fig. 23.

34. Volbach, *Elfenbeinskulpturen*, 83 noted this parallel.

35. F. Gerke, "Der neugefundene altchristliche Friessarkophag im Museo Archeologico zu Florenz," *Zeitschrift für Kirchengeschichte* 54 (1935): 18ff on the Florence sarcophagus; Wilpert, *Sarc. crist.*, 1: pl. XXXVIII (3), Gerke, "Friessarkophag," pl. 2, and Benoit, *Sarcophages*, p. 50 on the one in Arles. Benoit suggests that the woman may be Jairus's wife. Conceivably, she is the woman plagued by incessant hemorrhages whom Christ healed while on the way to Jairus's house (Matt. 9, 20-22, Mk. 5, 25-34, and Luke 8, 43-48). Mark reports that when she realized she had been cured, this woman "fell at Christ's feet." Accordingly, Early Christian depictions of the Miracle of the Woman with an Issue of Blood show the woman genuflecting before Christ (cf. Brescia lipsanotheca and plaques from an ivory diptych in the Louvre, Volbach, no. 113).

36. G. Stuhlfauth, *Die apokryphen Petrusgeschichte*, Berlin, 1925; T. Klauser, "Studien zur Entstehungsgeschichte der Christlichen Kunst 4, *Jahrbuch für Antike und Christentum* 4 (1961): 128f.; Sotomayor, *S. Pedro*, 58ff.; and C. Pietri, *Roma Christiana*, Paris and Rome, 1976, 316ff.

37. G. Bovini-M. Brandenburg, *Repertorium der Christlich-Antiken Sarkophage*, Wiesbaden, 1967, 1: 39ff.

38. E. Becker, *Das Quellwunder des Moses in der altchristlichen Kunst*, Strasbourg, 1909.

39. Benoit, *Sarcophages*, 53.

40. Volbach, *Elfenbeinskulpturen*, 83, still identifies the scene as Moses's water miracle.

41. Sotomayor, *S. Pedro*, 147ff.; Pietri, *Roma Christiana*, 316ff.

42. Hennecke, *New Testament Apocrypha*, 2: 322ff.

43. R. Bianchi Bandinelli, *Rome: The Late Empire*, New York, 1971, fig. 51.

44. *Repertorium*, 1: 416.

45. Benoit, *Sarcophages*, p. 72.

46. Waetzoldt, *Die Kopien*, Fig. 388.

47. Cf. e.g. the Cathedra of Maximianus (Volbach, *Elfenbeinskulpturen*, 93f.).

48. Waetzoldt, *Die Kopien*, Fig. 406. The healing of Publius's father in the *Sacra Parallela* (fol. 213ʳ) bears no resemblance to the ivory.

49. Eleen, "Acts Illustration," 257ff. I am grateful to Dr. Eleen for calling this manuscript to my attention and providing me with a photograph of the miniature. According to the chart in Eleen's article the Healing of Publius's Father is portrayed on folio 143ᵛ of the Giustiniani codex.

50. A fragment of a liturgical comb in the cathedral of Castellammare on which the Meeting of Peter and Paul is depicted in low relief has been published by Testini, "L'iconografia," 281ff. Because I know the Castellammare comb only from photographic reproductions, I cannot be certain of its date or place of origin. The comb is unrelated to the Roman ivories. Its iconography, which derives from the apocryphal *Acts of Peter and Paul*, seems to have a

118

parallel in the San Paolo frescoes (Waetzoldt, *Die Kopien*, Fig. 407); it is otherwise unknown in Early Christian art.

51. A. Goldschmidt, *Die Elfenbeinskulpturen aus der Zeit der karolingischen und sächsischen Kaiser*, Berlin, 1914, 1: 56, and P. Lasko, *Ars Sacra*, Baltimore, 1972, 70.

52. Cipolla, "La Pergamena," 10. Cf. also the Liège baptismal font of Rainer of Huy.

53. "Abbreviated Representations," *Age of Spirituality*. See also A. Grabar, *Christian Iconography*, Princeton, 1968, 7ff.

54. E. Cruikshank-Dodd, *Byzantine Silver Stamps*, Washington, 1962, 178ff.; K. Weitzmann, "Prolegomena to a Study of the Cyprus Plates," *Journal of the Metropolitan Museum of Art* 3 (1970): 97ff.; see also Kessler, *Tours*, 111ff.

55. Delbrueck, *Probleme der Lipsanothek*, 130ff.

56. *Life of St. Ambrose*, trans. J. Lacey, in *Early Christian Biographies* (ed. R. Deferrari), New York, 1952, 64.

57. Augustine, *The City of God*, trans. G. Walsh and D. Honan, New York, 1954, 432ff.

58. They may also represent a reaction to the claims of gnostic magic. Cf. A.A. Barb, "The Survival of the Magic Arts," in *The Conflict between Paganism and Christianity in the Fourth Century* (ed. A. Momigliano), Oxford, 1963, 100ff. For a reference to Paul's encounter on Malta, cf. 123.

59. H. Lietzmann, *Petrus und Paulus in Rom*, Bonn, 1927; C. Pietri, "Concordia apostolorum et renovatio urbis," *Mélanges d'archéologie et d'histoire* 73 (1961): 275ff.; J. Matthews, *Western Aristocracies and Imperial Court A.D. 364-425*, Oxford, 1975; and Pietri, *Roma Christiana*, 1537ff.

60. Pietri, *"Concordia,"* pp. 310ff and *Prudentius* (trans. H.J. Thomson), Cambridge, Mass., 1949-53, 2: 135f; subsequent references to Prudentius are from this edition.

61. "Plotinus-Paul," *Byzantion* 25-27 (1955-57): 485.

62. H. Bloch, "The Pagan Revival in the West at the End of the Fourth Century," in *Conflict between Paganism and Christianity in the Fourth Century*, 193ff. and most recently, E. Kitzinger, *Byzantine Art in the Making*, Cambridge, Mass., 1977, 34ff.

119

Joseph Iconography on Coptic Textiles

GARY VIKAN

p. 105, n. 4, line 9: the Greek should read.
Τὰ Κοπτικὰ ὑφάσματα τοῦ ἐν Ἀθήναις Μουσείου Κοσμητικῶν Τεχνῶν.

p. 106, n. 5, line 1: for note 6 read note 4.

Scenes from the Acts of the Apostles on Some Early Christian Ivories

HERBERT L. KESSLER

Figure 2 should have been reproduced as follows:

FIGURE 2.

Figure 7 should have been reproduced as follows:

FIGURE 7.

Figure 13 should have been reproduced as follows:

FIGURE 13.

p. 110, col. 1, line 30: after "this thesis" read (Fig. 14).

FIGURE 14. *Moses Receiving the Law, silver lipsanotheca, in Thessaloniki, Archeological Museum.*

p. 112, col. 2, line 16: after "rotulus" read (Fig. 15).

FIGURE 15. *Display of Shirts and Coats, and Raising of Tabitha,
rotulus in Vercelli, Biblioteca Capitolare.*

p. 113, col. 2, line 10: after "seventeenth century" read (Fig. 16).

p. 114, col. 2, line 3: after "copy" add (Fig. 17).

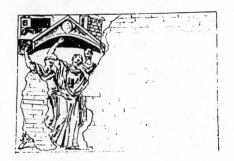

FIGURE 16. *Stoning of St. Paul, 17th century copy of fresco in San Paolo f.l.m., Rome.*

FIGURE 17. *Miracle of the Viper, 17th century copy of fresco in San Paolo f.l.m., Rome.*

101

1. THE LITURGICAL EDIFICE

ERNST KITZINGER

THE THRESHOLD OF THE HOLY SHRINE:
OBSERVATIONS ON FLOOR MOSAICS AT ANTIOCH AND BETHLEHEM

In 1935 excavations at Antioch brought to light a cruciform church which has been identified with a high degree of probability as the Martyrion of St. Babylas[1]. Erected shortly before 381 A.D., the building subsequently received in its four naves sumptuous yet sober floor decorations consisting of vast mosaic carpets of purely geometric design, while the central crossing – the focal area containing what was almost certainly the saint's tomb – was paved with *opus sectile*. Inscriptions in the north, west and south arms record the laying of the mosaics in the period of Bishop Flavianus (381–404 A.D.). The inscription in the north arm specifies the year 387 A.D. There is no inscription in the east arm, but its mosaic floor, which is on a slightly lower level, is certainly no later, though possibly a little earlier, than the other three. Here, too, the ornaments are exclusively geometric. The whole decoration is a prime example of a trend characteristic of Christian pavement decoration of the late fourth century in many areas, namely, the banishment from the floor of all representational and symbolic imagery and its replacement by purely abstract designs[2].

The mosaics of the Antiochene sanctuary do, however, comprise one minor and marginal element which is potentially meaningful. Jean Lassus, in his publication of the building, drew attention to the fact that the plain white border (or »surround«) of the mosaic of the east arm bears on its west side, where it adjoins the central square, a row of simple, equal-armed crosses made of double rows of red tesserae and measuring 18 by 18 centimeters each (fig. 1). Three such crosses, spaced at regular intervals, are preserved in the right (or northern) half of the border. A partially preserved motif which followed after a wider interval, a little to the left of the central axis of this border, may have been another, more elaborate cross. The left half of the border is not preserved[3].

Lassus, while not excluding the possibility that these crosses may have symbolic significance, was understandably cautious on this score[4]. Cruciform motifs are among a number of simple designs that tend to be scattered in loose sequences on the »surrounds« of late antique floor mosaics[5]. Certainly in many instances no special meaning attaches to these modest devices. But the present case is, after all, not quite in the same category.

---

[1] *Antioch-on-the-Orontes*, II: *The Excavations 1933–1936* (Princeton, London and The Hague, 1938), p. 5 ff. (J. Lassus); p. 45 ff. (G. Downey). J. Lassus, *Sanctuaires Chrétiens de Syrie* (Paris, 1947), p. 123 ff. D. Levi, *Antioch Mosaic Pavements* (Princeton, London and The Hague, 1947), I, p. 283 ff.; II, pl. 113–115, 139.

[2] See my paper in *La Mosaïque Gréco-Romaine* (Colloques internationaux du Centre National de la Recherche Scientifique, Paris, 29 Août–3 Septembre 1963, published 1965), p. 341 ff., esp. p. 343 f.

[3] *Antioch-on-the-Orontes*, II, p. 20 f. and fig. 19; p. 218 f., Plan IV.

[4] *Ibid.*, p. 20. In his subsequent discussion of these crosses in *Sanctuaires Chrétiens de Syrie* (p. 297), Lassus does attribute to them a religious significance.

[5] M. Avi-Yonah, *Mosaic Pavements in Palestine* (Reprinted from *The Quarterly of the Department of Antiquities in Palestine* [= *QDAP*], II and III), Oxford, n. d., p. 85. See also below, n. 36.

What we have before us is not merely a cruciform ornament but a row of plain, undisguised crosses. We are in a church, and in the mind of a fourth century worshipper the motif must have evoked specific associations no less than it would today. Furthermore, the crosses seem to be confined to one single place in the church: they marked what appears to have been in the original layout of the building the principal approach to the central square which was the actual shrine of the saint[6].

This last consideration, in fact, permits us to go beyond a generic *interpretatio Christiana* for these crosses and to assert with some confidence what their purpose was. In Early Christian times crosses placed more or less conspicuously on, or near, entrances served primarily an apotropaic function. They denied access to the powers of evil which were thought to lurk particularly at doorways and other openings[7]. There is ample evidence that by the late fourth century crosses were widely used for this purpose and nowhere more profusely than in Syria. St. John Chrysostom, in a sermon preached at Antioch itself within at most a few years of the laying of the floor in the church of St. Babylas, refers to the inscribing of the cross of Christ on houses, walls, and windows as an established custom[8]. He does not elaborate on the reasons for this custom, but in the light of other contemporary documentation – much of it from the same Syrian milieu – there can be no doubt that it had to do with widely held beliefs in the magic efficacy of the sign. At the outset two kinds of buildings were held to be particularly in need of protection – the house and the tomb[9]. Churches, however, soon followed suit, witness instances of crosses on lintels of church doors of the late fourth and early fifth centuries[10]. Since the Martyrion of St. Babylas was both a tomb and a church our mosaic crosses fit into this picture very well.

Their meaning and their purpose, then, are hardly open to dispute. They are unusual only in that they appear here not on a lintel or other upright feature of the architecture but on the threshold underfoot. Thresholds were indeed held to be in special need of apotropaia, and if they did not receive them as frequently as did door frames, walls, and vaults, it was because the desire for protection here came into conflict

---

[6] There certainly were no crosses in the corresponding borders of the north and south arms; see *Antioch-on-the-Orontes*, II, pl. 48, no. 66 (»Panel A«); pl. 49, no. 67. In the west arm this border is not preserved. But we can be sure that in the original layout of the church the main approach to the central square was from the east rather than from the west, witness the fact that the inscription of Bishop Flavianus in the west arm is placed so as to be read from the east (*ibid.*, p. 35; Levi, *op. cit.*, pl. 114b). The remains of a portico, which were found in front of the west arm, belong to a later phase of the building when there must have been a principal entrance on that side (*Antioch-on-the-Orontes*, II, pp. 22, 35).

[7] F. J. Dölger, »Beiträge zur Geschichte des Kreuzzeichens, VII«, *Jahrbuch für Antike und Christentum*, 7, 1964, p. 5ff., especially p. 23ff. Cf. also A. Grabar, *Martyrium* (Paris, 1946), II, p. 277ff.; P. Nautin, »La conversion du temple de Philae en église chrétienne«, *Cahiers Archéologiques*, 17, 1967, p. 1ff.

[8] In Matth. Homil. LIV, 4 (Migne, *PG*, 57, col. 537); for the date – probably after 388 and before November

393 – see H. Lietzmann, in Pauly-Wissowa, *Real-Encyclopädie*, IX, 2, col. 1817.

[9] For »Hausschutz« see Dölger, *op. cit.*; for tombs, Grabar, *op. cit.*, p. 279ff.

[10] I quote the following dated examples of the fourth and early fifth century from churches: Fāfirtîn, 372 A. D.: *Publications of the Princeton University Archaeological Expeditions to Syria in 1904–1905 and 1909*, Div. III, Section B, Part 6 (Leyden, 1922), no. 1199, p. 202; Bābiskā, 390 A. D.: *ibid.*, Div. III, Sect. B, Part 4 (Leyden, 1909), p. 167 and p. 166, fig. 177; Kasr Iblîsu, West Church, Baptistery, 431 A.D.: *ibid.*, p. 206f. and fig. 212; El-Hazimé, 390–391 A.D.: J. Lassus, *Inventaire archéologique de la région au nord-est de Hama* (Institut français de Damas, Documents d'études orientales, IV, 1935–1936), no 93, p. 163. There are many additional examples of later or uncertain date in Syrian churches. A. Grabar has connected this type of lintel decoration with Jewish antecedents (»Recherches sur les sources juives de l'art paléochrétien«, *Cahiers archéologiques*, 11, 1960, p. 41ff., especially p. 45ff.).

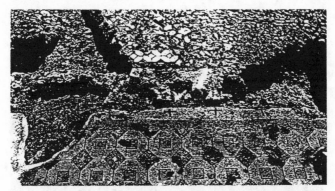

Fig. 1. Antioch, Cruciform Church. Border of Mosaic in East Arm, adjoining Central Square.

Fig. 2. Bethlehem, Church of the Nativity: View from the North with Steps descending to Grotto

Fig. 3. Bethlehem, Church of the Nativity. Mosaic Panel to the South of Steps shown in Fig. 2 (after Harvey).

Fig. 4. Bethlehem, Church of the Nativity. Mosaic Panel to the North of Steps shown in Fig. 2 (after Harvey).

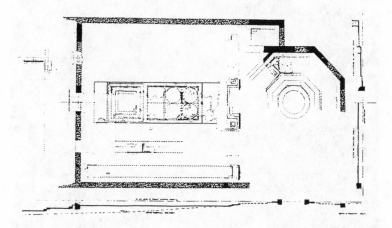

Fig. 5. Bethlehem, Church of the Nativity. Ground Plan of Constantinian Church, showing Position of Floor Mosaics (after Harvey).

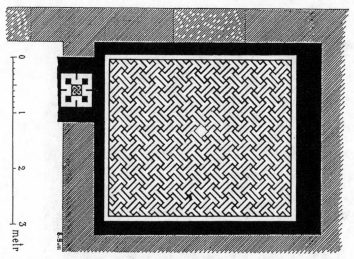

Fig. 6. Ostia. Ground Plan of Room in House, Reg. II, Ins. 6, showing Design of Floor Mosaics (after *Notizie degli Scavi*, 1908).

Fig. 7. Antioch. House of Phoenix, Upper Level. Room adjacent to Phoenix Floor.

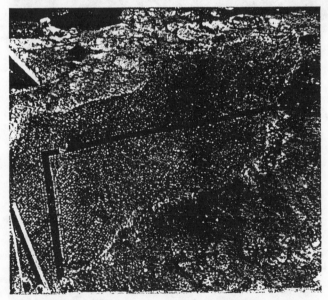

Fig. 8. Bethlehem, Church of the Nativity. Detail of Mosaic Floor to the North of Constantinian Octagon (after Harvey).

with the fear of desecration[11]. Placed in this position the sacred sign was liable to be trodden on. Undoubtedly this accounts for the fact that clearly meaningful and undisguised crosses are altogether not very frequent on mosaic pavements and that when they do occur they are usually in places not open to general traffic[12]. It is difficult to find another case where they are placed so squarely in the path of a person entering a building or precinct[13]. Yet the form of protection thus provided for the central area of the Antioch church does have a parallel elsewhere. Turning to another martyrion – a *locus sanctus* of far greater importance and renown than the shrine of St. Babylas – we find similar devices similarly incorporated in its floor decoration.

It was presumably during the first half of the fifth century – a few decades after the period of the St. Babylas floors – that the church which the Emperor Constantine had built over the Grotto of the Nativity in Bethlehem received its magnificent mosaic pavements[14]. A general compositional relationship of the great carpet in the nave of Constantine's basilica to that in the east arm of the Martyrion in Antioch has long been noted[15]. In my opinion the mosaics at Bethlehem represent a somewhat more advanced stage in the development of these carpets. Foliate motifs here begin to be used to break up and enrich the even flow of abstract motifs. The mosaics of the octagonal sanctuary which enshrines the Grotto itself include, in addition to a wedge-shaped unit with a vine rinceau, some panels with birds which intrude into the compact design of an otherwise geometric field. This is the beginning of an evolution which will eventually result in the appearance – or reappearance – of a much more lively and emphatic pictorial repertory on church floors. But it is only a beginning. Essentially the Bethlehem mosaics are still rooted in the tradition of those mute geometric floors which had been characteristic of the late fourth century[16].

---

[11] Dölger, *op. cit.*, p. 32 ff. See also below, p. 00.

[12] P. Gauckler, in: Ch. Daremberg and E. Saglio, *Dictionnaire des Antiquités Grecques et Romaines*, III, 2 (Paris, 1904), p. 2124; Avi-Yonah, *op. cit.*, p. 81. Finds of recent decades have added a number of examples. See, e. g., Salona-Marusinac, Basilica: *Forschungen in Salona*, III (Vienna, 1939), p. 76, n. 43 and fig. 94; Butrinto, Baptistery: L. M. Ugolini, in: *Rivista di Archeologia Cristiana*, 11, 1934, p. 265 ff., esp. p. 267, fig. 2, and p. 270 f.; Zahrani, Basilica: M. H. Chehab, *Mosaïques du Liban* (= *Bulletin du Musée de Beyrouth*, 14 and 15, Paris, 1958–59), p. 93 with fig. 6, pl. 47, and Plan 7 (cf. also the Chi-Rho monograms of cruciform design in the same mosaic, as well as in the pavements of the chancel: *ibid.*, pls. 45 f.); Damascus, Museum (from the region of Hama): S. Abdul-Hak and A. Abdul-Hak, *Catalogue Illustré du Département des Antiquités Greco-Romaines au Musée de Damas* (Damascus, 1951), p. 69, no. 12, and pl. 33, 2 (I owe this reference to Prof. G. M. A. Hanfmann); Shavei Zion, Basilica: *Revue Biblique*, 65, 1958, p. 420 f. and pl. 13 b (cf. the Unesco publication *Israel-Ancient Mosaics* [1960], pl. 4 and *Israeli Mosaics of the Byzantine Period* [1965], pl. 6; the full report on this site, published in 1967, was not accessible to me); Gerasa, »Glass Court« (see next footnote).

[13] A single cross is used in a somewhat comparable manner in the mosaics of the lower level of the so-called »Glass Court« at Gerasa. These mosaics, which also were laid in the second half of the fourth century when the court was remodelled to become an entrance to the Cathedral precinct, consist of a variety of geometric ornaments and are stylistically similar to those of the cruciform martyrion at Antioch. The motif which is of interest to us is directly in front of the steps giving access to the portico of the Cathedral. It is a large disk or whirl with an equal-armed cross in the center. See *Gerasa, City of the Decapolis* (C. H. Kraeling, ed., New Haven, 1938), pp. 217, 309 f., pl. 58 a, b, and Plans 31, 32; cf. J. W. Crowfoot, in: *Palestine Exploration Fund Quarterly Statement*, 1931, p. 143 ff., especially p. 147 f.

[14] W. Harvey, *Structural Survey of the Church of the Nativity, Bethlehem* (London, 1935), p. 21 f.; E. T. Richmond, in: *QDAP*, 5, 1936, p. 75 ff.; 6, 1938, p. 63 ff.; L. H. Vincent, in: *Revue Biblique*, 45, 1936, p. 544 ff.; 46, 1937, p. 93 ff.; W. Harvey and J. H. Harvey, in: *Archaeologia*, 87, 1937, p. 7 ff.; L. H. Vincent, in: *Atti del IV Congresso Internazionale di Archeologia Cristiana*, II (= Studi di Antichità Cristiana, 19, Rome, 1948), p. 65 ff.; B. Bagatti, *Gli antichi edifici sacri di Betlemme* (Jerusalem, 1952), p. 42 ff.

[15] *Antioch-on-the-Orontes*, II, p. 19, n. 15 (Lassus).

[16] For the evolution here sketched, and the place of

Here again, however, there is on the margin of the main composition one clearly meaningful feature. This is the word IXΘYC inscribed in the center of a square panel of meander ornament which is situated in splendid isolation in a large expanse of white mosaic in the eastern »surround« of the nave carpet. Measuring 72.5 x 72.5 cm., the panel containing the famous acrostic is in an oddly eccentric position to the left of a very slightly raised stone platform which is thought to be the lowest of three steps that led from the nave to the sanctuary. The Ichthys panel does have a pendant in a mosaic square of identical size and layout situated in a corresponding position to the right of this platform. But this second panel is made up entirely of conventional motifs. It contains in the center, in lieu of the inscription, a simple rendering of Solomon's knot and thus only adds to the seeming oddity of the arrangement (fig. 2–5).

To my knowledge, the Ichthys panel at Bethlehem has not been adequately explained. The late F. J. Dölger, who devoted to it a brief discussion shortly after it was discovered, cited a number of instances of the acrostic from houses and tombs in Syria and surmised that in churches, too, it must have been more common than the few extant examples would suggest, simply because of the significance attached to it »als der gedrängtesten Kurzform des christlichen Glaubensbekenntnisses«[17]. Yet it is to Dölger that we owe the fullest exploration of the protective and apotropaic properties which early Christianity often attributed to the Ichthys formula[18]. Primary evidence for this comes precisely from those buildings in Syria which have the word inscribed over their entrances and doors[19]. Surely at Bethlehem, too, the word is inscribed at an entrance. It is placed at the approach to the most sacred and most important part of the building, and, like the crosses at Antioch, it guards the threshold which gives access to it[20].

The companion panel on the south side (fig. 3) confirms this interpretation. Banal as its ornamentation seemingly is, it gains status and emphasis from the very fact that it is a counterpart to the Ichthys inscription. While the motif of Solomon's knot, which occupies the four corners as well as the center of the square, is among the most common in late antique floor mosaics, in this instance it clearly has a special role to play. What this role was is not hard to determine. The apotropaic use of knots is a recurrent phenomenon in the folklore of many countries and periods[21]. Obviously our inquiry here

---

the Bethlehem mosaics within this evolution, see my paper cited *supra* in n. 2 (especially p. 347, n. 29). My dating of the Bethlehem mosaics agrees substantially with that proposed by Père Vincent, who saw an additional argument in its favor in the fact that in two places the mosaic extends over worn parts of thresholds. This seems to indicate a considerable time-lag between the period of construction of the church and the laying of the mosaics (*Revue Biblique*, 46, 1937, p. 102 ff.). Harvey, on the other hand, contended that the mosaic areas in question are patches and not part of the original mosaic work which he considered to be Constantinian (*Structural Survey*, p. 18; see also *Archaeologia*, 87, 1937, p. 16). Granted that the mosaic covering the thresholds may be secondary – which seems to me far from certain –, it follows by no means that the original work must be as early as Harvey claimed.

[17] F. J. Dölger, *Antike und Christentum*, V (Münster i.W., 1936), p. 81 ff.

[18] *Id.*, *IXΘYC* (Münster i.W., 1910–1943), passim. See also J. Quasten, in: *Miscellanea G. Mercati*, I (= Studi e Testi, 121, 1946), p. 373 ff., especially p. 382 ff.

[19] Dölger, *IXΘYC*, I, p. 248 ff.; IV, pl. 205 f.

[20] Father Bagatti perhaps hints at this explanation when he says that the position of the inscription does not seem fortuitous (*op. cit., p.* 43).

[21] P. Wolters, »Faden und Knoten als Amulett«, *Archiv für Religionswissenschaft*, 8 (Beiheft gewidmet Hermann Usener), 1905, p. 1 ff.; J. Heckenbach, *De nuditate sacra sacrisque vinculis* (Giessen, 1911), p. 78 ff.; K.-H. Clasen, »Die Überwindung des Bösen«, *Neue Beiträge Deutscher Forschung, Wilhelm Worringer zum 60. Geburtstag*, ed. E. Fidder (Königsberg, 1943) p. 13 ff.; C. L. Day, *Quipus and Witches' Knots* (Lawrence, Kansas, 1967).

touches upon a wide field. Any broad generalization would be dangerous in view of the common – and surely often quite mechanical – use of the knot motif in the decorative arts of late antiquity and on floor mosaics in particular. I shall put the matter on the narrowest basis possible and merely quote two instances from other floor mosaics in which, because of the physical location and architectural context, Solomon's knot undeniably has a special function as an apotropaion guarding an entrance. One is the principal room of a small second-century house in Ostia paved with a diagonal meander pattern in black and white. On its threshold, against a black background, is a white square containing in its center a single Solomon's knot (fig. 6)[22]. The other is in the mosaics on the upper level of the House of the Phoenix at Antioch, attributed by Levi to the early sixth century. Adjoining on the northeast side the huge floor which has given the house its name is a room paved in mosaic with an all-over pattern of interlacing circles. The field is surrounded by a border of octagons containing squares. At one point, however, at or near the center of the side adjacent to the Phoenix floor, the monotony of this simple border pattern is broken. Here a sequence of three octagons contains respectively a Solomon's knot, a whirl, and another (square) Solomon's knot (fig. 7). There can be no doubt that this stretch of the border marks the threshold of the door which gave access to this room from the room – or, more probably, courtyard – with the Phoenix floor[23]. The whirl, it should be added in passing, is another apotropaion familiar from lintels[24].

It is not my intention with the foregoing remarks to open a floodgate of symbolic interpretations of innocent ornaments in late antique art. The perils are only too obvious. But one can err equally through an excess of skepticism. Certainly the two examples I have quoted are not the only ones, aside from Bethlehem, in which Solomon's knot was invested with a special meaning. I have chosen what I believe to be indisputable cases closely comparable to Bethlehem so far as the physical location of the motif is concerned, and spanning the period within which the Bethlehem mosaic was made. Other instances in which Solomon's knot was featured with special emphasis and a probably similar intent could easily be quoted. On the other hand, there are countless cases in which the motif clearly was used routinely and with little or no special purpose. Indeed, in the Bethlehem floors themselves it recurs repeatedly and in random positions in the nave and in the south aisle[25]. In surveying the material one soon becomes aware that a hard and fast determination is often impossible. Just as there were shades and degrees in the amount of emphasis which the motif received within a design, so there must have been shades and degrees in the amount of meaning that was attached to it in the designer's mind. Possibilities run the gamut from precise symbolism via the vaguely

---

[22] *Notizie degli Scavi*, 1908, p. 23, fig. 1; G. Becatti, *Mosaici e pavimenti marmorei* (= Scavi di Ostia, IV, Rome, 1961), p. 63f., no. 81, pl. 28.

[23] Levi, *op. cit.* (*supra*, n. 1), p. 351; pls. 83b, 135c. For the likelihood that the Phoenix floor was open to the sky see also R. Stillwell, in: *Dumbarton Oaks Papers*, 15, 1961, p. 54. The placing of the Phoenix motif itself shows that the main axis of the building was from southwest to northeast, so that the principal entrance to the room under discussion probably was on the side on which the special ornaments are. There seems to have been another threshold on the opposite

side, but it is not clear whether at that point, too, the border of octagons was enriched by special motifs.

[24] W. K. Prentice, *Greek and Latin Inscriptions* (= Publications of an American Archaeological Expedition to Syria in 1899–1900, III, New York, 1908), p. 18; cf., e. g., *Publications of the Princeton University Archaeological Expeditions to Syria in 1904–1905 and 1909*, Div. III, Section B, Part 4, no. 1081, p. 123 (456 A. D.), and no. 1089, p. 127f.

[25] *QDAP* 5, 1936, pls. 44, 46; *Archaeologia*, 87, 1937, pl. 7.

41*

meaningful to the purely ornamental. The notion of a »semantic range« within which meaning is determined by context is familiar from modern linguistics[26]. The principle has its application also in the visual arts. What precisely a motif signifies within a composition can depend on the context, in much the same way as does the meaning of a word in a sentence.

With this principle in mind we may touch briefly on another aspect of Solomon's knot as it appears at Bethlehem in the panel opposite the Ichthys inscription. The knot incorporates the shape of an X and might thus be considered to hold its own vis-a-vis the acrostic not only as another apotropaion but also as another reference to the name of Christ. The use of the X – sign as a »seal« of Christ – and as a reference to His cross – goes back to a very early period[27]. E. Dinkler in his recent searching studies of this subject, which have thrown much light also on the antecedent Jewish symbolism of the sign, has spoken of Solomon's knot in this connection and has pointed out that the history of this motif has yet to be written[28]. A short essay such as the present is not the place to fill the lacuna. It must suffice to point out that the situation at Bethlehem lends support to Dinkler's contention that Solomon's knot can serve as a substitute for X. Indeed, the X- shape seems to recur there in two guises in the Ichthys panel itself. The top right-hand square of that panel again shows Solomon's knot, as presumably did the corresponding square in the lower left where no mosaic is preserved. The other two corner squares are adorned with what at first sight appears to be a checker-board pattern which, however, may also incorporate a chiastic motif[29].

Whether or not the interpretation of these ornaments as disguised X-forms is justified we may hold fast to our principal contention, namely, that at Bethlehem Solomon's knot – specifically in its use as a pendant to the Ichthys inscription – served an apotropaic function. In terms of their meaning the two panels are equivalents. Together they guard the approach to the most sacred part of the building. In the purely formal sense, however, there remains a strange imbalance, and it is tempting to relate this asymmetry to the architecture of the area. Here again I touch upon a controversial subject and I do so with some hesitation, especially since I have had no opportunity to investigate the architectural remains myself. But the available descriptions, drawings, and photographs leave no doubt as to the essential data. I have already mentioned the fact that the two mosaic squares are situated on either side of a very slightly raised platform and that this platform is thought to be the lowest of three steps that led from the nave to the sanctuary. Indeed, on the right (or south) side a second riser was found still *in situ*[30]. On the left hand side, however, the platform has been cut through to accommodate a flight of steps leading down to the Grotto itself (fig. 2)[31]. W. Harvey and E. T.

---

[26] S. Ullmann, *The Principles of Semantics* (Glasgow and Oxford, 1957), p. 62f.

[27] E. Dinkler, »Kreuzzeichen und Kreuz«, *Jahrbuch für Antike und Christentum*, 5, 1962, p. 93ff. (with further references). The article is reprinted, with additions, in the author's recent book *Signum Crucis: Aufsätze zum Neuen Testament und zur christlichen Archäologie* (Tübingen, 1967).

[28] *Signum Crucis*, p. 53.

[29] I am judging from black and white illustrations, which may be misleading. No description of the colors employed for this pattern is available to me.

[30] Harvey, *Structural Survey*, fig. 65; *QDAP*, 5, 1936, pl. 41, fig. 2.

[31] Harvey, *Structural Survey*, p. 18 and figs. 61–64, 66; idem, in: *Archaeologia*, 87, 1937, p. 12 and pl. 10, 2; Richmond, in: *QDAP*, 5, 1936, p. 77f. and pl. 42 (= our fig. 2). At a later time these steps were narrowed by the insertion of a secondary wall clearly visible in the illustrations. They then started at a higher level, witness the additional riser to the left of that wall and well above the level of the Ichthys panel. Harvey's contention that from the outset these steps started on

Richmond, the discoverers of the remains of the Constantinian basilica, considered these steps secondary[32]. In the original layout of the church they thought access to the Grotto must have been gained by other means, but the suggestions they made in this respect were purely conjectural[33]. Father Bagatti, on the other hand, is of the opinion that the left or northern half of the platform enclosed from the outset a flight of descending steps and that only the southern – badly worn – end of the platform formed the base of a short flight of ascending steps leading up to the octagon. For the descent he reconstructs five steps leading transversely from left to right. At the foot of the fifth step he assumes a 90 degree turn to the east, with further steps leading down to a still existent – though walled up – entrance to the Grotto[34]. I see no reason to doubt Father Bagatti's contention that this was indeed the original solution devised by Constantine's architect to provide access from the nave to the Grotto as well as to the sanctuary. In any case, I believe that this must have been the arrangement in the early fifth century when the mosaics were laid and that it explains both the presence of the two square panels and their asymmetry. Both were placed close to the thresholds of what were then key openings in the circulation system of the building, but the one on the left was more important than the one on the right. It marked the point of access to the very spot where Christ was born. Here alone His name was articulated.

The fifth century floor decoration of the Church of the Nativity is imperfectly preserved and may have included other apotropaic devices. The extant part of the decoration comprises one further marginal element which possibly is meaningful, and which must be mentioned at least in passing. In the room flanking the octagon to the north (on the axis of the outer north aisle) a fragment of a white mosaic floor was found. The extant portion shows a simple black border marking the northwest corner of this room and, just inside the border, a sequence of three small cruciform motifs also in black (fig. 8)[35]. One is naturally reminded of the little crosses on the floor of the Martyrion of St. Babylas. But the situation is different here. The crosses are rendered ornamentally[36], and in the section of the wall which they adjoin there seems to be no trace of a threshold. In the circumstances it would be hazardous to interpret them as an apotropaion on the same order as the crosses at Antioch or the two panels at the east end of the nave at Bethlehem itself.

---

al evel above that of the mosaic floor is not borne out by his illustrations.

[32] See preceding footnote.

[33] Harvey and Richmond originally proposed a stairway in the longitudinal axis of the nave, descending from west to east and cutting through what they considered the central part of the steps leading up to the octagon (*QDAP*, 5, 1936, p. 81). Essentially, this was also the idea of Père Vincent, who incorporated it in his plan of the basilica suppressing in the process the existing transversal platform entirely (*Revue Biblique*, 45, 1936, p. 558 and pl. 2; *Atti del IV Congresso Internazionale di Archeologia Cristiana*, II, p. 69, fig. 2; p. 73f.). Richmond subsequently proposed an access to the Grotto through two flights of stairs within the octagon (*QDAP*, 6, 1938, p. 66 and fig. 1).

[34] Bagatti, *op. cit.* (*supra*, n. 14), p. 47 and figs. 16f.;

cf. also fig. 37, 1.

[35] Harvey, *Structural Survey*, p. 20 and figs. 89, 89.A. Cf. *Revue Biblique*, 45, 1936, pl. 7,2; *QDAP*, 5, 1936, pl. 39. Harvey remarks that the technique here is coarser than in the nave. This is not unusual for pavements in secondary areas and need not signify a difference in date.

[36] Cf., e. g., the surround of a mosaic in a villa at Baláca in Hungary attributed by A. Kiss to the third century (*La Mosaique Gréco-Romaine* – supra n. 2 –, p. 300 and fig. 15); also the surrounds of some of the panels of the pavement of the synagogue at Sardis (D. G. Mitten, *The Ancient Synagogue of Sardis* [New York, 1965], fig. 4; E. R. Goodenough, *Jewish Symbols in the Greco-Roman Period*, XII [New York, 1965], p. 195, fig. 5; *Bulletin of the American Schools of Oriental Research*, 187, October 1967, p. 31 ff., figs. 53f.).

I shall conclude these brief observations with a reference to the well-known Edict of 427 A. D. which forbad the representation of the »sign of Christ« on the floor[37]. Is it not possible that what prompted the imperial government to act in this matter was an increasing popularity of such signs not just on floors in general but on thresholds in particular? This is where the danger of desecration was greatest; and the examples from Antioch and Bethlehem show that signs of Christ had come into use in this position at precisely the time when the law was promulgated. In putting forward this suggestion I do not, however, mean to imply a safe *terminus ante quem* for the Bethlehem mosaics. Rather than being counted among the instances which provoked the Edict they could also be interpreted as a response to it. If *signum Christi* is construed narrowly to mean only a plain cross the special devices which were incorporated in the floor of the Church of the Nativity could be said to have been chosen in an attempt to comply with the letter, if not the spirit, of the law. In any case, the Edict was not entirely effective. There are plain crosses on floor mosaics which are undoubtedly later than 427 A. D.[38], and the prohibition had to be reaffirmed not only in the Code of Justinian but even as late as 692 A. D. when it was included among the canons of the Council in Trullo[39]. But whatever the precise chronological relationship of the Bethlehem mosaics to the Edict of 427 may be, it would certainly seem that the protection of the threshold had become a particular concern at that time[40].

This, however, was only part of a broader phenomenon which was to have a considerable future. Whether in our two sanctuaries in Antioch and Bethlehem similar protective devices were incorporated also in the superstructure we cannot say[41]. But

---

[37] » ... signum salvatoris Christi nemini licere vel in solo vel in silice vel in marmoribus humi positis insculpere vel pingere, sed quodcumque reperitus tolli« (Cod. Just. I, 8, 1; ed. P. Krueger [Berlin, 1954], p. 61).

[38] E. g., nos. 133 and 326 in Avi-Yonah's inventory cited *supra* n. 5; also the pavement in the baptistery at Butrinto (*supra*, n. 12) which is certainly of the sixth century.

[39] J. D. Mansi, *Sacrorum conciliorum nova et amplissima collectio*, XI (Florence, 1765), col. 975, no. 73.

[40] H. Brandenburg, in an important recent article (»Bellerophon christianus?«, *Römische Quartalschrift*, 63, 1968, p. 49 ff.), has discussed the Edict of 427 in a different context and has suggested that it was prompted primarily by an increasing use of »signs of Christ« on floors in private houses (*ibid.*, p. 85). His point of departure is the mosaic pavement of Hinton St. Mary which has as its central motif what appears to be a bust of Christ with a Chi-Rho-monogram behind its head. He recognizes a magic and apotropaic element in the depiction of the monogram of Christ when it occurs on floors in the private sector but is unaware of the indubitable presence of the same element on the floors of churches (*ibid.*, p. 79f.). A brief reference should here be added to an extremely interesting floor decoration first discovered more than thirty years ago by the University of Pennsylvania at Kourion in Cyprus. These mosaics, which still await publication, do belong to a secular building and their date must

be quite close to that of the Edict (see the preliminary notices by J. F. Daniel in *University Museum Bulletin*, 7, no. 2, March 1938, p. 4 ff., and by De Coursey Fales, Jr., *ibid.*, 14, no. 4, June 1950, p. 27 ff. The date proposed by Daniel is certainly too early; I owe to the kindness of Mr. Fales the information that a coin of Theodosius II was found beneath the mosaic illustrated in *Bulletin*, June 1950, pl. 8). The feature which is of special interest in the present context is a poetic inscription on one of the thresholds referring to »signs of Christ« which the house »has girded to itself«. It is tempting to relate to this inscription the four large cruciform motifs on which the ornamental design of the adjoining field is based and perhaps even the two fishes which – along with three birds – form part of the same design (*Bulletin*, March 1938, pls. 1, 3), though, of course, the inscription could also refer to »signs« that were incorporated in the superstructure. In any case, by implication the verses seem to attribute to the »signs of Christ« in this building apotropaic powers.

[41] Nothing is preserved of the superstructure of the Martyrion of St. Babylas. As for the Church of the Nativity, we might refer in this context to the little crosses which form part of the ornament of the abaci of the nave capitals (cf. A. Grabar, in *Cahiers archéologiques*, 11, 1960, p. 45 ff. and fig. 2). These capitals, however, are in all probability not those of the Constantinian church, even though they may be more or less faithful copies thereof; see Harvey, in: *Archaeo-*

we are able to glimpse in these floor mosaics the beginnings of an »uniconic« system of church decoration subsequently developed mainly on walls and vaults and providing vulnerable parts of the building with manifold »signs of Christ«[42].

HARVARD UNIVERSITY   CAMBRIDGE, MASS.

logia, 87, 1937, p. 13 f.; R. Krautheimer, *Early Christian and Byzantine Architecture*, (Baltimore, 1965), p. 189.

[42] Grabar, *Martyrium*, II, p. 280 ff.

Note: I am greatly indebted to Miss M. Katherine Donaldson for her assistance in the preparation of this paper; also to Professor Richard Stillwell and Miss Kaz Higuchi of the Department of Art and Archaeology of Princeton University for the photographs reproduced in figs. 1 and. 7.

THE CLEVELAND MARBLES

E. Kitzinger

The discovery in the early 1930s of the Christian community house at Dura Europos with its frescoed baptistery gave us for the first time a work of Christian pictorial art of indisputably pre-Constantinian date from any part of the ancient world east of Italy. The group of marble sculptures which will be discussed in this paper constitutes a second major find in this category. Totally different in character from the Dura frescoes, it adds an important, if isolated, piece to the jig-saw puzzle of pre-Constantinian Christian art. It helps a little to fill the Eastern half of that puzzle which is, of course, by far the larger one and which is still alarmingly empty.

In 1965 the Museum of Art in Cleveland, Ohio, acquired eleven small marble sculptures-five statuettes and six portrait busts. They were published and quite extensively discussed by William Wixom in the Cleveland Museum Bulletin [1] but have as yet received little attention internationally [2]. In part, no doubt, this is due to skepticism on the part of some scholars as to whether these pieces — and especially the statuettes, which do not fit readily into the accepted textbook image of Early Christian art — are authentic. Personally I have long since come to the conclusion that they are. In this paper, however, I shall not argue the case point by point. Instead I shall take up certain specific aspects of the Cleveland marbles, keeping in mind the general theme of " Craftsmanship " to which Mr. Ward Perkins' session is devoted and on which they have a de-

---

[1] W. D. WIXOM, *Early Christian Sculptures at Cleveland*, in *The Bulletin of the Cleveland Museum of Art*, 54, 3 (March 1967) (published 1968,) p. 67ff. (hereafter cited as *BullCMA* 1967). Thanks to the kindness of Dr. Sherman E. Lee, the Director of the Cleveland Museum, and Mr. Wixom, the Curator of Medieval Art, I was able to make a through study of the marbles in 1966. The principal results of the research I carried out at the time were incorporated in Mr. Wixom's article (cf. p. 71 and *passim*). I am very much indebted to him for providing for the present publication photographs of the marbles as well as of some of the comparative material illustrated in *BullCMA* 1967.

[2] See, however, P. DU BOURGUET, *Art paléochrétien*, Paris 1970, p. 108ff., with excellent illustrations of the five statuettes (p. 105ff.); also published in English as *Early Christian Art*, New York 1971.

117

finite bearing. In this discussion some of the principal reasons why in my
opinion these sculptures cannot be forgeries will emerge automatically.

I shall briefly introduce the pieces. Of the busts, which are of miniature size (ca. 31-35 cm.), three are male and three female (figs. 1-6).
The physiognomies in each set of three are very similar, and it seems to me
evident that the same two individuals are represented three times over,

Fig. 1-2 - Busts of men.

though there are some variations in dress. Of the statuettes, one represents
the Good Shepherd carrying a large ram on his shoulders (figs. 11, 12).[3]
The other four illustrate the story of Jonah — his being swallowed by
the ketos (fig. 7),[4] his being cast up (fig. 8),[5] his prayer (figs. 9, 20),[6]
and his repose under the gourd (fig. 10).[7] Allegedly busts and statuettes

[3] Height 50.3 cm.
[4] Height 51.7 cm.
[5] Height 40.7 cm.
[6] Height 47 cm.
[7] Height 32 cm.

were found together and there is nothing in the material evidence to contradict this. All eleven pieces are made of the same fine-grained, highly crystalline marble; all have the same golden-brown patina; and the incrustation from burial which many of the pieces bore proved identical when analyzed; also, granted the basic differences in subject matter and scale, portraits and statuettes share certain stylistic characteristics, for instance in the rendering of drapery.

Fig. 3 - Bust of man. Fig. 4 - Bust of woman.

The first question I shall take up is the date, though in the present context I cannot do more than draw attention to a few key indicators. An obvious starting point is offered by the portraits. The female heads can be dated fairly accurately on the strength of their hair style (figs. 4, 5, 6). With the hair combed back in simple waves that do not cover the ears and a highly developed *Scheitelzopf* brought up from the nape of the neck

119

to the top of the head, the coiffure of our busts has its closest parallels in coin portraits of Severina, the wife of Aurelianus (270-275), Magnia Urbica, the wife of Carinus (283-285), and Galeria Valeria, the wife of Galerius (d. 315)[8]. The men's fashion (figs. 1, 2, 3) is equally telling, for the com-

Fig. 5-6 - Busts of women.

bination of very closely cropped hair and luxuriant whiskers is characteristic of only a brief period--after Gallienus and before Diocletian, i.e. ca. 270-285. The portraits of the emperor Carinus (283-285) provide the closest parallels[9]. Thus examination of male and female busts independently leads to identical results.

---

[8] K. Wessel, *Römische Frauenfrisuren von der severischen bis zur konstantinischen Zeit*, in *Archäologischer Anzeiger*, 1946-47, col. 62ff., especially col. 65ff. and fig. III, (cf. *BullCMA* 1967, p. 74, fig. 20); see also H.P. L'Orange, in *Antike Kunst*, 4 (1961), p. 71 f.

[9] B.M. Felletti Maj, *Iconografia romana imperiale da Severo Alessandro a M. Aurelio Carino (222-285 d. C.)*, Roma 1958, pls. 57-59.

To find chronologically meaningful comparisons for the statuettes is more difficult. The Jonah sequence in particular stands out by its uniqueness. Statuettes of Good Shepherds, on the other hand, are common [10];

Fig. 7 - Jonah swallowed.

and although no precise chronology has yet been established for such figures, two points can be made. The pose of our shepherd--his freely turning torso and head and the action of his left hand, which firmly grips all

[10] For a catalogue of such figures (not entirely free of errors) see T. KLAUSER, in *Jahrbuch für Antike und Christentum*, 1 (1958), p. 45 f. The Cleveland statuette, associated as it is with representations of Jonah, shows that — contrary to Klauser's contention (*ibid.*, p. 35 ff.) — these figures of shepherds carrying a sheep or a ram on their shoulders were made for Christian contexts at an early date. See also Klauser's further discussion of the kriophoros theme in subsequent volumes of the same *Jahrbuch* [3 (1960), p 112 ff.; 5 (1962), p. 113 ff.; 7 (1964), p. 67 ff.; 8-9 (1965-66), p. 126 ff.; 10 (1967), p. 82 ff.]. In *Jahrbuch* 8-9 (1965-66), p. 127, n. 5, he lists additions to his catalogue of statuettes.

Fig. 8 - Jonah swallowed.

four legs of the sheep placed on his shoulders--recurs in a mirror reversal
on a well-known statuette in the Capitoline Museum, found in the 1880s
near the Porta Ostiense in Rome, which is certainly pre-Constantinian.[11]

---

[11] No. 25 in Klauser's catalogue cited in the preceding note. The best reproduction
is in *Bullettino di Archeologia Cristiana*, 1887, pl. 11; *ibid.*, p. 138 a view of the back
showing a satchel suspended in the same way as that of the Cleveland shepherd (cf. our
fig. 12). See also G. Bovini, *Musei Capitolini: I monumenti cristiani* (Cataloghi dei Musei Comunali di Roma), Roma 1952, p. 41 f., no. 14, and pl. 3. Bovini attributes the
statue to the second half of the third century, G. Gerke to the late Tetrarchic period
(*Die christlichen Sarkophage der vorkonstantinischen Zeit*, Berlin 1940, p. 252, n. 1).
It is interesting to note that the Roman statue has a close parallel in an unfortunately
badly battered figure found in the early 1960 s at Caesarea Maritima and now displayed in the open air on that site [cf. *Illustrated London News*, November 2, 1963,
p. 729, fig. 4, and p. 731; Klauser, in *Jahrbuch für Antike und Christentum*, 8-9
(1965-66), p. 127, n. 5]. The pose and even the design of the folds, of the tunic
are almost identical, though the Caesarea shepherd was carved without use of the

Fig. 9 - Jonah's prayer.

And the physiognomy of our figure, with its heavy jaw and full mane of hair, while differing from that of the Capitoline statuette, corresponds to that of Good Shepherds on certain sarcophagi which are undoubtedly of the second half of the third century (fig. 13) [12]. Since this quite

---

drill, so conspicuous in the Roman work, and belongs to the category of statues attached to pillars and supported by altar-like plinths which will be referred to below.

[12] For this facial type, best represented by the central figures of shepherds on sarcophagi in the Louvre and in the Palazzo dei Conservatori (G. WILPERT, *I sarcofagi cristiani antichi*, I, Roma 1929, pls. 66, 3, and 76, 2; cf. *BullCMA*, 1967, p. 87, figs. 45, 46), see GERKE, *op. cit.*, p. 253 f., n. 6. The sarcophagus in the Louvre belongs to the class of oval troughs with lion protomes and can hardly be later than the period of Gallienus [cf. G. RODENWALDT, *Römische Löwen*, in *La Critica d'Arte*, 1 (1935-36), p. 225 ff.; U. SCERRATO, *Su alcuni sarcofagi con leoni*, in *Archeologia classica*, 4 (1952), p. 259 ff.]. The sarcophagus in the Palazzo dei Conservatori has been attributed most recently to the third quarter of the third century; see *Repertorium der christlich-antiken Sarkophage*, I (F.W. DEICHMANN, ed.), Wiesbaden 1967, no. 816.

distinctive facial type never recurs subsequently, it constitutes an important chronological clue. O. Wulff long ago recognized the relationship of this type to the idealized portrait of Alexander the Great,[13] a relationship which in the Cleveland statuette is particularly evident (fig. 14)[14] and to which I shall come back later. Meanwhile let us be aware that consideration of the one statuette which lends itself readily to chronological comparisons — and all the statuettes in the Cleveland ensemble are clearly of one date — has led us to the same general period as the busts. In my opinion this

Fig. 10 - Jonah under the Gourd Vine.

fact alone strongly militates against these sculptures being forgeries. For a forger thus to satisfy the requirements of scholarship in what is after all a recondite field would be an unbelievable achievement. The years ca. 270-80 are a plausible date for the entire find.

At the time the marbles were acquired several different stories were in circulation regarding their provenance. The stories are mutually exclusive and none has been confirmed. Undoubtedly, however, the sculptures are of Eastern Mediterranean origin. The marble in all probability is from the Dokimian quarry in Phrygia;[15] and they were probably carved in

[13] O. WULFF, *Altchristliche und byzantinische Kunst*, I, Berlin-Neubabelsberg 1918, p. 107.

[14] Cf. *BullCMA*, 1967, p. 88 and figs. 41-43.

[15] Tests on the marble are pending. Meanwhile, Mr. John B. Ward-Perkins and other experts who have had a chance to examine the pieces in the original are agreed

southern Asia Minor, where both the male and the female portraits have their closest parallels. I cite for the male heads two portraits found at Side in Pamphylia; and for the female ones a head found at Alacami in the same province and now in the Museum at Antalya (fig. 15).[16] The facial

Figg. 11-12 - The Good Shepherd.

features of the Alacami head are so similar to those of our three female busts that one is almost tempted to recognize in it a portrait of the same person at a more advanced age.

Originally it was thought that all the marbles came from a single

on the likelihood of this provenance. For the Dokimian quarries see L. ROBERT, in *Iournal des Savants*, 1962, p. 23 ff.; J. RÖDER, in *Jahrbuch des Deutschen Archäologischen Instituts*, 86 (1971), p. 253ff.

[16] J. INAN and E. ROSENBAUM, *Roman and Early Byzantine Portrait Sculpture in Asia Minor*, London 1966, p. 194 ff., nos. 268, 268a, 269, with pl. 146 f.; cf. *BullCMA*, 1967, p. 72, fig. 15f., and p. 74, fig. 21.

context, most probably a Christian family tomb or columbarium whose decor included both commemorative portraits and biblical figures symbolic of resurrection and salvation. In my opinion this theory is rendered unlikely by the — to me indisputable — fact that male and female busts portray respectively the same individuals three times. It is hard to believe that any tomb decoration could have included such a multiple portrayal of a deceased couple. The survival of these six closely similar busts as a

Fig. 13 - The Good Shepherd (Photo M. Chuzeville).

single group can best be explained on the assumption that they were serially produced and not distributed. In other words, what has been found is not a functionally meaningful ensemble but a stockpile held either by the workshop which made the busts or by the persons portrayed. The implication is that these persons were prominent in public life and had occasion to commission multiple portraits of themselves for different purposes and locations. That their station in life was indeed exalted is borne out by their costume. [17]

[17] All three male busts show the sitter wearing the paludamentum or chlamys.

If, however, these marbles come from some kind of storage there need not be any functional connection at all between portraits and statuettes. According to one of the reports that were in circulation at the time they were acquired, all eleven pieces were found in one huge pithos. This report agrees well with the internal evidence, not only insofar as the serial character of the busts is concerned but also because it would explain the fact that all the marbles are in mint condition. Pithoi, of course, were in wide use for storage.

What I have just said does not amount to a conclusive proof that portraits and statuettes did not form (or were not intended to form) a single meaningful ensemble. But I think it is legitimate, in the light of the evidence I have cited, to leave the portraits out of account when inquiring into the purpose for which the statuettes were made.

Obviously, even if one disregards the busts one can make a case for the statuettes having been destined for a funerary context. One need only think of Roman catacomb art of the third century in which the Good Shepherd and the story of Jonah are the most common of all themes. But to me it seems probable that these marbles were meant for a more mundane use. Their most likely destination in my opinion was a small nymphaeum or decorative fountain.[19] In the framework of the present exposé it is not possible to argue this thesis in detail. In part it rests on an investigation of a well-known class of small scale marble sculptures of the third and fourth centuries mostly with mythological or idyllic subjects but including

Worn over a cuirass this is part of the full military uniform of emperors and generals. Worn over a tunic, as in the case of our busts, it is still a service costume, favored by the emperors of the second and subsequent centuries when not actually in battle and characterizing a non-imperial wearer as a high-ranking official, military or civilian [L.M. WILSON, *The Clothing of the Ancient Romans*, Baltimore 1938, p. 100ff.; cf. A. ALFÖLDI, in *Römische Mitteilungen*, 50 (1935), p. 43ff.; R. DELBRUECK, *Die Münzbildnisse von Maximinus bis Carinus*, Berlin 1940, p. 11 ff.]. A recent find at Aphrodisias enables us to identify a wearer of this costume as a provincial governor [I. SEVCENKO, *A Late Antique Epigram and the So-called Elder Magistrate from Aphrodisias*, in *Synthronon* (Bibliothèque des Cahiers Archéologiques, II), Paris 1968, p. 29 ff.]. The most notable element of the attire of the female busts is the broad band adorned with a rinceau which one of them shows draped over the left shoulder and across the chest (fig. 4). The precise meaning of this feature eludes us- - the problem is too complex to be discussed *in extenso* in the present context- -but there can be little doubt that the band denotes a specific rank or dignity. Among a number of parallels in female portraiture of the second and third centuries much the closest is afforded by the famous sarcophagus from Sidamaria in the Archaeological Museum in Istanbul. The lady who, with her husband, is portrayed reclining on the lid of this sumptuous tomb wears a band bearing the same ornament and draped in the same manner as that of our bust (H. WIEGARTZ, *Kleinasiatische Säulensarkophage*, Berlin 1965, p. 156 f. and pl. 34).

[18] *BullCMA*, 1967, p. 67.

[19] Actually, such a setting could conceivably be sepulchral at the same time; see below, n. 29.

also Christian pieces.[20]   A group with Orpheus charming the beasts which was found at Sabratha but must have been made in Eastern Mediterranean lands may serve as an example (fig. 16).[21]   Being provided with a distinctive

Fig. 14 - Alexander the Great.

type of plinth, reminiscent of an altar, and a short pillar at the back, these sculptures have often been considered supports for tables. But the available evidence rather suggests that they were fountain ornaments. In one

[20] *BullCMA*, 1967, p. 88 ff. figs. 47-50, 55. The class awaits comprehensive study and full publication. Principal references are: K. LEHMANN-HARTLEBEN, in *Römische Mitteilungen*, 38-39 (1923-24), p. 264 ff.; M. FLORIANI SQUARCIAPINO, in *Bullettino della Commissione Archeologica del Governatorato di Roma*, 69 (1941), Appendice, p. 61 ff.; CH. PICARD, in *Orientalia Christiana Periodica*, 13 (1947), p. 266 ff.; N. BONACASA, in *Archeologia Classica*, 12 (1960), p. 179 ff.; H. BRANDENBURG, in *Römische Quartalschrift*, 63 (1968), p. 31 with n. 6, p. 54f. with n. 12 f.

[21] SQUARCIAPINO, *op. cit.*; the group, which has been plausibly attributed to the third century A.D., is not without stylistic affinities with the Cleveland Jonah statuettes.

instance where an object of this class was found in a controlled excavation — an Orpheus group found at Byblos — the context was a nymphaeum; [22] another piece, found in the Case Giardino at Ostia and showing fishermen on a rocky seashore, is fitted out for actual water to spout through the rocks; [23] and years ago Strzygowski and others related the Good Shepherds,

Fig. 15 - Portrait from Side.

of which there are many among these pillared statuettes, to a famous passage in Eusebius' Life of Constantine in which the author, speaking of the founding of the city of Constantinople, mentions figures of the Good Shepherd — as well as Daniel and the Lions — as embellishments of public fountains. [24]

[22] J. LAUFFRAY, in Bulletin du Musée de Beyrouth, 4 (1940), p. 29 f. and pl. 5. Cf. PICARD, op. cit., p. 266 ff.; M. FLORIANI SQUARCIAPINO, in Bullettino della Commissione Archeologica Comunale di Roma, 72 (1946-48), p. 9 ff.; BRANDENBURG, op. cit., p. 54 f.

[23] M. FLORIANI SQUARCIAPINO, in Bollettino d'arte, 37 (1952), p. 29 ff. I owe this reference to Professor Irving Lavin. Unfortunately, the characteristic plinth on which the rocky landscape rests is not shown in the illustration accompanying the article.

[24] EUSEBIUS, Life of Constantine, III, 49 (Die griechischen christlichen Schriftsteller, vol. 7, ed. I. A. Heickel, Leipzig, 1902, p. 98). Cf. J. STRZYGOWSKI, in Römische Quartalschrift, 4 (1890), p. 97 ff.

Now this class of marble statuettes with pillars and plinths is relevant to the Cleveland pieces not only because it includes a sizable number of Good Shepherds.[25] It includes also a Jonah group which came to the Metropolitan Museum in New York in 1877 and which is said to have been found at Tarsus (fig. 17).[26] The iconography of this Jonah scene is quite different from that of our marbles (though the ketos with his wolf's head provides a good parallel for our ketoi), and the date is certainly not earlier than the fourth century. But, given its affiliation with pieces that are indisputably fountain ornaments, the New York sculpture does suggest that the Jonah story was indeed used in such a context, for which it was, of course, singularly appropriate. In effect it can now be argued, in the light of the Cleveland group, that the fourth century fountain sculptures with biblical themes[27] perpetuated or resumed a pre-Constantinian tradition. Needless to say, this third century precedent cannot have taken the form of public fountains but only of private ones.[28]

Whether or not one accepts this specific interpretation, the Cleveland statuettes certainly belong to a larger genus of which fountain ornaments are a part and which may be referred to as luxury decor. This entire genus, examples of which are scattered through the Roman world, still awaits comprehensive study.[29] Rooted in the tradition of Hellenistic baroque, it characteristically features subjects with an idyllic or genre-like flavor, complicated figure compositions and poses, and landscape elements such as rocks

---

[25] See, e.g., KLAUSER, op. cit. (above, n. 10), pl. 1, c, d; also the statuette in Caesarea Maritima cited above in n. 11, and another in Verona [P.L. ZOVATTO, in Felix Ravenna, 81 (1960), p. 106 ff.]. In many instances the pillar is incompletely preserved; and the base, along with the leg portion of the figure, is often missing entirely.

[26] W. LOWRIE, in American Journal of Archaeology, 5 (1901), p. 51 ff. Cf. BullCMA, 1967, pp. 75, 88c f. and fig. 55.

[27] Mention should also be made here of a fragmentary group, found in the Crimea in 1898, which has been interpreted as a representation of the Sacrifice of Isaac [cf. D.V. AINALOV, in Seminarium Kondakovianum, 1 (1927), p. 187 ff. and pl. 14, 1]. Like the New York Jonah group it may have come from a fountain, since it is equipped with the characteristic plinth (and, originally, a pillar?). There need not be anything exclusive about Eusebius' reference to Daniel and the Lions (cf. note 24 above). A variety of biblical stories may have come to be represented on fountains.

[28] For fountain statuary in general see B. KAPOSSY, Brunnenfiguren der hellenistischen und römischen Zeit, Zurich 1969.

[29] Professor N. Bonacasa has kindly informed me that he hopes to publish before long a corpus of certain types of genre figures- -shepherds, fishermen, etc.- -falling into this category (cf. the remarks on p. 172 of his article cited in n. 20 above). H.U. von Schönebeck [in Rivista di Archeologia Cristiana, 14 (1937), p. 301 ff.] has made interesting observations on relationships between statuary of this kind and sarcophagus reliefs, observations which suggest that « luxury decor » and funerary sculpture are not always and necessarily mutually exclusive categories. In this connection one should also keep in mind the existence of tomb gardens- -even with fountains [see W.F. JASHEMSKI, in The Classical Journal, 66 (1970-71), p. 97 ff.].

and trees. Sculpture belonging to this class tends to be under life size. Much of it clearly was meant for outdoor display in villas and gardens, and often there is some connection with water. Whatever the actual destination of the Cleveland statuettes may have been, this is the type of sculpture with which their creator was familiar and from which he drew his inspiration.

Fig. 16 - Orpheus charming the beasts.

It is because he operated within this established genre that his work — despite the seeming novelty, particularly of the Jonah sequence — has a distinctly routine character. This is not so much a personal and original vision of biblical figures and events as a skilful and ingenious transfer of types and motifs from another sphere.

I propose to demonstrate this point in some detail. The group of Jonah swallowed (fig. 7) makes an intriguing comparison with a group in the Naples Museum (in all likelihood from a fountain) showing a boy entwined

with a dolphin.[30] In this case the human figure's thrust-up legs domin-
ate the composition, whereas in the Cleveland group they are subordinate to the curled tail of the ketos that makes a characteristically baroque
crowning motif familiar from fountain ornaments.[31] The motif recurs in
the group of Jonah cast up (fig. 8); and the half-length figure of the prophet in this group — right side up as he emerges from the monster's jaws
— in all probability also is modelled on some fountain figure — a sea god
or triton. He may be compared, for instance, to the small and picturesque
figure of Pontos which nestles at the feet of a severely academic statue of
Tychè discovered in 1960 at Constanta, the ancient Tomis, on the Black
Sea coast of Roumania (fig. 18).[32] It is undoubtedly because he is modelled on a figure such as this that the Cleveland Jonah displays what is
by the common standard of Early Christian iconography such an unusual
physiognomy. As we shall see presently, the artist drew on models from
the same aquatic sphere for the features of Jonah also in the remaining two
statuettes, thus achieving internal consistency.

Of these two remaining pieces I shall first take up the resting Jonah
(fig. 10). Here the basic model clearly was a river god. The famous
statue of the Nile in the Vatican lends itself well for comparison, both
for the facial features and for the languid, relaxed pose.[33] It, of course, is of monumental size, but similar figures of reclining river gods are
common in miniature sculptures, being evidently a popular adornment for
small fountains and nymphaea.[34]

While river gods are normally fully awake, our Jonah is represented
somnolent with his eyes half-closed and his right arm folded over his head
in a pose familiar from mythological sleepers such as Endymion and Ariadne. Such figures, too, in under life-size renderings were favorite ornaments
for nymphaea and gardens.[35]

---

[30] A. RUESCH, Guida illustrata del Museo Nazionale di Napoli, I, 2nd ed., Napoli,
n.d., p. 159 f., no. 500 (6375); B. MAIURI, Museo Nazionale di Napoli, Novara
1957, p. 37.

[31] Cf., e.g., a bronze fountain spout in the shape of a dolphin from Constantinople
in the British Museum (H.B. WALTERS, Catalogue of the Bronzes, Greek, Roman, and
Etruscan, London 1899, p. 289, no. 1922). I owe an illustration of this object to the
kindness of Mr. Wixom (cf. BullCMA, 1967, n. 61).

[32] V. CANARACHE, A. ARICESCU, V. BARBU, A. RADULESCU, Tezaurul de Sculpturi
de la Tomis, Bucharest 1963, p. 16 ff. and figs. 4-9; p. 149 (English résumé). Cf.
BullCMA, 1967, p. 88² and figs. 56, 57.

[33] A. ADRIANI, Repertorio d'arte dell'Egitto greco-romano, Serie A, Vol. II, Palermo
1961, p. 52 ff., no. 194, with pls. 89-92.

[34] E.g., ibid., p. 55 ff., nos. 195, 196, with pl. 93. W.D. Wixom cites a number of
examples seen by him during his travels in Asia Minor (BullCMA, 1967, p. 83 and
fig. 60).

[35] See, for instance, the « Wilton House Ariadne »: H. HOFFMANN, Ten Centuries
that Shaped the West; Greek and Roman Art in Texas Collections (exhibition cata-

The fourth of the Cleveland Jonah statuettes (figs. 9, 20) calls for a general comment preliminary to a discussion of its visual sources. A praying Jonah is not part of the usual Jonah cycle as we know it from catacomb

Fig. 17 - Jonah Cast to the Whale.

paintings and sarcophagi. Normally only three phases of the story are depicted — the beginning of the ordeal (i.e. Jonah being cast overboard and being swallowed by the ketos); the casting out by the ketos; and the repose.

logue), Houston, Texas, n.d. [1970-71], p. 35 ff. and frontispiece. The figure, which measures 82 cm in length, is depicted resting on a rocky shelf at the water's edge and is thought to have been made for a grotto or nymphaeum. It has also been interpreted as a naiad [cf. M. MEISS, in *Proceedings of the American Philosophical Society*, 110 (1966), p. 350 and fig. 12]; and it certainly suggests that the use of the Ariadne type for fountain figures goes back to antiquity [for a different view--which, however, leaves the « Wilton House Ariadne » out of account-- see E.B. MACDOUGALL, in *Art Bulletin*, 57 (1975), p. 357 ff.]. Another relevant figure is the sleeping goatherd in the Sala degli Animali in the Vatican, which is thought to have been a garden ornament. It is of the same miniature scale as our Resting Jonah and also shows the characteristic position of the arms (W. HELBIG, *Führer durch die öffentlichen Sammlungen klassischer Altertümer in Rom*, 4th edition, I, Tübingen 1963, p. 81, no. 113).

In some catacomb chambers the system of decoration invited the addition of a fourth scene, but in these instances the moment chosen was not that of prayer.[36] It might be thought that the Cleveland figure does not represent Jonah at all but a generic orant. This possibility, however, is ruled out by the fact that the sculptor provided the figure with a satchel and a hefty

Fig. 18 - Tychè from Constanta.

walking stick, thus characterizing him as a traveler. Undoubtedly the statuette forms part of the Jonah cycle. At several points in the biblical story the prophet addresses the Lord. But his prayer *par excellence* is the great hymn of thanksgiving which he pronounces while being in the belly of the fish (Jon. 2, 3-10). This beautiful prayer was among the biblical texts which

---

[36] GERKE, *op. cit.* (above, n. 11), p. 158, n. 2; A. FERRUA, *Le pitture della nuova catacomba di Via Latina*, Città del Vaticano 1960, p. 43 ff. with pls. 6-8; p. 74 f. with pls. 70-71; ID., in *Rivista di Archeologia Cristiana*, 38 (1962), p. 8 ff., with figs. 2-5, and p. 69.

at an early date came to be recited in services; and in due course it became one of the liturgical odes appended to the psalter.[37] Thus it was that illustrations of the Jonah story were given a place in Byzantine psalter manuscripts such as the famous Paris Codex, Ms. gr. 139, of the tenth century.[38] Here a statuesque figure of the praying Jonah reappears as part of the story cycle and, indeed, as its most prominent part. The miniaturist, imbued with the Hellenizing taste of the Macedonian Renaissance, transferred the praying figure from the belly of the ketos onto dry land as our sculptor had done many centuries before.[39]

Attire, attributes and the somewhat dishevelled appearance of the Cleveland figure might suggest that it was modelled on a typical Hellenistic genre figure of a workingman or even a beggar. But I do not think so. There was a category of persons in the ancient world which adopted the appearance and life-style of such low class people but in its social role came much closer to a perambulating Jewish prophet, namely, the philosophers of the Cynic school. A figure from a Roman fresco, plausibly interpreted as a portrayal of Krates, may serve to illustrate the type (fig. 19).[40] A satchel and a walking stick were these men's proverbial attributes symbolizing their renunciation of all worldly riches.[41] The fact that our figure is equipped with these two objects strongly suggests that a representation of a beggar philosopher served as its model. Quite ingeniously the sculptor managed to retain the stick despite the orant gesture which he necessarily introduced. The prophet is seen propping the stick against his hip with his elbow as he raises his arm in prayer.[42]

---

[37] For this development see H. SCHNEIDER, in Biblica, 30 (1949), p. 28 ff. (especially pp. 40 f., 52); pp. 239 ff.; 433 ff.; 479 ff.

[38] H. BUCHTHAL, The Miniatures of the Paris Psalter, London 1938, p. 40 ff. and pl. 12.

[39] Cf. also a single leaf in the Benaki Museum, Athens, from a Psalter and New Testament Ms. of 1084 A.D., formerly Mount Athos, Pantokrator Ms. 49, now Dumbarton Oaks Ms. 3 [S. DER NERSESSIAN, in Dumbarton Oaks Papers, 19 (1965), pp. 159, 169 and fig. 17]. By contrast, in Byzantine psalters with marginal illustrations the miniatures accompanying the Ode of Jonah show the prophet inside the ketos; see S. DU-FRENNE, L'illustration des psautiers grecs du moyen âge, I, Paris 1966, pl. 32 (Mount Athos, Pantokrator Ms. 61, fol. 217v); S. DER NERSESSIAN, ibid., II, Paris 1970, pl. 112 (British Museum, Ms. Add. 19352, fol. 201r). Our statuette cannot be claimed to be a direct ancestor of the figure in the Paris Psalter. It does show, however, that the prophet's prayer had become part of the Jonah iconography at an early date and in a context other than text illustration.

[40] H. FUHRMANN, in Römische Mitteilungen, 55 (1940), p. 86 ff. and pl. 9; cf. K. SCHEFOLD, Die Bildnisse der antiken Dichter, Redner und Denker, Basel 1943, p. 162 f.; G.M.A. RICHTER, The Portraits of the Greeks, II, London 1965, p. 186 and fig. 1079.

[41] MARTIAL, Epigram 4, 53 (Loeb ed., I, p. 264 ff.). APULEIUS, Apologia (De Magia), 22 (ed. R. Helm, Leipzig, 1959, p. 25 f.). Cf. O. BRENDEL, in Römische Mitteilungen, 49 (1934), p. 157 ff., especially p. 163 f. and pl. 10.

[42] Cf. the well known ivory diptych of ca. 400 A.D. in Liverpool, on which Askle-

Face and countenance of our statuette also agree with its derivation from the figure of a vagrant philosopher. I have said earlier that the head, like the heads of the other two Jonahs in our series, is modelled on that of an inhabitant of the sea. No contradiction is involved, as witness Lucian's

Fig. 19 - Krates.

verbal portrayal of the Cynic philosopher Thrasycles: " With his beard spread out and his eyebrows uplifted, he marches along deep in haughty meditation, his eyes glaring like a Titan's and his hair ruffled up over his forehead, a veritable Boreas or Triton such as Zeuxis used to paint. "[43]

pios is shown supporting his club in a similar manner (F.W. VOLBACH, *Elfenbeinarbeiten der Spätantike und des frühen Mittelalters*, 2nd ed., Mainz 1952, pl. 15, no. 57). For the statuesque prototypes of this relief, which showed the god more definitely leaning on the club, see H. GRAEVEN, in *Römische Mitteilungen*, 28 (1913), p. 227 ff.

[43] LUCIAN, *Timon*, 54 (Loeb ed., II, p. 386 f.).

The description fits our praying Jonah admirably. Like his two companion figures, he has a physiognomic connection with the sea — only in this
case, I believe, it is an indirect one: the figure of a Cynic philosopher which
served as a model bore the facial features of a Triton.

For the manner in which our Jonah cycle came into being, the three
heads of the prophet are particularly revealing. As I have said, by model-
ling all three after bearded denizens of sea or river, physiognomic consistency was assured. But each of the three heads bears the signs of its
particular source. Thus there is a distinct difference between the head of
the praying Jonah — strong-boned and decidedly unkempt (fig. 20) — and
that of the resting Jonah, whose more elongated features and gently flowing
beard echo the countenance of a reclining river god. Conventional art
historical method might account for these different nuances within our
series simply by claiming that each statuette was done by a different hand. But each time the specific character of the head is so much
in keeping with the specific character of the prototype which we found
to be behind the figure as a whole that an explanation in terms of an artist's individual style does not seem adequate. The differences between the
heads is indicative of the extent to which this atelier operated with established prototypes and of the hold which these prototypes had over the
executant artist.

As models for recreating the biblical Jonah visually, these types were
a good deal more appropriate than the Endymion figure and other ephebic
nudes that usually served this purpose in Early Christian art. It is surprising, therefore, that, so far as extant material is concerned, the iconography
of the Cleveland Jonahs has neither precedent nor sequel. In all of Early
Christian art — even if I use that term in its widest sense — I can find only
one parallel for a bearded Jonah: namely, a miniature in the Rabula Gospels. [44] Even this example is not very relevant since it does not show the
specific characteristics of our marine type. For the moment we must accept
the physiognomy of the Cleveland Jonahs as a *hapax*.

This is not true of the physiognomy of the Good Shepherd. As I have
indicated earlier, shepherd figures that bear a facial resemblance to Alexander the Great have long been known to scholarship as a distinct group.[45]
Being confined to the pre-Constantinian period, this group has provided
us with a chronological clue for our marbles. I now want to make two
additional points concerning the Cleveland Shepherd's Alexander-like physiognomy. The first is that this particular type-casting is even more appropriate than the use of tritons and river gods as models for Jonah. The simile of the Good Shepherd had been a royal simile, an epithet of the good

---

[44] Florence, Laur. Ms. Plut. I, 56, fol. 6a. See C. CECCHELLI, G. FURLANI, M.
SALMI, *The Rabbula Gospels*, Olten and Lausanne 1959 (facsimile publication).
[45] See above, n. 12f.

ruler, long before it was used by Christ in reference to Himself; and the royal implications of the Gospel simile were well understood by Early Christian writers (notably Clement of Alexandria). Thus it is quite possible that these royal implications were in the minds of artists who endowed the figure of the Good Shepherd with the features of Alexander. [46]

My other point is that the occurrence of the Alexander type in figures of the Good Shepherd on a number of sarcophagi does constitute a tangible link between the Cleveland marbles and Early Christian art of the West

Fig. 20 - Head of praying Jonah.

(and sculpture in particular). Indeed, the Jonah series, too, with all its singularities, has certain aspects that are capable at least of a general correlation with sculpture in Rome of the same period. I do not suggest that there was any influence of the particular atelier that produced the Cleveland marbles on Western workshops. What I do mean is that certain developments in Christian sculpture in Rome in the late third century should now be re-examined and may turn out to reflect an Eastern development to which the Cleveland marbles bear witness. [47]

[46] F. DVORNIK, Early Christian and Byzantine Political Philosophy, Washington, D.C. 1966, II, p. 595 ff.; see also Index, s.v. « shepherd ».

[47] I am thinking particularly of the phenomenon of the story of Jonah being

But essentially these sculptures are an isolated find just as the paintings of the Dura Baptistery to which I referred at the beginning are an isolated find. Separated from the Dura paintings by almost half a century, our marbles offer insight into a formative stage of Christian image-making in an entirely different and far less peripheral part of the Eastern Mediterranean world. The process was one of assimilation and adaptation of pre-existent forms, as it was always bound to be wherever the themes of the new religion were to be rendered visually. And it may safely be assumed that the atelier that produced these marbles also worked for a pagan clientele, as the painters of the Dura Baptistery may have done and the painters of catacomb chambers and the sculptors of Christian sarcophagus reliefs in third century Rome certainly did. But the prototypes that were available in this particular Eastern workshop were quite different from those used in Dura or in Rome The traditions of Hellenistic baroque were still very much alive among these makers of luxury decor in the Greek East and the use they made of the types and forms handed down by this tradition was singularly sophisticated, bold and imaginative. As a result, Hellenistic exuberance and pathos appear here in a measure we did not previously know was ever attained in Early Christian art.

Presumably the impetus that gave rise to such work was cut short by the persecution under Diocletian. Examples of fourth century Christian statuary which can be shown to be in some way related are tame by comparison and are, in fact, only a belated echo of the pre-Constantinian vogue to which we owe the Cleveland marbles. [48] A comparable use of the sculptural medium for dramatic story-telling was not to be made again in Christian art until the age of the Counter-Reformation when Bernini and his contemporaires drew inspiration once again from Hellenistic models.

broadly developed over the entire front of Christian sarcophagi, a phenomenon unparalleled both earlier and later; cf. GERKE, op. cit. (above, n. 11), p. 38 ff. and pl. 1 f.; also M. LAWRENCE, in De artibus opuscula XL: Essays in Honor of Erwin Panofsky, New York 1961, p. 325 f. and pl. 100, 4 (sarcophagus in the British Museum). In one example--a fragment in S. Maria in Trastevere--the figure of Jonah in repose differs from normal Roman iconography by being clothed (GERKE, pl. 2, 2 and p. 49 f.). The rendering of the gourd in this fragment also is reminiscent of that of the corresponding feature in Cleveland; and it is curious to find that the figure rests on what appears to be an elaborately profiled pedestal as though it were a piece of sculpture in the round. Another element that may be mentioned in this context is the appearance in Christian sculpture in Rome in the late third century of the type of the Cynic philosopher, albeit not for Jonah (ibid., pl. 33 ff. and pp. 227 ff., 271 ff.).

[48] See above, p. 666 f. with notes 25-27 and fig. 17.

Engelbert Kirschbaum zum 6. 1. 1962

12. Die ältesten biblischen Motive der christlichen Grabkunst

Geht man der Frage nach, in welcher Häufigkeit biblische Motive aus dem Alten und Neuen Testament in der altchristlichen Sepulkralkunst vorkommen, so sieht es auf den ersten Blick so aus, als hätten die Bilder aus dem NT das Übergewicht. P. STYGER führt 1927 in einer statistischen Übersicht über die altchristliche Grabkunst insgesamt 78 biblische Einzelmotive auf[1]. Davon entfallen 27 auf das AT, aber 51 auf das NT. Dieses Übergewicht des NT scheint sich auch zu bestätigen, wenn man nicht die Motive zählt, sondern die Zeugen. Nach STYGER werden die 27 Themen aus dem AT durch insgesamt 778 Zeugen — 373 aus der Malerei, 405 aus der Plastik — vertreten. Demgegenüber entfallen auf die 51 neutestamentlichen Motive nicht weniger als 1158 Denkmäler, nämlich 299 aus der Malerei und 859 aus der Plastik.

Die statistischen Angaben STYGERS können freilich nur mit einigen Vorbehalten verwendet werden. Weniger wichtig ist, daß seit 1927 Neufunde und Erstveröffentlichungen von Katakombenmalereien und Sarkophagen den uns bekannten Bestand an Denkmälern vermehrt haben; denn im ganzen gesehen, wird sich das Zahlenverhältnis zwischen den Bezeugungen alttestamentlicher und neutestamentlicher Motive wohl kaum entscheidend verschoben haben. Wesentlicher ist folgender Umstand: In STYGERS Liste der neutestamentlichen Themen steht der »Gute Hirt« mit nicht weniger als 300 Darstellungen zu Buch, von denen 120 auf die Malerei und 180 auf die Plastik entfallen. Nun hat sich aber aus den Untersuchungen, die im ersten Bande dieses Jahrbuchs angestellt wurden, deutlich genug ergeben, daß der »Gute Hirt« auch in der heidnischen Kunst ein beliebtes Bildmotiv war und es auch im 4. Jh. noch gewesen ist[2]. Viele Denkmäler, welche nur dieses Motiv zeigen — ohne Beigabe eines spezifisch christlichen Elements —, werden also heidnisch sein. STYGERS Zahlen für das Vorkommen des »Guten Hirten« in der christlichen Kunst lassen sich daher sicher nicht aufrechterhalten. Die richtigen Ziffern werden sich freilich erst herausstellen, wenn durch weitere Einzeluntersuchungen die Geschichte der Christianisierung dieses Motivs geklärt ist.

Aber die Verwertung von STYGERS Zahlen muß noch an einen weiteren Vorbehalt geknüpft werden. In seiner Liste werden für die Darstellung des »Quellwunders des Petrus« 146 Bezeugungen gezählt, nämlich 26 aus der Malerei und 120 aus der Plastik. Nun ist aber bekannt, daß eine befriedigende Textunterlage für das »Quellwunder des Petrus« im Textbestand der neutestamentlichen Apokryphen bisher nicht nachgewiesen

[1] P. STYGER, Die altchristliche Grabeskunst. Ein Versuch der einheitlichen Auslegung (1927) 6/8. Die Verantwortung für die Zuverlässigkeit der Statistik muß STYGER überlassen bleiben; wir haben keinen Anlaß, an der Sorgfalt seiner Ermittlungen zu zweifeln. Eine ältere Statistik bietet

H. LECLERCQ: DACL 2,2,2476f. Man wird den Angaben des mit den Denkmälern vertrauten Schweizer Gelehrten mehr Vertrauen schenken als der Zusammenstellung des Schreibtischarchäologen LECLERCQ.
[2] JbAC 1 (1958) 20/51.

werden konnte[3]. Da außerdem die als »Quellwunder des Petrus« gedeuteten Darstellungen engste ikonographische Verwandtschaft mit jenen anderen aufweisen, die mit Sicherheit als Verbildlichungen des Quellwunders des Moses anzusehen sind, kann nach wie vor folgende Erwägung nicht von der Hand gewiesen werden: In einer Zeit wachsenden Interesses an der Person des Petrus, wohl im beginnenden 4. Jh., wird die Darstellung des Quellwunders des Moses als biblischer Hinweis auf Petrus, den Felsenmann, verstanden[4]; dieses typologische Verständnis führt seinerseits zur Bildung einer Legende, die von einem Wasserwunder des Petrus in Rom zu erzählen weiß. Die legendären Umstände des angeblichen römischen Petruswunders werden allmählich in die Darstellung des Moseswunders hineingetragen; aus den Israeliten werden Römer in militärischer Uniform.

Ist diese Überlegung richtig, so gehört das Quellwunder so lange zum alttestamentlichen Bilderschatz, wie das bloß typologische Verständnis der Mosesszene noch nicht zum Aufkommen der Legende und zu der damit zusammenhängenden Umwandlung der Begleitfiguren in römische Uniformträger geführt hat. Da aber in STYGERS Statistik die für das einzelne Motiv in Betracht kommenden Denkmäler nicht angeführt sind, läßt sich nicht sagen, ob er die Grenzlinie zwischen Moses- und Petrusszenen richtig gezogen hat, oder konkret gesagt, ob er nur solche Bilder als Darstellungen des legendären Petruswunders gerechnet hat, bei denen sowohl die Bärtigkeit des Wundertäters wie die römische Uniform außer Zweifel steht[5].

Wenn diese Erwägungen nahelegen, gegenüber den Zahlen für die Darstellung des Quellwunders des Petrus eine gewisse Zurückhaltung walten zu lassen, wird man nicht umhin können, ebenso bei einer anderen Szene zu verfahren, die gewöhnlich eng mit dem Quellwunder verbunden ist: der Szene der »Bedrängung« oder »Verhaftung«. Sie tritt in STYGERS Liste mit insgesamt 57 Zeugen unter den Rubriken »Flucht des Petrus« und »Bedrängung des Petrus« beim NT auf. Es bleibt auch in diesem Fall denkbar, daß zunächst der Exodus 17,2 und Numeri 20,2/6 angedeutete Vorgang der Bedrängung des Moses durch die verdurstenden Israeliten gemeint war, und daß auch dieser in der Zeit aufblühender Petrusverehrung als typologischer Hinweis auf eine Bedrängung oder Verhaftung des Apostels verstanden und entsprechend abgewandelt wurde[6].

---

[3] G. STUHLFAUTH, Die apokryphen Petrusgeschichten in der altchristlichen Kunst (1925) 60 verwies auf das Martyrium Petri a Lino conscriptum 5 (AAA 1,6,28f), wo von einem Wasserwunder des Petrus im mamertinischen Kerker die Rede ist. Aber dieser Text gehört wohl erst dem 6. Jh. an. Außerdem dient das hier geschilderte Wasserwunder der Taufe der Gefängniswärter, nicht der Tränkung verdurstender Soldaten oder Polizisten wie auf den Bildern. E. STOMMEL, Beiträge zur Ikonographie der konstantinischen Sarkophagplastik (1954) 84/87 versucht, die Spannung zwischen der Legende und der Darstellung durch die Annahme zu überbrücken, daß im Bilde symbolisch der Durst der Soldaten nach der Taufe ausgedrückt werde.
[4] Die typologische Erklärung des Moses-Quellwunders begründete eingehend E. BECKER, Das Quellwunder des Moses in der altchristlichen Kunst (1909) 141/45. Wenn G. STUHLFAUTH aO.

[5] 57 einwandte, die typologische Ausdeutung sei der altchristlichen Kunst fremd, so blieb er den überzeugenden Beweis schuldig.
[5] Ähnliche Überlegungen auch bei E. WEIGAND, Die spätantike Sarkophagskulptur im Lichte neuerer Forschungen: ByzZ 41 (1941) 129/33.
[6] Eingehende Behandlung der in Betracht kommenden Denkmäler bei G. STUHLFAUTH, Die apokryphen Petrusgeschichten in der altchristlichen Kunst (1925) 72/101. — Daß die Umwandlung der Mosesszenen in Petrusbilder in den Anfang des 4. Jh. fallen muß, ist nach den Untersuchungen von E. DINKLER, Die ersten Petrusdarstellungen. Ein archäologischer Beitrag zur Geschichte des Petrus-Primats: Marburger Jahrbuch für Kunstwissenschaft 11/12 (1938/39) 1/80, besonders 62f, nicht zu bezweifeln. Nur sollte man sie doch wohl nicht schon in die tetrarchische Zeit datieren, wie DINKLER aO. 60 es tut. Sie gehört u. E. eher in die Zeit nach 313, als Konstantin, sicher in Überein-

9 Antike und Christentum

Wenn wir also einen noch unbekannten, aber sicher erheblichen Teil der von STYGER in seine Rechnung aufgenommenen Zeugen für das Thema des »Guten Hirten« streichen und außerdem annehmen, daß die Beispiele des Quellwunders und der Bedrängung des Petrus weniger zahlreich sind, als STYGER meinte, sieht das Ergebnis der Motivstatistik schon anders aus, als es auf den ersten Blick schien: auf der Seite des NT sind bis zu 300 angebliche Zeugen für den »Guten Hirten« zu streichen, während andererseits vermutlich ein beträchtlicher Teil der 203 Beispiele der Bedrängung und des Quellwunders Petri dem AT zuzuweisen ist. Das NT hat also im Bilderschatz der altchristlichen Sepulkralkunst keineswegs ein Übergewicht; eher hat das AT einen gewissen Vorsprung[7].

Weil die Bemühungen um die genauere Datierung der altchristlichen Denkmäler zwar in den letzten Jahrzehnten große Fortschritte gemacht haben, aber noch nicht zu völlig abschließenden Ergebnissen gediehen sind, kann heute noch nicht daran gedacht werden, in der Motivstatistik auch die chronologische Seite durchgehend zur Geltung zu bringen, so sehr dies zu wünschen wäre. Erst, wenn wir eine solche, wenigstens nach Halbjahrhunderten gegliederte chronologische Übersicht über die Zeugen der biblischen Motive in der sepulkralen Denkmälerwelt besitzen, läßt sich das Auf und Ab der Beliebtheit alt- und neutestamentlicher Bildstoffe in der Grabkunst genauer verfolgen[8]. Immerhin kann man heute dank den Forschungen von F. WIRTH, H. U. VON SCHOENEBECK, F. GERKE, G. BOVINI, A. M. SCHNEIDER und J. KOLLWITZ mit dem Anspruch einer gewissen Wahrscheinlichkeit schon sagen, welche altchristlichen Sepulkraldenkmäler noch der vorkonstantinischen Zeit angehören[9]. Infolgedessen läßt sich wenigstens für diese frühe Periode der christlichen Kunstgeschichte das gegenseitige Verhältnis alt- und neutestamentlicher Bilder annähernd zuverlässig bestimmen. Das soll im folgenden versucht werden.

Der vorkonstantinischen Zeit werden heute von der Forschung folgende Katakombenmalereien mit biblischen Stoffen zugewiesen: die Bilder in den sogenannten Sakra-

---

stimmung mit der römischen Gemeinde, anfing, das Andenken des Petrus durch großartige Kirchenbauten zu ehren. Diese Ära beginnt mit der Errichtung der Basilika an der Via Appia; vgl hierzu TH. KLAUSER, Die römische Petrustradition im Lichte der neuen Ausgrabungen unter der Peterskirche (1956) 82f. Zur Frage der Datierung der Umwandlung der Mosesbilder in Petrusbilder erst in konstantinische Zeit vgl. auch die durch historische und formale Erwägungen bestimmten Bemerkungen von H. VON SCHOENEBECK in der Besprechung der DINKLERschen Arbeit: DLZ 1939, 1316/19.
[7] Dies behauptete schon, freilich ohne Nachweis, C. M. KAUFMANN, Handbuch der christlichen, Archäologie³ (1922) 198. Ebenso O. WULFF, Altchristliche und byzantinische Kunst 1 (1941) 60.
[8] P. STYGER hat seiner, mit chronologischen Erwägungen noch nicht beschwerten Statistik von 1927 (vgl. oben Anm. 1) später eine neue, diesmal chronologisch vorgehende Zusammenstellung folgen lassen und zwar in seinem Buch: Die römischen Katakomben (1933) 355/59. Er ist dabei von den Zeitansätzen ausgegangen, die er bei seinen verdienstlichen Untersuchungen zur Chronologie der

Katakomben gewonnen hatte. Die weitere Entwicklung der Forschung hat gezeigt, daß STYGERS vorkonstantinische Ansätze, so revolutionär sie gegenüber den bisher üblichen Frühdatierungen wirkten, immer noch durchweg um 50 oder 100 Jahre zu weit nach oben gegriffen waren.
[9] F. WIRTH, Die römische Wandmalerei (1934). H. U. VON SCHOENEBECK, Die christliche Sarkophagplastik unter Konstantin: RömMitt 51 (1936) 238/336; Die christlichen Paradeisossarkophage: RivAC 24 (1937). 289/343. F. GERKE, Die christlichen Sarkophage der vorkonstantinischen Zeit = Studien zur spätantiken Kunstgesch. 11 (1940), im folgenden abgekürzt: GERKE; Ideengeschichte der ältesten christl. Kunst: ZKG 59 (1940) 1/102; Der Trierer Agricius-Sarkophag (1949). G. BOVINI, I sarcofagi paleocristiani. Determinazione della loro cronologia mediante l'analisi dei ritratti (1949). A. M. SCHNEIDER, Die ältesten Denkmäler der christlichen Kirche: Festschrift zur Feier des 200-jährigen Bestehens der Akademie der Wissenschaften in Göttingen 2 (1951) 166/98. J. KOLLWITZ, Das Christusbild des 3. Jh. = Orbis antiquus 9 (1953); Christusbild: RAC 3 (1957) 4/15.

mentskapellen der Callistus-Katakombe[10], die Fresken in der Doppelkammer der Lucina-Region[11], zwei Bilder in der sonst heidnisch dekorierten Flavier-Galerie der Domitilla-Katakombe (die hier in Strichzeichnung vorgeführt werden sollen, s. Abb. 5)[12] und, freilich nicht mit gleicher Sicherheit, der Bilderschmuck in der sogenannten Cappella Greca der Priscilla-Katakombe[13].

Abb. 5. Rom, Domitilla-Katakombe, Flaviergalerie. a Arche Noes. b Daniel in der Löwengrube.

[10] Kapelle A²: G. B. DE ROSSI, Roma sotterranea 2 (Rom 1867) Tav. d'agg. C/D (unsere Taf. 6a); J. WILPERT, Malereien der Katakomben (1903), im folgenden abgekürzt: WM, Taf. 27,2; 38; 39, 1/2: Quellwunder des Moses (unsere Taf. 6a. 7a); Meerwurf des Jonas (unsere Taf. 6a. 7b); Ruhe des Jonas (unsere Taf. 6a); Taufe Jesu? (unsere Taf. 6a. 7b); Auferweckung des Lazarus (unsere Taf. 6a).— Kapelle A³: DE ROSSI aO. (unsere Taf. 6b); WM Taf. 26,2/3; 27,3; 29,2; 41,2: Opfer Abrahams (unsere Taf. 6b. 8a); Quellwunder des Moses (unsere Taf. 6b); Meerwurf des Jonas (desgl.); Ausspeiung des Jonas (unsere Taf. 6b. 7c); Ruhe des Jonas (desgl.); Taufe Jesu (unsere Taf 6b. 8b); Heilung des Gichtbrüchigen (desgl.); Samaritanerin am Jakobsbrunnen (unsere Taf. 6b). — Kapelle A⁴: R. GARRUCCI, Storia dell'arte cristiana (Prato 1873) Taf. 8, 1. 2. 3: Meerwurf des Jonas; Ausspeiung des Jonas; Ruhe des Jonas. — Kapelle A⁵: GARRUCCI, Storia Taf. 8, 4. 5. 6; WM Taf. 47, 1: Quellwunder des Moses: Ruhe des Jonas. — Kapelle A⁶: WM Taf. 46, 1/2; 47, 2: Quellwunder des Moses (unsre Taf. 9a); Meerwurf des Jonas (unsere Taf. 8c); Ausspeiung des Jonas (desgl.); Ruhe des Jonas (desgl.); Auferweckung des Lazarus (unsere Taf. 9b). — Zur Datierung WIRTH aO. 184 f; SCHNEIDER aO. 176/82; KOLLWITZ a.O (1953) 26. — Bedauerlicherweise fehlen immer noch gute neuzeitliche Weitwinkelaufnahmen der ältesten Zömeterialkammern; auch Gesamtaufnahmen der einzelnen Wände wären willkommen. Wer die Dekorationen einer Kammer untersuchen will, muß sie aus WILPERTS Einzelbildern erst mühsam rekonstruieren. Dabei leisten für die Sakramentskapellen A¹ und A³ immer noch gute Dienste DE

ROSSI aO. Taf. 11/13 und Tav. d'aggiunta C/D; vgl. für alle Sakramentskapellen die schematische Übersicht bei J. WILPERT, Die Malereien der Sakramentskapellen in der Katakombe des hl. Callistus (1897) 26f.33f und bei C. M. KAUFMANN, Handbuch der Christlichen Archäologie² (1922) 262f.

[11] WM Taf. 26,1; 29,1: Ruhe des Jonas; Daniel in der Löwengrube; Taufe Jesu. — Außer Betracht bleibt das zweimal auf der gleichen Wand begegnende Motiv des großen Fisches mit einem Korb, der mit Broten (»Kringelbroten«) gefüllt ist. Die Verdoppelung des Motivs an der gleichen Wand spricht u. E. nicht dafür, daß es sich um eine verkürzte Darstellung des Speisungswunders Jesu oder gar der Eucharistie handelt; eher soll auf ein Totenmahl hingewiesen werden. Vgl. auch DÖLGER, Ichth. 5,527/33. — Zur Datierungsfrage vgl. F. WIRTH aO. 175f.183f; A. M. SCHNEIDER aO. 180f; J. KOLLWITZ, Das Christusbild des 3. Jh. = Orbis antiquus 9 (1953) 6.

[12] WM Taf. 5,1; GARRUCCI, Storia 2 Taf. 19,2/3 (unsere Abb. 5). Daniel in der Löwengrube; Arche Noes. — Zur Datierung vgl. F. WIRTH aO. 170/74; A. M. SCHNEIDER aO. 185; J. KOLLWITZ aO. (1953) 7.

[13] WM Taf. 13; 14, 1/2. r.; J. WILPERT, Fractio panis (1895) Taf. 4. 5. 7. 8. 10. 11: Arche Noes; Opfer Abrahams; Quellwunder des Moses (unsere Taf. 10b); Jünglinge im Feuerofen (unsere Taf. 10b); Anklage der Susanna; Schwur im Susanna-Prozeß; Gebet Susannas und Daniels; Anbetung der Magier (unsere Taf. 10a); Auferweckung des Lazarus. — Zur Datierung zuletzt F. WIRTH aO. 213/15; A. M. SCHNEIDER aO. 189f.

9*

Zu den Denkmälern der Sepulkral-Plastik, die von der Forschung mehr oder weniger übereinstimmend der vorkonstantinischen Zeit zugesprochen werden, gehören die folgenden Sarkophage: der Sarkophag des ehemaligen Kaiser Friedrich-Museums[14], der Sarkophag von S. Maria antica[15], der Sarkophag Lateran 119[16], der Sarkophag Ny Carlsberg 832[17], ein soeben erst bekannt gewordener Sarkophag des Britischen Museums[18], der Sarkophag der Hertofile im Thermen-Museum[19], der Sarkophag der Iulia Iuliane im Lateran[20], der Noe-Sarkophag in Trier[21], der Sarkophag in Velletri[22], ein erst vor wenigen Jahren in die Forschung eingeführter Sarkophag in Belgrad[22a] und der Sarkophag von Mas d'Aire[23]. Weiter gehören in die vorkonstantinische Denkmälergruppe einige Riefelsarkophage, nämlich je ein Sarkophag im Thermen-Museum (von Via Lungara)[24] und in Lucca[25] und ein besonders bemerkenswertes Stück in Pisa[26]. Vorkonstantinisch sind auch mehrere Sarkophagdeckel, nämlich Stücke in S. Pretestato[27] und Villa Doria[28]. Sehr erheblich ist die Zahl vorkonstantinischer Sarkophagfragmente. Es handelt sich zunächst um Bruchstücke von Sarkophagkästen in Neapel[29], im Lateran[30], in S. Maria in Trastevere[31], im Thermen-Museum — die viel-

---

[14] G. WILPERT, I Sarcofagi cristiani antichi 1/3 (1929/36), im folgenden abgekürzt: WS, Taf. 54,3: Ruhe des Jonas (abgeb. JbAC 1 Taf. 8,3). — Zur Datierung GERKE 234/41.
[15] WS Taf. 1,2; 3,1 (JbAC 3 Taf. 6,2): Ruhe des Jonas (mit Schiff und Ketos); Taufe Jesu. — Zur Datierung GERKE 259/65; VON SCHOENEBECK: Riv. 241; M. LAWRENCE, Three pagan themes in christian art: Essays in honor of E. Panofsky (New York 1961) 324f.
[16] WS Taf. 9,3 (unsere Taf. 11a): Arche Noes; Quellwunder des Moses; Bedrängung des Moses (Ex. 17,3f); Meerwurf des Jonas; Ausspeiung des Jonas; Ruhe des Jonas; Auferweckung des Lazarus. — Zur Datierung VON SCHOENEBECK: RömMitt 1936, 245; GERKE 38,51.
[17] WS Taf. 59,3: Meerwurf des Jonas; Ausspeiung des Jonas; Ruhe des Jonas. — Zur Datierung GERKE 38,51.
[18] M. LAWRENCE aO. 325f u. Taf. 100f Fig. 4/5: bemanntes Schiff mit Ketos (Moment vor dem Meerwurf des Jonas); Ausspeiung des Jonas. — Zur Datierung M. LAWRENCE aO. 325f. Den gleichen Sarkophag behandelt die unten Anm. 92 genannte Arbeit von H. ROSENAU.
[19] WS Taf. 53,3: Ruhe des Jonas (mit Schiff und Ketos). — Zur Datierung GERKE 120/55; VON SCHOENEBECK: Riv. 325f.340; BOVINI 111f. 272.
[20] WS Taf. 57,5 (JbAC 3 Taf. 8a): Arche Noes; Meerwurf des Jonas. — Zur Datierung VON SCHOENEBECK: RömMitt 245; GERKE 84.339₂; BOVINI 155.293f.
[21] GERKE 300/306 u. Taf. 47,1: Arche Noes. — Zur Datierung BOVINI 150/289.
[22] WS Taf. 4,3 (JbAC 3 [1960] Taf. 7a) Adam und Eva; Arche Noes; Daniel in der Löwengrube; Meerwurf des Jonas; Ausspeiung des Jonas; Ruhe des Jonas. — Zur Datierung VON SCHOENEBECK: Riv. 325; GERKE 73/81. 188f.339.
[22a] GERKE, Agricius- Sark. Taf. 4,7: Meerwurf des

Jonas; Ausspeiung des Jonas. — Zur Datierung ebd. Tabelle 1.
[23] WS Taf. 65,5: Adam und Eva; Opfer Abrahams; Daniel in der Löwengrube; Tobias und der Fisch; Ausspeiung des Jonas; Auferweckung des Lazarus; Heilung des Gichtbrüchigen; Heilung des Besessenen (unsere Taf. 11b). — Zur Datierung GERKE 306/309.
[24] WS Taf. 19,3.5f: Taufe Jesu (Seitenfläche). — Zur Datierung VON SCHOENEBECK: Riv. 323/25; GERKE 66.143; BOVINI 99/102.267.
[25] WS Taf. 166,3: Daniel in der Löwengrube; Ruhe des Jonas. — Zur Datierung GERKE 168.
[26] WS Taf. 88,1/3.5/7: Ruhe des Jonas. — Zur Datierung VON SCHOENEBECK: Riv. 337; GERKE 165f. — Gegen den christlichen Charakter des Sarkophags könnte sprechen, daß der ruhende Jonas unter der Laube (rechte Nebenseite) ein Hirt mit Pedum, Hirtentasche und Schafen ist. Man denkt unwillkürlich an Endymion. Aber das Schiff mit den betenden Matrosen auf der linken Seite zeigt eindeutig, daß an der christlichen oder wenigstens biblischen Interpretation festzuhalten ist.
[27] RivAC 13 (1936) 214 Abb. 6; GERKE Taf. 29,2: Ruhe des Jonas. — Zur Datierung GERKE 126f. 173f.
[28] WS Taf. 10,1: Ruhe des Jonas (mit Schiff und Ketos). — Zur Datierung GERKE 152/55.
[29] WS Taf. 164,5 (Scheinsarkophag): Daniel in der Löwengrube. — Zur Datierung VON SCHOENEBECK: Riv. 338; GERKE 165/70; BOVINI 121f.276.
[30] WS Taf. 190,3 (JbAC 1 Taf. 6g): Himmelfahrt des Elias. Die Zugehörigkeit des Reliefs zu einem Sarkophag scheint nicht zweifelsfrei zu sein. — Zur Datierung GERKE 86/94.
[31] WS Taf. 161,2: Jünglinge im Feuerofen; Ruhe des Jonas (Jonas bekleidet; vgl. Anm. 26). — Zur Datierung VON SCHOENEBECK: Riv. 245; GERKE 49/51.

besprochenen polychromen Denkmäler 67606[32] und 67607[33]. Es handelt sich sodann um eine größere Anzahl von Deckelfragmenten, nämlich um die Stücke Antinori[34], Campo S. Teutonico I[35], Campo S. Teutonico II[36], Corsetti[37], Lateran[38], Louvre (aus S. Priscilla)[39], Neapel (vom Sarkophag der Cyriaca)[40], S. Severino I[41], S. Severino II[42], Thermen-Museum I[43], Thermen-MuseumII[44] und S. Priscilla[45]. Die Reihe der vorkonstantinischen Sepulkraldenkmäler aus dem Bereich der Plastik schließt mit einer reliefierten Loculusplatte im Konservatorenpalast[46].

Stellt man die biblischen Szenen aus dem Alten und Neuen Testament zusammen, die durch die oben aufgeführten Denkmäler der vorkonstantinischen christlichen Grabkunst bezeugt sind, so ergibt sich folgendes Bild (die Zahlen hinter den Motiven beziehen sich auf die Häufigkeit der Bezeugung):

Altes Testament

Belebung Evas	1
Adam und Eva	3[47]
Arche Noes	6
Opfer Abrahams	3
Bedrängung des Moses	1
Quellwunder des Moses	5
Himmelfahrt des Elias	1
Meerwurf des Jonas	13[48]
Ausspeiung des Jonas	9
Ruhe des Jonas	26[49]
Tobias und der Fisch	1
Drei Jünglinge im Feuerofen	3

[32] WS Taf. 220,1 r.: Heilung des Gichtbrüchigen I (Version Mc. 2,3 u. Par.); Brotwunder; Heilung des Gichtbrüchigen II (Version Mc. 2,12 u. Par.). — Zur Datierung GERKE 207/33.

[33] WS Taf. 220,1 l.: Heilung der Gekrümmten; Bergpredigt; Heilung des Blinden; Heilung des Lahmen. — Zur Datierung GERKE 207/33.

[34] WS Taf. 300,3: Ruhe des Jonas (mit Schiff und Ketos). — Zur Datierung GERKE 151/55.

[35] WS Taf. 164,1: Ruhe des Jonas (mit Schiff und Ketos) .— Zur Datierung GERKE 151/55.

[36] WS Taf. 176,2 (unsere Taf. 12 b): Jünglinge im Feuerofen; Meerwurf des Jonas. — Zur Datierung GERKE 176f.

[37] WS Taf. 163,1: Ruhe des Jonas. — Zur Datierung GERKE 126f.

[38] WS Taf. 8,2: Taufe Jesu. — Zur Datierung GERKE 142/46.

[39] WS Taf. 53,2: Ruhe des Jonas (mit Schiff und Ketos). — Zur Datierung GERKE 151/55.

[40] WS Taf. 185,1 (unsere Taf. 12 a): Belebung Evas; Adam und Eva. — Zur Datierung GERKE 190/201.

[41] WS Taf. 162,2: Meerwurf des Jonas. — Zur Datierung GERKE 175/78.

[42] WS Taf. 165,6: Ruhe des Jonas (mit Schiff und Ketos). — Zur Datierung GERKE 151/55.

[43] WS Taf. 84,4: Meerwurf des Jonas; Ruhe des Jonas. — Zur Datierung VON SCHOENEBECK: RM 245; BOVINI 146f.

[44] WS Taf. 163,3: Ruhe des Jonas (mit Schiff und Ketos). — Zur Datierung GERKE 151/55.

[45] WS Taf. 167,5: Ruhe des Jonas (mit Schiff und Ketos). — Zur Datierung GERKE 152/55.

[46] WS Taf. 3,4 (unsere Taf. 12 c): Auferweckung des Lazarus. — Zur Datierung VON SCHOENEBECK: RM 241; GERKE 284/95; BOVINI 141/43.284f.

[47] Es ist daran zu erinnern, daß dieses Motiv zwischen 232 und etwa 250 in gleicher Fassung auch im Kultraum von Dura an die Wand gemalt worden ist.

[48] Man beachte oben Anm. 18. Auf dem neuen Sarkophag des Britischen Museums ist nicht der Meerwurf selbst, sondern der Moment unmittelbar davor dargestellt: das Ketos schaut zu seinem Opfer, das noch an Bord des Schiffes steht, hinauf.

[49] Mehrfach sind Schiff und Ketos dem ruhenden Jonas sozusagen attributartig beigegeben. In diesen Fällen ist die Darstellung nur als Ruhe des Jonas gezählt worden. — Da das Bild sich vom Ruhelager erhebenden Jonas vielleicht nur eine Variante der Darstellung des ruhenden Jonas sein will und nicht Anspielung auf den Jon. 4,8f erwähnten Unmut des Jonas über das Verdorren der Staude, sind die beiden Motive hier nicht getrennt gezählt worden.

Daniel in der Löwengrube	6
Die Richter Susannas	1
Anklage gegen Susanna	1
Dankgebet der Eltern Susannas	1

Neues Testament

Huldigung der Magier	1
Taufe Jesu	6 (5?)
Bergpredigt Jesu	1
Gichtbrüchiger auf dem Bett getragen	1
Gichtbrüchiger, mit dem Bett davongehend	3[50]
Heilung des Besessenen	1
Brotwunder	1
Heilung des Lahmen	1
Heilung des Blinden	1
Heilung der Gekrümmten	1
Gespräch mit der Samaritanerin	1[51]
Auferweckung des Lazarus	6

Die Denkmäler der vorkonstantinischen christlichen Sepulkralkunst zeigen demnach, wie unsere Listen ausweisen, insgesamt 28 biblische Motive. In diesen 28 biblischen Motiven müssen wir den Grundstock der christlichen Grabkunst, sozusagen ihr Anfangskapital ganz oder teilweise erfaßt haben. Das NT ist mit nur 24 Zeugen vertreten, unter denen an Häufigkeit die Taufe Jesu, das Davongehen des sein Bett tragenden Gichtbrüchigen und die Auferweckung des Lazarus durch stärkere Bezeugung auffallen[52]. Das AT hat mehr als dreimal soviel Zeugen geliefert wie das NT. Aber dabei sind auffallende Unterschiede festzustellen. Nur neun Themen aus dem AT begegnen dreimal und häufiger, nämlich das Stammelternpaar, die Arche Noes, das Opfer Abrahams, das Quellwunder des Moses, der Meerwurf, die Ausspeiung und die Ruhe des Jonas, die drei Jünglinge im Feuerofen und Daniel in der Löwengrube. Aber in dieser Reihe bevorzugter Motive gibt es wiederum drei, die an Häufigkeit alles andere weit hinter sich lassen: die drei Etappen der Jonasgeschichte. Die Ruhe des Jonas steht ihrerseits mit ihren 26 Bezeugungen an der Spitze.

Unsere Annahme, daß mit den ermittelten biblischen Themen das Grundkapital der christlichen Grabkunst vollständig oder doch zu einem erheblichen Teil erfaßt sei, wird durch die Beobachtung bestätigt, daß die gleichen Themen auch in der nachkonstantinischen Zeit in der sepulkralen Malerei und Plastik nicht nur weiter verwendet werden, sondern auch hier noch eine dominierende Stellung einnehmen. Diese Beobachtung ergibt sich aus einem Vergleich der soeben vorgelegten Liste der biblischen Motive mit der schon einleitend herangezogenen Motivstatistik STYGERS vom Jahre 1927. Der Vergleich führt im einzelnen zu den folgenden Feststellungen.

[50] Dieses Bild wurde zwischen 232 und etwa 250 in gleicher Fassung im christlichen Kultraum in Dura auf die Wand gemalt.
[51] Eine wenig abweichende Darstellung dieses Themas auch im Kultraum von Dura.
[52] C. H. KRAELING, The Synagogue = Exca-vations at Dura Europos, Final Report 8, 1 (1956) 399 irrt also, wenn er meint, daß in der ältesten Katakombenkunst außer der symbolischen Darstellung des »Guten Hirten« keine historische Szene aus dem NT begegne und daß alle übrigen Dekorationsmotive aus dem AT stammten.

Von den Bildern aus dem AT behaupten auch nach Konstantin einen Vorrang die folgenden: das Stammelternpaar, die Arche Noes, das Opfer Abrahams, das Quellwunder des Moses, die Jonasgruppe, die Feuerofenszene, die Aussetzung Daniels in der Löwengrube. Diese Bilder sind erheblich stärker vertreten, als die beliebten neuen Motive wie die Darstellung des Dulders Job, des seine Sandalen lösenden Moses, des Durchgangs des Volkes Israel durch das Rote Meer und der Übergabe des Gesetzes an Moses.

Bei den neutestamentlichen Bildern scheint die Situation auf den ersten Blick nicht ganz so eindeutig zu sein; denn zwar sind die in vorkonstantinischer Zeit häufiger begegnenden Darstellungen des sein Bett davontragenden Gichtbrüchigen und der Auferweckung des Lazarus auch in der Folgezeit sehr beliebt; aber die dritte bevorzugte Szene unter den Bildern der vorkonstantinischen Zeit, die Taufe Jesu, ist nur noch selten anzutreffen. Dafür werden aber andere, in der vorkonstantinischen Zeit nur vereinzelt bezeugte Darstellungen in der Folgezeit, die ja überhaupt dem NT stärkeres Interesse schenkt, noch gerne verwendet: die Huldigung der Magier, das Brotwunder und die Blindenheilung. Vergleicht man aber schließlich innerhalb der nachkonstantinischen Periode der Sepulkralkunst die Häufigkeit des Auftretens der schon in der vorangegangenen Zeit begegnenden neutestamentlichen Themen mit der Häufigkeit der Bezeugung der vielen neuen Motive, so kommt man zu einem eindeutigen Ergebnis: die alten Bildthemen dominieren; nur das Bild der Taufe Jesu ist aus irgendeinem Grunde in den Hintergrund getreten.

Es ist nützlich, zum Abschluß dieser Überlegungen zwei Feststellungen zu machen. Erstens handelt es sich bei den biblischen Bildern der vorkonstantinischen Grabkunst nicht etwa um Motive, die sämtlich aus demselben einzelnen biblischen Buch entnommen wären. Es handelt sich auch nicht um eine Folge von offensichtlich zusammenhängenden Themen. Es handelt sich vielmehr um isolierte, in sich geschlossene Bildeinheiten[53], deren textlicher Hintergrund in den verschiedensten Büchern des Alten und Neuen Testament zu finden ist. Diese auffallende Zusammenhanglosigkeit eignet sogar denjenigen Bildern, die auf einer einzelnen Grabkammerwand oder auf einem und demselben Sarkophag nebeneinander aufgereiht sind. Alles in allem: es steht nicht ein Bildersystem vor uns, sondern, wie C. KRAELING sich einmal ausgedrückt hat, ein »Florilegium«[54].

Zweitens ist folgende, ebenso wichtige Feststellung zu treffen: Sämtliche Bilder der vorkonstantinischen Sepulkralkunst — wie denn auch die späteren — sind äußerst arm an Figuren. Nebenfiguren und detaillierte Hinweise auf den Raum, in dem sich der gemeinte biblische Vorgang abspielt, fehlen so gut wie ganz, es sei denn, solche Details wären für die Kennzeichnung der Szene selbst unentbehrlich[55]. Die Komposition der Bilder ist also in einem kaum noch überbietbaren Ausmaß konzentriert[56]. Man fühlt

---

[53] Eine Ausnahme scheint die Gruppe der drei Jonasbilder darzustellen; sie scheinen eine Ereignisfolge wiederzugeben. Es sei aber daran erinnert, daß diese drei Bilder ursprünglich, nämlich in den Malereien der Callistus-Katakombe, als selbständige Einheiten auftreten. Vgl. zur Entwicklungsgeschichte der Jonasbilder die scharfsinnigen Untersuchungen von A. STUIBER, Refrigerium interim (1957) 136/51.

[54] C. H. KRAELING aO. 400.

[55] Man denke an die Jonasbilder.

[56] Diese Eigenart, welche den Bildtypus der ältesten christlichen Sepulkralkunst scharf abhebt von dem ausführlichen Bildtypus des größeren Teils der Buchillustrationen und der gesamten Mosaikkunst, ist von der Forschung schon länger erkannt worden. Es sei verwiesen auf K. WEITZMANN, Die Illustration der Septuaginta: Münchener Jb. der bildenden Kunst 3,3/4 (1952/53) 96/120 und C. H. KRAELING aO. 401. Beide Gelehrte unter-

sich geradezu an die sogenannten Embleme der neueren Jahrhunderte erinnert, zu
denen freilich auch eine Inschrift gehört, die in unserem Falle fehlt[57]. Bei den Bildzei-
chen der Heraldik, an die man auch denken könnte, ist die Abstraktion freilich noch
weiter getrieben. Mit den Bildern der Emblematik und der Heraldik haben die frühchristlichen Sepulkralbilder aber außerdem gemein, daß sie sich in einen begrenzten
Raum einzufügen scheinen, dessen Andeutung freilich im Fall der Sepulkralkunst fehlt.

Über die letztgenannte Eigentümlichkeit der ältesten Bilder der christlichen Sepulkralkunst wird gleich noch mehr zu sagen sein. Aber schon jetzt sei aus dem oben fest-
gestellten doppelten Befund, dem der Isoliertheit und dem der knappen Fassung, ein
vorläufiger Schluß gezogen: Die Bilder dieser Grabkunst wollen nicht von einem biblischen Vorgang anschaulich berichten, sie wollen nicht unterhalten. Sie müssen vielmehr
als Erinnerungszeichen gedacht sein. Der Betrachter soll nicht bei den Bildern selbst
stehen bleiben. Er soll auf irgendeine Wahrheit oder irgendeine ethische Forderung, die
in dem im Bilde wiedergegebenen biblischen Vorgang mehr oder weniger deutlich enthalten ist, hingewiesen werden. Das aber heißt, daß die Bilder symbolisch gemeint
sind[58].

13. Die frühesten biblischen Kompositionen der christlichen Grabkunst. Neu-schöpfungen oder Entlehnungen?

Den biblischen Bildern der vorkonstantinischen Sepulkralkunst ist, wie soeben schon
bemerkt wurde, eigentümlich, daß ihre Komposition äußerst knapp gehalten ist. Der
gemeinte biblische Vorgang ist nur durch wenige Elemente angedeutet. Die Reduktion
des Bildes ist soweit getrieben, daß nur der Kenner der Bibel erraten kann, auf welche
Texte eigentlich hingewiesen werden soll. Aber wenn er auch das Motiv zu identifizieren
weiß, weiß er damit noch keineswegs, warum das betreffende Bild auf die Wand der
Grabkammer oder auf den Sarkophag gesetzt ist. Das weiß nur der, der den über sich
selbst hinausweisenden Sinn des Bildes, seine symbolische Bedeutung kennt.

Das Gesagte sei im einzelnen an den mehrfach bezeugten, also wohl beliebtesten
Motiven der vorkonstantinischen Grabkunst noch etwas näher verdeutlicht. Zunächst
an den Darstellungen aus dem AT: Ein Baum, um den sich eine Schlange windet und
neben dem ein Mann und eine Frau, beide nackt, stehen, bedeutet das Paradies oder
den Sündenfall (Taf. 11b. 12a). Ein mehr hoher, als breiter rechteckiger Kasten mit aufgeklapptem Deckel, aus dem ein Mann mit ausgebreiteten Armen, einer Taube mit Ölzweig entgegenblickend, herausschaut, weist auf das Sintflutereignis oder vielmehr auf
sein glückliches Ende hin (Taf. 11a). Die Darstellung des Isaakopfers zeigt als Haupt-
figur Abraham und neben ihm, kleiner wiedergegeben, Isaak, den Altar und den Widder,
während eine aus den Wolken herunterlangende Hand das Eingreifen Gottes oder
Gottes Stimme versinnbildet (vgl. Taf. 8a). Das Quellwunder wird durch zwei parallele

---

scheiden zwischen einer »symbolischen« und einer
»narrativen« Ausdrucksform in der altchristlichen
Kunst. Über die Differenzierungen innerhalb
dieser ausführlicheren, »narrativen« Bildform
handelt K. WEITZMANN, Narration in early
Christendom: Narration in ancient Art, a symposium. 57th General meeting of the Archaeological Institute of America: AmJournArcheol 61
(1957) 83/91.

[57] Über das Emblem vgl. die instruktiven Dar-
legungen von W. S. HECKSCHER und K. A. WIRTH:
RLDK 5,85/228.
[58] Vgl. H. L. HEMPEL, Zum Problem der Anfänge
der AT-Illustration: ZAW 69 (1957) 108, nach
dem die Knappheit der künstlerischen Formulierung die Zeichenhaftigkeit der Bilder unter-
streicht.

Körper dargestellt: den Felsen und den mit dem Stab auf den Felsen schlagenden Moses (Taf. 7a. 9a. 10b). Ein Segelschiff mit Bemannung, vor dem sich im Wasser ein Meerdrache tummelt, deutet den Sturm an, der mit dem Meerwurf des Jonas endet; der Meerwurf selbst wird auf jüngeren Darstellungen auch selbst wiedergegeben (Taf. 7b. 8c). Die Befreiung des Jonas aus dem Bauche des Meerdrachens wird dadurch angedeutet, daß das Ketos den Propheten aus seinem Rachen ausspeit (Taf. 7c). Ein unter einer Kürbis- oder Efeulaube ruhender nackter Mann weist, reichlich wenig biblisch, auf ein Ruhen des Jonas hin (Taf. 6a. 8c. 12b)[59]. Ein rechteckiger breiter Kasten, in dem drei Jünglinge mit ausgebreiteten Armen inmitten von lodernden Flammen stehen, soll an die Befreiung der drei jüdischen Jünglinge aus Todesnot erinnern (Taf. 10b). Ein zwischen zwei Löwen stehender betender Mann deutet die Errettung des den Tieren ausgesetzten Propheten Daniel an (Abb. 5b, Taf. 11b).

Die vorkonstantinischen Sepulkralbilder aus dem Neuen Testament sind ebenso knapp organisiert; wir begnügen uns damit, die beliebtesten kurz auf ihre Komposition zu prüfen: Eine auf einem Thronsessel sitzende Mutter, die ihr Kind auf dem Schoß hält und der sich, hintereinander aufgereiht, drei Männer im persischen Kostüm und in geneigter Haltung nähern, erinnert an die Anbetung des Kindes durch die Weisen aus dem Osten (Taf. 10a). Die Darstellung der Taufe Jesu beschränkt sich auf zwei parallel angeordnete menschliche Gestalten von verschiedener Größe und verschieden hohem Standort; die größere, mehr oder weniger bekleidete, die eine Hand ausstreckt, soll auf Johannes, die kleinere, nackte auf Jesus hinweisen (Taf. 7b. 8b). Verblüffend stark vereinfacht ist die Darstellung der Heilung des Gichtbrüchigen: man sieht einen davongehenden Mann, der auf den Schultern eine Bettstelle trägt (Taf. 8b. 11b). Eine Aedicula, vor der, mumienhaft verhüllt, eine männliche Figur steht, und eine andere männliche Gestalt, die einen Stab zur Aedicula hin ausgestreckt hält, weisen auf die Auferweckung des Lazarus hin (Taf. 7a. 9b. 11ab).

Aus diesen Hinweisen ergibt sich, daß in allen Fällen die gleiche Technik zum gleichen Ergebnis geführt hat: Der biblische Vorgang wird auf die äußerste Mindestzahl von Elementen zurückgeführt. Diese Elemente werden, wenn das möglich ist, in einer einzigen Achse angeordnet. Dies trifft zu auf die Darstellung Noes und des Gichtbrüchigen, wo die Bildachse senkrecht verläuft (Taf. 8b. 11a), und auf die Szene der Ausspeiung und der Ruhe des Jonas, wo eine waagerechte Bildachse vorliegt (Taf. 8c). Manchmal sind die Bildelemente in zwei parallele Achsen eingeordnet, senkrecht im Fall des Quellwunders (zB. Taf. 9a), der Taufe Jesu (zB. Taf. 8b) und des Lazaruswunders (zB. Taf. 9b), waagerecht auf jenem reiferen Jonasbild, das den Meerwurf selbst vergegenwärtigt (Taf. 8c). In einigen Fällen sind auch drei senkrechte Achsen gebildet, so beim Sündenfall (Taf. 12a), beim Feuerofenbild (Taf. 10b) und bei der Darstellung des in der Löwengrube betenden Daniel (Abb. 5b); hierher muß wohl auch die Darstellung des Abrahamsopfers gerechnet werden (Taf. 8a). Nur bei der Wiedergabe der Huldigung der Magier ist es zu einer vierachsigen Komposition gekommen (Taf. 10a); doch sind die Bildelemente in diesem Fall so straff zusammengefaßt, daß sie sich in ein niedriges Rechteck oder in ein flaches Oval einzufügen scheinen.

Angesichts dieses Befundes erhebt sich die Frage: Wie ist es zu erklären, daß für den Bildschmuck der christlichen Grabkammern und Sarkophage in vorkonstantinischer

---

[59] Vgl. hierzu A. STUIBER aO. 138.

Zeit ausnahmslos so extrem reduzierte biblische Kompositionen gewählt worden sind? Es ist doch höchst auffallend, daß die gleichzeitige heidnische Plastik auf der Front ihrer Sarkophage in der Regel nur ein einziges mythologisches Thema figurenreich entwikkelt[60], während die christliche Plastik eine Mehrzahl knapp formulierter biblischer Motive äußerlich aneinanderreiht[61] oder ein oder mehrere dieser so komprimierten biblischen Themen mehr oder weniger gewaltsam in eine aus der profanen Kunst übernommene bukolische oder maritime Szenerie hinein setzt[62]. Die Knappheit der biblischen Kompositionen in der Katakombenmalerei, so wird man vielleicht sagen, ist durch den Stil der Zimmermalerei des 3. Jh. diktiert, der inmitten der von schmalen roten und grünen Linien eingerahmten Wandfelder nur kleine und gewichtlose Bilder zu dulden scheint[63]. Aber diese Erklärung befriedigt nicht; denn die nichtchristliche Zimmermalerei kennt neben jenen zierlichen und figurenarmen Bildern auch vielfigurige größere Kompositionen[64]. Und in der Tat schaffen ja die christlichen Katakombenmaler, wenn sie es nicht mit biblischen Themen zu tun haben, auch figurenreiche Darstellungen wie zB. die des Totenmahls[65]. Der Schluß ist also unausweichlich: das Auftreten so stark vereinfachter biblischer Bilder in den Grabkammern und auf den Sarkophagen der vorkonstantinischen Zeit läßt sich mit dem, was man in der nichtchristlichen Malerei und Plastik der Zeit beobachtet, nicht in Einklang bringen. Die Erklärung für die Eigenart der christlichen Bildproduktion kann also nur in der Entwicklungsgeschichte der christlichen Kunst selbst gesucht werden.

Wäre nun aber die Entscheidung zugunsten der verkürzten Fassung biblischer Themen und die Schaffung eines Grundstockes ein für allemal festgeprägter Kompositionen erst in der christlichen Sepulkralkunst selbst erfolgt, so müßten wir die Spuren des Ringens um diese Entscheidung und um die Gewinnung eines Kanons überlieferter Bildformen in den Grabkammern und auf den Sarkophagen noch antreffen. Aber das ist nicht der Fall. Wohl hat einmal ein provinzieller Steinmetz für die Darstellung der Arche Noes eine eigenwillig abweichende Form gefunden[66], ebenso der Maler, der in der Callistus-Katakombe das Opfer Abrahams darzustellen hatte[67]; aber von solchen Ausnahmen abgesehen, treten die in der Zeit vor Konstantin bevorzugten biblischen Motive — wir können ja nur die mehrfach vorkommenden vergleichen — schon immer in der gleichen Gestalt auf, die sie dann auch im nachkonstantinischen Zeitalter behalten haben. Wir müssen also schließen, daß die Sepulkralkunst diese Kompositionen nicht selbst entwickelt hat. Sie waren ihr bereits vorgegeben. Aber woher stammen sie dann?

Ein wichtiger Anhaltspunkt für die Lösung dieses Problems scheint uns in der Bildform der biblischen Kompositionen zu liegen. Diese Form weist darauf hin, daß die Bil-

---

[60] Eine Übersicht über die heidnische Sarkophage findet man etwa bei F. CUMONT, Recherches sur le symbolisme funéraire des Romains (1942). Für die Frage der Auslegung dieser Sarkophage ist A. D. NOCK, Sarcophagi and symbolism: AmJournArch 50 (1946) 140/70 mit heranzuziehen.

[61] So auf den Sarkophagen Lateran 119 und Velletri (s. o. Anm. 16 und 22).

[62] Das ist der Fall auf den Sarkophagen Kaiser Friedrich-Museum, S. Maria antica, Ny Carlsberg und Britisches Museum (s. o. Anm. 14. 15. 17. 18).

[63] Vgl. hierzu die bei F. WIRTH, Römische Wandmalerei (1934) 104/228 behandelten Denkmäler.

[64] Vgl. F. WIRTH aO. 148 Abb. 76; 149 Abb. 77; 173 Abb. 188; ferner Taf. 48/51.

[65] Vgl. WM Taf. 15.41. Daß es sich bei den christlichen Mahlbildern in Grabkammern und auf Sarkophagen nicht um Jenseitsmahle oder um die Darstellung der Eucharistie oder gar um die wunderbare Speisung des Volkes durch Jesus handelt, braucht heute wohl nicht mehr bewiesen zu werden. Über diese Frage zuletzt A. STUIBER, Refrigerium interim (1957) 146,1.

[66] Vgl. o. Anm. 21.

[67] Vgl. o. Anm. 10. Die Eigenwilligkeit liegt hier nur in der frontalen Reihung der traditionellen Elemente.

der dieser Gruppe von Haus aus für einen ganz anderen Bildträger geschaffen waren, nämlich für einen Bildträger von geringerem Format und kreisrunder oder ovaler Gestalt. Man könnte an die Glasbecher mit dekoriertem Goldboden denken, die man sich im Altertum zu Neujahr, zum Geburtstag oder bei anderen Anlässen schenkte, die also ein Massenprodukt gewesen sein müssen. Aber es ist kaum anzunehmen, daß solche Geschenkbecher schon im 3. Jh. christianisiert, d. h. mit biblischem Dekor anstelle des profanen oder mythologischen versehen worden sind [68]; unsere bisherigen Beobachtungen zur Entstehungsgeschichte der frühchristlichen Kunst sprechen ja nicht dafür, daß gerade diese Glasbecher an der Wiege der christlichen Kunst gestanden haben [69]. Aber es gibt einen uns bereits bekannt gewordenen anderen Bildträger noch erheblich kleineren Formats, mit dem sich die Christen nach unseren Feststellungen schon erheblich früher befaßt haben: die Ringgemmen. Sie scheinen uns in der Tat die ursprüngliche Heimat der frühen biblischen Kompositionen der altchristlichen Sepulkralkunst gewesen zu sein.

Wir haben schon früher gesehen, daß in einer Zeit, als die christliche Kunst noch nicht existierte, nämlich im Zeitalter des Clemens von Alexandrien, auch die Strengen unter den Anhängern des christlichen Glaubens auf Siegelringe nicht verzichten konnten und mochten und daß sogar führende Männer der Kirche, wie eben Clemens, bei aller Abneigung gegen das Bild und vor allem gegen das Gottes- und Menschenbild, sich mit dem Bildschmuck auf den Siegelsteinen abfanden und nur forderten, man möge beim Einkauf eines Ringes neutrale, nicht verfängliche, mit der christlichen Ethik verträgliche Embleme wählen [70]. Es müßte merkwürdig zugegangen sein, wenn nicht dieser oder jener Christ auf den Gedanken gekommen wäre, statt nach einem neutralen, nach einem christlichen Siegelbild Ausschau zu halten. Das konnte natürlich, entsprechend dem runden oder ovalen Kleinformat der Gemmen und der Tradition der Glyptik, nur eine Darstellung sein, die in knappster Fassung irgendein Motiv aus der christlichen Glaubenswelt oder der christlichen Ethik weniger illustrativ als symbolhaft vergegenwärtigte. Wir kommen also im logischen Ablauf unserer Überlegungen unausweichlich zu der Hypothese, daß durch die Diskussion über das unentbehrliche Siegelbild die Verchristlichung dieses Siegelbildes eingeleitet und damit die christliche Kunst ausgelöst worden ist. Die Eigenart dieses Bildträgers würde also auch die Erklärung für die Besonderheiten des ältesten Repertoires der christlichen Kunst darstellen.

Setzt man einen solchen Ausgangspunkt für die christliche Kunst an, so hätte man zugleich eine Lösung für die Rätselfrage gefunden, wie es möglich war, daß sich die ältesten Kompositionen so rasch und gleichmäßig in Ost und West verbreitet haben [71].

---

[68] H. Vopel, Die altchristlichen Goldgläser (1899) 32/77 breitet das Material in chronologisch-sachlicher Ordnung aus. Die Verchristlichung der Becherdekoration scheint mit dem Zusatz »in Deo« oder »in Christo« zum Trinkspruch »Vivas« zu beginnen und dann erst zu christlichen und biblischen Motiven überzugehen. Vopel datiert die Blütezeit der christlichen Goldglasbilder erst in die zweite Hälfte des 4. Jh.; für die frühere Zeit kann er nur sporadisches Auftreten solcher Bilder feststellen (S. 59). Es ist wohl überflüssig, eigens anzumerken, daß die Datierung der Goldglasbilder sehr vorläufig ist. Abbildungen profaner oder heidnisch-mythologischer Bilder auf Goldglasböden bei A. Kisa, Das Glas im Altertum 3 (1908) 866. 867. 869. 871/3. 875; Abbildungen christlicher Goldglasbilder, welche die Übereinstimmung mit den Bildfolgen der sepulkralen Kunst deutlich machen ebd. 881/3. 887. 891; vgl. auch die Medaillons der Kölner Schale ebd. 893.

[69] Vgl. JbAC 1 (1958) 24/27.

[70] Vgl. JbAC 1 (1958) 21/23.

[71] Man denke vor allem daran, daß die Darstellungen der Stammeltern, des mit seinem Bett davongehenden Gichtbrüchigen und der Samariterin am Brunnen fast zur gleichen Zeit in den römischen Katakomben und im christlichen Kultraum zu Dura auftreten. Zu den Bildern in Dura vgl. O. Eissfeldt, Dura: RAC 4,365f.

Christliche Kaufleute, die Siegelringe mit solchen christlichen Bildern trugen, kamen von Land zu Land. Ihre Ringe mußten die Aufmerksamkeit der Glaubensgenossen erregen. In solchen Fällen war das Muster rasch kopiert.

Auf den Schatz der ältesten christlichen Gemmenbilder müßten dann diejenigen zurückgegriffen haben, die sich nach einem passenden Bildschmuck für ihre Grabkammern und Sarkophage umsahen. Sie konnten aus den Gemmenbildern diejenigen auswählen, die dem sepulkralen Milieu, also den christlichen Jenseitsvorstellungen und Totengebeten gemäß zu sein schienen[72]. Die in der sepulkralen Kunst des 3. Jh. auftretenden Bilder brauchen also nicht notwendig den ganzen Bildvorrat der christlichen Glyptik erschöpft zu haben; dieser könnte erheblich größer gewesen sein. Umgekehrt kann natürlich auch die Möglichkeit nicht ausgeschlossen werden, dass einzelne unter den in der Sepulkralkunst auftretenden Motiven — vor allem wird man dabei an die nur einmal bezeugten und auch später nicht mehr vorkommenden denken — wirklich Erfindungen des Auftraggebers oder des ausführenden Künstlers gewesen sind und nicht aus der Glyptik übernommen wurden.

Zur Bestätigung unserer Hypothese darf daran erinnert werden, daß wenigstens ein paar christliche Gemmen erhalten sind, die biblische Motive in der gleichen oder annähernd gleichen Fassung zeigen, wie sie in der vorkonstantinischen Grabkunst begegnen. Das Stammelternpaar mit Paradiesesbaum ist genau wie auf den Wänden der christlichen Grabkammern und auf den Sarkophagen, also in einer dreiachsigen Komposition, auf einem Nicolo des Britischen Museums dargestellt (Abb. 6a)[73]. Der betende Daniel zwischen den Löwen erscheint in der gleichen dreiachsigen Komposition wie in der Grabkunst auf mehreren Gemmen, nämlich auf einem Sardonyx des Wiener Kunsthistorischen Museums (Abb. 6c)[74], auf einem Nicolo aus Canossa (Abb. 6d)[75] und auf einem Jaspis des Museo Trivulzio in Mailand (Abb. 6e)[76]. Der Meerwurf des Jonas endlich begegnet auf einem Sardonyx des Bostoner Museums of Fine Arts, freilich mit Zutaten, die unseren Sepulkraldarstellungen fremd sind: rechts steht der offenbar inzwischen gerettete Jonas, wohl damit beschäftigt, für seine Rettung zu danken, links ruht er unter einem Baum von den Strapazen aus (Abb. 6b)[77].

Die Gemmensammlungen sind bekanntlich bisher viel zu wenig aufgearbeitet und veröffentlicht. Daher erscheint es durchaus möglich, daß in Zukunft noch weitere Stücke nachgewiesen werden, die als Belege für den von uns angenommenen Zusammenhang herangezogen werden können. Leider lassen sich die oben aufgeführten Denkmäler kaum datieren; nur bei dem Jaspis aus der Sammlung Trivulzio ist es wahrscheinlich, daß er erst im 4. Jh. bearbeitet worden ist, weil er auf der Rückseite das sogenannte konstantinische Christusmonogramm trägt. Aber wie es es auch um das Alter der aufgeführten Gemmen bestellt sein mag, sie vermögen zum mindesten anschaulich zu machen,

---

[72] Hierzu vgl. die wegweisenden Ausführungen von A. STUIBER, Refrigerium interim (1957) 167/175.

[73] DALTON, Catalogue Pl. 1 nr. 42; DACL 6, 1, 840 Fig. 5060.

[74] GARRUCCI, Storia 6 Tav. 478 nr. 24; DACL 6, 1, 842 Fig. 5067.

[75] GARRUCCI, Storia 6 Tav. 492 nr. 15; DACL 6, 1, 842 Fig. 5069. Die Umschrift ist nach E. PETERSON, H. TH. 83 zu lesen: εἷς θεὸς βοή(θ)ι.

[76] GARRUCCI, Storia 6, Tav. 478, Fig. 26; DACL 6, 1, 842 Fig. 5068.

[77] C. BONNER, Studies in magical amulets (1950) 312 u. Pl. 19 nr. 347; DACL 6, 1, 842 Fig. 5070 (seitenverkehrt?). — Eine andere Darstellung des Meerwurfs, mit der sich C. BONNER aO. 227f und 311 nr. 346 eingehend beschäftigt, soll hier beiseitebleiben, erstens, weil es sich nur um die Nachahmung einer Gemme in geringwertigem Material und zweitens um ein sehr spätes Machwerk, etwa des 5. Jh., handelt.

Abb. 6. Christliche Gemmen.
a. London, Brit. Mus., Nicolo. Adam und Eva. b. Boston, Sardonyx. Jonas. c. Wien, Kunsthist. Mus., Sardonyx. Daniel. d. Nicolo aus Canossa. Daniel. e. Mailand, Sammlung Trivulzio, Jaspis. Daniel.

wie überzeugend sich die Kurzfassungen der biblischen Motive der frühchristlichen Sepulkralkunst im Oval oder Rund dieser Gemmen ausnehmen. Die Gemmen, so meinen wir also aus allen unseren Beobachtungen schließen zu müssen, müssen der Ursprungsort dieser Kompositionen gewesen sein.

Haben die christlichen Gemmenschneider des beginnenden 3. Jh. die Kurzfassung der biblischen Motive des Alten und Neuen Bundes selbst erdacht? Sicher die neutestamentlichen. Wie weit sich die christlichen Erfinder dieser neutestamentlichen Kompositionen an verbreitete Motive der nichtchristlichen Glyptik angelehnt haben, ist eine Frage für sich, der hier und jetzt nicht nachgegangen werden kann. Um die Gestaltung der alttestamentlichen Motive aber brauchten sich die christlichen Gemmenschneider nicht erst selbst zu bemühen. Wie die Christen waren auch die Juden von Haus aus bildfeindlich; aber wie die Christen und schon vor ihnen — so wird man sich sagen müssen — werden auch sie früher oder später die mit den antiken Lebensverhältnissen verknüpfte Notwendigkeit empfunden haben, sich nach Siegelringen und Siegelbildern umzusehen. Und wenigstens in der jüdischen Diaspora wird man sich dieser Notwendigkeit nicht lange ängstlich verschlossen haben[78]. Dieselben Erwägungen, die Clemens von Alexandrien dazu geführt haben, seinen Glaubensgenossen die Benutzung von Siegelringen zu gestatten[79], werden die Rabbinen genötigt haben, ihren Gläubigen das

---

[78] Zur Frage der liberalen Haltung des Diaspora-Judentums vgl. E. Schürer, Geschichte des jüdischen Volkes 3⁴ (1909) 135f. 420ff.; A. Baum-

stark, Bild: RAC 2,290/92.
[79] Vgl. JbAC 1 (1958) 21/23 und die ergänzenden Bemerkungen von L. Eizenhöfer: ebd.3 (1960) 68f.

gleiche Zugeständnis zu machen. Auch die Rabbinen werden zunächst wie Clemens neutrale Motive für die Siegelsteine empfohlen, dann aber auch mit biblischen Motiven sich abgefunden haben. Und auch in diesem Fall sahen Auftraggeber wie Steinschneider sich genötigt, die biblischen Motive, die sie für die Ringe zu verwenden dachten, äußerst zu vereinfachen, weil das geringe Format des Steines es so verlangte. So wird wohl bei den Juden der Diaspora ein Grundstock von biblischen Themen in Kurzform entstanden sein, noch ehe Christen an verchristlichte Siegelbilder dachten.

Aber auch hier brauchen wir nicht bei theoretischen Überlegungen stehenzubleiben. Es gibt einen, wenn auch vorerst nur schwachen Beweis dafür, daß bei den Juden solche biblischen Bilder bekannt und verbreitet waren, welche die charakteristische Vereinfachung des Gemmenbildes aufweisen. Der Beweis stützt sich auf einige Kleindenkmäler: eine kleinasiatische Münzprägung und eine Gemme.

Die Münzprägung, an die hier gedacht ist, ist im phrygischen Apameia zu Hause[80]. Wie die erhaltenen Exemplare durch ihre Kaiserporträts auf der Vorderseite verraten, wurde diese Prägung in der ganzen ersten Hälfte des 3. Jh. verwendet; ob auch schon vorher, wissen wir nicht (Abb. 7). Das Rückseitenbild zeigt das Ende der Sintflut,

Abb. 7. Münzen von Apameia in Phrygien, geprägt unter Septimius Severus und Philippus Arabs. Noe in der Arche.

und zwar auf allen Emissionen in unveränderter Fassung, nur mit jeweils anderer Umschrift, die außer dem Ortsnamen den jeweils verantwortlichen Beamten nennt. Im Bild sieht man wie in den Darstellungen der frühchristlichen Grabkunst die Arche als hohen Kasten mit aufgeklapptem Deckel dargestellt, auf den von links eine Taube mit Ölzweig zufliegt. Aus der Öffnung des Kastens schaut in diesem Fall freilich nicht Noe allein heraus, sondern mit ihm sein Weib; beide sehen der heranfliegenden Taube entgegen und beide halten ihre Arme abwärts. Auf dem Deckel rechts oben sitzt, ebenfalls abweichend von der christlichen Darstellung, der Rabe der biblischen Erzählung[81]. Links neben dem Kasten steht das Ehepaar noch einmal, auch diesmal nach links gewendet, aber nun betend. Anscheinend erheben die beiden nur den rechten Arm, wie es in der klassischen und hellenistischen Kunst häufig vorkommt[82]. Die Errettung aus der Sintflut und die Danksagung für diese Errettung, die in der christlichen Grabkunst, wohl nach dem Vorbild der christlichen Glyptik, in einem einzigen Bild zusammen-

[80] Vgl. zum folgenden F. W. Madden, On some coins of Septimius Severus, Macrinus and Philipp I, struck at Apameia in Phrygia, with the legend Noe: NumChron NS 6 (1866) 173/220; H. Leclercq, Apamée: DACL 1,2,2509/18 mit Literatur; E. Schürer, Geschichte des jüdischen Vol-

kes 3⁴ (1909) 18f; V. Schultze, Altchristliche Städte und Landschaften 2,1 (1922) 454/56.
[81] Vgl. Gen. 8,6.
[82] Vgl. C. Sittl, Die Gebärden der Griechen und Römer (1890) 188/90.

gefaßt war, findet sich also hier noch in zwei Etappen zerlegt. Nun wissen wir, daß die Stadt Apameia, vielleicht nach einem Vorort, den Beinamen Kibotos trug. Die Erläuterung dieses Beinamens muß der Bevölkerung durch die jüdischen Mitbürger geliefert worden sein. Diese haben darauf hinweisen können, daß Apameia deswegen den Beinamen Kibotos führe, weil hier die Arche Noes, die κιβωτός der Septuaginta, gelandet sei[83]; das Nähere, so werden sie gesagt haben, könne man in ihrem heiligen Buch nachlesen. Daß die jüdische Gemeinde in Apameia und Umgegend stark und vermögend war, ergibt sich aus der Tatsache, daß der von Cicero verteidigte Propraetor Flaccus bei der jüdischen Bevölkerung von Apameia und Umgegend fast 100 Pfund Gold beschlagnahmen lassen konnte, die als Abgabe an den Tempel in Jerusalem geliefert werden sollten[84]; das war schon im Jahre 61 vC. Außerdem erinnert eine jüdische Inschrift der Kaiserzeit diejenigen, welche vielleicht die Grabesruhe einer bei Apameia beigesetzten Frau zu stören im Sinne hatten, daran, daß das »Gesetz der Juden« derartige Akte unter strenge Strafe stelle; die Stadtbehörde von Apameia muß also wegen der Bedeutung der jüdischen Gemeinde Anlaß gehabt haben, das jüdische Gesetz ausdrücklich anzuerkennen[85]. Wie die Juden als erste die Landung der Arche ihrer Sintflutgeschichte in Apameia lokalisiert haben müssen, so werden sie auch eine bei ihnen entwickelte und geläufig gewordene Darstellung dieses Ereignisses in Umlauf gebracht und damit die Anbringung des Bildes auf der Münze veranlaßt haben. V. SCHULTZE hat vermutet, daß die Juden ein solches Bild in ihren illustrierten Pentateuch-Handschriften fanden[86]. Aber auf den Münzen finden wir eben nicht den erzählerischen Stil, welcher der Buchmalerei eignet; was wir auf den Münzen vor uns haben, ist die knappe, nur andeutende Sprache, wie sie den Kompositionen des symbolischen Stils eignet. Es ist also wahrscheinlicher, daß das Sintflutbild der Münzen von Apameia auf jüdische Siegelbilder zurückgeht. Von diesen aus wird das Bild in noch stärkerer Vereinfachung auf die christlichen Siegelringe und von da aus in die christliche Sepulkralkunst des 3. Jh. übergegangen sein.

Das zweite Beweisstück für die Abhängigkeit der christlichen Glyptik von der jüdischen ist ein ovaler Lignit aus der Sammlung Newell (Abb. 8)[87]. Er zeigt in der Mitte Abraham, der nach links zur Hand Gottes hinaufschaut. Rechts von ihm sieht man den Altar und Isaak, links den Widder und einen Baum. Die Darstellung entspricht also der uns aus der christlichen Grabkunst vertrauten dreiachsigen Kompo-

Abb. 8.
Sammlung Newell,
Lignit. Opfer Abrahams.

---

[83] Diese Lokalisierung ist nicht nur durch die Münze von Apameia bezeugt, sondern auch durch literarische Quellen, nämlich durch Iulius Africanus: Georg. Syncell. p. 38 Dindorf und Orac. Sibyll. 1,262/65.
[84] Cicero pro Flacco 28. Die römische Staatsverwaltung hatte gegen die Ausfuhr der Tempelsteuer nach Jerusalem wie in diesem Fall auch sonst hin und wieder Bedenken; vgl. E. SCHÜRER aO. 34 (1902) 13.
[85] Die Inschrift bei W. RAMSAY, The cities and bishoprics of Phrygia 1,2 (1897) 528.
[86] V. SCHULTZE aO. 455.
[87] C. BONNER, Studies in magical amulets (1950)

310 pl. 18 nr. 343; die gleiche Gemme Newell bei E. R. GOODENOUGH, Jewish symbols in the greco-roman period 3 (1953) nr. 1039. Dieselbe Gemme kehrt wieder bei C. H. KRAELING, The Synagogue = Excavations at Dura Europos, Final Report 8,1 (1956) Pl. 40,4. Da der Verfasser bemerkt, daß diese Gemme sich in der Sammlung Torray befinde und bisher unpubliziert sei, könnte es sich um ein zweites Exemplar handeln. Auffällig wäre dann freilich, daß beide Stücke, das Exemplar Newell und das Exemplar Torray, nachträglich, sicher um die Gemme als Amulett verwendungsfähig zu machen, durchlöchert worden sein müßten.

sition. Bei dem Lignit der Sammlung Newell läßt sich die jüdische Herkunft einwandfrei beweisen: auf der Rückseite steht ein mit hebräischen Lettern geschriebener, wenn auch noch nicht gedeuteter, vielleicht magischer Text[88]. Wenn die Inschrift tatsächlich magisch wäre, würde sie zeigen, daß von irgendeinem Zeitpunkt an die Darstellung dieses wichtigen Ereignisses der israelitischen Geschichte, das in der jüdischen Theologie und Kulttradition stets eine zentrale Stellung innehatte[89], nicht bloß an die heroische Glaubenstat eines vorbildlichen Israeliten erinnern sollte, sondern nach der Meinung vieler zugleich auch magische Kräfte ausstrahlen konnte; eine solche Gemme diente also zugleich auch als ein im Ring immer mitgeführtes Amulett.

Wenn C. BONNER einen runden Sardonyx des Pariser Cabinet des Médailles mit gleicher, wenn auch gröberer Darstellung, gleichfalls unter die jüdischen Denkmäler einreiht[90], tut er es wohl deswegen, weil er mit der Existenz christlicher Gemmen dieser Art nicht gerechnet hat. Nach allem, was hier ausgeführt wurde, muß aber ernstlich daran gedacht werden, daß das Pariser Stück, an dem kein Zeichen jüdischen Ursprungs festzustellen ist, christlicher Herkunft sein könnte.

Abb. 9.
Nicolo. Jason und Medea

Wenn mit dem Gesagten einigermaßen warscheinlich gemacht ist, daß Christen jüdische Gemmen mit alttestamentlichem Bildschmuck nachahmten oder gar kurzerhand solche Gemmen jüdischen Ursprungs für ihre Siegelringe erwarben, so darf doch nicht übersehen werden, daß es auch unter den heidnischen Gemmen solche gab, deren Bildschmuck jüdische wie christliche Gemmenschneider mit geringen Änderungen übernehmen konnten. So hat schon A. FURTWÄNGLER einen Nicolo veröffentlicht, der eine der christlichen — und wohl auch jüdischen — Darstellung der Stammeltern sehr nahestehende Komposition zeigt (Abb. 9): links und rechts neben einem Baum, um dessen Stamm sich eine Schlange windet, stehen Jason und Medea. Medea gibt der Schlange ein Zaubermittel zu trinken, während Jason sich das goldene Vlies vom Baum herunternimmt[91].

Das Ergebnis aller Erwägungen zusammenfassend wird man etwa folgendes sagen dürfen: Die merkwürdig verkürzten biblischen Darstellungen aus dem Alten und Neuen Testament, die in der christlichen Sepulkralkunst von Anfang an in stereotyper Form auftreten, können nicht erst für die christlichen Grabkammern und Sarkophage er-

---

[88] C. BONNER aO. 310f.

[89] Darüber einiges bei C. H. KRAELING aO. 58f und R. MEYER, Betrachtungen zu den Fresken der Synagoge von Dura Europos: ThLZ 74 (1949) 29/34. Vgl. auch J. DANIÉLOU, Sacramentum futuri (Paris 1950) 97/111; A. STUIBER aO. 178/82; J. VAN GOUDOEVER, Biblical calendars ² (1961) 68.156f.

[90] C. BONNER aO. 311 nr. 344.

[91] A. FURTWÄNGLER, Die antiken Gemmen. Geschichte der Steinschneidekunst im klassischen Altertum 1 (1900) Taf. 62 nr. 27; DACL 1,2,2701 Fig. 890. Ausführlichere Fassungen der Szene wie

zB. auf dem Campana-Relief ROHDEN 115 = REINACH, Rép. des Rel. 2,264 und auf dem Sarkophagfragment Ludovisi = REINACH aO. 3,280,3 geben die Möglichkeit, die Verdichtung der Szene in der Glyptik genauer zu studieren; vgl. auch den Sarkophag in Wien bei REINACH aO. 2,140,4. — Ein Becher im Vatikan zeigt, wie ein Monstrum von der Art des Ketos Jason ausspeit; s. REINACH, Rép. des Vases 3,102,1; ein solches Rundbild könnte jüdischen oder christlichen Gemmenschneidern als Vorlage für die Darstellung der Ausspeiung des Jonas gedient haben.

funden worden sein. Sie scheinen ausgewählt zu sein aus einem Schatz von biblischen Bildern, die in einer zu vermutenden Ringstein-Glyptik zu Anfang des 3. Jh. entwickelt worden waren. Es spricht manches dafür, daß diese christliche Glyptik ihre altchristlichen Motive ihrerseits ganz oder zum Teil von einer vorausgegangenen jüdischen Steinschneidekunst übernommen hat[92]. Diese dürfte ihrerseits wieder Anleihen bei der heidnischen Gemmenfabrikation gemacht haben, ähnlich wie es vermutlich auch die christliche Glyptik bei der Schaffung ihrer neutestamentlichen Bildtypen getan hat[93].

BONN   THEODOR KLAUSER

[92] Für eine Abhängigkeit der christlichen von der jüdischen Kunst haben sich in den letzten Jahren aufgrund ihrer Beobachtungen mehrere Gelehrte ausgesprochen. Es seien hier genannt: G. WODKE, Die Malereien der Synagoge in Dura u. ihre Parallelen in der christl. Kunst: ZNW 34 (1935) 51/62. K. WEITZMANN, Die Illustration der Septuaginta: Münchner Jb. d. bildenden Kunst 3, 3/4 (1952/53) 119/20. R. DELBRUECK, Probleme der Lipsanothek in Brescia (1952) 89/95; hierzu zustimmend und weiterführend J. KOLLWITZ: ByzZ 49 (1956) 145f. Vgl. ferner J. GUTMANN, The jewish origin of the Ashburnham Pentateuch miniatures: Jewish Quart. Rev. 44 (1953/54) 55/72; vgl. hierzu A. BAUMSTARK, Bild (jüdisch): RAC 2,299. E. R. GOODENOUGH, Jewish symbols in the greco-roman world = Bollingen Series 37,1 (1953) 3. C. H. KRAELING, The Synagogue = Excavations at Dura Europos, Final Report 8,1 (1956). 398/402. H. L. HEMPEL, Zum Problem der Anfänge der AT-Illustration: ZAW 69 (1957) 103/31. C. O. NORDSTRÖM, Spätjüdische Reminiszenzen in der altchristl. u. byzantin. Kunst: Actes X⁰ Congrès int. d'études byzantines (Istanbul 1957) 150f; Some jewish legends in byzantine art: Byzantion 25/27 (1955/57) 487/508; The water miracles of Moses in jewish legend and byzantine art: Orientalia Suecana 7 (1958) 78/109; Rabbinica in frühchristlichen und byzantinischen Illustrationen zum 4. Buch Mose: Figura NS 1 (Uppsala 1959) 24/47. A. FERRUA, Una scena nuova nella pittura catacombale: RendicPontAccArch 30/31 (1957/59) 107/116. O. PÄCHT, Ephraimillustration, Haggadah u. Wiener Genesis: Festschrift K. M. Swoboda (1959) 213/21. A. GRABAR, Recherches sur les sources juives de l'art paléochrétien: CahArch 11 (1960) 41/71. H. L. HEMPEL, Das Problem der Anfänge der AT-Illustration: ZAW 73 (1961) 299/302. H. ROSENAU, The Jonah sarcophagus in the British Museum: Journ. Archaeol. Association 3,24 (1961) 60/66 — Die Frage, nach welchen Gesichtspunkten die Motive für die christliche Sepulkralkunst aus dem Bilderschatz der christlichen Ringgemmen ausgewählt wurden, soll mit den oben gemachten Andeutungen keineswegs abschließend erledigt werden. Es ist z. B. durchaus nicht ausgeschlossen, daß auch die Erinnerung an die Katechese mitgesprochen hat; vgl. dazu A. G. MARTIMORT, L'iconographie des catacombes et la catechese antique: RivAC 25 (1949) 105/14.

[93] Für freundliche Hilfe und Hinweise ist der Verfasser verpflichtet den Herren H. Brandenburg, K. Rischar, A. Stuiber und K. Weitzmann.

10 Antike und Christentum

DANIEL DE LACO LEONIS

TRIS PVERI DE ECNE CAMI

SVSANA DE FALSO CRIMINE

DIVNAN DE VENTRE QVETI LIBERATVS
EST

ABRAM ETET EVAM

DOMNVS LAIARVM *resuscitat*

Petrus virga percouuouset

fontis ciperunt quorere

cf. C.I.L. 3, supp. 1-3, 10190

Insc. Lat. Chr. Vet.² n. 2426

NOTES AND COMMENTS

THE PODGORITZA CUP

The Podgoritza cup was discovered about 1870 near the site of Doclea in Dalmatia, a town founded by Vespasian or one of his sons.[1] It was immediately recognized to be a fascinating and unique christian monument, and started at once on an odyssey. From Doclea it went to Podgoritza (the nearest town), and then southward to Scutari, to the Italian consul's collection, where it was seen by Dumont,[2] the director of the French school at Athens. It was bought from the Italian consul by Colonel Basilewsky from Paris, one of the greatest nineteenth-century collectors of christian antiquities, who went to Albania to fetch it. During the journey from Scutari to Paris it was slightly chipped. By this time de Rossi himself knew of it, and published it with a sketchy drawing given to him by Dumont.[3] He too had gone to Albania to see the cup, but the Italian consul had moved to Sarajevo, and the Balkan war, which broke out soon afterwards, made further investigations impossible. De Rossi in fact found the Podgoritza cup by chance on a visit to Basilewsky's collection in Paris, and at once republished it with a better drawing.[4] But the first important advance in its interpretation, which remains the most serious work yet done on it, was the thin but fundamental *Étude sur les sarcophages chrétiens de la ville d'Arles*, by E. Le Blant.[5]

At the sale of the Basilewsky collection, the Podgoritza cup was bought for St Petersburg. It survived the revolution and there, on display in the very rich Byzantine collection of the Hermitage Museum, it still is. The Leningrad collections have been rather neglected by Western scholars: they were ignored in the expensive publication of the Vatican gold-glass, and the most recently issued catalogue of Christian inscriptions[6] still hopefully lists the Podgoritza cup as 'exstat Parisiis' although its whereabouts had been known to Dom Leclercq in 1914.[7] No photograph of it has ever appeared.[8]

The cup is a clear glass patera with no base, about eleven inches across and two inches deep, engraved by a freehand technique with ornaments and inscriptions. (These need not necessarily be of the same date as the bowl itself or as

[1] *C.I.L.* 3, Supp. 8287-8.
[2] *Bull. de la soc. nat. des ant. de France*, 1873.
[3] *Boll. Arc. Crist.*, 1874.
[4] *Boll. Arc. Crist*, 1877.
[5] Paris, 1878.
[6] *Insc. Lat. Chr. Vet.*, Diehl ed. Moreau 1961, n. 2426.
[7] DACL s.v. 'Coupe'.
[8] For this photograph I am indebted to the great kindness of Dr A. Bank, of the Hermitage Museum, Leningrad, and to the Soviet Ministry of Culture. and (for its enlargement) to Dr D. B. Harden and the photographer of the London Museum; also to Mr Robin Milner-Gulland, for an interesting preliminary photograph and for some measurements.

55

each other.) Certain features of its style[1] and iconography are apparently unique: but the comparative scarcity of similar glass-ware and the parallels that can be brought piecemeal for most of its eccentricities are sufficient to comfort the faintest-hearted of archaeologists about a date being fixed in the fourth century.

It was already apparent to Le Blant that this particular series of images, Jonas, Susanna, Daniel, the *tres pueri* in the furnace, Adam and Eve, Christ and Lazarus, the sacrifice of Isaac and Peter (?) striking water from a tree, was not only to be associated with a similar cycle found, for example, on the Arles sarcophagi, but that these images directly recall one of the earliest prayers of the ritual, which occurs in the *Ordo commendationis animae*.[2]

The prayer can be analysed in several ways; its roots are equally Greek and Jewish. The gradually intensifying symbolism of the ambiguous, repeated 'deliver ... as thou didst deliver ... ' would not have been unfamiliar to a Stoic. The repeated examples (in Greek usually introduced by καὶ γάρ) follow one of the simplest and oldest patterns of prayer, but the emphasis on the word 'deliver' is a notorious feature of late Stoicism: a play on this word is the mainspring of one of the finest and most terrible poems of Horace.[3] 'Ipse deus simul atque volam me solvet.' Opinor hoc sentit, Moriar. Mors ultima linea rerum est.

The roots of the prayer in the Old Testament are obvious at a glance. But further, this sort of prayer is a commonplace of Jewish religious tradition; it can be traced in the Old Testament,[4] in Philo[5] and in the Epistle to the Hebrews,[6] and often in Jewish iconography,[7] so that we can be as certain about the origins of this prayer as we can about the image-types on this cup,[8] that they were in some form pre-Christian. Here is yet another case where we can see that both the literary and the visual tradition derive not from a christian mixture of Jewish and pagan, but from Jewish sources which were already expressed in classical terms before the formation of Christianity.

There are two interesting prayers related to the one in the *Ordo commendationis* which enumerate the same cycle of primary images of salvation. They survive because they were falsely attributed to St Cyprian, but since they were quite evidently not written by him they have attracted little attention. Their early

---

[1] I hope later to complete a more technical study of this cup. The lines that such a study should be on can easily be seen from Dr D. B. Harden's full comparative study of the Wint Hill hunting bowl (*Journal of Glass Studies*, II [1960], pp. 45-81).

[2] Deliver O Lord the soul of thy servant as thou didst deliver Enoch and Elias ... Noah ... Abraham ... Job ... Isaac from the sacrificing hand of his father ... Lot ... Moses ... Daniel from the lions' den ... the three children ... Susanna ... David ... Peter and Paul out of prison ... and as thou didst deliver St Thecla.

[3] Ep. 1. 16. 78-9.

[4] Cf. Ps. 105 (106), 1 Macc 4:30, etc.

[5] His list is like Paul's and even affects his literary form.

[6] Heb 11.

[7] E.g. on the Noah coins of Apamea in Phrygia around 200 A.D.

[8] The sacrifice of Abraham occurs on a wall of the Beth Alpha synagogue (cf. E. R. Goodenough, *Jewish Symbols in the Greco-Roman Period* [Bollingen Series XXXVII] III, 638), Daniel on a synagogue mosaic, Susanna is an ordinary 'orans', Peter and Christ are versions of Moses of Doura-Europos and elsewhere, etc., etc.

date can be established by the existence of versions in Arabic, Ethiopian, Syriac and Slavonic (the last two fragmentary), and in Greek,[1] by some reminiscences of the *Te Deum* and of Cyprian *de mortalitate* (26) and with even greater confidence by their rhythm.[2]

In the first prayer the examples of salvation are Sara, Tobias, the *tres pueri*, Daniel, and the miracles of Christ. The prayer then continues: 'assiste nobis sicut apostolis in vinculis, Theclae in ignibus, Paulo in persecutionibus, Petro in fluctibus, Qui sedes super septem thronos ad dexteram patris, respice nos et libera nos de aeternae mortis interitu.' The prayer ends with a resounding acclamation. The second prayer is at once more subjective and more profuse: surely a rather later composition. Its examples are Israel in Egypt, the people of Niniveh, the *tres pueri*, Daniel, Tobias and Sara, Ezechias, Thecla ('libera me de medio saeculi huius sicut liberasti Theclam de medio amphitheatro'), and the miracles of Christ, ending 'qui Petro labenti manum tradidisti'.

In such a series as this no instance is definitive; the list varies each time it occurs. The persistent inclusion of Thecla, for example, is chiefly in the literary sources, though she occurs in association with the apostles and with Moses striking the rock, on a fourth-century Roman ivory panel in the British Museum.[3] The Apostles, the *tres pueri*, Ezechias, and Moses striking the rock occur together on a piece of *dignitas amicorum* gold-glass in the Wilshere collection,[4] with another scene conjecturally and very oddly interpreted as the martyrdom of Isaias.[5] Sarcophagi often include Cana and Peter's crowing cock: the most persistent image of all is that of Moses or his successor Peter striking the rock.[6]

It may be that the oldest written source for the series of prayers on which this cycle of images depends is the Sunday prayer in the *Constitutiones Apostolicae*.[7] It ends with two *Paradigmagebeten*, the first a list of twenty-nine accepted prayers of the patriarchs, including Noah, Moses, Elias, Ezechias, Daniel, Jonas and the *tres pueri*, the second based on the phrase 'in generation after generation'. In the first prayer everything is Jewish, and in the second the end of the list is Christ 'in our days'.[8] Not even the apostles are allowed to intrude into the canon of examples: everything is still Jewish.[9]

---

[1] *Oriens Christianus* t. 3, 1903.

[2] A heavily marked rhythm like that of *laudes* and of theatrical acclamations can often be recognized in the fragments of early public prayers, in the wording of epitaphs, for example (Wilpert, *Catac. Rom.* t. 183, 1) and in the liturgy reported by Cyril of Jerusalem.

[3] *B.M. Catalogue of Ivories*, n. 8.

[4] Formerly at Pusey House, now in the Ashmolean Museum, Oxford.

[5] Like most gold-glass, this piece may probably be deteriorating. In spite of every possible care the British Museum gold-glass is visibly crumbling. T. B. L. Webster (J.R.S. XIX [1929], p. 150) notes that part of Isaias' martyrdom got lost in the nineteenth century.

[6] Cf. E. Becker, *Quellwunder des Moses* (Strasbourg, 1912). (His list is not exhaustive.)

[7] Cc. 37-8.

[8] Cf. Heb 1: 2.

[9] On the contemporary Jewish preoccupation with Enoch and Elias, who are invoked in the *Ordo commendationis*, cf. Erik Peterson's essay in *Frühkirche, Judentum und*

E

The central question of iconography about the Podgoritza cup is the question of Peter as a second Moses, striking not a rock but a tree. Unfortunately this involves several uncertainties, including an awkward problem of epigraphy. Distinguishing Peter from Moses on monuments where the types are identical can be done only on general grounds. The presence or absence of a beard can hardly be a safe criterion, since once a beardless figure began to do service as Peter on christian monuments, it could equally well have served as Moses. (The inscription of names may often be later than the rather conventional heads they fit).[1]

At any rate it can be said that Moses certainly occurs on christian monuments, striking a rock from which men in Jewish hats and trousers are drinking. Where a cycle of images belongs chiefly to the Old Testament but includes Peter doing what Moses did, then Peter stands in the place of Moses, and there must at some time have been an original Jewish cycle in which Moses figured, and Christ and Peter were excluded.

The Latin inscriptions on the Podgoritza cup are in two hands. These were distinguished by Le Blant as a good majuscule and a bad and much later minuscule.[2] It will be seen that the supposedly very late inscription is the one which tells us about Peter. (It also adds the word *resuscitat* to Christ and Lazarus.) Early scholars found it very hard to decipher, but the writing becomes quite clear in an enlarged photograph, and a modern epigrapher might even prefer this small but distinguished hand to the clumsier capitals. I am not myself entirely convinced that the hands are different. The minuscule is at least as good as that of the potter Acaunissa.[3] Its closest parallels are probably on the glass from Doura-Europos, which I have never seen.[4]

The tree and the water have been variously but not at all satisfactorily explained. The passages cited range from a remark of Cyprian, 'quotiescumque autem aqua sola in scripturis sanctis nominatur, baptisma praedicatur',[5] and one of Innocent I about Peter,[6] 'natalis fons unde aquae cunctae procedunt', to various symbolic statements about trees. But no one mentions the tree and the water together. While it may be true that the fathers are full of enthusiastic *laudes aquae*,[7] the one crooked beam of light on the water in this picture comes from the catacombs,[8] where a similarly strange liberty is taken with traditional

[1] Cf. C. R. Morey, *Early Christian Art* (Princeton, 1942), p. 217.

[2] *Étude sur les sarcophages chrétiens de la ville d'Arles*, table 35.

[3] Acaunissa's signed bowls have been found at Birdoswald in Cumberland, at Mainz and at Cologne. He probably worked at Vichy under Hadrian.

[4] C. R. Morey, op. cit.

[5] Ep. 63.8 (CSEL III, 706).

[6] Petrus Coustant, *Epp. Rom. Pont.* (Paris, 1721) 86b.

[7] Tert. Bapt. 3, Theoph. Ant. as Ant. 1, 12, etc.

[8] Wilpert, *Cat. Rom.*, tav. 252.

Gnosis (Freiburg, 1959). To this add Jerome in Gen 4:23 'Et putant mortem atque peccatum in septima progenie sabbatizasse, quando Enoch raptus est, *et non inveniebatur, quia transtulit illum Deus*': *Op. Hieron.* (Paris, 1693-1703), vol. II, t.2, pp. 265-6

imagery: the acclaimed Lamb, labelled IORDAS (the Mandaean word for water), is standing on a hill-top from the bottom of which run seven rivers. Whatever text stands directly behind this scene must be apocryphal;[1] it has not survived.

It has been suggested that the rock Horeb has become a tree by a simple mistake of drawing. This is a suggestion of despair, and no enumeration of curled or semi-foliated 'Asiatic' rocks can make it acceptable.[2] To suppose a mistake like this implies a contempt for the drawing on this cup like that expressed by Dom Leclercq:[3] 'Le latin des légendes servant à expliquer les compositions est déplorable et au niveau de l'art qui n'est guère qu'un griffonnage.' But the iconography is very careful, the tree above Jonas is a gourd, the tree of knowledge is an accurate and characteristic fig-tree, and Peter's or Moses' tree looks like a date-palm. There was a widespread pre-christian and apocryphal tradition that the date-palm was the tree of life.

The question therefore arises whether the three scenes of Adam and Eve, Christ and Lazarus, and Peter and his tree are meant to be seen together. Reference to the cross ('in ligno quoque vinceretur') can be ruled out of the discussion, since the trees are different and the raising of Lazarus is not the crucifixion. The three scenes are not even necessarily related, since Adam and Eve occur on similar glass bowls with only Daniel and Susanna,[4] or even alone.[5] Yet how did Adam and Eve, complete with their serpent, become part of this cycle of images? I can only assume they were a late addition (they occur more often in engraved glass than on stone) and that the reference is in fact to a fully christian theory of salvation. The substitution of Peter for Moses striking the rock is another indication of this meaning. The rock was already supernatural in Jewish tradition, but from the time of St Paul the rock was Christ.[6]

But the central difficulty obstinately refuses to dissolve. Neither Moses nor Peter ever struck water out of a tree. The inscription and the type of Peter with the wand relate the picture clearly to Moses[7] and the rock which was Christ.[8] If any literary text directly explains this iconographic development, as far as I know it has perished. We can be reasonably secure about the identity of the date-palm with the tree of life, and we have one further crumb of comfort.

And I entered in further and saw a tree planted, out of whose roots flowed waters, and out of it was the beginning of the four rivers, and the spirit of God rested upon that tree, and when the spirit breathed, the waters flowed forth (Apocalypse of Paul, c. 45).[9]

The garden was watered by a river; it came out from the place called the place of Delight, and went on to divide into four branches (Gen 3:10).

[1] Cf., of course, Apoc. 21:6 and 22. For seven rivers cf. Enoch cc. 24, 55 and 77.
[2] The knobbly 'Asiatic' form of rock occurs often on gold-glass both for Horeb and for Lazarus' tomb.
[3] DACL 3, 2, 3009.
[4] Louvre, fig. 32 in D. B. Harden, in *Journal of Glass Studies* quoted above.
[5] Cologne, fig. 33 in D. B. Harden, op.cit.
[6] 1 Cor 10:4.   [7] Cf. Num 20:11.
[8] Cf. Cyprian Ep. 63.8 later in the chapter.
[9] Tr. M. R. James, *The Apocryphal New Testament* (Oxford, 1924).

In this account God goes on to show Paul the tree of good and evil, 'This is the tree whereby death entered into the world', and the tree of life. The three trees are distinct. One might compare a passage in the Apocryphal Gospel of Bartholomew: 'But the devil said ... "I took a vial in mine hand and scraped the sweat from off my breast and the hair of mine armpits, and washed myself in the springs of the waters whence the four rivers flow out, and Eve drank of it and desire came upon her: for if she had not drunk of that water I should not have been able to deceive her." Then Bartholomew commanded him to go to hell' (4, 59-60).[1]

It seems then that Daniel, the *tres pueri*,[2] Susanna, Jonas and Abraham and Isaac,[3] perhaps Adam and Eve, and certainly Lazarus are examples of those whom God has delivered. The addition of Lazarus and the central position of Isaac point the meaning we can refer to in the *ordo commendationis*. These images have to do with God saving the just from death. The exact meaning of Moses and the rock was uncertain, and the meaning of Peter and the tree is still not precise: but given the context we can suppose the water means immortality.[4] Adam and Eve may be related (through Christ and Lazarus?) to this image.

The date of the Podgoritza cup seems likely from every point of view to be in the fourth century. No other surviving glass can be attributed to the same workman.[5] It seems unlikely to have been made locally; the nearest glass-making was in Italy. It could hardly have been ornamented by an amateur. The inscription is not by a native Latin speaker.[6] The cup was almost certainly designed to be used in celebrating the memory of the dead, and as such Christian gold-glass was probably used. Whether the celebration was in some way liturgical is a question outside the scope of this note, though the history and iconography of this class of object might help to solve it.

PETER LEVI

[1] Tr. M. R. James, *The Apocryphal New Testament* (Oxford, 1924).

[2] At Wadi Sarga the *tres pueri* are used for a martyr-shrine, perhaps as figures of intercession, but much later than this.

[3] It should be stressed that the meaning of this image in this context is the saving of Isaac and not the idea of sacrifice.

[4] Cf. John 4:10 ff. Jewish grave-inscriptions have been found in Alexandria praying for water from Osiris.

[5] Considering the tiny remains of ancient glass that have survived this is not surprising. The first Byzantine stained glass and the first classical painted glass vessel ever to be discovered have both turned up only in the last two years.

[6] Neither is this surprising. A last faint echo of these prayers can be heard in Roland's dying words in the *Chanson de Roland:*

Veire Paterne, ki unkes ne mentis,
Seint Lazaron de mort resurrexis
E Daniel des leons guaresis ... (2384 - 6)

THE TOMB OF THE APOSTLES AD CATACUMBAS

HANS LIETZMANN

UNIVERSITY OF JENA

IN the number of this REVIEW for January 1921, Dr. George La Piana discussed, in the light of the most recent discoveries at Rome, the several hypotheses which have been put forward in regard to the ancient tradition connected with the church of San Sebastiano at Rome. He there controverts the view proposed in my *Petrus und Paulus in Rom* (1915) that a translation of the relics of Peter and Paul to the Catacumbae, that is to the site of the later basilica of San Sebastiano, took place on June 29, 258, and defends the opinion, held also by eminent archaeologists in Rome, that what took place ad Catacumbas in the year 258 was only the establishment of a memorial festival in honor of the two apostles. His acute argument skilfully detects the weak points of my position, and at the same time contains so much that is new as to give me a welcome opportunity for a reëxamination of the evidence. A necessary preliminary to this was a journey to Rome and the personal inspection of the excavations, which I was able to make late in April 1922.

It may be taken as accepted that the original text of the Filocalian Calendar is not that found in the corrupt manuscripts of the Chronographer of 354, but is to be arrived at through a combination with the Martyrologium Hieronymianum.[1] The true text should read: *III Kal. Jul. Natale sanctorum apostolorum Petri et Pauli: Petri in Vaticano, Pauli vero in via Ostensi, utriusque in catacumbas. Basso et Tusco cons.* The consular year named is 258 A.D.

La Piana is entirely correct in remarking that nothing here directly attests a translation of the bodies of the apostles; the supposition that in the year 258 a memorial festival of the apostles was established would fully satisfy the wording of the

---

[1] La Piana, pp. 60 f., and Lietzmann, Petrus und Paulus in Rom, pp. 81 f.

text. But when he adds (p. 61): "On the contrary, this origin [a translation] is implicitly excluded by the assumption that the 29th of June is the *dies natalis* of the apostles," he proves too much for the good of his theory. It is generally admitted that in the fourth century the 29th of June was celebrated as the *dies natalis* of the two apostles, but it is also more than probable that this day cannot have been the actual historical day of their martyrdom. The Roman liturgical tradition betrays no knowledge of days of martyrs' deaths before the year 200.[2] On the other hand the date in question did not arise from a liturgical constructive theory, as appears to be the case with the oriental festival of Peter and Paul on the 28th of December.[3] Therefore the 29th of June must have some historical significance, and it is most natural to connect it with the year mentioned in the tradition, and to regard June 29, 258, as the day on which the liturgical festival in honor of the apostles Peter and Paul was initiated — and in fact both initiated and observed for the first time.[4]

So far my learned critic might agree with my argument, for the difference between us here is slight; but he would then ask me, with all the greater emphasis, why I assume a translation of the apostolic relics, which Filocalus does not mention, and against which, as I myself acknowledge, considerable arguments can be urged. My answer is: first, because of the testimony of Damasus; secondly, because of the archaeological facts; thirdly, because of the general principle that in antiquity church festivals were not instituted by an arbitrary decree, but arose out of some tangible liturgical act, which in this case is most easily conceived as a translation.

The verses of Damasus read as follows:

> *hic habitasse prius sanctos cognoscere debes,*
> *nomina quisque Petri pariter Paulique requiris.*

La Piana's statement (p. 65), "It cannot be denied that the

---

[2] This I think I have shown; Petrus und Paulus in Rom, pp. 90 ff. La Piana also (p. 65) considers the date June 29 as not historical.

[3] Petrus und Paulus in Rom, pp. 92 ff.

[4] La Piana (p. 90, note 32) characterizes this view as "not improbable," but in so doing he destroys his own argument in the text (p. 61).

verb *habitare* is found in the epigraphic terminology in the meaning *to be buried*," does not cover the ground. I still find my argument [5] convincing, that the phrases which follow reflect the customary expressions of Damasus, and that therefore the poet intended here by *habitasse* to express the same idea which he habitually expresses in such a connection, namely: 'Here were the martyrs buried.' Parallels are more significant in the case of Damasus than with other poets because he is fond of repeating both ideas and language.

Accordingly, while it is, to be sure, "not impossible," as La Piana proposes, to interpret *habitasse*. here "in its primary meaning 'to dwell' of a living person," yet the interpretation is not free from objection, and I cannot accept as "very likely" the theory that Peter "found a refuge while living in Rome" in the villa whose walls have been brought to light beneath the church of San Sebastiano. For if La Piana refuses to admit a translation in the year 258, on the ground that such translations cannot be proved to have taken place in Rome before the latter part of the fifth century, he ought to have still stronger objections to the supposition of a local tradition about an apostle's place of residence which wholly lacks liturgical support, and which (since it must have arisen in the first century) presupposes a curiosity about such matters very strange for that time and with analogies only at distinctly later dates. To my mind such a tradition, even if it were attested for the fourth century, which is not the case, would be quite incredible. La Piana's praiseworthy caution in rejecting (p. 89, note 22a) Wilpert's use of the graffito *domus Petri* in one of the excavated chambers, need not rest for its justification solely on the date in the fifth century assigned to the graffito on palaeographical grounds, for Franchi de' Cavalieri in another connection [6] has called attention to a pseudo-damasine inscription (No. 82 Ihm) in which the burial chamber of St. Hippolytus is designated as *domus martyris Hippolyti*. That agrees perfectly with the frequent pagan designation of the grave as *domus aeterna*.[7] More-

---

[5] *Petrus und Paulus in Rom*, pp. 107 f.　　[6] *Note agiografiche* 5 (1915), p. 123.

[7] See Dessau, *Inscriptiones latinae selectae* III. 2, Index, p. 939; *Carmina epigraphica*, ed. Buecheler, No. 662. 1.

over La Piana has to assume an inaccuracy on the part of
Damasus. The latter says *hic habitasse sanctos*, and names
Peter and Paul with emphasis, so that both apostles would
have to be supposed to have resided ad Catacumbas. This
strikes La Piana as legendary, and he explains the legend as
having arisen from the later habitual combination of the two
apostles as a pair — "a binomial like Castor and Pollux." So
he cuts the statement of Damasus in halves, and supposes Peter
to have dwelt ad Catacumbas, while Paul was added later by
the legend. That is perhaps not impossible, but certainly not
obvious; and clearly this explanation sacrifices the exact interpretation of the text of Damasus, which my view, I hope,
preserves. Equally beside the mark is Delehaye's objection [8]
that Damasus ought to have said:

> *corpora quisque Petri pariter Paulique requiris,*

instead of *nomina*, if he intended to refer to the place of burial.
Requiris here does not mean 'thou seekest,' but 'thou askest.'
Damasus means, 'Here once Saints lay buried; if thou askest
their names, I answer, "Peter and Paul."' This is the meaning
in Damasus 10, 2 (ed. Ihm): *hic soror est Damasi, nomen si
quaeris, Irene.* For *requiris* Ihm compares appropriately Carmina epigraphica (ed. Buecheler), No. 748. 28, *nomina sanc-
tarum, lector, si forte requiris,* and such phrases are common
enough in the language of metrical epitaphs. For instance
Carm. epig. 696. 3, *nomen dulce, lector, si forte defunctae requiris;*
1357. 3, *quae tegitur tumulo, si vis cognoscere, lector;* Damasus,
carm. 34. 1, *quisque vides tumulum, vitam si quaeris opertae,* etc.
This very common form is in our case varied to read: 'If thou
askest after the persons (*nomina*) Peter and Paul, know that
they were buried here.' We find *nomen* used in this way in
the pseudo-damasine inscription, No. 87, *hic votis paribus tumulum duo nomina servant Chrysanthi Dariae.*

Accordingly our inscription can hardly be understood in any
other sense than as I have interpreted it: 'Here once the two
apostles lay buried.' To what date Damasus assigns the burial,

---

[8] H. Delehaye, Les origines du culte des Martyrs (1912), p. 308, cited by La Piana, p. 90, note 28.

— whether he believed it to have taken place immediately after their martyrdom under Nero or in the year 258 — cannot be determined from the *prius* of the text; and also that Damasus was correct in what he states is not proved by the mere existence of the inscription, of which indeed the original is no longer extant. La Piana presents impressively the view that the verses which follow are colored by the antagonism which divided Rome and the East in the time of Damasus and came to a climax in 381; but the parallel phrases of poems No. 52 and No. 46 make it seem doubtful whether the words have here any such peculiar significance.

We may now turn to the examination of the archaeological facts. To the full bibliography of the excavations at San Sebastiano given by La Piana I can add but little. The results of the work down to April 1916 are contained in the fundamental publication of Dr. Styger in the *Dissertazioni della Pontificia Accademia Romana di archeologia*, ser. II, vol. XIII (1918), with most careful descriptions and abundant figures, plans, and plates. On the later excavations articles have appeared in the *Studi Romani* and in the *Nuovo Bullettino d'archeologia*, and Dr. Styger gives a good summary in the *Zeitschrift für katholische Theologie*, vol. XLV, pp. 549–572 (Innsbruck, 1921). Plate I of the present article combines all the previous drawings in a single outline sketch and Plate II gives a vertical section.

The history of the site has been briefly as follows. The locality consists of a cliff of tufa enclosing a semicircular valley which descends steeply to a depth of about 8 meters. In the last quarter of the first century after Christ a row of columbaria was constructed on the flat top of the cliff. At about the same time, or perhaps a little later, three extensive burial chambers (32, 33, 34) were cut in the cliff, on the level of the bottom of the valley. These had façades of masonry and were decorated on the interior with stucco ornaments and various paintings, including pictures of banquets. Inscriptions show that these chambers were used for pagan burials as late as 238 A.D. To the right of these large structures two smaller tombs (35 and 36)

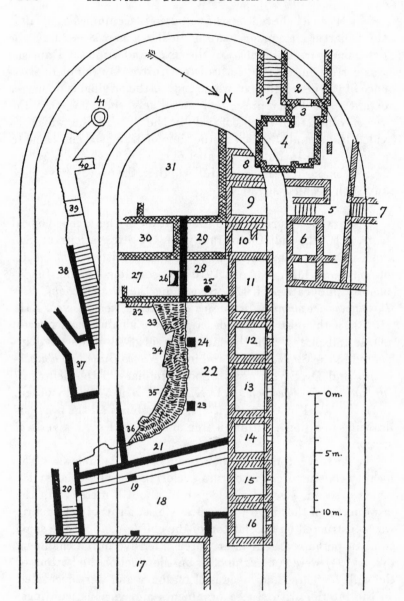

PLATE I. PLAN OF THE EXCAVATIONS AT SAN SEBASTIANO

4, Burial chamber with light-shaft. 6, 8, 10–16, Columbaria. 9, Ustrinum. 18, Triclia. 22, Court. 25, Oil-column. 26, Cathedra. 27–31, Roman villa of the time of Hadrian. 32, 33, 34, Façades of the three large tombs in the valley. 35, 36, Crypto-christian inscriptions. 38, Stairs leading to underground passage and well. 39, Reservoir with stuccoed wall. 41, Well.

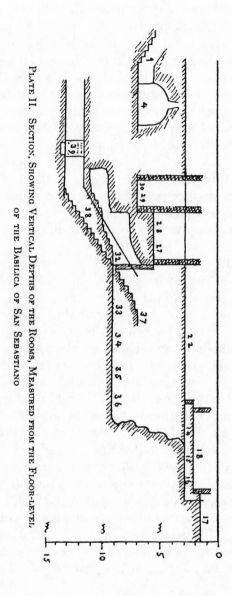

Plate II. Section, Showing Vertical Depths of the Rooms, Measured from the Floor-level, of the Basilica of San Sebastiano were made in the rock. But side by side with the preponderating pagan characteristics of all these tombs are Christian features, which were probably not evident to pagans but revealed their true nature only to the initiate. In one chamber of tomb 33 we find scratched in the stucco of the wall ΙΤΧΘΥΣ, that is, the confessional symbol (ΙΧΘΥΣ) with the cross (T). In the rock-wall near tombs 35 and 36 are two grave-stones the wording of which is entirely "neutral," but which by fish and anchor, palm and crown, indicate the Christian profession of the dead. About the time of Hadrian a villa was built above tomb 32, extending back as far as the row of columbaria and with its east wall resting partly on the façade of tomb 32. One of its rooms (29) made necessary the destruction of part of a columbarium. Styger has lately expressed the opinion that these rooms were not the dwelling-rooms of a villa but pagan meeting-places of a sepulchral character.[9]

In the middle of the third century the villa was destroyed; its lower (basement) rooms and the valley were filled with earth; and the long rear wall of the columbaria (11–16), as well as the wall of a building (17) which has not yet been fully examined, were used to form the back of a colonnade (18) opening toward the south-west, and of an enclosed court (22) roofed over on the north side. This court extended also over the demolished walls of the villa. At that time, apparently, the east wall of room 27 was reërected with fragments of tufa and bricks,[10] and a cross-wall carried from east to west across the space 27–28. A cathedra (26) and an oil-column (25) testify to the ritual use of the new rooms. On the east wall of the so-called *triclia* (18) are the numerous graffiti invoking Peter and Paul and mentioning *refrigeria*. La Piana prints the texts of these (pp. 78 f.), and Styger gives excellent photographs of all of them.[11] This whole reconstruction, as is admitted on all hands, was evidently undertaken by Christians for the purpose of celebrating the commemoration of the apostles, and no doubt, as the archaeological indications suggest, in the year 258 of which the Filo-

---

[9] Zeitschrift für katholische Theologie XLV, p. 567.
[10] Styger, Dissert. Pont. Acc., p. 93.
[11] Dissert. Pont. Acc., plates I–XXV.

calian Calendar speaks. The triclia was specially intended, like the well-known portico of the Catacomb of Domitilla, for the ritual banquets, a custom to which we find many literary allusions.[12]

This structure, however, did not long stand, for the *basilica apostolorum*, as San Sebastiano was originally called, was built before the middle of the next century, and in its turn covered up all the remains of this earlier building. The terminus ante quem for the erection of the church is fixed by the grave-stone of a child, let into the level surface of the pavement and found in situ.[13] The child died *VIII Kal. Octob[res] Costantio Agusto* S [. . . *et J] uliano [Caes. conss.*], that is, on the 24th of September, 356 or 357 (according as we supply SII = 8 or SIII = 9). The graffiti in the triclia suit best the second half of the third century, by reason both of their matter and of the forms of the scratched letters; the Constantinian monogram for Christus ☧ does not occur.

These discoveries rejoiced the heart of the archaeologists, who were looking for the tomb of the apostles; but as the excavations brought one surprise after another, their disappointment must have been equally great. Not a trace of the tomb of an apostle has so far been found. The columbaria can yield nothing, even where they were altered to admit coffins. The burial-chambers in the valley were closed by ruins. The other rooms, such as the *"Platonia"* and the *"domus Petri"*[14] or the cubiculum with a light-shaft (4 of our plan), are too far from the centre of interest, and give no evidence of the burial of an apostle. An ingenious suggestion has been made by O. Marucchi[15] with regard to a flight of steps (38) on the south side of the court, which lead to a depth of four metres below the level of the bottom of the valley into a horizontal passage leading to an old well (41). At the point marked 39 on the Plan the wall of the passage is entirely covered with stucco,

---

[12] Bullettino d'archeologia cristiana, 1865, p. 96; Cabrol, Dictionnaire d'archéologie chrétienne I, 809 ff.

[13] Figured in Styger, Diss. pont. acc., p. 27.

[14] See La Piana, p. 70, plan I, A and N.

[15] Nuovo bullettino 26 (1920), pp. 12 ff.

on which are graffiti with invocations of the apostles. At this point, Marucchi thinks, the passage was once closed by a cross-wall, and in the time of Nero the bodies of the apostles were temporarily concealed here. But this cross-wall is entirely hypothetical, and another explanation of the strange piece of plastering is more natural. A branch of the spring, namely, opens into the passage at this point and still fills with water the trough-shaped hollow floor. This was the reservoir from which the water needed for the triclia above was fetched. The wall about it was given the distinction of a coat of stucco, and this was covered with graffiti by Christians who came down to draw water. These inscriptions contain the Constantinian monogram, and are therefore later than the greater part of those in the triclia. It may be added that the presence of the branch of a spring in the chamber makes it highly unlikely that bodies were hidden there.

From these facts many scholars, among them La Piana, have concluded that there never was any apostles' grave here, and consequently no translation. Their conclusion does not seem to me justified. Styger's first report led me to surmise that the burial place of the apostles was to be sought in room 17.[16] The idea met at first with strong opposition, but competent judges in Rome have recently declared it quite probable. At any rate, this structure appeared on Styger's first investigation[17] to be a rebuilt sepulchral monument originally of the first or second century, and it still awaits thorough excavation and study. Let us then reserve our judgment, for nothing but a complete clearing of the whole area can fully account for the architectural plan of San Sebastiano, in particular for the lack of orientation by points of the compass and for the position of the apse over the remains of the villa.

Nevertheless La Piana thinks that at any rate in 258 no translation took place, because, first, there was no reasonable occasion for it, and secondly, because such translations were

---

[16] Petrus und Paulus in Rom, pp. 120, 182. I spoke only of the rooms, not of the sarcophagi; La Piana (p. 74) misunderstood the bearing of the passage. The coffin of "Fabianus" with its mediaeval inscription was merely a guide for the tradition of a later age. [17] Diss. pont. acc., p. 49.

not then customary. He points out (p. 67), following Delehaye, that by Roman law the violation of graves was liable to a heavy penalty and that for every translation a special permit would have been required. That is true, but it proves nothing, for all Christian worship was subject to heavy penalties, indeed to the death penalty, and more than usually so in the year 258. The unquestionable erection of a place of worship ad Catacumbas and the undoubted observance there of religious ceremonies were quite as much prohibited and dangerous as the removal of revered relics for ritual purposes.[18] A few weeks later, on the 6th of August, 258, Bishop Sixtus found this out at the cost of his life. We are justified in assuming that the Christians of Rome in the third century had enough courage, when the interests of the church required, to undertake translations without fear of the Roman police. A shrewd and, if necessary, open-handed diplomacy would have been able to smooth the way to the attainment of their desires.

But what would have been the motive for the removal? La Piana is quite right in saying (p. 67), "There is no example in Rome of the tombs of the martyrs ever being molested by the government even in times of fierce persecutions. The Christians therefore had nothing to fear for the tombs of the Apostles." It was not for fear that the graves would be violated by public officials that the relics were transferred ad Catacumbas. A more probable reason can be suggested.

In the first half of the third century the ritual veneration of martyrs developed in the Christian church at Rome, and the impossibility of such worship at the graves of the chief apostles and first martyrs of the church must soon have been painfully felt. No trace has been found of a Christian cemetery in the neighborhood of the grave either of Peter or of Paul. The entire surroundings of both graves are purely pagan, and near Peter's grave pagans were buried as late as in the second half of the third century. The funeral chapel of Anacletus had its origin in the legendary fancies of the sixth century.[19] The

---

[18] Cf. Acta Cypriani i, 8, *praeceperunt etiam ne in aliquibus locis conciliabula fiant nec coemeteria ingrediantur.*

[19] For the proofs see Petrus und Paulus in Rom, p. 152.

reports of all the excavations testify that before the time of Constantine private worship was perhaps possible at the graves of both apostles, but never any liturgical church worship. That would seem to me a sufficient reason why, soon after the middle of the third century, a suitable place of worship should have been built, necessarily withdrawn from the surveillance of the police, to which the relics were transferred. And even if it were true that such translations were not customary in Rome at that date or for a long time afterward, that would not be a valid objection to this view, for no other martyr can be compared in importance with Peter and Paul, and in no other case was the translation for purposes of religious veneration so imperative a necessity.

But that no translations took place in the earlier years is by no means so certain. De Rossi's theory of a translation of the bodies of Sts. Parthenius and Calocerus rests chiefly on the fact that both the Martyrologium Hieronymianum and a graffito in their tomb mention a second day of commemoration, the 11th of February, in addition to their regular holy-day of May 19. What event took place on February 11, if not a translation? The case is the same with regard to St. Bassilla, and only topographical considerations create difficulty; here also two dates of commemoration are recorded, September 22 and June 11. The strong probability then remains that in the other two cases (beside that of the year 258) where Filocalus mentions years, he refers to translations, namely that of Sts. Parthenius and Calocerus on February 11, 304, and that of St. Bassilla on June 11, 304. To Franchi de' Cavalieri's objection [20] that under the merciless persecution of Diocletian in the year 304 the Christians had other things to think about than translations of martyrs, it may be answered that even the bloodiest year of persecution included many weeks and even months of peaceful freedom from disturbance, and that we do not know the particular circumstances of time and place which were finally controlling.

La Piana, however, brings forward another argument which is calculated to make much impress on the reader's mind. "If,"

[20] Note agiografiche V, pp. 123 f.

he says, "the translation of the bodies to their original resting places had taken place after Constantine, such a great event would certainly have left some trace in the records of the time" (p. 82). From this he draws the conclusion that even if there was a translation ad Catacumbas, — whether in 64 or in 258 makes no difference, — the bodies in any case "remained ad Catacumbas for a very brief time — one or two years. It has to be admitted therefore that the *refrigeria* were held ad Catacumbas *absente cadavere*," and so as mere commemorative meals in honor of the apostles, contrary to the usual meaning of the term.

Let us examine this reasoning in detail. In the first place, it is hazardous to assert that an event of this kind must necessarily have left some trace in the tradition, and from the lack of such a trace to infer that there was no such event. For instance, the rebuilding of the church of St. Paul is attested, as it happens, for the years 384–390, by certain documents preserved wholly by accident; [21] we have even by a lucky chance the dedicatory column with the inscription of Pope Siricius. But the Liber pontificalis, which should have made official record of such things, says nothing at all about it. Indeed, if we should draw up a list of events of interest for church history which certainly took place and yet of which we have no information, it would be a long one.

But in the case before us the tradition is by no means so devoid of traces of the translation as La Piana avers. The Martyrologium Hieronymianum records for the 12th of December an *inventio corporis sancti Pauli apostoli;* and for the 25th of January a *translatio Pauli apostoli* which later, under New Testament influence, became the feast of the Conversion of St. Paul. One could hardly in reason expect more from the tradition than that; these are the dates of the identification of the body of St. Paul in the burial-chamber ad Catacumbas, and of the transfer to the rebuilt church of St. Paul. [22] But we have no corresponding dates recorded for St. Peter! Well, if the great church of St. Peter was finished later than the (oldest)

[21] On these see Zeitschrift für die neutest. Wissenschaft XXI (1922), p. 148.
[22] Cf. Petrus und Paulus in Rom, p. 164, note 2.

small church of St. Paul (and it surely was), that is not surprising. A special *inventio corporis sancti Petri* doubtless did not take place after the body of Paul had been identified and removed. But a translation must have taken place; why then is its date not preserved?

The dedication of St. Peter's is believed (since what date I cannot here show) to have taken place on November 18; and the great new church of St. Paul, consecrated in 390, observes as its own the same dedication-day. The date of St. Paul's was perhaps influenced by that of St. Peter's, since it might have been desired to celebrate both dedications on the same day, because of the common commemoration of the two apostles on June 29. That would have been a natural consequence of the combination of the two apostles into a "binomial," on which La Piana has laid so much stress (p. 65). Accordingly, so far as I can see, nothing stands in the way of assigning to November 18 the dedication of the Constantinian church of St. Peter, which meant also the translation of the body of St. Peter to the new church. In that case we could understand why no special date is recorded for the translation of St. Peter. But the point must again be emphasized that even without any such trace in tradition, the idea of a translation would be historically justified, provided other grounds for it exist, and I think I have been able to produce such.

The graffiti, too, testify to the strong probability that when they were written the apostles actually lay buried near the triclia. Both the acclamations, with prayer for the apostles' intercession, and the mention of the *refrigeria* point to the bodily presence of the saints addressed. La Piana (pp. 79 ff.) tries to overthrow this argument by affirming that the formula, *Petro et Paulo Tomius Coelius refrigerium feci*, must be understood as meaning, '*In honor of* Peter and Paul, I, Tomius Coelius, celebrated a refrigerium,' not '*as an offering for the eternal rest of* Peter and Paul' (p. 83). He infers from this that the word *refrigerium* "has lost its original meaning and its connection with a funeral rite which was the essential part of that meaning," and "that the word *refrigerium* had come in the popular use to signify merely a banquet, having a loose religious connection and celebrated in a place dedicated to the memory of a martyr." Continuing, he refers to Augustine, epist. 29, 10, where the writer deplores the *quotidianae vinolentiae exempla* reported from Rome *de basilica beati apostoli Petri*, which no prohibitions succeed in preventing, *quod remotus sit locus ab episcopi conversatione.* Such prohibitions, says La Piana, would have primarily affected the poorer people, who would then perhaps have withdrawn their *refrigeria* to the secluded spot ad Catacumbas. Augustine's letter is from the year 392; the prohibitions of which he speaks "must have been felt strongly at least from the middle of the century. Now, according to Dr. Styger, explorer of the triclia, the graffiti might have been written during the second half of the century, and not very long before the destruction of the triclia" (p. 85). La Piana has here fallen into a pardonable error. The prohibitions of which Augustine speaks may, it is true, go back to 350 — we know nothing further about them — but the triclia was built about 250, and the graffiti, according to Styger's correct opinion,[23] were written during the second half of the *third* century, that is, from half-a-century to a century earlier. Moreover, since the basilica of San Sebastiano was built before 356, not much time remains for the existence of the triclia in the fourth century. And not only is it a questionable procedure to assume without compelling reasons that the word *refrigerium* has here another sense that the funereal, but a positive refutation is at hand in the inscription [24] *at Paulo et Pet[ro] refri[geravi]*. That can only be translated: '*in the presence of* Peter and Paul I have celebrated a refrigerium,' and must be understood by every unprejudiced reader to mean '*at the grave of* Peter and Paul.' That some one might have written *Petro et Paulo refrigerium feci*, which La Piana with perfect propriety

[23] Styger, Diss. pont. acc., p. 88: "Possono essere assegnate alla seconda metà del III secolo. Ciò è fuori di ogni dubbio, perchè mancano affatto in esse i caratteri della decadenza, che già si rivelano nel IV secolo avanzato." He expresses the same opinion in his earlier publications.

[24] Styger, Diss. pont. acc., plate II, on the right, below. Styger, p. 61, reads *Paulu[m]*, but the *o* is clearly recognizable. The sense is the same with either reading; *at* is equivalent to *ad*, and, as often, is construed with an ablative; cf. Diehl, Vulgärlateinische Inschriften (Kleine Texte 62), Nos. 1293 ff.

renders 'in honor of Peter and Paul,' is by no means inconsistent with my contention. It is well known that martyrs were chiefly venerated at their graves; but that *refrigeria* were celebrated in their honor anywhere else than at or very near their graves has never been proved or even made probable.

I agree with my critic in his conclusion that we are "still far from having the positive proof of the assumed translation." But I still believe that by the recent excavations ad Catacumbas the probability of the view which I have urged has been considerably increased, and I hope that the future work of the spade will confirm the results reached by study of the written documents.

THE DOMED CHURCH AS MICROCOSM:
LITERARY ROOTS OF AN ARCHITECTURAL SYMBOL[1]

KATHLEEN E. McVEY

In discussion of the domed, centrally-planned church typical of the Byzantine period, historians of art and architecture commonly refer to the "dome of heaven" and to the notion of the church as microcosm.[2] An important step in the application of these interpretations to sixth-century church buildings in general, and especially to Hagia Sophia in Constantinople, is provided by a Syriac hymn on another Hagia Sophia, the cathedral church of Edessa.[3] This hymn was most probably composed for the occasion of the dedication of the church after its Justinianic reconstruction, com-

pleted *ca.* A.D. 543–554.[4] It is the earliest extant document which associates the central dome (and other architectural features) of a Christian church with cosmology and mystical theology. Hence the hymn provides the first literary evidence for the popularization of the notion of the "dome of heaven" among Christians of the mid-sixth century.

Given the importance of this hymn for interpretations of Byzantine architecture, it is perhaps inevitable that it should be seen by some (e.g., E. A. Baldwin Smith) as typically Syrian and Near Eastern, whereas others (e.g., A. Grabar) see it as Syriac in language only but Greek in spirit.[5] The same dichotomy that characterizes the discussion of Byzantine art history in general is present in the discussion of this piece. While recognizing the interest and importance inherent in this discussion of the larger cultural context, I will attempt here to look more closely at the immediate literary and intellectual environment of this hymn, deliberately avoiding the presupposition of either a Near Eastern or a Greek background. This approach seems to me to be the most fruitful, given the complex cultural ambiance of sixth-century Edessa.

[1] An earlier version of the present paper was delivered at the Spring Symposium at Dumbarton Oaks, May 1980. I have benefited from discussions of this subject with too many persons to be able to name them all here. I am especially grateful to Ernst Kitzinger for suggesting that I undertake this study, and to Thomas Mathews, Glen Bowersock, and Corby Finney for numerous helpful suggestions and criticisms.
[2] E. A. Baldwin Smith, *The Dome of Heaven* (hereafter, *Dome*) (Princeton, 1950), 88 f.; K. Lehmann, *Art Bulletin*, 27 (1945), 1 ff.; A. Grabar, *The Art of the Byzantine Empire: Byzantine Art in the Middle Ages* (hereafter, *Byzantine Art*) (New York, 1966), 68 f., 77, 106; H. Kähler and C. Mango, *Hagia Sophia* (London, 1967), 11; W. L. MacDonald, *Early Christian and Byzantine Architecture* (New York, 1962), 33; J. B. Ward Perkins, *Proceedings of the British Academy*, 51 (1965), 198 ff.; R. Krautheimer, *Early Christian and Byzantine Architecture*, 3rd ed. (Baltimore, 1979), 230. For a recent critique of Lehmann's view, cf. T. F. Mathews, "Cracks in Lehmann's 'Dome of Heaven,'" *Source: Notes in the History of Art*, 1, no. 3 (Spring 1982), 12–16.

[3] Explicit references to this hymn in Smith, *Dome*, 74, 89–91 *et passim*; Grabar, *Byzantine Art*, 106; and Krautheimer, *op. cit.*, 230; and in R. W. Thomson, "Architectural Symbolism in Classical Armenian Literature," *JThS*, n.s., 30 (1979), 102–14, mention of the Syriac hymn, 111. For the Syriac text, translations, and studies of the Edessa Hymn: Syriac text, German translation, and the history of the building, by H. Goussen, "Über eine 'sugitha' auf die Kathedrale von Edessa," *Le Muséon*, 38 (1925), 117–36; another German translation with comments by A. M. Schneider, "Die Kathedrale von Edessa" (hereafter "Die Kathedrale"), *OrChr*, 36 (1941), 161–67; French translation and textual commentary by A. Dupont-Sommer with a study by A. Grabar, "Le témoignage d'un hymne syriaque sur l'architecture de la cathédrale d'Édesse au VIᵉ siècle et sur la symbolique de l'édifice chrétien" (hereafter, "Le témoignage"), *CahArch*, 2 (1947), 29–67; Eng. trans. C. Mango, *The Art of the Byzantine Empire* (Englewood Cliffs, New Jersey, 1972), 57–60.

[4] For discussion of the date, cf. notes 123 f. *infra*; Averil Cameron, "The Sceptic and the Shroud" (hereafter "Shroud"). Inaugural Lecture, Departments of Classics and History, King's College (London, April 29, 1980), 23 f. note 46, argues for a later date, 553/4.
[5] Cf. works cited in notes 2, 3 *supra*. On Grabar's views, cf. Appendix 1.

I. The Syriac Text[6]

ܣܘܓܝܬܐ ܐܚܪܬܐ[1]

ܐܝܬܝܐ ܕܫܪܐ ܒܗܝܟܠܗ̇ ܩܕܝܫܐ 1
ܕܫܘܒܚܗ ܡܢܗ ܗܘ ܒܟܝܢܗ̇.
ܗܒ ܠܝ ܡܘܗܒܬܐ ܕܪܘܚܩܘܕܫܐ
ܕܥܠ ܗܝܟܠܐ ܕܒܐܘܪܗܝ ܐܡܠܠ.
ܒܨܠܐܝܠ ܡܫܟܢܐ ܥܒܕ ܠܗ 2
ܒܛܘܦܣܐ ܗܘ ܕܠܗ ܡܢ ܡܘܫܐ.
ܘܐܡܝܕܘܢܝܣ ܘܐܣܦ ܘܐܕܝ
ܗܝܟܠܐ ܫܒܝܚܐ ܒܢܘ ܠܟ ܒܐܘܪܗܝ.[2]
ܓܠܝܬ ܕܝܢ ܒܗ ܐܝܪܐ[3] 3
ܘܐܫܬܬܐܣܬ[4] ܘܕܡܫܒܚܬܐ.
ܘܐܝܟ ܕܫܡܝܐ ܡܬܦܫܛܬ
ܗܕܝܪܐ ܡܐܬܠܐ ܒܚܘܪܬܗ.[5]
ܘܡܕܒܪܐ ܗܘ ܕܝܢ ܥܒܝܪܬܐ. 4
ܐܝܟ ܕܠܟܠܗܐ ܪܘܚܐ ܕܩܘܕܫܗ.[6]
ܠܐ ܒܡܫܘܚܬܐ ܐܠܐ ܒܛܘܦܣܐ.
ܘܐܝܟ[7] ܝܡܐ ܡ̈ܝܐ ܚܕܪܝܢ ܠܗ.
ܗܐ ܬܛܠܝܠܗ ܡܬܬܚ ܐܝܟ ܫܡܝܐ 5
ܘܕܠܐ ܥܡܘ̈ܕܐ ܟܦܝܦ ܘܦܫܝܛ.
ܘܨܒܝܬ[8] ܬܘܒ[9] ܒܦܣܦܣܐ ܕܕܗܒܐ
ܐܝܟ ܪܩܝܥܐ[10] ܒܟܘܟ̈ܒܐ ܢܗܝ̈ܪܐ.
ܘܦܪܘܠܘܣ[11] ܕܠܗ ܠܟܠܐ. 6
ܠܥܠ ܫܡܝܐ ܗܘ[12] ܡܬܕܡܐ.[13]
ܘܟܒܫܬܐ[14] ܣܘܪܬܐ ܡܫܬܟܚܬ[15]

1 ܥܠ ܥܕܬܐ ܕܐܘܪܗܝ B
2 ܐܦ ܐܕܝ. ܥܠܝܐ ܘܐܡܘܕܘܢܣ B
3 ܐܝܪܐ ܕܝܢ ܒܗ ܘ B
4 i < B
5 ܒܚܙܬܗ B
6 ܕܠܠܟܠܐ ܕܪܒܐ ܐܘܬܗ B
7 ܕܐܝܟ B
8 i < B
9 ܕܟ B
10 ܪܩܝܥܐ B
11 ܘܦܪܘܠܘܣ B; lege ܦܪܘܠܐ
12 < B
13 + ܗܘ B
14 i < B
15 ܕܡܫܒܚܐ B

[6] The text of the hymn was published by Goussen, *op. cit.*, 119 f., based on Vat. Syr. 95 (folios 49v–50v), a thirteenth-century collection of hymns in a serto hand. (Cf. S. E. Assemani, *Bibliothecae Apostolicae Vaticanae codicum mss. catalogus in tres partes distributus*, Part I, vols. 2 and 3 [Rome, 1758–59; repr. Paris, 1926], where, however, the MS is incorrectly identified as being in an estrangelo hand.) As published, however, the text of the hymn contains numerous errors. That the errors are simply misprints is shown by Goussen's translation, which agrees in all essential respects with my own. Since the textual errors have caused some confusion in subsequent studies of the piece, it seems useful to present an accurate text here. Further, a second MS of the hymn is to be found in Br. Lib. Add. 17,141 (fols. 109b–110a), a collection of hymns ascribed to Ephrem, Isaac of Antioch and Jacob of Sarug. This MS dates to the eighth or ninth cent., but the Edessa Hymn has been added by a later hand, which Wright did not attempt to date (cf. W. Wright, *Catalogue of the Syriac Manuscripts in the British Museum acquired since the year 1838*, 2 vols. [London, 1870–72], 362). The Vatican MS remains a more appropriate choice as the basic MS since the British Library MS (identified in the apparatus as B) contains several lacunae and errors. B's variant readings have been incorporated into the critical apparatus; orthographic errors have been ignored; the general method of edition is as in the *Corpus Scriptorum Christianorum Orientalium*. I am grateful to Aelred Cody for examining the Vatican MS for me when I began this study. Although I was subsequently able to view both MSS myself, his preliminary assistance and observations were most valuable.

[Syriac text, verses 16–37]

---

16 i + ܢ B
17 [Syriac] err B
18 [Syriac] B; lege as if [Syriac] but modified for the sake of the alphabetic acrostic
19 [Syriac] B
20 [Syriac] B
21 [Syriac] B
22 [Syriac] B
23 < v. 8 err B
24 cum punct. fem. B
25 i < B
26 i + ܢ B
27 [Syriac] B
28 i + ܐ B
29 [Syriac] B
30 < v. 11 c, d err B
31 interlin 1° m. B
32 cum punct. fem. B
33 cum suff. fem. B
34 [Syriac] B
35 [Syriac] B
36 [Syriac] B
37 lege + [Syriac] B

15

16

17

18

19

20

21

22

---

38 < v. 13 c, d et 14 err B

39 ܟܚܒܝ B

40 ܂ < B

41 ܒܪ ܢܚܒ B

42 ܘܚܒ ܚܒܢ ܚܒܝ ܚܒܠ B

43 ܐܚܒܪ B

44 ܒܪ ܢܒ B

45 ܟܚܒܘܬܚܒ B

46 ܗܒܢܒܝ B

47 ܐܚܒܢܗܕ B

48 ܒܪ ܢܚܒ ܗܘܘ B

49 < v. 19-22 err B,
   ܗܘܢܐ ܒ ܚܒܪ ܕܢܚܒ ܒܝܪ ܚܒܪܬܚܒܕ ܐܚܒ B

II. Translation

ANOTHER SOGITHA

1 Oh Being Itself who dwells in the holy Temple, whose glory naturally [emanates] from it,
Grant me the grace of the Holy Spirit to speak about the Temple that is in Urha.

2 Bezalel constructed the Tabernacle for us with the model he learned from Moses,
And Amidonius and Asaph and Addai built a glorious temple for You in Urha.

3 Clearly portrayed in it are the mysteries of both Your Essence and Your Dispensation.
He who looks closely will be filled at length with wonder.

4 For it truly is a wonder that its smallness is like the wide world,
Not in size but in type; like the sea, waters surround it.

5 Behold! Its ceiling is stretched out like the sky and without columns [it is] arched and simple,
And it is also decorated with golden mosaic, as the firmament [is] with shining stars.

6 And its lofty dome—behold, it resembles the highest heaven,
And like a helmet it is firmly placed on its lower [part].

7 The splendor of its broad arches—they portray the four ends of the earth.
They resemble also by the variety of their colors the glorious rainbow.

8 Other arches surround it like crags jutting out from a mountain,
Upon, by and through which its entire ceiling is fastened on the vaults.

9 Its marble resembles an image not [made] by hands, and its walls are suitably overlaid [with marble].
And from its brightness, polished and white, light gathers in it like the sun.

10 Lead was put on its roof so it would not be damaged by streams of rain;
There is no wood at all in its ceiling, which is as if entirely cast from stone.

11 It is surrounded by magnificent courts with two porticoes composed of columns
Which portray the tribes of Israelites who surrounded the [temporal] Tabernacle.

12 On every side it has the same façade; the form of the three of them is one
Just as the form of the holy Trinity is one.

13 One light shines forth also in its sanctuary by three open windows,
And announces to us the mystery of the Trinity, of the Father and the Son and the Holy Spirit.

14 And the light of its three sides abides in many windows.
It portrays the apostles, Our Lord, the prophets, martyrs and confessors.

15 The ambo is placed in the middle of [the church] on the model of the Upper Room at Zion,
And under it are eleven columns, like the eleven apostles that were hidden.

16 The column that is behind the ambo portrays Golgotha in its form,
And fastened above it is the cross of light, like Our Lord between the thieves.

17 Five doors open into [the church] like the five virgins,
And the faithful enter by them, gloriously like the virgins to the bridal couch of light.

18 Portrayed by the ten columns that support the Cherubim of its altar
Are the ten apostles, those who fled at the time that our Savior was crucified.

19 The structure of nine steps that are placed in the sanctuary of [the church] together with the *synthronos*
Portrays the throne of Christ and the nine orders of angels.

20 Exalted are the mysteries of this temple in which heaven and earth
Symbolize the most exalted Trinity and our Savior's Dispensation.

21 The apostles, [the church's] foundations in the Holy Spirit, and prophets and martyrs are symbolized in it.
By the prayer of the Blessed Mother may their memory abide above in heaven.

22 May the most exalted Trinity that strengthened those who built [the church]
Keep us from all evils and preserve us from injuries.

III. Commentary on the Text and Translation

TITLE

Another Sogitha:
While the Vatican manuscript has simply "another sogitha," the British Museum manuscript says, "On the great church of Urha." Neither is likely to be the original title, if there was one—the first, for obvious reasons; the second, because the hymn consistently refers to the "temple" rather than the "church."

STR. 1.

Being Itself:
The Syriac word used here (*îthyâ*) occurred in Ephrem's *Commentary on Genesis* and in Narsai's *Homilies on Genesis* with the specific meaning of "Being Itself" applicable only to God. In Ephrem's commentary (especially Intro. 4; I,2 and I,16) God as "Being Itself" is contrasted with the five elements created *ex nihilo* (heaven, earth, fire, water, and wind), as well as with the rest of the material world, made from these first five elements.[7] Either from Ephrem or, more probably, from Theodore of Mopsuestia, Narsai adopted the same exclusive use of the term for God and further specified that not even the three persons of the Trinity might be referred to as *îthyê* (pl.), but only the Godhead in its unity is "Being Itself."[8]

In contrast, Stephen bar Sudaili used a transliteration of the Greek οὐσία for the Deity as well as for all creatures, rational and irrational.[9] This is as one might expect in Stephen's ontologically fluid Origenistic system. On this point the Edessa Hymn has no apparent Origenistic heritage.

Dupont-Sommer had suggested that "Essence" (οὐσία) rather than "Being" was an appropriate translation of *îthyâ* here. Grabar then argued that this was one of the Pseudo-Dionysian features of the hymn.[10] But the use of the term by Ephrem and Narsai indicates that a Pseudo-Dionysian connection is not self-evident. The influence of Ephrem or of the Antiochene School is most probable here.

Temple:
The choice of the Syriac word *hayklâ* (temple, palace, or church) here is provocative. Either *'idhthâ* (assembly, congregation, church = ἐκκλησία) or *knûšthâ* (congregation, synagogue) would have been acceptable from the metric standpoint. Most probably the choice was deliberate, emphasizing the building as a holy place, independent of the presence or absence of a congregation. The cosmic temple is a common theme in Hellenistic Greek literature which was appropriated by early Christian writers, at first primarily as a description of the individual believer or of the believing community and eventually, in Eusebius' speech on the church at Tyre, to describe the church building.[11]

Some connection with early Jewish mysticism is possible. Among the most important literary remains of early Jewish mysticism are the *Hekhaloth Books*, so named because they contain descriptions of the seven heavenly palaces (*hekhaloth*) through which the visionary passes en route to the vision of the throne of glory. Some of these materials date to the second century and were edited in the fifth or sixth century A.D. to their present form. The texts were being edited and translated by Gershom Scholem, but their history and literary context are not yet clear.[12]

On the basis of John 2:19,21, Dupont-Sommer suggested that the Temple is not primarily the church building but Christ.[13] This is an interesting hypothesis but needs corroboration in contemporaneous sources.

Whose glory . . . from it:
The Syriac text here allows four distinct translations:

[7] R. M. Tonneau, ed. and Latin trans., *Sancti Ephraem Syri in Genesim et Exodum Commentarii*, CSCO, 152, 153 (Louvain, 1955); Ephrem's use of the word is discussed by Nabil El-Khoury in *Die Interpretation der Welt bei Ephraem dem Syrer*, Tübinger Theologische Studien, 6 (Tübingen, 1976), 65–81.

[8] P. Gignoux, ed., trans., intro., *Homélies de Narsaï sur la Création* (hereafter, *Homélies de Narsaï*), PO, 34 (Paris, 1968), 433 ff., 465, 472, and all references to "L'Etre par soi" in the index, 709.

[9] F. S. Marsh, ed., trans., *The Book which is called The Book of the Holy Hierotheos with Extracts from the Prolegomena and Commentary of Theodosius of Antioch and from the "Book of Excerpts" and other works of Gregory Bar Hebraeus* (London-Oxford, 1927), 230. Further on Stephen, cf. notes to strophe 19 *infra*. For an example in Jacob of Sarug, cf. notes to strophe 12 *infra*.

[10] Dupont-Sommer, *op. cit.*, 32 f. (*supra*, note 3), and Grabar, "Le témoignage," 55.

[11] On the Hellenistic τόπος of Temple-House-Cosmos, cf. A. J. Festugière, *La Révélation d'Hermès Trismégiste*, II, *Le Dieu cosmique* (Paris, 1949), 233–38. For early Christian use of this theme, cf. R. Bornert, *Les commentaires byzantins de la divine liturgie du VII' au XV' siècle* (hereafter, *Commentaires*), AOC, 9 (Paris, 1966), 99 f.; for a more extensive treatment, cf. P. C. Finney, "TOPOS HIEROS und christlicher Sakralbau in vorkonstantinischer Überlieferung," *RQ* (forthcoming).

[12] For an introductory discussion, cf. G. Scholem, *Major Trends in Jewish Mysticism* (Jerusalem, 1941), 42–78; and more recently, cf. *idem*, *Kabbalah* (New York, 1974), 14–20, 373–76. For an enumeration of the sources, cf. *idem*, *Jewish Gnosticism, Merkabah Mysticism and Talmudic Tradition* (New York, 1960), 5–7.

[13] Dupont-Sommer, *loc. cit.* (*supra*, note 3).

1. God's glory [emanates] naturally from Himself
2. God's glory [emanates] naturally from the Temple
3. The glory of the Temple [emanates] naturally from God (Dupont-Sommer, Mango)
4. The glory of the Temple [emanates] naturally from itself (Goussen, Schneider)

The second possibility—that God's glory flows forth naturally from the Temple, i.e., from the church building—is both simple and internally consistent with the rest of the hymn. Proceeding from his Christological interpretation of the Temple, Dupont-Sommer argued for the third translation (above) as a statement of the divinity of the Son. He added further that the verse as a whole thereby gains a Trinitarian interpretation, the Father being the Divine Essence, the Son the Temple, and the Holy Spirit mentioned as such.[13a] His interpretation is ingenious but not compelling.

Similar phrases occur in Narsai's *Homilies on Creation*, though his intent is more clearly anti-Origenistic. Without rejecting the immanence of God altogether, Narsai is clearly concerned to emphasize His transcendence over the creation:

"His glory is in His nature
and His majesty is with His Essence.
He neither decreases nor increases,
for His nature is too great for these things."
(III, 376 f.)
"By the power that (flows) from Me,
I made heaven and earth and all that is in them."
(God to Moses; III, 18)
(Also cf. V, 363–380 on the glory of God.[14])
The theological position of the Edessa Hymn on this point is not discernible.

Urha:
The Syriac uses the Semitic name of the city, Urha, rather than the Hellenistic Greek name, Edessa.[15]

STR. 2.

Bezalel:
Bezalel was the artisan chosen by God to direct the construction of the Tabernacle according to the instructions given by God to Moses (Exodus 35:30 ff.).

[13a] *Ibid.*
[14] Ginoux, *Homélies de Narsaï*.
[15] For the history of the city and its name, cf. E. Kirsten, "Edessa," *RAC*, 4, 552–97, or J. B. Segal, *Edessa: the Blessed City* (hereafter, *Edessa*) (Oxford, 1970), 1–6 *et passim*.

Tabernacle:
The description of the construction of the Tabernacle in Exodus 25–27 was the focus of cosmological speculation for both Jews and Christians in the early Christian centuries. A portion of this speculative exegetical literature forms the matrix of the symbolism of the present hymn. Scholars are divided on the question of the dating of some of the important Jewish materials. While Scholem thinks the Shekinah as a full feminine counterpart to Yahweh develops only in the medieval Kabbalah, Patai argues that this notion dates to the Midrashic period.[16] Comprehensive discussion of the Jewish materials has not been attempted here, not only because of the difficulties inherent in that subject, but also because it is fairly unlikely that they exercised any direct influence on a Christian hymn composed as late as the mid-sixth century c.e.[17] The Christian materials will be discussed in the body of the paper.

Model:
Like its Greek cognate, τύπος, the Syriac *ṭûpsâ* means "form," "model," "representation," or "image." Dupont-Sommer noted that it was a *terminus technicus* of theology, but he did not specify its importance in the context of early Christian biblical interpretation.[18]

Even before the fifth-century translations into Syriac of the commentaries of Theodore of Mopsuestia and Diodore of Tarsus, this terminology was established in Syriac literature. Both Aphrahat and Ephrem use the Syriac *ṭûpsâ* synonymously with *râzâ*, mystery (= Greek μυστήριον), giving both words primarily the force of a Christological symbol.[19] The symbolism may have Scripture as its primary matrix with various figures from the Old Testament interpreted as types of Christ. Or Christ as the Paschal Lamb may be interpreted in a sacramental matrix

---

[16] G. Scholem, *On the Kabbalah and its Symbolism* (New York, 1965), 104 f.; R. Patai, *The Hebrew Goddess* (New York, 1967), 137–56. For a recent discussion, cf. M. Pope, *The Song of Songs, A New Translation with Introduction and Commentary*, The Anchor Bible, VII, c (New York, 1977), 153 ff., esp. 158–61.
[17] S. Brock, "Jewish Traditions in Syriac Sources," *JJS*, 30 (1979), 212–32, esp. 226–28.
[18] Dupont-Sommer, *op. cit.*, 33. The considerable literature on the history of exegesis which has appeared since Dupont-Sommer's work cannot be cited here. But a fundamental understanding of the use of the term "typos" in Greek Christian exegesis may be gained from the following works: G. W. H. Lampe and K. J. Woollcombe, *Essays on Typology* (London, 1957); *The Cambridge History of the Bible*, I, *From the Beginnings to Jerome*, ed. P. R. Ackroyd and C. G. Evans (Cambridge, 1970), esp. essays by R. P. C. Hanson and M. F. Wiles, 412–509.
[19] E. Beck, "Symbolum-Mysterium bei Aphraat und Ephräm" (hereafter, "Symbolum"), *OrChr*, 42 (1958), 19–40.

as the central mystery of salvation symbolically realized in the sacraments (eucharist, baptism, and myron). Ephrem extends the use of the term mystery (*râzâ*) to the names of the Trinity as well.[20]

The language of typology and symbolism recurs throughout the Edessa Hymn, specifically:

ṭûpsâ translated as "model," "type," or "form" in strophes 2, 4, 12, and 15

ṭps (also from Greek τύπος) translated "symbolize" in strophes 20, 21

râzâ, "mystery" in strophes 3, 13, 20

ẓwr, "portray" in strophes 7, 11, 14, 16, 18, 19

dmʾ, "resemble" in strophes 6, 7

ṭbʿ, "resemble" in strophe 9

ʾaykh, "like" in strophes 4, 5, 6, 8, 9, 16, 17d

bʾdhmôth "like" in strophe 17b

ʾaykanâ d, "just as" in strophe 12

Amidonius, Asaph, and Addai:

Goussen's suggestions that Amidonius was the thirty-eighth Bishop of Edessa (Amazon)—a Chalcedonian—and that Asaph and Addai were the architects, have won general acceptance.[21]

STR. 3.

Essence:

The Syriac word *îthûthâ* may be used for either οὐσία or ὑπόστασις in Greek.

Dispensation:

The Syriac word is the equivalent of Greek οἰκονομία. The distinction between theology and economy is common in the Patristic period. Since it continues to play an important role for all three parties in the Christological controversies,[22] its prominence here does not help to define the theological commitment of the hymn's author.

will be filled with wonder:

A sense of awe is awakened in the viewer of God's mysteries as revealed through the building. A similar notion with more explicit anagogical overtones is found in Procopius' *On Buildings*, I.I.61: "And whenever anyone enters this church to pray, he understands at once that it is not by any human power or skill, but by the influence of God that this work has been so finely turned. And so his mind is lifted up toward God and exalted, feeling that He

cannot be far away, but must especially love to dwell in this place which He has chosen."[23]

STR. 4.

like the wide world:

That the cosmos is like a building and, conversely, that certain buildings—house, temple, and palace—are like the cosmos, was a popular notion widespread in the ancient Near East.[24] This tradition continued especially in the exegetical tradition of Christian Antioch, where the cosmos was commonly portrayed as a building, often a two-storeyed structure.[25]

Waters surround it:

The church was actually situated between two streams and adjacent to a pond.[26] The entire city of Edessa itself was, in a sense, surrounded by water. The River Skirtos (Daiṣan) ran through it, and several springs and pools were within—some of them reputed to have healing properties and containing fish sacred to Atargatis.[27]

This topographical reality corresponded readily to the popular cosmology of the Near East. Of the Sumerians, for example, Harrelson observes: "The abode of the gods was the upper heavens, a region quite distinct from the world of men. The earth, conceived of as a disc surrounded by waters and anchored to mountain peaks below its surface, was separated from heaven by the open sky and especially by the firmament, a solid substance holding the upper waters in place and preventing their rushing in upon the earth. The underworld contained vast seas and land areas as well, the latter containing the abode of the dead."[28] The biblical accounts of creation, especially the Priestly account, share this basic cosmology.[29]

---

[20] Cf. notes to strophe 13 *infra*.

[21] Goussen, *op. cit.*, 121 f.

[22] Cf. J. Pelikan, *The Spirit of Eastern Christendom (600–1700)* (Chicago, 1974), 76 *et passim*.

[23] Noted by A. Cameron, in F. C. Corippus, *In laudem Iustini Augusti minoris*, bk. IV (London, 1976), 207.

[24] For general discussion of Near Eastern cosmology as well as the notion of heavenly archetypes and their relation to worship, cf. W. Harrelson, *From Fertility Cult to Worship* (New York, 1969), esp. 1–18.

[25] W. Wolska, *La Topographie Chrétienne de Cosmas Indicopleustes. Théologie et Science au VIᵉ siècle* (hereafter, *Topographie*) (Paris, 1962), esp. 136–42. Also cf. Part VII of the present study.

[26] Segal, *Edessa*, 189 and Plan I, 262 f.

[27] *Ibid.*, 6–8, 48 f., 54–56.

[28] Harrelson, *op. cit.*, 2.

[29] For a translation of the *Enûma Elish*, the Babylonian creation myth, with discussion of its relation to the account in Genesis 1–2, cf. Alexander Heidel, *The Babylonian Genesis. The Story of the Creation* (Chicago, 1942). The extensive secondary literature on this subject cannot be fully cited here, but particularly useful at an introductory level are: Nahum Sarna, *Understanding*

This cosmology was maintained in the early Christian period by the Antiochene school of exegesis. In Alexandria in the mid-sixth century, cosmology became an explicit subject of debate between representatives of the Antiochene and Alexandrian Christian traditions. Cosmas Indicopleustes, a Nestorian, representing the biblical cosmology and the Antiochene theological system, contended against John Philoponus, a Monophysite, who defended the Ptolemaic cosmology and, implicitly, the Alexandrian tradition.[30] Even Cosmas' views had been affected by a variety of Greek and other influences.[31] Unlike the created order described in Genesis, his cosmos is suspended over nothingness rather than over water. Cosmas still thinks of the earth as surrounded by water, but now it is the land mass surrounded by the ocean on a disc, all of it suspended over the void.[32] Jacob of Sarug is in agreement with Cosmas on this point.[33]

STRS. 5–6.

ceiling . . . sky; dome . . . highest heaven:

Citing strophe 8 where the entire ceiling is said to be supported by the arches, Grabar argued that the ceiling and the dome are synonymous, as are the sky and the highest heaven which they represent.[34] This identification is necessary if the form of the church is a cube surmounted by a dome, as Grabar contended. But the language of the hymn itself does not support this interpretation. Instead the ceiling, which represents the sky, and the dome, which represents the highest heaven, seem, both architecturally and symbolically, to be two different entities. On this point Schneider's interpretation is more acceptable.

STR. 5.

without columns:

For Grabar this phrase stresses the contrast between the structure of this church and the basilicas as well as most contemporaneous domed churches which utilized columns to support the dome.[35] Whatever the architecture, a literary allusion to the Hexaemera of the Antiochene School is likely. It is a commonplace of this tradition to contrast God's manner of building with the human approach, since God constructed the cosmos from the top downward, first miraculously suspending the ceiling, then adding the lower structures.[36] The absence of columns or other supports under the earth is also stressed by both Cosmas and Jacob—a rejection of the Ionian cosmology.[37]

mosaic:

Dupont-Sommer corrected the previous translations at this point.[38]

STR. 6.

helmet:

Smith suggested that the helmet is another cosmological symbol, in this case connected with the cult of the Dioskuri as well as with Hittite mythology. He adduced parallels in Josephus on the miter of the High Priest, and in Paul the Silentiary on the dome of Hagia Sophia of Constantinople.[39]

STR. 7.

The splendor of its broad arches:

Here the translation differs from earlier renderings, because of the correction of the text. The manuscripts have "broad" in the plural, thus modifying "arches" (pl.) rather than "splendor" (sing.). Word order and meter support the plural reading as well. *Zalgûthâ*, a word unattested elsewhere, is apparently to be taken as *mazlᵉgûthâ*. The exigencies of the alphabetical acrostic best explain the poet's neologism as well as the odd phraseology.

This strophe, together with strophes 12 and 14, provides the principal evidence for Schneider's reconstruction of the building as a cruciform church, since they seem to indicate that there are four arches

---

Genesis: The Heritage of Biblical Israel (New York, 1966); and S. H. Hooke, *Middle Eastern Mythology* (Baltimore, 1963), esp. 117–21.

[30] Wolska, *Topographie*, esp. 147–92. The sixth-century discussion did not settle this issue for Byzantine Christians. For a twelfth-century description of Hagia Sophia of Constantinople which shares the Edessa Hymn's interest in cosmology and architectural mysticism but differs in choosing the Ptolemaic rather than the Antiochene biblical cosmology, cf. C. Mango and J. Parker, "A Twelfth-century Description of St. Sophia," *DOP*, 14 (1960), 233–45, esp. 237 ff.

[31] Wolska, *Topographie*, 219–44.

[32] *Ibid.*, 260 ff.

[33] Jacob's homilies in hexaemeron are discussed in detail in part VII of this paper.

[34] That is, *ṭlilâ* = *ṭrûllôs* and *šmay* = *šmay šmayâ*; cf. Grabar, "Le témoignage" (*supra*, note 3), 45.

[35] *Ibid.*

[36] T. Jansma, "L'Hexameron de Jacques de Saroug" (hereafter, "Hexameron"), *OrSyr*, 4 (1959), 18 f., 21, 39, 41, 282.

[37] Cf. Wolska, *Topographie*, 220 f.

[38] Dupont-Sommer, *op. cit.*, 33 f.

[39] Smith, *Dome*, 77–79.

opening in the four cardinal directions. Dupont-Sommer agreed with this interpretation and added the suggestion that the arches most probably owed their colorful splendor to mosaic decoration.

Numerical symbolism appears in this strophe and then figures significantly in strophes 11–19. Early Christian exegesis in general included symbolic interpretation of numbers. Pythagorean lore made its way into Christian exegesis through Philo and the Alexandrian Christian exegetes to Augustine in the West.[40] Less elaborate numerology found a place in the hexaemera of Basil of Caesarea and others, whose influence is felt in Jacob of Sarug's Syriac homilies in hexaemeron.[41] More intricate and esoteric numerical speculation entered the Syriac-speaking environment with the writings of Evagrius of Pontus.[42] The Pseudo-Dionysian writings, while sharing this interest with the hymn's author, as Grabar noted,[43] merely share a commonplace. The hymn's numerological allusions do not correspond consistently with any particular school of thought. The number four is almost universally a sacred number. Its association with the "ends of the earth" is typical of the language of the Bible and does not necessarily imply the rejection of a spherical cosmos.[44]

STR. 8.

Other arches . . . ceiling:

Dupont-Sommer and Grabar argued that these arches were the squinches which supported the central dome of the church and that, therefore, the "ceiling" mentioned here must actually be the dome.[45] An interpretation which maintains a distinction between the ceiling and the dome would

be preferable.[46] The Syriac here translated "arches" could be read as "vaults" or "hollows," allowing even the possibility that the half-domes of a cubic triconch are meant.[47]

STR. 9.

Its marble resembles an image not [made] by hands:

This phrase has provoked considerable discussion. Since Edessa was the home of one of the most famous ἀχειροποίητοι of the Byzantine period, scholars have assumed that this is an allusion to that icon and that, therefore, the date of discovery of the icon provides a terminus post quem for the hymn or, conversely, that the hymn provides a terminus ante quem for the icon.[48] This assumption led Goussen to translate *ṭbiᶜ b* as "set in": "Eingelassen in seinen Marmor ist das ohne Hände gemachte Bild."[49] Schneider followed Goussen on this point.[50] Dupont-Sommer proposed a very different translation: "Son marbre est semblable à l'Image non faite de main."[51] Mango adopted this interpretation,[52] as I have also.

Dupont-Sommer correctly observed that the earlier translations transposed the subject and object of the preposition. If *ṭbiᶜ* were taken in its literal sense, the marble would be "set into" the "image not [made] by hands" rather than vice versa—a translation which is scarcely adequate. Segal avoids this problem by translating: "Its marble bears the

---

[46] Cf. remarks on strophes 5–6 *supra*.

[47] Cf. remarks on strophe 12 *infra*.

[48] Apart from the present hymn, the earliest allusion to the *acheiropoïetos* of Edessa is in Evagrius, *Historia ecclesiastica*, IV.27, ed. J. Bidez and L. Parmentier (London, 1898; repr. Amsterdam, 1964). The classic study of the Image of Edessa is E. von Dobschütz, "Das Christusbild von Edessa," Kap. 5 of *Christusbilder: Untersuchungen zur Christlichen Legende, TU,* ser. 2, III (Leipzig, 1899), 102–96. Others are S. Runciman, "Some Remarks on the Image of Edessa," *Cambridge Historical Journal,* 3 (1931), 238–52; A. Grabar, *L'Iconoclasme byzantin* (Paris, 1957), 31 ff.; E. Kirsten, "Edessa" (*supra,* note 15), esp. 568–74; *idem,* "Edessa. Eine römische Grenzstadt des 4. bis 6. Jahrhunderts im Orient," *JbAChr,* 6 (1963), 145 ff.; P. Devos, "Égérie à Edesse. S. Thomas l'Apôtre. Le Roi Abgar," *AnalBoll,* 85 (1967), 381–400; Segal, *Edessa,* 76–78, 189, 250, *et passim*; H. J. W. Drijvers, "Hatra, Palmyra und Edessa," *Aufstieg und Niedergang der römischen Welt,* II.8 (Berlin, 1977), 893–906; Averil Cameron, "Images of Authority: Elites and Icons in Late Sixth-Century Byzantium," *Past and Present,* 84 (1979), 23 f. For a recent reassessment of the dating of the image of Edessa, with attention to the Edessa Hymn, cf. Cameron, "Shroud" (*supra,* note 4). For some additional bibliography, cf. *The Teaching of Addai,* trans. G. Howard, SBL Texts and Translations, 16 (Ann Arbor, 1981), viii f.

[49] Goussen, *op. cit.* (*supra,* note 3), 120, 122.

[50] Schneider, *op. cit.* (*supra,* note 3), 162.

[51] Dupont-Sommer, *op. cit.,* 31, 35.

[52] Mango, *Art of the Byzantine Empire* (*supra,* note 3), 58.

---

[40] V. F. Hopper, *Medieval Number Symbolism. Its sources, meaning and influence on thought and expression* (New York, 1938); Marie Comeau, *Saint Augustin, exégète du quatrième Evangile,* 2nd ed. (Paris, 1930), 127–42; M. Pontet, *L'exégèse de S. Augustin prédicateur* (Paris, 1945), 278–303.

[41] Jansma, "Hexameron," 4–43, 129–62, 253–85, esp. 40–42.

[42] A. Guillaumont, *Les 'Kephalaia Gnostica' d'Evagre le Pontique et l'Histoire de l'Origénisme chez les grecs et chez les syriens* (hereafter, *Kephalaia et l'Origénisme*), Patristica Sorboniensia, 5 (Paris, 1962), 34 f.

[43] Grabar, "Le témoignage," 56 f.

[44] For discussion and further bibliography, cf. Wolska, *Topographie,* 133–36. Numerical symbolism was popular among Armenian Christians as well. For a survey of Armenian interpretations with "possible sources and parallels in Greek or Syriac texts which were known in Armenia," cf. R. W. Thomson, "Number Symbolism and Patristic Exegesis in Some Early Armenian Writers," *Handes Amsorya,* 90 (1976), 117–138; on the number four, cf. 120–24.

[45] Dupont-Sommer, *op. cit.,* 34 f. (*supra,* note 3) Mango accepts this interpretation, *Art of the Byzantine Empire,* 58.

impress of the portrait [of Jesus, made] without [mortal] hands."[53] But M. Mundell has noted a difficulty with any translation which portrays the icon as attached to the wall of the church: such icons were not normally placed on permanent display.[54] Despite the issue raised by Mundell, Cameron has argued that the literal sense is more common and therefore to be preferred.[55]

The correct translation is the one proposed by Dupont-Sommer. In justification of his translation, he cited Brockelmann's entry of *similis* as the translation of *ṭbiᶜ b*.[56] Brockelmann had offered two references to Ephrem's *Commentary on Genesis* in support of this translation.[57] In the first Ephrem observed that Seth, in resembling Adam, prefigured the Son's likeness to the Father. In the second he simply said that Ishmael resembled his mother. The context of biblical commentary and the specific meaning of the first reference suggest that the connection between the literal and figurative meanings of *ṭb* is analogous to the meanings of the Greek τύπτω and τύπος, from which the notion of typological exegesis is derived. The Greek τύπτω has the literal meaning "to stamp, mold, impress," with reference to a coin or seal. From this the theological and philosophical meanings are derived. The Syriac Christian writers, in translating the Greek notions of biblical typology, most frequently used the cognate denominative verb *ṭapes* (from *ṭupsa* = Gk. τύπος). But occasionally at least Ephrem used *ṭbᶜ*, the literal Syriac equivalent of τύπτω. The author of the hymn has followed the latter course here.

Although our translation is compatible with the contemporaneous cult of icons, we must consider the possibility that the phrase in question does not allude at all to the famous icon. It is reasonable to construe the phrase *zûrthâ dlâ bʾidhîn* as an icon "not made by hands." Like its Greek counterpart, ἀχειροποίητος, however, the expression *dlâ bʾidhîn* oc-curs in the New Testament and in other early Christian writings in contexts which have no direct connection with the later cult of images.[58] Since the Edessa Hymn dates to the formative period of this piety,[59] we should not assume that the reference here is to be construed according to the Byzantine usage rather than according to the earlier Christian usage. That is, we should not assume that this is a reference to an icon or to the icon of Edessa without consideration of the possibility that it is a more general allusion to things not made by human craft, whether from the natural rather than the civilized world or from a heavenly rather than an earthly context. Since Syriac does not distinguish a definite from an indefinite article, this strophe could refer to the famous image of Edessa, as is usually assumed, or it could equally refer only to the general notion of an ἀχειροποίητος, as I have interpreted it here. In the latter case the line means that the pattern in the marble was like a picture made without human agency.[60]

STR. 10.

Lead . . . stone:

It is difficult to evaluate this strophe as an actual description of the architectural features involved. Grabar makes some suggestions but does not ad-

[53] Segal, *Edessa*, 189.

[54] M. Mundell, "Monophysite Church Decoration," in A. Bryer and J. Herrin, eds., *Iconoclasm* (Birmingham, 1977), 59–74, esp. 65.

[55] Cameron discusses this in "Shroud," 10, 25 note 47. Without addressing the grammatical difficulty noted by Dupont-Sommer, she cites the opinions of S. Brock, H. J. W. Drijvers and J. B. Segal in favor of the literal sense.

[56] C. Brockelmann, *Lexicon Syriacum* (Göttingen, 1928), 267b.

[57] *Ephraemi Syri opera omnia*, ed. P. Benedictus (Rome, 1737–43), 47c, 75E; cf. *Sancti Ephraem, Syri in Genesim et in Exodum commentarii* V.1 and XVIII.1, ed. and trans. R. M. Tonneau, CSCO (Louvain, 1955), v. 152, 54; v. 153, 43: In Seth autem, qui omnino similis fuit Adae, similitudo Filii figurata est qui *signatus* a *Patre*, suo genitore, sicut Seth ab Adam qui progenuit eum. v. 152, 82; v. 153, 68: Sara autem, quae vidit quantum *conformaretur matri eius Ismael*. . . .

[58] Von Dobschütz argued that there were four uses of ἀχειροποίητος distinct from and mostly antecedent to any reference to icons: (1) natural things, made by God rather than by human craft; (2) the human body; (3) heavenly things as opposed to their earthly images in a Platonic or Philonic context; (4) spiritual, as opposed to physical things. These uses, especially the latter two, are attested in the New Testament and in Patristic literature, notably in scriptural commentary on the New Testament passages (Mark 14:58; 2 Cor. 5:1, Col. 2:11; Heb. 8:2, 9:11, 9:23 ff.). The specific notion of icons as ἀχειροποίητος, according to von Dobschütz, does not occur until the Justinianic period (*op. cit.* [*supra*, note 48], esp. 37–39, 118*–122*). In most New Testament passages where the Greek uses ἀχειροποίητος, the Peshitta uses a phrase similar to or identical with the phrase used here in the Edessa Hymn: (1) *dlâ ᶜbidh bʾidhâyâ* in Mark 14:58, Heb. 9:11 and Heb. 9:24 (with slight modification); (2) *dlâ baᶜbâdh ʾidhâyâ* in 2 Cor. 5:1; (3) *dlâ bʾidhîn* in Col. 2:11. Other examples in Syriac which antedate the Edessa Hymn are unknown to me; cf. only R. Payne Smith, *Thesaurus Syriacus* (Oxford, 1979, 1901), 1547 (on *ʾidhâyâ*) and 2769 (τὰ χειροποίητα = *idola*, for the opposite to our phrase).

[59] E. Kitzinger, "The Cult of Images in the Period before Iconoclasm," *DOP*, 8 (1954), 85–150; *idem*. "Byzantine Art in the Period between Justinian and Iconoclasm," *Berichte zum XI. Internationalen Byzantinistenkongress* (1958), 41–50; A. Grabar, *L'Iconoclasme byzantin* (*supra*, note 48), 21 ff.; P. Brown, "A Dark-Age Crisis: Aspects of the Iconoclastic Controversy," *EHR*, 88 (1973), 1–34; Cameron, "Images of Authority" (*supra*, note 48).

[60] Mango (*Art of the Byzantine Empire*, 58 note 14) suggested the allusion was to the pattern in the marble but did not infer from this, as I do, that there was no allusion to the icon.

duce any parallels.[61] Smith infers from this strophe that the "pre-Justinianic church had a wooden cosmic dome like those on the Syrian martyria."[62] Early Christian speculation on the Tabernacle suggests a symbolic significance either alongside or in place of a literal significance. Gregory of Nyssa's description of the Tabernacle in his *Life of Moses*, 170 stresses the use of precious metals and very little wood.[63] Even that wood which is used is said to be "wood that does not rot."

STR. 11.

. . . columns Which portray the tribes of Israelites . . . :
This and similar statements in strophes 15 and 18, have parallels in Gregory of Nyssa's *Life of Moses*, 184, where apostles, teachers, and prophets and "all those who themselves support the Church and become lights through their own works are called 'pillars' and 'light.'"

STR. 12.

On every side it has the same façade:
Schneider translated this, "Jede Seite hat ein und dieselbe Fassade," and suggested that the church was cruciform. Grabar took essentially the same translation, "De chaque côté il possède une façade identique," but from it he argued that the church must be cubic rather than cruciform, or there would be more than three identical sides.[64] But the word they translated as "side" (Seite, côté) could equally be rendered "region, quarter, district" or, as in my translation, "part." (The same word was used in strophe 7 in the sense of the four "ends" of the earth.) Then Schneider's architectural interpretation would be as acceptable as Grabar's on this point. Neither reconstruction takes into account, however, the fact that the five doors (str. 17) make it impossible for the north, west, and south sides of the church to be the same. Both Schneider and Grabar assume that the unique side is the east, which would have an apse. An interesting alternative solution, mentioned by Grabar but hastily dismissed, is the cubic triconch, a cubic structure with central dome and three semicircular apses surmounted by half-domes, such as the churches at Mren and Ar-

tik in Armenia.[65] The three identical sides would then be the north, the south, and the east; the west side would differ in having doors rather than an apse. This type of church would also provide another interpretation of the "other arches" mentioned in strophe 8; they would be the three half-domes upon which the central dome was supported.

the form of the three . . . Trinity is one:
The number three served to remind many early Christian authors of the Trinity, from Theophilus of Antioch to Augustine and Jacob of Sarug.[66] Theophilus, in his description of the creation of the world, says, "the three days prior to the luminaries are types of the triad of God and his Logos and his Sophia."[67] In a similar context, his homilies in Hexaemeron, Jacob of Sarug reflects on the Nicene Trinity in a manner analogous to the hymn's: "The number three . . . is as fair as the first number, and it resembles it and comes from it and stands firm and exists. Three is one and thus also there are one. One is Being Itself (*îthyâ*) and one is the Trinity."[68]

STRS. 13–14.

One light shines forth . . . by three open windows:
The light shining through three windows as symbolic of the Trinity has partial parallels in Ephrem the Syrian, Pseudo-Dionysius, and Stephen bar Sudaili. Ephrem used the image of light or fire, heat and light, to represent the Trinity.[69] Grabar noted that Pseudo-Dionysius used the idea of light shining through several windows, yet remaining one.[70] Pseudo-Dionysius did not, how-

---

[61] Grabar, "Le témoignage," 44 (*supra*, note 3).
[62] Smith, *Dome* (*supra*, note 2), 90 f.
[63] For bibliography on Gregory's *Life of Moses*, cf. note 171 *infra*.
[64] Grabar, "Le témoignage," 46 note 3.

[65] *Ibid.*, 47. Grabar brings the Armenian churches back into the discussion as useful examples of the dome unsupported by columns, but rejects their plan and façade as a parallel to the church at Edessa, *ibid.*, 51. The reasoning seems circular. The possibility of Armenian architectural parallels is especially intriguing given the symbolic interpretation of church buildings in Armenian literature; see Thomson, "Architectural Symbolism" (*supra*, note 3).
[66] The number three as symbolic of the Trinity is simply taken for granted by Augustine, cf. G. Bonner, "Augustine as Biblical Scholar," *Cambridge History of the Bible*, I, eds. P. R. Ackroyd and C. F. Evans (Cambridge, 1970), 541–63, esp. 560.
[67] *Ad Autolycum* 15, ed. and trans. R. M. Grant, Oxford Early Christian Texts (Oxford, 1970), 52 f: καὶ αἱ τρεῖς ἡμέραι πρὸ τῶν φωστήρων γεγονυῖαι τύποι εἰσὶν τῆς τριάδος, τοῦ θεοῦ καὶ τοῦ λόγου αὐτοῦ καὶ τῆς σοφίας αὐτοῦ.
[68] *Homiliae selectae Mar Jacobi Sarugensis* (Paris-Leipzig, 1905–1910), 3, 141–42; cf. Jansma, "Hexaemeron" (*supra*, note 36), 40 f.
[69] *Hymnes de fide* 13.5 and 40.9–10. For discussion of the imagery, cf. E. Beck, "Symbolum" (*supra*, note 19), 19–40.
[70] *De divin. nominibus* II, 4; cf. Grabar, "Le témoignage," 56.

ever, relate this notion to the Trinity. An instance of imagery very similar to Pseudo-Dionysius' occurs in the *Book of the Holy Hierotheos* IV, 21: "For as at the time of sunrise, there may be found some wall facing the east, and therein, in turn, be many windows distinct from each other; in proportion to their multitude they also distribute the rays of the sun in separate beams, and the rays are numbered in proportion to the distinction of the windows. But if thou remove the essence (οὐσία) which causes distinctions, then all the separated rays return to be commingled in each other and in the essence that produced them."[71]

STR. 13.

the mystery of the Trinity, of the Father and the Son and the Holy Spirit:

For Ephrem the names of the Trinity are veiled revelations, or, as both he and the author of the hymn would express this notion, they are "mysteries" (*râzê*).[72]

STR. 15.

ambo:

As described here, the ambo (*bêma*) functioned as in Byzantine liturgical usage, i.e., it is a raised platform used only for chanting of litanies and readings, not for the seating of the clergy as in the East Syrian liturgical tradition.[73] This is clear because the altar and certainly the σύνθρονος are not on the *bêma* (cf. strs. 18, 19).

. . . the Upper Room at Zion . . . the eleven apostles that were hidden:

The allusion to the Upper Room and to the eleven hidden apostles suggests Acts 1:13 ff., the Pentecost narrative, or, more strongly, John 20:19 ff., which is also a commissioning of the apostles. In either case the emphasis is on apostolic and episcopal authority. Mark 14:15 ff. and parallels might suggest a eucharistic interpretation for the Upper Room, but there are twelve apostles present, and they are not in hiding.[74]

STR. 16.

column . . . portrays Golgotha:

The placement of a cross on a pillar behind the ambo (or *bêma*) is unattested in literary sources for the Byzantine and East and West Syrian liturgical traditions.[75] The Byzantine and West Syrian traditions placed the cross with the altar in the sanctuary (in the apse), while the East Syrians placed both on the *bêma* in the center of the church and thus at the symbolic center of the earth. These are the arrangements described by the eleventh-century Monophysite Yahya Ibn Jarir: "Le bîma, c'est-à-dire l'ambon (*al-manbar*) qui est au centre de la nef est la figure du Temple (*bayt al-maqdes*) qui se trouve au centre de la terre, et il est la figure du lieu ou notre Seigneur a été crucifié. Il est connu [sous le nom] de Golgotha, [ce lieu] ou la tête de notre père Adam était enterrée. . . . La croix qui se trouve sur le bîma, les Nestoriens l'y placent pour symboliser la crucifixion du Christ sur le Golgotha. La placer, d'après les autres confessions et sectes, sur l'autel, au sanctuaire, symbolise le Christ."[76]

The three liturgical traditions agree with the hymn in associating cross, altar or *bêma* with Golgotha, though the Nestorian liturgical arrangement is most compatible with their cosmological interpretation of Golgotha: "The temple then is the whole world. The *bêma* that is in the middle of the temple is the place of Jerusalem that is in the middle of the earth. The altar that is in the middle of the *bêma* fills the place of Golgotha.[77]

An earlier literary tradition underlies the interest of the liturgical commentaries in Golgotha. Cyril of Jerusalem interpreted Ps. 74:12, "Yet God my King is from of old, working salvation in the midst of the earth," to mean that Golgotha was the center of the earth, thereby emphasizing the cosmic dimension of the death of Christ (Cat. 13.28). This notion occurs also in the Syriac *Cave of Treasures*, a fifth- or sixth-century work, which adds that the skull for which Golgotha was named is Adam's skull, thus concretizing the second-Adam theme of Cy-

---

[71] *Book of Hierotheos*, ed. Marsh, 126 trans., 114 text. Further on Stephen bar Sudaili, cf. remarks on strophe 19 *infra*.

[72] For examples and discussion, cf. Beck, "Symbolum," esp. 35–37.

[73] For a review of the discussion and selected recent literature, cf. R. F. Taft, "Some Notes on the Bema in the East and West Syrian Traditions," *OCP*, 34 (1968), 326–359, esp. 349. Grabar and Smith assumed that the East Syrian type of *bêma* was meant here, cf. Grabar, "Le témoignage," 63, and Smith, *Dome*, 137, 143 f., 149 f.

[74] Pace Smith, *Dome*, 137, 143 f, 149 f.

[75] The written record may be in disagreement with the archeological record on this point, cf. Grabar, "Le témoignage," 63 f.

[76] G. Khouri Sarkis, "Le Livre du Guide de Yahya Ibn Jarir," *OrSyr*, 12 (1967), 303–54, 421–80; contains French translation from the Arabic of chaps. 29–31; passages quoted are chap. 29.11 ad 29.23, pp. 325, 328. For a sketch of the arrangement of the Nestorian church, cf. R. H. Connolly, ed. and trans., *Anonymi Auctoris Expositio Officiorum Ecclesiae*, CSCO, 64 (= Scr. Syr. 25,28 = 1), 72 (= Scr. Syr. 29, 32 = II) (Paris, 1911–15), I, 196–7 (trans.).

[77] Connolly, *op. cit.*, I, 114 text.

ril's comments (cf. Cat. 13.28). The Edessa Hymn shows awareness neither of this cosmic interpretation nor even of the second-Adam theme in relation to Golgotha.

our Lord between the thieves:

The new Testament tradition of the two thieves crucified on either side of Jesus (Mark 15:27 and parallels) and especially the story of the forgiveness of the "good thief" (Luke 23:39–43) play a significant role in Syriac liturgical and literary traditions. Yahya Ibn Jarir (cited above) continues: "Les deux flabelles placés à droite et à gauche [de l'autel] représentent les deux personnes crucifiées avec lui [le Christ]. On dit aussi qu'ils figurent les deux chérubins qui étaient dans le sanctuaire des Israelites."[78] That the "good thief" was first to enter Paradise is a favorite theme in Ephrem's Diatessaron commentary; he managed even to wring from it another of his favorite themes, the rejection of the Jews.[79] Cyril of Jerusalem used the thief who is saved as an example of grace.[80] Closer to the chronological and geographical setting of the Edessa Hymn, Jacob of Sarug employed the example of the good thief to refute the argument of the Origenist Stephen bar Sudaili against eternal rewards and punishments.[81] Stephen himself interpreted this passage allegorically.[82] For him, the three crosses represent the three essences which comprise a human being: body, soul, and spirit. Although all three are crucified, the one in the middle (the mind) and the one on the right (the soul) live; only the body dies. Against this, Jacob emphasized the literal and moral interpretation of the thief as paradigmatic of the free grace of salvation. In his *sôgîthâ* of the cherubim and the thief, Jacob emphasized, as Cyril had, the paradoxical working of grace which admits the thief to Paradise even before the prophets and leaders of the Old Testament.[83] Again, the Edessa Hymn shows no awareness of the broader tradition on the thieves.

STR. 17.

five doors:

Goussen argued that there were three doors in the east façade, one each in the south and west façades.[84] Mango suggested five doors on the west or three on the west with one each on north and south.[85] Others have declined to comment on this issue, which is particularly difficult if strophe 12 is taken literally.[86]

like the virgins to the bridal couch of light:

The allusion is to the five wise virgins of Mt. 25:1–13. Goussen's printed text erroneously reads *legyon* instead of *lagnôn*, though his translation, "ins Lichtgemach," reflects my reading of the text.[87] Dupont-Sommer followed Goussen's text rather than correcting it and so arrived at the erroneous translation, "troupe lumineuse."[88] The correct reading attests one of the more typically Syriac themes of the hymn, the "bridal couch of light," a symbol both of the baptistery and of heaven in Syriac literature from the *Acts of Thomas* to Ephrem and Narsai.[89] The bridal chamber appears as an eschatological symbol in the Manichaean and Gnostic literature as well.[90] Greek Christian writers from the New Testament onward, especially in the Alexandrian tradition, applied nuptial imagery to the relation between the individual soul and Christ or between a pre-existent or personified Church and Christ.[91]

---

[78] *Loc. cit.* (*supra*, note 76).
[79] R. Murray, *Symbols of Church and Kingdom: A Study in Early Syriac Tradition* (Cambridge, Eng., 1975), 64, 258.
[80] *Catecheses*, 13.30–31.
[81] For the text and translation of the letter, cf. A. L. Frothingham, *Stephen bar Sudaili, the Syrian mystic and the Book of Hierotheos* (Leyden, 1886), 10–27; reedited by G. Olinder, CSCO, 110, Scr. Syr. 57 (Paris, 1937), 2–11. For discussion, cf. Guillaumont, *Kephalaia et l'Origénisme* (*supra*, note 42), 302 ff.
[82] Marsh, ed., trans., *Book of Hierotheos* II, 20–22.
[83] Trans. F. Graffin, "La soghita du Cherubin et du Larron," *OrChr*, 12 (1967), 481–90. This hymn became a regular part of the Syriac Paschal Vigil, cf. *ibid.*

[84] Goussen, *op. cit.* (*supra*, note 3), 6 f.
[85] Mango, *Art of the Byzantine Empire* (*supra*, note 3), 59.
[86] Schneider's diagram, *op. cit.*, (*supra*, note 3), 167, bears no indication of doors; Dupont-Sommer explicitly declines placing the doors, *op. cit.*, 38. Further, cf. our discussion of strophe 12 *supra*.
[87] Goussen, *op. cit.*, 119, 121.
[88] Dupont-Sommer, *op. cit.* (*supra*, note 3), 38.
[89] For specific citations, cf. A. F. J. Klijn, *The Acts of Thomas* (Leiden, 1962), 173 f., and for further related material, 67 f., 71, 168–79, 192–95. For a similar reference in another fifth-century Syriac composition written for the rededication of a church building, cf. Appendix 3.
[90] *Ibid.* The Greek version of the *Acts of Thomas* is a Gnostic document, and the original Syriac version may also have been Gnostic. On the versions and Gnosticism, cf. Klijn, *op. cit.*, 1–16; G. Bornkamm, "Acts of Thomas," in *New Testament Apocrypha*, ed. E. Hennecke and W. Schneemelcher, trans. R. McL. Wilson (Philadelphia, 1965), II, 425–41, with postscript by D. Georgi, 441 f. The debate over the nature of early Syriac Christianity need not detain us here. For a balanced account of the problem in Edessa, cf. H. J. W. Drijvers, "Edessa und das jüdische Christentum," *VChr* 24 (1970), 4–33; for discussion of the issue of Syriac Christian origins in Adiabene as well, cf. Murray, *Symbols*, 4–24.
[91] Cf. note 173 *infra*.

STR. 18.

the Cherubim of its altar:

The "Cherubim of its altar" was probably a ciborium over the altar adorned with carved depictions of a pair of cherubim. A ciborium or baldachino is a free-standing canopy, either flat or curved, erected over a throne, altar, tomb, ambo, stream, or pool.[92] The ciborium occurs in ancient Near Eastern contexts (Iran, Babylonia, Egypt, Israel) as well as in Hellenistic, Roman, and Early Christian settings, and has cosmological and sacred connotations, essentially indicating that the person or object beneath is representative of the ruler of the cosmos.[93] Early pictorial representations in a Christian context show the ciborium bedecked with flowers, plants, and birds.[94] However, an illustration of the Ark of the Covenant in the *Topography of Cosmos Indicopleustes* shows a ciborium surmounted by two cherubim.[95] Two sources (one approximately contemporaneous with Cosmas, the other from the twelfth century) attest that cherubim adorned the ciboria over altars in northern Mesopotamian Christian churches: A description of a church at Qartamin mentions the figure of a cherub over the altar (or perhaps over the bishop's throne);[96] and an account of the Muslim capture of the Jacobite church of St. Jacob in Aleppo alludes to the destruction not only of the altar and of the icons but also of the figures of cherubim above the altar.[97] The Edessa Hymn's reference to the "cherubim of the altar" probably indicates that a

ciborium supported by ten columns and ornamented with carved representations of a pair of cherubim was erected over the altar.[98]

ten apostles . . . who fled:

The misprint in Goussen's Syriac text (*danraqw* instead of *da'raqw*) misled Dupont-Sommer into an ingenious but erroneous translation.[99] The allusion is to Mark 14:50 ff. and parallels, combined with John 19:26, assuming the popular identification of the apostle John with the "beloved disciple."

STR. 19.

nine orders of angels:

The earliest references to a ninefold angelology in extant Christian literature are in John Chrysostom's *Homily on Genesis* and in the fifth of the *Mystagogical Catecheses* attributed to Cyril of Jerusalem.[100] It is possible that these two examples are indicative of a broader acceptance of a ninefold angelology in the late fourth or early fifth century. Best known to modern scholars is the ninefold angelology of Pseudo-Dionysius, who used the same names for the angelic orders as the earlier examples but modified their sequence and fitted them into the triadic framework of his neo-Platonic system.[101] The *Book of the Holy Hierotheos*, a Syriac work

---

[92] For definition, cf. Krautheimer, *op. cit.* (*supra*, note 2), 541; more extensively, T. Klauser, "Ciborium," *RAC*, III (1955), 68–86.

[93] Klauser, *op. cit.*

[94] T. Klauser, "Das Ciborium in der älteren christlichen Buchmalerei," *NachrGött* (1961), no. 7, 191–207; repr., with some remarks on further bibliography, in *JbAChr*, Suppl. 3 (1974), 314–27.

[95] Cosmas Indicopleustes, *Topographie Chrétienne*, ed., trans., intro., and notes by W. Wolska-Conus, SC, 141, 159, 197 (Paris, 1968, 1970, 1973), II, 64 ff. (illustration accompanying Bk. V, 36); a similar structure, though without the cherubim, takes the place of the Tabernacle in the Sinai MS at Bk. V, 55, cf. *ibid.*, I, 195 (fig. 10). Grabar noted this parallel and assumed, perhaps too readily, that Cosmas' illustration shows the placement of cherubim above Christian church altars in the sixth century, cf. Grabar, "Le témoignage," 64 note 3.

[96] From the reign of Emperor Anastasius (491–518 C.E.), cf. E. Sachau, *Verzeichnis der syrischen Hss. der Königlichen Bibliothek zu Berlin* (Berlin, 1899), 585; it is cited by Goussen, *op. cit.*, 123 note 11, who dismisses the possibility that the cherubim are actually above the throne, i.e., the bishop's chair. This may be too hasty a conflation of the evidence, cf. note 105 *infra*.

[97] I. E. Rahmani, "Ein Blatt aus der Geschichte der Kirchen Aleppos im Mittelalter," *ThGl*, 4 (1912), 268; again, cited by Goussen, *op. cit.*, 123 note 11.

[98] This is Grabar's conclusion and it seems most plausible. Basing his view on the ongoing practice of the Armenian Church and the restored practice of the Syrians, Goussen had argued that a curtain embroidered with cherubim was meant, *op. cit.*, 123 note 11. For some evidence in favor of Goussen's hypothesis, cf. W. Cramer, *Die Engelvorstellungen bei Ephräm dem Syrer*, *OCA*, 173 (Rome, 1965), 172, and R. Taft, *The Great Entrance: A History of the Transfer of Gifts and other Pre-anaphoral Rites of the Liturgy of St. John Chrysostom*, OCA, 200 (Rome, 1975). 39 note 95. For the roots and symbolic significance of such a curtain, cf. T. Klauser, "Der Vorhang vor dem Thron Gottes," *JbAChr*, 3 (1960), 141 f.; repr. in *ibid.*, Suppl. 3 (1974). 218–20 with brief response to O. Hofius, *Der Vorhang vor dem Thron Gottes. Eine exegetisch-religionswissenschaftliche Untersuchung zu Hebr. 6.19f und 10.19f*, WUNT, 14 (Tübingen, 1972), q.v.

[99] Goussen, *op. cit.*, 119, 121; Dupont-Sommer, *op. cit.*, 38.

[100] John Chrysostom, *Hom. in Gen.* IV,5 (PG, 53–54, 44) and Cyril of Jerusalem, *Cat.* 23,6 (PG, 33, 1113B). For critical edition of the latter, cf. *Catéchèses Mystagogiques*, Introduction, texte critique et notes de A. Piédagnel, traduction de P. Paris, SC, 126 (Paris, 1966), 159–52; discussion of authorship and date of the mystagogical catecheses by Piédagnel, 21–40. Both Chrysostom and Cyril are cited by R. Roques in "Pierre l'Ibérien et le Corpus dionysien," *RHR*, 145 (1954), 69–98, esp. 87–96.

[101] *Hier. Cael.* VI,2. For a general discussion of the angelology of Pseudo-Dionysius, cf. R. Roques, *L'univers dionysien* (Paris, 1954), 135–67. For comparison with the earlier examples, cf. *idem*, "Pierre l'Ibérien," 87–96. Grabar considered the hymn's reference to a ninefold angelology a clear indication of dependence on the Pseudo-Dionysian literature, cf. "Le témoignage," 56.

of the early sixth century, attributed to Stephen bar Sudaili, also presumes a ninefold angelology.[102] Although this work was put into final form and entitled by someone familiar with the Pseudo-Dionysian corpus, the background of the bulk of the work is the *Kephalaia Gnostica* of the Origenist, Evagrius of Pontus.[103] The reference in the Edessa Hymn is too general to determine literary dependence on any of these earlier works.[104] It is most likely that all are indebted to a broader tradition of liturgical and exegetical interpretation.

throne of Christ . . . angels:

Ezekiel 1:1–26, which portrays God enthroned above the cherubim, was interpreted by early Christians to imply that Christ was enthroned above the cherubim after the ascension.[105] The arrangement of the Edessa Hymn seems at first to conflict with this tradition, since the cherubim are associated with the altar while Christ is enthroned above the nine orders of angels rather than only above the cherubim. By the fourth century, however, it was commonplace to identify the altar with the throne of Christ.[106] The hymn's portrayal apparently results from acceptance of this identity combined with the development of a ninefold angelology. The hymn's conception is not readily identifiable with a particular line of exegesis.

STR. 20.

heaven and earth:

In an Antiochene exegetical tradition this expression is the equivalent of "the cosmos." In the sixth-century Alexandrian Christian framework, with its Ptolemaic cosmology, "heaven" alone would be the cosmos, since it would be understood as a sphere enclosing the earth and the space around it.[107] The hymn's meaning here is closer to the Antiochene tradition.

STR. 21.

apostles . . . and prophets and martyrs:

As in strophe 14, the leaders of the church are represented by parts of the church building.[108]

IV. The Building

The church building described by the hymn was destroyed in 1031 C.E.[109] Archeological exploration of the site has not yet been permitted. In contrast to the architecture of the Syrian countryside, the ecclesiastical architecture of major cities like Edessa is relatively unknown.[110] In the absence of external evidence about the architecture of the church, reconstruction of the plan of the church building is dependent only on the sparse data within the hymn. A precise reconstruction of the architecture of the church would be useful in two respects: first, in determining whether the background of the building is primarily Justinianic imperial architecture or regional Syrian architecture; second, in determining the applicability of the hymn's symbolism to other Byzantine churches.

Two types of church have been proposed as most compatible with the hymn's description.[111] Schneider suggested that the cathedral was a cruciform church with a central dome and arched, not domed, ceilings in the shallow arms of the cross.[112] Grabar argued for a substantial modification of this reconstruction.[113] In his view the church was of the cross-in-square type.[114] He conjectured that massive exterior walls enclosed the cruciform inner structure of the church. By means of squinches, these exterior walls supported a single dome which covered the entire church.[115] From the exterior, the church

---

[102] Marsh, ed., trans., *Book of Hierotheos*, I, 10–12; on Stephen as the author, cf. 222–32.

[103] Guillaumont, *Kephalaia et l'Origénisme*, 302–32, esp. 318 ff.; also Guillaumont, "Etienne bar Soudaili," in *Dictionnaire de Spiritualité* (Paris, 1961), col. 1487.

[104] Even the rejection of nine spheres and nine heavens by later Antiochenes such as Cosmas Indicopleustes cannot provide a criterion of literary dependence, since rejection of nine spheres or heavens does not necessarily imply rejection of nine orders of angels; cf. Wolska, *Topographie* (*supra*, note 25), 88 note 2, 103 note 1, 169, 201.

[105] This interpretation appears in Philo, Irenaeus, and Ephrem; since it is not prominent in Clement or Origen, Cramer concludes that it is a Syrian rather than an Alexandrian tradition; cf. Cramer, *Engelvorstellungen*, 102 f., 132–34. Further, cf. G. W. H. Lampe, *A Patristic Greek Lexicon* (Oxford, 1961), 655b.

[106] T. Klauser, "Altar," *RAC*, I, 353.

[107] Wolska, *Topographie*, 138, 173.

[108] Further on this theme and its roots, cf. note 11 *supra* and note 176 *infra*.

[109] Goussen, *op. cit.*, 133.

[110] Krautheimer, *op. cit.*, 147.

[111] These reconstructions are based primarily on the information in strophes 5–8, 12–13, 17 of the hymn; cf. the commentary on those strophes for a more detailed discussion.

[112] Schneider, *op. cit.*, (*supra*, note 3), 166 f., with a plan, fig. 2, 167. He suggests the Church of Mary at Farqîn as a parallel, cf. G. L. Bell, *Churches and Monasteries of the Tûr 'Abdîn*, *Zeitschrift für die Geschichte der Architektur*, Suppl. 9 (Heidelberg, 1913), 88, fig. 28.

[113] Grabar, "Le témoignage" (*supra*, note 3), 44–51.

[114] Among others, Grabar cites the example of St. Clement at Ankara, cf. Krautheimer, *op. cit.*, 302, fig. 249.

[115] Since the dome was stone, Grabar's reconstruction requires that the overall dimensions of the building be fairly small—a requirement which is, as he noted, not incompatible with the Arab reckoning of the church as one of the wonders of the world, since architectural wondrousness flows neither solely nor necessarily from magnitude; cf. Grabar, "Le témoignage," 41, 47 f.

would have the appearance of a simple cube surmounted by a dome, although the interior would be more complex.

It has been generally accepted that, given the inadequacies of the hymn's description of the building, Grabar's reconstruction is a reasonable proposal.[116] But it remains a hypothetical reconstruction and is not without difficulties.[117] In the wealth of architectural forms of the East Syrian environment there are likely to be other solutions which are equally feasible.[118] As Schneider wrote in 1941, the most sensible solution to this problem would be an excavation of the probable site of the building.[119] But this possibility apparently remains as remote now as when he raised the issue almost half a century ago.

V. Historical Setting and Date

The church described in the hymn is the so-called "Great Church."[120] The *Chronicle of Edessa* reports that its construction was begun in 313 c.e. and completed in 325–328 c.e.[121] The church building was destroyed by the fourth recorded flood of the Daisan (Skirtos) River in April 525 and was rebuilt with the financial assistance of the Emperor Justinian.[122] Amidonius, mentioned in the second strophe of the hymn, is apparently identical with Amazon, mentioned by Jacob of Edessa as the thirty-eighth bishop of Edessa; according to Michael the Syrian, the Chalcedonian Bishop Amazon "rebuilt and decorated the Great Church."[123] The present

hymn appears to be the foundation hymn sung on the occasion of the dedication of the new building, an event which probably took place about the middle of the sixth century.[124]

In order to ascertain an appropriate literary environment for the hymn, it is important to look more closely at the contemporaneous ecclesiastical politics.[125] Christological allegiances shifted rapidly in the turbulent atmosphere of sixth-century Edessa. Paul, Bishop of Edessa from 501 to 519 c.e., had written to Flavian, Patriarch of Antioch, assuring him of his acceptance of the "synod of Chalcedon." When Severus succeeded Flavian as Patriarch of Antioch, however, he demanded Paul's retraction of the statement of allegiance to Chalcedon, and Paul complied. Paul of Edessa remained faithful to the Monophysite position during the persecutions which followed Severus' deposition.[126] Twice exiled for his Monophysite allegiance, Paul was replaced during his second exile by Asclepios bar Malaha. A zealous Chalcedonian, Bishop Asclepios participated in the general persecution of Monophysites in the east. A Monophysite source claims that God's wrath at Asclepios' persecution of a group of monks was the cause of the great flood which eliminated one third of the population and destroyed all the major buildings of Edessa in April 525.[127]

---

[116] Full acceptance by Smith, in *Dome* (*supra*, note 2), 91, citing Grabar's statement that the Edessa Church is "du type 'carré dans carré' ou en croix inscrite," in *Martyrium. Recherches sur le culte des reliques et l'art chrétien antique*, 2 vols. and plates (Paris, 1946), I, 327. Partial or hesitant acceptance in Wolska, *Topographie*, 295, where she assumes that the church is on a square rather than rectangular plan (and has a dome) and is therefore incompatible with the drawings of Cosmas Indicopleustes; Mango, *Art of the Byzantine Empire* (*supra*, note 3), 60 note 13, agrees that the "other arches" of strophe 8 are "probably" squinches, but does not treat the dome and ceiling of strophes 5 and 6 as identical; Krautheimer, *op. cit.*, 253, says the plan of the cathedral of Edessa was "apparently" of the type "of a domed cross enclosed in a square and resting on the walls of corner chambers."
[117] They are discussed in the comments on strophes 5–8, 12–13, and 17, *supra*.
[118] Cf. Krautheimer, *op. cit.*, 143–65, 271–86.
[119] Schneider, *op. cit.*, 167.
[120] It is to be distinguished from the "Savior Church" also known as the "Old Church" of Edessa; cf. Goussen, *op. cit.*, 123 ff. For the probable site of the church, cf. Segal, *Edessa* (*supra*, note 15), Plan I, 262 f.
[121] Goussen, *op. cit.*, 125 f.
[122] *Ibid.*, 129.
[123] The identification was suggested by Goussen, *op. cit.*, 128 f. and has been generally accepted. It is based on the witness of

two primary sources: Jacob of Edessa in *Chronica Minora*, ed. E. W. Brooks, I. Guidi, and I.-B. Chabot, pt. 3, CSCO, 5 (Louvain, 1905), 321 text, 243 trans.; and Michael the Syrian, *Chronique de Michel le Syrien*, ed. J. B. Chabot (Paris, 1901), II, 246b. Michael's reference is to the twenty-fifth year of Justinian, the twenty-second year of Chosroes of Persia, which means Amazon became the thirty-eighth bishop in 543. Cameron asserts that Jacob of Edessa implies a date of 553–560, but her reasons are not clear. Coupled with the date of 554 for Procopius' *On Buildings*, which mentions the rebuilt church, this gives her a date of 553/54 for the reconstruction; cf. Cameron, "Shroud" (*supra*, note 4), 23 f. and note 46. My own estimate would be broader, between 543 and 554.
[124] This is the date and setting of the hymn suggested by Dupont-Sommer, *op. cit.*, 29, whereas in his portion of their joint article Grabar argued for a late seventh-century date, "Le témoignage," 58 *et passim*. Grabar's dating has been widely accepted, but it is erroneous, as Cameron argues, in "Shroud," esp. 23 f. and note 46, and as the present article is intended to demonstrate. Further on Grabar's theory concerning literary dependency and dating, cf. Appendix 1 of this article.
[125] The following reconstruction of events is based on E. Honigmann, *Évèques et évechés Monophysites d'Asie antérieure au VIème siècle*, CSCO, 127 (Louvain, 1951), 48 ff.; J. Lebon, *Le Monophysisme sévérien* (Louvain, 1909), 39 ff.; and Segal, *Edessa*, 93–103.
[126] For a balanced view of Justin's persecution of the Monophysites, using both Chalcedonian and Monophysite sources, cf. A. A. Vasiliev, *Justin the First: An Introduction to the Epoch of Justinian the Great*, DOS, I (Cambridge, Mass., 1950), 221–41.
[127] Segal, *Edessa*, 96 f.

Perhaps Asclepios believed in his own culpability for this disaster; or perhaps the anger of a disgruntled Monophysite populace in search of a scapegoat was sufficient to dampen his enthusiasm for the episcopacy. Whatever his reasons, Asclepios fled, and Justinian accepted Paul's reappointment as Bishop of Edessa. Paul was required first to accept the "synod of Chalcedon," and his final stint as Bishop of Edessa lasted only a few months, until his death in October 526.[128] So while his reinstatement constituted a moral victory for the Monophysite cause, it was a limited and temporary success.

Asclepios had also died in 526, so Justinian appointed a new bishop, Amazon.[129] Information about Bishop Amazon is quite meager. Even precise dates for his episcopacy are lacking. We know only that he was an adherent of the Chalcedonian formula and that he supervised the reconstruction of the church building. From Procopius' account it is clear that the restoration of the church was an important aspect of a major building program financed by Justinian and apparently begun immediately after the flood; even the diversion of the course of the river for the sake of preventing future floods was included in the task assigned to the imperial engineers.[130]

Although Justinian made some unsuccessful attempts at reconciliation with the Monophysites in 531 and 535–536 at Constantinople, the Monophysite Christology was definitively condemned in 536 at the Council of Constantinople.[131] This decision was followed by the most severe persecutions of the Monophysites under Severus' third successor at Antioch, Patriarch Ephrem bar Afyana, a native of Amida. Patriarch Ephrem visited several cities in the East during the winter of 536–537, Edessa among them.[132] Nevertheless, the Monophysites continued to rely on the Empress Theodora for assistance, and in 542 she saw to the consecration of Jacob Baradaeus as Bishop of Edessa. The assiduous labors of Jacob Baradaeus, Theodore of Arabia, and Theodosius of Alexandria resulted in the successful reestablishment of a Monophysite hierarchy and priesthood throughout the East.[133] Still, Jacob Baradaeus never sat openly on the episcopal throne of Edessa, and his

revived church was, as Honigmann has said, "une communauté illégale de fidèles qui s'opposait secrètement à l'Église chalcédonienne, qui jouissait, elle, des faveurs du pouvoir et était fermement établie dans tous les éveches de l'empire."[134] So we may surmise that as the middle of the sixth century drew near, there was an official attitude of inflexible adherence to the Chalcedonian formula, though this may have been coupled with an uneasy awareness that the Monophysite Church, far from being dead, had become a powerful underground force.

Other theological and even cosmological disputes of the time were closely related to the Christological controversies. The Emperor Justinian issued a decree anathematizing certain opinions of Origen in January 543.[135] The following year, at the prompting of two Monophysites who were also Origenists, Theodore Askidas and Domitian of Ancyra, Justinian issued a second decree, this one against the "Three Chapters," certain writings of Ibas of Edessa and of Theodoret of Cyrrhus, and the substance of the Christological opinions of Theodore of Mopsuestia. Theodore of Mopsuestia was not only the most important representative of the Antiochene, "Diophysite" Christology, but also the primary opponent of the allegorical method of exegesis as practiced at Alexandria especially since the time of Origen.[136]

A decade after these imperial decrees, the Council of Constantinople in 553 condemned both Origen and Theodore of Mopsuestia. In the intervening years, in Alexandria at least, the debate shifted from Christology to cosmology. Cosmas Indicopleustes undertook the defense of Theodore's theological system without mentioning his name and without emphasizing Christology. Instead he argued for the Antiochene cosmological system for which he claimed Scriptural authority, and he flatly stated that those who did not subscribe to this cosmology

---

[128] Honigmann, *op. cit.*, 49 f.
[129] *Ibid.*, 50 note 1.
[130] *On Buildings*, II, 7,6.
[131] Honigmann, *op. cit.*, 149–52.
[132] *Ibid.*, 149.
[133] *Ibid.*, 157–245.

[134] *Ibid.*, 244.
[135] In general on the Origenistic Controversies, cf. F. Diekamp, *Die Origenistische Streitigkeiten im sechsten Jahrhundert und das fünfte allgemeine Concil* (Münster, 1899); especially for the relation between the Origenistic controversies of the fourth and the sixth centuries, cf. Guillaumont, *Kephalaia et l'Origénisme*, and for the date given, *ibid.*, 132.
[136] On the "collusion" of Origenists and Monophysites against the tradition of Theodore of Mopsuestia, cf. Guillaumont, *Kephalaia et l'Origénisme*, esp. 128–36, 173–75. On the theology of Theodore himself, cf. R. Devreesse, *Essai sur Theodore de Mopsueste* (hereafter, *Essai*), ST, 141 (Vatican, 1948); and on Theodore's general principles of biblical interpretation, cf. M. F. Wiles, "Theodore of Mopsuestia as Representative of the Antiochene School," *Cambridge History of the Bible*, I (Cambridge, 1970), 489–509.

were not really Christians. Cosmas' opponent in the debate was John Philoponos, a Monophysite and proponent of the Ptolemaic cosmology, whom Cosmas accused of Origenism.[137]

Reverberations of every aspect of these theological discussions were felt in Edessa. The Christological issues and the competing exegetical traditions which constituted their background, Origenism, and cosmological speculation were all part of the intellectual environment of Syriac-speaking Christians in the early sixth century. In general, the discussion at Edessa and in its environs was less sophisticated than in Alexandria, but all the same issues were there. Occasionally the peculiar intellectual history of Edessa and its surroundings—a combination of exposure to many ideas with provincial lack of sophistication—allowed for the intermingling of ideas that were theoretically incompatible. In the case of the Edessa Hymn, this confusion produced a striking architectural symbol. In order to trace this development we must first consider the literary genre of the hymn.

VI. Literary Analysis

a. Structure of the Hymn

In general structure, the hymn falls into three main sections: (1) introduction (strophes 1–4), (2) main body (strophes 5–19), and (3) closing (strophes 20–22). The introductory section begins with an invocation of divine aid (str. 1). The foundation information follows (str. 2), presented typologically in anticipation of the main theme. That is, Moses, Bezalel, and the Tabernacle are types for Amidonius, the bishop, for Asaph and Addai, the architects, and for the church building, respectively. Since the Tabernacle was understood, as we shall see, as a cosmological symbol, this typology is also an anticipation of the main theme. That theme is presented in the following two strophes: the building represents, on the one hand, the mysteries of the Godhead and the economy of salvation, and, on the other hand, the cosmos (strs. 3–4).

The central portion of the hymn (strs. 5–19) is at once a symbolic interpretation of the architectural details of the building in accordance with the announced theme and an elaboration of cosmological and ecclesiological dimensions of the theme. The symbolic interpretation of the building proceeds from the cosmological theme first to the Tabernacle, then to the Trinity, and finally to the earthly dispensation of the Savior and his exaltation. Specifically, architectural features are related to heaven, earth, and the sun, i.e., the cosmos, in strophes 5–9,[138] to the Tabernacle in strophes 10–11, and to the Trinity in strophes 12–13. Strophes 14–19 relate architectural and liturgical features to the Dispensation of Christ, his prophets, apostles, martyrs, confessors, and virgins, ending with the image of the exalted Christ enthroned above the nine orders of angels.

The description of the architectural features proceeds generally, but not exclusively, from the higher parts of the building to the lower and then to the major liturgical furnishings. Strophes 5–10 concern the ceiling, dome, and arches, but also the marble revetment of the walls. Strophes 11–14 pertain to the courts, façades, and the windows of the sanctuary and façades. Strophes 15–19 touch upon the major liturgical furnishings of the building: ambo, altar, and σύνθρονος. The doors, also included here, might be considered to have a liturgical function if processions enter through them. The fact that the hymn is an alphabetical acrostic probably accounts for its rather haphazard approach to describing the building.

The final three strophes constitute a mirror-image of the first four. So the twentieth strophe recapitulates the main theme, that the building represents the cosmos and the Godhead both in Itself and in relation to the world. The ecclesiological dimension of the theme is given emphasis in the following strophe (21a). Finally, the invocation of the first strophe is mirrored by the prayer for protection in the last verses (strs. 21b–22).

b. Genre of the Hymn

Both known manuscripts, which date to the thirteenth and sixteenth centuries respectively, classify the Edessa hymn as a sôgîthâ (plural sôgyâthâ).[139] This is not the hymn in the form of a dramatic dialogue that is discussed in the standard histories of Syriac literature under this title. It belongs instead to the type of sôgîthâ commonly found in the Maronite daily office. Like many sôgyâthâ of this type, the Edessa Hymn is in the form of an alphabetical acrostic; its twenty-two strophes begin with the

---

[137] Wolska, Topographie, esp. 63 ff., 191 f.

[138] Cf. note 107 supra.

[139] For a discussion of this genre and its characteristics, cf. Appendix 2. For information on the MSS and their dating, cf. note 6 supra.

consecutive letters of the Syriac alphabet. Each strophe of the Edessa Hymn has four hemistichs, each of which has, in turn, eight syllables. This is the meter which G. Khouri-Sarkis named the "Maronite meter," except that each strophe has twice the number of syllables as the usual Maronite *sôgîthâ*.[140]

In a broader sense the hymn on the Church of Edessa may be appropriately characterized as architectural θεωρία, a contemplation of the church building.[141] The fundamental theological postulate underlying the hymn is that God is a mystery, who is both revealed and hidden (str. 3). Although beyond the comprehension of creatures, God may be truly known if approached through three modes of contemplation: (1) theological: the Godhead in Itself, the Trinity (strs. 12–13); (2) Scriptural: God as Savior revealed in the Bible (strs. 11, 14–19); (3) cosmological: God as Creator revealed through the creation (strs. 4–8). Each of these three ways of contemplating the mysterious God is accessible through the contemplation of the church building (strs. 3, 20–21). Consideration of each of the architectural features of the building—the structural components as well as the major liturgical furnishings—leads to one of the three essential ways of knowing God. So the building is a prefatory means of contemplation, which leads to the three major routes to the mystery of the Godhead Itself.[142]

The term θεωρία, or contemplation, occurs in the context of early Christian biblical commentaries and Byzantine liturgical commentaries.[143] In both cases it refers to contemplation of the sacred text or of the sacred actions at the highest level, the spiritual or anagogical level. Hence the synonym for θεωρία in the Byzantine liturgical commentary is μυσταγωγία.

The Edessa Hymn, as an architectural θεωρία, resembles the mystagogical commentaries on the liturgy in one respect but differs in another. Like the liturgical commentaries, the hymn derives from the tradition of θεωρία as it had developed throughout the Patristic period, especially since Origen, as a manner of biblical interpretation. Both the hymn and the commentaries take this tradition of contemplation from its Scriptural context and apply it to an object or action. The object or action is then understood to be a means of ascent to God. The fundamental difference between the architectural θεωρία of the hymn and the liturgical θεωρία of the commentaries is that the hymn contemplates an object—the church building—while the commentaries contemplate an action—the public worship of the Christian community. The two remain closely related since the place of the action (the building) and the instruments of the action (clergy, vestments, altar, ambo, vessels) are closely related to the actions themselves.

Liturgical θεωρία is rooted in Patristic typological and spiritual interpretations of the Jewish Temple cult and of the Jewish Scripture.[144] Early Christian writers, by claiming Jewish Scripture as their own, forced themselves to find Christian explanations not only for the events of Jewish history but also for the ceremonial of Jewish religion insofar as it was attested in Scripture. By the third century Origen had begun to apply the same method of spiritual interpretation of cultic actions directly to the Christian liturgy, so that what had begun as an apologetic necessity attained independent theological significance. For Origen, Scripture, the Church, and the Eucharist are all mysteries. That is, they are temporal or material phenomena in which the Divine Reality is present by participation.[145] These mysteries simultaneously reveal and conceal the Divine Reality.

Others followed Origen's lead. Gregory of Nyssa, especially, began with the image of the Tabernacle

---

[140] G. Khouri-Sarkis, "Note sur les mètres poétiques syriaques," *OrSyr*, 3 (1958), 63–72, esp. 64–66, 70; also J. Puyade, "Composition interne de l'Office syrien," *ibid.*, 2 (1957), 77–92; 3 (1958), 25–62, esp. 44 note 12 (notes by Khouri-Sarkis).

[141] The term "architectural θεωρία" is used here analogously with the term "liturgical θεωρία" as used by Bornert, *Commentaires* (*supra*, note 11), 35–39, 90 ff. Bornert's work, in turn, rests on the studies of H. de Lubac and J. Daniélou, as he indicates. Smith (*Dome*, 91) suggests a similar notion with his term "architectural mysticism," applied both to Eusebius' speech on the Church at Tyre and to the Edessa Hymn.

[142] Although the presentation is not systematic, these conceptions are presupposed. Similar understandings of θεωρία occur throughout the eastern Christian tradition from Origen to the sixth century and beyond, especially among the Cappadocians, Origenists, and Monophysites. Briefly on Origen, Gregory of Nyssa, Evagrius, and Pseudo-Dionysius, cf. L. Bouyer, *The Spirituality of the New Testament and the Fathers* (London, 1960), 355, 384, 410. On Severus of Antioch, Philoxenus of Mabbug and Jacob of Sarug, cf. R. Chesnut, *Three Monophysite Christologies: Severus of Antioch, Philoxenus of Mabbug and Jacob of Sarug* (Oxford, 1976), 37–44, 105–11, 139. On Maximus the Confessor, Bornert, *Commentaires*, 93 ff.

[143] For discussion of the Byzantine liturgical commentaries in relation to the Patristic literature, cf. Bornert, *op. cit.*, esp. 47–82.

[144] The following discussion of liturgical θεωρία is based on the work of Bornert, *loc. cit.*

[145] More precisely, the temporal or material phenomena participate in varying degrees in God. Further, cf. D. L. Balas, "The idea of participation in the structure of Origen's thought: Christian transposition of a theme of the Platonic tradition," *Origeniana*, ed. H. Crouzel *et. al.*, Quaderni di Vetera Christianorum, 12 (Bari, 1975), 257–75.

and developed the Christological and ecclesiological dimensions of its *interpretatio christiana*. Gregory's interpretation of the Tabernacle provided the background for the Pseudo-Dionysian ecclesiastical and celestial hierarchies. Pseudo-Dionysius carried out the anagogical emphasis as it had become prominent in the Alexandrian line, especially in Origen himself and in the Origenists.[146] In these later Alexandrian writings the anagogical contemplation of liturgical actions, personages, and objects takes place without emphasis on the Tabernacle or other Jewish antecedents. In some cases the Old Testament antitype has completely disappeared and the Christian contemplation of heavenly reality proceeds directly from Christian liturgy.

As represented in the writings of Cyril of Jerusalem, John Chrysostom, Isidore of Pelusium, and Theodore of Mopsuestia, the Antiochene line of Scriptural interpretation followed a similar development, through the interpretation of Jewish Scripture and ceremonial, especially the Tabernacle, to the interpretation of Christian liturgy as the analogue of the angelic liturgy. But the Antiochenes also emphasized the interpretation of Christian liturgy as the reenactment of the life and death of Christ. Further, while clearly subordinating the Old Testament antitypes to their type, Christ, this line of interpretation is less likely to omit the Jewish antecedents entirely from the discussion. Both Alexandrian and Antiochene schools share Origen's fundamental notion of a mystery as something which simultaneously reveals and conceals spiritual reality, though the Antiochenes are more influenced by Aristotelian epistemology than are the more Platonic Alexandrians. The more obvious distinctions between the two approaches are the Antiochene interest in the liturgical mysteries as representative of the events, persons, and places associated with the life of Jesus of Nazareth and the greater Alexandrian inclination toward anagogy which bypasses Jewish antecedents.[147]

Architectural θεωρία, such as we find in the Edessa Hymn, may be expected to follow the same general pattern of development as liturgical θεωρία—from the *interpretatio christiana* of a Jewish model to a Christian contemplation of either the Alexandrian or Antiochene type. That is, in its more developed phase the contemplation might proceed directly from Christian temporal reality (the church building) to heavenly reality (the preexistent Church), or it would clearly subordinate the Jewish antitype (the Tabernacle) to its type (the Church). If this analogy with the liturgical commentaries is sound—and it would seem to be—then the Edessa Hymn represents a relatively early stage in the development of architectural θεωρία, since the Jewish intermediary, the Tabernacle, is quite prominent in the first eleven strophes of the hymn. Further, the latter half of the hymn, with its emphasis on New Testament events, personages, and places, would seem to indicate an Antiochene provenience for the hymn.

If the Edessa Hymn represents a relatively early stage of architectural θεωρία, its literary roots should be traceable to the contemporaneous exegetical literature of Christian Edessa. In order to elucidate this literary background, we turn now to a brief history of the exegetical traditions at Edessa, followed by a discussion of the notion of the Tabernacle in each of those traditions.

VII. Exegetical Traditions in Sixth-century Edessa

There were three major strands of exegetical tradition in Edessa by the early sixth century: (1) the Syriac traditions stemming from Ephrem of Nisibis; (2) the Antiochene tradition, especially as represented by the commentaries of Theodore of Mopsuestia; (3) the Alexandrian tradition, represented by Gregory of Nyssa, Evagrius of Pontus, and perhaps some earlier writers.[148] The works of Ephrem had constituted the core of the theological and exegetical curriculum of the School of the Persians at Edessa from the late fourth to the early fifth century. In the early fifth century Ibas, director of the school and later Bishop of Edessa, had the works of Theodore of Mopsuestia and Diodore of Tarsus translated from Greek to Syriac for use in the School of the Persians.[149] These new translations were so successful that they virtually sup-

---

[146] Gregory of Nyssa and Basil of Caesarea fall into this line to a limited extent; more fully, Evagrius of Pontus; cf. Bornert, *Commentaires*, 52, 64–66, 71.

[147] For the similarities and differences in general approach between the Alexandrians and the Antiochenes with respect to liturgical θεωρία, cf. *ibid.*, esp. 47, 52, 72–75, 82; for the ongoing significance of both approaches, 267 f.

[148] Barhadbešabba Arbaya, *La cause de la Fondation des écoles*, ed. and trans. A. Scher, PO, 4 (1908). 382; also, A. Vööbus, *History of the School of Nisibis* (hereafter, *Nisibis*), CSCO, 266 (Louvain, 1965), 14.

[149] Barhadbešabba, *op. cit.*, 382 f.; also, Vööbus, *Nisibis*, 14 ff.; Lebon, *op. cit.*, 39 ff.; E. R. Hayes, *L'École d'Édesse* (Paris, 1930), 154–55; A. Vööbus, *A History of Asceticism in the Syrian Orient*, II, CSCO, 197 (Louvain, 1960), 410–14.

planted the indigenous tradition of Ephrem's exegesis.[150] In 489, however, after a series of struggles
between Nestorians and Monophysites in Edessa,
the School of Persians was closed.[151] Narsai, a Nestorian who had previously fled from Edessa to Nisibis, had become the director of the newly established School of Nisibis.[152] So the school at Nisibis
fell heir to the Antiochene style of exegesis.[153]

These events put an end to substantial Nestorian
leadership in Edessa.[154] Nevertheless, the Antiochene manner of exegesis, which had permeated the
curriculum until 489, continued to exercise a profound influence on Christians in the area through
the Monophysites who had studied at the School
of Edessa. Foremost among them were Philoxenus
of Mabbug and Jacob of Sarug. Both Philoxenus
and Jacob attempted to expunge the effects of their
Antiochene schooling.[155] Philoxenus, who may have
been instrumental in the closing of the School of
the Persians in 489, was especially determined in
this regard.[156] While deliberately returning to the
exegetical tradition of Ephrem, the Syrian Monophysites apparently looked to Alexandrian sources
as well.[157] Even strongly Origenistic currents were

felt at Edessa by this time, thanks to the dissemi-
nation of the writings of Evagrius of Pontus and
Stephen bar Sudaili.[158]

An appropriate context for studying the symbolic meaning of the Tabernacle in the Edessa Hymn
is the following: (a) the literary corpus of Ephrem
of Nisibis; (b) the works of Antiochene exegesis
known to have been translated into Syriac before
the mid-sixth century, especially the works of
Theodore of Mopsuestia insofar as they survive;
(c) works of the Alexandrian exegetical tradition
which are known to have been translated into Syriac before the middle of the sixth century; (d) works
of the Syriac writers of the later fifth and early sixth
centuries, especially those associated with Edessa.

a. Ephrem the Syrian

The most striking example of the interpretation
of the Tabernacle in the works of Ephrem the Syrian
is his cycle of Hymns on Paradise.[159] These employ
an extensive system of symbols relative to the Tabernacle. In the third hymn the Tabernacle is the
symbol of Paradise: the Tree of Life is the Holy of
Holies; the Tree of Knowledge is the veil separating the Holy of Holies from the rest of the Tabernacle; eating the fruit of the Tree of Knowledge is
the pulling aside of the veil, an action which gives
to Adam and Eve two kinds of knowledge: "the
glory of the intimate Tabernacle" and the "misery"
of seeing their bodily condition.[160] In the sixth hymn
Ephrem sets forth the Church on earth as a type
of Paradise.[161] In passing, he compares the original creation, Paradise before the Fall, with a house
built by God.[162]

Implicit in the Hymns on Paradise is the comparison of the Tabernacle with the Church on earth
and with the created order. Since the world is also
like a house, all these conceptions could have been
fused to conclude that the Christian church build-

[150] Vööbus, Nisibis, 24 ff.

[151] Ibid., 30–32.

[152] Further on Narsai, cf. ibid., 57–121. For a general introduction to the life and work of Narsai, cf. P. Gignoux, Homélies
de Narsaï (supra, note 8), esp. 419–516.

[153] This is the line through which the Antiochene exegesis
was transmitted to Cosmas Indicopleustes, cf. Wolska, Topographie, 63–85.

[154] Yet even in the early sixth century there were still some
Nestorians in Edessa, such as Thomas of Edessa who is supposed to have helped Mar Aba translate the works of Theodore
of Mopsuestia into Syriac, cf. Wolska, Topographie, 66.

[155] On Jacob's studies at Edessa and his later view that through
the works of Diodore, Theodore, and Theodoret the School of
the Persians had "corrupted the whole Orient," cf. P. Martin,
"Lettres de Jacques de Saroug aux moines du Couvent de Mar
Bassus, et à Paul d'Edesse," in ZDMG, 30 (1876), 220–22 (text),
224 f. (trans.); G. Olinder, Iacobi Sarugensis Epistulae quotquot su-
persunt (Paris, 1937; repr. Louvain, 1952), CSCO, 110, 58–61;
discussed by Jansma, "Hexameron" (supra, note 36), 264 f., and
by A. de Halleux, Philoxène de Mabboug, Sa vie, ses écrits et sa
théologie (Louvain, 1963), 30. For the importance of the School
tradition for Jacob's homilies in Hexaemeron, cf. Jansma, op.
cit., 278.

[156] On Philoxenus' education and "conversion" at Edessa, cf.
de Halleux, op. cit., 22–30. For the anti-diophysite polemical intent of Philoxenus' scriptural work, cf. ibid., 131 f., but for his
continued dependence on what he had been taught, cf. ibid., 30
note 52.

[157] Or perhaps the influence, at least in Philoxenus' case, ought
to be more narrowly identified as Evagrian; on this, cf. de Halleux, op. cit., 440 f. et passim, also A. Guillaumont, Kephalaia et
l'Origénisme, 213, for the view that Philoxenus was the probable
translator of the expurgated version of the Kephalia Gnostica of
Evagrius. I suspect a broader interest in Alexandrian tradition
at this time as evidenced by the translation of the Commentary on
the Song of Songs of Gregory of Nyssa between 450 and 550, cf.

note 169 infra. This, rather than earlier as Jansma suggested
("Hexameron," 268 f.), is the time when unexpected traditions
of exegesis enter into Jacob of Sarug's exegesis. A fuller examination of this question would be useful but cannot be undertaken here.

[158] Guillaumont, Kephalaia et l'Origénisme, esp. 196–337.

[159] Syriac text with German translation by E. Beck, Des Heili-
gen Ephraem des Syrers Hymnen de Paradiso und Contra Julianum,
CSCO, 174–75 (Louvain, 1957). French translation, Éphrem de
Nisibe, Hymnes sur le Paradis, trans. R. Lavenant, intro. and notes
F. Graffin, SC, 137 (Paris, 1968). Partial English translation by
S. Brock, Harp of the Spirit, Studies Supplementary to Sobornost
4 (London, 1975).

[160] Hymn 3, 5–7, et passim.

[161] Hymn 6, 7–12.

[162] Hymn 13, 2.

ing is symbolic of the cosmos and of the Tabernacle and of Paradise. So Ephrem provides a basis from which the ideas stated explicitly in the Edessa Hymn might have developed. But Ephrem never explicitly equated his images of Paradise with one another, nor did he apply them to a church building.

b. Antiochene Exegesis

The primary exponent of the second major exegetical strand present in Edessa, the Antiochene, is Theodore of Mopsuestia.[163] The Tabernacle played a major role in Theodore's theological and exegetical system. He conceived of the Tabernacle as the true type of the visible creation.[164] That is, just as God indwells the visible created order, He also dwelt in the Mosaic Tabernacle. The Tabernacle was given to the Jews to stress that their God, in contrast to the idols of the pagans, was the creator and sustainer of the entire cosmos. The Tabernacle, divided by the veil into an inner and an outer area, is the exact model of the cosmos, which is divided by the firmament into two καταστάσεις or conditions.[165] The distinction between the two καταστάσεις is at once temporal and spatial. The first κατάστασις, the lower world, was created even before the Fall to be the temporal dwelling place of human beings. The second κατάστασις, the upper world, is the dwelling place for angels at present, but it is also the eschatological home of humankind.

For Theodore, the furnishings of the Tabernacle are not types, but only symbols of lesser theological significance.[166] These furnishings are symbols of the seven days of the week, or of the four corners of the earth, but not of the members of the Church. Instead, Theodore's preferred ecclesiological metaphor is the Body of Christ.[167] So Theodore's understanding of the Tabernacle provides a parallel for the cosmological dimension of the symbolism of the Edessa Hymn but not its ecclesiological dimension. Theodore's interpretation of

the Tabernacle as a cosmological symbol implies comparison of the cosmos with a tent or building. But the absence of the ecclesiological metaphor for the Tabernacle means that Theodore also fails to apply the symbolism to a particular church building. This strand of exegetical tradition, like the works of Ephrem, provides some of the background of the Edessa Hymn, though not all of it.

c. Alexandrian Exegesis

The symbolic interpretation of the Tabernacle has a long and fairly complex history in the Alexandrian school of exegesis from Philo through Origen to Gregory of Nyssa.[168] With one exception these works either were not translated into Syriac, or the translations have not survived or have yet to be discovered. The sole exception is Gregory of Nyssa's *Commentary on the Song of Songs*, which was translated in the late fifth or early sixth century by an unknown Syrian Monophysite.[169] Although it is possible that another of the surviving interpretations of the Tabernacle was known in Syriac, Gregory's commentary is the most probable point of contact between this aspect of Alexandrian exegesis and Edessene Christianity of the early sixth century.[170]

In his *Life of Moses*, which does not exist in a Syriac translation, Gregory laid out a complex but fairly clear interpretation of the Tabernacle and its furnishings, based on Exodus 25–26 and Hebrews 8–9.[171] Gregory was aware of the cosmological in-

---

[163] Fragments collected and studied by R. Devreesse, *Essai* (*supra*, 136); for discussion of the surviving corpus of Theodore in Syriac and Greek, cf. Vööbus, *Nisibis*, 19 f., and Gignoux, *Homélies de Narsaï*.

[164] Devreesse, *Essai*, 25ff.

[165] On the two *catastases* in Theodore's thought, cf. Devreesse, *Essai*, 89 f., 100 f.; also Wolska, *Topographie*, 37 ff.; and Cosmas Indicopleustes, *Topographie*, III, 406–10. Further, esp. on the difference between this and the Origenistic view, cf. Guillaumont, *Kephalaia et l'Origénisme*, 184 f.

[166] On types vs. other symbols in Theodore's system, cf. Devreesse, *Essai*.

[167] *Ibid.*

[168] Philo, De Vita Mosis 2.15.71 – 27.140 and Quaest. Ex. 2.51–106; Epistle of Barnabas 16; Clement of Alexandria, Strom. 5.6.32–40; Origen, In Ex. hom. 9 and Comm. Cant. 2.1; Ps. Justin, Coh. ad Graecos (MG 6.296 B–C); Gregory Nazianzen Or. 28.31 (MG 36.72 A); Gregory of Nyssa, Vit. Mos. 2.170–188 and Comm. Cant. Or. 2 *passim* and Or. 14, esp. H. Langerbeck, ed., *Gregorii Nysseni in Canticum Canticorum, Gregorii Nysseni Opera*, ed. W. Jaeger, VI (Leiden, 1960), 415: 14 ff. Strictly speaking, the Epistle of Barnabas and the oration of Gregory of Nazianzus may not be "Alexandrian," but the point has little relevance to the discussion here.

[169] C. Van den Eynde, *La version syriaque du commentaire de Grégoire de Nysse sur le Cantique des Cantiques: Ses origines, Ses témoins, Son influence*, Bibliothèque du Muséon, 10 (Louvain, 1939), esp. 21 f., 37–42, 61–66; and see Langerbeck, *op. cit.*, lxi–lxvii. Also R. H. Connolly, in *JThS*, 41 (1940), 84–86.

[170] Seventeen of Gregory of Nazianzus' orations survive in Syriac, but have not been edited; possibly the twenty-eighth is among them. For the MS, see I. Ortiz de Urbina, *Patrologia Syriaca* (Rome, 1965), 234, or A. Baumstark, *Geschichte der syrischen Literatur* (hereafter, *Geschichte*) (Bonn, 1922), 77 f.

[171] *Gregorii Nysseni de Vita Moysis*, ed. H. Musurillo, in *Gregorii Nysseni Opera*, ed. W. Jaeger, H. Langerbeck, VII, pt. I (Leiden, 1964); *La Vie de Moïse*, ed. and trans. J. Daniélou, SC, 1 bis (Paris, 1955); Gregory of Nyssa, *The Life of Moses*, trans., intro., and notes by A. J. Malherbe and E. Ferguson, Classics of Western Spirituality (New York, 1978).

terpretation of the Tabernacle as passed on by Philo
and Origen.[172] The elaboration of Christological and
ecclesiological dimensions for the symbol had been
begun by Origen and Methodius of Olympus as
well.[173] Gregory incorporated their notions and
further refined the Christological interpretation.
For Gregory, Christ as the preexistent power and
wisdom of God, the Logos, is the heavenly Tabernacle; the Logos incarnate is the earthly Tabernacle.[174] The furnishings of the heavenly Tabernacle represent the angels.[175] The furnishings of
the earthly Tabernacle are the members of the
Church in their various liturgical roles and in their
ascetic and spiritual lives.[176] Philo had already said
that the "divine powers" were housed in the heavenly Tabernacle.[177] Drawing on the Pauline image
of the Church members as members of the Body
of Christ, Origen had added to this the parallel notion that the Church members are represented by
the furnishings of the earthly Tabernacle.[178] Gregory combined the two notions in a manner which
anticipates the Pseudo-Dionysian hierarchies.[179]
These same ideas, though less fully and systematically presented, may be found in Gregory of Nyssa's *Commentary on the Song of Songs.*[180]

[172] For a discussion of Gregory's sources and especially his relation to Philo and Origen on the Tabernacle, cf. Malherbe and
Ferguson, *op. cit.*, 179 ff.
[173] The Bride in the Song of Songs represents for Origen three
realities: the Church of the circumcision, the Church of the
Gentiles and the individual soul (Comm. Cant. 2.3). With less
than total consistency, Origen says that the Bride of the Canticle
represents the wife of Moses, while Moses represents the spiritual Law and hence Christ as Logos (Comm. Cant. 2.1). Origen
makes occasional references to the Tabernacle (esp. in Comm.
Cant. 2.1). The Incarnation is the house that Wisdom/Sophia
built for herself (Comm. Cant. 2.1), with the bishops, priests,
and deacons represented in it. Again, she is the churches
throughout the world. In Comm. Cant. 2.8 the Bride is the
preexistent Church, beloved of the preexistent Christ. On the
preexistent Church in Origen's predecessors, cf. J. Beumer, "Die
altchristliche Idee einer präexistierenden Kirche und ihre theologische Anwendung," *Wissenschaft und Weisheit*, 9 (1942), 13–
22; in Origen, A. Lieske, *Die Theologie der Logosmystik bei Origenes*
(Münster i.W., 1938), 88 ff.; J. C. Plumpe, *Mater Ecclesia. An Enquiry into the Concept of the Church as Mother in Early Christianity*
(Washington, D.C., 1943), chap. 5; C. Chavasse, *The Bride of Christ.
An Enquiry into the Nuptial Element in Early Christianity* (London,
1940), 172 ff. Discussion of these and other sources in R. P.
Lawson, trans., Origen, *The Song of Songs, Commentary and Homilies*, Ancient Christian Writers, 26 (New York, 1956), 14, 98,
106, 149, 311, 338, 349 *et passim*. For Methodius on the Tabernacle and Church, cf. Sym. 5.7.
[174] Gregory of Nyssa, Vit. Mos. 2.174.
[175] *Ibid.*, 2.179.
[176] *Ibid.*, 2.184.
[177] Quaest. Ex. 2.62; Malherbe and Ferguson, *op. cit.*, 180 note
230.
[178] Cf. note 173 *supra*.
[179] Daniélou, *op. cit.*, (*supra*, note 171), 89 note 2; Malherbe
and Ferguson, *op. cit.*, 181 note 240.
[180] The Incarnation is the construction of the true Tabernacle
(Greg. In Cant. 5.9; Langerbeck, 381: 1ff.). The apostles,

The particular contribution of the Alexandri-
ans, especially Gregory of Nyssa, to the interpre-
tation of the Tabernacle is the development of its
Christological and ecclesiological aspects. The
Christological dimension is not present in the Edessa
Hymn, but the ecclesiological interpretation of the
Tabernacle is one of its principal themes.

d. Syriac Writers of the Later Fifth and Early Sixth Centuries: Narsai and Jacob of Sarug

Since the Antiochene exegesis was taught at
Edessa during the time of Narsai's studies there,
and since Narsai, a Nestorian, remained faithful to
his Antiochene heritage, it is not surprising to find
the influence of Theodore of Mopsuestia in Narsai's *Homilies on the Creation.*[181] In his exegesis of the
Genesis account of creation Narsai describes the
visible world as a huge building. In addition to this
building, which is described as the "lower building" and "suitable for mortals," there is also an upper building for the "spiritual beings." This bipartite creation is a clear reflection of the two
καταστάσεις of the cosmological system of Theodore of Mopsuestia.[182] The following is Narsai's
description of the cosmos:

> The Creator constructed a great building for
> humankind,
> And He placed its foundations on liquid water
> which He made solid.
> He stretched out over it a roof of liquid water,
> And above it He piled up the water as in a res-
> ervoir.
> He suspended lamps from the ceiling of His
> building: the sun and moon;
> And He poured out oil, the sign of His power,
> and lit them.
> Glorious is the Creator, sublime His creation,
> immense His foreknowledge,

prophets, teachers, and pastors make up the Body of Christ
(Greg. In Cant. 5.9; Langerbeck, 382:14 ff., drawing on Eph.
4:11 ff.). Together, these two notions mean that the Tabernacle,
which is the Body of Christ, consists of the members of the
Church. Elsewhere, Gregory says that the life of the virtuous
person is represented by the furnishings of the Tabernacle (Greg.
In Cant. 1,4; Langerbeck, 44:9 ff.). A full exposition of this imagery in Gregory's commentary would be useful here, but is beyond the scope of this article.
[181] Gignoux, *Homélies de Narsaï*. Unlike Gignoux, Jansma is
convinced that Ephrem as well as Theodore had a significant
impact on Narsai; cf. Jansma, "Etudes sur la pensée de Narsai.
L'homélie n° XXXIV: essai d'interprétation," *OrSyr*, 11 (1966),
147–68, 265–90, 393–429; further, "Narsai and Ephraem: Some
Observations on Narsai's Homilies on Creation and Ephraem's
Hymns on Faith," *Parole de l'Orient*, 1 (1970), 49–68. The main
point at issue, the motif of the "*docta ignorantia*," does not bear
directly on my subject here.
[182] Cf. Gignoux, *Homélies de Narsaï*, 444.

Who knew in advance, before it had been cre-
ated, what His creation needed.
The One Who established all things made two
buildings for the creation;
He created two dwellings and constructed two
worlds.
He rendered the lower one suitable for mortals;
He gathered it up and filled it with fruits appro-
priate to corporeal beings.
He made of the upper one a beautiful building
full of delights,
So that the spiritual beings might enjoy it spiri-
tually.
For the terrestrial beings, He made terrestrial
things;
For the celestials, He promised celestial benefits.
The Omniscient contemplated the two build-
ings,
And He saw them before heaven and earth ex-
isted,
Because the will of His love was prior to His cre-
ation,
And the works that He did were outlined by His
will for Him.
He built and constructed heaven and earth like
a vast building;
He accumulated and heaped up immense wealth
for the one who would live there.[183]

In the homilies on creation, Narsai, a Nestorian,
clearly reflects the κόσμος-οἶκος notion typical of
Antiochene exegesis.[184] His description of the creation of the world is rooted in his notion of the
Tabernacle, since Moses' vision of the Tabernacle
(Genesis 24:12 ff., esp. 25:30) with the accompanying instructions constitute the basis for Moses' account of the creation of the world (i.e., Genesis 1
ff.).[185] The revelation of the Tabernacle is at once
a revelation of the mysteries of the cosmos and of
God's nature as Creator; God's nature can be known
by mortal creatures only indirectly, through His
creation.[186] The human being, made in the image
of God, is the sole vehicle of the revelation of God's
hidden nature. This is not because people share in
God's nature itself, but because the production of
Eve from Adam's side is a type of the generation
of the Son from the Father and because Adam is
made the lord of creation.[187] In the Incarnation,

Christ restores and fulfills the promises of this image.[188]

In sum, for Narsai, the cosmos is a great two-
storey building, which reveals God as Creator. God's
inner Trinitarian nature cannot be known through
the cosmos but only through human beings and
especially through Christ. The cosmos is in the image of the Tabernacle, but Narsai equates neither
Tabernacle nor cosmos with the Christian Church,
whether as ecclesiological concept or as architectural actuality.

The surviving literary corpus of Jacob of Sarug
provides an extensive exploitation of the Tabernacle imagery, which includes both cosmological and
ecclesiological dimensions. In this, he, being a Syrian
Monophysite, shows the influence of both the Antiochene and Alexandrian exegetes.

In his *Homilies in Hexaemeron*, Jacob portrays the
cosmos as a building, as expected of one schooled
in Antiochene exegesis.[189] Jacob's two-storey cosmos has a firmament which divides the waters above
from those below, sheltering the material creation,
the dwelling-place of humankind:

The firmament came to exist in the middle of
the waters on the second day,
As the Lord commanded it by a gesture of His
creativity,
And it became a limit between the waters for the
waters above.
And it became a shelter [*mṭalthâ*] for this dry place
beneath.
And it became a tent [*maškna* = Tabernacle] for
the pounded depth of the whole world,
And in its shadow [*ṭlâlâ*] dwells and rests the entire Creation.
It became the ceiling [*taṭlîlâ*] for the great house
of humankind,
That the gesture of the Deity built from nothing.
It became like a vault [*kaphthâ*] that hangs and
stands without foundation,
And not columns but a gesture supports it.[190]

This same firmament that forms the ceiling of the
human habitation, is the floor of the upper world.
"Stretched out like a garment under the habitations of the Deity,"[191] it separates the corporeal world
from the incorporeal. The firmament is solid and

[183] *Ibid.*, 1:83–104; for other examples cf. 444 note 64.
[184] Wolska, *Topographie*, 113–18, 121–27; and Cosmas Indicopleustes, *Topographie*, ed. Wolska-Conus, IV.2 note 1.
[185] Gignoux, *Homélies de Narsaï*, III, 1–30.
[186] *Ibid.*, III, 87–100.
[187] *Ibid.*, I, 135–44, 295 f.; III, 245 ff., 281–99, cf. discussion
of Gignoux, 449–53; at times it seems Adam alone is in the
image of God.

[188] *Ibid.*, III, 299, and Gignoux in the introduction, 449 f.
[189] Jansma, "Hexameron," 4–43, 129–62, 253–85 (contains
partial translation of Jacob's text). For the Syriac text, cf. P. Bedjan, ed., *Homiliae selectae Mar Jacobi Sarugensis* (Paris-Leipzig,
1905–1910), III, 1–151
[190] Bedjan, *op. cit.*, III, 34:12–35:2.
[191] *Ibid.*, III, 38:3.

material, but all that is above it is nonmaterial, an unlimited "sea of light," the present dwelling place of angels and future home of human beings.

All this is compatible with the Antiochene exegesis and proceeds from Jacob's early exegetical training at Edessa. But equally as well established as the κόσμος-ὄικος notion for the Antiochenes was the explicit rejection of a spherical firmament. Both Diodore of Tarsus and Severian of Gabala oppose the biblical terms καμάρα and σκηνή to the pagan term σφαῖρα, eschewing the use of the latter term.[192] Jacob of Sarug—whether in blissful ignorance of this issue or deliberately returning to the compromise of Basil of Caesarea—juxtaposes the traditional Antiochene language (tent, ceiling, shelter, vault) with "sphere," thus suggesting a compromise with the Ptolemaic cosmology:

> All of the creation of bodies and shades
> Like a sphere [= Gk. σφαῖρα] is placed, all of it, in the midst of nothing.
> There is no body above or below it
> Or surrounding it except the power that supports it.
> It is suspended and stands like a flying creature in the midst of nothing.[193]

In the middle of the sphere is a disc upon which the material creation rests. The angelic powers dwell in a "wilderness of light" which is above the disc and also seems to be above the firmament which encloses the material world from above:[194]

> There is in the middle the troubled world [ʿalmâ] full of motions,
> And above this disc [gîglâ; also = sphere] bearing bodies,
> A wilderness of light in which dwell the powers.
> Beneath these [is] this firmament like a sphere [sphayrâ]
> In which are closed up these corporeal bodies.
> [The firmament is] pitched like a tent for the habitation of races and tribes.
> There dwell in it many peoples with their natural dispositions
> And the Wisdom of the Exalted One made it firm and it came to exist on the second day,
> Like a ceiling [taṭlîthâ] for the whole world [ʿalmâ] of people.[195]

Jacob's treatment of the cosmos shows a unique combination of influences from Antioch and Alexandria—the κόσμος-οἶκος idea of Antioch coupled with the acceptance of a spherical cosmology typical of Alexandria.

In addition to the cosmological notions related to the Tabernacle, Jacob reflects an ecclesiological interpretation of the Tabernacle. The latter shows again the probable influence of Alexandrian thought on Jacob. The vision of Moses on Mt. Sinai, which prepared him for the construction of the Tabernacle, was, in Jacob's interpretation, a vision of the preexistent Church:

> Through Moses the Church was imprinted by a mystery.
> And the Tabernacle was designated as the type (of the Church).
> He who was not truly her Lord [i.e., Moses] did not create her.
> He stamped her imprint mysteriously and left and passed away.
> For the elect Church was built from eternity,
> And Moses testifies that he saw her image on Mount Sinai.[196]

Jacob's primary concern is to identify the vision of Moses as the preexistent Church and thereby to emphasize the subordinate status of Moses and the Old Covenant to Christ and the New Covenant. But it is equally clear that the vision provided the precise model by which the Tabernacle was constructed by Bezalel:

> Unless Moses saw with his eyes the Church that was built,
> He would not have been able to make all of its ornament.
> For with the image that was seen by him on Mount Sinai
> He came down and completed the construction without confusion.[197]

Thus the content of Moses' vision is at once the heavenly archetype of which the Tabernacle constructed by Bezalel is a mere earthly copy, and it is the preexistent Church. Like Gregory of Nyssa, Jacob holds that the object of Moses' vision has a

---

[192] Wolska, *Topographie*, 131; cf. also 129–32, 170 f.
[193] Bedjan, *op. cit.*, III, 40:10–14.
[194] Since the angelic "powers" are not corporeal, they may be above the sphere of the firmament without contradicting Jacob's previous statement that "there is no body above or below it."
[195] Bedjan, *op. cit.*, III, 40:15–41:4.

[196] *Ibid.*, I, 40:7–11; the citation is from Jacob's homily entitled, "On the consecration of the Church and on Moses the prophet"; for the Syriac text, cf. *ibid.*, I, 38–48. In this homily Moses is presented as a type of Christ, not primarily as lawgiver or as leader of the people from bondage in Egypt, but as the prophet who saw the eternal preexistent Church of the elect.
[197] *Ibid.*, I, 41:9–22.

higher degree of reality than its earthly imprint, the Mosaic Tabernacle. But whereas Gregory identifies this heavenly reality with the Logos, the preexistent Christ, Jacob identifies it with the preexistent Church.

Jacob's account of Moses' vision of the Tabernacle takes the form of a fiery female figure whose womb is the dwelling place of the several ranks of heavenly beings. She awaits the arrival of the "corporeal beings," the members of the Church. Rather than identifying her with the cosmos, Jacob says that the created order is "made a footstool for her feet, and she like a noblewoman bore herself grandly in the height. (Moses) saw her seated above the limits of all the high places, and her Lord alone rules over her." [198]

Like Gregory of Nyssa, Jacob sees the Tabernacle as a personification and as the dwelling place of all the angels, but whereas in Gregory's *Life of Moses* the Tabernacle represents the Logos, for Jacob it is the preexistent Church, Bride of the Logos. The image of the Church as Bride is common in the Alexandrian Christian tradition of commentaries on the Song of Songs, represented by Origen as well as by Gregory of Nyssa.[199] Gregory's *Commentary on the Song of Songs* or the general influx of Origenistic teachings could be the source of Jacob's imagery.[200] The source here cannot be Antiochene since Theodore of Mopsuestia explicitly rejected the allegorical interpretation of the Song of Songs.[201] It is conceivable, though not likely, that Jacob was inspired by rabbinic speculations on the Shekinah as the feminine counterpart of Yahweh; these notions might have reached Jacob either directly from Jewish contacts or through earlier Syriac Christian sources which do not survive.[202]

Whatever his precise sources, Jacob of Sarug

---

represents a point of convergence of cosmological and ecclesiological traditions related to the Tabernacle. Jacob's *Hexaemeron* reflects the typical Antiochene interest in the Tabernacle as cosmological symbol and the accompanying notion of the κόσμος-οἶκος, represented in the Syriac realm also by Narsai of Nisibis; but by his use of the term "sphere" for the firmament, Jacob also shows an Alexandrian modification of that cosmology. Finally, Jacob is influenced by the ecclesiological and mystical speculations on the Tabernacle and on the Song of Songs, probably mediated by the earlier Alexandrian Christian exegetes.

e. Conclusions

The examination of a variety of traditions about the Tabernacle in the main lines of Christian exegetical tradition at sixth-century Edessa has led to their convergence in the homilies of Jacob of Sarug. Jacob broadly exploits the imagery which had developed in both the Antiochene and Alexandrian exegetical schools. From the former he drew an emphasis on the Tabernacle as a cosmic house; from the latter, the vision of the Tabernacle as the (female) personification of the preexistent Church. Jacob was in an almost unique position among Patristic exegetes. As an early Syrian Monophysite, he had been trained in the Antiochene exegesis, yet his disaffection with the Antiochene Christology turned him toward the older Syriac sources and to Alexandrian traditions. So his exegesis was a hybrid, sometimes holding in tension essentially incompatible concepts.

VIII. Conclusion: From Scriptural Θεωρία to Architectural Θεωρία

The complex exegetical heritage of Jacob of Sarug has direct bearing on the problem of the interpretation of the domed church building as microcosm. By the sixth century C.E. only the Antiochene school maintained and emphasized the tradition of the cosmos as building. The Antiochene exegetical tradition was also explicitly opposed to the notion of the cosmos as a sphere. The notion of the spherical cosmos and the related idea that the firmament is a hemisphere (or that they are sets of spheres or hemispheres) were the preferred views in the Alexandrian tradition of exegesis. Yet the cosmic building and the hemispherical dome together constitute the basis for the interpretation of domed church buildings in cosmological terms and

---

[198] *Ibid.*, I, 42:22–43:3.
[199] Cf. note 26 *supra*.
[200] On the spread of Origenism in the Syriac-speaking environment, cf. Guillaumont, *Kephalaia et l'Origénisme*, 173 ff. The preexistent Church as the Bride of Christ is a prominent theme in Jacob's writings. For other examples, cf. F. Graffin, "Recherches sur le thème de l'Église-Épouse dans les liturgies et la littérature patristique de langue syriaque," *OrSyr*, 3 (1958), 317–36, esp. 322–36; also, J. Babakhan, "Essai de Vulgarisation des Homélies Métriques de Jacques de Saroug, Évêque de Batnan en Mésopotamie (451–521)," *ROChr*, 17 (1912), 410–26; 18(1913), 42–52, 360–74; idem, "Homélie de Jacques de Saroug sur le Voile de Moïse," *Vie spirituelle ascétique et mystique*, 91 (1954), 142–56; and M. Albert, *Jacques de Saroug: Homélies contre les juifs*, PO, 38, (1976),19 *et passim*.
[201] Devreesse, *Essai* (*supra*, note 136).
[202] M. Pope, *The Songs of Songs* (*supra*, note 16), 158 ff. *et passim*, on the Shekinah. On this and on the question of direct Jewish influence, cf. notes 14, 15 *supra*.

their domes (as distinct from vaults, canopies, or other curved but not spherical surfaces) as representations of the heavens. Smith tried to reconcile the Antiochene cosmology with Syrian architecture by proposing that the Antiochene firmament—the "lower heaven"—was tentlike, while the upper heaven was spherical. The lower heaven would then be represented by the vaulted ceiling while the upper heaven was represented by the dome. This corresponds well with the Edessa Hymn, as he noted. But as Wolska has shown, Smith's conception cannot be rooted in the Antiochene hexaemera with their explicit rejection of the term σφαῖρα.[203] The transposition of scriptural θεωρία to architectural θεωρία seems inadequate as an explanation of the cosmological interpretation of the domed church building, if Greek Christian traditions alone are taken into account.

Our consideration of certain homilies of Jacob of Sarug shows that this Syrian Monophysite exegete mixed the two major Greek traditions to produce a scriptural θεωρία which happened to be suitable for transposition into the architectural θεωρία of the Edessa Hymn. The discrepancy in theological perspective between Jacob of Sarug and Bishop Amazon, who rebuilt the church at Edessa, might seem to be a barrier to the interpretation proposed here, viz., that the homilies of Jacob of Sarug provide the immediate background of the Edessa Hymn. But this apparent difficulty is not actual. A hymnographer writing a dedication hymn for the Chalcedonian bishop of Edessa might draw upon the scriptural interpretation of a Syrian Monophysite like Jacob of Sarug for three reasons: (1) Syriac literary models of some kind were necessary.[204] (2) Provided that Christological issues were not directly addressed, this could be a subtle means of reconciling the substantial Monophysite populace of Edessa to the Chalcedonian bishop. (3) Jacob's hybrid exegetical tradition could be taken to represent a compromise similar to the views espoused by the Greek neo-Chalcedonians of the later sixth century, such as Leontius of Byzantium.[205] The Edessa Hymn appears to be the earliest sur-

viving example of architectural θεωρία in Syriac, but it has a notable precedent in Greek Christian literature, Eusebius' speech on the Church at Tyre.[206] Eusebius' speech shows that the notion of the cosmic house or temple had been applied to a Christian basilica by the end of the fourth century.[207] The Edessa Hymn's application of this notion to a domed church building rather than a basilica represents a variation on the theme of the cosmic temple. At first glance the hymn appears to be only a minor modification of the theme, due to a shift in architectural style. But behind this change stands a lengthy and controversial process of integrating features of a new cosmology into the interpretation of Scripture and into an overall theological perspective. This process was being executed by the numerous hexaemera composed from the late fourth to the sixth century.

Jacob of Sarug's hybrid solution to the cosmological problem was especially appropriate to the interpretation of the domed church building. The Edessa Hymn, emerging from the same geographical environment about a quarter of a century after Jacob's death, presupposes Jacob's cosmology. The Edessa Hymn constitutes the transposition of this scriptural θεωρία into an architectural θεωρία and pinpoints this transition at Edessa in the mid-sixth century. From there the diffusion of the architectural θεωρία could take place without further specific reference to the scriptural interpretations of the Tabernacle and of the opening chapters of Genesis which had given it birth.

Appendix 1. André Grabar's Study of the Symbolism of the Edessa Hymn

André Grabar's study of the Edessa Hymn in 1947 brought this relatively unknown piece of Syriac literature into the limelight of Byzantine architectural his-

---

[203] Smith, Dome, 88 f.; Wolska, Topographie, 129–31, esp. 131.

[204] For a Syriac example which might have provided the formal but not the thematic model for the Edessa Hymn, cf. Appendix 3.

[205] Jacob's theological stance was sufficiently ambiguous to produce a lengthy scholarly discussion. For the basic literature, cf. Ortiz de Urbina, Patrologia Syriaca, 107 f; to this may be added: T. Jansma, "Encore le credo de Jacques de Saroug," OrSyr, 10 (1965), 75–88; 193–236; 331–70; 475–510; and the general assessment of Jacob's Christology in R. Chesnut, Three Monophysite Christologies (supra, note 142).

[206] Eusebius of Caesarea, Ecclesiastical History X.IV, esp. 2–9, 63–68, 69–72. Although the earliest Syriac MS, dated to 462 C.E., does not contain the tenth book, it probably was known in Syriac by the mid-sixth century. For the Syriac text, cf. P. Bedjan, Histoire ecclésiastique d'Eusèbe de Césarée. Version syriaque éditée pour la première fois (Leipzig, 1877); and W. Wright and N. McLean, The ecclesiastical history of Eusebius in Syriac, edited from the ms with collation of the ancient Armenian version (Cambridge, 1898); trans. E. Nestle, TU, 25; on the age of the individual chapters, E. Nestle, Syrische Grammatik, 2nd ed. (Berlin, 1888), 44; E. Nestle, in ZDMG, 56, 559–64; E. Lohmann, Der textkritische Wert der syrischen Übersetzung der Kirchengeschichte des Eusebios (diss. Halle, 1899); W. Wright, Journal of Semitic Languages, 9, 117–36; 10, 150–64.

[207] Smith argues that the Church at Tyre must have been a domed structure, cf. Dome, 92. A recent study points out the literary context of Eusebius' description, cf. J. Wilkinson, "Paulinus' Temple at Tyre," JÖB, 32 (1982), 553–61.

tory.[208] In that study Grabar argued that the hymn had a bipartite provenience.[209] On the one hand, the verses pertaining to the furnishings of the church building and to liturgical functions were interpreted in terms of biblical prototypes in the manner of the Byzantine liturgical commentaries attributed to Cyril or Sophronius of Jerusalem and Germanus of Constantinople.[210] On the other hand, the verses pertaining to the architecture itself, and especially to the dome, were interpreted in the manner of the Pseudo-Dionysian writings. Traditional biblical interpretations from Palestine were retained for the liturgical commentary, but the newer mystical trends of Greek Neo-Platonism were used for interpreting the new domed architecture.

Grabar questioned neither that Syriac was the original language of the hymn, nor that its place of origin was Edessa, nor that it was composed in honor of the Justinianic reconstruction of the church building, completed in the mid-sixth century.[211] Nevertheless, he argued that the cosmic and mystical symbolism of the hymn was "Greek" rather than "Syriac," because its literary roots were to be found in three Greek Christian works of the sixth and seventh centuries: (1) the Pseudo-Dionysian corpus, (2) the *Topography* of Cosmas Indicopleustes, and (3) the *Mystagogy* of Maximus the Confessor.[212] Dependence on Maximus the Confessor (d. 662) necessitates a seventh-century date for the hymn, although one would otherwise assume that a hymn composed in honor of a building was intended to be used on the occasion of its dedication and hence contemporaneous with the completion of construction.[213] Grabar's analysis of the literary roots of the Edessa Hymn's symbolism and, consequently, his dating of the hymn have been generally accepted.[214]

The present study of the literary roots of the hymn leads to substantial modification of Grabar's analysis. Grabar correctly recognized that the Byzantine liturgical commentaries and the Pseudo-Dionysian writings are fundamentally similar to the Edessa Hymn. Subsequent research on the history of exegesis and the history of the liturgy, especially the work of Bornert on the Patristic exegetical background of the Byzantine liturgical commentaries, indicates a close relationship among scriptural, liturgical, and mystical commentaries.[215] A strict dichotomy between biblical and Neo-Platonic interpre-

tations is misleading in this context. Middle and Neo-Platonic philosophy strongly influenced early Christian biblical interpretation, especially in the Alexandrian tradition. The Pseudo-Dionysian writings and the *Mystagogy* of Maximus the Confessor are themselves examples of scriptural and liturgical θεωρία.[216]

It is now clear that Grabar's suggestions about the lines of literary influence leading to the Edessa Hymn are erroneous. First, since it has become clear that both Pseudo-Dionysius and the Edessa Hymn belong to a broader context in which mystical and cosmological interest are not uncommon, these affinities are not sufficient to show the literary dependence of the Edessa Hymn on Pseudo-Dionysius. Not even the nine orders of angels is exclusively Dionysian.[217] Second, the *Topography* of Cosmas Indicopleustes belongs in the context of early Christian exegetical literature. It is the product of the same Antiochene exegetical tradition that survives in the commentaries and homilies of Theodore of Mopsuestia and Narsai of Nisibis, and in part, in the homilies of Jacob of Sarug. Cosmas transmitted the Syriac version of Antiochene hexaemeral literature back into the Greek-speaking world.[218] He is not the source but another branch of the tradition reflected in the Edessa Hymn. Third, Maximus the Confessor's *Mystagogy* shares the hymn's mystical and ecclesiological themes, but emphasis on the actual church building is less explicit in Maximus than in the hymn. The homilies of Jacob of Sarug provide a sufficient literary background for the hymn in Syriac rather than Greek and at a date more compatible with the external evidence. If there is any literary dependence between Maximus and the Edessa Hymn, it is more probable that Maximus is the recipient.

Appendix 2. The Genre of the *Sôgîthâ*

The term *sôgîthâ* is used to identify four distinct types of Syriac hymn. According to Baumstark, the *sôgîthâ* is most characteristically a dialogue: it may be a dramatization either of biblical events or of a theological debate.[219] Some *sôgyâthâ* dramatizing biblical events, all of them attributed to Narsai, consist of conversations between Cain and Abel, the Archangel Gabriel and Mary, Mary and the Magi, John the Baptist and Herod, the Pharisees and Jesus.[220] Another group of three *sôgyâthâ*

[208] Grabar, "Le témoignage" (*supra*, note 3), 41–67.

[209] *Ibid.*, esp. 59–63.

[210] For a recent discussion of the authorship and date of these works and further bibliography, cf. Bornert, *Commentaires* (*supra*, note 11), 125 ff., esp. 128 note 4.

[211] Grabar, "Le témoignage," 54, 52.

[212] *Ibid.*, 54, 57–79.

[213] *Ibid.*, 41, 52, 58, for Grabar's dating of the hymn. For the argument that the hymn is a foundation hymn, cf. Cameron, "Shroud" (*supra*, note 4), 10.

[214] For example, Wolska, *Topographie*, 295 f. Smith, *Dome*, 89–91. C. Mango and J. Parker, "A Twelfth-century Description of St. Sophia," *DOP*, 14 (1960), 241. Cameron, ed., Corippus, *In laudem Justini*, 207.

[215] Bornert, *Commentaires*, esp. 35 f.

[216] *Ibid.*, 66–72, on Pseudo-Dionysius as sacramental θεωρία; 90–104, on Maximus' *Mystagogy* as liturgical θεωρία.

[217] Cf. comments on strophe 19, *supra*.

[218] On Cosmas and the Antiochene exegesis, cf. Wolska, *Topographie*, esp. 31 note 1, 32, 37–85.

[219] Or a combination of the two, cf. Baumstark, *Geschichte* (*supra*, note 170), 39 f. and note 5; also cf. R. Duval, *Anciennes Littératures Chrétiennes* II, *La Littérature Syriaque*, 2nd ed. (Paris, 1900), 23 f.; and E. Wellesz, "Early Christian Music" and "Music of the Eastern Churches" in *Early Medieval Music up to 1300*, ed. Dom A. Hughes, The New Oxford History of Music, II (London, 1954), 1–57, esp. 9.

[220] F. Feldmann, *Syrische Wechsellieder von Narses* (Leipzig, 1896), Syriac text with German translation.

includes discussions among Abraham, Sarah, Isaac, and God.[221] Examples of the second type of dramatic dialogue, the theological debate, are encounters between the Church and the Synagogue,[222] between Cyril of Alexandria and Nestorius,[223] or between a persecuting king and a group of martyrs.[224] Several of the biblical subjects chosen by the authors of *sôgyâthâ* have an element of conflict as well.[225]

Whether their purpose was the simple edification or the theological instruction of the listeners, the dialogue form seems to be an essential feature of these hymns. They were probably sung by a combination of two soloists and two choirs.[226] Robert Murray and Sebastian Brock have suggested that this controversial type of *sôgîthâ* stands in a direct line from the Mesopotamian contest poem to the western medieval tenson.[227] The alphabetical acrostic is a second device which is not always present in these hymns.

There is a third group of *sôgyâthâ*, which Baumstark classified as akin to ballads, and which may be the forerunners of the dialogical types of *sôgîthâ*.[228] Baumstark suggested that the essential feature of these hymns is their dramatic quality. They generally consist of a monologue put into the mouth of a single biblical character. One extant example comments on the story of the Prodigal Son.[229]

G. Khouri-Sarkis identified a fourth type of *sôgîthâ*, the Maronite type, which occurs frequently in the daily office of the Maronite rite. This type is closely related both by content and by meter to the *bâ'ûthâ*, a hymn of supplication, in the meter of Jacob of Sarug. It is often in the form of an alphabetical acrostic. The Edessa Hymn is essentially of this type, although its metrical pattern differs slightly: it has twenty-two strophes, each with four eight-syllable hemistichs rather than the usual twenty-two strophes, each with four four-syllable hemistichs.[230]

Although some *sôgyâthâ* are attributed in the manu-

script traditions to such well-known Syriac authors as Ephrem, Narsai, and Jacob of Sarug, some of these attributions are uncertain or erroneous; others are without attribution; still other extant examples remain unpublished. As a result, the history of the development of the *sôgîthâ* and especially the interrelationship of the four types has not been delineated. It is unclear, therefore, how the Maronite type of *sôgîthâ* is related to the dialogical types, if it is related at all.[231]

Appendix 3. Balai's *madrâšâ* on the dedication of the church at Qenneŝrîn

A *madrâšâ* on the rededication of the church at Qenneŝrîn (Beroea) composed by Balai in the early fifth century, A.D., is extant and provides certain parallels to the Edessa Hymn.[232] There are formal similarities between the two pieces, although the manuscripts entitle them differently, i.e., the one as a *sôgîthâ*, the other as a *madrâšâ*. Both have strophes consisting of four octosyllabic hemistichs; but in contrast to the Edessa Hymn, Balai's composition has sixty-eight strophes and is not an alphabetical acrostic.

There are also some thematic parallels. The anagogical tendency is present in Balai's poem: The church is called the dwelling place of God and "heaven on earth," while the service of the priests is compared with the ministry of the angels (strs. 1–7). The theme of the κόσμος-οἶκος is also represented, though only implicitly, in the statement, "[God] built us the world, and we [have built] Him] a house" (strs. 31–32). Yet a greater emphasis is on the congregation or on the heart or mind (*lebbâ*) of the Christian, especially of the priest or bishop, as the Temple, the dwelling place of God (strs. 23–26).[233] Further, it is Solomon's Temple rather than the Mosaic Tabernacle that is invoked as the model of the church (strs. 27–30).

Some architectural features (the foundations, doors,

---

[221] B. Kirschner, "Alphabetische Akrosticha in der syrischen Kirchenpoesie," *OrChr*, 6 (1906), 1–69; 7 (1907), 254–91.

[222] *Ibid.* Also Br. Lib. Add. 17141 and 17190, noted by S. Brock, "The Dispute Poem: From Sumer to Syriac," *Bayn al-Nahrayn* (Mosul), 7(28) (1979), 417–26, esp. 421; and Albert, *op. cit.*, PO, 38 (1976), 160–81, but one MS identifies this as a *mêmrâ* rather than a *sôgîthâ*.

[223] Feldmann, *op. cit.*

[224] *Ibid.*

[225] For example, Christ and the Pharisee, Christ and John the Baptist, John and Herod, cf. *ibid.*

[226] Wellesz, *op. cit.*, 9; Baumstark, *Geschichte*, 40.

[227] R. Murray in *Annual of the Leeds University Oriental Society* (1980), cited by Brock, "Dispute Poem," 421.

[228] Baumstark, *Geschichte*, 40.

[229] Kirschner, *op. cit.*, classified the six *sôgyâthâ* he studied as either elegies or tensons, depending on their content. Another *sôgîthâ* is "On impiety," also in Kirschner, *op. cit.* Neither Baumstark nor Jeannin includes the acrostic type unless it is also a dialogue, cf. J. Jeannin, *Mélodies liturgiques syriennes et chaldéennes* (Paris, 1928), 2, 17.

[230] For references, cf. note 140 *supra*. Earlier studies of the Edessa Hymn have not commented on its literary structure, nor has it been noted previously that the hymn is an acrostic.

[231] In addition to the works of Duval, Jeannin, Baumstark, Wellesz, Brock, and Khouri-Sarkis cited in notes 140, 170, 219, and 222, cf. I. H. Dalmais, "L'apport des Églises syriennes à l'hymnographie chrétienne," *OrSyr*, 2 (1957), 243–61. For general bibliography on Syriac liturgical music, cf. H. Husmann, *Die Melodien des Wochenbreviers* (Shimta), Österreichische Akademie der Wissenschaften 6.9; Sitzungsberichte, Phil.-His. Kl. (Vienna, 1969), I, 213–16. For discussion of the internal structure of this type of verse, cf. G. Hölscher, *Syrische Verskunst*, Leipziger Semitische Studien, 5, n.f. (Leipzig, 1932), 54–73, 128 ff.

[232] For the Syriac text, cf. J. J. Overbeck, *S. Ephraemi Syri, Rabulae Episcopae Edesseni, Balaei Aliorumque Opera Selecta* (Oxford, 1865), 251–58; German trans. G. Bickell, *Ausgewählte Gedichte der syrischen Kirchenväter: Cyrillonas, Baläus, Isaak von Antiochien und Jakob von Sarug*, BKV (Kempten, 1872), 74–82, and Landersdorfer in BKV, 6 (Kempten, 1912), 63–70. Strophe numbers here refer to Overbeck's Syriac text.

[233] This is the only context in which Balai uses *haŷklâ*, temple, though Bickell and Landersdorfer translate both *haŷklâ* and *bêth qûdšâ* as "Tempel." *Bêth qûdšâ*, in strs. 6–10, would better be translated as "sanctuary." The German translations obscure a distinction which is clearly present in the Syriac text.

courts, sanctuary [? *'athrâ*], and altar), are enumerated and interpreted, but not in cosmological terms. Here, apart from a general reliance on biblical imagery, the only similarity to the Edessa Hymn is in the use of nuptial imagery: "The [holy] place (*'athrâ*) is adorned, crowned with glory, since it is the day of the festival and the wedding feast, the new bridal couch [for ?] Christ the Bridegroom. ." (str. 14). In this section we can see the difference between Balai's emphasis and the Edessa Hymn. The culmination of Balai's enumeration of architectural features of the church at Qennešrîn is the altar, this because it is the place where the eucharistic elements are consecrated. The notion of the Divine presence in the building and the ascent to heaven which God's descent has made possible is a central feature of Balai's poem (strs. 30–34), but it is not contemplation of the building as microcosm which mediates this ascent. It is clearly the eucharistic meal (strs. 35–37); God's presence is in the sanctuary (str. 41). The theological explanation that Balai offers is a kenotic Christology with emphasis on the Incarnation, especially on the Nativity and Epiphany (strs. 38–66), rather than on the Creation account of Genesis or the Mosaic Tabernacle.

In conclusion, it is clear that certain formal similarities exist between Balai's composition on the church at Qennešrîn and our unknown author's hymn on the church at Edessa. Further, there are thematic parallels in the notion of the κόσμος-οἶκος and in the interpretation of the building in terms of Biblical materials. Yet the specific focus of the Edessa Hymn on Genesis 1 and on the Mosaic Tabernacle is almost entirely absent from Balai's composition, which emphasizes instead the Incarnation and the eucharistic meal. Although some architectural features are mentioned by Balai, a dome is not among them; so the very features which make the Edessa Hymn significant for architectural iconology are absent from Balai's poem on the church at Qennešrîn. Still his poem is an interesting representative of θεωρία in Syriac, but one which is closer in emphasis to the liturgical commentaries than to the Edessa Hymn.

Princeton Theological Seminary

ART AND THE EARLY CHURCH

IT is universally held to be a fact that the early Church was hostile to art.[1] The view recently received confirmation in a *relazione* to the Ninth International Congress of Christian Archaeology which met at Rome in 1975, and has also been made the basis for an assessment of the background to the Byzantine iconoclastic controversy in a recent book by L. W. Barnard.[2] However, it is the purpose of this paper to investigate whether this accepted fact has any foundation in reality, or whether it is simply an example of the phenomenon by which repeated assertion raises to the level of established truth what was initially a matter of scholarly opinion.

The reason why a matter of conjecture should appear to be a matter of fact is not hard to find: repetition has not only standardized the content of the theory, but the form in which it receives presentation has by now become classical.[3]

Although it receives slight modification as it is rehandled, nevertheless the basic outline and content remain the same, and it may be briefly summarized as follows. From its origins in Judaism Christianity inherited its pure and spiritual worship of God 'in spirit and in truth' and along with this therefore a hostility to religious artistic representation

[1] In direct discussions in the field of Christian archaeology itself, e.g. J. Beckwith, *Early Christian and Byzantine Art* (London, 1970), p. 37. In indirect discussions among church historians, e.g. the section on Christian art in the most recent and widely read history of the early Church, H. Chadwick, *The Early Church* (Pelican history of the Church, 1967), pp. 277–84, esp. p. 280. In Byzantine studies, e.g. the first two chapters on early Christian images in P. J. Alexander, *The Patriarch Nicephorus of Constantinople* (Oxford, 1958), pp. 1–53.

[2] J. D. Breckenridge, 'The Reception of Art into the Early Church', in *Ueberlegungen zum Ursprung der fruehchristlichen Bildkunst* (IX Congresso Internazionale di Archeologia Cristiana, Rome, 1975, preliminary acts), pp. 29–38, esp. p. 31, 'an absolutely monolithic opposition to imagery existed among responsible ecclesiastics from the earliest days of the Christian era through at least the reign of Constantine . . .' and p. 30, where he echoes the view of G. B. Ladner, 'The Concept of the Image in the Greek Fathers and the Byzantine Iconoclastic Controversy', *D.O.P.* vii (1953), pp. 3–34 and p. 5, that the founders of Christian theology were 'anything but friendly to the images of art'. L. W. Barnard, *The Graeco-Roman and Oriental Background of the Iconoclastic Controversy* (Leiden, 1974), pp. 51–64, esp. p. 53 and pp. 89–91.

[3] It is found, for example, in Chadwick and Alexander and see also E. Kitzinger, 'The Cult of Icons before Iconoclasm', *D.O.P.* viii (1954), pp. 85–150, esp. pp. 88–9.

[Journal of Theological Studies, N.S., Vol. XXVIII, Pt. 2, October 1977]

which both religions identified with pagan practice. The second of the Ten Commandments had forbidden Israel the making of any graven image and the authoritative leaders of the Christian community such as Tertullian, Clement of Alexandria, Eusebius, and Epiphanius right up to Augustine considered this prohibition as absolute and binding on Christians also. Yet by the end of the second century Christians were expressing their faith in artistic terms in a movement gathering evermore momentum. Nevertheless the older and purer strain of religion was not lost for it remained operative at the official level, among the church authorities, who continued to manifest their disapproval in the matter. Originally, artistic displays had been shy of portraying Christ and of making representations of the central mysteries of the Christian religion, particularly of the Cross and Resurrection. But by the fourth century, if not earlier as is sometimes said, any sense of restraint or inhibition had vanished, and images or icons representing individual persons had become the characteristic form of personal piety. They had thus entered the Church from below against the older form of austerity which was always present at a higher level, and mistrust of the icon erupted in the eighth century into the bitter struggle of the iconoclastic controversy which ended ultimately in 843 with the icon triumphant over the purer spirit of Christianity.

When the theory is summarized in this way it becomes clear what the problem was to which it addressed itself: there appears to be a divergence between the art and the literature of the early Church. And since the material remains are evidently in conflict with the texts of the Fathers a hypothesis was necessary which would explain it. So the difficulty was resolved by making the art originate with the laity in opposition to the clergy. One can only say that the solution looks extremely neat; it covers all eventualities and is apparently foolproof. It is unsurprising therefore that despite the wealth of new material which has been discovered in the interim, it has remained unexamined for more or less fifty years.

Who invented it is a fascinating question, and a search for its origin appears to lead to Renan, who made Christianity a normatively iconophobic religion because of its Jewish matrix.[1] In his view the early Church was completely opposed to images prior to the third century when, as the result of its transplantation to a Greco-Roman environment friendly to art, it lost its essentially aniconic nature through pressure to conform. Since this was basically deviationist in terms of the

[1] See E. Renan, *Histoire des origines du christianisme 7: Marc Aurèle et la fin du monde antique*, 6th edn. (Paris, 1891), pp. 539 f.

initial purity, Renan made Gnosticism the origin of Christian art.[1] The presupposition here is obvious: as Judaism was hostile to art, so any religion of which it was the source must automatically be hostile too. This same presupposition also underlies the monumental work of von Dobschütz.[2]

Von Dobschütz was the scholar from whom the classical presentation of the theory received its framework, with its opening sentence describing Christianity as the worship of God in spirit and in truth according to John iv. 24, and the reference to the Decalogue prohibition, which has been repeated ever since. Von Dobschütz too seems to have been the first to compose the standard list of patristic texts regarded as supporting the view of a rigorous official attitude towards art.[3]

But the major substantiation, giving the hypothesis the general acceptance it has had ever since, came with the analysis of the literary evidence made by Koch and Elliger.[4] Their study led them to conclude that a continuous thread of official hostility to art could be traced in leading churchmen from the beginning to Augustine. In a second exhaustive monograph Elliger attempted to co-ordinate his literary analysis with the archaeological evidence so as to make clear the factors favouring or retarding the development of Christian art and to define the contributions of the various regions of the Roman empire to it.[5] Both scholars worked from Renan's and von Dobschütz's viewpoint of a purely spiritual definition of Judaism and Christianity and the adherence of the Christian leadership to the second commandment. This question of the Decalogue prohibition was probed more deeply still by Klauser, and he elaborated yet more fully the theory that Christian art was the product of certain circles of the laity who opposed themselves to the teaching authority of the Church.[6] In constructing

---

[1] For Renan Christianity was 'une grandiose maison de la prière, voilà tout', op. cit., p. 539.
[2] E. von Dobschütz, *Christusbilder* (T.U. 18, Leipzig, 1899). Both scholars derived their assumption from Harnack who had begun the publication of his *History of Dogma* a few years earlier (1885). Von Dobschütz was in fact discussing one category of Christian images only, the so-called *acheiropoietai*—those not made by human hands, but his profound study led him to consider all manner of general questions connected with religious images; he discussed art in the early Church in his second chapter.   [3] Belege, pp. 98*–122*.
[4] H. Koch, *Die altchristliche Bilderfrage nach den literarischen Quellen* (Forsch. zur Relig. und Lit. des A. und N. Testaments, x, Göttingen, 1917); W. Elliger, 'Die Stellung der alten Christen zu den Bildern in den ersten vier Jahrhunderten', *Studien über christliche Denkmäler*, xx (Leipzig, 1930), pp. 1–98.
[5] 'Zur Entstehung und frühen Entwicklung der altchristlichen Bildkunst', ibid. xxiii (1934), pp. 1–284.
[6] Th. Klauser, 'Erwägungen zur Entstehung der altchristlichen Kunst', *Z.K.G.* lxxvi (1965), pp. 1–11.

his view he acknowledged his debt to the literary work of Koch and Elliger.[1]

Elliger's interpretation of the patristic evidence finally became canonical with the use made of it by Ernst Kitzinger in a magistral article on the cult of icons before iconoclasm, in the section in which he dealt with the centuries of the Church before Justinian.[2] And it is Kitzinger's study, based on the interpretation of the literature made by Elliger, which is now regarded as authoritative in all subsequent discussions, including those of Breckenridge and Barnard.[3]

Why this should be so may at first appear to be surprising when it is remembered that Kitzinger's work was not in the main concerned with the early period. His purpose was to analyse the cult of images at a time already recognized as crucial,[4] the period between Justinian and Iconoclasm. But it was in order to throw into relief the phenomena new at this time that he went back to look at the attitude of the early Church, with the intention of setting out the maximum amount of textual evidence witnessing to an intensification of cult practices then and to explore the motives for their development. He took his evidence from the by now standard treatment of Elliger[5] and arrived at the view that 'an undercurrent of at least potential iconoclasm does in fact run through the entire history of the Church in the intervening centuries'[6] and to the necessity of thinking in terms of a continuing conflict which finally 'erupted into an explosion of well-nigh world historical import'.[7]

Ultimately he reached a thesis 'of practice, opposition and apologetic theory' as characteristic not only of the sixth to the ninth centuries but of the third and fourth as well.[8]

Kitzinger's authority is not therefore to be wondered at since what he has done is to add a further dimension to the hypothesis. In seeing the whole sweep of antagonism to art from the beginning of the Church to the iconoclastic controversy as a genetic and organic development, he has linked it indissolubly with Byzantine iconoclasm. And in doing so has carried it out of the field of early church history into that of Byzantine studies where it remains as the accepted interpretation of the attitude of the early church in any discussions connected with the iconoclastic controversy. The patristic evidence therefore has changed its context.

---

[1] p. 4 n. 19.　　　　　　　　　　　　　　[2] pp. 85–160, cf. section I.
[3] For their acknowledgements see Breckenridge, p. 37 n. 27: Barnard, p. 52 n. 5.
[4] By von Dobschütz *passim*, and esp. p. 35, and A. Grabar, *Martyrium*, ii (Paris, 1946, repr. 1972), pp. 343 f.
[5] For example, p. 86 nn. 5 and 6; p. 87 n. 7.
[6] p. 85.　　　　　　　　　　[7] Ibid.　　　　　　　　　　[8] p. 86.

It will be noted from the foregoing historical sketch that there are, so to speak, two peak periods of presentation of the hypothesis—the initial one at the end of the nineteenth century, which gave it the presuppositions upon which it is based,[1] and the confirmation in the work of Kitzinger which provided it with a new content; both are associated, though in different ways, with crises in the discussion of images. So although the theory ultimately stands or falls according to whether the documentary evidence from the Fathers, normally adduced in support of it, has in fact been correctly interpreted, nevertheless since the interpretation rests on these presuppositions about the nature of Christianity as understood by the Fathers of the early period, and about the unbroken link in the matter of attitude of the early Church with the Byzantine Church, it is first of all necessary to discover whether these presuppositions are correct. For if it is found that they are not historically representative of the social context in which the literary evidence was composed then the interpretation of the texts becomes seriously weakened from the outset. From the point of view of the literary evidence as it touched on matters of art, the essentially spiritual nature of Christianity was regarded as proved by the continual attempt to enforce the second commandment. So a short examination is needed of what is actually known of the use of the Decalogue in the early Church to get the context right, and to see if there is any ground for continuing to believe that the prohibition of the second commandment was taken seriously at the 'official level' since all agree that it was disregarded at the 'popular level'.

It seems clear from the study made by Grant[2] that there was no real theological analysis of the meaning of the Old Testament Law as it should be reinterpreted in the life of the Church until the mid second century and then it was made by the Valentinian heretic, Ptolemy.[3]

---

[1] On the notion of Christian art as part of what J. B. Bury, *History of the Later Roman Empire*, i (London, 1923), p. 372, called 'the pagan transmutation of Christianity', see A. Harnack, *Lehrbuch der Dogmengeschichte*, ii, 4th edn. (Tübingen, 1909), p. 467, who speaks of 'Christentum zweiter Ordnung', and *Mission und Ausbreitung*, i⁴ (Leipzig, 1924), pp. 300–1; and Elliger, 'Zur Entstehung', p. 272 and passim for 'Ethnisierung'. On churches as sacred objects see Koch, pp. 93–9, and on the relationship of acheiropoietai with image worship, see von Dobschütz, pp. 277–9 and passim.

[2] R. M. Grant, 'The Decalogue in Early Christianity', *Harv. Theol. Rev.* xl (1947), pp. 1–17.

[3] See the *Letter to Flora* in R. M. Grant, *Gnosticism—an Anthology* (London, 1961), pp. 184–90, which synthesizes the sayings of Jesus as found in the gospel of Matthew with the varying levels of inspiration in the Old Testament; part of the Law is from God, part from Moses, part from the Elders, a part mixed with evil, and a purely typical or symbolical part. The example of the pure

Indeed if Grant's theory of the origin of the *Shepherd of Hermas* is true,[1] the whole of the Jewish Law was in disrepute in Rome in the earliest, sub-apostolic centuries and the Decalogue itself had fallen out of use among Christians at this time. Justin's *Apology* i. 14–17 makes no explicit use of the Decalogue in this collection of sayings on particular virtues;[2] and even in the case of converts instructed by Christian Jewish leaders, where apparently the Decalogue seems to be superficially of high value, the content is quietly altered.[3] Clement of Alexandria, writing for the more elementary pupils of the *Paedagogus* iii. 89, observes that the Decalogue was proclaimed openly and not through enigmas, that is, it does not need allegorization, but when it comes to the *Stromateis* vi. 133–48, written for the more advanced, his real opinion comes out and he explains almost all of it symbolically. The true Christian does not need the Decalogue but it is useful for proving the divine origin of Christian gnosticism.[4] As regards the specific prohibition of the second commandment, the Fathers do not seem to have had any clear idea about the interpretation of Mosaic texts, and so their explanations are not always coherent. A clear example can be seen in the case of Tertullian, normally regarded as proof of the rigorous attitude of church leaders on the point. For a sound principle of approach we have his *Adv. Marc.* ii. 22: representation is not illegal because it is not idolatrous; yet *De Spect.* xx. 3 and *Adv. Marc.* iv. 22 seem to suggest that Exodus xx. 4 forbids representation of all living things. What we have is not really Tertullian's

---

legislation of the Law of God is the Decalogue, but even this did not reach perfection, it needed the fulfilment of the Saviour.

[1] He considers it was written to bring back the Roman community to a sense of the importance of the ten commandments, see 'Decalogue', p. 11.

[2] For Justin as here representing the standard and traditional teaching see W. Bousset, *Jüdisch-christliche Schulbetrieb in Alexandria und Röm* (Göttingen, 1915), pp. 282–308.

[3] Theophilus of Antioch offers great praise but in iii. 9 the first and second commandments consist of 'piety' and the third and fourth are simply omitted. *Theophilus of Antioch*, ed. R. M. Grant (Oxford, 1970).

[4] In other words the pattern at Alexandria reflects that in Rome: *Strom.* vi. 147, theft is the imitation of true philosophy; 146, adultery means leaving the true knowledge to be found in the Church for vain opinion. According to Stählin, G.C.S. ii, pp. 499–508, Clement is much indebted here to the Jewish tradition of allegorization found in Aristobulus and Philo. See also P. Heinisch, *Der Einfluss Philos auf die älteste christliche Exegese* (Münster, 1908), pp. 273–7. For the ban imposed on the daily recital of the Decalogue in the synagogues by the Jewish authorities, some time in the early Christian period after the destruction of the Temple, in order to restrain heretics from claiming its pre-eminence over the rest of the Law, see C. K. Barrett, *The Gospel of John and Judaism* (London, 1975), p. 49.

own view about the legality of making images, but a confusion of exegesis resulting from the inability to harmonize one part of the Old Testament with another. Scholars, and in particular Klauser, have credited the Fathers with a consistency in the matter which they do not have. It seems therefore that the protagonists of the hostility theory have begun with a wrong assumption. This is further borne out if one looks briefly at the supposition underlying this assumption: that historical Judaism itself was aniconic because of continuous enforcement of the same legal prescription. Presumably this idea is also to be related to theories held in Germany at the end of the nineteenth century; for the standard view of the Jewish attitude towards images at the time when the analysis of the Christian one was being made was based on that of Harnack's friend Schürer, who stated categorically that 'Judaism rejected all images of men and animals',[1] and regarded the prohibition as founded on the mosaic law. That this view of the matter could have been held at all seems extraordinary in view of the fact that the history of the Old Testament itself shows that the law was never interpreted as completely forbidding images. The descriptions of the Temple and the palace of Solomon immediately come to mind, the fashioning of the Brazen Serpent also;[2] though admittedly there is no mention of sculptured statues, and classical Hebrew has no word for 'to paint', and certainly the commandment was strictly enforced in that, so far as we know, Judaism never made an image of God.[3] What is more surprising, however, is that when Schürer made that statement in 1907 there was already well-known and published a wealth of Jewish archaeological evidence from the Jewish catacombs of Rome.[4]

The Vigna Randanini already explored in the sixties of the nineteenth century has chickens, bulls, and rams engraved on its doors; one bull is on a sepulchral tablet of a doctor of the Law. There is also a chamber adorned with paintings in which birds appear, and the same catacomb has yielded fragments of a sarcophagus on which winged griffins are combined with specifically Jewish emblems. Still richer in

---

[1] E. Schürer, *Geschichte das Jüdischen Volkes im Zeitalter Jesu Christi*, ii, 4th edn. (Leipzig, 1907), p. 65.

[2] For the flowers, palms, and cherubim of the Temple see 1 Kgs. vi–vii. For the lions of Solomon's throne, ibid. x. 18–20. For the brazen serpent, Num. xxi. 8–9.

[3] None has ever been found. For the celebrated Yahweh hoax at the beginning of the century see H. Vincent, 'Pseudo-figure de Iahvé récemment mise en circulation', *Rév. Biblique* (1909), pp. 121–7.

[4] See R. Garrucci, *Cimitero degli antichi Ebrei scoperto recentemente in Vigna Randanini* (Rome, 1862).

painting is the Villa Torlonia[1] where side by side with Jewish symbols (roll of the Law, seven-branched candlestick, etc.) are dolphins, lion's heads, peacock, ram, sun, and moon. However, the most serious contradictory piece of evidence is the sarcophagus of a Jew whose profession was that of 'zoographos' 'painter of living things'.[2] Finally, at Gamart in Tunisia, near the site of ancient Carthage, Jewish sepulchral chambers have been discovered decorated with painted stucco figures in relief. These represent winged genii, horsemen, and a vintage scene with men carrying amphorae, and a female figure.[3] The representation in human form on the Jewish sarcophagi and in the catacombs presented a problem for Elliger, and he was forced to conjecture that they were made for proselytes who had been pagans.[4]

This is possible, although we do not really know, but it seems unnecessary, for even if the cases so far referred to are explained away as pieces executed for Jewish individuals who were indifferent in matters of religion, such an explanation will not cover the representations of animals and men and even the hand of God, found in the public synagogues—above all that of Dura-Europos, where all the evidence points to the orthodox and pious nature of the Jewish community there and the official sponsoring of its amazing decoration.[5] All these products of Jewish art in the Christian period prove conclusively that, however the second commandment was interpreted, it was not regarded as literally prohibiting artistic representations of anything either on, above, or beneath the earth, or of human beings. All these images are

---

[1] See H. W. Beyer and H. Lietzmann, *Die jüdische Katakombe der Villa Torlonia in Rom* (*Studien zur spätantiken Kunstgeschichte 4, Jüdische Denkmäler*, i, 1930). Elliger disputed the dating: 'Entstehung', pp. 22 f. The generally accepted view is that the Jewish catacombs date from about, but slightly after, the first Christian catacombs; for the dating of these see F. Wirth, *Römische Wandmalerei vom Untergang Pompejs bis ans Ende des dritten Jahrhunderts* (Berlin, 1934).

[2] It was found in the Vigna Randanini and is inscribed: Ἐνθάδε κιτε (κεῖται) Εὐδόξιος ζωόγραφας ἐν εἰρήνη (without iota subscript) ἡ κύ[μησις] (κοίμησις) [αὐτοῦ]. It was originally published by Garrucci in *Civiltà Cattolica Series V*, vol. vi (1863), p. 104, and is now accessible in J. B. Frey, *Corpus Inscriptionum Judaicarum*, vol. i, *Europe* (1936–52), no. 109, p. 76.

[3] See P. Delatte, *Gamart ou la nécropole juive de Carthage* (1895). Note also the Jewish sarcophagus in the Museo Nazionale, Rome, with the menorah supported by victories and seasons; see F. van der Meer and C. Mohrmann, *Atlas of the Early Christian World* (Edinburgh and London, 1958), fig. 36.

[4] 'Entstehung', p. 15.

[5] On the Jewish synagogues in general see E. L. Sukenik, *Ancient Synagogues in Palestine and Greece* (London, 1934). For Dura see C. H. Kraeling, *The Excavations at Dura-Europos. Final Report VIII*, Part I: *The Synagogue* (Yale, 1956), and E. R. Goodenough, *Jewish Symbols in the Graeco-Roman Period*, vol. ix (Bollingen Series XXXVII, 1964). On the orthodoxy of the community see A. Perkins, *The Art of Dura-Europos* (Oxford, 1973), p. 56.

two-dimensional, flat and of a narrative character. The question of a cult image does not come in. It must mean therefore that the prescription was understood as qualified by the second part which forbade the adoring or serving of them[1]—that is, what was being forbidden were idolatrous images. The question of art therefore for Judaism seems to have been one of forbidden and permitted images, not of blanket prohibition.

So we seem to have arrived at a point in the discussion of the second commandment where it has become clear that in the early Christian period the prohibition was regarded in contemporary Jewish circles as definitely modified, while by Christians it was regarded as irrelevant save in matters of Old Testament exegesis. Therefore it cannot be used as a background for supporting a spiritual view of Christianity necessitating a hostile interpretation of Christian texts with regard to matters of Art. The conceptual framework within which the first presentation of the theory was expressed may therefore be regarded as outmoded.

But since the modern presentation of the hypothesis is now within the context of the iconoclastic controversy let us begin again from this point, and with the large and explicit body of evidence for the religious views of the period, and most notably with the Definition of the iconoclastic Council of Hiereia of 754 together with its discussion among the iconodules of the Second Council of Nicaea in 787, and also with the Horos of the iconoclastic Council of 815,[2] in order to be clear about the

---

[1] The wording of the commandment is ambiguous, since what in a classical or modern language would be grammatically represented by a subordinate clause in logical dependence on the first clause, Hebrew often renders by simple sequence. The commonest rabbinic interpretation appears to have been that it was wrong to make an image intended for worship but that an image might be made of any living creature save a human being; this also seems to have been the opinion of the medieval Jewish philosopher, Maimonides; see J. B. Frey, 'La Question des Images chez les Juifs à la lumière des Récentes Découvertes', *Biblica*, xv (1934), pp. 265–300. Some rabbis considered it impious to portray the dragon; why is unclear, but W. A. L. Elmslie, *The Mishna on Idolatry*, '*Aboda zara* (T.S. viii. 2, 1911), pp. 46–7, plausibly suggests that it was because the worship of a sea-monster (the kētos from which Perseus rescued Andromeda) was established at Joppa and presented a problem of conduct to the local Jewish community. That in England also, in the Middle Ages, the understanding of the prohibition was more or less tempered by a sense of reasonable necessity is seen from the figure of the rampant lion, in two representations, on the seal of Jacob the Jew on a document of 1267 transferring Halegod's house in Merton Street, Oxford, to Walter de Merton (*Merton College Record*, 188). For the text see H. W. Garrod and P. S. Allen, *Merton Muniments*, p. 20; for the iconography of the seal see R. Highfield, *Early Rolls of Merton College* (O.H.S. 1964, N.S. vol. xviii), p. 406. I would like to express my thanks to Dr. Highfield and the authorities of Merton for allowing me to examine the seal.

[2] Available in ed. H. Hennephof, *Textus Byzantini ad iconomachiam pertinentes* (Leiden, 1969), nos. 200–64, 265–86, pp. 61–78, 79–84, extracted from J. D.

position and attitude to art expressed then and so to see whether these can really be read back into the period of the early Church, as is usually done by scholars seeking always to understand the earlier origins of the iconoclastic movement.[1] The case made is very reasonable and apparently well supported. For, in the first place, Iconoclasm seems to have been a crisis within Christianity itself; recently converging studies of its origins are becoming increasingly cautious of invoking the influence of any non-Christian culture.[2] It was this recognition of Iconoclasm as a Christian phenomenon which led Kitzinger to link the 'uniconic [sic] phase of early Christianity' with Byzantine Iconoclasm.[3] But, as he made very clear in his study, it was the rise of the cult of icons in the sixth and seventh centuries, and not the origin of the movement, which is the central problem of the controversy. And, as we have seen, his explanation of this central problem was based on the opposition of church leaders in contradistinction to the 'naive animistic attitudes of the masses',[4] whose adherence to magical belief had resulted in the production of and semi-idolatrous attitude towards works of art. This attitude he was able to isolate as going back to the time of the

Mansi, *Sacrorum Conciliorum nova et amplissima Collectio*, xiii (Florence, 1759 ff.), pp. 205–364. See also the relevant pages in C. Hefele–H. Leclercq, *Histoire des Conciles*, ii. 2 (Paris, 1907 ff.), pp. 693–709.

[1] As done, for example, by Ladner, who considers Basil's fourth-century anti-Arian treatise *On the Holy Spirit*, xviii, p. 45, Gregory of Nyssa's *de Opificio Hominis* v, and Basil's *Twenty-fourth Homily against Sabellius and the Arians* as characteristic of the whole relationship between orthodox Byzantine image doctrine and patristic thought, see op. cit., pp. 4–5.

[2] On Byzantine-Arab relations in the eighth century see A. Graber, *L'Iconoclasme byzantin: dossier archéologique* (Paris, 1957) and P. Lemerle, *Le Premier Humanisme byzantin* (Paris, 1971); on Islamic attitudes to images see K. A. C. Cresswell, 'The Lawfulness of Painting in Early Islam', *Ars Islamica*, xi–xii (1946), pp. 159–66, and U. M. de Villard, *Introduzione allo Studio dell'archeologia islamica* (1966), esp. pp. 249–75. For the position of Jews see A. Sharf, *Byzantine Jewry from Justinian to the Fourth Crusade* (1971), pp. 61–81. For a consideration of the early Church and images based on the standard view of hostility see N. H. Baynes, 'Idolatry and the Early Church', *Byzantine Studies and other Essays* (London, 1955), pp. 116–43, and cf. also his, 'The Icons before Iconoclasm', *Harv. Theol. Rev.* lxiv (1951), pp. 93 f. For the discovery of an iconoclastic movement in Christian seventh century Armenia see S. der Nersessian, 'Une Apologie des Images du Septième Siècle', *Byzantion*, xvii (1944–5), pp. 58–87, and P. J. Alexander, 'An Ascetic Sect of Iconoclasts in Seventh Century Armenia', *Late Classical and Medieval Studies in Honor of Albert Mathias Friend Jr.*, ed. K. Weitzmann (Princeton, 1955), pp. 151–60. For an interpretation in socio-religious terms see P. R. L. Brown, 'A Dark Age Crisis: Aspects of the Iconoclastic Controversy', *Eng. Hist. Rev.* lxxxviii (1973), pp. 1–34, and its critique and supplement by P. Henry, 'What was the Iconoclastic Controversy About?', *Church History*, xlv. 1 (1976), pp. 16–31.

[3] p. 85.

[4] p. 146.

early Church. It was the final resistance to pressure on the part of church authorities which, in the late sixth century, was a major factor in the development of the outbreak.[1] In the second place, it is also true, that whatever the root cause underlying their rise, the controversy was undoubtedly about images; or at least it is perhaps more exact to say that it focused on images. For if one asks what in essence the controversy was about, when stripped of all the learned explanations given, and theological subtleties of expression, the fundamental concern was with idolatry. As the Horos of 754 says—the basic sin of mankind is idolatry.[2] Here we begin to approach the heart of the matter, for this is the text which provides the clue to the reason for the assembling, by both sides, in the dispute, of biblical and patristic texts which would support a doctrine about images; for idolatry had been the besetting sin of Israel, and also of the pagan milieu against which the Fathers had struggles. And it seems clear, as far as one can tell from the literature preserved, that the iconoclasts, on their side, genuinely believed that the early Church has been hostile to images.

The whole iconoclastic case rested on an appeal to antiquity in which of course the scriptural proofs were paramount. The major proof was taken to be the Old Testament prohibition of images which became, as is clear from the literature, the real hub of the theological debate.[3]

There was plenty of material to hand since there had been prior to the outbreak of iconoclasm a Jewish-Christian controversy on the point and Byzantine apologists had compiled testimonia to vindicate the Christian position.[4] It was to be expected therefore that in the literature of the

---

[1] pp. 119-20.

[2] Hennephof, nos. 202-6, pp. 61-2, esp. no. 205, p. 62. The Horos had begun with an account of creation, the corruption of man by Lucifer, the inventor of idolatry, the incarnation which had liberated man from idol-worship, the renewed introduction of idolatry under the cover of Christianity and of the first six Ecumenical Councils which had established the doctrine of Christ's two natures in one hypostasis.

[3] The influence of the Old Testament on the public image of the Byzantine empire had been growing since the early seventh century, see the evidence in Brown (p. 25) where it is attributed, along with other wider-world examples, to the sense of the threat of Islam as God's punishment for Christian apostasy in the form of idolatry.

[4] Fragments dating from c. 630 of John, bishop of Thessalonica (610-49) were read at the Second Council of Nicaea, apparently from a comprehensive work called *Contra Paganos et Judaeos*, see Mansi, xiii. 164-8; and also from the *Fifth Speech in Defence of Christianity against the Jews* of Leontius, bishop of Neapolis in Cyprus (582-602), see Mansi, xiii. 44-53 and *P.G.* xciii, 1597-1609. This text gives the main outline of the Jewish attack as based on the Torah prohibition of idolatry (Exod. xx. 4-5; Lev. xxvi. 1; Deut. v. 8) while Leontius argued the existence of another legal tradition: the divine command to fashion

iconoclastic controversy much space should be devoted to the theological meaning of the second commandment.

However, in the totally Christian context of this latter debate it was the appeal to the Fathers, the other witnesses of antiquity, which made more sense, and in the whole exposition of the theory of identification of or distinction between icons and idols, it was the use of the texts of the Fathers which provided the evidence; and immense trouble was taken to assemble florilegia, regardless of the original context from which the passages came.[1] Now in fact we have arrived at the position of seeing how the Byzantine Church got its information about the early period. The collection of evidence assembled for the Council of 754 was state-organized and extensive and, because the Fathers in their own contexts had said little on the subject of images, very attentively made. An illustration of the care taken is most interestingly found in *The Admonition of the Old Man concerning the Holy Images*, which dates from between 750 and 754.[2] It describes a dispute which took place between the iconodule monk George of Cyprus and the iconoclastic bishop Cosmas who used the early writers Epiphanius of Salamis, George of Alexandria, and Severus of Antioch in support of his case, and says that their writings were perused in the palace every day. But since, as George of Cyprus pointed out, George of Alexandria and Severus of Antioch were both heretics,[3] there was the problem of orthodoxy; and since, as he also stated, the writings attributed to Epiphanius were the fabrications of the Novationists, there was also the problem of authenticity.[4]

two gold cherubim (Exod. xxv. 18), God's vision to Ezekiel of a temple with palms, lions, men, and cherubim (Ezek. xli. 18), and Solomon's decoration of the Temple with all manner of carved and molten images.

[1] From the fifth to the seventh century church councils had relied increasingly on patristic testimony in the form of florilegia; the trend is particularly evident at the Lateran Council of 649 and even more markedly at the Sixth Ecumenical Council, and so the tradition of assembling extracts can be traced back before Iconoclasm. There is surprisingly little evidence that John Damascene's work on images was known at the council of 787; see P. Van den Ven, 'La Patristique et L'Hagiographie du Concile de Nicée de 787', *Byzantion*, xxv–xxvii (1955–7), pp. 325–62, esp. pp. 332–8.

[2] Ed. B. M. Melioranskij, *Georij Kiprijanin: Ioann Ierusalimljanin* (St. Petersburg, 1901). The text is the record of one of the *silentia* or propaganda meetings arranged in 752–3 by the Emperor Constantine V in which he explained, or had explained by his sympathizers, his theological views; see Theophanes, *Chronographia*, 427, 19 f. de Boor.

[3] p. xxviii. George, bishop of Alexandria (356–61) was a radical Arian; Severus, Patriarch of Antioch (d. 538) was monophysite.

[4] Pp. xxvii–xxviii. Ὁ γέρων περὶ τοῦ μακαρίου Ἐπιφανίου ψευδεπιπλάστως αὐτοῦ χρᾶσαι· Ναυατιανοὶ γὰρ, σπεύσαντες τὰ εὔλογα τῆς αἱρέσεως αὐτῶν στῆσαι, τὸ ὄνομα τοῦ θεοφόρου κεφαλὴν τοῦ λόγου ἐχρήσαντο. Asia Minor, the home of the first

That this was quite serious the Acts of the Second Council of Nicaea show, where scrupulous attention was given to the patristic texts quoted, because falsification, according to the Fathers of Nicaea, had been characteristic of the Council of 754.[1] It must be noted here, although for the moment only in passing, that some of the crucial patristic passages alleged in favour of the hostility theory only survive here in these iconoclastic florilegia.

The point which emerges from this brief review of the iconoclastic background to the hypothesis is that in any polemic about idolatry at any period, emphasis will automatically fall on material objects. And what seems to have happened in the Byzantine period is that the iconoclastic controversialists took up these sort of emphases from patristic polemics against idolatry and used them to construct a theory about the making of material objects themselves. What they have done is to tie down patristic references to idolatry to matters of art and Christian worship. It is the failure to observe this on the part of modern scholars that has resulted in the identification of what was in the early Church a statement, possibly an overstatement of the case against idolatry in general, with the Byzantine controversy about the rightness of the use of images for religious purposes within the Christian Church itself.

It seems essential then to detach the literary evidence from a preconceived notion of Christianity, and also from the Byzantine context in which it has become lodged, both things which automatically have coloured its interpretation, and to see if it will still, in its own right, support the standard view of art and the early Church; for so far it seems to have become entangled in the various accidents of controversy.

iconoclastic bishops, Thomas of Claudiopolis and Constantine of Nacoleia, had large Novationist communities and George's assertion which is extremely direct and goes unchallenged by Cosmas offers an attractive possibility; no one has yet, so far as I know, explored this hypothesis.

[1] The Acts of the Council of 787 are compelling reading. The Fathers alleged that at Hiereia in 754 the iconoclasts did not produce the original books but circulated extracts on loose sheets referred to as πιττάκια, extracts which were sometimes falsified or taken out of context, cf. Mansi. xiii. 36E, 37B–C, 173D. The two bishops who had taken part in the iconoclastic council, Gregory of Neocaesarea and Theodosius of Amorium, and who, by what appears to modern sensitivity as sheer cruelty, were asked to read the Horos, were repeatedly questioned about these sheets and their own failure to demand to see the books. They had no reply save that their minds were darkened (37B). This time the Nicene Fathers insisted on the production of the actual codex in each case; the lector began with the incipit and then read the relevant passage. The Acts cry out for a critical edition. On this value of Mansi see H. Quentin, *Jean-Dominique Mansi et les grandes collections conciliaires* (1900); resumé by S. Vailhé, *E.O.* iv (1900–1), pp. 235–8.

Before a re-examination of the texts is made, a few relevant pre-liminary observations must be put forward in summary form. Firstly, it is normally the same passages which are repeated from scholar to scholar, although a few which obviously lack seriousness lose them-selves on the way.[1] Secondly, the number of the Fathers represented in the evidence, and also the number of passages from their works is remarkably small in view of the weight given to them. Thirdly, because of the supposition that a continuous stream of hostility can be traced from one Father to another through the centuries, the method employed in discussion is always to treat them chronologically, and end with the immediate pre-iconoclastic period into which they are considered to feed. Fourthly, evidence from those writers who may be understood as not merely non-inimical to, but positively receptive of, artistic representation are omitted; as are passages from apparently 'hostile' Fathers which in fact support an opposite view. This is particularly true in the case of Origen. Fifthly, Fathers like the Cappa-docians who are too important to be omitted but not sufficiently hostile, are explained away on other grounds. Sixthly, passages in a writer, known to be hostile, which seem to conflict with each other are always explained away in terms of pressure from below.

The theory also presupposes two more things: (a) that the views of any Christian writer, however idiosyncratic he is known historically to be, for example Tertullian, automatically reflect the view of the whole Church because of his eminent position, and (b) that only the church leaders represent genuine Christianity and therefore constitute the essence of the Church, a view which overlooks the fact that, far from being mere ciphers or naïve animistic masses, the laity were responsible in view of their baptism for electing the official leaders of their own community.[2] It is beginning to emerge from the outset therefore that the evidence is not quite so clear-cut as the normal interpretation presumes, and needs to be taken away again from another preconception: this time an idea of a monolithic Church which gives no credit to differences of temperament, interest, theological stand-point, geography, or time. It needs to be examined carefully piece by piece. But here again it must be remarked that in fact the handling of these pieces is a delicate and difficult matter because of the way the sources survive. Some of the pieces we still have intact in the context in

[1] For example the fragments of Porphyry's περὶ ἀγαλμάτων preserved in Eusebius' *Praep. Ev.* iii. 7–13, which were regarded by von Dobschütz, p. 106, as going back to a gnostic source.

[2] From the earliest days the voice of the laity had been substantially more than mere assent in the election of their bishop, as in the paradigm case of the election of Ambrose of Milan by popular acclaim as late as 374.

which they were written, and so they can be checked without difficulty in the actual works of the Fathers who wrote them. But others, and this applies to the key pieces on which the theory rests, do not—as was noted earlier, they survive only in iconoclastic florilegia. Since the purpose of the examination is to re-appraise the content of the passages and therefore of the theory, it seems best from the methodological point of view not to proceed chronologically, as is usually done, but to treat the evidence in terms of minor and major pieces: for not all are of the same importance, and some may be dealt with briefly, whereas others require longer discussion.

Finally, this preamble may be concluded by saying that no protagonist of the hostility theory has yet been able to produce one single clear statement from any early Christian writer which says that non-idolatrous artistic representation is wrong.

The only text which might seriously be regarded as supporting this view is the 36th Canon of the Council of Elvira, though even here again the question of worship is involved.

The Fathers of Elvira, the Roman city of Illiberis in southern Spain, near modern Granada, who met in a synod about the year 300, laid it down: 'picturas in ecclesia non debere, ne quod colitur et adoratur in parietibus depingatur': which means literally that there ought to be no pictures in a church (or in the Christian Church) lest what is worshipped and adored be depicted on walls.[1] And round that sentence has grown up a voluminous controversial literature. It has been claimed that the canon does not forbid representation completely or that it forbids a certain kind of bad church art which had come into vogue in Spain about A.D. 300.

Funk years ago disposed of the more spectacular kinds of argument and recognized quite clearly that the canon really does forbid pictorial representations of religious content.[2] This certainly seems to be

[1] The exact date is unknown. For the text see J. Vives, Concilios Visigóticos e Hispano-Romanos (España Cristiana, i, Barcelona–Madrid, 1963), p. 8.

[2] F. X. Funk, Kirchengeschichtliche Abhandlungen und Untersuchungen, i (1897), pp. 346–52. A. Harnack, Die Mission und Ausbreitung des Christentums in den ersten drei Jahrhunderten, ii, 4th edn. (Leipzig, 1924), p. 925, tried to read into the language a declaration against offering homage to pictures but this is unquestionably a mistake. The canon is saying that what is worshipped is not to be painted on walls, not vice versa. Bevan's solution is even more extraordinary. He believes that underlying the prohibition was the 'current' idea that a picture was essentially derogatory to the divine because it was made of perishable material; since he could produce no Christian evidence for the idea he relies on Buddhist evidence from Gandhara, see p. 115. But there is no trace of any connection of the canons of Elvira with Buddhist theological ideas current on the North West Frontier at an imprecisely defined period. The Kushan patrons of

unquestionable, and should be taken as the one clear piece of evidence which forbids representations in churches. But because the circumstances to which it refers are lost, and because it comes only from a local synod and not a major church council, one can only guess what lies behind it and no conjectures can be made on the basis of it with any degree of security. What therefore is it possible to say by way of interpretation without indulging in any extremity of view and without departing from the text? The *ne quod* of the wording appears to refer to a divine person, perhaps Christ, because whoever it is is adored and worshipped.

Secondly, the emphasis seems to be against depicting this person on the walls of churches—that funerary monuments are excluded is proved by the series of the Spanish sarcophagi which still survive.[1] Thirdly, there seems to be missing the reason for which it is forbidden to put what is holy on walls. Now all these observations may be drawn together and a tentative conclusion arrived at if one remembers that, archaeologically speaking, the Council belongs to the period of the house-church; and this may be why the Council is emphatic about the walls of churches. Such houses are known to have been vulnerable: to raids by the imperial police; or in the case of Elvira, where judging from the other canons which imply an atmosphere which the fathers found threatening, to desecration by pagans; or even to use by some Christians for purposes of black magic now known to have been operative in Spain at the time.[2] If the Christian building at Dura is

Buddhism had used the services of journeying Eastern Roman craftsmen to produce a form of late antique art dedicated to Buddhism, i.e. Graeco-Roman form and Indian iconography. This so-called 'Gandhara Art' flourished from the first to the fifth centuries A.D. when in Gandhara proper it came to an end with the invasion of the Huns, but its style survived in Kashmir and in isolated Buddhist establishments in Afghanistan as late as the seventh or eighth centuries. For art in India see B. Rowland, *The Art and Architecture of India*, 3rd edn. (London, 1967), esp. pp. 73–90; for Afghanistan see P. Levi, *The Light Garden of the Angel King* (London, 1972), passim.

[1] See G. Bovini, *I Sarcofagi paleocristiani della Spagna* (Rome, 1954). 'The Saragossa sarcophagus' (there are in fact two) was particularly difficult for Koch to explain, see p. 37 n. 1. Of early Christian Spanish antiquities, apart from these sarcophagi, scarcely anything survives. For the Visigothic period see P. de Palol and M. Hirmer, *Early Medieval Art in Spain* (London, 1967), esp. fig. 23, illustrating a very interesting piece: a sixth–seventh century bronze terret four inches high, showing a figure of the Good Shepherd with a lamb on his shoulder, now in the Museo Arqueólogico in Madrid, which must reflect earlier Romano-Christian influence.

[2] See H. Chadwick, *Priscillian of Avila, the Occult and the Charismatic in the Early Church* (Oxford, 1976). The 6th Canon excommunicates those responsible for causing death by sorcery. Whatever the ultimate reason for the prohibition of the 36th Canon it is virtually certain that it was neither a refined theological

typical, and if the later villa of Lullingstone in Kent is accepted as containing a house church,[1] then it is known that these churches were painted and some included figures of Christ. Beyond this it is impossible to go and in the absence of knowledge of the original circumstances what was in fact in question we cannot know.

Minor Pieces of Evidence

Tertullian

Two quotations from Tertullian's treatise on idolatry are usually taken as showing in him a hostile attitude to art.[2] But *de Idol.* iv. 1 is speaking clearly of the making of an idol and cannot support any inference that he regarded it as wrong to make images not intended for worship. The same is true of the later sentence where there is a reference to the second commandment, normally taken to express an attitude supporting the prohibition. But the context here—a discussion on whether the profession of a sculptor or painter is open to a Christian is again concerned with idolatry not art. Tertullian fears that such a Christian may be associated with the production of something which may become an idol.

Early Church Orders

Von Dobschütz had omitted the idolatry passages from Tertullian but listed the following extracts from the early Church Orders as

one nor due to lay-official tension on the question of art in Spain; for the style and quality of the Spanish bishops in the fourth century and their almost total lack of theological training see Chadwick, p. 11. For Koch's view of the prohibition as due to reverence for the second commandment, see pp. 39–40, and for confirmation of it, Elliger, p. 34; Klauser, p. 4.

[1] For the Christian building at Dura see Kraeling, *Final Report VIII, II, the Christian Building.* For the Roman villa at Lullingstone with its enigmatic painted figures and chi-rho symbol see J. M. C. Toynbee, *Art in Britain under the Romans* (Oxford, 1964), pp. 220 f. and pls. liii–lv. There is no evidence at Lullingstone of a figure of Christ, but the polychrome mosaic of an uncertain date in the fourth century from Hinton St. Mary appears to contain a bust of Christ with the chi-rho monogram behind the head. See J. M. C. Toynbee, *J.R.S.* liv (1964), pp. 7–14. Its position on the floor makes it impossible as an icon. Likewise the bearded and nimbate bust of Christ on the east wall of the fourth-century hall at Ostia, a simple element in an architectural design, is in the wrong position for a cult image. As Becati suggests, it is probably only a symbol of protection. See G. Becati, *Scavi di Ostia*, vi. (1969), *Edificio in opus sectile fuori Porta Marina*, pp. 161–5, and pls. 53, 55, 56.

[2] *De Idol.* iv. 1, viii. 1–2; cf. iii. See Koch, p. 3; cf. Klauser, p. 2.

forbidding art.[1] The *Syriac Didascalia* says: no oblations may be
received from those who paint with colours, from those who make
idols, or workers in silver and bronze. And in the *Pseudo-Clementine
Church order*, a painter is put into the same list with a harlot, a brothel-
keeper, drunkard, actor, and athlete. But it is possible that in these
two cases, as in the passage from Tertullian, what is understood by a
painter is meant a painter of idolatrous images. That this is virtually
certain seems clear if it is interpreted in the light of the *Egyptian
Didascalia* which says clearly: if anyone is a sculptor or a painter let
him be instructed not to make idols; he must either cease from doing
so or be expelled from the Church. This seems to distinguish between
artists and the makers of idols and renders the position clear.

These passages then may be taken as evidence of hostility to the
making of idols but not necessarily to the making of images of art.

Clement of Alexandria

Here is a positive quarry for passages regarded as hostile to the
making of images,[2] and one text, made much of by Bevan,[3] may be
singled out as an illustration of the standard kind of interpretation.
This is *Strom.* vi. 16. 147, 'The artist would rob God: he seeks to
usurp the divine prerogative of creation and by means of his plastic
or graphic art pretends to be a maker of animals or plants.' As was
said earlier, this passage is part of the allegorization of the Decalogue
and so, apparently, evidence for the enforcement of the Old Testament
prohibition by Clement. But in fact the commandment under discussion is the eighth: thou shalt not steal, and the substance is really a
somewhat inflated prohibition about not robbing the creator God of
his glory. While superficially it may look like a prohibition of art,
Clement can scarcely have meant it to be taken at its face value, in view
of the reason he gives for it: no artist ever claimed to be a maker of
plants and animals. It is rather, then, a curious line of argument,

---

[1] pp. 100*–101*. For the *Syriac Didascalia* he refers to A. Harnack, *Geschichte
der altchristl.—Litteratur*, I. i, pp. 456 f. For the *Pseudo-Clementine Church
order* to the edition of P. de Lagarde, *Reliq. Iuris Eccles. antiq. graece* (1856,
repr. 1967), p. 87. For the *Egyptian Didascalia* to H. Achelis (T.U. 6, 4), pp. 78 f.
Repeated by Koch, pp. 12–13. The 'Egyptian Didascalia' referred to is the
Sahidic church order (ed. Leipoldt and Till, T.U. 58) which drew on the
'Apostolic Tradition' of Hippolytus (ch. 16, p. 34, Botte) or the work of
the third century commonly so described. For the *Syriac Didascalia*, see
R. H. Connolly's edition (Oxford, 1929, repr. 1970), p. 158.
[2] According to Elliger, p. 38, we pass with the great Alexandrians into the
clear air of spirituality.
[3] E. Bevan, *Holy Images* (London, 1940), p. 87.

unusually expressed and based on the platonic doctrine of ideas and theory of imitation. Yet even though it has no connection, save by way of incidental illustration, with the question of art: being concerned to emphasize the transcendence of God, Bevan regards it as evidence that Clement went even further than the Moslem view in the matter of aniconism. Unlike Islam, Clement even forbids the portraying of plants. But this is obviously preposterous and to make Clement into the forerunner of Islam seems to be carrying solemnity of interpretation a little too far.

But it does serve to make us aware of where misinterpretation of other passages in the Alexandrians,[1] normally brought forward, have occurred. As we have seen, the passage from the *Stromateis* is rhetorical language stressing the transcendence of God in a context allegorizing the whole of the Decalogue. And it should be recognized that language used in a depreciative way of images in comparison with direct apprehension of the invisible, does not necessarily imply that the use of images is wrong or forbidden. The language is relative only and the result of the Platonic background from which the Alexandrian Fathers drew their thinking. What either of them would have said on the general question of artistic representation cannot be known, it was never a question they considered. It is important therefore to be cautious in taking language expressive of a relative depreciation of material symbols to be an absolute repudiation of their use at all.

---

[1] For Origen the standard texts alleged are *C. Celsum*, iv. 31 (answering the charge that the Jews were runaway slaves who never did anything important), vi. 66 (on passing into the radiant light of the knowledge of God), vii. 64 (the second commandment forbids idolatry), viii. 17–19 (discussion of anthropology); none of which are directly discussing the question of art. But Koch concludes his examination, p. 22, by saying that Origen unmistakably enforces the second commandment and considers artistic representation to be dead, unnatural, and deceitful. One wonders what he would have made of a passage like *In Gen. Hom.* xiii. 4. 119 f., if he had discussed it, where Origen treats of man, the image of God, a painting painted by Christ the best painter (G.C.S. vi, pp. 119 f.). Whether this form of the idea is original with Origen is uncertain, but it appears to be part of an old theological tradition of God as artist, see 'Excursus XXI Gott als Bildner', in E. R. Curtius, *Europäische Literatur und Lateinisches Mittelalter* (Bern, 1948), pp. 529 f., which goes back at least to the demiurge of the *Timaeus*. Cf. also Origen's contemporary the elder Philostratus', *Life of Apollonius of Tyana*, ii. 22, where the conception of God as painter could blend with that of the divine image in the human soul according to *C. Celsum*, viii. 17–19. A similar idea is to be found in Methodius of Olympus, e.g. *Symp.* 1. 4 (G.C.S. xiii), who frequently uses metaphors from the realm of art to emphasize the full reality of the incarnation and man's bodily resurrection. Christ assumed a human body as if he had painted his picture for us so that we might imitate him its painter, cf. *de Res.* I. xxxv. 3–4; II. x. 7–12; III. vi.

Major Pieces of Evidence

Now let us turn to the more serious passages and comparatively rare occurrences in which the Fathers do discuss the case of a material image in a non-idolatrous context and are apparently antagonistic towards it.

Tertullian, De Pud. VII. x. 12

The first and most famous of these is Tertullian and the Good Shepherd cups.[1] Close examination of the context here makes clear that it will not be the standard interpretation of showing Tertullian as hostile to art. The context is one of rhetorical mockery. Tertullian had a particular hatred of the *Shepherd of Hermas* because it allowed the readmission of fornicators, if penitent, to communion and so the figure of the Shepherd was associated in his mind with a plea for moral laxity in the Church. He describes it as the 'idol of drunkenness and the sanctuary of adultery', and Christians who at the Eucharist drank from a cup with the Good Shepherd on it, while relying on the freedom to sin afforded by a second repentance, had chosen their symbol well. In other words, this is not an example of Tertullian's rigorism in the matter of art but the treating of a particular symbol with contempt because it was used by Christians for whom he felt contempt.

Clement, Paedagogus III. 12. 1

Here, according to the normal view, is a passage which shows Clement making a concession to pressures being forced on him from below, in the matter of the designs to be put on signet-rings. It is pointed out, to save him from inconsistency with his usual hostility, that the wearing of signet-rings was essential in antiquity and that he only concedes the representation of inanimate things or those of neutral content: ship, lyre, anchor. Bevan expresses surprise that he allows

---

[1] Koch, pp. 9–10, explains Tertullian's hostility to art here as excessive reverence for the Eucharist. Elliger (pp. 28 f.) felt Koch had not used Tertullian sufficiently to illustrate the dogmatic connotations of hostility and developed these further. For Klauser, pp. 2–3, the passage was an example of compromise in the matter of the second commandment in Christian lay circles in Carthage *c*. 213 and official opposition to it; it was also the proof that the passages from the *de Idol.* were not merely reactionary and peculiar opinion on Tertullian's part. No examples of these chased cups survive from the early period but an idea of the type may be gained from the silver-gilt Great Chalice of Antioch in the Metropolitan Museum, New York, variously dated between the fourth and sixth centuries because of its damaged and rubbed condition and provincial execution. It is decorated with twelve seated figures: including two representations of Christ, the four evangelists and six apostles set between vine-scrolls, vases, and birds. For an illustration see Beckwith (above p. 303 n. 1), fig. 47.

a dove or a fish—good Moslems should not—but salvages Clement's reputation by adding that it seems unlikely he would have allowed a human figure.[1] For Klauser the passage was crucial as indicative that the laity were really beginning to get out of hand. The mass production of Good Shepherd cups in the Mediterranean had already begun to force the issue against authority as the passages from Tertullian, in Klauser's view, already show. And here in Clement's reluctant concession, the forced introduction of art into the early Church in spite of official prohibition is clearly seen.[2]

But reference to the original context shows that the opposition is the other way round. The hesitancy about design is on the part of inquiring Christian converts, used to the iconographic oddities of gnostic gems, and this is encouragement from Clement as to what can cheerfully be admitted. What has been lost in wrenching the passage from its context is the tone of Clement's voice. There seems to be good indication elsewhere that Clement had a positive appreciation of art and that in fact it is a passage from his *Protrepticus* which may well lie behind the figure of the Christian Orpheus in the catacomb of St. Callixtus.[3]

Asterius of Amaseia

Klauser omitted from his evidence another passage which had been brought forward by Koch.[4] Asterius of Amaseia refers in one of his sermons (c. A.D. 400) to the fashion for Christians of his day to have woven on their robes representations of the Gospel scenes: Christ with the disciples, the raising of Lazarus.

[1] p. 87. He seems to be unaware of the fisherman-apostle seal of *Paed.* iii. 59. 2.

[2] p. 4. The neutrality of content is stressed as a desperate effort on Clement's part to salvage some sort of religion out of the compromise. For examples of ancient signets both pagan and Christian, Britain is extremely well placed, see H. B. Walters, *Catalogue of the Engraved Gems and Cameos in the British Museum* (B.M., 1926) and M. Henig, *A Corpus of Roman Engraved Gemstones from British Sites, parts I and II*, B.A.R. 8 (1974), and *The Lewis Collection of Engraved Gemstones in Corpus Christi College, Cambridge*, B.A.T.–Sl. (1975).

[3] See Sister C. Murray, 'The Christian Orpheus', *Cahiers Archéologiques* (to appear).

[4] pp. 64–7, cf. von Dobschütz, Beilagen, p. 102, for his view of the passage as a humorous and satirical treatment showing Asterius' opposition to biblical or at least Christian images. For the *Homily on the Rich Man and Lazarus* see *Homilies I–XIV*, ed. C. Datema (Leiden, 1971). For an illustration of the kind of robe in question, cf. the portrait of the Empress Theodora (probably c. 547) in the apse of San Vitale, Ravenna, where her purple chlamys is embroidered in gold with figures of the three Magi. See G. Bovini, *Ravenna Mosaics* (London, 1957), fig. 33 (uncoloured).

If they take my advice they will sell such garments and pay honour to the living images of God. Do not paint a picture of Christ. That of his humiliation when he took upon himself our humanity for our sakes of his own will is enough. Rather carry about within your soul in a spiritual way the immaterial Logos. Do not have the paralytic man of the Gospel upon your clothes, but go and visit those who are bedridden. Do not look so steadfastly on the sinful woman at the feet of the Lord but have contrition for your own sins and shed tears yourself for them . . .

Yet the same bishop gives an emotional description of the martyrdom of Euphemia depicted in her basilica at Chalcedon, and also speaks of it as customary in his time to offer homage to the Cross.[1] The discrepancy in attitude which troubles Koch is found not to exist when reference is made back to the sermon from which the passage came. The title of the homily is itself sufficiently instructive: it is *On the Rich Man and Lazarus* and appears to have been addressed to a wealthy audience. Reading of it shows that it is not a discussion of the legitimacy of art but a moral exhortation to virtuous living and avoidance of luxury: the demands of Christian service to God are not satisfied by wearing his image but by active love of one's neighbour. It does not reflect, as it is supposed to do, any official opposition to art at the beginning of the fifth century. The Cappadocians could not on any score be made into opponents of art, nor could they be ignored as representing the official level of the Church, so they are explained away by the hypothesis as 'fleeting references'[2] to a more positive approach. And this gets over difficulties like the passage in Basil's sermon on the Martyr Balaam in which he calls upon all proficient painters to depict the martyr's sufferings and those of the Master who ordains and judges the contest, Christ. Gregory of Nyssa also described a picture of Christ Agonothetes in another representation of martyrdom;[3] and John Chrysostom inconveniently kept a picture of St.

---

[1] For the whole question of Euphemia see F. Halkin, *Euphémie de Chalcedoine*, Subsidia Hagiogr. 41 (Brussels, 1965). For the literary genre of ecphrasis, which was a standard form of exercise in late antique rhetoric, see the lovely description of Hagia Sophia by Paul the Silentiary in ed. P. Friedländer, *Johannes von Gaza, Paulus Silentarius und Prokopios von Gaza: Kunstbeschreibungen justinianischer Zeit* (Hildesheim, 1969). And for a discussion, see H. Maguire, 'Truth and Convention in Byzantine Descriptions of Works of Art', *D.O.P.* xxviii (1974), pp. 113–40. On the homage to the cross see *Homily XI in Praise of St. Stephen*. Kitzinger, p. 90 n. 13, includes this reference to proskynesis as evidence for the paving of the way of image worship in the fourth century, but omits the passage from the sermon and the ecphrasis of H. Euphemia.

[2] Kitzinger, p. 86, following as he admits (p. 87 n. 7) Koch, pp. 69 f. and Elliger, pp. 60 f.

[3] That of the martyr Theodore, see *P.H.* xlvi. 737CD.

Paul before him, according to John Damascene.[1] But these texts are glossed over in the standard treatments; they are omitted by Klauser, explained away by Koch and Elliger, and alluded to by Kitzinger. There are two other passages which also appear to have been wrongly interpreted and so made to support the theory.

Augustine, de Moribus Ecclesiae Catholicae I. 34

Augustine's famous passage reads: 'novi multos esse sepulchrorum et picturarum adoratores, novi multos esse qui luxuriosissime super mortuos libant et epulas cadaveribus exhibentes, super sepultos seipsos sepeliant, et voracitates ebrietatesque suas deputent religioni.'

On this passage Kitzinger says: 'It is from St. Augustine that we first hear in unambiguous terms of Christians worshipping images. Among those who had introduced superstitious practices in the Church, he mentions "sepulcrorum et picturarum adoratores", thus linking the cult of images to the cult of tombs.'[2]

It will be noticed that he has quoted only one phrase from the passage and this may well have reference to abuses at the tomb during the funeral cult, and to the worshipping of structures and their painted decoration. What it will not do is support any idea of Augustine's attitude to art, as can be seen if it is put back into its context. Augustine is not singling out the adoration of pictures for condemnation, much less the making of them. The passage refers to the practice of a particular set of Christians only, in the context of the funeral cult, whose banquets in Augustine's opinion are a scandalous indulgence of the sensual appetite for food and drink. Wrongful indulgence at banquets is the point. When he uses the phrase quoted by Kitzinger to describe these people it is to imply depreciation of this method of honouring the dead; the presence of the pictures and their worship, if more than rhetorical emphasis of description is intended, he simply accepts as facts. Since this passage would not support Elliger's thesis in an entirely specific way, he tried to reinforce his point by bringing in, irrelevantly, Augustine's attitude to church music as an example of the danger of the appeal of the senses in religion.[3] Augustine is known from the *Confessions* to have been by temperament as sensitive to the appeal of music as to that of language, and his view of the legitimacy of it fluctuated because he was always alive to the possibility of danger for himself. But he seems to have been much less stirred by the appeal of visual art.[4]

[1] Ed. B. Kotter, *Die Schriften des Johannes von Damaskos III* (P.T.S. 17, Berlin, New York, 1975), p. 161.   [2] p. 92.   [3] pp. 86 f.
[4] See esp. x. 33. 49–50. For a generalized discussion of art, x. 34. 53.

Paulinus of Nola, Carm. XXVII. 542 f.

Paulinus in his poem is naming particular churches richly decorated with biblical personages and scenes. When he describes them as executed 'raro more' Koch tries to understand the phrase to mean that at that time pictorial decoration in churches was still uncommon.[1] But given Paulinus' enthusiasm for church decoration recorded elsewhere, it is far more likely that Paulinus took pleasure in these paintings because they were exceptionally good. He even mentions a representation of the Trinity in mosaic.[2]

Paulinus is from the fourth century and a most influential member of the 'official church' who is omitted, unsurprisingly, by Klauser and Kitzinger.

However, with the fourth century we have reached the key pieces of evidence on which the whole hypothesis of hostility really rests and which are apparently irrefutable. Eusebius, bishop of Caesarea, and Epiphanius, bishop of Salamis, really seemed to have thought it wrong to make representations of religious things and personages, notably of Christ.

We seem to have in Eusebius of Caesarea an important and influential figure at the beginning of the fourth century who categorically opposed himself to the making of representations of Christ. The evidence is, of course, in the celebrated letter to the Empress Constantia which figures prominently in all discussions of the subject and yet surprisingly is never itself submitted to discussion. It is always referred to but never analysed; presumably because it is regarded as self-evidently hostile to art. Since it obviously supported his view and therefore required no comment, Koch gives a brief summary of its contents and then devotes the remainder of his section on Eusebius to a long discussion of the cross and the labarum. Elliger says almost nothing and,

---

[1] Koch, p. 74, 'pingere sanctas raro more domos animantibus adsimulatis'. For the frequent use of 'rarus' in the sense of 'outstanding' see Lewis and Short, *Latin Dictionary* (Oxford, 1879).

[2] For the Trinity in mosaic see *Ep.* xxxii. 10 to Sulpicius Severus. The representation avoided human figures: the Father was symbolized by some emblem which stood for the voice of thunder from heaven, the Son by a lamb, the Spirit by a dove. One would give much to know how one represents a voice in mosaic. This apse mosaic from Paulinus' famous church of St. Felix at Nola is lost, but for an attempted reconstruction see Wickhoff, illustrated as fig. 77 in M. Lawrence, *The Sarcophagi of Ravenna* (New York, 1945). Wickhoff represents the Father by a hand. For a major analysis of the culture and mind of Paulinus see W. H. C. Frend, 'The Two Worlds of Paulinus of Nola' in *Religion Popular and Unpopular in the Early Christian Centuries* (London, 1976), pp. 100–33. On the basilicas see H. Belting, *Die Basilica der SS. Martiri in Cimitile* (Wiesbaden, 1961).

astonishingly, makes his few references in a Latin translation and not to
the Greek original as it is given by Pitra and Mansi. Bevan repeats
Koch more emphatically, Kitzinger refers to the letter in passing, and
for Klauser it was a fundamental example of his thesis.[1] However,
as I hope to show, had the letter ever been subjected to critical analysis
a very different view of it might have been taken, and a much greater
reserve employed in the matter of regarding it even as indicative of
Eusebius' personal opposition to imagery, much less that of the whole
Church; because, for Klauser and Bevan Eusebius was a representative
figure, and his witness was crucial as proof of the universal attitude of
the Church in the fourth century.[2] Neither in fact say why; one
assumes that what is implied is that Eusebius was the Constantinian
bishop *par excellence*,[3] and at a time when art was evidently beginning
to run mad. What then may be learned of the letter when careful
investigation is undertaken?

The first, fundamental and completely astonishing fact to emerge, and
of capital importance not merely for the purposes of this paper but
also for other issues for which it is a vital piece of evidence, is that not
only is there no critical edition of the text but the manuscript tradition
of the letter has never in fact been examined.

The text as it stands at the moment is not an ancient but a modern
one, first put together in the eighteenth century and reprinted with
additions in the nineteenth, its latest reprinting being in Hennephof's
collection of documents published in 1969. There is no trace of it in
the fourth century among the authentic works of Eusebius and presumably this is why it has been omitted from the volumes of his work
in the Berlin corpus. Further, the text nowhere exists in its entirety,
nor is there any trace or reference to the letter from the empress to
which this is supposed to be the reply. Boivin and Pitra assembled it
piecemeal from a passage in the iconoclastic florilegium of 754 which
was read and refuted by the orthodox in 787, who dismissed it on the
grounds that Eusebius was an Arian, and gave no attention to the
question of its authenticity, as they did to the passages alleged from
the orthodox Epiphanius. This passage is not to be found in the other
florilegium, attributed to the ninth century, belonging to the Church
of Rome and surviving in the Paris codex gr. 1115, where the

---

[1] Koch, pp. 41–58; Elliger, pp. 47–53; Bevan, pp. 111–12; Kitzinger, p. 93
n. 28; Klauser, pp. 4–5.

[2] Klauser, p. 5; Bevan, p. 111.

[3] Yet Ossius of Cordova was Constantine's chief ecclesiastical adviser; see
V. C. de Clerq, *Ossius of Cordova: A Contribution to the History of the Constantinian Period* (Cath. Univ. America Studies in Christian Antiquity 13. Washington, 1954).

correspondence of hagiographic texts with that of 754 is remarkable, but not that of the patristic passages. It was also omitted from the florilegium of the iconoclastic council of 815. Other parts were added from the work of Nicephorus of Constantinople and Pitra printed the whole thing as chapter nine, book four, of his edition of the *Antirrhetici* of Nicephorus. It is quite certain therefore in the circumstances of the text as we have it at present we cannot even be sure which sentence consecutively follows which, even if the letter is in fact authentic.[1]

For the textual problem immediately raises the question of authenticity. In all discussions this normally passes unquestioned, and the few scholars who do mention the possibility of spuriousness do so in order to dismiss it without any solid reason being given.[2] Only an examination of the manuscript tradition, which I have undertaken and hope to publish later, will finally settle this problem. In sum therefore all that can be said of the letter from the point of view of the text itself is that there is no mention of it earlier than the eighth century when it comes into play at the time of the iconoclastic controversy in a source hostile to the making of images. Accordingly, since at the moment there is no evidence to show that, if it ever existed as an entire composition, it was composed in the fourth century, it cannot be taken as evidence of the view of the historical Eusebius towards art, and even less as a testimony to the general view of the official church in the fourth century.

But suppose for the sake of argument this matter is allowed to rest and

---

[1] For the extract from the Horos of 754 quoted at Nicaea in 787 see Hennephof, p. 72 no. 242 and Mansi, xiii. 313ABCD. For Boivin see in *Nicephori Gregorae Byzantina Historia Graece et Latine* (cum annotationibus H. Wolfi, Car. Ducangii, Io. Boivini et Cl. Caperonnerii), ed. L. Schopen, vol. ii (=*Corpus Scriptorum Historiae Byzantinae*, vol. 31, Bonn, 1829). In his note, p. 1300, Boivin assembles a text of the letter based on the Labbe edition of the conciliar *acta* (actio vi, p. 494), and also on a source which he produces for the first time and gives as Cod. Reg. 1980, fols. 191 f. A letter from M. Astruc informs me that this number should read 1989. It therefore needs correction in the Bonn edition of Nicephorus Gregoras and in Migne, *P.G.* xx. 1545 n. 1. The manuscript in question is the present *Parisinus gr. 910*. I would like to express my thanks to M. Astruc for his help in locating Boivin's manuscript. For Cardinal Pitra and his additions see *Spicilegium Solesmense Sanctorum Patrum*, i (Paris, 1852), pp. 383–6. For his unreliability as an editor of the *Antirrhetici* see Alexander, *Nicephorus*, pp. 173–8.

[2] K. Holl, 'Die Schriften des Epiphanius gegen die Bilderverehrung', *Gesammelte Aufsätze zur Kirchengeschichte II, der Osten* (Tübingen, 1928), p. 387 n. 1, asserted that it was undoubtedly genuine since style, standpoint, and understanding all agreed with the works of Eusebius. This was repeated by G. Florovsky, 'Origen, Eusebius and the Iconoclastic Controversy', *Church History*, xix. 2 (1950), pp. 77–96 at p. 84 n. 21, in which he quoted Holl verbatim. Neither attempted to substantiate the statement.

it is assumed, until shown otherwise, that the letter is authentic, what can be said of it from the point of view of the hostility theory? First of all and clearly, it is not a manifesto opposing religious artistic representations in general. The point is specific: it is speaking of an image of Christ, and what appears to be objected to is the idea of an icon, as a true portrait claiming to represent the actual features of Christ. Presumably Eusebius had in mind some large-scale rendering of the head and shoulders—something like the seventh-century icon of St. Peter from Mt. Sinai. That it was portable is clearly shown from the fact that it was to be sent to Constantia.

Yet of icons of this type, portable representations of historical figures, there is so far no trace in the fourth century.[1] In third- and fourth-century art Christ appears either as a symbolic figure: good shepherd, fisherman, or in the painted and sculpted scenes where he is shown in the teacher/philosopher type not really differentiated from the surrounding figures. He never appears isolated, as a cult image, and there is no attempt to depict him as a real and distinctive personality. This is true not only of the Christ figures on the crowded frieze sarcophagi but also of the more beautiful and distinctive representations of him with the Apostles on those of S. Ambrogio and Ravenna. There are indeed portraits in the strict sense on the sarcophagi, but they are those, usually framed in shells or medallions, of the dead interred within: but even here where the idea is to represent definite individuals, it is unlikely that realistic personal features were carved.

Still they are more sharply contrasted with the personally neutral character of Christ and the biblical figures, and this is because the religious scenes are incidental: they are only the background to the

[1] See K. Weitzmann, M. Chatzidakis, K. Miatev, and S. Radojčić, *Icons from South Eastern Europe and Sinai* (London, 1968), p. 13, who date it to the seventh century. See also E. Kitzinger, 'On Some Icons of the Seventh Century' in *Late Classical and Medieval Studies* (as above p. 312 n. 2), pp. 132–50 at p. 136 and pl. xx, fig. 7. The earliest surviving icons are in the collection from the Monastery of St. Catherine on Mount Sinai, and none is firmly dated. On stylistic grounds the earliest tentative date is given to a Virgin and Child between two saints with two very hellenistic-looking angels; it is attributed to the sixth century. Dating is the major problem in the study of icons, which is still in its infancy, particularly with regard to those of the Byzantine period. The few icons preserved in Rome are old but it is unlikely that any were earlier than the sixth century. On the chronology and provenance and for a catalogue of the major icons see D. and T. Talbot-Rice, *Icons and their Dating* (London, 1974). However, it is pointed out to me by Dr. H. Chadwick that the portrait in question may rather have been in the nature of a simple souvenir from the bazaar such as the likenesses of apostles painted on gourds mentioned by Jerome, *in Ionam*, iv. 6 (425 Vallarsi), and I would like to thank him warmly for the suggestion.

illustrious dead whose portraits occupy the central position and the centre of interest in the designs.[1] Again, this is in keeping with the fact that in late antiquity religious art is always allegorical and symbolic.

Secondly, there are two other passages in the undoubted works of Eusebius which mention religious representations and with which this letter may be compared. The *Vita Constantini*, iii. 48 f., speaks with zest of the representations of the Good Shepherd and Daniel with the lions with which Constantine adorned the fountains in the public squares of Constantinople, figures made of brass and resplendent with gold-leaf and the *Church History*, vii. 8, mentions the bronze group of Paneas, thought in Eusebius' time to be a representation of Christ and the woman with the issue of blood. This group was again a fountain ornament, described by Eusebius with sympathy and interest.

For some reason these figures had made an impression on him, for he refers to them again in his fragmentary commentary on Luke viii.[2] But the rights and wrongs of making the images he does not consider at all, simply considering the group as an offering made in the manner of pagan votive statues on the part of the woman. The positive approval of the *Vita*, the absence of hostile comment in the *Church History* compared with the sharply hectoring tone of the *Letter* was a difficult

[1] For the complete catalogue of subjects so far discovered in the Roman catacombs see A. Nestori, *Repertorio Topografico delle Pitture delle Catacombe Romane* (Rome, 1975) and for the illustrations see J. Wilpert, *Die Malereien der Katakomben Roms* (Freiburg-im-Breisgau, 1903). For the sarcophagi of Rome and Ostia see F. W. Deichmann, *Repertorium der christlich-antiken Sarkophage, Texte und Tafeln* (Wiesbaden, 1967). For Ravenna see M. Lawrence (above p. 326 n. 2); for S. Ambrogio see D. Strong, *Roman Art* (London, 1976), pl. no. 225. For a very characteristic example of the portraits of the deceased see the sarcophagus of Adelphia in the Archaeological Museum at Syracuse, and that so-called of the Two Brothers, in the Vatican, both illustrated in Beckwith, figs. 27 and 29.

[2] The authenticity of the *Vita* is generally accepted though the bibliography on the question is long. Much of it was covered when the authenticity was defended by N. H. Baynes, *Constantine and the Christian Church* (Proc. Brit. Acad. xv, 1929, and separately, repr. 1972). I. A. Heikel, G.C.S. i., Einleitung (1902) also accepted the authenticity which is still doubted, however, by W. Seston, *J.R.S.* 1947, pp. 127–31, and H. Grégoire, *Byzantion*, 1938, pp. 551–60 and 561–83, who made some very pertinent comments, chiefly as they affect the military campaigns of Licinius; the archaeological passages normally go unquestioned. Though these fountain ornaments are lost, they must have been similar to the Orpheus fountain figures of Istanbul, Athens, and Sabratha, see J. M. C. Toynbee, *Animals in Roman Art* (London, 1973), pp. 290–2. If the Cleveland Jonas figures are also accepted as coming from a nymphaeum, then further evidence of the type in question is available, see W. D. Wixom, 'Early Christian Sculptures at Cleveland', *Bulletin of the Cleveland Museum of Art*, liv (March 1967), pp. 66–88 k.

inconsistency for the hostility theorists, particularly Klauser, who was reluctant to think that Eusebius, and with him the whole church, had changed their minds about art in the ten years which he regarded as lying between the (undated) *Letter* and the *Church History* and *Vita*. So he fell back on a theory of interpolation into the text of the *Vita* at the end of the fourth century without stopping to prove it.

Nevertheless he seems really to think that Eusebius did change his mind, for on the following page he speaks of 'Eusebius' memorable change of position'.[1] Bevan's explanation is a little more low-level. He believes that either Eusebius considered Good Shepherds inoffensive, or his adulation of Constantine got the better of him: which amounts to a personal aspersion about Eusebius' integrity.[2]

Of course if the truth is that Eusebius never was an opponent of art then explanation is unnecessary since there is no inconsistency of attitude; the *Letter* is objecting only to one kind of artistic form. So much therefore seems to be relevant about the fact of representation of Christ according to the *Letter*: the portrait in question appears to be an icon.

Now it is necessary to examine on what grounds the *Letter* condemns such a portrait. The reasons given are theological, and they differ according to whether Constantia requires 'the true, unalterable image which bears his essential characteristics', that is his divinity—but Eusebius feels the empress is not referring to this—'or his image as a servant that of the flesh he put on for our sake', that is Christ's humanity.[3] The theological problem of representation in this case is, according to the *Letter*, that 'the flesh was so mingled with the glory of the divinity that the mortal part was swallowed up by life even when he was on earth', as the Transfiguration proves. But how is it possible to represent the transfigured countenance 'when even the superhuman disciples could not bear the sight'. If the incarnate form of Christ possessed such power, it was even less susceptible to painting after the Resurrection. And when one arrives at the idea of 'form' as applicable to the divine and human essence 'one is left like the pagans to the representation of things that bear no possible resemblance to anything, for this is what their cult figures are'. But Constantia knows perfectly well that if the subject of the request is really a picture of the historic Christ on earth not only is it forbidden by the second commandment but there are no such examples to be found. 'Have you ever heard anything of the kind yourself in church or from another person? Are

---

[1] pp. 5 and 6.
[2] p. 111.
[3] For the translation see C. Mango, *The Art of the Byzantine Empire 312–1453, Sources and Documents* (Englewood Cliffs, 1972), pp. 16–18.

not such things banished and excluded from churches all over the world; and is it not common knowledge that such practices are not permitted to us alone?'

The presentation of the arguments can scarcely be called clear but it seems possible to unpack them eventually. To take the 'archaeological' argument first—that Constantia is asking for a representational innovation. If the *Letter* does refer to a Byzantine style icon, then quite clearly it is an innovation since, as already indicated, there is no evidence of such icons in the fourth century. But what rather seems to be the point is that because the second commandment forbids representation of the earthly Christ altogether, no representations of him are to be found at all in fourth-century churches; in other words, Eusebius seems to be denying the existence of material representations of Christ in the fourth century. If this really is the point of the passage, it can be disproved as historically inaccurate by the use of one spectacular example: the emperor's sister, and Eusebius himself, can scarcely have been unaware of the five foot high, hundred and twenty pounds weight, silver figure of Christ with the Apostles and Angels which adorned the 'fastigium' of the Basilica Constantiniana, the Lateran.[1]

Ignorance of a production like this must have been impossible in the fourth century; it must have caused a sensation when it was first installed and revealed. So far then, it appears that Eusebius' denial of the existence of the material objects such as those he refers to in his *Letter* is at variance with the archaeological material of the fourth century as it is recorded or survives: we do not have the icons and there are images of Christ.

To test the theological argument it is necessary to see if it is consistent with what is known of the theological position of the historical Eusebius. Basic to the reasoning of the *Letter*, and to the hostility theory built on it, is the enforcement of the obligation of the second commandment; a prohibition already seen as neglected by the early Church but figuring prominently in Byzantine discussions. What of

---

[1] According to the *Liber Pontificalis*, vol. i, ed. L. Duchesne (Paris, 1886, repr. 1955–7), p. 172, in the record under the Life of Sylvester, a structure of hammered or beaten silver weighing 2025 lb., a 'fastidium' or 'fastigium', was given to the Lateran Basilica. It had in front a seated figure of the Saviour 5 feet high, weighing 120 lb. and figures of the twelve apostles each 5 feet and weighing 90 lb. with crowns of pure silver. Behind, looking into the apse, was a figure of the Saviour enthroned, made of pure silver, 5 feet high, weighing 140 lb. and four silver angels, each again 5 feet and 105 lb. weight with gems set in their eyes and holding spears. The exact purpose, position, and form of it remain a mystery; for a discussion and attempted reconstruction see M. Teasdale-Smith, 'The Lateran Fastigium. A Gift of Constantine the Great', *Riv. A.C.* xliv (1970), pp. 149–75.

Eusebius? As Wallace-Hadrill clearly shows, it was crucial to the whole theological position of the historical Eusebius to discount the Mosaic Law as of significance for Christians. It interfered with his interpretation of history.[1] History was the proof of the truth of the Gospel for Eusebius, because the truth must be materially demonstrable. So his four major works form a unit,[2] setting out the history of mankind from remote antiquity to the persecutions of his own day, and drawing the theological lesson from the historical process through which God makes himself known.

Since the axis of history is along the line Abraham, Christ, Constantine, he had to show that the roots of Christianity lay not in Judaism founded on the Mosaic Law but further back in the age of the Patriarchs.[3]

The Mosaic Law was local, temporary, applicable to Jews and only to Palestinian Jews at that. It was a lower and less perfect way and the destruction of the Temple by the Romans signified the destruction of the Mosaic dispensation altogether. The keeping alive of imperfect Jewish ideals was pointless in view of the Incarnation of the Word.[4] Because of this historical dimension, the Incarnation was central to his thinking and this meant therefore that for history the evidence of scripture was primary. And it is here that the link comes with what is of great interest to the purpose of this discussion; for not only did Eusebius write commentaries on scripture but he allied with them 'archaeological field-work', if one may be permitted so to call it. His interest in identifying and developing the archaeological sites most closely linked with the historical associations of Christianity, as recorded in the narrative of the scriptures, and to which he gave expression in his topographical works such as the *Onomasticon*, was meant to be the material reinforcement of the documentary evidence, which proved the truth of his view of history.[5] And this, despite his so-called Origenism, 'gave the humanity of Christ an importance for him that it had never had for Origen, and centred his theology in the Incarnation'.[6]

A further point should be added here as fundamental to this outlook and yet usually dismissed as some sort of sycophancy or adulation of

[1] D. S. Wallace-Hadrill, *Eusebius of Caesarea* (London, 1960), pp. 171–2.

[2] i.e. *The Chronicle, History, Preparation for,* and *Demonstration of the Gospel.*

[3] See *D.E.* I. iii. 40 and cf. *Proph. Ecl.* ii. 5; *Comm. Is.* xlv. 19. 24 (on the temporary nature of the Law); *D.E.* I. vi. 39 (destruction of the Temple); *P.E.* I. v. 1 (the incarnation as the bright intellectual daylight of the truth).

[4] Wallace-Hadrill, ibid.

[5] The *Onomasticon,* ed. E. Klostermann (G.C.S. ii. 1, Euseb. iii. 1, 1966) is, in essence a record of all the memorials still extant of the great biblical figures; notably of the site of the oak of Abraham, which was of vital importance as concrete evidence of the ancestor of Christian mankind. [6] p. 97.

Constantine, this is the lavish praise bestowed on the emperor as the material founder of the Church. When it is recollected that what gave Eusebius his motivation towards a theological interpretation of history was personal experience of what persecution could do to the Church[1] and that the persecution had had for its aim the destruction of scripture —the documentary proof of God's work in history—and the material monuments of the Church,[2] then the amount of space devoted to church buildings,[3] decorated canon-tables,[4] and religious statues appears as what it really is: a major theological theme.

The material restoration of the Church was essential as part of the visible proof of God's culminating historical work in Constantine. Quite clearly the *Vita* and the concomitant *Laus* are works of serious thought and not sycophancy.[5] Quite clearly also, therefore, a theological

---

[1] See *H.E.* viii and *Mart. Pal.* According to A. Momigliano, 'Pagan and Christian Historiography in the Fourth Century A.D.' in ed. Momigliano, *The Conflict between Paganism and Christianity in the Fourth Century* (Oxford, 1963), pp. 79–99, see pp. 89–93, it is the theological interpretation of history which distinguishes Eusebius as a historian in the strict sense from an annalist.

[2] For a discussion of the Edict of Diocletian and the course and consequences of the Great Persecution see W. H. C. Frend, *Martyrdom and Persecution in the Early Church* (Blackwell, Oxford, 1965), pp. 477 f.

[3] Churches from various provinces, built under varying patronage illustrate the vast variety of Constantinian church planning. See, for example, the double cathedral of Aquileia, G. Brusin, *Aquileia e Grado* (Aquileia, 1956); the rectangular form at Orléansville, S. Gsell, *Les Monuments antiques de l'Algérie*, ii (Paris, 1901). For the christological martyria of the Holy Land see J. W. Crowfoot, *Early Churches in Palestine* (London, 1941), and for the buildings of Jerusalem, L. H. Vincent and F. M. Abel, *Jérusalem Nouvelle*, ii. 1 and 2 (Paris, 1925)— this latter especially for the building of the terebinth of Mambre. Of the lavish decorations of the interiors, recurrent commonplaces in contemporary prose and poetry, nothing survives save the vault mosaics of the ambulatory of S. Costanza, see H. Stern, 'Les Mosaïques de l'église de Sainte-Constance à Rome', *D.O.P.* xii (1958), pp. 157–258, and nine of the 'barley-sugar' columns of Old St. Peter's, see J. B. Ward-Perkins, 'The Shrine of St. Peter and its Twelve Spiral Columns', *J.R.S.* xiii (1952), pp. 21–33.

[4] See *V.C.* iv. 36. 37. The decorative, illuminated ornamentation of the Eusebian canon-tables, produced in Caesarea in the second quarter of the fourth century, became known in Italy slightly later, through the Vulgate of St. Jerome; the oldest extant date from sixth century, see C. Nordenfalk, *Die Spätantiken Canontafeln* (Göteborg, 1938). St. Jerome refers to purple codices in terms of contempt, partly because he found them not always textually accurate and partly because he found them difficult to read; see his preface to Job. An extant example which appears to date from the middle of the sixth century is the Vienna Genesis, a manuscript de luxe in which the parchment is painted purple and the script in silver with the illuminations executed in a singular and refined style. It is now only a quarter of the original. See W. Ritter von Hartel and Fr. Wickhoff, *Die Wiener Genesis* (Vienna, 1895).

[5] Accepting with A. H. M. Jones, *The Later Roman Empire 284–602*, i (Blackwell, Oxford, 1973), p. 77, the authenticity of the *Laus*. Both works seem

theme of such major importance must be taken to be representative of the attitude of the historical Eusebius towards matters of Christian imagery and art. So far from being antagonistic, the stress on the monumental evidence of Christianity was for Eusebius as essential as that on the literary evidence for the demonstration of, and propagation of, the truth. It is no accident that he wrote four books on archaeology of which only the *Onomasticon* is extant.[1]

Turning back to the theology of the *Letter* one cannot fail to observe that the whole christological thrust is curious in one who has been celebrated through the centuries as an Arian; for the basic tenet of Arianism, whatever its variety of manifestation, was that in the relationship between the Father and the Son the latter was in some way subordinate.

Yet the emphasis throughout is on the true nature of Christ as divine and therefore the impossibility of representing him in portrait form. Nor is there, if the foregoing statement of Eusebius' theology is true, any trace of Origenism in the historical Eusebius, as it is understood by Florovsky to be characteristic of the *Letter*, which he used as evidence in an influential article attempting to trace the roots of Iconoclasm to Origenism through Eusebius.[2]

A minor point, this time concerning Eusebius' style and habit of mind, may finally be added to this survey. It is the *Vita* and the *Laus* again which provide some means of judging his normal and deeply

to combine unrestrained eulogy and religious interpretation of Constantine's significance. I. A. Heikel (G.C.S. i. 1), p. xlv, draws attention to the correct title of the work as being not 'the Life of Constantine' but 'on the life of Constantine' ('Jedenfalls wird die Arbeit nicht als ein βίος Κωνσταντίνου sondern als eine Schrift Εἰς τὸν βίον Κωνσταντίνου de Vita Constantini . . . . . genannt.')

[1] The lost works are the *Interpretation of Ethnological Terms*, the *Chorography of Ancient Judaea*, and the *Plan of Jerusalem*.

[2] See, for example, p. 87, 'The Origenistic character of the letter in question is beyond doubt . . . . . We could not fail to observe the close and intimate resemblance between Origen's ideas and those of the Letter of Eusebius to Constantia. Origen's christology was the background and presupposition of Eusebius.' Origen's position he defines thus: 'the whole set of his (Origen's) metaphysical presuppositions made it very difficult for him to integrate the Incarnation as a unique, historical event, into the general scheme of Revelation. Everything historical was for him but transitory and accidental. Therefore the historical Incarnation had to be regarded only as a moment in the continuous story of permanent theophany of the Divine Logos—a central moment in a sense, but still no more than a central symbol. . . . The historical was, as it were, dissolved into the symbolic.' His thesis was accepted and developed by P. J. Alexander, 'The Iconoclastic Council of St. Sophia (815) and its Definition (Horos)', *D.O.P.* vii (1953), pp. 35–66, esp. p. 51, and M. V. Anastos, 'The Ethical Theory of Images Formulated by the Iconoclasts in 754 and 815', *D.O.P.* viii (1954), pp. 151–60, esp. p. 154.

respectful method of address to the members of the imperial family; and in his discussion of *Theophany* ii. 4, Wallace-Hadrill is able to remark that it is one of the few passages where Eusebius' scorn goads him to one of his rare exhibitions of vigorous and effective prose.[1]

In keeping with this, his hesitations and sufferings at the Council of Nicaea, dismissed by ancient authorities and modern scholars alike,[2] may very well be interpreted rather as the hesitations of a scholarly mind which disliked being forced by pressure into a decision on a matter of first importance without due opportunity for calm and objective thought. Yet the language of the *Letter* has been described by Professor Mango as 'vitriolic' and by Klauser as 'irritiert'.[3] Once more we seem to encounter a discrepancy with what is known from the authentic works. But this brings the discussion back to its starting-point. After passing the evidence in review one is forced to conclude that the *Letter* seems to be of so uncertain a nature, in so many areas, that it cannot be used as evidence of an attitude of general hostility to art on the part of Eusebius and through him of the entire fourth-century Church. And since its origin is so completely obscure, and its content so much at variance with what is known of the views of Eusebius himself, even its authenticity is doubtful. If it is, in spite of all, genuine, the most that can be said is that it relates specifically to an icon of Christ and could therefore be considered to suggest a demand for them in the fourth century, from which there are no actual known examples.

Epiphanius of Salamis, Letter to John of Jerusalem

If the ultimate problem of the Letter of Eusebius is one of authenticity, the case of the passages from Epiphanius is quite different: it is this time one of interpretation.

The authenticity of the fragments attributed to Epiphanius by the iconoclasts in 754 and 815 has been controverted since the time of the iconoclastic controversy itself, and they have been discussed exhaustively from this point of view in more recent times by Holl and Ostrogorsky.[4] Ostrogorsky denied the authenticity of all but the

---

[1] *V.C.* and *Laus* passim. Wallace-Hadrill, p. 145.

[2] The Fathers of 787, having heard Epiphanius the Deacon read Jerem. ii. 13, welcomed it as apposite in the case of Eusebius who was an Arian and double-minded in the manner of James i. 8, see Mansi, xiii. 316, cf. B.C.D. For Eusebius' hesitancy as a commonplace of modern theological discussion see J. Stevenson, *Studies in Eusebius* (Cambridge, 1929), p. 77, and C. N. Cochrane, *Christianity and Classical Culture* (Oxford, 1940), p. 218.

[3] Mango, p. 4; Klauser, p. 5.

[4] Holl, op. cit., and G. Ostrogorsky, *Studien zur Geschichte des byzantinischen Bilderstreites: Historische Untersuchungen*, Heft 5 (1929, repr. Amsterdam, 1964), pp. 61–113.

Testament of Epiphanius and Holl accepted the attribution of them all. The argument on both sides turned in the last analysis on the christology contained in the fragments and to Holl the witness of Epiphanius was essential as proof of a dogmatic connotation of the whole problem of images which he believed to be present as early as the fourth century; this was the reason why he discussed the authenticity at all. Ostrogorsky's work was severely reviewed after its publication, and he capitulated on the authenticity of the *Letter to John of Jerusalem*.[1] The question with regard to the fragments still remains obscure.

But one fact which is of the highest importance for the purpose of this paper has emerged from the controversy, and it concerns the text of this letter to John of Jerusalem. It is now known that the Greek original of the famous curtain episode, preserved in the Latin translation of St. Jerome and believed to be lost does in fact survive.[2] As will appear this is crucial with regard to the use of this letter as evidence of Epiphanius' 'taking up the matter of Christian religious images as an issue' and the fact that 'even the most sceptic do not doubt that Epiphanius was an opponent of Christian religious imagery'.[3] For it is the letter which is the real basis of this view.

It is the tearing down of the curtain with its figured representation from the church door of a village in Palestine that is regarded as the *locus classicus* for Epiphanius' iconophobia. For this reason the less important fragments are left aside in discussions of his supposed hostility to art, particularly as there is always the possibility that they are spurious; the curtain passage seems to be undoubtedly authentic

[1] See F. Dölger in *Göttingische Gelehrte Anzeigen*, 1929, pp. 353 f.; H. Grégoire, *Byzantion*, iv (1927–8, published 1929), pp. 769 f.; V. Grumel, *E.O.* xxix (1930), pp. 95 f. Ostrogorsky, see *B.Z.* (1931), p. 389.

[2] The question is complicated. The letter is first found in Latin in the translation in *ep.* 51 of Jerome, secondly and partially in the *Libri Carolini*, iv. 25; thirdly in Greek in the work of Nicephorus of Constantinople against the Council of 815. D. Serruys, 'Les Actes du Concile Iconoclaste de l'An 815', *Mél. d'Arch. et d'Hist.* xxiii (École Française de Rome, 1903), pp. 345–51, first drew attention to the Greek text when he discovered the codex 1250 in the Bibliothèque Nationale. The letter is quoted by Nicephorus with a series of passages from Epiphanius attributed to him by the Iconoclasts; all these texts figured in a list of patristic extracts alleged in their florilegium by the Council of 815. The writings of Epiphanius from which these passages are taken are the Testament, the Letter to John of Jerusalem, a dogmatic encyclical, and a letter to Theodosius II. For the texts see Hennephof, pp. 44–51, nos. 111–39, but consult also Ostrogorsky, op. cit., pp. 73 f. and Alexander, 'The Iconoclastic Council . . .' (fragment 30D), p. 65, for the text of Nicephorus' quotation of the letter. See also P. Maas, 'Die ikonoklastische Episode in dem Brief des Epiphanius an Johannes', *B.Z.* xxx (1929–30), pp. 279 f., who proves the existence of a ninth-century archetype for the two manuscripts of Nicephorus' *Refutatio et Eversio*.   [3] Kitzinger, pp. 92–3, repeated by Barnard, p. 89.

because of the contemporary witness of St. Jerome. However, so far as I know, the Greek and Latin texts have never been compared in order to see what Epiphanius actually wrote, and if therefore the usual interpretation is correct.

The scholarly tradition with which this paper is concerned has always based its interpretation only on the Latin text of St. Jerome and this appears to be the basic mistake which has led to misinterpretation. Koch was writing before Ostrogorsky's work, although Serruys had isolated the Greek text before his publication; Elliger published his monograph much later but ignored Serruys and Ostrogorsky and relied entirely on Holl.[1] Klauser too makes reference only to the Latin text,[2] and Schneemelcher who wrote the article on Epiphanius in the *Reallexicon* also relied on Jerome for his statement of the traditional view of Epiphanius and imagery; Dr. Kelly relied on Schneemelcher, and this may be how he was led into an error of fact in his recent discussion of the passage.[3] Before comparing the two texts some remarks are perhaps in order. It is not usually made clear when Jerome's text is used that there is a question of his having, if not falsified, at least tampered with the letter of Epiphanius which he was translating. The question was so pointed that it drew from Jerome a reply in the form of a letter on the principles of good translation. It should be further noted that the substance of the accusation was that he had failed to reproduce the courteous and quiet tone of the original.[4]

In addition it is important to emphasize, from the archaeological point of view, that the curtain episode has a context. It is in essence an apology for not sending sooner a curtain to replace the one he had pulled down—for it should be observed that the immediate criticism made of Epiphanius' action by the people involved was not a protest that he had destroyed an image of Christ but that he had removed a valuable curtain and not replaced it. Epiphanius excused the delay

[1] p. 53.

[2] p. 6 n. 27.

[3] See W. Schneemelcher, 'E. und die Bilder', *R.A.C.* v, pp. 925 f. and cf. P. Nautin, 'Épiphane-ouvrages contre les images', *D.H.G.E.* xv, 628. See J. N. D. Kelly, *Jerome* (London, 1975), p. 20: 'He had noticed a curtain embroidered with a portrait of Christ or of a saint hanging before a church door and . . . in his iconoclastic zeal had pulled it down and torn it in pieces', and p. 201 n. 24: 'Epiphanius tells the story without a blush, in letter 51. 9. He was one of the leading denouncers of the cult of images in the fourth century: see W. Schneemelcher . . .'. But when Epiphanius had pulled down the curtain he did not tear it in pieces, he directed that it should be given to some poor dying man as a shroud. Dr. Chadwick, *Early Church*, p. 281, thinks there was more than one figure on the curtain: 'a curtain in a church porch with a picture of Christ and some saints'—but this is unsupported either by the Latin or the Greek.

[4] Jerome, *Ep.* 57.

because he wanted to find a really good one and so felt it better to send to Cyprus for one of the right quality as well as of religious acceptibility. It is the detaching of the episode from its context and the loss of the over-all courteous presentation and excusing of his action that has caused attention to be focused on a rabid tearing down of curtains and, according to the Latin, a sharp reminder about the second commandment, resulting in the standard picture of Epiphanius as a raving iconoclast.

Another matter of context, this time of social context, should also be considered here, for context seems to disappear altogether whenever Epiphanius and art are discussed. It is well to be reminded of the background against which Epiphanius moved so as to have a perspective from which to approach the literary evidence; the works of St. Jerome are a mine of information about Epiphanius and enable us to see him in his own time.

As a visitor to Rome he was a welcome friend of Damasus, the Pope famous in his own day and since for the care and money he lavished on the material monuments of the Church, in particular the Catacombs. Sunday walks through the Catacombs with their painted decorations, so conducive to meditation, were a favourite form of recreation with Jerome and his friends; works of art were essential to the piety of aspirants to the priesthood in official church circles in the fourth century—although this seems to have escaped the attention of the hostility theorists. Epiphanius is known to have received hospitality from, and given it to, the cultured and wealthy lady Paula, and he also preached in the Anastasis at Jerusalem on the feast of the Dedication. Yet in all this there is no surviving record that he felt himself threatened by revolutionary images put up by the laity in the teeth of the bishops and clergy.[1]

Does the literary evidence then confirm the traditional view of Epiphanius' attitude to art or not? In *Ep.* 51. 9 of Jerome we read that on entering the village of Anablata and seeing a lamp burning and learning that there was a church in the place, he went in to pray and:

inveni ibi velum pendens in foribus eiusdem ecclesiae tinctum atque depictum et habens imaginem quasi Christi vel sancti cuiusdam, non enim satis memini, cuius imago fuerit. Cum ergo hoc vidissem, in ecclesia Christi contra auctoritatem scripturarum hominis pendere

---

[1] Ibid., *Ep.* 127. 7 (Epiphanius' visit to Rome); *Comm. Ez.* xl. 5–13 (walks through the Catacombs); *Ep.* 108. 6–14 (Epiphanius and Paula), cf. *Apol.* 3. 22; *Against John*, 11. 14 (Epiphanius in Jerusalem). For the work of Damasus who became Pope in 366 and whom Jerome was later to serve as secretary (*Ep.* 123. 9) see A. Ferrua, *Epigrammata Damasiana* (Rome, 1942).

imaginem, scidi illud et magis dedi consilium custodibus eiusdem loci, ut pauperem mortuum eo obvolverent et efferrent. Illique contra murmurantes dicere: 'si scindere voluerat, iustum erat, ut aliud daret velum atque mutaret . . .'

The Greek reads: εὕρομεν βῆλον ἐν τῇ θύρᾳ βαπτόν, ἐν ᾧ ἐζωγράφητο ἀνδροείκελόν τι εἰδωλοειδές· ὃ ἔλεγον τάχα, ὅτι Χριστοῦ ἦν τὸ ἐκτύπωμα ἢ ἑνὸς τῶν ἁγίων· οὐ γὰρ μέμνημαι. Ἐγὼ θεασάμενος καὶ εἰδώς, ὅτι μῦσός ἐστιν ἐν ἐκκλησίᾳ τοιαῦτα εἶναι, διέρρηξα αὐτὸ καὶ συνεβούλευσα ἀμφιάσαι ἐν αὐτῷ πένητα τελευτήσαντα. οἱ δὲ γογγύσαντες ἔλεγον· ἔδει αὐτὸν ἀλλάξαι ἐκ τῶν ἰδίων τὸ βῆλον πρὶν ἢ αὐτὸν σχίσῃ.

The fact which emerges plainly here is that while the Latin speaks of an 'image' as of Christ or some saint, identifying (although not very clearly) apparently a Christian image, the Greek makes quite clear what it was. It was an idol in the shape of a man; and furthermore it was only alleged to represent Christ or one of the saints by the bystanders, not by Epiphanius. This too is missing in the Latin. In other words what seems to have been on the curtain was not a Christian figure at all, and was recognized as such by Epiphanius. It would be quite consistent with known Christian practice for the Christian community of this church to have bought what they regarded as a beautiful curtain for their church regardless of the design. Examples of the extraordinarily pagan things which Christians made use of are the Projecta casket from the Esquiline Treasure and now in the British Museum, or the Traprain Treasure in Edinburgh. These all fall into the class of luxury objects; and from what is known of the manufacture, geographical distribution, and expense of high-quality textiles in the Roman world this curtain of Anablata should perhaps be put into the same class.[1]

[1] Luxury craftsmanship whether in the service of individuals or of the Church consistently illustrates this marriage of pagan and Christian. For the Projecta casket, see Strong, pl. 248; on the lid a chi-rho monogram precedes an inscription exhorting Projecta and Secundus to live in Christ, but the decoration represents Venus, nereids, tritons, and sea monsters. The Traprain Treasure contains a flagon with biblical scenes and two fragmentary flasks of pagan mythological content, see Toynbee, pp. 312–14. For the Mildenhall dishes—the large, famous one with the head of Oceanus and the smaller Bacchic platters—and the five inscribed Christian spoons see J. W. Brailsford, *The Mildenhall Treasure* (B.M. 1947) and K. S. Painter, 'The Mildenhall Treasure: A Reconsideration', *B.M. Quarterly*, xxxvii (1973), pp. 154–80. But for the most startling piece of supporting evidence, of undoubted religious and not secular use and now known to be the earliest Christian silver hoard (third-fourth century) see the newly discovered Water Newton Silver. K. S. Painter, 'A Fourth Century Christian Silver Treasure found at Water Newton, England in 1975', *Riv. A.C.* li. 3–4 (1975),

It would therefore scarcely be surprising that the authorities took a dim view of Epiphanius' removal of, and slowness in replacing, such an object. If, on the other hand, the representation was Christian, as is usually thought, then it seems to imply a single figure, frontally placed, of the type found in pagan cultic representations but of which there is no evidence in fourth–fifth-century Christian art. The implication therefore seems to be again, as in Eusebius' Letter, that it was an icon. Epiphanius does not appear to mind what it represents, it was the possibility of its interpretation as a cult figure to which he objected.

The second point made clear in the comparison of the two texts is that only the Latin speaks of the authority of scripture forbidding human representation. While the exact prescription is not specified, Klauser and other scholars are surely right in identifying here the prohibition of the second commandment.[1] But the Greek simply says that mounting of idols is a hateful practice in the Church and omits all mention of scripture. The Greek passage therefore will not support the traditional view here either: that Epiphanius was hostile to the making of images on the grounds of the second commandment.

This discussion of the evidence from Epiphanius may be concluded with reference again to the study of Kitzinger.[2] As quoted earlier, he believed Epiphanius to be an opponent of Christian, not merely pagan, imagery. And when he wished to find confirmation of this from a text about which no questions of authenticity could be raised he looked to the *Panarion* 27. 6. 10, the Greek of which he quotes: στήσαντες . . . τὰς εἰκόνας τὰ τῶν ἐθνῶν ἔθη λοιπὸν ποιοῦσι. This he translates as: 'when images are put up the customs of the pagans do the rest'.

And he comments, 'This surely reflects the experience of his own age.' Unfortunately it does not. Consultation of the original context of the *Panarion* shows that the sentence comes from a passage in which

pp. 333–45. Its most arresting feature is a number of silver religious votive plaques of a type known all over the Roman Empire but hitherto only found in pagan contexts; these are the first to be discovered with Christian symbols and inscriptions. For what is known of Christianity in Britain in general see M. J. Green, *The Religions of Civilian Roman Britain*, B.A.R. 24 (1976), pp. 60–4. For Christian miniatures as part of the whole field of book illumination see those of the fourth century Quedlinburg Old Testament, H. Degering and A. Boeckler, *Die Quedlinburger Italafragmente* (Berlin, 1932). For one of the finest and earliest Christian ivories see the so-called Lipsanotheca, now in the Museo Cristiano at Brescia, an oblong box richly carved with episodes from the scriptures, probably late fourth century, whose real purpose is unknown; illustrated, Beckwith, fig. 35. Ancient textile fabrics and the methods used to produce them are badly documented; for what is known of them in the Roman period see J. P. Wild in *Roman Crafts*, ed. D. Strong and D. Brown (London, 1976), pp. 167–77.   [1] p. 6. Koch, p. 59.   [2] p. 93 and n. 30.

Epiphanius, following Irenaeus, is simply giving information about the Carpocratian gnostics and saying that when they have put up their images, then pagan customs complete the matter. Not only has Kitzinger misunderstood the reference of the passage but, as can be seen, he has also mistranslated it; and by turning the aorist active participle into a passive, he has made into a generalization about images what in Epiphanius was a specific reference to a specific group of heretics, and not a discussion of imagery at all. Both the mistranslation and the misconception have been adopted by Barnard.[1]

Finally, how very slender the case for Epiphanius' hostility really is may be judged from one more piece of evidence. Holl, and following him Kitzinger, interpreted the writings and activities of Epiphanius against the background of the passage from Augustine discussed earlier.[2] But as the primary reference is to excessive eating at funeral meals, and perhaps to real idolatry, practised by a group of deviant Christians in Africa, it cannot well be used as the 'logical background' for a supposed antagonism to Christian art on the part of Epiphanius.

In conclusion, therefore, if the foregoing analysis of the literary evidence is correct, it seems a reasonable assessment of the case to say that there is very little indication indeed that the Fathers of the early Church were in any way opposed to art.

Since then, according to the traditional view taken of the literature so many difficulties and inconsistencies have to be explained away, to say nothing of explaining away the art itself, it seems far simpler and far more in accord with what the Fathers actually wrote, to conclude that there never was a dichotomy between the art and the literature of the early Church; and an apparently insoluble problem proves never to have been a problem at all. It does seem impossible to believe, nor does there now seem to be any evidence for doing so, that all the wealth of art which survives was produced in the face of the Church authorities. Some of the Dura paintings are, if one considers it, remarkably sketchy, and although Christ is represented there, there is no question of portraiture. Nor could the innumerable figures on the sarcophagi and in the Catacombs be considered in any way objects of worship. There is no question of idolatry arising in connection with the art as we have it; yet idolatry was what the iconoclasts feared and what the modern interpretation makes the basis of the hostility to Christian art in the authorities of the Church. It would be unhistorical to consider that these works provided such a possibility.

[1] p. 91, where he quotes Kitzinger verbatim; in view of S. Gero's review in *B.Z.* lxix, Heft 1 (1976), pp. 103–5, this book must be regarded as a less than independent study of the subject.   [2] pp. 384 f. Kitzinger, p. 92.

Also it is extremely puzzling, if the standard hypothesis is correct, that all this art should suddenly spring up at the end of the second century, despite the Pope, in the official burying-ground of the Roman church; for that the Catacombs were official we know beyond doubt from Hippolytus.[1]

At the risk of possible overstatement the point of view opposite to that normally adopted in discussions of Christian art needs stating, and it is therefore very necessary to emphasize the universal character of this art as it is found in the Catacombs and on sarcophagi, etc. from all over the Roman empire—and its completely non-idolatrous character.

With this also should be put forward the major piece of literary evidence which unequivocally supports a positive attitude to art at the unequivocally official level. Unlike any of the pieces of literary evidence alleged for the opposing view, the 82nd canon of the Council in Trullo (A.D. 692)[2] which, while later than the period under discussion, nevertheless presupposes an earlier artistic tradition, provides evidence of an art which accords with the material remains as they survive. It regards the art of the earlier period as symbolic. From the theological point of view the canon is extremely important, since it gives a doctrinal basis for the representation of images: it repudiates the symbolic art of the early Church in favour of the icon.

The Council forbids the symbolic representation of Christ as the Lamb; apparently it was objecting to a semi-historical scene in which John the Baptist pointed to the coming of Christ and Christ represented symbolically. It is the reason for the prohibition which is highly instructive—the Lamb is a 'typos' or an 'image' or 'figure' of the coming grace which signifies the very Lamb, Christ.[3]

Now while types and shadows, that is symbols and signs, must be respected, priority belongs to grace and truth which is the fullness of the Law. The Council therefore prescribes that Christ should be depicted as a man, instead of the 'ancient lamb', in remembrance of his Incarnation, Passion, and redeeming Death, and of the universal redemption

[1] *Philosophumena*, ix. 12.   [2] Mansi, xi. 977 f.

[3] For important remarks about language and texts concerning concepts like imago, figura, etc. see H. de Lubac, *Corpus Mysticum* (Paris, 1949), pp. 210 f., 248 f. For the development of the concept of figure (τύπος, figura) in the Latin West with some notice of corresponding Greek terms such as τύπος, μορφή, εἶδος, σχῆμα, see E. Auerbach, 'Figura' in *Neue Dantestudien, Istanbuler Schriften*, v (Istanbul, 1944). There is not, so far as I can discover, a detailed investigation of the Greek patristic terms such as χαρακτήρ in their relationship to the image concept, or a linguistic study of the word εἰκών, apart from that in Kittel, *T.W.B.* ii (Stuttgart, 1933–35), p. 387, under *eikon* (Kleinknecht).

thereby accomplished. It is a doctrinal programme and a true preamble to all the subsequent literature on holy images. For while the case the Council refers to seems to be a special one, it nevertheless lays down a theological principle. What is remarkable is that the painting of icons is linked with the contrast between 'types' and 'historical truth'. So it seems then to be an encouragement of the new 'historical' art so foreign to that of the earlier period which it is rejecting.

Nothing perhaps could illustrate more completely the real gulf between the thought world of the early Church where types and shadows can be used as description in a book devoted to the study of the Fathers,[1] and that of the Byzantine Church. In archaeological terms the same gulf is exemplified in the iconography of the fourth-century Sarigüzel sarcophagus in Istanbul and that of the late-sixth-century Riha and Stuma patens.[2] It is perhaps to be explained because the link between the two worlds was not the texts of the Fathers read in their entirety but the catenae of quotations made from them in the period before Iconoclasm. The library resources of Constantinople were not large and the copying of manuscripts was expensive.[3]

Clearly the 'genetic' theory of a continuously hostile tradition to art which finally erupted into Iconoclasm cannot be maintained, and the linking of discussions of early art to the period of Iconoclasm has been mistaken.

It seems, therefore, that what has happened is that the materials of church history have been mistaken for the history of the Church itself; because church history, in this matter, has been regarded primarily as based on written documents. The material remains, ignored by church historians, have been left to the analysis of art historians, Roman and Byzantine social historians, or sub-departments of classical archaeology. Yet the purpose of all this art was religious and therefore it is the theological dimension which in the end is paramount; discussions of types, origins of motifs, etc. are only ancillary, though essential, studies. Perhaps therefore it may be pleaded that the monuments of the Church

---

[1] J. Daniélou, *From Shadows to Reality. Studies in the Biblical Typology of the Fathers* (tr. W. Hibberd, London, 1960).

[2] See J. Beckwith, *The Art of Constantinople*, 2nd edn. (London, 1968), p. 21, pls. 23-6, and pp. 46-7, pls. 58 and 59. Basically the difference is that the iconography of the patens, which depict the communion of the apostles, seeks to avoid any sense of weight or volume which might suggest a third dimension and so give a naturalistic appearance to the figures, while that of the sarcophagus with angels bearing the monogram of Christ in a garland and the apostles on either side of a plain cross is entirely classical in spirit and expression.

[3] See C. Mango, 'The Availability of Books in the Byzantine Empire, A.D. 750-850' in *Byzantine Books and Bookmen* (Dumbarton Oaks, 1975), pp. 29-45.

should be put back into the context of church history alongside the literary remains in order to arrive at a more rounded estimate of matters of fact in the early Church. There is after all an excellent precedent in the practice of Eusebius.   Sister CHARLES MURRAY

A FOURTH-CENTURY CHRISTIAN SILVER TREASURE

FOUND AT WATER NEWTON, ENGLAND, IN 1975

In February, 1975, a treasure of one gold and 27 silver objects was found at Water Newton, near Peterborough, in central England (fig. 1). On September 10th, 1975, a court declared the the treasure to be the property of the state, and it is now in the British Museum. The treasure is important both as a discovery in its own right, and also because it is an example of one of the main themes of the *relazione* presented to the Ninth Congress of Christian Archaeology by Professor Ward Perkins, that the ancient craftsman adapted and supplied objects from his regular repertoire for his customer, and that the customer gave significance to the objects by his choice of details and by his use of the objects [1]. The Water Newton Treasure constitutes evidence for this hypothesis because the objects are not individual finds but can be interpreted on the basis of their relationship within the group.

The discovery was made by an amateur archaeologist, just after ploughing by the farmer, in a field which is known to be part of the small Roman town of Durobrivae. Its defences enclose about 17.3 hectares. Durobrivae lies on the main Roman road between Lincoln and York to the north and London and Colchester to the south. It grew up outside the military fort built in the first century A. D. to defend the bridge across the River Nene. The importance of Durobrivae is belied by its size. Dr Wild has pointed ont, « The residential and commercial buildings so tightly packed within the defences were merely the centre of a much more extensive zone of industrial, commercial and religions enterprise which spread

---

[1] J. B. WARD-PERKINS, *'The Role og craftsmanship in the Formation of Early Christian Art'* (1975).

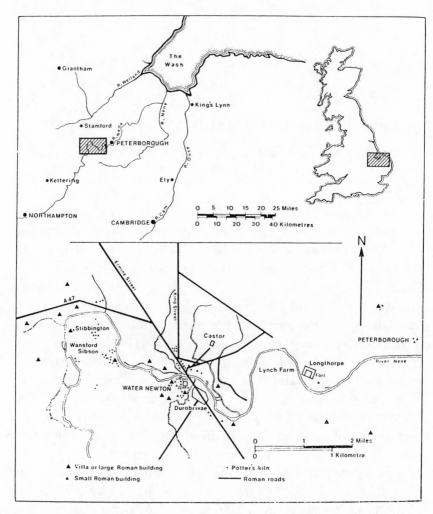

Fig. 1   Durobrivae. Location map. (*Drawn by P. Compton*).

over the old fort site west of the town and across Normangate Field, Castor, north of the river. The suburbs covered at least 100 hectares, an area comparable in size with some of the large towns of Roman Britain... The suburbs had begun to grow in the Flavian period and reached their apogee in the fourth century» [2].

The treasure includes nine vessels and nineteen plaques. Some

[2] J. P. WILD, '*Roman Settlement in the Lower Nene Valley*', in *Archaeological Journal*, 131 (1974), pp. 140-170.

of the objects are damaged; but of the vessels six are more or less complete.

One item, a circular disc, is of gold. The other objects are of silver, of a purity of about 96 or 97 per cent. The objects are:

1. Plain bowl Broken. Diameter, c. 16 cm.

2. Mouth and neck of a spouted jug. Height, 10.5 cm.

3. Large dish with Chi-Rho and omega in central roundel. Diameter, 27 cm. (fig. 2).

Fig. 2 — Large dish. Diameter, 27 cm.
(Photograph, British Museum).

4. Bowl decorated with facets. Diameter, c. 10 cm. (fig. 3).

5. Decorated jug. Height, 20.3 cm. (fig. 4).

6. Cup with two detached handles. Height, 12.5 cm. (fig. 5).

7. Strainer with handle. Decorated at the end of the handle with a Chi-Rho and alpha and omega. Length, 20.2 cm. (fig. 6).

8. Cup, partly lost, inscribed round the rim, « (Chi-Rho with alpha and omega) INNOCENTIA ET VIVENTIA ... RVNT ». Height, c. 12.4 cm. (fig. 7).

Fig. 3   Bowl decorated with facets. Diameter. 10 cm. (*Photograph, British Museum*).

9. Cup or bowl, inscribed in the same style of lettering on the base and round the rim: (a) on base, « PVBLIANVS »; (b) round the the rim, « Chi-Rho with alpha and omega) SANCTVM ALTARE TVVM D(Chi-Rho with alpha and omega)OMINE SVBNIXVS HONORO ». This inscription forms a dactylis hexameter. Height, 11.5 cm. (fig. 8).

10-19 Triangular plaques with veins like leaves. Heights, 3.8 cm. — 7.8 cm.

20-26 Triangular plaques, each with veins like leaves, and also with a Chi-Rho stamped in relief in a central roundel (fig. 9). All except one have in addition an alpha and omega. One

Fig. 4 — Decorated jug and fragment of handle. Height, 20.3 cm.
(*Photograph, British Museum*).

Fig. 5 — Cup with two handles. Height, 12.5 cm. (*Photograph, British Museum*).

has an extra inscription at the top, « . . . ANICILLA VOTVM QUO(D) PROMISIT CONPLEVIT » (fig. 10). Heights, 4.9 cm — 15.7 cm.

27. Gold disc with Chi-Rho and alpha and omega. Diameter, 4.9 cm.

28. Fragments of undecorated silver plaques or sheet.

No precise indication of date is available from within the group in the way in which some discoveries are dated by inscriptions or coins. The date of manufacture of certain of the objects, however, can be ascertained approximately by comparison with other discoveries: 4, bowl decorated with facets, late 3rd century A. D.; 5, decorated jug, late 3rd or possibly 4th century A. D.; 6, cup with two handles, 3rd century A. D.; 7, strainer, 3rd century A. D.; 10-27, votive plaques, 3rd century A. D. in type.

There is evidence that the vessels were not abandoned but were put away in antiquity with the intention of being recovered. First, the finder described how the vessels lay carefully arranged in the large dish, and his evidence is confirmed by markings on the dish. The bright patches, for example, show that some of the plaques lay directly on the dish. Second, scientific examination of the broken edges of the objects shows that the majority of the

Figg. 6 — Strainer, Length. 20.2 cm.
(*Photograph, British Museum*).

breaks are recent and are likely to have occurred during ploughing or the removal of the objects from the soil. All the objects, therefore, were probably in a usable condition when they were put away in antiquity. The combination of these two factors suggests that the objects were deposited with intent to recover.

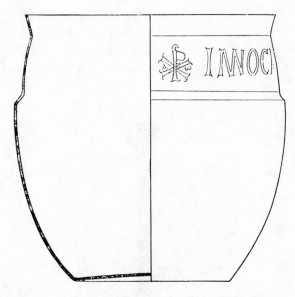

Fig. 7 — Cup, inscribed round the rim. Height, 12.4 cm.
(*Drawing, P. Compton*).

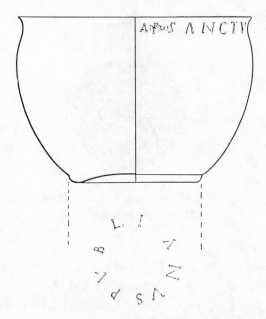

Fig. 8 — Cup, inscribed on the base and round
the rim. Height, 11.5 cm. (*Drawing, P. Compton*).

The earliest possible date of deposition of the group is the latter part of the third century or the early part of the fourth century. The group was not deposited later than some time in the fourth century, for it does not include types of vessels found in the outstanding fourth-century silver hoards, such as (a) that from the Eastern Roman Empire, now in the Staatliche Münzen-

Fig. 9 — Plaque, with gilt roundel.
Height, 15.7 cm. (*Photograph, British Museum*).

sammlung in Munich, deposited about A. D. 321/322; (b) the Kaiseraugst Treasure, deposited in A. D. 350; and (c) the Mildenhall Treasure, deposited about A. D. 360 [3]. The reason for putting

---

[3] (a) B. OVERBECK, *Argentum Romanum, Ein Schatzfund von spätrömischem Prunk-geschirr* (Munich 1973); (b) R. LAUR-B ELART, *Der spätrömische Silberschatz von Kaiseraugst* (Basel 1963); (c) J. W. BRAILSFORD, *The Mildenhall Treasure* (British Museum 1947), and K. S. PAINTER, 'The Mildenhall Treasure: A Reconsideration', in *British Museum Quarterly, XXXVII* (1973), pp. 154-180.

away the Water Newton Treasure could have been to protect it
against theft or confiscation, or perhaps to keep the objects safe
in a period of danger. One of the earliest occasions when such
hiding might have been necessary is the Great Persecution of
Diocletian in A. D. 303-304; but there are many other possibili-

Fig. 10 — Plaque, with roundel and inscription at top.
Width. 9.5 cm. (*Drawing, P. Compton*).

ties and the particular reason is not now likely to be known [4].

In character and purpose the treasure is religious and not
secular. There is no apparent reason why any of the vessels should
not occur as types in any of the secular hoards of the period.
Indeed, the facetted bowl comes from the same workshop as that
in the treasure of Chaource in France, a treasure famous because
it is probably a full set, or *ministerium*, of table silver, dated

---

[4] Protection against theft by Mensurius, Bishop of Carthage, c. A. D. 308: OPTATVS
On the schism of the Donatists, I, 15-19. Great Persecution, action at Cirta, 19 May
303, *Gesta apud Zenophilum* in *Corpus Scriptorum Ecclesiasticorum Latinorum, XXVI,*
pp. 186-188,

around A. D. 270 [5]. The plaques in the Water Newton Treasure, however, can only be religious. Such plaques are known from the western to the eastern ends of the Roman Empire [6]. All previous discoveries, however, are pagan. The Water Newton plaques are of exactly the same type; but they are the first to be discovered with Christian symbols and inscriptions. The Water Newton plaques are votive, and the inscriptions on two of the vessels show that they too were dedicated as offerings. The three votive inscriptions and the use, fifteen times, of the Chi-Rho device demonstrate that the whole Water Newton Treasure is religious and Christian.

The use of the Water Newton Treasure is problematical. The plaques were clearly votive, payments to God for requests fulfilled. The group of vessels, however, must be compared with those in other major hoards of the period. They resemble the important religious hoard from Berthouville in France, in that they have dedicatory inscriptions [7]. The vessels from Berthouville, however, wehe old and more or less worn when the dedications to Mercury were added in the third century A. D. The major secular hoards, however, were all usable when deposited. The Water Newton Treasure, by contrast, was both religious and in good usable condition when deposited. Unlike the secular pieces, however, no vessel has inscriptions of possession or weight scratched on it. It seems likely, therefore, that the treasure was in the possession of, and being used by, a practising Christian group, perhaps for *refrigeria* or for baptisms or for communion. Jungmann has pointed out that before the third century the material gifts of bread and wine by the laity were hardly ever mentioned, only the thanksgiving over them, but that from the third century it is precisely the material side which is stressed [8].

---

[5] H. B. WALTERS, *Catalogue of the Silver Plate, Greek, Etruscan and Roman, in the British Museum* (London 1921), nos. 144-182.

[6] Britain: J. M. C. TOYNBEE, *Art in Britain under the Romans* (Oxford, 1964), pp. 328-331. Rhineland: O. DOPPELFELD (ed.), *Römer am Rhein* (Cologne 1967), pp. 246-248. Other areas: R. NOLL, 'An den Silbervotiven aus dem Dolichenusfund von Mauer a. d. Url', in *Jahreshefte des Österreichischen archäologischen Instituts in Wien*, *XXXVIII* (1950), cols. 125-146.

[7] E. BABELON, *Le Trésor de Berthouville* (1920).

[8] J. A. JUNGMANN, *The Early Liturgy to the Time of Gregory the Great* (London 1960, pp. 117-118.

Bread and wine are referred to, for example by Cyprian, as the *sacrificium* [9]. Could it be that new recruits to Christianity felt encouraged to bring offerings of pagan type, their *oblationes*, to place within the *altare*, not the altar, but the sanctuary or sacred place? [10]. Could the objects from Water Newton be the hint of a practice, not previously suspected, transitional between paganism and Christianity?

It cannot be known without excavation whether the Water Newton silver was in a shrine or church at Durobrivae. It is important, however, that Durobrivae lies on the main road between Lincoln and York to the north and London and Colchester to the south. The objects, therefore, may have been hidden while in passage between any of the places. Publianus, Innocentia, Viventia and Anicilla may not even have had a particularly close connection with the province of Britain at all. It is clear, however, from the names — Publianus, Innocentia and Viventia are Roman, as also is Anicilla — and from the use of Latin that the treasure belongs in the western half of the Roman Empire even though the type of Chi-Rho device used suggests an eastern origin for the workmanship [11].

Before the descovery of the Water Newton Treasure the two earliest known Christian treasures were those of Canoscio in Umbria, and of Kumluca in south-west Turkey, both of the sixth century A. D. [12]. The Water Newton silver is not later than the fourth century A. D. The group includes religious plaques which are pa-

---

[9] CYPRIAN, *De Opere et Eleemosynis* (c. A. D. 253), c. 15.

[10] Altare in the sense of 'shrine', 'sanctuary', 'sacred place': J. M. C. TOYNBEE and J. B. WARD-PERKINS, *The Shrine of St. Peter and the Vatican Excavations* (London 1956), pp. 212 ff.; A. FERRUA, *Epigrammata Damasiana* (Vatican 1942), p. 122, 1.5; GREGORY of TOURS, *De Gloria Martyrum XXVII* (MIGNE, *Patrologia Latina LXXI*, cols. 728-9), and *Historia Francorum* II, 14 (MIGNE, *Patrologia Latina LXXI*, col 213). Oblations: IRENAEUS, *Adversus Haereses*, ed. W. W. HARVEY (Cambridge 1857), *IV*, 21, 5; JUNGMANN, *l. c.*; A. H. COURATIN, *Liturgy*, in R. P. C. HANSON (ed.), *Historical Theology* (Penguin Books 1969), pp. 153-154.

[11] ALISON FRANTZ, 'The Provenance of the Open Rho in the Christian Monograms', in *American Journal of Archaeology*, end series, *XXXIII* (1929), pp. 10-26.

[12] Canoscio: E. GIOVAGNOLI, 'Una Collezione di Vasi Eucaristici Scoperti a Canoscio', in *Rivista di Archeologia Cristiana* XII (1935), pp. 313-328; E. GIOVAGNOLI, *Il Tesoro Eucaristico di Canoscio* (Città di Castello 1940). Kumluca: N. FIRATLI, '*Un Trésor du sixième siècle trouvé à Kumluca, en Lycie*', in *Akten des VII Internationalen Kongresses für Christliche Archäologie*, Trier 1965, pp. 523-525.

gan in type and vessels which are ordinary secular types used for Christian religious purposes. The objects throw light on areas of the history of Christianity of which we know almost nothing. The Water Newton Treasure is the earliest known group of Christian silver from the whole Roman Empire and is a discovery of international importance.

K. S. PAINTER

The Painting of the Good Shepherd at Dura-Europos

JOHANNES QUASTEN

DURING the excavations of the city of Dura-Europos, conducted by Yale University in 1932, C. Hopkins[1] discovered close to the west wall an ancient Christian baptismal chapel[2] the walls of which are decorated with fairly well preserved frescoes. The frescoes on the side walls present the scenes of David and Goliath, of the paralytic, of Peter walking on the water, and of the prudent virgins;[3] on the rear wall which forms a kind of apse, one sees on the lower portion a picture of Adam and Eve, and on the upper portion, one of the Good Shepherd with his flock. Baur gives the following description of the latter:

> The Good Shepherd is depicted in frontal view, and stands behind his flock. On his shoulders he carries a huge ram, holding the hind leg of the animal with the right hand against his chest, and grasping the foreleg with the left hand close to his shoulder. He is painted in dark red; the details of his feet are not clear. The girt tunic is yellowish-brown with dark edgings. Slung over his right shoulder is the strap of a bag which hangs at his left side. The head is represented with a band of dark hair; the eyes are dark dots; nose and mouth are scarcely distinguishable. In front of him is a flock of seventeen rams huddled together, and as difficult to count as a real flock of sheep. They are of the oriental fat-tailed variety with long, curving horns. The leader of the flock and some of the other rams lower their heads to drink at a brook beyond which reeds grow. Behind the Good Shepherd on the left side of the picture, are a number of trees. From one of these trees, which probably indicate the celestial paradise, the paint ran down, making a streak on the face of Adam.[4]

The private dwelling, of which the baptismal chapel is a part, was covered up in the year 256, when the Romans hastily converted the border stronghold of Dura into a breastwork against the Parthians. The frescoes must therefore have been installed before that year. Thus we have here the picture of the

---

[1] See M. J. Rostovtzeff, *The Excavations at Dura-Europos. Preliminary Report of Fifth Season of Work,* October 1931-March 1932 (New Haven, 1934).

[2] In this connection see M. Aubert, 'Les Fouilles de Doura-Europos, Notes sur les origines de l'iconographie chrétienne', *Bull. Monum.* (1934) n. 4; A. von Gerkan, 'Die frühchristliche Kirchenanlage von Dura', *Römische Quartalschrift* 42 (1934) 219 ff.; W. Seston, 'L'Eglise et le baptistère de Doura-Europos', *Ann. de l'Ec. d. Hautes Et. de Gand* I (1937), 161 ff.; M. Rostovtzeff, *Dura-Europos and its Art* (Oxford, 1938) 130 ff.; A. J. Pelekanides, *To protochristianikon baptisterion tes Douras-Europou kai hai toichographiai autou: Nea Sion* 31 (1936), pp. 50-57; 138-49; 209-220; 282-291. The theory of P. V. C. Baur, 'Les peintures de la chapelle chrétienne de Doura', *Gazette des Beaux-Arts* 65 (1933) 66, that the rectangular depression in the floor of the chapel is not the *piscina* of a baptistry, but a place used for the preservation of relics, is untenable. The position in the city, on which J. Kollwitz, *Jb. f. Liturgiewiss.* 13 (1935) has already

commented, the steps which lead down from three sides to the floor of the basin, and the frescoes, all disprove this view. Baur believes that the basin was probably covered with a stone slab upon which the *mensa* used for the celebration of the Eucharist was erected. The condition of the basin, however, shows that it never was covered. There is just as little trace of Baur's supposed stone slab for the altar. Baur's objection that the space could not have served for the administration of Baptism since the *piscina* is only 0.95 m. deep, is refuted by a comparison of this with the other baptistries which we possess. For example, the *piscina* of the baptistry of Fréjus is only 0.82 m. in depth. Cf. Pfister, 'Il battistero di Fréjus', *Rivista di archeologia cristiana* 5 (1928), 352.

[3] Regarding this matter see O. Casel, *Jb. f. Liturgiewissenschaft* 13 (1935), 311, note 1; E. Weigand, *Byzantin. Zeitschr.* 37 (1937), 240, is in agreement.

[4] P. V. C. Baur, in M. J. Rostovtzeff, *The Excavations,* p. 259. See the reproduction on plate XLIX and our plate I.

[1]

Good Shepherd in a baptistry which comes from the middle of the third century.
A twofold question arises: first of all, can the picture of the Good Shepherd be found in other baptistries? Second, why did early Christian thought associate the Good Shepherd with the liturgical room in which the ceremony of baptism was performed?

About a century and a half later than Dura-Europos we find a picture of the Good Shepherd in a baptismal room in the West. The baptistry of *San Giovanni in Fonte* in Naples contains among the mosaics[5] which decorate its interior room, not less than four representations of the Good Shepherd. The artist has arranged them according to the laws of symmetry on the slanting surfaces above the corners, thus giving them a place of prominence. The Good Shepherd stands in the center of each of the four mosaics,[6] but one recognizes without difficulty that the two diagonally opposed pictures are complementary in composition. Twice the Good Shepherd is presented between two harts, which are refreshing themselves from a spring which flows from the rocks, and twice he is represented as standing between two sheep which are hastening toward him. In the first two scenes the Good Shepherd stands between the fountains which break from the rocks, supporting himself on his staff, gesturing invitingly toward the spring, in one picture with his right[7] and in the other with his left hand.[8] In both mosaics which picture him between the two sheep the scenery is entirely different, if we exclude the palms and the birds which form a sort of frame work. The Shepherd is placed not in a rocky landscape but in a blooming meadow, and in one picture he carries a lamb on his shoulders[9] and in the other he is resting among colorful flowers with his arm out-stretched, beckoning to his flock.[10]

The mosaics of *San Giovanni in Fonte* in Naples were, until the discovery of the baptismal chapel of Dura-Europos, the sole example preserved to us of the representation of the Good Shepherd in an ancient Christian baptistry. It would be a mistake, however, to conclude from this, that the picture of the Good Shepherd in ancient Christian baptistries was as rare as the examples which have been preserved. The mosaics of the old portico of the Lateran baptistry,[11] the so-called chapel of Rufina and Secunda, derive from approximately the same period[12] as those of the baptistry of *San Giovanni in Fonte* in Naples. Opposite the still extant mosaic of the eastern apse, which shows on a blue background a gigantic acanthus vine, the golden branches of which fill the entire surface of

---

[5] For a description of these see R. Garrucci, *Storia della arte cristiana nei primi otto secoli della chiesa* IV (Prato, 1877), pp. 79 ff.; E. Muntz, 'Notes sur les mosaïques chrétiennes de l'Italie', *Revue archéologique* I (1883) 21 ff.; J. Wilpert, *Die römischen Mosaiken und Malereien der kirchlichen Bauten vom IV. bis XIII. Jahrhundert* I (Freiburg, 1916), pp. 214-229; G. Stuhlfauth, 'Das Baptisterium San Giovanni in fonte in Neapel und seine Mosaiken', *Reinhold-Seeberg-Festschrift* II (Leipzig, 1929), 181-212.

[6] See the reproduction by J. Wilpert, *op. cit.*, III (Volume of Illustrations) plates 36; 37, 1; 38, 1; and 38, 2.

[7] See the reproduction given in our plate II.

[8] See plate III.

[9] See plate IV.

[10] See plate V.

[11] J. Wilpert, *op. cit.*, 1, p. 246 is of the opinion that the mosaics are from the second half of the fourth century, and believes that the date of the mosaics must be placed "toward the beginning of that period rather than at the end." G. Stuhlfauth *art. cit.*, 206

assigns their origin to the early fifth century on the grounds that the mosaics are of a formal artistic kind. The mosaics cannot be assigned to a later date, because of certain parts of the garments worn by the Good Shepherd, principally the shoulder cape. As G. Rodenwaldt, 'Eine spätantike Kunstströmung in Rom', *Römische Mitteilungen* 36/37 (1921-22), 58-100 has pointed out, this shoulder cape is a characteristic piece of clothing peculiar to Roman dress among the rural population of the fourth century, and one introduced into the West under the influence of Roman culture. A typical example of this outside Rome is the representation found in the mosaic paving of the Basilica of Aquileia. See the reproduction of this in: *La Basilica di Aquileia a cura del comitato per le ceremonie celebrative del IXᵒ centenario della basilica* (Bologna, 1933), plate 30.

[12] Regarding this see J. Wilpert *op. cit.*, I, pp. 250-268; G. B. Giovenale, *Il Battistero Lateranense* (Studi di antichità cristiana I, Rome, 1929), pp. 121 ff.

[2]

I

Painting in the Baptistry at Dura-Europos

The Good Shepherd and his flock.

(Rostovtzeff)

275

II

III

Mosaics in the Baptistry of S. Giovanni in Fonte at Naples

II. The Good Shepherd inviting to the waters of Baptism.

III. The Good Shepherd and the hart at the fountain.
(Wilpert)

IV.

V.

Mosaics in the Baptistry of S. Giovanni in Fonte at Naples

   IV. The Good Shepherd carrying the lamb.
    V. The Good Shepherd among flowers inviting his sheep.
                   (Wilpert)

the mosaic, there was formerly another one in the western apse, which, if we may judge from the attention given to it in the old descriptions, must have been, from the artistic point of view, the more important of the two. According to the description of this mosaic given by A. *Ciacconio*, it also contained a picture of the Good Shepherd: *Christus ter armentarii, semel pecuarii habitu cernitur, caetera quae olim superius exstabant temporis iniuria collapsa sunt, nec potest aliud videri.*[13] The copies which he added[14] to his manuscript notes have of course only a relative value, since according to his own words the mosaic was already at his time in a state of decay. They give four representations of the Shepherd in the midst of his flock. The position which he assumes reminds us strongly of the representations in *San Giovanni in Fonte* in Naples. In both instances he stands leaning on his staff with his legs slightly crossed. O. Panvinio describes it as follows: *In dextera sunt picti pastores, armenta pascentes cum ovibus aviariisque, emblematibus scite expressis.*[15] From these words, as well as from the description and the drawings given by Ciacconio, it may be concluded that the representations of the Shepherd in the one-time mosaic of the Lateran baptistry had taken on a highly ornamental character which relegated the thought associated with the picture into the background.

Through the description given us by Prudentius of the arrangement and decoration of the baptistry which Pope Damasus had erected near the Vatican Basilica[16] we know that here also the picture of the Good Shepherd appeared in the cycle of the mosaics. Prudentius describes the picture in the following words: "The Shepherd himself there refreshes with the fluid from the cool spring the sheep, which he sees panting after the waters of Christ".[17]

Since Prudentius adjoins these words to his description of the richness of color and the splendor of the mosaics, the presumption is justified that he intended to describe the content of the picture also. His words remind us spontaneously of the representations in the baptistry of *San Giovanni in Fonte* in Naples. Probably here in the baptistry of the Vatican Basilica the Good Shepherd was also represented as inviting his sheep to the fountain.

In the early Christian baptistry of Mainz, the Good Shepherd appeared not in a picture but in the form of an inscription which has been preserved by Venantius Fortunatus.[18] The intitial verses of this inscription which in classical form pay a final tribute to Christian antiquity[19] deserve to be reproduced here:

> Ardua sacrati baptismatis aula coruscat
> quo delicta Adae Christus in amne lavat
> Hic pastore Deo puris grex mergitur undis,
> ne maculata diu vellera gestet ovis.[20]
> Traxit origo necem de semine, sed pater orbis
> purgavit medicis crimina mortis aquis.[21]

[13] A. Ciacconio, *Vita Bonifacii VIII.*, vol. II col. 302; Codex Vaticanus 5407, pp. 195-200.
[14] See the reproductions by Ch. Rohault de Fleury, *Le Latran au moyen-âge* (Paris, 1877), pl. 43; J. Wilpert, op. cit., III (Volume of Illustrations), p. 256, fig. 72 and p. 257, fig. 73; G. B. Giovenale, op. cit., p. 124, fig. 71 and p. 125, fig. 72.
[15] O. Panvinio, *De septem Urbis ecclesiis* (Roma, 1570), p. 158.
[16] For a description of this baptistry see J. Zettinger, 'Die ältesten Nachrichten über Baptisterien der Stadt Rom', *Römische Quartalschrift* 16 (1902), 331-336; A. de Waal, 'Das Baptisterium des Papstes Damasus bei St. Peter', *Römische Quartalschrift* 16 (1902) 58-61.

[17] Prudentius, *Peristephanon* 12, 43 (456 Dressel):
Pastor oves alit ipse illic gelidi rigore fontis videt sitire quas fluenta Christi.
[18] Venantius Fortunatus, *Carmina* 2, 12. See also the verse of another hymn which goes back to Fortunatus: Accedite ergo digni/ ad gratiam lavacri/ quo fonte recreati/ refulgeatis agni. A. S. Walpole, *Early Latin Hymns* (Cambridge, 1922), p. 192.
[19] See W. Neuss, *Die Anfänge des Christentums im Rheinlande* (Bonn,[2] 1933), p. 25.
[20] See Petrus Chrysologus, *Sermo* 173, (PL 52, 651A): vos filioli dominici gregis portio copiosa niveo et divino vestita iam vellere.
[21] The complete inscription may be found

[3]

What thought did Christian antiquity associate with this picture of the Good Shepherd in the baptistries? H. Achelis[22] in answer to this question has pointed out that the baptismal chapel is a place "in which the forgiveness of sin was imparted". He applies to the mosaics of the baptistries his general interpretation of the pictures of the Good Shepherd, which he explains from the controversies regarding the sacrament of penance. However, this interpretation cannot be easily reconciled with the paintings in the catacombs. This is still more true of such representations of the Good Shepherd in the baptism room. The connection of the picture of the Good Shepherd with the room used for the baptismal ceremony is much more deeply rooted in the mysteries of Christianity.

Even in the period before the coming of Christ, the Good Shepherd was the symbol of the σωτήρ, the author of salvation.[23] Thus also in the Gospel of St. John (x, 28) he guarantees the σωτηρία: "And I give them life everlasting and they shall not perish forever, and no man shall pluck them out of my hand." It is significant that the parable of the Good Shepherd, which is given both by St. Matthew (xviii, 12-14) and by St. Luke (xiv, 4-7) who places his lost sheep on his shoulders and carries it back with joy to the flock, was applied by the ancient authors consistently to the σωτὴρ τοῦ κόσμου, Christ, who bears his lost sheep, humanity, on his shoulders, and brings it back to the heavenly fold, to the host of the angels.[24] According to the Christian conception the σωτηρία which the Good Shepherd brings, is the "salvation of the world". For the individual this salvation begins with Baptism. It is for this reason that ancient Christianity associated the picture of the Good Shepherd with the mystery of rebirth. In his *Exhortation to the Heathens*, Clement of Alexandria exclaims:

σπεύσωμεν εἰς σωτηρίαν, ἐπὶ τὴν παλιγγενεσίαν· εἰς μίαν ἀγάπην συναχθῆναι οἱ πολλοὶ κατὰ τὴν τῆς μοναδικῆς οὐσίας ἕνωσιν σπεύσωμεν.[25]

Clement uses side by side various names for Christ such as "the author of salvation", "the life", "the leader", "the illuminator", "the living water", and "the shepherd of the sheep". He states:

εἰκότως ἄρα σωτῆρος μὲν οἱ νοσοῦντες δεόμεθα, οἱ πεπλανημένοι δὲ τοῦ καθηγησομένου καὶ οἱ τυφλοὶ τοῦ φωταγωγήσοντος καὶ οἱ διψῶντες τῆς πηγῆς τῆς ζωτικῆς, ἀφ' ἧς οἱ μεταλαβόντες οὐκέτι διψήσουσιν, καὶ οἱ νεκροὶ δὲ τῆς ζωῆς ἐνδεεῖς καὶ τοῦ ποιμένος τὰ πρόβατα καὶ οἱ παῖδες τοῦ παιδαγωγοῦ, ἀλλὰ καὶ πᾶσα ἡ ἀνθρωπότης Ἰησοῦ.[26]

---

in: *Die christlichen Inschriften der Rheinlande* I, by F. X. Kraus (Freiburg i. Br., 1890), Nr. 46.
[22] H. Achelis, 'Altchristliche Kunst IV', *ZNW* 16 (1915), 23.
[23] Further information on this subject will be provided in a forthcoming article.
[24] Cf. Origen, *In Gen. Hom.* 9.3. (GCS Orig. VI 92 Z.5 Baehrens): necesse habuit "pastor bonus" relictis in supernis nonaginta novem, descendere ad terras et unam ovem, quae perierat, quaerere inventamque eam et humeris revectam, ad supernum perfectionis ovile revocare. Irenaeus, *Adversus haereses* III 22,2 (124 Harvey): Necesse ergo fuit, Dominum ad perditam ovem venientem, et tantae dispositionis recapitulationem facientem, et suum plasma requirentem, illum ipsum hominem salvare, qui factus fuerat secundum imaginem et similitudinem eius, id est Adam adimplentem tempora eius

condemnationis. Additional passages will be found in F. J. Dölger, *Ichthys* II (Münster, 1922), p. 467.
[25] *Exhortation to the Heathen* 9, No. 88, 2 (GCS Clem. I 65Z. 27 Stählin): Let us hasten to salvation, to rebirth. Let us who are many hasten that we may be gathered into one flock, according to the unity of the one being.
[26] *The Instructor* I, 9, No. 82, 3 (GCS Clem. I, 139 c. 2 Stählin): Naturally we who are sick stand in need of the author of salvation, having wandered, one to guide us, being blind, one to bring us to the light, being thirsty (we stand in need of) the living fountain, of which if anyone partakes he shall no longer thirst; being dead, we stand in need of life, the sheep of the shepherd, the children of the instructor, while all humanity stands in need of Jesus.

[4]

He explains the σωτηρία which the Good Shepherd brings as the eternal life which begins with Baptism:

> We can learn if you will, the perfect wisdom of the holy shepherd, of the instructor, of the almighty logos of the Father, when he represents himself in figure as the shepherd of the sheep; for he is the instructor of the children. For he tells us through Ezechiel, addressing himself to the Elders, and setting before them the salutary example of his prudent solicitude: 'And that which is wounded I will bind up, and that which is ailing I will heal, and I will pasture them on my holy mountain' (*Ezechiel* xxxiv, 14, 16). These are the promises of the Good Shepherd. Guide us, the children, like sheep. Yea, Lord, satiate us with pasture, the pasture of righteousness! Yea, Instructor, lead us to the pastures of thy holy mountain, the Church, which rises aloft, which towers above the clouds, which reaches the heavens! 'And I will be', he says, 'their shepherd; and I will be as near to them as the garment to their skin' (*Ezechiel* xxiv, 23). He wishes to redeem my flesh by enveloping it in the garment of immortality and he hath anointed my skin.[27]

It is even more important for the interpretation of the painting of the Good Shepherd at Dura Europos that in the *Acts of Thomas*, which originated about the year 200 in Syria, before the baptism of King Gundafor and his brother Gad, the Apostle says the following prayer which pictures Christ as the Good Shepherd who through Baptism becomes for man the σωτήρ and φύλαξ:

> And now at my supplication and request, do thou receive the king and his brother and join them unto thy fold, cleansing them with thy washing and anointing them with thine oil from the error that encompasseth them; and keep them also from the wolves, bearing them into thy meadows. And give them also drink out of thine immortal fountain which is neither fouled nor drieth up; for they entreat and supplicate thee and desire to become thy servants and ministers, and for this they are content even to be persecuted of thine enemies and for thy sake to be hated by them, and to be mocked and to die, as thou for our sake didst suffer all these things, that thou mightest preserve us, thou that art Lord and verily the Good Shepherd.[28]

The connection between the picture of the Good Shepherd and Baptism arises therefore from the fact that in early Christianity the ποιμὴν καλός was a favorite symbol of the redeemer and author of salvation.[29] One can readily understand why early Christian mysticism extended the use of this picture also to Baptism. The ancient Christian name for Baptism, *Sphragis*, (seal) contributed much to this process.

As F. J. Dölger[30] has proved, the oldest indisputable evidence for the designation of Baptism as a seal, σφραγίς, is met in Hermas in the first half of the second century.[31] Since, however, this designation of Baptism appears almost simultaneously in Asia Minor, in Lyon, in Carthage, in Alexandria, and in Rome, about the middle of the second century, Dölger rightly concluded that this term

---

[27] *The Instructor* I, 9, No. 84, 1-3 (GCS Clem. I, 139, Z 11-25).
[28] *Acts of Thomas* 25; translation into English by M. R. James, *The Apocryphal New Testament* (Oxford, 1924). p. 375.
[29] On the meaning of the mystery of redemption in ancient Christian art, see O. Casel, 'Aelteste christliche Kunst und Christus-mysterium', *Jb. f. Liturgiewiss.* 12 (1932), 1-86.
[30] F. J. Dölger, *Sphragis. Eine altchristliche Taufbezeichnung. Studien zur Geschichte und Kultur des Altertums* 5, 3-4 (Paderborn, 1911) pp. 70 ff.
[31] *Pastor Hermae*, Sim. 9, 16, 2-7 (PA I, 2, 608 f Funk): Sim. 9, 17, 4 (PA I, 2, 610 f. Funk): Sim. 8, 6, 3 (PA I, 2, 566 f. Funk).

[5]

must have been in use previously for a considerable time.[32] The concepts which the Christians of antiquity associated with this name for Baptism, are extraordinarily rich in content, according to the multiplicity of meaning given to the word *Sphragis* in the profane and religious culture of antiquity. One of the most interesting uses of the word, and one which led to its application to baptism, is its use in the sense of a mark of identification for property; proprietors branded their animals with such a mark in order to make deceit and theft more difficult, and to facilitate the process of sale. Attaching this sign of ownership to an animal was usually done in the form of a stamp with a branding iron. In the case of small animals the mark was applied as a rule by means of a weather proof paint or tax. The sign or mark was called the *nota* or *signum*, and the branding iron was called χαρακτήρ and καυτήριον. The branding was known as χαράσσειν or σφραγίζειν. One meets both terms in the documents of sale which we possess in the papyri. This brand usually consisted in an abbreviated signature which was meant to represent in a kind of monogram, the name of the owner.

In order to be able to evaluate the importance of the picture of the Good Shepherd in the liturgy and art of antiquity, a picture which was a general favorite with the authors of antiquity, one must be familiar with the custom of branding animals as it was then practiced. For the Christians, to be baptized meant to be stamped with the indelible mark of the name of Christ. And since Baptism meant the designation of a human being as God's property, this figure of the branding of animals was borrowed from contemporary custom and Baptism was called *Sphragis*. We find this comparison already in the *Excerpta ex Theodoto*:

καὶ τὰ ἄλογα ζῷα διὰ σφραγῖδος δείκνυσι τίνος ἐστὶν ἕκαστον, καὶ ἐκ τῆς σφραγῖδος ἐκδικεῖται. οὕτως καὶ ἡ ψυχὴ ἡ πιστὴ τὸ τῆς ἀληθείας λαβοῦσα σφράγισμα "τὰ στίγματα τοῦ Χριστοῦ" περιφέρει. οὗτοι εἰσὶν τὰ παιδία τὰ ἤδη ἐν τῇ κοίτῃ συναναπαυόμενα "καὶ αἱ παρθένοι αἱ φρόνιμοι," αἷς αἱ λοιπαὶ αἱ μέλλουσαι οὐ συνεισῆλθον εἰς τὰ "ἡτοιμασμένα ἀγαθά, εἰς ἃ ἐπιθυμοῦσιν ἄγγελοι παρακύψαι".[33]

In the *Acts of Thomas* which originated at the same time and in the same country as the painting of Dura, this figure becomes still more clear. Here there is no longer question of animals in general, but it is the baptized who are designated as the sheep of God. Of King Gundafor and of his brother Gad, it is said:

ἐδεήθησαν δὲ αὐτοῦ ἵνα καὶ τὴν σφραγῖδα τοῦ λόγου δέξωνται λοιπὸν καὶ αὐτοί, λέγοντες αὐτῷ· Σχολαζουσῶν τῶν ψυχῶν ἡμῶν καὶ προθύμων ἡμῶν ὄντων περὶ τὸν θεόν, δὸς ἡμῖν τὴν σφραγῖδα· ἠκούσαμεν γάρ σου λέγοντος ὅτι ὁ θεὸς ὃν κηρύσσεις διὰ τῆς αὐτοῦ σφραγῖδος ἐπιγινώσκει τὰ ἴδια πρόβατα.[34]

Here, as is apparent from the accompanying text, the anointing with oil in the form of a cross before Baptism, is considered a seal, and similarly in other places in the *Acts,* it is unmistakably applied to Baptism. So, when Siphor begs the Apostle for himself and his wife:

[32] Cf. F. J. Dölger, 'Profane und religiöse Brandmarkung der Tiere in der heidnischen und christlichen Antike', *Antike und Christentum* 3 (1932), 25-61.
[33] *Excerpta ex Theodoto* 86, 2 (GCS Clem. Alex. 3, 133 Stählin): Also irrational animals show through their brand to whom they belong, and according to their mark they are assigned to their owners. In the same

manner the believing soul carries, after the reception of the seal of truth, the stigmata of Christ.
[34] *Acta Thomae* 26 (2, 2, 141 Bonnet): And they besought him (the Apostle) that they also might henceforth receive the seal of the word, saying unto him: 'For we have heard thee say that the God whom thou preachest knoweth his own sheep by his seal.'

[6]

δέομαί σου ἡμᾶς τὴν σφραγῖδα δέξασθαι παρὰ σοῦ, ἵνα γενώμεθα τῷ θεῷ τῷ ἀληθινῷ λάτραι καὶ ἐναρίθμιοι τοῖς αὐτοῦ ἀρνίοις καὶ ἀμνάσιν.[35]

Accordingly, through the Sphragis one is accepted into the flock of Christ. In one of his baptismal catecheses, Cyril of Jerusalem addresses the candidates for baptism as follows:

Προσέλθετε εἰς τὴν μυστικὴν σφραγῖδα, ἵνα εὔγνωστοι ἦτε τῷ δεσπότῃ· συγκαταριθμήθητε τῇ ἁγίᾳ καὶ λογικῇ τοῦ Χριστοῦ ποίμνῃ, εἰς τὰ δεξιὰ αὐτοῦ ἀφορισθησόμενοι, καὶ κληρονομοῦντες τὴν ἡτοιμασμένην ὑμῖν ζωήν.[36]

Just as the faithful sheep of Christ carry the name of their great Shepherd and Redeemer as a sign, so too the heretics have marked the flock of their followers with their name, but it is the "sign of the thieves". In his Hymn 56 "Against the Heretics", Ephraem, the Syrian, explains:

His flock, Bardaisan has signed and named according to his name. According to his name, the flock of Mani is also called. Like stolen sheep they are signed with this ugly sign of thieves. According to the name of the Redeemer, his sheep are marked; it is Christ who has collected them; the sheep (therefore) are (called) Christians . . . Therefore, depart you rams, and lambs, and sheep, you who have been stolen from the heretics, and renounce the markings and the name of thieves; come and let yourselves be called Christians, in order that according to that sign and name you may be in every regard a Christian flock.[37]

In the background of this entire exposition there stands the figure of the branding of the flock with the name of their owner. For Ephraem, Baptism is the source through which the lambs and the flocks of the Church multiply. It is in this sense that he places the following petition to God in the month of the Church: "increase my lambs and flocks, on the great stream of my fountain".[38] The sign which the Christians receive through anointing before Baptism is at the same time the mark of property ownership and protection. It puts the devilish adversary to flight. Ephraem makes use of this thought in the picture of the flock, which by having received the seal of their Lord, is protected from the attacks of the wild animals: "Through thy seal has the wicked one been put to flight. Through thy seal evil things have been driven away. Come ye sheep, receive your seal, through which those who try to devour you will be put to flight."[39]

A thought which is very similar to this is developed by Basil in his homily On Baptism:

οὐδεὶς ἐπιγνώσεταί σε, εἰ ἡμέτερος εἶ ἢ τῶν ὑπεναντίων, ἐὰν μὴ τοῖς μυστικοῖς συμβόλοις παράσχῃ τὴν οἰκειότητα, ἐὰν μὴ σημειωθῇ ἐπὶ σε τὸ φῶς τοῦ

---

[35] Acta Thomae 131 (2, 2, 239 Bonnet): I beseech that we may receive of thee the seal and become worshippers of the true God and numbered among his sheep and lambs. In this connection see W. Heitmüller, Sphragis. G. Heinrici zum 70. Geburtstag dargebracht (Leipzig, 1914), pp. 51 ff.

[36] Cyril of Jerusalem, Catecheses 1, 2, (30 Reischl): Approach to the mystical seal in order that the Lord may recognize you Let yourself be joined to the holy and spiritual flock of Christ, in order to be placed on his right hand and in order to inherit the life prepared for you.

[37] A. Rücker, Des heiligen Ephräm des Syrers Hymnen gegen die Irrlehren aus dem Syrischen übersetzt: BKV 61 (Munich, 1928), pp. 188 ff.

[38] Th. J. Lamy, Sancti Ephraemi Syri hymni et sermones I (Mechliniae, 1882), 105, 7. See also B. Schmidt, Die Bildersprache in den Gedichten des Syrers Ephräm I. Teil (Breslau Diss., 1905), p. 30.

[39] Ephraem. Hymnus 3, 24 (I, 42 Lamy): Signo tuo halus in fugam actus est, signo tuo iniquitates dissipatae sunt. Venite oves, accipite signum vestrum quo fugantur qui vos devorare quaerunt.

[7]

προσώπου κυρίου. Πῶς ἀντιποιηθῇ σου ὁ ἄγγελος; πῶς δὲ ἀφέληται τῶν
ἐχθρῶν, ἐὰν μὴ ἐπιγνῷ τὴν σφραγῖδα; πῶς δε σὺ ἐρεῖς· τοῦ θεοῦ εἰμι, μὴ
ἐπιφερόμενος τὰ γνωρίσματα; ἢ ἀγνοεῖς ὅτι τὰς ἐσφραγισμένας οἰκίας ὁ
ὀλοθρευτὴς ὑπερέβαινεν, ἐν δὲ ταῖς ἀσφραγίσταις κατεφόνευε τὰ πρωτοτόκα;
ἀσφράγιστος θησαυρὸς εὐεπιχείρητος κλέπταις· πρόβατον ἀσημείωτον ἀκινδύνως
ἐπιβουλεύεται. [40]

In the baptismal catecheses of Theodore of Mopsuestia once used in Syria, and
recently discovered by A. Mingana, the rite of imposing the seal on the forehead
before Baptism is explained in the following words:

> And he signs you on the forehead with the oil of anointing, and he says
> at the same time. 'N. is sealed in the name of the Father, and of the Son,
> and of the Holy Ghost.' It is this sealing through which you are now signed
> as sheep of Christ . . . Because when a sheep is bought it is marked with a
> seal in order that one may recognize the owner to whom it belongs.[41]

In his treatise on the *Consecration of the Oils of Anointing* George, the bishop of
the Arabs, explains:

> Baptism is completed through the same (oil) and thus becomes the mother
> which brings forth the children of light to the Father who is in heaven;
> and the baptized will also be signed with him and sealed, and become
> spiritual lambs in the flock of the son.[42]

In another place he says:

> He cleansed us with the pure water of baptism, we have been baptized in
> his name, we have put him on as is written (*Gal.* iii, 27). He anointed us and
> sealed us with the pure and sweet smelling oil of anointing and gave us
> the guarantee of the Holy Spirit in our hearts. He made us to be lambs and
> sheep endowed with reason, in his great flock.[43]

Therefore he praises the Church:

> Hail to thee, O Church, that the day of thy sterility is passed. And behold,
> baptism gives birth to new children for thee. Hail to thee, O Church, that
> the Lord of the flock impressed his sign upon thee, in order that he who
> comes to thee becomes a pure lamb through anointing.[44]

The symbolism which finds expression in these texts of the oriental authors,
was however, not limited to the Orient. It is well known in the Occident also.
Augustine refers to it several times: *Et vos oves Christi estis*, he says on one

[40] Basil, *Hom. 13 in s. baptisma* 4 (PG 31,
432): No one will recognize whether you
belong to us or to the enemy if you do not
prove it through the mystical sign of your
membership, if the light of the faith of the
Lord is not found upon you as a sign. How
will the angel protect you? Will he save you
from the hands of the enemy if he does not
recognize the seal? How can you say 'I
belong to God' if you do not carry his sign
(on you)? Or know you not that the de-
stroying angel passed by those houses which
were marked, but destroyed the first-born
in those which were not? A treasure which
is not sealed is easily stolen by thieves, a
sheep which is not branded may be molested
with impunity. See also Gregory Nazianzen,
Oratio 40, n. 15 (PG 36, 377).

[41] Theodore of Mopsuestia, *Sermones cate-
chetici* (3 177 Mingana). Cf. Rücker, *Ritus
baptismi et missae quem descripsit Theo-
dorus ep. Mopsuestenus* (Opuscula et Textus
series liturgica, fasc. 2, Monasterii, 1933), p.
15: Et signat te in fronte oleo unctionis et
dicit: "Signatur N. in nomine Patris et Filii
et Spiritus Sancti": Est enim haec signatio,
qua nunc signaris. signum, quo obsignaris
ut ovis Christi . . . Nam ovis, cum acquiritur,
signatur sigillo, ut cognoscatur, cuius domini
est.
[42] *Uber das Salböl* I, 99-102 in: V. Ryssel,
*Georgs des Araberbischofs Gedichte und
Briefe* (Leipzig, 1891) p. 11.
[43] *Uber das Salböl* I, 196-201; *loc. cit.*, pp. 12
ff.
[44] *Uber das Salböl* II, 591-594; *loc. cit.*, p. 30.

[8]

occasion, *characterem dominicum portatis in sacramento quod accepistis.*[45] The *character dominicus* is the mark of ownership of their lord, which the "sheep of Christ" have received at Baptism. Referring to the validity of the Baptism of heretics he explains in one place:

> etiam ovem, quae foris errabat et dominicum characterem a fallacibus depraedatoribus suis, foris acceperat, venientem ad christianae unitatis salutem ab errore corrigi, a captivitate liberari, a vulnere sanari, characterem tamen in ea dominicum agnosci potius quam inprobari.[46]

With regard to the winning of the Donatists for the true Church he says:

> Annon pertinet ad diligentiam pastoralem, etiam illas oves quae non violenter ereptae, sed blande leniterque seductae, a grege aberraverint, et ab alienis coeperint possideri, inventas ad ovile dominicum si resistere voluerint, flagellorum terroribus, vel etiam doloribus revocare . . . ? Sic enim error corigendus est ovis, ut non in ea corrumpatur signaculum redemptoris.[47]

Thus from Oriental as well as from Occidental testimony one can see how the designation of Baptism as *Sphragis* helps to interpret the picture of the Good Shepherd as a symbol of Christian initiation. We are not surprised to find therefore that early Christian mysticism and liturgy look upon that Psalm which praises the loving care of God for man as a hymn of thanksgiving for initiation into the Christian mysteries. The exegesis of the Psalms and the historical sources of the liturgy of Christian antiquity supply sufficient proof of this.

As St. Jerome tells us,[48] Origen composed a homily on Psalm 22. Unfortunately it has not been preserved for us. Still, in his commentary on the *Canticle of Canticles* he gives us an interpretation of the entire Psalm. To Origen Christ is the Shepherd who initiates souls in his mysteries. The Royal Psalmist speaking about the "waters of refreshment" points to the fact that the waters which the Shepherd has provided for his sheep are not only "flowing over" but "salutary" and "refreshment for all".[49] In the language of the discipline of the secret, which Origen likes to use, these expressions point clearly to the sacrament of Baptism. He calls the bringing of the sheep to the "waters of refreshment" and "to the green pastures" the "instruction in beginnings".[50] Through this Christ, the Good Shepherd bestows upon the soul the first token of his great goodness. This is the real conversion of the soul, its introduction to the "path of justice".[51] In the same manner, the "anointing of the head with oil" and the "preparation of the table" and the "chalice which inebriates" are all mystical secrets to Origen.[52] In these words he sees indicated the μυστικὸν χρῖσμα and the σεμνὰ τῆς Χριστοῦ τραπέζης θύματα, the mysteries which follow immediately after Baptism.

---

[45] Augustine, *Epistula* 183, 2 (PL 33, 754).
[46] Augustine, *De baptismo* 6, 1, 1 (CSEL 51, 298 Z. 12-17, Petschenig).
[47] Augustine, *Epistula* 185, 26, 23 (CSEL 57 22, Z. 2-17, Goldbacher).
[48] Jerome, *Epistula* 33, 4 (CSEL 54, 253 Hilberg).
[49] Origen, *Homiliae in Canticum Canticorum* II (GCS Orig. 8, 138 1, 7 Koetschau): de hoc optimo pastore Domino dicit: "in loco viridi, ibe me collocavit; super aquam refectionis educavit me" ostendens pastorem hunc non solum abundantes "aquas" ovibus suis sed et salubres ac puras, et quae per omnia reficiant, providere.
[50] *Loc. cit.*, 1, 27: Illa prima, id est pas-

toralis, institutio initiorum fuit, ut "in loco viridi collocatus super aquam refectionis educaretur".
[51] *Loc. cit.*, 1, 10: Sed quoniam ab hoc statu, quo ut ovis sub pastore deguerat, conversus ad rationabilia et celsiora profecit idque adeptus est per conversionem, subjungit et dicit: "animam meam convertit; deduxit me super semitas iustitiae propter nomen suum".
[52] *Loc. cit.*, 1, 21. Hinc vero, ubi se a pastoralibus videt pascuis ad rationabiles cibos et mystica secreta translatum, addit et dicit: "Parasti in conspectu meo mensam adversus eos, qui tribulant me; impinguasti in oleo caput meum, et poculum tuum inebrians quiam praeclarum est".

[9]

Athanasius calls Psalm 22 a song of the nations proclaiming their gladness that the *Kyrios* is their shepherd, enabling them to participate in the "mystical banquet".[53] For him, too, the "waters of refreshment" are the waters of holy Baptism which take away the burden of sins.[54] For the words "he has converted my soul" he gives the explanation: "From the imprisonment of the devil he led my soul to himself, and on the path of his commandments, and thus he led her from death to life."[55] Accordingly, he explains the words "Thou hast anointed my head with oil" as indicative of the Sacrament of Confirmation: "This is the mystical Chrism."[56] The "prepared table" is the $\tau\rho\alpha\pi\acute{e}\zeta\alpha$ $\mu\nu\sigma\tau\iota\kappa\acute{\eta}$,[57] an expression which, in the language of the time, meant the Holy Eucharist.[58]

In this interpretation the Psalm becomes an exquisite hymn of thanksgiving for the reception of the mysteries of Easter Eve. The exegesis of Origen and Athanasius is not at all sporadic. Eusebius, for instance, gives the same interpretation He says:

> When a man has dropped the whole burden of his old sins, he may in truth say, 'He has brought me to the waters of refreshment'. Waters of refreshment are certainly those waters through which one casts off the heavy and tiring burden of sins oppressing his soul.[59]

Therefore the baptized may actually say, "He has converted my soul".[60] The oil is that of the Holy Spirit, the table is the "mystical food offered by Him who came as Shepherd and Bridegroom".[61]

To Cyril of Alexandria, the Good Shepherd of the Psalm is Christ, the Archshepherd, in distinction to other shepherds like Moses.[62] The pasture is Paradise from which we were driven, but to which Christ has led us back, and in which He placed us through the "waters of refreshment," i.e. through Baptism.[63] "Because we are baptized in the death of Christ, even Baptism itself should be called 'shadow and imitation of death', which are not to be feared".[64]

Consequently, Cyril interprets even the words "Though I should walk in the midst of the shadow of death, I fear no evil" as referring to the mystery of Baptism, in which we are buried together with Christ. For the "table prepared before me" he gives the explanation: "But even this mystical table, the flesh of our Lord, makes us strong against the passions and the demons because Satan is afraid of those who participate worthily in these mysteries".[65]

St. Augustine declares in his *Enarratio* on Psalm 22: The Church says to Christ, 'The Lord rules me, and I shall want nothing'. The Lord Jesus Christ is my shepherd, and therefore I shall want nothing. 'He has brought me to the waters of refreshment,' i.e. He has brought me to the waters of Baptism in which those are restored who had lost their innocence and vigor.[66]

In a commentary on the Psalms, edited among the works of St. Athanasius, but which according to the researches of M. Faulhaber[67] and G. Mercati,[68] was

---

[53] Athanasius, *Expositio in Psalmum 22* (PG 27, 140).
[54] *Loc. cit.*
[55] *Loc. cit.*
[56] *Loc. cit.*
[57] *Loc. cit.*
[58] Cf. F. J. Dölger, 'Die Heiligkeit des Altares und ihre Begründung im christlichen Altertum', *Antike und Christentum* 2 (1930), 172.
[59] Eusebius, *In Psalmum 22* (PG 23, 17).
[60] *Loc. cit.* (PG 3, 216).
[61] *Loc. cit.* (PG 23, 219).
[62] Cyril of Alexandria, *In Psalmum 22* (PG 69, 840).

[63] *Loc. cit.* (PG 69, 841).
[64] *Loc. cit.*
[65] *Loc. cit.*
[66] Augustine, *In Psalmum 22 Enarratio* (PL 36, 182): Ecclesia loquitur Christo: Dominus pascit me, et nihil mihi deerit. Super aquam refectionis educavit me: super aquam baptismi quo reficiuntur qui integritatem viresque amiserant, educavit me.
[67] Cf. M. Faulhaber, *Isaiasglossen des Hesychius* (Freiburg, 1900), pp. XVI ff.
[68] Cf. G. Mercati, *Note di letteratura biblica e cristiana antica* (Studi e Testi 5, Rome, 1906) 145-179.

[10]

composed by Hesychius of Jerusalem, the "Lord" of verse one is described as the Good Shepherd who gave His life for us.[69] "In a place of pasture" means according to Hesychius, "in the Church of God in which His saints flower".[70] "He has brought me to the waters of refreshment" means the grace of the Holy Ghost.[71] He remarks on "Thou hast prepared a table before me": "The Psalmist calls the mystery of immortality the heavenly table".[72] Finally, as Hesychius interprets the oil as the "grace of the Holy Pneuma"[73] it is evident that he also conceives the Psalm as a hymn of thanksgiving for the sacramental initiation, the reception of Baptism, Confirmation and the Holy Eucharist.

How deeply it was felt that this Psalm was a fitting prayer of the baptized is further shown by the interpretation of Theodoret of Cyrus. "Here are obscurely symbolized", he says, "the waters of regeneration, in which the person to be baptized, longing for grace, puts off the old man of sin and receives youth in place of old age".[74] Again he writes: "Thou hast prepared a table for me against those who afflict me. Thou hast anointed my head with oil: and my cup which inebriates me, how goodly it is. This is clear to the baptized, and it needs no explanation, for they know the spiritual oil with which they anointed the head, as well as the inebriating but not weakening cup, and the mystical food which the Shepherd and Bridegroom offers us."[75]

Cassiodorus gives a similar exegesis in his *Expositio* on Psalm 22. "The waters of refreshment are the bath of Baptism in which the soul, barren through the dryness of sin, is bedewed with divine gifts to produce good fruits." And fittingly he adds, "He has gradually nourished me like new born babes and reborn men, as the Apostle Peter says, 'As new born babes, desire spiritual milk unadulterated, that thereby you may grow unto salvation (*1 Peter* ii: 2).'" Furthermore, he says:

> He has converted my soul because after Baptism the sinner has become righteous, the unclean radiantly pure, the blemished without blemish; as the Apostle says, 'That he might present the Church to himself a glorious Church, not having spot or wrinkle' (*Eph.* v, 27)! He justly congratulates himself that his soul, which was so long a slave of the devil, was converted to Christ . . . 'Thou hast prepared a table', i.e. Thou hast predestined the holy altar which the whole Church sees, around which all Christian people throng. *Mensa* is derived from *mensis*, because on the same day the pagan banquets were celebrated. But the table of the Church is the gathering of the faithful, joyous feasting, spiritual satisfaction, heavenly food. 'The cup that inebriates,' that is a new gift of the blood of the Lord which inebriates so as to heal the soul, preserves from crimes and prevents sins.[76]

In view of the great variety of interpretation found in the ancient Christian commentaries on the Psalms, the uniformity of explanation given Psalm 22 is surprising. The reason for this can only be that this prayer of the Old Testament had a prominent place in the liturgy of the Christian service. Perhaps it was already in the liturgy of Baptism in the time of Origen. At least it is remarkable that in the sermons to the newly baptized this Psalm is so often cited.

Cyril of Jerusalem addresses his audience in such a sermon: "You also say with the Psalmist, 'The Lord rules me and I shall want nothing; He has set me

---

[69] Athanasius, *De titulis psalmorum* 22 (PG 27, 79).
[70] *Loc. cit.*
[71] *Loc. cit.*
[72] *Loc. cit.*
[73] *Loc. cit.*

[74] Theodoret of Cyrus, *Interpretatio Psalmi* 22 (PG 80, 1025).
[75] *Loc. cit.* (PG 80, 1028).
[76] Aurelius Cassiodorus, *Expositio in Psalmum* 22 (PL 69, 168).

[11]

in a place of pasture. He has brought me to the waters of refreshment; He has converted my soul'."[77] In his fourth *Mystagogical Catechesis*, he points out more clearly the relation of this Psalm to the mysteries of Easter Eve:

> The blessed David shall advise you of the meaning of this saying, 'Thou hast prepared a table before me against those who afflict me'. What he says is to this effect: before Thy coming the evil spirits prepared a table for men, polluted and defiled and full of devilish influence; but since Thy coming, O Lord, 'Thou hast prepared a table before me'. When man says to God, 'Thou hast prepared a table before me' what does he mean but that mystical and spiritual table which God has prepared for us . . . in opposition to the evil spirits? And very truly; for that led to communion with devils, but this with God. 'Thou hast anointed my head with oil'. With oil He anointed your head, upon the forehead for the seal which you have of God; that you may be made 'the engraving of the signet, Holiness unto God' (*Ex.* xxviii, 32), and 'Thy cup inebriates me, how goodly it is!' You see that cup here spoken of which Jesus took in His hands and gave thanks and said. 'This is my blood of the new covenant which shall be shed for many unto the remission of sins.' "[78]

It is more than likely that this interpretation of Psalm 22, addressed by Cyril to the newly baptized can be atributed to the use it had in the liturgical ceremonies of Easter Eve. It is not known when this Psalm was recited by the newly baptized in Jerusalem, though it may have been during the procession from the baptismal font to the altar.

On this subject we have better information concerning the liturgy of Milan. In the *De Mysteriis* of St. Ambrose, a western counterpart to the *Mystagogical Catecheses* of Cyril of Jerusalem, the procession of the newly baptized from the font to the altar is described thus:

> Enriched with these adornments, the cleansed people hasten to the altar of Christ saying, 'And I will go unto the altar of God, unto God who gives joy to my youth'; for putting off the slough of long-standing sin, renewed in the youth of the eagle, the soul hastens to approach that heavenly banquet. She comes, therefore, and seeing the holy altar duly ordered cries, and says, 'Thou hast prepared a table before me'. She it is whom David represents as the speaker in the words, 'The Lord is my shepherd, and I shall want for nothing. He has set me in a place of pasture. He has brought me to the waters of refreshment. For though I walk in the midst of the shadow of death, I fear no evil; for Thou art with me, Thy rod and Thy staff have comforted me. Thou hast prepared a table before me against those who afflict me. Thou hast anointed my head with oil, and the cup which inebriates me, how goodly it is'!"[79]

Judging from this interpretation of St. Ambrose, the newly baptized recited this Psalm when they approached the altar for the first time. It is impossible to give a different meaning to the words: *Venit igitur et videns sacrosanctum altare compositum, exclamans ait.* Even in *De Sacramentis*, another collection of mystagogical lectures, the author of which is, according to the latest researches, also St. Ambrose, the description of the procession from the baptismal font to the altar mentions Psalm 22.

[77] Cyril of Jerusalem, *Catecheses* 1, 6, (36 Reischl).
[78] Cyril of Jerusalem, *Catech. mystagogica* 4, 7, (376 Rupp).

[79] Ambrose, *De mysteriis* 8, 43: J. Quasten, *Monumenta eucharistica et liturgica vetustissima* (Bonn, 1937), pp. 131 ff.

Therefore you have come to the altar, you have received the body of Christ. Hear again what sacraments you have obtained. Hear holy David speaking. He, too, foresaw these mysteries in the spirit and rejoiced and said that he 'lacked nothing'. Why? Because he that has received the body of Christ shall never hunger. How often have you heard the twenty-second Psalm and not understood! 'The Lord is my shepherd, and I shall want for nothing. He has brought me to the waters of refreshment. He has converted my soul. He has led me on the paths of justice for his own name's sake. For though I should walk in the midst of the shadow of death, I fear no evil; for Thou art with me. Thy rod and Thy staff have comforted me.' Rod is rule, staff is passion; that is the eternal Divinity of Christ, but also His passion in the body. The one created, the other redeemed. 'Thou hast prepared a table before me against those who afflict me. Thou hast anointed my head with oil. The cup which inebriates me, how goodly it is!' Therefore, you have come to the altar, you have received the grace of Christ, you have obtained the heavenly sacraments.[80]

The investigation of the place of Psalm 22 in the catechumenate and the baptismal liturgy leads further to the pseudo-Augustinian *Sermon 366*, which according to the words *Qui ad Christi baptismum properatis*, is addressed to the catechumens. The preacher says here:

We present his Psalm to you, beloved, who are hastening to the Baptism of Christ, in the name of the Lord, so that you may keep it in your heart. But it is necessary that we reveal its mystery under the inspiration of divine grace because this Psalm contains in a special manner the regeneration of fallen mankind, the order of the holy Church, and at the same time the sacraments. The ears of your heart, therefore, may open in silence to hear, and the seed of the word may fall in furrows prepared through complete recollection, so that what the thirsty earth receives now, may at the opportune time, bedewed with the blood of Christ, sprout into high stalks and bring forth fruit in abundance.[81]

In these words of the sermon a *traditio* of the Psalm to the audience is mentioned. That reminds us at once of the *traditio symboli*, and the *traditio orationis dominicae* to the catechumens during Lent. It is a fact that there was a *traditio psalmorum* to the catechumens. At least this was true of the liturgy of Naples, as we know from the investigations of G. Morin.[82] The immediate preparation for Baptism began in the second week of Lent, with the listing of the persons to be baptized, and it ended in the three Masses of "scrutinies". In the first of these, celebrated on "Oculi Sunday", the solemn delivery of the Psalms to the catechumens took place. In the second, on "Laetare Sunday" the Our Father was given to them. And in the third, on Passion Sunday, the Creed was delivered. According to current opinion, this order represents a peculiarity of the rite of Naples, for which no parallel has been found. During the solemn delivery of the Psalms to the catechumens, the Psalter was placed in the hands of the catechumens. The text of two of the Psalms was read to them. It is of importance for our investigation to observe that one of these Psalms was that of the Good Shepherd. On the occasion the bishop interpreted Psalms 22 and 96.[83] The catechumens were admonished to learn the text by heart, and to assimilate the contents.

[80] Ambrose, *De sacramentis* V. 3, 1-14: J. Quasten, *loc. cit.* pp. 165 ff.

[81] Augustine, *Sermo* 366, 1 (PL 39, 1646).

[82] G. Morin, 'Etude sur une série de dis-

cours d' un évêque (de Naples?) du VIe siècle', *Revue Benedictine* II (1894), 392.

[83] Cf. F. Wiegand, *Die Stellung des apostolischen Symbols im kirchlichen Leben des*

[13]

A sermon delivered on such an occasion is preserved in manuscript form in the Library of State at Munich. The sermon is here attributed to St. Augustine, while the old edition of Venice declares St. John Chrysostom to be its author. According to G. Morin,[84] however, a bishop of Naples of the sixth century must be regarded as its author. In this sermon Psalm 22 is mentioned and the catechumens are admonished: *Hos versiculos psalmi memoria tenete, ore reddite . . . Tenete traditum vobis psalmum cum tenueritis lingua, reddideritis vita, vocibus et moribus.* Judging from these words there was not only a *traditio* but even a *redditio psalmorum* as there was in the case of the Our Father and the Creed.[85] F. Wiegand[86] has maintained that only Psalm 22 was delivered to the catechumens on the occasion of the *traditio psalmorum* at Naples. He pointed to the fact that this Psalm more than any other reflects the religious mentality of the early Church. But after the above investigation of the place of this Psalm in the ancient Christian cult, and in the liturgy of Baptism, this explanation is far too weak. The Psalm was rather the great hymn of thanksgiving for the reception of Baptism, Confirmation and the Holy Eucharist. It was for this reason that it was presented to the catechumens to be learned by heart. The Our Father was given them because it expresses better than any other prayer the filial relation to God which the Sacrament of Baptism conferred upon them. Like the Our Father, Psalm 22 was probably recited immediately after the reception of Baptism. This is made likely by the fact that even in the liturgy of Milan this Psalm was a hymn of thanksgiving for the newly baptized.

Thus our investigation takes us back to the baptistry of *San Giovanni in Fonte* in Naples. The mosaics depicting the Good Shepherd inviting to Baptism require no further elucidation. They belong, as we saw, to about the beginning of the fifth century. From the manuscript of the homilies in Munich, which according to G. Morin must be attributed to a bishop of Naples, the *traditio psalmorum* to the candidates for Baptism can be traced back to the sixth century. It is not entirely certain that, at the time of the completion of these mosaics, the solemn tradition of the Psalms with which the Psalm of the Good Shepherd was so intimately connected was already in practice. But even if this were not the case, the mosaics with their fourfold repetition of the picture of the Good Shepherd at the fountain of water, and the rite of the *traditio psalmorum* with the Old Testament song of the Good Shepherd who leads his sheep to "The waters of refreshment", are both executed in one and the same spirit. The mosaics receive their meaning from the traditional interpretation of Psalm 22. We are therefore not in the least surprised to find in another baptistry of fifth century Italy, the baptistry of the Orthodox church at Ravenna, the following inscription instead of the picture of the Good Shepherd at the fountain of water:[87]

IN LOCUM PASCVAE IBI ME CONLOCAVIT

suPER AQVAm REFECTIONIS EDOCAVIT ME

The picture of the Good Shepherd and the flock has remained alive in the liturgy. In the liturgy of St. James Psalm 22 is the communion song. The Oriental

---

Mittelalters. (Studien zur Geschichte der Theologie und Kirche, 4 Band, 2 Heft, Leipzig, 1899), 171 ff.

[84] Cf. G. Morin, loc. cit. p. 392.

[85] According to these facts, *Sermon 366,* printed by Migne among the *Sermones dubii,* must be attached to Naples. Its open-

ing words leave no doubt that it points to a *traditio psalmorum* known only in the pre-baptismal rites of Naples.

[86] Cf. F. Wiegand, loc. cit. p. 172.

[87] Cf. E. Brightman, *Liturgies Eastern and Western* I (Oxford, 1906), p. 63.

[14]

baptismal liturgies display a special fondness for this picture. In the Armenian rite Psalm 22 is recited before Baptism is administered.[88] In the Syrian ritual of Baptism of Severus of Antioch the picture of Shepherd and flock have been kept in the baptismal formula. It reads: "N. is baptized that he may be a lamb in the flock of Christ in the name of the Father and of the Son and of the living Holy Spirit unto eternal life."[89] After Baptism the deacons sing a hymn in which the verse occurs: "Stretch out thy wings, O holy Church, and take up the humble lamb which the Holy Spirit has begotten from the waters of Baptism. We salute thee, O Lamb and Son born of Baptism, whom I have brought forth from the water in the name of the Holy Trinity."[90] In a prayer which is said later by the priest over the baptized we read:

> The holy God, the author of all holiness with whose seal thou art sealed, and the seal of whose holy and sweet smelling and vivifying chrism thou hast been marked, himself make thee worthy to receive zealously his body with purity, and to drink his blood in holiness and be numbered among his divine flock, an heir to his eternal kingdom, and be protected finally through his victorious cross.[91]

When the candidate is anointed with oil the priest says:

> "Behold in the Church, the humble lambs who have come unto Baptism, shall be anointed with oil".[92]

The picture of the Good Shepherd appears most frequently in the baptismal liturgies of the Orient in connection with the idea of *Sphragis*. Thus in the Marionite rite of Baptism of James of Sarug at the rite of the *Signatio* the priest says: "Good Shepherd, Thou who findest those who are lost, whom thou hast marked as thy sheep, with the seal of the Holy Trinity, that they may be protected from the ravening wolves, protect them through thy glorious name".[93] After a prayer for strength in time of battle there follows: "May the humble lamb of thy flock be marked, and through thy seal may it be numbered in thy spiritual flock, may it enter into thy sheep-fold, and be thy own, and be protected from all evil; and do thou sanctify it by the seal of the most Blessed Trinity, and may it be reborn with praise and thanksgiving".[94] Then the priest anoints with the sacred oil in the form of a cross the head of the baptizand who is facing the east. Meanwhile, the priest prays: "Thou shalt be sealed N. as a lamb in the Christian fold, with the oil of holy anointing in the name of . . ."[95]

---

[88] *Ritus baptismi et confirmationis apud Armenos I, 1 Ordo baptismi et confirm. ex Maschdoz impresso*: H. Denzinger, *Ritus orientalium, Coptorum, Syrorum et Armenorum in administrandis sacramentis* I (Wirceburgi, 1863), p. 386.

[89] *Ordines baptismi et confirmationis Jacobitarum.* 4a. *Ordo apostolicus a Severo Antiocheno ordinatus* (H. Denzinger, *loc. cit.* p. 307): Et demittit eum in craterem, conversa ad orientem quidem baptizandi facie, sacerdotis vero ad occidentem, et dexteram suam capiti eius imponens, sinistra ex aquis, quae coram baptizando sunt, attollit et fundit super caput eius, dicens: "Baptizando sunt, attollit et fundit super caput eius, dicens: "Baptizantur N., ut sit agnus in grege Christi in nomine Patris." Et ex iis, quae sunt a tergo eius, et fundit super caput eius, dicens: "Et filii". Et accipit ex aqua, quae est ad dexteram et sinistram ipsius, funditque super caput eius dicens: "Et Spiritus vivi et

Sancti in vitam saeculi saeculorum."

[90] Cf. H. Denzinger *loc. cit.* p. 308.

[91] *Loc. cit.* pp. 308 ff.

[92] *Loc. cit.*

[93] *Ordo baptismi et confirmationis Jacobi Sarugensis* (H. Denzinger *loc. cit.* p. 347): Pastor bone et perditorum inventor, qui Trinitatis signaculo oves tuas obsignasti, ut a lupis rapacibus custodirentur, glorioso tuo nomine eas conserva. Cf. also S. 356.

[94] *Loc. cit.* p. 348: Signetur agnus simplex gregis tui et per signaculum tuum connumeretur cum spirituali grege tuo, ingrediatur tuum ovile, commisceatur cum tuis ovibus tuusque sit, et custodiatur ab omnibus malis, ac illum sanctifica sigillo Trinitatis gloriosae, veniatque ad regenerationem. gloriam canens et gratiarum actionem attollens.

[95] *Loc. cit.* See the same formulary in the *Ordo brevissimus Philoxeni Mabugensis*: H. Denzinger I, 320.

[15]

The deacon anoints the body of the candidate. The priest accompanies the candidate into the water of the baptistry and baptizes him with the words: "I baptize thee N. as a lamb in the fold of Christ in the name of . . ."[96] When the newly baptized Christian has donned the white garment "the priest makes him a partaker in the holy mysteries and says: 'Be thou, O Lord, the protector of this lamb, which is accepted into thy fold, baptized with thy Baptism, and sealed in the mystery of the Most Blessed Trinity, that it may be reared and may grow in the true faith in Thee and be a sharer of thy love'."[97]

In the ritual of Baptism of the Jacobites, which is ascribed to James of Edessa, we read the following words in the prayer which precedes the blessing of the water:

> Good Shepherd, who has gone in search of the erring sheep which through the cunning of the hostile serpent had fallen from the number of the enlightened . . . liberate now, O Lord, and redeem for the sake of thy grace and bounteous mercy all our souls from every stain and defilement of sin . . .[98]

While the anointing is performed by the priest, the deacons sing: "The oil anoints the exterior; Christ seals the interior of his new and spiritual lambs, his flock namely, whose adornment is twofold; its conception from the oil and its birth from the water."[99]

In the Nestorian baptismal liturgy the Good Shepherd is besought, in one of the first prayers with which the ceremony begins, to withdraw his sheep from the maze of the world into his fold, by means of holy Baptism: "Bring us back to Thee, in thy mercy, and make us members of thy household, O Thou Good Shepherd, who hast come forth in search of us and found us lost, and hast been propitious to us upon our return to Thy grace and mercy, O Lord of All, Father, Son and Holy Spirit in all eternity."[100]

After the entry into the baptistry the following prayer is said: "Gather us unto Thee and bring us into thy fold and mark us with thy seal, and make our childishness to be wise through thy truth, that we may honor thy holy name at all times O Lord of all."[101] Here Baptism, in harmony with the ancient Christian concept, is thought of as a *Sphragis*, with which all the lambs of the Good Shepherd are branded upon their reception into the fold. The same is true of the prayer which precedes the imposition of hands:

> Accept, My Lord, in thy mercy, these sheep, these lambs, and these newly-born, which have been branded with the holy sign, and inscribe their names in the Church of the first-born in heaven, that they may acknowledge and honor thy Blessed Trinity, at all times, O Lord of all . . .[102]

The picture of the Good Shepherd no longer exists in the baptismal ritual of the Roman Church. But in the liturgy for Quadragesima, which is still strongly pervaded with the thought of the preparation of the catechumens for the reception of the holy mysteries during Easter night, we still find many traces of it. On the Monday after the first Sunday of Lent, on which day in the ancient Church the names of the candidates for Baptism were entered on the lists, the catechumens are presented in the Epistle with the picture of the Good Shepherd who calls his sheep to him from the darkness of paganism:

---

[96] *Loc. cit.* p. 349.
[97] *Loc. cit.* p. 350.
[98] *Ordinis baptismi et confirmationis Jacobi Edesseni*: H. Denzinger, *loc. cit.* p. 292.
[99] *Loc. cit.* p. 294.

[100] G. Dietterich, *Die nestorianische Taufliturgie ins Deutsche übersetzt* (Giessen, 1903), p. 6.
[101] G. Dietterich, *loc. cit.* p. 10.
[102] G. Dietterich, *loc. cit.* p. 26.

[16]

Thus saith the Lord, Behold I Myself will seek my sheep and will visit them. As the shepherd visiteth his flock in the day when he shall be in the midst of his sheep that were scattered, so will I visit my sheep and will deliver them out of all the places where they have been scattered in the cloudy and dark day. And I will bring them out from the peoples, and will gather them out of the countries, and will bring them to their own land; and I will feed them in the mountains of Israel, by the rivers, and in all the habitations of the land. I will feed them in the most fruitful pastures, and their pastures shall be in the high mountains of Israel; there shall they rest on the green grass, and be fed in fat pastures upon the mountains of Israel. I will feed my sheep and I will cause them to lie down, saith the Lord God. I will seek that which was lost; and that which was driven away I will bring again; and I will bind up that which was broken; and I will strengthen that which was weak; and that which was fat and strong I will preserve; and I will feed them in judgment, saith the Lord Almighty. (*Ezech.* xxxiv, 11-16).

The Mass for the Saturday of the fourth week of Lent is entirely inspired by the picture of the Good Shepherd, who invites his sheep to the fountains of water, just as in the scene we have seen depicted in the mosaics of *San Giovanni in Fonte* in Naples. The Introit begins with the words: *Sitientes, venite ad aquas.* In the lesson the catechumens are promised fountains of water and abundant pastures by their shepherd:

Super vias pascentur, et in omnibus planis pascua eorum. Non esurient, neque sitient, et non percutiet eos aestus, et sol, quia miserator eorum reget eos, et ad fontes aquarum potabit eos.

The *Communio* begins with the initial words of Psalm 22, which was so popular in the ancient christian sermons addressed to the newly baptized, *Dominus regit me* . . . The Wednesday after Passion Sunday contains in its Gospel the classical description of the Good Shepherd from the New Testament, (*John* x, 22-38), in which the Good Shepherd promises his catechumens the Sacrament of Life. The fourth responsory of Matins for the Saturday before Easter presents the picture of the Good Shepherd and the fountain: "Our Shepherd goeth away, the fountain of living water, at whose death the sun hid his face." The second responsory of Matins on Easter Monday recalls the Good Shepherd who lays down his life for his sheep. In the *Liber Responsalis* of St. Gregory the newly baptized are compared to lambs in a responsory for the Wednesday following Easter. Here they are pictured as coming forth from the fountain in which they have been made immaculate: "These are the young lambs who have announced the alleluia; they but now come to the fountain where they were filled with light."[103] Th Roman liturgy makes use of this text on the Saturday after Easter, the day on which it was customary for the newly baptized to lay aside their white garments. Here we are dealing with ancient christian symbolism as we learn from the *Catechesis* of Cyril of Jerusalem[104] and from the *De Mysteriis* of St. Ambrose.[105] It is noteworthy that these same words are used at the rite which accompanies the distribution of the blessed *Agnus Dei* which are given to the newly baptized on the Saturday of Easter week in remembrance of their Baptism.[106] In the Roman *Caeremoniale*[107] it is prescribed that on these days after

---

[103] *Liber responsalis S. Gregorii,* ed. Bened. (Paris, 1705) III, 787.
[104] Cyril of Jerusalem, *Catecheses,* 3, 16 (86 Reischl).
[105] Ambrose, *De mysteriis* 7, 38 (Quasten).

[106] Cf. H. Grisar, *Das Missale im Lichte römischer Stadtgeschichte* (Freiburg i. Br., 1909), p. 566.
[107] *Caermoniarum sacrarum sive rituum ecclesiasticorum s. Romanae ecclesiae, liber*

[17]

the Communion, the tray holding the previously blessed *Agnus Dei* be received in solemn procession. Then it continues:

> Cum fuerint intra ostium capellae, genuflectunt omnes et subdiaconus cantat competenti voce ita ut ab omnibus audiatur, dicens: Pater sancte, isti sunt Agni novelli, qui annuntiaverunt vobis alleluia, modo veniunt ad fontes, repleti sunt claritate, alleluia.

Thereupon, the *Agnus Dei* are distributed by the Pope. The newly baptized took the small waxen lambs to their homes as a remembrance of their enrollment in the fold of Christ through the *Sphragis* of Baptism on Easter night.

In the Mass of the Second Sunday after Easter, the text of which expresses gratitude for the accomplishment of the redemption, Christ appears again before the liturgical community in the form of the Good Shepherd. In the Epistle we read the words taken from the First Epistle of St. Peter: "For you were as sheep going astray; but you are now converted to the Shepherd and Bishop of your souls."[106] The second alleluia verse reads: *Ego sum pastor bonus, et cognosco oves meas, et cognoscunt me meae, alleluia.* The same words of Holy Scripture are repeated in the communion prayer. The Gospel repeats the classical passage describing the Good Shepherd (*John* x, 11-16), which contrasts the conduct of the hireling with that of the true shepherd at the approach of the wolf. The hymn at Matins, however, sings at Eastertide the song of the eternal Shepherd who cleanses his flock with the waters of Baptism.

> Qui Pastor aeternus, gregem
> Aqua lavas baptismatis:
> Haec est lavacrum mentium;
> Haec est sepulchrum criminum.

Thus the presence of the Good Shepherd in the baptistry of Dura-Europos is by no means accidental. It has deep roots in ancient Christian art, mysticism and liturgy which associated this parable with the ceremony of Baptism throughout the early centuries as the baptistries of Naples, Rome, Ravenna and Mainz prove. But the painting of Dura is the oldest example of this association and therefore of the highest importance.

II (Venetiis, 1852) c. 6 Bl. 177. Cf. A. Franz *Die kirchlichen Benediktionen im Mittel-* alter I (Freiburg i. Br., 1909), p. 566.
[106] *I Peter* ii, 25.

[18]

LA CHRONOLOGIE

DE LA PEINTURE PALÉOCHRÉTIENNE.

NOTES ET RÉFLEXIONS

Le terrain commun qui vit s'illustrer par leurs contributions fondamentales les deux Maîtres auxquels ce volume est dédié, est sans conteste celui de la peinture cémétériale paléochrétienne. Le Rev.me Père A. Ferrua S. J. a amplement élargi le champ de nos connaissances par la découverte d'hypogées et de nouvelles régions de catacombes riches en décoration picturale. Citons parmi les trouvailles les plus récentes et les plus importantes l'hypogée de la voie Latine et les nouvelles zones des cimitières des SS. Pierre et Marcellin et de Commodilla [1]. Par ses études récentes, que nous examinerons de plus près dans ces pages, Mgr. L. De Bruyne a ouvert de nouvelles perspectives à l'histoire de la peinture paléochrétienne, tout spécialement dans le domaine crucial de la chronologie [2].

Une de ces études a été présentée au VIIᵉ Congrès d'archéologie chrétienne à Trèves en 1965. Ce Congrès réserva une attention spéciale à la peinture paléochrétienne. En effet, en plus de Mgr. L. De Bruyne, deux autres savants, J. Kollwitz et S. Pelekanidis ont

---

[1] A. FERRUA, *Le pitture della nuova catacomba di Via Latina*, Città del Vaticano, 1960. — A. FERRUA, *Scoperta di una nuova regione della catacomba di Commodilla*, dans *Riv. Arch. Crist.*, 33 (1957), p. 7-43 et 34 (1958), p. 5-56. — A. FERRUA, *Una nuova regione della catacomba dei SS. Marcellino e Pietro*, dans *Riv. Arch. Crist.*, 44 (1968) (= *Miscellanea Enrico Josi*, vol. III), p. 28-78 et 46 (1970), p. 7-83.

[2] Ainsi L. DE BRUYNE, *La peinture cémétériale constantinienne*, dans les *Akten des VII. Internationalen Kongresses für Christliche Archäologie, Trier 5-11 September 1965* (= *Studi di Antichità Cristiana*, vol. XXVII), Città del Vaticano — Berlin, (1969), p. 159-214. — L. DE BRUYNE, *L'importanza degli scavi Lateranensi per la cronologia delle prime pitture catacombali*, dans *Riv. Arch. Crist.*, 44 (1968) (= *Miscellanea Enrico Josi*, vol. III), p. 81-113. — L. DE BRUYNE, *La « Cappella greca » di Priscilla*, dans *Riv. Arch. Crist.*, 46 (1970), p. 291-330.

traité de la peinture de l'époque constantinienne, tandis que H. G. Thümmel examinait la question des débuts [3]. D'autre part, ces dix dernières années plusieurs travaux de caractère général sur la peinture romaine tardive et paléochrétienne ont été publiés: citons les ouvrages de M. Borda, de W. Dorigo, de P. du Bourguet, ainsi que la réédition en 1968 du travail de F. Wirth [4]. A quoi il faut encore ajouter les aperçus clairs et utiles de G. Bovini et P. Testini dans lesquels ces auteurs ont classé chronologiquement les peintures principales [5]. Nous ne pouvons mentionner ici toutes les études de détail. Signalons néanmoins deux secteurs de recherche qui méritent l'attention. Tout d'abord, les fresques de l'hypogée de la voie Latine ont suscité de multiples contributions qui se succèdent à un rythme difficile à suivre et qui concernent surtout l'iconologie. En second lieu, les premiers monuments de la peinture chrétienne continuent, comme on a pu déjà le remarquer, à jouir d'une faveur toute spéciale. L'étude étendue de L. Pani Ermini sur l'hypogée des Flaviens le confirme, une fois de plus [6].

Cet aperçu rapide peut suffire, je l'espère, à montrer que les recherches sur la peinture cémétériale chrétienne ont connu pendant cette dernière décennie un élan notable, qui était d'ailleurs bien nécessaire. Car le retard à rattraper dans ce secteur de l'archéologie, était considérable: on s'en rend facilement compte lorsqu'on fait la comparaison avec, par exemple, le domaine de la sculpture paléochrétienne, où la plupart des problèmes qui se posaient sur

[3] J. KOLLWITZ, Die Malerei der konstantinischen Zeit, dans Akten VII. Int. Kongr. Christl. Arch. Trier, p. 29-158. — S. PELEKANIDIS, Die Malerei der konstantinischen Zeit, dans Akten VII. Int. Kongr. Christl. Arch. Trier, p. 215-235: cet article présente un nombre de peintures retrouvées récemment en Grèce. — H. G. THÜMMEL, Die Anfänge der Katakomben-malerei, dans Akten VII. Int. Kongr. Christl. Arch. Trier, p. 745-752.

[4] M. BORDA, La pittura romana, (= Le grandi civiltà pittoriche), Milano, 1958. — W. DORIGO, Pittura tardoromana, Milano 1966. — P. DU BOURGUET, La peinture paléochrétienne, (= Le livre-musée), Paris, 1965. — F. WIRTH, Römische Wandmalerei vom Untergang Pompeijs bis ans Ende des dritten Jahrhunderts, 1e éd., Berlin, 1934; 2e éd., Darmstadt, 1968.

[5] G. BOVINI, Monumenti tipici del linguaggio figurativo della pittura cimiteriale d'età paleocristiana, dans Corsi di cultura sull'arte ravennate e bizantina, Ravenna 31 Marzo — 13 Aprile 1957, Fascicolo I, Ravenna, 1957, p. 9-30. — P. TESTINI, Le catacombe e gli antichi cimiteri cristiani in Roma, (= Roma cristiana, vol. II), Bologna, 1966, p. 285-307.

[6] LETIZIA PANI ERMINI, L'ipogeo detto dei Flavi in Domitilla, dans Riv. Arch. Crist., 45 (1969) (= Miscellanea Enrico Josi, vol. IV) p. 119-173 et 48 (1972) (= Miscellanea L. De Bruyne e A. Ferrua, vol. I), p. 235-269.

les reliefs des sarcophages, pour rester dans l'art sépulcral, avaient déjà été examinés dans une longue série d'études pendant la période d'entre deux guerres. Parmi les causes de ce retard se trouve le fait que la recherche sur les peintures des cimetières chrétiens est gravement handicapée par un problème de chronologie dont on a parfois l'impression qu'il est insoluble. En 1936 déjà, G. Rodenwaldt déclarait que la chronologie de la peinture des catacombes romaines se trouvait au milieu d'une crise [7]. Depuis, la situation ne s'est pas beaucoup améliorée, s'il faut en croire les trois rapporteurs qui traitèrent de la peinture constantinienne au Congrès de Trèves. Il doit y avoir en effet quelque chose qui, fondamentalement, ne va pas, si l'on considère avec quelle facilité on fait voyager à travers les quatre premiers siècles de notre ère certaines peintures, et non des moindres comme celles de la *Cappella greca*, des Cryptes de Lucine, du *Cubicolo del Buon Pastore* à Domitille, lorsqu'on voit aussi les datations divergentes proposées pour des ensembles picturaux aussi importants que ceux du cimetière des SS. Pierre et Marcellin. Cela ne signifie toutefois pas que notre ignorance soit totale. En simplifiant à l'extrême, on pourrait dire qu'on peut bien distinguer les phases initiale et finale du développement, mais que le brouillard règne sur la peinture de la deuxième moitié du IIIe siècle et de la première moitié du siècle suivant. Ajoutons aussi que si l'on tombe d'accord pour reconnaître les fresques qui appartiennent à la phase initiale, on ne s'entend plus lorsqu'il s'agit de les situer avec quelque précision dans la période qui va de 170 à 250 ap. J.-C. Ce fut donc une bonne initiative de demander à deux des meilleurs connaisseurs des monuments chrétiens de Rome de faire un exposé sur la peinture constantinienne au Congrès de Trèves. Ce fut aussi pour ces rapporteurs une tâche particulièrement ardue, puisqu'ils avaient à évoluer sur des sables mouvants.

Avant d'examiner de plus près les développements pris par les recherches des dernières années, il n'est peut-être pas superflu de voir où en étaient les choses avant le Congrès de Trèves, dont les Actes ont paru en 1969. Parmi les publications récentes que nous

---

[7] G. RODENWALDT, *Zur Kunstgeschichte der Jahre 220 bis 270*, dans *Jahrb. Dt. Arch. Inst.*, 51 (1936), p. 82.

avons mentionnées plus haut, figure la *Römische Wandmalerei* de F. Wrth. La réédition de cet ouvrage en 1968 est symptomatique de l'importance et de l'influence qu'il a exercées depuis sa première parution en 1934. A ce moment, le livre de F. Wirth avait marqué un tournant décisif. L'auteur était le premier à avoir examiné systématiquement la peinture romaine postpompéienne du IIe et du IIIe siècle. Il avait eu aussi le mérite de renverser la barrière artificielle que l'on avait édifiée entre les peintures romaine et paléochrétienne. Les fouilles d'Ostie confirmèrent d'ailleurs de façon définitive sa façon de voir en livrant au jour dizaines de parois de maisons, de sanctuaires, d'édifices publics décorés et peints dans le même style linéaire rouge-vert que les chambres sépulcrales des catacombes. Il n'y avait plus aucune raison de croire alors à la thèse d'un style spécifiquement chrétien, encore brillamment défendue par M. Dvořák en 1924 [8].

Avant la publication de l'ouvrage de F. Wirth prévalait pour la peinture paléochrétienne la chronologie proposée par G.-B. De Rossi et J. Wilpert, qui en faisant remonter les débuts au premier siècle et à la première moitié du IIe. Une première attaque contre cette chronologie, devenue traditionnelle, fut lancée par P. Styger. En se basant sur ses études topographiques des plus anciennes catacombes romaines et sur des critères d'ordre stylistique, cet auteur arriva à la conclusion que « dans aucun des cimetières paléochrétiens connus, il n'y avait de peintures conservées datant d'avant la moitié du IIe siècle ». En outre, une partie considérable des peintures cémétériales fut située au IVe siècle [9]. Cette prise de position de P. Styger annonçait une nouvelle tendance dans la recherche.

---

[8] M. Dvořák, *Katakombenmalereien. Die Anfänge der christlichen Kunst*, dans *Kunstgeschichte als Geistesgeschichte*, 2e éd., München, 1928, p. 3-40.

[9] P. Styger, *Die altchristliche Grabeskunst, Ein Versuch einheitlicher Auslegung*, München, 1927, p. 83-94. — P. Styger, *Die altchristliche Kunst. Grundlegende Erörterungen über die Methode der Datierung und Auslegung*, in *Zeitschr. Kath. Theol.*, 53 (1929), p. 545-563. — P. Styger, *Ursprung und Wesen der altchristlichen Kunst*, dans *Die römischen Katakomben*, Berlin, 1933, p. 353-362; voir aussi aux p. 14-18. Vers le même temps que P. Styger, A. W. Bijvanck (*De datering der schilderingen in de Romeinse katakomben*, dans *Med. Ned. Hist. Inst. Rome*, S. II, 2 (1932), p. 45-78) situait aussi les plus anciennes fresques des catacombes romaines vers le milieu du IIe siècle, mais, d'un autre côté plusieurs de ses datations correspondent, comme il écrit lui-même à la p. 73, n. 1, à celles de J. Wilpert.

Elle avait, en tout cas, le mérite du point de vue méthodologique, de tenir compte de la situation topographique des fresques.

F. Wirth alla plus loin. Il proposa une chronologie révolutionnaire en reculant les premières peintures chrétiennes jusq'aux années 220-250. La place importante que l'ouvrage de F. Wirth a occupée et occupe encore toujours dans la recherche, nous incite à nous arrêter un moment aux méthodes appliquées et aux résultats concrets obtenus. Pour cet érudit également, la question chronologique était primordiale. Il estimait que la solution du problème de la peinture romaine dépendait en grande partie du choix de la méthode qui pourrait nous permettre de dater les peintures et de retrouver les différentes phases du développement [10]. Faute d'une méthode valable et généralement adoptée, F. Wirth a ébauché sa propre méthode dans un chapitre introductif de son ouvrage [11]. Sur ce terrain encore, il trace de nouvelles voies. Jusqu'alors, on n'avait surtout eu d'yeux que pour les aspects iconographiques de la peinture des catacombes. F. Wirth par contre adoptait un point de vue exclusivement stylistique.

En se basant sur la psychologie de l'art de E. Wundt et sur les théories de A. Riegl (le *Kunstwollen*) et de H. Wölfflin (les *kunstgeschichtliche Grundbegriffe*), F. Wirth a élaboré une méthode d'analyse stylistique. Dans celle-ci les catégories « représentation imitative » et « représentation expressionniste », « pictural » et « linéaire » et l'examen du tracé (net ou flou) des lignes jouent un rôle primordial, et doivent permettre de distinguer les grandes époques artistiques (*Kunstepochen*) et les périodes stylistiques (*Stilperioden*). En établissant la succession de ces périodes, on arrive à dresser un cadre chronologique.

F. Wirth ne limitait pas l'examen du style à l'analyse de la forme extérieure. Suivant la théorie de A. Riegl selon laquelle le style naît du *Kunstwollen* d'une période, qui à son tour surgit de l'idéologie (*Weltanschauung-Zeitgeist*) du temps en question, F. Wirth reconnaît dans les formes artistiques ou stylistiques, — et celles-ci peuvent se réduirent même aux moindres petits traits ou à une irrégularité, — des manifestations d'un fond spirituel,

---

[10] P. WIRTH, *Römische Wandmalerei*, p. 3.
[11] P. WIRTH, *Römische Wandmalerei*, p. 1-22.

d'une tournure mentale. Il explique les formes *geistesgeschichtlich* [12].

Regardons maintenant un instant les résultats auxquels cette méthode stylistique l'a conduit. F. Wirth discerne dans la peinture postpompéienne les styles ou les périodes stylistiques suivantes: le style flavien jusqu'en 100 ap. J.-C.; le style philhellénique de 100 à 160 ap. J.-C.; le style antoninien de 160 à 220 ap. J.-C.; le style illusionniste de 220 à 260 ap. J.-C.; la periode de Gallien de 260 à 270 ap. J.-C.; le début du *Spätantike* vers 270 ap. J.-C.

Ce qui nous intéresse en particulier dans ce système, ce sont les dates qui délimitent les différentes périodes stylistiques et la façon dont elles ont été obtenues. Prenons les dates qui concernent la peinture paléochrétienne, donc celles de la période dite illusionniste et des deux périodes stylistiques suivantes. Chacune de ces dates a été fixée, en fin de compte, sur la base des changements stylistiques constatés dans les portraits des monnaies romaines, et surtout dans la coiffure [13]. Une telle façon de procéder surprend. Certes, ces portraits reflètent dans une certaine mesure les tendances générales de l'évolution stylistique, et ils offrent le très grand avantage de constituer une documentation cohérente, qui s'étend sur plusieurs siècles et qui procure des dates certaines et précises. Tout cela n'implique cependant pas que ces seules représentations, et surtout celle de la coiffure, soient assez représentatives de l'art en général, et puissent servir de critère de datation pour ainsi dire unique pour distinguer les étapes stylistiques des autres branches de l'art comme la peinture par exemple. Un système chronologique établi de cette façon ne peut pas inspirer beaucoup de confiance.

Cette méfiance (de principe) ne fait que se confirmer lorsqu'on contrôle de près chacune des périodes stylistiques proposées pour le IIIᵉ siècle. Pourquoi insérer, comme F. Wirth le fait, la prétendue Renaissance de Gallien, qui n'est qu'un intervalle classicant

---

[12] L'esprit novateur de F. Wirth apparaît aussi dans l'application qu'il fait de la technique murale comme critère chronologique (*Römische Wandmalerei*, p. VII et 21-22). A cette fin, il se base sur les recherches de ESTHER VAN DEMAN, *Methods of determining the date of Roman concrete monuments*, dans *Am. Journ. Arch.*, S. II 16 (1912), p. 230-251 et p. 387-432. Évidemment, ce critère, valable pour les peintures d'Ostie et de la villa d'Hadrien à Tivoli, est peu applicable aux peintures des catacombes, ordinairement exécutées sur les parois de tuf.

[13] F. WIRTH, *Römische Wandmalerei*, p. 101-2, 160, 162, 164, 199, 206-208, 222.

perceptible dans la sculpture pendant à peine une dizaine d'années, comme une période stylistique indépendante dans le développement de la peinture du IIIe siècle, surtout que F. Wirth ne peut lui attribuer qu'une seule fresque [14]?

F. Wirth consacre aussi un chapitre aux débuts de ce qu'on pourrait peut-être appeler — faute de terme convenable — l'art subclassique tardif (*Spätantike*). Il en fixe la date en 270 selon le procédé déjà expliqué, c'est-à-dire en se basant sur le style fortement « expressionniste » qui après Gallien se manifeste sur les monnaies romaines, et qui, selon F. Wirth, est le reflet d'un esprit transcendental qui existait déjà depuis longtemps, mais qui s'exprima clairement à cette époque par la proclamation du dieu-Soleil par Aurélien (270-275) en tant que dieu protecteur de l'Empire romain [15]. Nous ne devons plus dire pourquoi une date établie de telle façon, ne nous paraît pas acceptable.

Ce qui est sourtout étonnant, c'est que la peinture des dernières décennies du IIIe siècle ait été si peu traitée. Alors que l'auteur a réservé à ce sujet tout un chapitre établi sur la même trame que les autres, il limite son exposé sur la peinture proprement dite de cette période — une page et demie — à soulever la question de savoir si le système décoratif linéaire de l'époque précédente s'est maintenu. Pourtant, la période de plus de quarante ans entre la persécution de Valérien et celle de Dioclétien, pendant laquelle l'Église profita d'une longue paix, et pendant laquelle les cimetières chrétiens prirent une extension considérable, a dû être particulièrement favorable à l'éclosion de la peinture cémétériale chrétienne. Les rapports que L. De Bruyne et J. Kollwitz ont présentés au Congrès de Trèves l'ont confirmé. L'absence d'un exposé sur la peinture cémétériale chrétienne de la deuxième moitié du IIIe siècle est la lacune la plus grave dans l'ouvrage de F. Wirth, qui de fait se termine avec le style dit illusionniste en 260.

Au total donc, c'est uniquement dans le chapitre réservé à ce style, situé entre 220 et 260, qu'on trouve dans l'ouvrage de F. Wirth un exposé assez nourri sur la peinture cémétériale chrétienne. La plus grande partie des fresques considérées habituelle-

[14] F. WIRTH, *Römische Wandmalerei*, p. 211-213, 216.
[15] F. WIRTH, *Römische Wandmalerei*, p. 219 et 222.

ment comme les plus anciennes, y ont trouvé place. Nous devons nous borner ici à quelques remarques rapides sur certaines datations. Il nous est impossible de suivre F. Wirth dans sa manière d'argumenter avec les éléments topographiques et historiques lorsqu'il veut dater les fresques des Cryptes de Lucine et de la région des Papes du cimetière de Callixte [16]. Nous nous permettons de renvoyer à ce que nous avons déjà dit ailleurs sur ce sujet [17]. Il est surprenant de voir comment les fresques de l'hypogée des Flaviens, dont F. Wirth dit que, d'après la technique murale, elles pourraient déjà dater d'environ 200 ap. J.-C., sont retardées de trente ans pour devoir être insérées dans le cadre chronologique préétabli du style illusionniste [18]. Et quels sont les arguments pour dater de vers 250 ap. J.-C. le *Cubicolo del Buon Pastore* du cimetière de Domitille [19]? Pour la datation de la *Cappella greca* du cimetière de Priscille, F. Wirth n'a pas trouvé de solution définitive. C'est presque par exclusion d'autres possibilités qu'il propose de la situer provisoirement dans la prétendue Renaissance constantinienne des années 320-350 [20]. Avec des datations pareilles, il est difficile de dire qu'on se trouve sur un terrain stable. Nous avons dû porter un jugement similaire sur l'ensemble du système chronologique de F. Wirth. Nous n'avons pas manqué d'indiquer les grands mérites de l'ouvrage de cet auteur, mais nous nous voyons obligé de conclure que, du moins en ce qui concerne la peinture cémétériale chrétienne et la peinture du IIIe siècle en général, il n'offre pas de solution acceptable pour les problèmes de chronologie.

En 1938, J. de Wit publia un ouvrage sur les peintures des catacombes romaines que l'on pourrait considérer comme le complément de l'ouvrage de F. Wirth [21]. L'archéologue néerlandais ne prend pas en considération les fresques les plus anciennes, mais il prolonge, d'autre part, ses recherches jusqu'à la fin du IVe siècle. Comme F. Wirth, J. de Wit se place d'un point de vue exclusive-

---

[16] F. WIRTH, *Römische Wandmalerei*, p. 167-170.
[17] L. REEKMANS, *La tombe du pape Corneille et sa région cémétériale*, (= *Roma sotterranea cristiana*, vol. IV), Città del Vaticano, 1964, p. 192-194.
[18] F. WIRTH, *Römische Wandmalerei*, p. 174.
[19] F. WIRTH, *Römische Wandmalerei*, p. 176-177.
[20] F. WIRTH, *Römische Wandmalerei*, p. 213-215.
[21] J. DE WIT, *Spätrömische Bildnismalerei. Stilkritische Untersuchungen zur Wandmalerei der Katakomben und verwandter Monumente*, Berlin, 1938.

ment stylistique. Il distingue les courants stylistiques suivants qui, dans leur ordre de succession, forment un cadre chronologique pour la peinture paléochrétienne : l'impressionnisme des derniers Sévères à Gallien, le réalisme d'après Gallien ; l'expressionnisme de la Tétrarchie, l'expressionnisme constantinien, la période de transition de ce que l'on a dénommé le « beau style », le classicisme du temps de Valentinien, le maniérisme théodosien.

Il faut le dire, J. de Wit n'est pas exhaustif. Le système décoratif des chambres sépulcrales n'a pas été repris dans ses recherches. Il restreint ses analyses (stylistiques) aux têtes des figures bien conservées. Il justifie cette limitation en insistant sur l'importance de la tête par rapport au corps dans les recherches stylistiques sur l'art romain ; et cela vaudrait encore plus pour l'art du IIIe et du IVe siècle ap. J.-C. A quoi s'ajoute, toujours selon J. de Wit, que ce sont les portraits des monnaies et ceux en marbre qui fournissent la documentation permettant d'établir le cadre du développement stylistique de cette période [22]. On comprend alors pourquoi la confrontation stylistique avec la sculpture (portraits, sarcophages, monnaies) est essentielle dans la méthode de J. de Wit, et pourquoi les caractéristiques des têtes (peintes) prennent une valeur décisive comme critère de datation des peintures.

Toutefois, la validité de tels rapprochements entre peintures et sculptures est, pour le moins, fort discutable. La restriction de l'analyse aux seules têtes exclut trop d'éléments valables. Il faut dire aussi que J. de Wit ne tient pas assez compte — exception faite peut-être pour les fresques au cimetière des SS. Pierre et Marcellin —, de la situation topographique des peintures dans les catacombes. En somme, J. Kollwitz, qui remarque encore que les contextes iconographiques n'ont pas été pris en considération, a raison lorsqu'il estime qu'on ne peut pas faire l'histoire de la peinture du IIIe et IVe siècle sur une base aussi étroite [23]. Et lorsqu'il trouve que l'exposé de J. de Wit est peu convaincant, je dois le suivre dans cette opinion, puisque je ne parviens pas à reconnaître, en feuilletant les illustrations, tous les styles annoncés dans les titres des chapitres et énumérés plus haut.

---

[22] J. DE WIT, *Spätrömische Bildnismalerei*, p. 20.
[23] J. KOLLWITZ, *Die Malerei der konstantinischen Zeit*, p. 30.

Cependant, si les ouvrages de F. Wirth et de J. de Wit ne peuvent plus donner entière satisfaction, nous ne pouvons pas oublier que ces historiens de l'art ont eu la sagacité de discerner la grande lacune qui existait et l'urgence de la combler, et qu'ils ont eu le courage de s'atteler à une tâche particulièrement difficile et ingrate. Quelle que soit la valeur des solutions proposées par eux, ils ont mené la recherche sur de nouvelles voies. On peut même dire qu'ils ont influencé grandement l'opinion des archéologues jusqu'à ce jour.

* * *

Après les ouvrages de F. Wirth et de J. de Wit, publiés dans les années trente, il faut attendre les rapports sur la peinture constantinienne que Mgr. L. De Bruyne et J. Kollwitz ont présentés au Congrès de Trèves en 1965 pour voir paraître de nouvelles études originales et de grande envergure sur le développement de la peinture paléochrétienne [24]. Dans l'amosphère d'incertitude et on peut même dire de confusion qui règnait, une nouvelle tentative de jeter une base solide sur ce terrain difficile ne pouvait être que la bienvenue.

Dans son rapport de Trèves, J. Kollwitz a fait une étude approfondie de la peinture romaine de la période tétrarchique aux années 360, c'est-à-dire pour la période pour laquelle les problèmes sont les plus nombreux et qui est aussi la moins bien étudiée [25]. Quoiqu'il ne se limite pas à la peinture cémétériale, le corps de son exposé est formé par l'analyse détaillée des fresques des cime-

[24] Le livre de M. BORDA, La pittura romana, (= Le grandi civiltà pittoriche), Milano, 1958, n'est pas un travail de recherche analytique mais un ouvrage de synthèse Cet excellent instrument de travail a le mérite d'être le premier traité de la peinture romaine à rassembler les fragments importants de peinture trouvés sur toute l'étendue de l'empire romain, et à englober aussi bien la peinture de la période républicaine que celle du Bas-Empire et la peinture chrétienne. Pour la chronologie de cette dernière. on notera que M. Borda reprend largement les thèses de F. Wirth et de J. de Wit. Quant à l'étude de H. G. THÜMMEL, Die Anfänge der Katakombenmalerei, dans Akten VII. Intern. Kongr. Christ. Arch., p. 745-752, il paraît préférable d'attendre la publication du travail complet, dont cet article s'annonce comme un résumé.

[25] J. KOLLWITZ, Die Malerei der konstantinischen Zeit, dans Akten des VII. Internationalen Kongresses für Christliche Archäologie, (= Studi di Antichità Cristiana, vol. XXVII), Città del Vaticano- Berlin, (1969), p. 24-158.

tières des SS. Pierre et Marcellin et de Domitille, les deux catacombes les plus riches et les plus importantes en ce qui concerne la peinture.

Ce qui frappe immédiatement dans le travail de J. Kollwitz, c'est le progrès considérable dans la méthode qu'il annonce. Pour donner une base aussi large que possible à sa méthode de classement et de datation des peintures, J. Kollwitz se propose, comme il explique dans l'introduction de son rapport, de tenir compte d'abord de la topographie des catacombes (surtout pour la chronologie relative), puis de la structure, de l'organisation et du système décoratif des chambres sépulcrales, enfin d'arguments iconographiques et de rapprochements stylistiques [26].

Le rapport de Trèves de J. Kollwitz est une construction impressionnante. Par une analyse minutieuse et en étalant une richesse d'idées et une maîtrise de la matière étonnante, il a éclairci une période compliquée de la peinture romaine jusque dans les plus petits coins. D'autre part, il est regrettable qu'il n'ait pas tracé plus fermement les lignes maîtresses de sa construction : on regrette une carence de synthèse. Le rapport de J. Kollwitz restera encore longtemps un instrument de travail de premier ordre. Il serait souhaitable qu'on le rende disponible en tirage à part — et de la sorte sous un volume plus maniable —, et qu'on l'assortisse d'un index, qui rendrait plus facile l'exploitation de cette mine si riche.

A la question qui surgit spontanément de savoir si le travail de J. Kollwitz offre un cadre assez solide pour la chronologie de la peinture de la periode envisagée, il vaut mieux, je crois, répondre d'abord par une autre question : est-ce que la base sur laquelle repose le système de J. Kollwitz est assez solide? En toute sincérité, je crains de ne pas pouvoir répondre par l'affirmative, et cela surtout parce que J. Kollwitz ne se trouvait pas dans la possibilité d'appliquer de façon suffisante la méthode qu'il préconisait lui-même. En lisant son exposé, il apparaît que son argumentation, dans le fond, repose sur des rapprochements stylistiques et iconographiques. Une fois de plus, nous devons constater que des arguments de ce genre ne suffisent pas à eux seuls pour constituer la base d'une chronologie de la peinture paléochrétienne. Dans ce domaine, en

---

[26] J. KOLLWITZ, *Die Malerei der konstantinischen Zeit*, p. 33-35.

effet, rien ne peut se faire sans un examen préalable et exhaustif de la topographie (le développement de l'excavation) de la catacombe, qui doit offrir une série de monuments datés par des critères extérieurs. J. Kollwitz voyait bien la nécessité de procéder ainsi; il l'a clairement dit en expliquant sa méthode dans l'introduction de son rapport. Seulement, on constate que, de fait, la topographie ne joue pas chez lui le rôle que lui-même lui avait attribué. Mais qui osera le lui reprocher, lorsqu'on voit que les catacombes dont les fresques formaient la documentation fondamentale de son étude, celles des SS. Pierre et Marcellin et celle de Domitille notamment, n'ont pas encore été convenablement publiées. Nous touchons ici le noeud du problème, nous y reviendrons plus bas. Nous ne pouvons pas essayer ici de faire en détail le bilan de ce que nous croyons être positif ou négatif dans le rapport de J. Kollwitz. Mais il est évident que cette étude marque une étape importante dans la recherche.

En passant, dans les Actes du Congrès de Trèves, du rapport de J. Kollwitz à celui que Mgr. L. De Bruyne y a également présenté sur la peinture constantinienne, il est frappant de voir que ce dernier, qui fréquente depuis plus de trente-cinq ans les catacombes romaines, commence par expliquer qu'il renonce à faire une synthèse, parce que « les temps ne sont pas mûrs » en constatant que « l'iconographie et l'histoire de l'art paléochrétien ne sont pas encore complètement sorties de la voie des approximations » [27]. « Afin de découvrir où et comment naît la peinture constantinienne, ce qu'elle doit au passé, quel est son apport propre et nouveau », Mgr. L. De Bruyne examine à son tour les fresques du cimetière des SS. Pierre et Marcellin, et parvient ainsi à dégager et à élucider de façon nuancée la transition entre la peinture chrétienne du IIIe siècle et celle du IVe, qu'on a l'habitude, toujours selon Mgr. L. De Bruyne, de considérer trop comme « deux blocs aux contours trop vagues, au contraste trop brutal » [28].

Dans le rapport de Mgr. L. De Bruyne également, on est tout de suite agréablement surpris par des nouveautés méthodologiques.

---

[27] L. De Bruyne, *La peinture cémétériale constantinienne*, dans *Akten des VII. Internationalen Kongresses für Christliche Archäologie, Trier 5-11 September 1965*, (= *Studi di Antichità Cristiana*, vol. XXVII). Città del Vaticano-Berlin, (1969), p. 159-214.

[28] L. De Bruyne, *La peinture cémétériale constantinienne*, p. 159, 161, 170, 211.

Bien conscient de l'insuffisance et des dangers inhérents aux critères chronologiques habituels, Mgr. L. De Bruyne est sans doute le premier à avoir exploité systématiquement, de pair avec les données de l'iconographie, les indications chronologiques qu'offrent les motifs purement ornementaux, pour lesquels il donne aussi une série de tableaux synoptiques suggestifs [29]. Il met toutefois clairement l'accent sur l'importance fondamentale des indications topographiques comme critère chronologique [30]. Ces données topographiques forment toujours la base de son argumentation. C'est grâce à un contact long de toute une vie, qui lui a donné une connaissance personnelle parfaite de la catacombe des SS. Pierre et Marcellin sous tous ses aspects, que Mgr. L. De Bruyne a pu mettre, malgré l'absence de publications de base suffisantes, ce fondement disons topographique à son étude de la peinture constantinienne.

Les résultats auxquels Mgr. L. De Bruyne est arrivé dans le rapport de Trèves, s'accordent remarquablement avec tout ce que le Rev. Père A. Ferrua S. J. a expliqué dans son rapport de fouilles de la nouvelle région de l'Agape qu'il a découverte au cimetière des SS. Pierre et Marcellin, et qui — encore une fois — est particulièrement riche en peintures [31]. Après la découverte sensationnelle de l'hypogée de la voie Latine, cette nouvelle trouvaille constitue une autre contribution fondamentale du Rév. Père A. Ferrua à l'histoire de la peinture chrétienne de la deuxième moitié du IIIe siècle et de la première du IVe. Par cette publication, nous disposons maintenant, du moins pour une région de cette catacombe, dont il est superflu de vanter l'importance qu'elle a pour l'histoire de la peinture chrétienne, d'une description, faite selon les règles, qui offre toutes les données présentes. Mettant à profit tous les éléments qu'on peut tirer de la topographie, des usages cémétériaux, des inscriptions, des monnaies, le Rév. Père A. Ferrua a pu conclure que la nouvelle région du cimetière des SS. Pierre et Marcellin est antérieure au IVe siècle ap. J.-C., et que, en général, l'utilisation du réseau souterrain de cette catacombe a probable-

---

[29] L. De Bruyne, *La peinture cémétériale constantinienne*, p. 161 et 169, fig. 114-127.

[30] L. De Bruyne, *La peinture cémétériale constantinienne*, p. 161, 170, 211.

[31] A. Ferrua, *Una nuova regione della catacomba dei SS. Marcellino e Pietro*, dans *Riv. Arch. Crist.*, 44 (1968) (= *Miscellanea Enrico Josi*, vol. III), p. 24-78, et dans *Riv. Arch. Crist.*, 46 (1970), p. 7-83.

ment cessé vers le milieu du IVe siècle [32]. En établissant ce fait, A. Ferrua a fourni une donnée d'une importance capitale pour l'histoire de la peinture paléochrétienne.

Les rapports de Trèves de J. Kollwitz et de L. De Bruyne et les éditions de l'hypogée de la voie Latine et de la nouvelle région de l'Agape de A. Ferrua forment un groupe d'études sur une période-charnière de la peinture paléochrétienne qui ouvre une nouvelle phase dans la recherche. Espérons que les trois dernières en date provoquent — comme l'hypogée de la voie Latine — de nombreuses réactions, confrontations, études de détail, et que le résultat en soit une riche moisson de faits définitivement acquis.

Entre-temps, Mgr. L. De Bruyne s'était déjà tourné ces dernières années vers une autre période de la peinture chrétienne à la fois très problématique et très discutée, à savoir celle des débuts. Dans un premier article, il a attiré l'attention sur la valeur de repère chronologique des peintures murales en style linéaire, retrouvées sous la basilique de St. Jean-du-Latran, et qui d'après les données d'une inscription ne peuvent pas être postérieures à 196 ap. J.-C. La parenté stylistique présentée avec les fresques des plafonds des chambres X-Y des Cryptes de Lucine, conduit Mgr. L. De Bruyne à dater celles-ci de la dernière décennie du IIe siècle [33]. Cela signifie que ces célèbres fresques des chambres X-Y, généralement considérées comme se rangeant parmi les plus anciennes peintures chrétiennes connues, ont pu être placées environ trente ans plus tôt que ne le proposa F. Wirth, dont l'opinion, nous l'avons vu, s'était largement répandue.

Un deuxième article de Mgr. L. De Bruyne dans ce contexte est consacré à la *Cappella greca* du cimetière de Priscille, dont les fresques occupent une place de première importance dans les discussions concernant les débuts de la peinture chrétienne, mais dont

---

[32] A. FERRUA, dans *Riv. Arch. Crist.*, 46 (1970), p. 81-83.

[33] L. DE BRUYNE, *L'importanza degli scavi Lateranensi per la cronologia delle prime pitture catacombali*, dans *Riv. Arch. Crist.*, 44 (1968) (= *Miscellanea Enrico Josi*, vol. III), p. 81-113. — A une datation similaire (règne de Septime Sévère ou 190-210 ap. J.-C.) est arrivé, par d'autres voies cependant, L. REEKMANS, *La tombe du pape Corneille et sa région cémétériale*, (= *Roma sotterranea cristiana*, vol. IV), Città del Vaticano, 1964, p. 191-194 et 227. A tort L. PANI ERMINI (*L'ipogeo detto dei Flavi in Domitilla*, dans *Riv. Arch. Crist.*, 45 (1969), p. 172, n. 111) pense que dans cet ouvrage les chambres X et Y des Cryptes de Lucine sont datées « de la deuxième décennie du IIIe siècle ».

les datations tellement divergentes sont d'autre part bien significatives de l'impasse dans laquelle on se trouve avec la chronologie de la peinture paléochrétienne. Après avoir donné un aperçu des datations proposées et après avoir démantelé les datations tardives, Mgr. L. De Bruyne arrive, par une analyse iconologique et stylistique poussée, à la conclusion que les fresques de la *Cappella greca* doivent se situer dans les années 170-180 [34].

A peu près au même moment que Mgr. L. De Bruyne, F. Tolotti fait paraître un ouvrage important sur le cimetière de Priscille. Il y propose, en se basant sur une analyse topographique et technique approfondie, de dater la *Cappella greca* des premières décennies du IVe siècle [35].

Cette situation est bien typique. D'une part, on se trouve devant une argumentation convaincante qui repose sur des critères stylistiques et iconographiques, et qui conduit à une datation « haute » vers les années 170-180. D'autre part, on rencontre une analyse de la succession des travaux entrepris dans et aux environs immédiats de la *Cappella greca*, qui semble diriger inévitablement vers une datation « basse » ou tardive. S'il faut donner, en principe, la préférence à une argumentation basée sur des critères externes, on peut se demander à quelles conditions les critères stylistiques et iconographiques possèdent encore quelque valeur dans l'étude de la peinture romaine et paléochrétienne. Tel est, à notre sens, le centre du problème.

* * *

Qu'il nous soit permis de formuler encore, en guise de conclusion, quelques réflexions qui nous sont venues à l'esprit lors de la lecture des études passées en revue dans les pages précédentes. Certaines de ces réflexions paraîtront peut-être trop évidentes pour être confiées au papier. Ne sont-ce pourtant pas ces vérités que nous négligeons le plus facilement?

Commençons par dire immédiatement que si la chronologie de la peinture chrétienne constitue depuis si longtemps un problème

---

[34] L. DE BRUYNE, *La « Cappella greca » di Priscilla*, dans *Riv. Arch. Crist.*, 46 (1970), p. 291-330.

[35] F. TOLOTTI, *Il cimitero di Priscilla. Studio di topografia e architettura*, (= *Collezione « Amici delle catacombe »*, vol. XXVI), Città del Vaticano, 1970, p. 258-275.

sans solution, c'est avant tout, croyons nous, parce que certaines conditions préalables et nécessaires ne sont pas remplies. Comment pourrait-il être possible d'étudier ces peintures sur une base suffisante, alors que la publication et l'étude des monuments dans lesquels elles sont placées, c'est-à-dire les catacombes, sont si peu avancées, alors que pour la plupart de ces mêmes catacombes, il n'existe même pas de plans dignes de confiance? Ces insuffisances constituent un obstacle majeur à l'établissement d'un système chronologique valable de la peinture paléochrétienne; ce système devra se faire, comme nous expliquerons plus loin, à base de critères extérieurs fournis par l'examen topographique des cimetières.

Tout aussi nécessaire, comme condition préalable, est l'existence d'une ample documentation photographique relative aux monuments picturaux. Parmi les photographies publiées et disponibles manquent en général les représentations des systèmes décoratifs dans leur ensemble. La même carence se constate en ce qui concerne les photographies de détails de figures et de systèmes décoratifs, qui rendraient de grands services pour le travail d'analyse et de comparaison. Depuis la publication du répertoire de J. Wilpert en 1903, un grand nombre de nouvelles fresques a été trouvé [36]. Le temps semble venu d'entamer la composition d'un nouveau *corpus*, à l'exemple de ce qui se fait pour les sarcophages. Ce serait en même temps l'occasion d'entreprendre l'enregistrement photographique complet et détaillé de toute la peinture cémétériale chrétienne à Rome et ailleurs. Les Congrès d'archéologie chrétienne de Ravenne (1962) et de Trèves (1965) ont d'ailleurs émi un vœu dans ce sens [37].

Le problème de la chronologie de la peinture cémétériale chrétienne est avant tout un problème de méthode. Depuis les ouvrages de F. Wirth et de J. de Wit, l'examen stylistique a joué un rôle prépondérant, quoique L. De Bruyne et J. Kollwitz, dans leurs rapports du Congrès de Trèves, aient attiré l'attention sur

---

[36] J. WILPERT, *Die Malereien der Katakomben Roms*, 2 vol., Freiburg-im-Breisgau, 1903.

[37] *Atti del VI. Congresso Internazionale di Archeologia Cristiana, Ravenna 23-30 Settembre 1962*, (= *Studi di Antichità Cristiana*, vol. XXVI), Città del Vaticano 1965, p. XCVII — *Akten des VII. Internationalen Kongresses für Christliche Archäologie, Trier 5-11 September 1965*, (= *Studi di Antichità Cristiana*, vol. XXVII), Città del Vaticano-Berlin, (1969), p. XLIV.

l'importance des rapprochements iconographiques. Si les principes de base de la critique stylistique sont clairs, les applications provoquent parfois des réserves. Personne ne niera la valeur et les grandes possibilités de la recherche stylistique, mais comment ne deviendrait-on pas méfiant, lorsqu'on constate que les datations effectuées au moyen d'arguments stylistiques divergent si souvent et si fort. Enumérons vite encore quelques points faibles de cette méthode.

Lorsqu'on veut employer des données stylistiques comme critère chronologique, il s'agit, en fin de compte, de savoir sous quelles conditions des similitudes stylistiques permettent de conclure à une simultanéité, ou une différence de style à une antériorité ou une postériorité. Ici surgissent d'abord des difficultés inhérentes aux styles de tous les temps. Les différences de génération, de formation, de tempérament (progressistes et conservateurs, minutieux et négligents), de capacités (les vrais artistes créatifs et les décorateurs de routine) font que plusieurs peintres peuvent travailler fort différemment au même moment. Même les différences de prix peuvent se refléter dans des diversités de forme. Deux têtes peuvent différer sensiblement en exécution par le simple fait d'une différence en grandeur. Tous ces phénomènes sont bien connus, mais vu notre documentation déficiente, il est rare qu'on puisse les reconnaître clairement dans l'art antique.

De plus, l'art romain, dont la peinture paléochrétienne fait partie, offre un terrain particulièrement dangereux pour l'application de caractéristiques stylistiques comme critère chronologique vu le mélange et la confusion des styles qui lui sont propres. Il suffit de penser à la peinture pompéienne et, en sculpture, à la base de la colonne d'Antonin le Pieux et à la base des Décénales. Le caractère hétérogène de l'art romain et le retour presque continuel de soi-disant Renaissances interdit même d'établir une chronologie relative sur la base unique de critères stylistiques.

Devant une situation pareille, on ne peut établir un cadre chronologique que sur des critères extérieurs. Cela signifie dans le cas de la peinture paléochrétienne qu'il faut d'abord fixer, par une étude topographique approfondie, la chronologie des cimetières où les fresques se trouvent. Une fois ce point atteint, la topographie, les tombeaux, les maçonneries, les inscriptions des cimetières pourraient fournir les critères objectifs pour la chronologie, aussi bien relative qu'absolue, des peintures. On pourrait examiner alors dans quelle mesure le style des fresques peut jouer un rôle de critère chronologique. Malheureusement, la chronologie des catacombes elles-mêmes reste toujours problématique. Aussi longtemps qu'une série de nouvelles études n'aura pas porté remède à cette situation, la chronologie de la peinture paléochrétienne restera une question sans solution définitive.

C'est devenu une habitude de désigner les diverses tendances stylistiques reconnaissables dans l'art romain à l'aide des termes empruntés à l'histoire de l'art européen et moderne. Pour certains, tels « réalisme, naturalisme, classicisme, baroque », qui indiquent des tendances fondamentales revenant régulièrement dans l'évolution des arts de tous les temps, cela ne présente pas de grands inconvénients. Mais cela ne semble pas être le cas, par exemple, pour « expressionnisme » ou « impressionnisme », qui sont des termes conventionnels désignant des courants bien spécifiques de l'art moderne. Cela ne favorise pas la clarté de les appliquer à des tendances artistiques antiques qui, tout au plus, ne ressemblent que de loin au courant moderne, surtout lorsqu'on se trouve sur un terrain embrouillé comme celui de l'art romain. Le terme « style illusionniste », lui aussi, employé pour la peinture de la première moitié du III᷃ siècle, ne paraît pas bien exprimer ce qu'il devrait indiquer. Il faut conclure que la terminologie habituelle ne satisfait pas tout à fait. Une revision des termes existants et la création de nouveaux termes mieux appropriés aux phénomènes stylistiques romains pourraient être bien utiles. Ce besoin se manifeste d'ailleurs aussi dans d'autres sciences.

Sur le terrain confus de l'art romain et paléochrétien et pour un problème aussi épineux que celui de sa chronologie, certaines méthodes de critique stylistique ne paraissent pas favoriser la clarté et la certitude. Nous ne voulons pas prendre position ici pour ou contre l'une ou l'autre méthode de recherche stylistique. Mais nous devons tout de même dire qu'il nous est impossible, par exemple, de reconnaître systématiquement, avec F. Wirth, un nouveau sentiment stylistique ou une nouvelle conception artistique dans de simples irrégularités (cfr. la *Schiefwinkligkeit* de F. Wirth), dans ce qui apparemment sont des formes négligées, déficientes ou tout simplement de moindre qualité, comme on trouve en tous temps. Nous ne pouvons encore moins y reconnaître, comme F. Wirth, l'expression de nouvelles forces spirituelles, alors de préférence transcendentales [38]. Au risque de passer pour un matérialiste, nous préférons, au moins lorsqu'il s'agit d'une entreprise risquée comme une datation, nous limiter à ce qui est constatable par les yeux.

Parlant plus en général, nous devons dire que nous ne pouvons échapper à l'impression que trop souvent les arguments stylistiques employés comme critère de datation paraissent trop subtils, trop superficiels, trop accidentels et trop subjectifs, de façon que la conclusion qui en est tirée ne semble pas assez fondée. Mais il faut avouer qu'il n'est parfois pas facile de trouver des arguments de poids, vraiment valables, qui ont une force démonstrative suffisante.

Il faut parler dans le même sens du procédé devenu courant qui consiste à chercher des critères de datation pour les fresques dans les comparaisons avec les sculptures, surtout de sarcophages, pour lesquels on croit disposer déjà d'un cadre chronologique plus sûr et plus élaboré. Nul ne niera, encore une fois, qu'il existe un parallélisme stylistique entre les différentes branches de l'art. Mais on ne peut pas oublier, d'autre part, la différence fondamentale entre la peinture et la sculpture. Mieux vaut être exigeant et se limiter ici à rapprochements vraiment évidents et frappants. D'ailleurs, il paraît prudent de prendre la même attitude pour les rapprochements entre peintures.

A ce propos, il est étonnant que si peu de rapprochements se fassent entre les peintures des catacombes romaines et les fresques

---

[38] Voir par exemple F. WIRTH, *Römische Wandmalerei*, p. 110, 115, 131, 140. 175-6, 181, 197-99, 225. Nous ne pouvons pas manquer de citer ici les paroles de Mgr. L. De Bruyne, dans *Riv. Arch. Crist.*, 44 (1968), p. 86, n. 8: « Per quanto riguarda poi la volta del gruppo occidentale, di cui parleremo fra poco (figg. 5-6), si osservi che i tratteggi che stanno nella direzione longitudinale della volta sono ben curati, perché per essi si poteva usare la riga, mentre quelli trasversali sono più irregolari perché tracciati a mano libera. La « Schiefwinkligkeit » non dipende quindi necessariamente da una questione di stile, ma spesso dalla situazione in cui si lavora, dall'importanza secondaria dell'ambiente (nel nostro caso sembra trattarsi di un corridoio), dal temperamento o dalla fretta dell'artista, ecc. Comunque, darle troppa importanza nelle proprie valutazioni cronologiche è esporsi a rischiose impressioni soggettive ».

d'Ostie. Ceci est d'autant plus curieux que ce site est le seul où l'on trouve une documentation abondante et continue pour la peinture romaine du IIe au IVe siècle ap. J.-C., et où des critères externes, comme la technique de la construction murale et des inscriptions, offrent une base de chronologie assez solide. Cette absence de rapprochements s'explique probablement par le fait que la publication des fresques ostiennes est encore peu avancée et qu'on ne dispose pas d'une étude d'ensemble approfondie. En attendant cette étude, l'esquisse que C. C. van Essen a donnée pour la chronologie de la peinture pariétale d'Ostie peut rendre de grands services [39].

D'autre part, grâce au grand nombre de peintures cémétériales retrouvées dans le rayon limité des catacombes d'une même ville, il doit être possible d'arriver à l'aide de la critique stylistique et de la méthode comparative, à des résultats positifs. Dans un cimetière comme celui des SS. Pierre et Marcellin, où la densité des fresques est si grande, on peut espérer pouvoir les grouper dans une certaine mesure par « ateliers », et même reconnaître des « mains » individuelles d'artistes en appliquant judicieusement la méthode de Morelli. Mgr. L. De Bruyne l'a prouvé dans son rapport de Trèves [40].

Jusqu'à présent, l'attention des archéologues s'est presque exclusivement concentrée sur les figures et les scènes figuratives. Les systèmes décoratifs des chambres sépulcrales, par contre, sont restés négligés, quoique une étude approfondie de la typologie et du développement de cet élément serait certainement fructueux, notamment pour le problème de la chronologie. On pourrait penser que ce manque d'intérêt trouve son origine dans le fait que, à l'intérieur des chambres sépulcrales des catacombes, le système décoratif des parois était gâché per l'insertion de tas de tombeaux. Toutefois, pour les systèmes décoratifs des plafonds, il faut constater une même carence d'études systématiques. Il n'existe, que je sache, qu'une seule étude consacrée à ce sujet, celle de P. Markthaler [41].

[39] C. C. VAN ESSEN, *Studio cronologico sulle pitture parietali di Ostia*, dans *Bull. Comun.*, 76 (1956-58), p. 155-181.

[40] Voir par exemple L. DE BRUYNE, *La peinture cémétériale constantinienne*, dans *Akten VII. Int. Kongr. Christl. Arch.*, p. 197-198, 200, 210-211.

[41] P. MARKTHALER, *Die dekorativen Konstruktionen der Katakombendecken Roms*, dans *Röm. Quartalschr.*, 35 (1927), p. 53-111.

D'autres carences plus ou moins voyantes pourraient être encore énumérées. Bornons-nous à en mentionner rapidement une : l'examen technologique de la peinture cémétériale chrétienne qui, à ma connaissance, doit encore être entamé. De telles recherches ouvriraient probablement des possibilités et des perspectives insoupçonnées, par exemple pour obtenir des certitudes en matière de similitude et de différence, avec toutes les conséquences pour la datation qui en peuvent découler.

Les quelques réflexions consacrées, dans les pages précédentes, à l'application de la méthode stylistique dans le domaine de l'art romain et de la chronologie de la peinture paléochrétienne en particulier, nous ont obligé à parler de tant de dangers, de tant de difficultés, de tant de carences, qu'il faut bien conclure que les possibilités de solution sont fort restreintes, que les problèmes, et certainement celui de la chronologie, ne sont solubles que dans une certaine mesure. Dans une situation comme celle de la peinture paléochrétienne, il paraît dérisoire de vouloir dater une fresque, uniquement sur la base d'arguments stylistiques à cinq ans près. Mieux vaut se contenter de datations approximatives qui laissent une large marge de sécurité.

Bien que les derniers développements de la recherche sur la chronologie de la peinture paléochrétienne justifient certains espoirs, il s'écoulera tout de même encore un bon nombre d'années avant qu'un cadre chronologique plus ou moins définitif et assez élaboré ne soit établi. Ne serait-il pas utile d'ébaucher entre-temps, peut-être par le biais d'un colloque de spécialistes en la matière, un schéma provisoire et de caractère général. Il pourrait être composé de peintures qui sont typiques au point de vue style et iconographie, et pour lesquelles il serait possible, grâce entre autres à l'étude topographique localement assez avancée ou à d'autres critères extérieurs, de fixer une date avec une certitude suffisante. Il s'agirait donc d'un schéma composé de points de repère sûrs. Nous croyons que ce serait un instrument très précieux, quoique provisoire, pour beaucoup d'archéologues.

LOUIS REEKMANS

242

Louis Reekmans

Zur Problematik der römischen Katakombenforschung

Von den letzten Jahrzehnten des 2. Jh. bis zu den ersten Jahrzehnten des 5. Jh. n.Chr. begruben die Christen von Rom ihre Verstorbenen gewöhnlich in unterirdischen Gängen und Kammern, die aus den Tuffschichten, aus denen der Boden von Latium besteht, herausgehauen waren (Abb. 1)[1]. Diese Grabstätten werden traditionell, zum ersten Mal — wie es scheint — im 9. Jh.,[2] „Katakomben" genannt. Dieser Ausdruck war im Altertum jedoch nicht gebräuchlich. Die Christen des Altertums bezeichneten ihre Grabstätten meistens mit dem griechischen Wort κοιμητήριον, das „Ruheplatz" bedeutete und in das Lateinische direkt als „coemeterium" übernommen wurde. Dieser Ausdruck spiegelt die neue christliche Auffassung von Tod und Jenseits wieder, die z.B. in den frühchristlichen Grabinschriften von Makedonien deutlich zum Ausdruck kommt in der Formel κοιμητήριον ἕως ἀναστάσεως, Ruheplatz in der Erwartung der Auferstehung.[3]
Es muß nebenbei darauf hingewiesen werden, daß die Christen in der Antike nur in einigen Teilen Italiens, Siziliens und in Nordafrika ausgedehnte unterirdische Grabstätten anlegten und daß sie anderwärts, wie alle anderen Einwohner auch, oberirdisch oder auch in kleinen Hypogäen begruben. Das ist durchaus keine neue These oder übertriebene Behauptung, sondern ein überall seit langem an den Befunden feststellbares Faktum. Auch in Rom verschwand selbst im 3. und 4. Jh. nicht die Beerdigung sub divo, das heißt unter freiem Himmel. Die mehr als tausend dort gefundenen frühchristlichen Sarkophage, die mit Reliefs verziert sind, bewiesen das.[4] Sarkophage fanden tatsächlich nur ausnahmsweise einen Platz in den Katakomben; normalerweise waren sie in den oberirdischen Grabkammern und Mausoleen aufgestellt.
Heute zählt man rund um Rom ungefähr sechzig frühchristliche unterirdische

Vortrag gehalten an der Universität Münster/Westf. am 15. Dezember 1983. Ich danke besonders Frau E.Stupperich für die sorgfältige Übersetzung des ursprünglich niederländischen Textes ins Deutsche.

1) G.-B. De Rossi, La Roma sotterranea cristiana I-III. Roma 1864-1877; M.Armellini, Gli antichi cimiteri cristiani di Roma e d'Italia. Roma, 1893, Nachdruck o.O. 1978; O.Marucchi, Le catacombe romane, Roma[2] 1932; P.Styger, Die römischen Katakomben. Berlin 1933; L.Hertling — E.Kirschbaum, Die römischen Katakomben und ihre Märtyrer. Freiburg-Wien 1950 (engl. Hrsg. v.M.J.Costello, The Roman Catacombs and their Martyrs. London[3] 1975); P.Testini, Le catacombe e gli antichi cimiteri cristiani in Roma. Roma cristiana II. Bologna 1966; L.Reekmans, Vroegkristelijke begraafplaatsen in Rome, Spiegel Historiael 4(1969), 514-522 u. 676-682; ders., Die Situation der Katakombenforschung in Rom. Rhein.-Westf. Akad. Wiss. G 233. Opladen 1979.

2) De Rossi, Roma sotterranea I, 87; C.Ducange, Glossarium mediae et infimae latinitatis II. Paris 1842, 232.

3) H.Leclercq, Dict.Arch.Chrét.Lit. I[1] (1924), 338f. s.v. Achaïe Abb. 65; ders., ebd. III[2] (1948), 1625f. s.v. Cimetière.

4) J.Wilpert, I sarcofagi cristiani antichi I-III. Roma 1929-1936; F.W.Deichmann — G.Bovini — H.Brandenburg, Repertorium der christlich-antiken Sarkophage I. Wiesbaden 1967.

Grabstätten, die die Stadt in einem Ring von ungefähr 3-4 römischen Meilen oder
ca. 5 km Breite umgeben und an allen aus der Stadt führenden Wegen entlang angelegt sind. Diese Grabplätze bestehen aus einem Netz von unterirdischen Gängen,
an denen meistens in größerer oder kleinerer Zahl Grabkammern (cubicula) liegen. Solch ein unterirdisches Netz kann sich auf einzelne, kürzere Gänge beschrän-

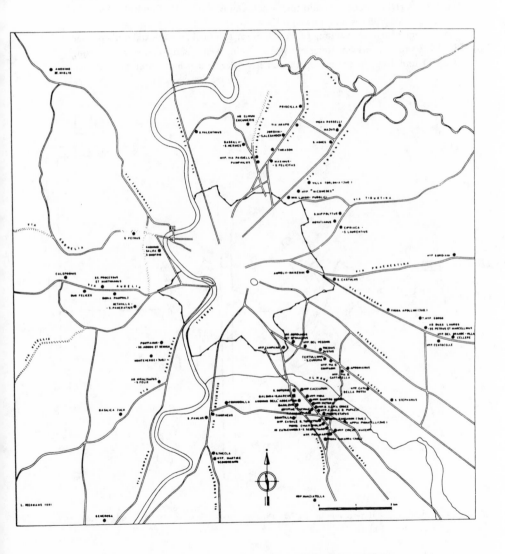

Abb. 1 Plan der frühchristlichen Nekropolen von Rom

ken – dann spricht man besser von einem Hypogäum. Als Beispiel sei das Hypogäum genannt, das 1956 an der Via Dino Compagni, d.h. an der alten via Latina,
ans Licht kam und das bald wegen seiner zahlreichen und bemerkenswerten Wandmalereien (Abb. 2) berühmt wurde[5]. Typisch für die frühchristlichen unterirdischen Grabplätze von Rom, Neapel, Chiusi, Syrakus und Sousse (Tunesien) ist
aber ihre enorme Ausdehnung bis zu kilometerlangen Gangnetzen. Der Ausdruck
„Katakomben" wird daher am besten dieser letzteren Serie besonders umfangrei-
cher Grabplätze vorbehalten. Zu den eindrucksvollsten Beispielen gehören die römischen Katakomben St. Callixtus, Praetextatus (Abb. 3), Domitilla, Priscilla,
Petrus und Marcellinus und die Majus-Katakombe.

Nach einer neueren Schätzung sollen schon ca. 150 bis 175 km Katakombengänge
im Untergrund von Rom freigelegt worden sein. Wenn man von dieser Schätzung
ausgeht und dazu die durchschnittliche Dichte der Gräber betrachtet, kommt man

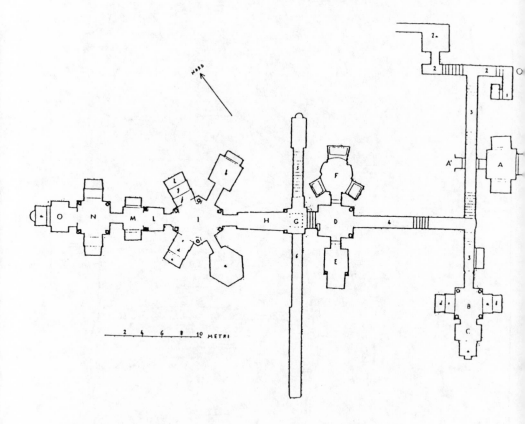

Abb. 2 Grundriß des Hypogäums in der Via Dino Compagni bzw. an der via Latina (Foto
P.C.A.S. – Din Z I).

5)   A.Ferrua, Le pitture della nuova catacomba di via Latina. Città del Vaticano 1960.

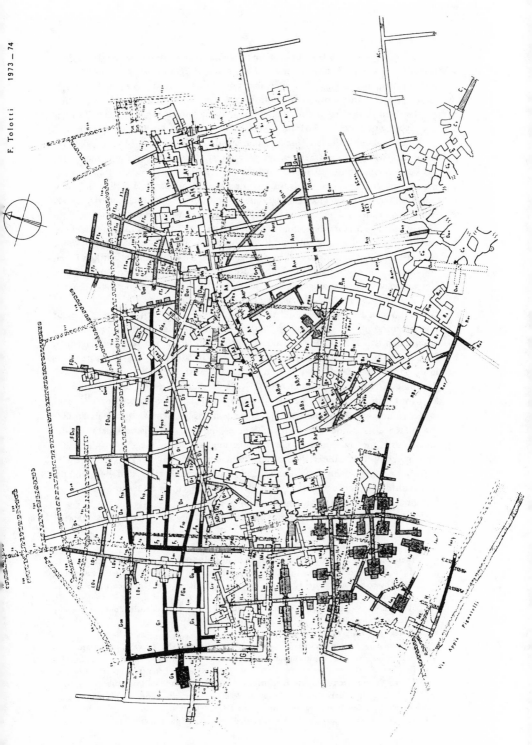

Abb. 3 Grundriß der Praetextatuskatakombe an der via Appia (Zeichnung F.Tolotti)

319

246

auf mindestens 750.000 Gräber.[6] Es ist unmöglich, auch nur annähernd zu schätzen, wieviel km an Katakombengängen noch unausgegraben im römischen Untergrund ruhen, auf jeden Fall sind es aber noch etliche -zig-km. Auf der Verbreiterungskarte der frühchristlichen Grabstätten Roms gibt es noch mehrere weiße Flecken von terrae incognitae, u.a. entlang der via Latina, am nördlichen Teil der via Appia und der via Ardeatina und entlang der via Portuensis. Daneben ist auch aus den schriftlichen Quellen, u.a. aus den Pilgerführern, bekannt, daß ansehnliche Grabplätze mit zahlreichen Märtyrergräbern noch nicht gefunden sind, z.b. das coemeterium ad septem palumbas, auch ad caput Sancti Johannis genannt, an der via Salaria vetus.[7] Das ändert aber nichts daran, daß die römischen Katakomben wohl den größten Begräbniskomplex der Welt ausmachen, der außerdem auch relativ gut erhalten und bekannt ist. Wenn man durch dieses endlose Netz von Gängen läuft, bekommt man auf eingängige Art einen Eindruck von der riesenhaften Bevölkerungszahl, die Rom noch im 4. Jh.n.Chr. gehabt haben muß. Im krassem Gegensatz dazu stehen die heidnischen Grabstätten des antiken Rom, von denen – merkwürdig genug – bis heute sehr wenige aufgefunden worden sind. Um sich davon zu überzeugen, genügt es, den Artikel „Roma" in der Enciclopedia dell' Arte Antica einmal durchzublättern.[8] Die römischen Katakomben bilden eine homogene Monumentgruppe, die nicht nur enorm groß, sondern die auch in historischer Hinsicht außerordentlich aufschlußreich ist. Denn diese Grabstätten liefern den ältesten zusammenhängenden Komplex von materiellen Zeugnissen über das Christentum, der mindestens bis in die letzten Jahrzehnte des 2. Jh.n.Chr. zurückgeht. Nebenbei sei erwähnt, daß das früheste christliche Monument von Rom die Ädikula ist, die um die Mitte des 2. Jh. auf dem Vatikan über dem Grab des Apostels Petrus errichtet wurde[9]. In den römischen Katakomben sind außerdem, grob geschätzt, mehr als 25.000 Inschriften aufgefunden worden. Sie bieten eine unerschöpfliche Quelle für die Christianisierung, quer durch alle Bevölkerungsschichten, für das Studium des christlichen Volksglaubens, für das Studium der Christenverfolgung, für die Untersuchung von Lebensverlauf und Lebensdauer, von Familie und Berufen, für sprachkundliche und namenskundliche Untersuchungen, und für das Studium der frühchristlichen Ikonographie und Monumente.[10] Die Bedeutung der römischen Katakomben in kunstgeschichtlicher Hinsicht wird

6) Diese mündlich mir mitgeteilten Zahlen beruhen auf Schätzungen der Pontificia Commissione di Archeologia Sacra, die für das Auffinden und den Unterhalt der Katakomben Italiens verantwortlich ist; s. auch L.Hertling – E.Kirschbaum, The Roman Catacombs (s. u. Anm. 1), 31 f.

7) R.Valentini – G.Zucchetti, Codice topografico della città di Roma II. Fonti per la storia d'Italia. Roma 1942, 40 f, 60, 74, 118, 201.

8) F.Magi u.a., EAA VI (1965), 856-899 s.v. Roma.

9) J.Toynbee – J.Ward Perkins, The Shrine of St. Peter and the Vatican Excavations. London[2] 1958, Abb. 17; E.Kirschbaum, Die Gräber der Apostelfürsten, St. Peter und St. Paul in Rom. Frankfurt a.M.[3] 1974, Abb. 26; D.W. O'Connor, Peter in Rom. The Literary, Liturgical and Archaeological Evidence. New York – London 1969, Abb. 36; J.Ruysschaert, Les premiers siècles de la tombe de Pierre. Une discussion dégagée d'une hypothèse, Revue des Archéologues et Historiens d'Art de Louvain 8 (1975), 7-47 Abb. 4.

10) A.Ferrua, Enciclopedia Cattolica V (1950), 429-440 s.v. Epigrafia cristiana.

deutlich, wenn man bedenkt, daß sich in ihnen die übergroße Mehrheit aller spätrömischen Wandmalereien erhalten hat.[11] Die vielen hundert Fresken, die vor allem die Grabkammern und Arkosolgräber schmücken, bilden das grundlegende Material für die römische Malerei der Zeit von ca. 175-425 n.Chr.

Schließlich enthalten die römischen Katakomben eine ganze Anzahl von Papst- und Märtyrergräbern.[12] Mehr als fünf Jahrhunderte hindurch sind diese Gräber durchgehend von Pilgerströmen, die aus allen Gegenden des orbis christianus antiquus kamen, besucht und verehrt worden. Diese Gräber haben im Rahmen der Heiligen-Verehrung die Entwicklung des Christentums bis in Karolingische Zeit in grundlegender Weise beeinflußt.

Außer ihrer historischen Bedeutung an sich haben die Papst- und Märtyrergräber auch einen besonders großen Stellenwert für die Untersuchung der römischen Katakomben. Diese Katakomben stellen meist keine schweren Probleme, was ihre Identifikation und ihre allgemeine Sinngebung betrifft. Ihre Bedeutung ist klar, weil ihr historischer Hintergrund gut bekannt ist.[13] Ungelöst sind dagegen die grundlegenden Fragen nach dem Ursprung und dem Ende, anders ausgedrückt, nach den Gründen für das unterirdische Bestatten in Rom. Warum haben die Christen und auch die Juden in Rom seit der 2. Hälfte des 3. Jh. ihre Toten in großer Anzahl im Untergrund begraben und warum hörten sie etwa um 400 damit auf? Über das Problem des Ursprungs ist schon viel geschrieben worden, und ich habe auch selbst unlängst versucht, eine vorläufige Antwort zu finden[14]. Für das Problem des Nachlassens der unterirdischen Bestattung in Rom ist meiner Meinung nach beim heutigen Stand der Forschung keine Lösung möglich, vor allem weil die römischen Bestattungsplätze des 5., 6. und 7. Jh. nicht bekannt sind. Das wichtigste und auch dringendste Problem aber, das die Untersuchung der römischen Katakomben seit fast 150 Jahren stellt, ist das der Chronologie. Aufgrund von internen Kriterien, d.h. von morphologischen und technischen Argumenten, kann man die letzte Phase der Katakomben-Ausarbeitung ziemlich gut erkennen, und an einigen Grabstätten erkennt man auch die frühesten Gänge und Kammern. Grundsätzlich ist es natürlich auch möglich, die relative Chronologie, d.h. die aufeinander folgenden Stadien in der Ausarbeitung und in den Bauten festzustellen. Giovanni-Battista und Michele-Stefano De Rossi haben das schon im vorigen Jahrhundert für die Callixtus-Katakombe getan, aber die Lösung, die sie

11) J.Wilpert, Die Malereien der Katakomben Roms I-II. Freiburg i.Br. 1903; M.Borda, La pittura romana. Milano 1958.

12) P.Styger, die römischen Märtyrergrüfte. Berlin 1935; L.Reekmans, Les cryptes des martyrs romains. État de la recherche, in: Atti del IX Congresso Internazionale di Archeologia Cristiana, Roma 1975. I Studi di antichità cristiana 32. Città del Vaticano 1978, 275-302.

13) Natürlich gibt es Unklarheiten, aber sie sind nicht von wesentlicher Bedeutung. In diesem Zusammenhang ist z.B. die Diskussion über die Interpretation der mensae zu nennen, über die weiter unten noch gesprochen werden soll. Über die Erklärung der Darstellungen auf den Wandmalereien der Katakomben und den frühchristlichen Monumenten im allgemeinen ist seit mehr als einem Jahrhundert eine Diskussion im Gang, für deren Ende durchaus nicht abzusehen ist, die die allgemeine Sinngebung der frühchristlichen Grabstätten aber nicht berührt.

14) L.Reekmans, Spätrömische Hypogea, in: Festschrift F.W.Deichmann (im Druck).

vorschlugen, ist heute nicht mehr haltbar[15]. In den 20er und 30er Jahren unseres
Jh. entwarf Paul Styger eine neue allgemeine Methode, die er A u s g r a b u n g s-
t h e o r i e nannte, um die aufeinander folgenden Phasen der Ausgestaltung einer Katakombe zu erkennen; aber dieser Versuch ist schließlich gescheitert[16] Eine
gut fundierte relative Chronologie ist zur Zeit nur für sehr wenige Katakomben
aufgestellt. Das ist vor allem durch die Tatsache zu erklären, daß die Durchfüh-
rung einer gründlichen und genauen Analyse der Monumente erst in letzter Zeit
mehr oder weniger allgemein begonnen worden ist.

Es bereitet fast unüberwindliche Mühen, für die frühchristlichen Grabstätten Roms
eine einigermaßen genaue absolute Chronologie festzulegen. Die verfügbaren
Kriterien, sowohl interne als auch externe, sind unzulänglich oder fehlen vollständig. Auf den ersten Blick kann das wohl Verwunderung hervorrufen, da doch
viele tausend Inschriften in den Katakomben aufgetaucht sind. Bis in die Zeit
Konstantins aber blieben datierte christliche Inschriften sehr selten, und es ist
sozusagen keine einzige in situ geblieben. Erst um die Mitte des 4. Jh. wurden datierte Inschriften zahlreicher[17]. Das hat zur Folge, daß sie nur zur Datierung der
letzten Phase in den römischen Katakomben helfen. Zwar kann die Entwicklung
der Formulierung und der Namensgebung in den frühchristlichen Grabinschriften
mitunter einen einigermaßen zuverlässigen Hinweis für die Datierung geben, aber
immer unter der Bedingung, daß diese Kriterien mit großer Vorsicht und sehr wei-
tem Spielraum verwendet werden.

Auch die zahlreichen Wandmalereien, die sich in den Katakomben befinden, liefern nicht das gewünschte externe Kriterium für eine sichere Datierung. Im Gegen-
teil, die Chronologie der Katakomben-Malerei stellt insgesamt ebenfalls ein unge-
löstes Problem dar. Es ist deutlich, daß stilistische und ikonographische Argumente
hier als chronologisches Kriterium fehlen. Sie lassen höchstens zu, innerhalb von
sehr weiten Grenzen eine früheste und eine letzte Periode in der Malerei der Katakomben zu unterscheiden. Aber eine mehr oder weniger sichere und genaue Datierung der großen Mehrheit der Katakomben-Fresken, die vermutlich in die Zeit
von 225 bis 350 gehören, bleibt ein offenes Problem.[18]

Es ist noch darauf hinzuweisen, daß Keramik und Münzen, zwei in allen Bereichen
der klassischen Archäologie außerordentlich wichtige Datierungsinstrumente, in
den Katakomben fehlen. Keramik gibt es nicht, weil die Christen ihren Toten
keine Grabbeigaben mitgaben. Und Münzen trifft man in den Katakomben nur
sehr selten an, und wenn, dann als Erkennungszeichen in der frischen Mörtel der
Grabplatten eingedrückt.[19]

15) s. die Kritik an der Darstellung von G.-B. und M.-S. De Rossi bezüglich der area I der
    Callixtuskatakombe in P. Styger, Die römischen Katakomben, 35-46, und bezüglich der
    sog. Lucinagrüfte und der Callixtusgrabstätte in L.Reekmans, La tombe du pape Cor-
    neille et sa région cémétériale. Roma sotterranea IV. Citta del Vaticano 1964, 185-226.

16) P.Styger, Die römischen Katakomben, 5-8 u. 24. – Kritik an der Ausgrabungstheorie von
    P.Styger in L.Reekmans, La tombe du pape Corneille, 4 f. u. ders., Die Situation der Ka-
    takombenforschung, 32.

17) A.Ferrua, in: Enciclopedia Cattolica V (1950), 436 s.v. Epigrafia cristiana.

18) L.Reekmans, La chronologie de la peinture paléochrétienne. Notes et réflexions. RACrist
    49 (1973), 271-291.

19) Ders., Die Situation der Katakombenforschung, 33.

Wenn man nicht warten will, daß neue Funde vielleicht neue Datierungsmöglich-
keiten mit sich bringen, bleibt meiner Meinung nach eigentlich nur ein Weg, das
allgemeine Datierungsproblem der römischen Katakomben einer Lösung näher zu
bringen, und das ist die Untersuchung der Grüfte, in denen in den Katakomben
Päpste und Märtyrer begraben lagen und die seit G.-B. De Rossi „historische
Grüfte" (cripte storiche) genannt werden. Nur diese Grüfte kommen – abgesehen
von einigen seltenen Ausnahmen – als hinreichend fundierte Anhaltspunkte für
eine absolute Datierung in Betracht, an die dann eventuell die unterschiedlichen
Entwicklungsphasen der Katakomben, oder zumindest einige von ihnen, fest an-
gehängt werden können. Die Todesdaten der Päpste des 3. und späterer Jahrhunderte sind alle bekannt. Die Gräber der Märtyrer gehören in jedem Fall in die Zeit
vor dem Kirchenfrieden von 313, nicht selten in die Christenverfolgung Diokletians (303-311) und einige in die Christenverfolgungen aus der Mitte des 3. Jh.
unter Decius (249-250) oder unter Valerianus (257-259).

Die Gräber der Päpste wie auch der Märtyrer wurden seit ihrer Anlage bis in die
Karolingische Zeit, als die Gebeine in die Kirchen intra muros gebracht wurden,
durchgehend besucht und verehrt. Sie machten also die gesamte Entwicklung der
Begräbnisstätten mit – die Anfangsphase hier und da ausgenommen –, und folg-
lich können sie mithelfen, die gesamte Entwicklung zu datieren. Im Laufe dieser
langen Existenz von mehr als fünf Jahrhunderten erfuhren diese „historischen
Grüfte" allerhand eingreifende Umwandlungen, durch die sie, wie man das nennt,
monumentalisiert wurden. Nun scheinen überall dieselben Umformungen und dieselben Elemente der Monumentalisierung vorzukommen. Sie haben den Märtyrergrüften ihre eigene Physiognomie gegeben, das es erlaubt, sie durchweg ziemlich
leicht zu erkennen und so das erste Problem zu lösen, das das Studium dieser Monumente stellt, nämlich das der Lokalisierung und der Identifizierung.

Welches waren die Umformungen, die Elemente der Monumentalisierung, die den
römischen Papst- und Märtyrerkrypten ihr eigenes Aussehen gegeben haben?

Zuerst sei festgestellt, daß Päpste und Märtyrer gewöhnlich unter den anderen
Gläubigen in einem gewöhnlichen Grab beigesetzt wurden, d.h. in einem loculus,
der in die Tuffwand eines Katakombenganges eingetieft war, oder in einem
arcosolium (Bogengrab) in einer Grabkammer. Die loculi der Hlg. Petrus und Marcellinus in der Grabstätte ad duas lauros an der via Labicana (Taf. 14,1) und
das arcosolium des Hl. Crescentionus in der Priscilla-Katakombe an der via Salaria (Taf. 14,2) sind Beispiele dafür. Dazu muß man noch bemerken, daß die meisten Päpste des 3. Jh. zusammen in einer Kammer begraben lagen, in der sog.
Papstgruft der Callixtuskatakombe (Taf. 16,1).

Soweit wir nach dem heutigen Stand der Erhaltung und der Forschung darüber
urteilen können, scheinen die verehrten Gräber anfänglich, d.h. im 3. Jh.n.Chr.
oder, anders gesagt, vor dem Kirchenfrieden wenig oder keine besondere Ausstattung oder Ausschmückung bekommen zu haben. Die Wände der Grabkammer
oder des Ganges um das Grab herum waren mit weißem Stuck verputzt und einfach im sog. rot-grünen Streifenstil bemalt. Erst im 4. Jh. und besonders unter
dem Einfluß des Papstes Damasus (366-384) fing man an, reichere Ausschmük-
kung anzubringen. Diese bestand aus einer Wandverkleidung in Marmor und Mosaik, marmornen Einfriedungen, Porphyrsäulen, großen figürlichen Fresken und
Ehreninschriften, darunter vor allem von Damasus verfaßten Epigrammen. Als

Beispiel nennen wir das Grab des Papstes Cornelius (+ 253) in den Lucinagrüften an der via Appia (Taf. 17,1), das Grab mit Porphyrsäulen in der Spelunca magna der Praetextatuskatakombe (Taf. 14,3), neuerdings als Grab des Hl. Januarius identifiziert, und die Gruft der Hlg. Felix und Adauctus in der Commodillakatakombe an der via Ostiensis (Taf. 14,4)[20].

Die Ausstattung der Gräber der Päpste und Märtyrer erfolgte im Hinblick auf die Verehrung und den starken Besuch, und dazu waren oft radikale Umformungen nötig. Neben das verehrte Grab setzte man nicht selten eine mensa, d.h. einen runden Block aus Mauerwerk. Solch eine mensa steht u.a. neben dem Grab des Papstes Cornelius (Taf. 17,1), und neben dem des Papstes Callixtus in der Calepodius-Katakombe an der via Aurelia (Taf. 17,5). Die Funktion einer solchen mensa ist unklar und umstritten. Nach Meinung der einen trug sie Lampen oder eine Schale, gefüllt mit Öl, in dem brennende Dochte aus Papyrus trieben. Andere glauben, daß eine solche mensa bei den Mahlzeiten am Grab verwendet wurde.[21] Ab und zu wurde gegenüber oder auch auf dem verehrten Grab ein Altar aufgestellt. Das schönste und auch besterhaltene Beispiel ist der Altar, der über das Grab des Hl. Alexander am 7. Meilenstein der via Nomentana gesetzt ist (Taf. 15,1). Hier erhebt sich die Frage, wann die Verbindung von Altar und verehrtem Grab gebräuchlich geworden ist.[22]

Andere Maßnahmen waren mehr von praktischer Art. Um den verehrten Gräbern, die 8 bis 20 m unter der Erdoberfläche lagen, direkte Belüftung und Tagesbeleuchtung zu geben, hub man von oben aus durch die starken Tuffschichten einen breiten Lichtschacht, der über dem Grab mündete. Solche Lichtschächte kommen z.B. in der Papstkrypta vor, in den Grüften der Hll. Cornelius und Eusebius (Taf. 17,2).

Um für die vielen Besucher den Zugang zu den Krypten zu erleichtern, baute man — öfter quer durch vorher schon bestehende Gänge — breite Treppen, die direkt zu dem verehrten Grab führten. Manchmal bekamen solche Treppen monumentale Ausmaße, mitunter baute man sogar zwei. Das waren die gradus ascensionis et descensionis, wie im Liber pontificalis die Treppen genannt werden, die zu dem unterirdischen Grab des Hl. Laurentius führten.[23] Eine solche monumentale

20) Ders., La tombe du pape Corneille, 125-184; F.Tolotti, Ricerca dei luoghi venerati nella Spelunca magna di Pretestato, RACrist 53 (1977), 71-87; B.Bagatti, Il cimitero di Commodilla o dei martiri Felice ed Adautto. Roma sotterranea cristiana II. Citta del Vaticano 1936, 101-120.

21) A.M.Schneider, Mensae oleorum oder Totenspeisetische, RömQSchr 35 (1927) 287-301; L.Reekmans, La tombe du pape Corneille, 151-153; H.Brandenburg, Das Grab des Papstes Cornelius und die Lucinaregion der Calixtus-Katakombe der Calixtus-Katakombe, JbAChr 11-12 (1968-1969), 52-53. P.-A.Fevrier, Le culte des morts dans les communautés chrétiennes durant le IIIe siecle, in: Atti del IX Congresso Internazionale di Archeologia Cristiana I. Roma 1975, 211-274.

22) F.Wieland, Mensa und Confessio. München 1906; ders., Altar und Altargrab der christlichen Kirchen im 4. Jh. Leipzig 1912; F.W.Deichmann, Das Mausoleum der Kaiserin Helena und die Basilika der Heiligen Marcellinus und Petrus an der via Labicana vor Rom, JdI 72 (1977), 92-109; R.Krautheimer, Mensa-Coemeterium-Martyrium, CArch 2 (1960), 15-40; F.W.Deichmann, Märtyrerbasilika, Martyrion, Memoria und Altargrab, RM 77 (1970), 144-169.

23) L.Duchesne, Le Liber pontificalis I. Hrsg. v. C.Vogel. Paris 1955, 181, 1.5-6.

Treppe führte z.B. zur Krypta der Hll. Petrus und Marcellinus in der Nekropole
ad duas lauros (Taf. 14,1) und zur Gruft der Hll. Felix und Adauctus in der
Commodilla-Katakombe bei der via Ostiensis.

Um einer großen Anzahl von Besuchern gleichzeitig den Zugang zu einem Märtyrergrab zu ermöglichen, wurde in verschiedenen Fällen der Gang oder die Kammer, in der sich das Grab befand, vergrößert, indem man die Tuffwand ringsum
aushöhlte. Auf diese Weise hat man in dem schon genannten Grab mit Porphyrsäulen in der Spelunca magna der Praetextatuskatakombe eine geräumige Apsis
oder Exedra in der gegenüberliegenden Wand angelegt (Taf. 14,3).

Nicht selten aber wurden die Wände der Galerie oder des cubiculum, in dem sich
das Grab befand, ganz weggehauen, um einen länglichen Raum, mit oder ohne
Apsis, herzustellen, dessen Wände dann meistens mit Mauerwerk oder Stuck über-
zogen wurden. So entstand ein kleines unterirdisches Heiligtum. Gute Beispiele
dafür bieten die Gruft der Hll. Petrus und Marcellinus im Friedhof ad duas lauros,
die der Hll. Felix und Adauctus in der Commodillakatakombe (Taf. 14,4), die
des Hl. Hippolytus an der Via Tiburtina (Taf. 16,2) und der Hl. Thecla an der via
Laurentina (Taf. 15,2). Mit solchen weitgehenden Umgestaltungen befinden wir
uns bereits im 4. und 5. Jh.

Die Anlage von Gängen, Kammern, Gräbern, Lichtschächten und Treppen ebenso
wie die nachfolgenden Umbauten hatten die unterirdischen Tuffmassen oft derart
ausgehöhlt, daß der Einsturz drohte oder unvermeidlich wurde. Das hatte zur
Folge, daß mehrere Grüfte in den römischen Katakomben heute wie Grotten aussehen. So ist es andererseits auch zu erklären, daß man schon im Altertum die
hohen Tuffwände und die Gewölbe verstärkte und unterstützte, indem man
schwere Pfeiler errichtete, die mit Bögen verbunden wurden, und indem man mit
Mauerwerk die Wände bedeckte und die Gräber auffüllte. Auch die Wände der
Gänge, die zu einem verehrten Grab führten, wurden zuweilen vollkommen mit
Mauerwerk verkleidet. Dabei wurden die Seitengänge und Grabkammern abge-
schnitten, so daß ein langer Weg von der Treppe bis zum Grab völlig abgeschlos-
sen war, damit fremde Besucher sich nicht in dem endlosen Netz von Gängen ver-
irren konnten. Diese Stützbauten gehören zu den charakteristischsten Elementen
der Begräbnisbereiche, in denen verehrte Gräber liegen. Beispiele dafür bieten die
Grüfte des Hl. Cornelius, und der Hl. Thecla (Taf. 15,2), der Päpste Gajus und
Eusebius und der lange gemauerte Gang, der in der Katakombe ad duas lauros zur
Gruft der IV. Coronati führt (Taf. 17,4).

Die römischen Märtyrergräber wurden — wie schon gesagt — bis in das 8. und 9.
Jh.n.Chr. sehr stark besucht, d.h. bis zu dem Augenblick, wo die Gebeine der
Märtyrer in die Stadt überführt wurden. Viele Besucher schrieben ihre Namen auf
die Wände der Grüfte, um sich so mit den Märtyrern zu verbinden. Ab und zu
fügten sie dabei den einen oder anderen Wunsch oder ein Gebet hinzu. Das sind
die graffiti, die bei einem Märtyrergrab stets zu finden sind und archäologisch eine
wichtige Rolle spielen, u.a. bei der Lokalisierung und zuweilen auch bei der Identifizierung des verehrten Grabes. Wände mit graffiti sieht man am Eingang der
Papstgruft in der Callixtus-Katakombe, in der Memoria Apostolorum des Coeme-
teriums von S. Sebastiano an der via Appia, wo graffiti aus der Mitte des 3. Jhs.
zigmal die Namen der Apostel Petrus und Paulus nennen, weiter in und bei der
Gruft der Hll. Petrus und Marcellinus und beim Grab des Hl. Crescentionus in
der Priscilla-Katakombe (Taf. 17,3).

Die frühen Christen legten größten Wert darauf, dicht bei den Märtyrern bestattet zu werden. Dazu wurden alle Möglichkeiten benutzt und ausgeschöpft. Nicht nur, daß die Wände der Grüfte und der Gänge ringsum immer besonders dicht mit Gräbern besetzt sind, in der unmittelbaren Nachbarschaft des verehrten Grabes wurde auch der Boden der Gruft und der Gänge immer in seiner ganzen Oberfläche und z.T. sehr tief (bis zu 3-4 m) mit formae oder Bodengräbern bedeckt. Das konnten wir bei der Ausgrabung der Grüfte der Päpste Cornelius, Gajus (Taf. 16,4) und Eusebius und der Märtyrer Calocerus und Parthenius feststellen.

Um neue Bestattungsmöglichkeiten rings um die Märtyrergräber zu schaffen, wurden die Gebeine der Gläubigen aus den alten, nicht mehr besuchten Gräbern herausgenommen und in ossuaria beigesetzt. Ganz nahe beim Grab des Papstes Cornelius sammelte man Gebeine in einer Grube, die dann zugemauert wurde (Abb. 4).

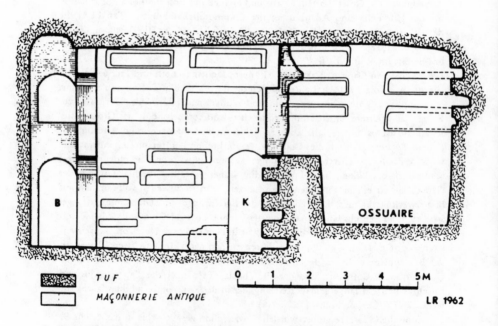

Abb. 4: Lucinagrüfte. Längsschnitt von Gang G, in der Nähe des Grabes des Papstes Cornelius. Der hinterste Teil in ein o s s u a r i u m umgewandelt.

Unmittelbar hinter dem verehrten Grab öffnete man oft auch einen neuen Raum für Bestattungen durch die Anlage einer Kammer oder sogar eines kleinen Gangsystems, das hier und da mit einem cubiculum versehen war. Eine solche Erweiterung wird gewöhnlich retro sanctos genannt. Hinter der Gruft des Papstes Gajus (Taf. 15,3) und nahe bei der der Hll. Felix und Adauctus in der Commodillakatakombe, findet man deutliche Beispiele dafür.

Immer mit demselben Ziel, nämlich Platz für Bestattungen in der Nähe des verehrten Grabes zu schaffen, grub man sogar rings um das Papst- oder Märtyrergrab ein neues Netz von Gängen. Als Beispiel kann das Gangnetz des späten 4. Jh. dienen, das wie ein Kranz rings um das Grab des Papstes Cornelius (Abb. 5) angelegt wurde.[24]

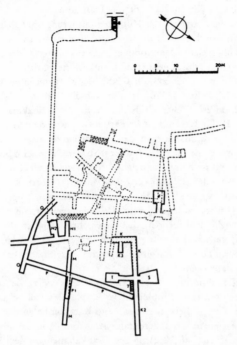

Abb. 5: Lucinagrüfte. Mit dicken Linien sind die Gänge eingetragen, die im späten 4. Jh. rings um das Grab von Papst Cornelius (L) gegraben wurden.

Alle diese zusätzlichen Gräber, Einbauten, Dekorationen und Umbauten unterschiedlichster Art sind während des langen Zeitraums von fünf bis sechs Jahrhunderten, in dem die Märtyrer-Gräber besucht wurden, in mehreren Phasen aufeinander gefolgt. Das Aufspüren und das Voneinandertrennen all dieser Elemente der Monumentalisierung sowie das Feststellen ihrer Reihenfolge oder relativen Chronologie ist eine der wichtigsten Aufgaben des Archäologen in den römischen Katakomben. Wegen des fortschreitenden Verfalls, in dem die historischen Grüfte der Katakomben sich befinden, ist es zugleich auch eine der mühsamsten Aufgaben. An diesem Verfall liegt es auch, daß nur eine aufs genaueste durchgeführte Analyse auch der kleinsten, scheinbar unwichtigsten Besonderheiten Aussicht hat, zu irgendeinem Resultat zu führen. Daneben hat uns die Erfahrung der letzten Jahre aber auch gelehrt, daß in einigen, wenn auch seltenen Fällen die verehrten Gräber und die Räume ringsum im Aussehen und in der Ausstattung immer einfach geblieben sind, was die Wiedererkennung dann aber problematisch machen

---

24)   L. Reekmans, La tombe du pape Corneille, 215-217 u. Taf. 11.

kann. Solche einfach belassenen verehrten Gräber und Grüfte sind u.a. die Grabkammer der Hll. Calocerus und Parthenius in der Callixtuskatakombe (Taf. 15,4),
das verehrte Grab am Ende von Gang A in der Lucina-Gruft und das im Hypogäum A bei der Gruft der Hl. Thecla an der via Laurentina.[25]
Im allgemeinen sind die Elemente der Monumentalisierung aber so zahlreich und
deutlich, daß die historischen Grüfte vernältnismäßig einfach zu erkennen sind.
Doch dann kann es überraschend vorkommen, daß es schwierig oder sogar unmöglich ist, das verehrte Grab selbst in der monumentalisierten Gruft zu erkennen und
zu lokalisieren. Wo befinden sich z.B. die Gräber der Märtyrer in der Gruft des Hl.
Hermes und der der Hl. Felicitas? Wo befinden sich die Gräber der Hl. Nereus und
Achilleus in der halbunterirdischen Grabeskirche der Domitillakatakombe an der
via Ardeatina (Taf. 18,1)? Wo sind die verehrten Gräber in dem martyrologischen
Zentrum der Pontianus-Katakombe an der via Portuensis zu erkennen? Für die
Lokalisierung des Grabes des Papstes Callixtus in der Calepodius-Katakombe an
der via Aurelia schwankt man immer noch zwischen zwei loculi (Taf. 17,5)[26].
Die Schwierigkeiten bei der Lokalisierung von Märtyrergräbern können verschiedene Ursachen haben. Angelegt in bröckeligen Tuffwänden, gingen sie bei dem
starken Verfall der Grüfte, in denen sie sich befanden, gemeinsam mit unter. Man
muß auch mit der Möglichkeit rechnen, daß die verehrten Gräber, die ursprünglich
sehr einfach waren, später vielleicht gründlich umgestaltet wurden. Schließlich
kann das verehrte Grab auch wegen unzulänglicher Ausgrabung der umgebenden
Gruft unerkannt geblieben sein.
Öfter noch als die Lokalisierung eines verehrten Grabes bietet die Zuweisung an
einen dort bestatteten Märtyrer Probleme. Das ist u.a. der Fall bei den Märtyrergräbern in dem sog. Treppenheiligtum der Majus-Katakombe an der via Nomentana, in der Spelunca magna der Praetextatus-Katakombe, in der sog. anonymen
Basilika der via Ardeatina (Taf. 18,2), in der Grabkammer mit dem Blockaltar in
der Pamphiluskatakombe (Taf. 18,3), in der Gruft an der 'via Laurentina, die traditionell der Hl. Thecla zugewiesen wird (Taf. 15,2). Es ist schließlich der Fall bei
den Märtyrern, die in dem Doppelgrab der sog. Tricora occidentale oberhalb der
Callixtuskatakombe bestattet sind.[27]
Die wichtigste Ursache für die Unmöglichkeit, die dort begrabenen Märtyrer zu
identifizieren oder hinreichende Sicherheit dafür zu bekommen, ist die Tatsache,
daß die Grabinschriften und die Ehreninschriften entweder verloren oder nicht am
Grab selbst gefunden worden sind. Die graffiti, die allerdings in großer Zahl bei
verehrten Gräbern angebracht worden sind, teilen oft nicht den Namen des dort
bestatteten Märtyrers oder Papstes mit. Auch die Angaben der Pilgerführer sind
zuweilen nicht genau genug, um eine Identifizierung mit ausreichender Sicherheit

---

25) Ebd. 37-39; 41f. u. 224f.; U.M.Fasola, Il complesso catacombale di S.Tecla, RACrist 40
   (1966), 19-50.

26) s. L.Reekmans, Les cryptes des martyrs romains, 278, 279f., 294, 298f., 300f.; dort wird
   auch die frühere Literatur genannt.

27) Ebd. 279, 283f, 289f, 292, 296-298, wo auch die frühere Literatur zu finden ist: s. weiter
   E.Josi, Il cimitero di Panfilo, RACrist 1 (1924), 86-108; F.Tolotti, a.O. (s.o. Anm. 20),
   7-102; U.M.Fasola, Indagini nel sopraterra della catacomba di S.Callisto, RACrist 56
   (1980) 221-278, s. bes. 224f. u. 267-278.

zu erlauben. Das ist z.B. der Fall bei der Identifizierung des verehrten Doppelgrabes in der soeben erwähnten Basilica anonima dell'Ardeatina. Andererseits sind diese Texte aber auch besonders wertvoll im Hinblick auf die Papstgräber in der Cripta ottagonale der Priscillakatakombe (Taf. 16,3).[28]

Wer die schon freigelegten Märtyrergrüfte in den römischen Katakomben untersuchen will, findet diese Monumente in dem Zustand gut erhalten auf, in dem sie sich unmittelbar nach der Ausgrabung und Restaurierung befanden, die meistens schon viele Jahrzehnte und nicht selten sogar mehr als ein Jahrhundert zurückliegen. Dabei gerät man jedoch durchaus in etwas, was man als archäologisches Vakuum wird bezeichnen dürfen. Ausgrabungstagebücher, Zeichnungen, Fotos, mit einem Wort, die archäologische Dokumentierung, die nach heutiger Auffassung verpflichtend ist und nach festgelegten Normen bei der Ausgrabung zusammengestellt werden muß, fehlen für beinahe alle römischen Märtyrergräber sozusagen vollständig. Jedesmal wieder fällt es auch auf, wie wenig diese Monumente bis heute untersucht wurden und wie wenige Publikationen darüber erschienen sind. Das Fehlen von Denkmälerpublikationen selbst ist dabei die schwerwiegendste Lücke.

Den heutigen Stand der Forschung zu den römischen Katakomben und den Märtyrergrüften haben wir schon anderswo näher dargelegt.[29] Hier weisen wir zur Illustration nur noch auf eine durchgehend anzutreffende Lücke in diesen Untersuchungen hin, die einem Archäologen besonders überraschend und zugleich unbegreiflich erscheint. Nirgends wird in den Publikationen darüber gesprochen, woraus der Boden der Märtyrergrüfte gebildet war. Man entledigte sich dieser Frage gewöhnlich mit dem stereotypen Satz, daß „der Boden der Krypta wie immer mit Gräbern besetzt ist". Dabei fehlt in der Regel selbst eine rudimentäre Skizze von diesen Bodengräbern oder formae. Dennoch bilden diese Gräber ein wichtiges Glied innerhalb der Entwicklung der Märtyrergrüfte, vor allem im Übergang von der Anfangsphase der Bestattung zur darauf folgenden Phase der Monumentalisierung. Das völlige Fehlen der Bodengräber in den Publikationen überrascht umso mehr, als wir in den Grüften, die wir ausgraben konnten, jedesmal feststellen mußten, daß der Boden schon früher durch die Fossoren der Pontificia Commissione di Archeologia Sacra gänzlich geleert worden war. Für einen Archäologen, der eine Märtyrergruft ernsthaft untersuchen will, bleibt also nichts anderes übrig, als ihren Boden von neuem gänzlich auszugraben — und natürlich auch die unmittelbare Umgebung.

In einer solchen Situation, so dachten wir, kann die Untersuchung von mehr als 50 bis jetzt freigelegten Papst- und Märtyrer-Gräbern und ihren Grüften am besten weitergeführt werden, wenn man diese Monumente zuerst einmal systematisch aufmißt, zeichnet und fotografiert. Eine angemessen zusammengestellte graphische Dokumentation ist doch das absolut notwendige Instrument, nicht

---

28) F.Tolotti, Il cimitero di Priscilla. Collezione „Amici delle catacombe" 26. Città del Vaticano 1970, 237-257; ders., Le cimetière de Priscille. Synthèse d'une recherche, Rev. Hist. Eccl. 78 (1978), 2, 281-314, s. bes. 311-314; L.Reekmans, Les cryptes des martyrs romains (s.o. Anm. 12) 281-282.

29) L.Reekmans, Die Situation der Katakombenforschung in Rom; ders., Les cryptes des martyrs romains.

allein um ein Monument in einer Publikation darzustellen, sondern auch, um die Möglichkeit zu schaffen, ein Monument in einer Publikation mit allen Aspekten und auch in allen archäologisch wichtigen Details kennenzulernen und zu untersuchen.

Aus früherer Erfahrung hatten wir gelernt, daß solch eine Arbeit, wenn sie mit den traditionellen Meß- und Zeichenmethoden durchgeführt wird, mehrere Jahrzehnte dauern würde, was mit dem verwickelten Charakter der Märtyrergrüfte, dem großen Rückstand in der Untersuchung und den jeweils kurzen Anwesenheitszeiten in Rom zusammenhängt. Darum haben wir beim Institut für Photogrammetrie und Topographie der Universität Karlsruhe angefragt, das auf archäologische Photogrammetrie spezialisiert ist. Dort waren Prof. Dr. M.Döhler, Prof. Dr. W.Hofmann und Ing. K.Ringle — zu unserem Glück — sehr an einer fotogrammetrischen Aufnahme der Papst- und Märtyrergrüfte in Rom interessiert. Darüber hinaus haben uns die Pontificia Commissione di Archeologia Sacra und die Römische Abteilung des Deutschen Archäologischen Instituts stets tatkräftig und auf vielerlei Weise unterstützt.[30]

Im Verlauf von vier Kampagnen, die in den Jahren 1974, 1976, 1977 und 1978 — während zusammengenommen dreieinhalb Monaten Anwesenheit in Rom — unternommen wurden, konnten 21 Grüfte und Komplexe mit Gräbern von Päpsten und Märtyrern in den römischen Katakomben photogrammetrisch aufgenommen werden. Prof. Dr. H.Brandenburg ergriff bei dieser Gelegenheit die glückliche Initiative, die area I der Callixtuskatakombe aufmessen zu lassen[31]. Zugleich wurde am Institut für Photogrammetrie in Karlsruhe mit der Auswertung begonnen, d.h. mit der maschinellen Umsetzung der in situ aufgenommenen Stereophotos in Linienzeichnung (Abb. 6). Diese zweite Phase geht in diesen Wochen zu Ende. Allerdings müssen diese Auswertungen in den Teilen der Grüfte ergänzt werden, die für die photogrammetrische Kamera nicht erreichbar waren, entweder weil sie hinter anderen Elementen versteckt saßen oder weil es unmöglich war, die Kamera aufzustellen. Auch die Teile der Grüfte, die sehr stark restauriert, in der Struktur einfach oder wenig informativ sind, werden am besten mit den gewohnten Zeichenmethoden ergänzt. Dazu kommt schließlich die Ergänzung der photogrammetrischen Linienzeichnungen selbst durch konventionelle Zeichen zur Andeutung von verschiedenen Materialien (Tufflagen, verschiedene Arten von Einbauten, Vermauerung, Wandmalereien und Marmorinkrustationen). Diese Arbeit wird zuerst in situ in Rom und auch weiter in Zusammenarbeit mit Frau Dipl.-Ing. U.Hess, Assistent am Institut für Baugeschichte in München, durchgeführt, die auch eine klare, archäologisch fundierte und technisch korrekte Darstellung entwerfen wird. Die abschließende Ausarbeitung und die Aufbereitung der Zeichnungen für den Druck findet in der Abteilung für Archäologie der katholischen Universität Löwen statt.

30) L.Reekmans, Essais photogrammétriques dans les cryptes des martyrs romains. Rend PontAcc 47 (1974-1975), 129-138.
31) H;Brandenburg, Photogrammetrische Bauaufnahme der Area I der Callixtus-Katakombe in Rom, in: Photogrammetrie in der Architektur und Denkmalpflege. Symposium Wien 16.-19. September 1981. Wien 1983, 171-180.

Auf einzelne besondere Aspekte und Eigenschaften der photogrammetrischen Untersuchungen in den römischen Katakomben muß noch kurz hingewiesen werden. Die Anwendung der Photogrammetrie in diesen unterirdischen, oft weit abgelegenen, engen, sehr feuchten und absolut dunklen Räumen war 1974, als wir damit begannen, ein Experiment. Die Ingenieure aus Karlsruhe standen vor einer gänzlich neuen Aufgabe, einer technischen Herausforderung, und das war wohl auch der Hauptgrund, warum sie auf die Bitte eingingen, mit in die Katakomben herunterzugehen. Prof. M.Döhler aus Karlsruhe entwickelte eine neue Methode, die sog. Linienmethode, speziell für die photogrammetrischen Aufnahmen der römischen Märtyrergrüfte.[32] Diese Methode hat inzwischen auch auf anderen Gebieten Anwendung gefunden. Während der zweiten Kampagne von 1976 gelang es Prof. M.Döhler und Ing. K.Ringle, die Probleme bei Aufnahmen von hohen und schmalen Katakombengängen technisch zu lösen und so den Anwendungsbereich der Photogrammetrie unverhofft stark auszuweiten. In Karlsruhe erfand Ing. K.Ringle eine neue Methode für die Auswertung der photogrammetrischen Aufnahmen, die in engen Katakombenräumen gemacht worden waren. Neue Methoden brachten auch die Anpassung der Instrumente und sogar den Entwurf neuer Instrumente mit sich.

Gleichzeitig wurde seit 1978 durch Ingenieure aus Karlsruhe auf unser Drängen hin in den Katakomben mit der Orthophotographie experimentiert, einer neuen Technik, die noch in voller Entwicklung ist und spektakuläre Ergebnisse zu liefern verspricht. Orthographische Photos, d.h. Photographien, die in allen Punkten eine geometrisch genaue Darstellung bieten und ebenfalls auf der Basis der photogrammetrischen Aufnahmen hergestellt worden sind, geben selbstverständlich eine viel reichere Information als die detaillierteste Linienzeichnung.[33] Soweit wir wissen, gehören die Experimente mit der Orthophotographie, die 1978 in den Grüften von Papst Cornelius und dem großen Komplex von St. Alexander an der via Nomentana durchgeführt worden sind, zu den allerersten im Bereich der Archäologie (Taf. 18,4).Im Augenblick macht man am Institut für Photogrammetrie in Karlsruhe Versuche mit neuen Meßkameras, mit neuen analytischen Methoden der Auswertung, mit der sog. digitalen Bildverarbeitung.[34]

32) M.Döhler, Photogrammetrische Aufnahme und Kartierung römischer Märtyrergrüfte, RendPontAcc 47 (1974-1975), 139-161; ders., Verwendung von Pass-„Linien" anstelle von Pass-„Punkten" in der Nahbildmessung, in: Festschrift K.Schwidefsky. Karlsruhe 1975, 39-45; ders., Erfahrungen mit der Photogrammetrie bei archäologischen und baugeschichtlichen Objekten, Bildmessung und Luftbildwesen 42,5 (1974), 138-148 ; ders., Photogrammetrische Bestandsaufnahme kulturhistorischer Objekte. Erfahrungen und Vorschläge, in: Architekturphotogrammetrie III. Landeskonservator Rheinland, Arbeitsh. 18. Köln 1977, 53-72.

33) E.Seeger, Das Orthophotoverfahren bei der Bauaufnahme am Beispiel Schloß Linderhof, Bildmessung und Luftbildwesen 42,5 (1974), 148-154; ders., Erfahrungen mit der Orthophototechnik in der Architekturphotogrammetrie, in: Architekturphotogrammetrie II. Internationales Symposium für Photogrammetrie in der Architektur und Denkmalpflege, Bonn 1976. Landeskonservator Rheinland, Arbeitsheft 17. Köln 1976, 149-156; ders., Orthophotography. Architectural Photogrammetry, Photogrammetric Engineering 42 (1976), 625-635.

33) H.-P.Bähr, Einsatz digitaler Bildverarbeitung in der klassischen Photogrammetrie am Beispiel eines Architekturobjektes, Bildmessung und Luftbildwesen 48,3 (1980), 85-93;

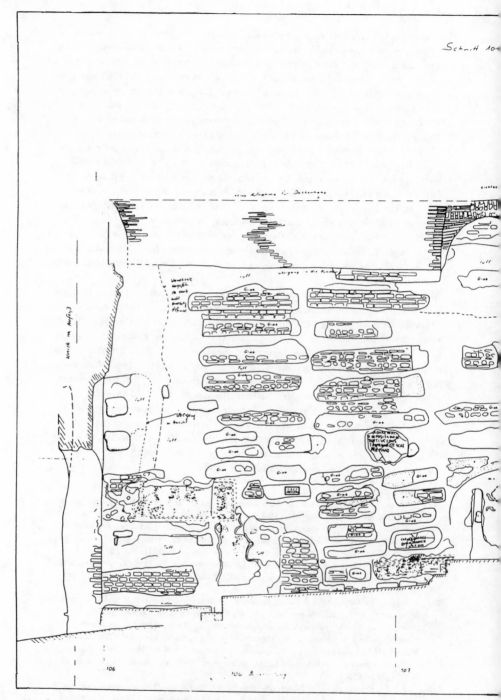

Abb. 6: Krypta von St. Felix und Adauctus in der Commodillakatakombe, westliche Längs-
wand, photogrammetrische Auswertung, ohne Zusätze.

Photogrammetrie ist, allein betrachtet, wohl sehr kostspielig, aber das wird weit aufgewogen durch die erheblichen und anders gar nicht erreichbaren Vorteile, die diese Methode bietet. Es hat sich nämlich gezeigt, daß die photogrammetrische Methode gestattet, die römischen Papst- und Märtyrergräber 15 bis 25 mal schneller aufzunehmen und zu zeichnen, als das mit den traditionellen Meßmethoden der Fall wäre. So bringt die Photogrammetrie, aufs Ganze gesehen, eine ansehnliche finanzielle Einsparung mit sich. Diese enorme Zeiteinsparung bietet natürlich auch einen bedeutenden Vorteil für die Ingenieure und die Archäologen, die nur eine kurze Zeit vor Ort arbeiten können. Darüber hinaus garantiert die Photogrammetrie eine absolute geometrische Genauigkeit in allen drei Dimensionen, die bei den traditionellen Meßmethoden nicht gegeben war.

Während die Photogrammetrie also einerseits eine beinahe ideale Lösung bot, den hoffnungslos großen Rückstand einzuholen und darüber hinaus technisch perfekte Zeichnungen zu bekommen, hat die Erfahrung der letzten Jahre uns doch auch die Grenzen gezeigt, die der Anwendung dieser Methode in den römischen Katakomben gezogen sind. In manchen Fällen, besonders bei den Märtyrergrüften, die sehr stark restauriert waren oder die nur eine begrenzte Informationsdichte bieten, kann man, wie bereits gesagt, häufig auf befriedigende Weise und auch billiger mit den traditionellen Methoden ausmessen und zeichnen. In anderen Fällen ist es dann wiederum angezeigt, die photogrammetrische und die traditionelle Meßmethoden zu kombinieren. Aus diesen Gründen haben wir das Zeichenbüro der Pontificia Commissione di Archeologia Sacra, das unter Leitung des Ing. M.Santa Maria und des Architekten F.Balzani steht, darum gebeten, nach unseren Angaben sieben Grüfte mit den gewohnten Instrumenten aufzumessen und zu zeichnen.

Zum Schluß sei dazu noch gesagt, daß wir die römischen Märtyrergrüfte nicht nur das erste Mal aufgemessen und gezeichnet, sondern auch systematisch und im Detail photographiert haben. In Zusammenarbeit mit Prof. Dr. H.Brandenburg und mit A.Reale, Berufsphotograph in Rom und Spezialist für archäologische Photographie, wurden diese Monumente in 400 neuen Photographien festgehalten. Die meisten Aufnahmen, die in diesem Beitrag erscheinen, gehören zu dieser neuen Dokumentation, abgesehen von denen, wo ein anderer Ursprung ausdrücklich vermerkt ist.

Das Hauptziel dieser systematischen Aufmessung, Zeichnung und photographischen Dokumentation ist die Zusammenstellung eines vollständigen graphischen Archivs der historischen Grüfte in den römischen Katakomben. Ein solches Archiv wird hoffentlich eine zuverlässige wissenschaftliche Basis für weitere Untersuchungen bieten. Diese graphische Dokumentation wird auch die Grundlage bilden für das allgemeine topographische Repertorium der römischen Papst- und Märtyrergräber, das wir im Rahmen des Martyrium-Projekts in Löwen vorbereiten.

G.Schweinfurth, Herkömmliche und neuartige Verfahren für photogrammetrische Bauaufnahmen, in: Photogrammetrie in der Architektur und Denkmalpflege. Symposium Wien 16.-19. September 1981. Wien 1983, 181-200. J.Wiesel, Didak, A Digital Image Processing System, in: Proceedings International Symposium on Image Processing – Interactions with Photogrammetry and Remote Sensing. Graz, October 3-5, 1977. Graz 1977, 219-221 (DIDAK = Digitales Daten- und Auswerte-System Karlsruhe).

HINTON ST. MARY, DORSET : PANEL OF FOURTH-CENTURY MOSAIC PAVEMENT FEATURING MALE BUST WITH CHI-RHO AND POMEGRANATES (see p. 8)

Photograph by Royal Commission on Historical Monuments, England. Copyright W. J. White

A NEW ROMAN MOSAIC PAVEMENT FOUND IN DORSET

By J. M. C. TOYNBEE *

(Frontispiece and plates I–VII)

In Memoriam Margerie Venables Taylor

The Roman polychrome mosaic, which forms the subject of this paper, came to light on 12th September, 1963, at the village of Hinton St. Mary in northern Dorset, 1½ miles north of Sturminster Newton. The field in which the pavement lies is the property of Mr. W. J. White, general engineer, blacksmith, and welder, who recognized as Roman the *tesserae* revealed by the postholes that were being dug for the foundations of a building near his forge. Mr. White immediately reported the discovery to the authorities of the Dorset County Museum, Dorchester, and invited them to direct the clearance of the whole mosaic with the help of a group of local archaeologists and amateurs. Mr. R. A. H. Farrar, of the Royal Commission on Historical Monuments (England), also took part in the work of clearance ; and the vertical photographs reproduced here, of which Mr. White holds the copyright, were taken at his request by the Commission with the aid of an 18-foot gantry.

The excavation disclosed a rectangular room measuring 28 ft. 4 in. by 19 ft. 6 in., and with its long axis running east and west. The pavement (fig. 1), which was found 15 inches at its shallowest point and 30 inches at its deepest point below the modern ground-level, covers the whole of the floor of the room, which is divided into two distinct and unequal portions by two short cross-walls (now mostly robbed out) that project at right-angles from the long walls and are linked, in the central area of the chamber, by a mosaic panel of *peltae* pattern. The eastern and larger portion (pl. II) consists of a square edged by a narrow border of guilloche and flanked to north and south by a wider border of double plait. Extensions of the narrow guilloche border run round the inner ends of the cross-walls and continue right round the mosaic panels of the western portion, thus binding intimately together both parts of the mosaic carpet. In the centre of the eastern square is a roundel framed by four concentric borders, which (to pass from the innermost to the outermost border) are filled with wave, single plait, fret, and guilloche patterns. Four half-circles, the chord of each of which is flush with one side of the square, and each of which is framed by narrow borders of guilloche and fret, surround the central circle ; and in each corner of the square is a quarter-circle framed by a narrow guilloche border. Four narrow borders of guilloche link the central circle with the quarter-circles and would, if projected inwards, form a St. Andrew's cross, with its arms intersecting at the centre of the roundel. The eight remaining spaces are occupied by boat-shaped panels each of which contains a running floral scroll.

The western and smaller portion of the room (pl. III) is of oblong shape and comprises a central square in which is inscribed a circle made up of a roundel framed by an inner, wider border containing a running floral scroll (of the same type as that of the eight scrolls in the eastern portion of the chamber) and by an outer, narrower border of guilloche. In each of the four corners of the square, outside the circle, is a two-handled chalice flanked by tendrils. To north and south of the square is an oblong panel framed by a guilloche border. As can be clearly seen from a drawing (fig. 1), or from a vertical photograph of the whole layout, the western portion is not quite symmetrically planned. The panel between the two cross-walls is not truly centred in the room ; the oblong panel to south of the square is wider than that to north of it ; and the small filling panel inserted just to west of the northern end of the *peltae* panel is wider than that at the south end. The general mosaic scheme closely resembles that of the most famous of the Roman mosaic pavements

* I should like to thank all those who have helped me in the study of this mosaic by discussing it with me and supplying me with references, notably Prof. Sir Ian Richmond and the late Miss M. V. Taylor of the Society for the Promotion of Roman Studies, Mr. H. S. L. Dewar and Mr. R. N. R. Peers of the Dorset Natural History and Archaeological Society, Mr. R. A. H. Farrar and Dr. R. M. Butler of the Royal Commission on Historical Monuments (England), Mr. R. M. Harrison of the University of Newcastle upon Tyne, Professor Ernst Kitzinger of the Center for Byzantine Studies, Dumbarton Oaks, Washington, and the Director of the Index of Christian Art, Princeton University. I am also very grateful to Mr. D. R. Wilson, Assistant Editor of the *Journal*, for preparing the drawing reproduced as fig. 1. The thanks of the Society are also due to the Jowett Trustees for their generous grant of £150 for the illustrations to this paper, given specifically in memory of Miss Taylor.

found at Frampton, north-west of Dorchester.[1] There, too, the smaller portion of the room consists of a central square flanked by two oblong panels, and is linked to the larger portion by a mosaic panel of *peltae* connecting the inner ends of two short, projecting cross-walls ; while the larger portion of the room is a square with a central circle surrounded by four half-circles, although the corners of the square are filled with small squares, in place of the quarter-circles used at Hinton St. Mary, and one side of the square throws off an apse, with the well-known instance of the Chi-Rho monogram placed in the centre of the running floral scroll in the narrow panel on its chord. The lay-out of this Frampton pavement shows an asymmetry similar to that on the new mosaic, with one small filling panel in the same position in the smaller portion of the room.

The close correspondence between the schemes of these two compositions, combined with the similarities in style and content shown by the Hinton St. Mary mosaic and all three mosaics at Frampton, suggests the possibility that the same firm of mosaicists was responsible for the pavements on both of these Dorset sites. Most of the similarities in details will be mentioned later. But at this point it may be noted that the method of merging two converging bands of guilloche is the same on the Frampton pavements as on the pavement at Hinton St. Mary. It is, furthermore, interesting to observe that the general scheme of the eastern portion of the new mosaic and the style of its running floral scrolls are closely paralleled on one of the mosaics from the villa at Fifehead Neville (some 3½ miles south of Hinton St. Mary, and also the source of two rings bearing the Chi-Rho monogram), a mosaic now lost, but known to us from drawings. Those mosaics, too, may be the same firm's work.

We turn now to the subjects of the pictures that occupy the two roundels, the four half-circles, the four quarter-circles, and the two oblong panels of the Hinton St. Mary mosaic.

In the roundel of the eastern portion (frontispiece) is the bust, facing east, worked with especial care, and very well preserved, of a fair-haired, clean-shaven man with dark, rather penetrating eyes. He is heavily draped in an inner and an outer garment, *tunica* and *pallium*, and has the Chi-Rho monogram behind his head and a pomegranate in the field on either side of him. Four of the strokes of the monogram terminate in serifs ; but the mosaicist has omitted to put in a serif at the bottom of the stroke of the Chi on the spectator's left. The man's hair is combed forward on to the brow in straight, neat strands and it falls in curly locks, with red shading, on either side of the neck. The drapery is coloured orange, white, black, grey, and purple. The man has a slightly cleft chin, as have also the four male busts each of which occupies one of the quarter-circles. These busts, which face outwards, have each one garment only, a cloak fastened by a brooch on the right shoulder and leaving one, somewhat wizened, arm exposed. The cloaks are bright red and so is the four men's hair, which shows in each case three or four upstanding, wind-blown locks on the crown of the head. Two of these busts have two large, red, rosette-like flowers in the field, one on either side (pl. v, 2) ; the other two busts have, in the same positions, two pomegranates (pl. v, 1). The bust in the north-west quarter-circle is slightly smaller than the rest and was not, perhaps, by the same hand as that which worked the other three busts. In the half-circle immediately below the central bust is a large, spreading tree with grey-blue leaves (pl. iv, 3). In each of the other three half-circles is an animal-hunt scene enacted in a setting of trees with grey-blue leaves—on the south, a dog confronting a stag, on the west, a dog pursuing a stag (pl. iv, 1), on the north, a dog pursuing a hind (pl. iv, 2). All the dogs wear collars.

In the roundel in the western portion of the pavement (pl. i) is the scene, facing west, of Bellerophon on Pegasus galloping towards the right and thrusting with his spear at the goat's head emerging from the centre of the back of the lion-headed, serpent-tailed Chimaera which also speeds rightwards. Both the horse and the monster are vigorously drawn. Pegasus has a flowing mane and a feathery tail. There are now no traces of his wings, if, indeed, this mosaicist ever gave him any. The Chimaera's mane is rendered by alternating

---

[1] S. Lysons, *Reliquiae Britannico-Romanae* i (1813), pl. 5. For the present position as regards the Frampton pavements, see *Proceedings of the Dorset Natural History and Archaeological Society* LXXVIII, 1956 (1957), 81–3.

HINTON ST. MARY, DORSET: PANEL OF FOURTH-CENTURY MOSAIC PAVEMENT SHOWING BELLEROPHON SLAYING THE CHIMAERA (see p. 8)

Photograph by Royal Commission on Historical Monuments, England. Copyright W. J. White

PLATE II

HINTON ST. MARY, DORSET : E. PORTION OF PAVEMENT, WITH SCALE IN FEET (see p. 7)
Photograph by Royal Commission on Historical Monuments, England. Copyright W. J. White

PLATE III

HINTON ST. MARY, DORSET : W. PORTION OF PAVEMENT, WITH SCALES IN FEET (see p. 7)
Photograph by Royal Commission on Historical Monuments, England. Copyright W. J. White

HINTON ST. MARY, DORSET : THREE OF THE FOUR HALF-CIRCLES ON THE E. PORTION OF THE PAVEMENT (see p. 8)

Photographs by Royal Commission on Historical Monuments, England. Copyright W. J. White

HINTON ST. MARY, DORSET : (1, 2) TWO OF THE FOUR QUARTER-CIRCLES IN E. PORTION OF MOSAIC ; (3) PANEL S.
OF BELLEROPHON IN W. PORTION OF MOSAIC (see pp. 8, 10)

Photographs by Royal Commission on Historical Monuments, England. Copyright W. J. White

PLATE VI

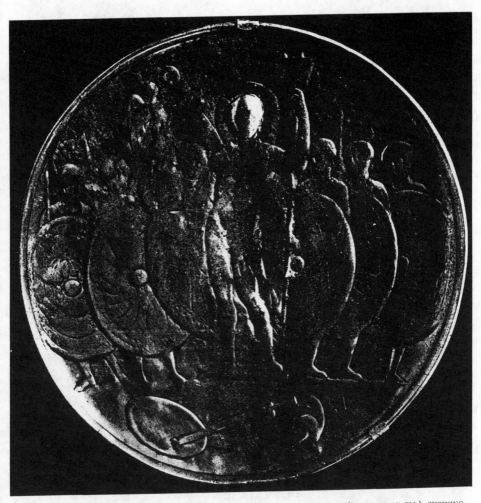

MUSÉE D'ART ET D'HISTOIRE, GENEVA : FOURTH- OR FIFTH-CENTURY SILVER PLATE (DIAMETER 27 CM.), SHOWING EMPEROR WITH NIMBUS BEARING CHI-RHO BETWEEN ALPHA AND OMEGA (INV. NO. C1241) (see p. 11)

Photograph by courtesy of Musée d'art et d'histoire, Geneva. Copyright reserved

345

(1) METROPOLITAN MUSEUM OF ART, NEW YORK : FRAGMENT OF FOURTH-CENTURY GOLD-GLASS MEDALLION SHOWING DRAPED BUST (PROBABLY ST. LAURENCE) WITH CHI-RHO BEHIND HIS HEAD (INV. NO. 18. 145. 3). (2) BRITISH MUSEUM, LONDON : FOURTH-CENTURY GOLD-GLASS MEDALLION WITH BUST OF YOUTHFUL CHRIST BETWEEN FOUR OTHERS. (3) S. SABINA, ROME : PANEL OF FIFTH-CENTURY WOODEN DOOR, SHOWING CHRIST WITH CHI-RHO BEHIND HIS HEAD, BETWEEN ALPHA AND OMEGA. (4) S. LORENZO, MILAN : FIGURE OF CHRIST WITH NIMBUS BEARING CHI-RHO BETWEEN ALPHA AND OMEGA, ON FIFTH-CENTURY MOSAIC ON THE VAULT OF CAPPELLA DI S. AQUILINO (see pp. 12, 13).

Photographs by courtesy (1) *of Metropolitan Museum,* (2) *of Trustees of the British Museum,*
(3) *of Foto Anderson. Copyright reserved*

FIG. I. HINTON ST. MARY, DORSET : SIMPLIFIED DIAGRAM OF DECORATIVE SCHEME OF PAVEMENT red and white lozenges. The head and chest of Bellerophon have been so badly worn that only their outlines can now be discerned ; and in ancient times a large, flat stone was placed as the filling of an ugly gash where his waist and abdomen should be. The hero seems to be naked save for a flying cloak. In the panel to the north of Bellerophon a hound, wearing a collar, chases a stag towards the right amid trees ; in the panel to the south of him a hound, again collared, pursues, again through trees, this time leftwards, a stag and a hind (pl. v, 3). These hunting-scenes, like those in the eastern portion of the pavement, are distinguished by a lively and naturalistic style.

The colours and materials used in this mosaic are (1) yellow, red, orange, purple, and fawn of baked tile of very fine texture ; (2) black, grey, white, blue, coarse buff, and grey-blue of stone. There are also (1) a sandy tile used in the Chimaera ; (2) a grey-blue tile used for the tip of Bellerophon's spear and for the setting of the brooch of the bust in the south-east quarter-circle.

The only other certain instance of Bellerophon slaying the Chimaera on a pavement from Roman Britain is that in the fourth-century *triclinium* of the villa at Lullingstone in Kent.[2] The scene in the central roundel of the larger portion of the Frampton Chi-Rho pavement would seem to be that of a hunter pursuing a lion or panther, not that of Bellerophon spearing the Chimaera ; for the back and the rear line of the neck of this feline are shown in Lysons's drawing (assuming it to be correct) as well preserved and there is no trace of a goat's head sprouting from the centre of the back. On the other hand, it is difficult to explain the elongated yellow feature in front of the right leg of the rider except as the beginning of one wing of Pegasus ; and if this were Bellerophon, again associated with a Chi-Rho, it would indeed be interesting. The Hinton St. Mary hunting scenes, of animals without human hunters, are closely paralleled by the scene in a panel on one of the Frampton mosaics.[3] There, too, the central roundel in the smaller portion of the pavement has much the same borders, of wave, plait, and fret patterns, as those that surround the Chi-Rho bust at Hinton St. Mary. The four busts in the quarter-circles of the latter pavement recall the two sets of four busts of Wind Personifications on two of the Frampton mosaics. On one of these the winds have red hair and cleft chins, but are naked and equipped with head-wings and conches ;[4] in the other set they are again naked and furnished with conches, but they are without head-wings and have red hair with upstanding, wind-blown locks very similar to those of the Hinton St. Mary busts.[5] It would seem that these new busts are basically modelled on Wind Personifications, but with rosettes and pomegranates as adjuncts substituted for the usual Wind attributes. For the great spreading tree in a scene all to itself I know of no mosaic parallel of fourth- or fifth-century date. But a sixth-century mosaic pavement in the cemetery church at Teurnia (St. Peter-im-Holz) in Austria has in one of its central panels a much more stylised solitary tree with birds perched on and below its branches ; and a fourth-century Eucharistic silver spoon found at Cologne has engraved on the interior of its bowl an extremely stylised tree with a Eucharistic loaf at its foot.[6]

The general style of the Hinton St. Mary mosaic indicates that it was laid during the fourth century, to which period most rural figured pavements in Britain of comparable elaboration do, in fact, belong. This dating is confirmed by the scale and the position of the Chi-Rho monogram as rendered in the central eastern roundel. It is, of course, well known that symbols like, and even identical with, the Chi-Rho monogram were in use in pre-Christian times and that the monogram appeared before, and even, perhaps, occasionally during and after, the Constantinian era in pagan contexts as an abbreviation or ligature for, or in, Greek words beginning with, or containing, the letter X and P juxtaposed—χρηστός, χρεωφύλαξ, ἄρχων, to cite some known examples.[7] It was, then, only natural that the Christians should have adopted that sign as an abbreviation of Χριστός. The Chi-Rho is found in a few third-century Christian inscriptions in Asia Minor ;[8] and it must have been

[2] G. W. Meates, *Lullingstone Roman Villa* (1955), pls. 3, 7.
[3] Lysons, o.c. (n. 1), pl. 4.
[4] ibid.
[5] Lysons, o.c. (n. 1), pl. 7.
[6] Teurnia mosaic: R. Egger, *Teurnia* (ed. 3, 1963), 35, fig. 7 ; Cologne spoon: F. Witte, *Die*

liturgischen Geräte der Sammlung Schnütgen in Cöln (1913), pl. 13, fig. 9.
[7] e.g. F. Cabrol and H. Leclercq, *Dictionnaire d'Archéologie Chrétienne et de Liturgie* III, 1 (1948), s.v. *Chrisme*, cols. 1481–4 ; *JRS* XVI (1926), 74.
[8] ibid., 73–74.

current among Christians in the West before 313, when the persecutions ended and Christianity could be openly professed. There is, indeed, a Christian Latin epitaph from Rome with the consular date 269, which bears the ☧ ligature of the initial letters, I and X, of Ἰησοῦς Χριστός, and other undated epitaphs containing the ☧ ligature and coming from the oldest galleries in the Roman catacombs have, with good reason, been assigned to the third century.[9] It was obviously because he knew it to be in Christian use that Constantine I, when he decided to seek the patronage of Christ, adopted the monogram as his official badge, on his own helmet (in both the ✗ and the ☧ form) [10] and on the shields of his soldiers and on the *labarum*, his own imperial standard (in the ☧ form)—whatever truth or untruth may lie behind the story of the emperor's vision. From that moment onwards the monogram became ubiquitous in Christian inscriptions, on Christian works of art, and as an emblem on the coins, medallions, etc., of Christian emperors. It was, in fact, normally recognized throughout the Christian Roman Empire as standing specifically for Χριστός. Like many other Christian symbols and motifs the Chi-Rho had a pre-Christian origin. But I cannot quote any rendering in art of an unequivocally pagan person with the monogram behind his head. The new mosaic must have belonged to a Christian *milieu*.

It is important to remember that by the fourth century the representation in art of the traditional Graeco-Roman myths, gods, and personifications and of many motifs from daily life (such as hunting scenes) had increasingly tended to assume an allegorical and quasi-religious meaning. This is particularly evident in the sphere of funerary iconography. But there can be little doubt that the selection of themes for domestic paintings, mosaics, and other forms of decoration was not infrequently determined by ideas concerning death and the life beyond the grave, to which a spiritual rebirth in this world forms the prelude. Such ideas are likely to have lain behind the choice for the Hinton St. Mary mosaic of the Bellerophon story, of the Wind Personifications, of the great tree, and of the hunting scenes ; and it is in the light of its place in a context of this kind that we should interpret the most important and the most impressive of all the figure-subjects on the pavement—the bust with the Chi-Rho behind his head. Who is he ?

Could the bust be that of some local Christian person ? Portraits which are probably those of donors occur on fourth-century mosaic pavements in the one-time cathedral and in private house-oratories at Aquileia.[11] Those in the former cathedral show men and women of various ages ; one of the private oratory portraits depicts a youthful woman. None of these has the monogram behind the head. The Chi-Rho seen behind the head of an imperial bodyguardsman wearing civilian dress, on a fifth-century ivory diptych in the Museo Civico at Bologna, turns out to be the device on his shield, of which the upper rim is clearly visible.[12] I do not know of any rendering in early Christian art of an ordinary Christian, clerical or lay, dead or living, with an independent Chi-Rho monogram in this position.

Could the bust be that of a Christian emperor ? The rather heavy face and neck, and the somewhat bold and confident expression, might, indeed, suggest that the mosaicist had used as his model some imperial portrait ; and I know of one work of art, the silver plate of fourth- or fifth-century date in the Museum of History and Art at Geneva, on which an emperor, identified by some as Valentinian I or II, is shown with the Chi-Rho on the nimbus behind his head, presumably in his capacity as Christ's vice-gerent in the realm of secular government (pl. VI).[13] But whereas the emperor on the plate appears in a wholly political setting, surrounded by his bodyguard, the setting of the bust on the mosaic is, as

---

[9] e.g. Cabrol and Leclercq, o.c. (n. 7), cols. 1483–1492.

[10] e.g. *JRS* XXII (1932), II, pl. IV, no. 17 (bronze coin from the Siscia mint) ; H. Kähler, *Rome and her Empire* (' Art of the World ' series, 1963), 212 (silver medallion, from the Ticinum mint, at Munich).

[11] G. Brusin and P. L. Zovatto, *Monumenti paleocristiani di Aquileia e di Grado* (1957), figs. 34–36, 92, 92a, pls. 3, 6.

[12] R. Delbrueck, *Die Consulardiptychen* (1929), no. 47.

[13] R. Delbrueck, *Spätantike Kaiserporträts* (1933), pl. 79. The letters A and ω flanking the monogram are invisible on photographs, but are said to exist on the original (*Schweizerische Altertumskunde* XXII,

1920, 26, n. 2). The Chi-Rho, flanked by A and ω, above the head of a child emperor being crowned by two senior emperors on a gem in Leningrad (*Germania* XIV, 1930, 38–39 with fig. ; Delbrueck, o.c., pl. 111, fig. 1) does not designate the boy as assimilated to Christ as His vice-gerent—if it did, the senior emperors would surely have been shown with it too : it simply means that the whole scene is taking place under the patronage of Christ, who looks down in symbolic guise, as it were from heaven, on the ceremony. Similarly, on the bronze roundel from Richborough depicting an emperor, probably Magnentius (*Richborough* IV, 1949, 140–1, pl. 42, no. 171), with a large Chi-Rho above his raised right hand (not, I think, held in his hand, as the text says, we have seen, mythological and allegorical, with no particular relevance to an emperor. Again, the emperor on the plate wears the imperial military costume, as Constantine I, for instance, does on many of his portraits, whether in the round or on coins and medallions, his portrait on a *solidus* of the Ticinum mint, struck *c.* 315, in the Ashmolean Museum, Oxford, being one of many examples.[14] The mosaic bust, on the other hand, has not only no imperial insignia, such as a diadem, a laurel-wreath, a globe, or a sceptre, but also no imperial dress, whether military or ceremonial: it does not wear a cuirass and *paludamentum* nor a *toga picta* and *tunica palmata*, in which emperors are frequently arrayed, as on a gold medallion of Constantine I, of the Trier mint, in Stockholm.[15] Furthermore, I do not know of any rendering of an emperor with pomegranates, well-known symbols of immortality, as his adjuncts or with a large tree associated with him. Finally, I can cite no certain representation of an emperor on a mosaic floor. The popular identification as Maximianus of the principal figure in the central group in the ' Great Hunt ' mosaic in the villa near Piazza Armerina in Sicily [16] has been vigorously disputed and is, to my mind, untenable. A. Ragona's view that these mosaics date from the second half of the fourth century and that this personage is Claudius Mamertinus, Prefect of the West under Julian the Apostate, has much to commend it [17]—if, indeed, the owner of the villa was not, as I myself am inclined (in the light of the prevailing content of these figured pavements) to think that he may have been, a man who had made an enormous fortune by supplying the arenas of the Roman world with performers in wild beast hunts and shows and in other spectacles of an athletic or dramatic character. Nor am I at all convinced by H. Kähler's attempt to identify the busts on the floor of the fourth-century Aquileia cathedral as those of Constantine I and members of his family.[18] His so-called Constantine [19] does not strike me as bearing much resemblance to that emperor ; and his so-called Fausta [20] seems to me to be wearing an embroidered veil, not an empress's diadem. The dresses of these men and women appear to me to indicate that they were, not imperial personages, but members of some aristocratic, consular family. Taking everything into consideration, I believe that the interpretation of the Hinton St. Mary bust as that of a Christian emperor is unlikely to be the right one. The bust must be that of a religious figure.

Could it be that of a Christian saint ? Three renderings of saints in early Christian art with the monogram behind the head are known to me. Among the fifth-century paintings in the Naples catacombs is the figure of St. Januarius standing in the Orans attitude, with his name inscribed above him and the Chi-Rho accompanied by A and ω on his nimbus.[21] A fragmentary gold-glass medallion of fourth-century date in the Metropolitan Museum of Art, New York, shows the draped bust of a man holding a long cross, flanked by A and ω, and with the Chi-Rho, without a nimbus, as at Hinton St. Mary, behind his head (pl. VII, 1) : from the inscription LAVRENTIO beside him the natural (but not certain) inference is that the person depicted is not Christ, but the martyr St. Laurence.[22] Again, on the lid of a sixth-century circular silver pyx in the Cathedral Treasury at Grado the Blessed Virgin

since there seems to be a gap between it and the fingers), the monogram merely indicates his Christian allegiance. The setting of the scene on the Leningrad gem, at any rate, would appear to be politico-historical. But neither on the gem nor on the roundel is the use of the Chi-Rho parallel to the use of it on the Geneva plate ; and neither work supports the notion that the Dorset mosaic bust represents an emperor. (I should like to thank Mr. Martin Biddle, of Exeter University, for suggesting to me that the Leningrad gem ought to be mentioned in the context of the Hinton St. Mary pavement). A position similar to that of the Chi-Rho on the Leningrad gem, and a similar significance, must be assumed for the σωτήριον σημεῖον which Eusebius (*Vita Constantini* III, 3) describes as *above* (ὑπερκείμενον) the head of Constantine in a picture of him displayed at the entrance to the imperial residence. It is clear that in this passage, as in several others, Eusebius was thinking, not of the monogram, but of the Cross—erroneously, it seems, since Lactantius (*De morte persecutorum* XLIV, 5-6) states that Constantine's sign was the monogram ; and it is the monogram, not the Cross, that normally appears in fourth-century

Christian art and inscriptions. We cannot, of course, check the accuracy of Eusebius' description of the picture ; and in any case, this passage offers no support to the view that the mosaic bust is that of Constantine.

[14] M. Alföldi, *Die constantinische Goldprägung* (1963), pl. 5, no. 68.
[15] J. M. C. Toynbee, *Roman Medallions* (1944), pl. 4, fig. 3.
[16] e.g. G. V. Gentili, *La villa erculia di Piazza Armerina* (1962).
[17] *Il proprietario della villa romana di Piazza Armerina* (1962).
[18] *Die Stiftermosaiken in der konstantinischen Suedkirche von Aquileia* (1962).
[19] Brusin and Zovatto, o.c. (n. 11), pl. 3.
[20] ibid., 81, fig. 35.
[21] C. M. Kaufmann, *Handbuch der christlichen Archäologie* (ed. 3, 1922), 396, fig. 184 ; *Enciclopedia Cattolica* VI (1951), pl. 2.
[22] C. R. Morey (ed. G. Ferrari), *The Gold-Glass Collection of the Vatican Library* (1959), 75, no. 460, pl. 36.

is enthroned facing the spectator, with the Child on her lap, a cross-sceptre in her right hand, and the ✗ form of the sacred monogram on her nimbus.[23] In all these three cases (assuming that the gold-glass does represent St. Laurence) the identity of the saint in question is unequivocally indicated, the saint having 'put on Christ' and being thus assimilated to Him. But the bust on the mosaic has no inscription and no feature to identify it as that of some particular saint ; and the conclusion would seem to be that the bust is that of the Person for whom the Chi-Rho properly stands in a religious context, namely Christ Himself.

A number of renderings of Christ with the monogram behind the head normally, but not always, on a nimbus, can be found in the art of the fourth and fifth centuries. In a fourth- or fifth-century painting in the Roman catacomb of SS. Peter and Marcellinus Christ has the ρ form on his nimbus.[24] The ✗ form appears on the nimbus of a medallion bust of Him on a silver flagon in the Vatican Library (Museo Sacro), dating from the second half of the fifth century ; [25] on the nimbus of figures of Him on three fifth-century sarco-phagi at Ravenna, one in the Museo Nazionale,[26] one in the Cathedral,[27] and one in the church of San Vitale (Adoration of the Magi) ; [28] and on the nimbus of a figure of Him on a fourth- to fifth-century sarcophagus in the Cathedral at Ferrara.[29] The vault mosaic, generally assigned to the middle of the fifth century, in the Cappella di Sant' Aquilino in the church of San Lorenzo at Milan shows Christ with the Chi-Rho and A and ⍵ on a species of ' open-work ' nimbus, with the golden background showing through the spaces between the letters and the circle that contains them (pl. VII, 4).[30] One of the panels of the fifth-century wooden doors of the church of Santa Sabina in Rome depicts a bearded Christ addressing three Apostles, with the Chi-Rho and A and ⍵ behind His head, this time without a nimbus (pl. VII, 3), as at Hinton St. Mary.[31] And the same form of Chi-Rho with A and ⍵, again without a nimbus, appears behind the head of the centrally placed bust on the Pontia sarcophagus in the Palazzo Comunale at Terni : here the face is entirely, the body largely, destroyed, but the figure holds an open book and is very likely to be Christ.[32] It is true that most of these monuments are of the fifth, not of the fourth, century. But there are certainly more known examples of Christ with the Chi-Rho behind the head than there are of any other type of person with the monogram in that position.

The treatment of the hair on the Hinton St. Mary bust can be paralleled in representa-tions of Christ on fourth- and fifth-century works of art, for example, on a fourth-century gold-glass medallion in the British Museum, where the main, central bust is clearly labelled CRISTVS (sic) and has the hair combed forward neatly on to the brow and falling on either side of the neck in curly locks somewhat more luxuriant than those on the mosaic (pl. VII, 2) : the four smaller, inward-facing busts, which surround Christ, are possibly intended to represent the Four Evangelists.[33] The garments worn by the mosaic bust, tunica and pallium, are normally those of Christ in the art of this epoch, although the mosaicist does not seem to have completely understood how the folds of the pallium should go. The bust's iconography is thus wholly consistent with the interpretation of it as Christ, despite the fact that its facial features are less refined and gentle than those of most con-temporary ' portraits ' of Him ; and this interpretation is supported by the two pome-granates, recognized symbols of eternal life (cf. p. 8), in the field on either side of the bust. Whether or no the artist consciously borrowed for his bust the features of some imperial portrait (cf. p. 11) is a question that we obviously cannot answer : nor does it affect the issue.

The most serious objection that can be urged against the interpretation of the Hinton St. Mary bust as Christ is the apparent unsuitability of placing a rendering of Him on the floor, where it risked being trodden on. I must admit that I cannot quote any other ' straight ' representation of Christ on a mosaic pavement. But at Aquileia there are no fewer than three renderings of the Good Shepherd on mosaic pavements—one in what was

[23] *Aquileia Nostra* XXIV–XXV (1953–54), fig. on p. 119.

[24] J. Wilpert, *Die Malereien der Katakomben Roms* (1903), pls. 252, 253.

[25] *Art Bulletin* XX (1938), 195, fig. 1.

[26] W. F. Volbach, *Early Christian Art* (1961), no. 176.

[27] ibid., no. 177.

[28] ibid., no. 179.

[29] *Studi Romani* II (1914–15), 402, pl. 24, fig. 1.

[30] Volbach, o.c. (n. 26), no. 138.

[31] *Rivista di Archeologia Cristiana* XXXVII (1961), 43, pl. 30 ; Alinari photo. no. 27591.

[32] R. Garrucci, *Storia della arte cristiana* V (1879), pl. 401, fig. 6.

[33] Morey, o.c. (n. 22), 52–53, no. 305, pl. 29.

once the fourth-century cathedral, where He appears in peasant guise and with a sheep on His shoulders, as in catacomb paintings and on sarcophagi ; [34] the second, badly damaged, in a fourth-century private oratory (the so-called Oratorio del Fondo della Cal), where He is shown in the same peasant costume, but with two sheep at His feet ; [35] the third, also of the fourth century in an aristocratic private house (known as del Fondo Cossar).[36] Although it could be argued that these are not direct, but symbolic, representations, it is clear that this third Good Shepherd was quite explicitly intended to portray Christ. Here the Shepherd has a blue nimbus and wears the richly embroidered, pearl-edged tunic, the purple, pearl-edged mantle, the blue leggings, and the patrician shoes that mark Him out as *Dominus*. His right hand originally held a *syrinx*, the tip of which remains ; but this hand was subsequently altered and the Shepherd now makes with it the gesture of greeting or benediction. There is, moreover, the decree of the emperors Theodosius and Valentinian, dated 427, forbidding the rendering of the Cross on mosaic floors and ordering the removal of any such renderings as already existed : [37] ' signum Salvatoris Christi nemini licere vel solo in silice vel in marmoribus humi positis insculpere vel pingere, sed quodcumque reperitur tolli.' This text implies that the Cross had appeared on mosaic pavements at an earlier date (if, indeed, *signum Salvatoris Christi* means the Cross, and not the Chi-Rho monogram)—and, if the Cross (or monogram), perhaps occasionally a ' straight' portrayal of Christ. It is at any rate probable that the Roman building and mosaic at Hinton St. Mary would have been abandoned before the decree was promulgated. If not, news of the decree could easily, at that date, have failed to penetrate to Dorset.

If the Hinton St. Mary bust be accepted as being probably that of Christ, the other motifs on the pavement fall into place in His context, when we recall the kind of significance that they would bear on many funerary and some domestic monuments (cf. p. 11). Bellerophon slaying the Chimaera would be an allegory of the overcoming of death and evil, a Christianized pagan allegory drawn from that traditional storehouse of Graeco-Roman mythology that was the fourth-century Christian's cultural heritage. And it is of interest to remember that in the Lullingstone villa the Christian paintings (the three Chi-Rhos and the Orans, etc. figures) were in a room adjacent to that in which was laid the Bellerophon mosaic and that the paintings and the mosaic were probably contemporary.[38] The animal hunting scenes would allude to the natural world as created by God or to the teeming life of paradise : the dogs chase, but do not wound, the stags and hinds. The great tree immediately below the bust could be the Tree of Life. The four corner busts would seem to be ' played down ' versions of the pagan Wind Personifications, their rosettes and pomegranates being emblems of life and immortality. Could there possibly be in these busts some suggestion of the Four Evangelists, whose Gospels are carried to the earth's four corners ? St. Irenaeus, writing *c*. 185, related the number of the Gospels to that of the number of the four main winds and of the earth's four regions, to which is wafted the life-giving message of the word of God.[39] The whole scheme of the eastern portion of the pavement could be regarded as the reflection of a ' dome of heaven ' ceiling design, with a central roundel, groins, lunettes, and squinches, projected on to the floor of the chamber. This would give an appropriate setting for the bust of Christ as Cosmocrator in the centre of the vault of heaven, with the winds at the world's four corners.[40]

To sum up, Hinton St. Mary would seem to enjoy the distinction of having yielded the earliest representation of Christ so far known to have been made in Britain.

Oxford

Postscriptum. We must not wholly overlook the possibility that the two portions of the Hinton St. Mary room, which face in opposite directions and between which a curtain could have been suspended, belonged respectively to Christian and pagan members of the same family, each group honouring its own saviour (here Christ or Bellerophon), as may have been the case with the two adjacent chambers O and N at the end of the new fourth-century Via Latina catacomb, the one with Christian, the other with pagan (Herculean) paintings (A. Ferrua, *Le pitture della nuova catacomba di Via Latina*, 1960 ; M. Simon in *Mullus : Festschrift Theodor Klauser*, 1964, 327–35).

[34] Brusin and Zovatto, o.c. (n. 11), 91, fig. 38.
[35] ibid. 210, figs. 92, 92a.
[36] *Fasti Archaeologici* XIII (1960), pl. 37, fig. 107 (no. 6502) ; G. Brusin, *Due nuovi sacelli cristiani di Aquileia* (1961).

[37] *Corpus Iuris Civilis* II : *Codex Iustinianus* i, 8.
[38] See n. 2 above.
[39] *Adversus Haereses* III, xi, 8.
[40] I owe this suggestion to Mr. Manfred Bräude of the Museum of Classical Archaeology, Cambridge.

Joseph Iconography on Coptic Textiles

GARY VIKAN
Dumbarton Oaks

FIGURE 1. *Joseph Roundel; Pushkin Museum, Moscow.*

FIGURE 2. *Joseph Roundel; The Metropolitan Museum of Art, New York.*

Much of what we know of the actual appearance of early Christian garments we owe to the dry climate of Egypt and to the conservative burial practices of the Copts, which together have preserved for us tens of thousands of tunics, tunic fragments, and embroidered tunic decorations dating from the Late Roman period into Islamic times.[1] Yet surprisingly, a survey of this vast body of material reveals that Coptic weavers, like Coptic sculptors, only occasionally chose Christian figurative subjects, and even more rarely attempted to organize those subjects into multi-scene, narrative compositions.[2] One Old Testament hero, however, does stand out for the frequency with which he appears on Coptic textiles and for the almost unique narrative breadth of his portrayal: the Patriarch Joseph.[3] The same basic nine-scene Joseph cycle recurs on an extensive, though closely-interrelated series of plied-warp woolen roundels and rectangles, the former of which were customarily attached near the hem or at the shoulder of a linen tunic and the latter on the sleeve.[4] Usually dated between the sixth and eighth centuries, and characterized by brilliant colors and strong, highly abstract designs,

these textiles differ from one another only in their relative degree of stylization and in the completeness of their cycles. One of the most naturalistic and well-preserved of the group is textile 5174 in the Pushkin Museum, Moscow (Fig. 1),[5] while somewhat more abstract and angular (and reversed left to right) is textile 63.178.2 in the Metropolitan Museum, New York (Fig. 2).[6]

Both textiles show the complete nine-scene cycle beginning in the central medallion and continuing from the top center around the circle – clockwise for the Moscow roundel and counter-clockwise for that in New York. 1. *Joseph's Dreams (Genesis 37.5-7, 9):* Joseph's second prophetic dream is clearly portrayed in both central medallions. The sun and moon, as stylized faces, and rows of triangular stars (eleven in Moscow but only five in New York) pay hommage to Joseph as he lies sleeping on a large mattress. For evidence of the first dream we must turn to yet another roundel, that in the Städtisches Museum, Trier, which in its relative naturalism

99

*GESTA XVIII/*1 © The International Center of Medieval Art 1979

FIGURE 3. *Joseph's two dreams; detail of a roundel in the Städtisches Museum, Trier.*

and state of preservation is equal to the Moscow textile (Fig. 3).[7] In the central medallion of the Trier roundel, just above Joseph's feet, may be seen eleven small squares – undoubtedly an allusion to the eleven symbolic sheaves of grain which make obeisance to Joseph (Genesis 37.7). By extension, the semicircular form just above the center of Joseph's body (with two white squares) is probably his sheaf, toward which the others bow. 2. *Joseph's Departure for Shechem (Genesis 37.13-14):* At the top center of both roundels is the nimbed, bearded figure of Jacob seated on a cushioned throne (facing right in Moscow and left in New York). He raises his hand in speech toward his nimbed son Joseph who, already having turned to depart, looks back over his shoulder. Actually, two closely-sequential phases of the same narrative context are here combined: Jacob's Instruction to Joseph (Genesis 37.13-14), and Joseph's Departure for Shechem (Genesis 37.14).[8] 3. *Joseph's Arrival to His Brothers (Genesis 37.17-18):* The same figure of Joseph plays the central role in a second, "conflated" episode of the story, for while looking back at his father in Hebron he raises his right hand to greet the foremost of his brothers in Dothan – obviously a physical impossibility. That brother, who extends a hand to receive Joseph, has long black hair and supports a staff over his shoulder. Here, as in the next four scenes, the limited space of the roundel has forced the weaver to eliminate all but one of Joseph's brothers.[9] 4. *Joseph is Removed from the Well (Genesis 37.28):* Joseph, nude save for a flying cape around his neck, is being drawn up from a high masonry well by a single brother who grasps him by the wrist.[10] 5. *Joseph's Coat is Stained with Blood (Genesis 37.31):* Although the weavers have obviously misunderstood and corrupted this scene, its essential elements can still be recognized, especially in the Moscow textile. One brother, wearing a short, dark garment, lowers himself onto one knee while holding a highly-

abstracted goat (?) over the other knee (note the eye, ear, and muzzle in Fig. 1). A second brother, incongruously given light hair and a nimbus like Joseph, stands opposite holding forth the cloak which, we must assume, is being stained with blood dripping from an unseen wound. 6. *Joseph is Sold to the Ishmaelite Traders (Genesis 37.28):* A black Ishmaelite with a pointed hat sits to one side looking at a single brother who stands opposite, one arm raised in speech and the other grasping a staff. Between them is the diminutive figure of Joseph. Standing frontally, he looks back toward his brother while extending his arms toward the Ishmalite's knees 7. *Reuben's Lamentation (Genesis 37.29):* Reuben, returning to an empty well, rents the clothes from his chest. Surprisingly, he looks not at the well but rather away, back toward the preceding scene. 8. *Joseph is Brought Down to Egypt (Genesis 37.28; 39.1):* Seated behind an Ishmalite on a highly-stylized camel (?) Joseph turns, extending his arms emphatically – assumedly back toward his brothers. 9. *Joseph is Sold to Potiphar (Genesis 37.35; 39.1):* Potiphar, seated to one side, raises an arm to pass money over the head of Joseph who stands before him, his arms extended toward the knees of his new master. Opposite, a black Ishmaelite with a spear in one hand extends an arm to receive payment.

The foregoing analysis has shown that the nine scenes customarily found on Coptic Joseph textiles actually evoke eleven distinct episodes from the 37th chapter of Genesis, since both dream one (of the sheaves) and dream two (of the stars) are combined in the first scene, and the instruction and departure of Joseph are combined in the second. A narrative picture cycle of such density (eleven episodes to only the first of thirteen Joseph chapters!) was not likely invented within the context of mass-produced textiles for the ornamentation of clothing; in fact, the corruption of scene 5 suggests that the weavers understood little of what they were portraying. Rather, one would suspect that such a cycle originated in a more favorable medium, of which, as Kurt Weitzmann has shown, manuscript illumination would be the most likely candidate.[11] Forty years ago Ernst Kitzinger published a short article devoted to Coptic Joseph Textiles wherein he concluded that it was impossible to demonstrate an iconographic link between them and any of the famous medieval Joseph cycles; indeed, he went on to reiterate J.J. Tikkanen's much earlier contention that no distinctive iconographic groupings could be established among the illustrations of Joseph's youth in Early Christian Art.[11a] Weitzmann has been able to distinguish at least four independent iconographic traditions for the illustration of the book of Genesis, and, more specifically, for the story of Joseph.[12] These traditions are exemplified by the Cotton Genesis (and the closely-related mosaics in the Basilica of San Marco),[13] the Vienna Genesis,[14] the illustrated Middle Byzantine Octateuchs,[15] and by the Joseph page in the famous Paris Gregory Nazianzenus manuscript, codex 510.[16] Whether our Joseph textile cycle may be linked to any one of these traditions is, of course, quite another question. In order

100

FIGURE 4. *Joseph's two dreams; detail of a mosaic in San Marco, Venice.*

FIGURE 5. *Joseph's departure for Shechem; tracing from British Library cod. Cotton Otho. BIV f.73r, London.*

to establish such a bond, two conditions must be satisfied: first, the four known recensions must be iconographically distinguishable in a significant number of the episodes found on the textiles; and second, the textiles' cycle must show a pattern of iconographic agreement with one tradition to the exclusion of the others.

Scene 1, Joseph's Dreams: In the mosaic cycle at San Marco, as in our textile cycle, Joseph's two dreams are combined into a single composition which marks the beginning of the narrative (Figs. 3, 4).[17] Joseph lies frontally on a large mattress with his symbolic sheaf centered over his body and those of his eleven brothers over his feet. Finally, as in our textiles, the sun and moon at San Marco are evoked by a pair of faces which, along with the eleven stars, are suspended over the mattress.[18] By contrast, the Vienna Genesis manuscript narrates the dreams in successive miniatures, begins its cycle with an earlier phase of the story, aligns the symbolic sheaves in a single row on the ground beside Joseph's bead, and evokes the sun and moon by busts and not by faces.[19] The Octateuchs, on the other hand, show Joseph *relating* his dreams to his brothers, but not actually in bed dreaming; moreover, the arc of heaven is in the upper right background of the miniature and the sheaves are spread out over a hillock.[20] The Paris Gregory, finally, begins its Joseph cycle not with the dreams sequence but rather with the departure for Shechem.[21]

Scene 2, Joseph's Departure for Shechem: Like our Coptic textiles, the illustrated Octateuchs provide evidence of both moments of the action; Joseph receives his instructions, and Joseph turns to depart.[22] And like almost every visualization of the episode, Jacob sits at the left while Joseph stands (or walks) at the right. The Octateuchs differ basically from the textiles, however, by the fact that Benjamin is shown standing at Jacob's knee. Joseph's youngest brother also appears in the Vienna Genesis version of the episode, and in that case Joseph bends down to kiss him goodbye, while an unidentified woman looks on from the right.[23] Furthermore, as Joseph departs he is led away by an angel, and sorrowfully looks back toward Benjamin (portrayed a second time). The Paris manuscript, finally, does not show Benjamin in the departure scene but, like the Vienna Genesis, includes an unidentified woman.[24] Unfortunately, the miniature in the Cotton Genesis which most likely portrayed the instruction phase of the narrative is so severely damaged as to preclude reconstruction,[25] while the San Marco cycle surprisingly lacks any trace of either the instruction or the departure. The following miniature in the Cotton manuscript, however, does again show clear traces of a figure striding forward while looking back over his shoulder (Fig. 5).[26] This is most likely Joseph going "out of the vale of Hebron" (Genesis 37.14), and thus bears comparison with the departing Joseph on our textiles. That there is indeed a specific link to the Cotton Genesis tradition is substantially affirmed by the fact that a significant number of Joseph cycles which, on other grounds have been brought into the iconographic orbit of that manuscript, show a combined "instruction-departure" scene very much like that on our Coptic textiles. An excellent example is provided by a Post Byzantine Joseph manuscript in a private American collection whose iconographic derivation from the Cotton tradition is demonstrable through the entirety of its dense cycle (Fig. 6).[27]

101

355

FIGURE 6. *Joseph's departure for Shechem; Greeley Collection, f.6v, San Francisco.*

FIGURE 7. *Joseph's arrival to his brothers; detail of mosaic in the Baptistry, Florence.*

Scene 3, Joseph's Arrival to His Brothers: Here again there is a clear iconographic distinction among the four Joseph traditions and good reason for suggesting a Cotton recension link for our textiles. The Vienna Genesis[28] and the Octateuchs[29] both show the receiving brothers scattered

102

over a hilly landscape in various seated poses and a dog at Joseph's feet, while in Paris 510 he is accompanied by a donkey and the brothers are seated around a table.[30] Monuments of the Cotton tradition, on the other hand, typically show the brothers close by, standing in a tightly-knit group among their sheep and extending their hands in gestures of greeting. An especially good comparison is provided by the Joseph mosaic cycle in the dome of the Florence Baptistry (Fig. 7),[31] whose arrival scene closely parallels the San Marco version.[32] We need only imagine the group behind the foremost brother as having been deleted by the weaver for lack of space.

Scene 4, Joseph is Removed from the Well: The Octateuchs[33] and the Paris Gregory manuscript[34] differ basically from the version of this episode found on the Coptic textiles insofar as both show a low, earthen pit with equal groups of brothers aligned to either side. Moreover, Joseph is clothed and is suspended frontally by both arms.[35] The Cotton Genesis (Fig. 8)[36] and San Marco mosaics (Fig. 9),[37] on the other hand, include a composition whose core is much like that of our roundels: primarily through the efforts of a single brother Joseph (nude, at least in San Marco) is being drawn out by the arm toward the side of a raised masonry well. Indeed, the brick construction of our well almost exactly matches that which appears in the Joseph cycle on the ivory cathedral of Maximianus, a sixth-century monument whose iconographic link to the Cotton tradition has been demonstrated by Kurt Weitzmann.[38]

Scene 5, Joseph's Coat is Stained with Blood: This episode is to be found neither among the surviving folios of the Vienna Genesis nor the Cotton Genesis, and was never included in the San Marco cycle. Moreover, the morphology of the action as it is rendered in the Octateuchs[39] and in Paris Gregory 510[40] is basically distinct from that of the textiles since in both a brother attacks the goat from behind, forcing a knee into its spine and pulling back its head in order to cut its throat. While this iconographic scheme also appears on the Maximianus cathedra,[41] there are other, medieval Joseph cycles with ties to the Cotton tradition which show a formula closer to our roundels. For example, among the Joseph episodes on a romanesque capital in the east wing of the cloister at Monreale is a staining scene wherein a brother, kneeling slightly, holds the goat upside down between his legs, wounding it in the neck and allowing its blood to flow onto a cloak held forth by another brother.[42] An arrangement like this may well lie behind the confused rendition of the textiles where at least we may be certain that, unlike the Octateuchs and Paris 510, the slaughtered animal is being held off the ground.[43]

Scene 6, Joseph is Sold to the Ishmaelite Traders: The most distinctive iconographic feature of this scene, the fact that the Ishmaelite is seated, is unparalleled in any of the Joseph cycles associated with the four known traditions.[44] Moreover, the elements which remain, a brother standing behind a small figure of Joseph and raising his hand to strike

FIGURE 8. *Joseph removed from the well; tracing from British Library, cod. Cotton Otho. B.IV, f.74r, London.*

FIGURE 9. *Joseph removed from the well; detail of mosaic in San Marco, Venice.*

the bargain, are so universal as to preclude meaningful comparison. The Octateuch version of this scene is like ours in that the Ishmaelites are portrayed as blacks, but differs basically in showing the foremost of Joseph's new masters already leading him away by the hand. On several of the Joseph armbands with reduced cycles the sale to the Ishmaelites is compositionally juxtaposed with the later sale to Potiphar (scene 9).[45] Since, as we shall see below, a seated Potiphar is consistent with more than one Joseph tradition while a seated Ishmaelite is apparently unique to our textiles, it is indeed not improbable that the latter was an internal creation of the Coptic weaving industry, developed for no other reason than to compositionally balance the sale to Potiphar.[46]

Scene 7. Reuben's Lamentation: Although this episode is found in neither the Vienna Genesis, the Octateuchs, or Paris 510. it does appear at San Marco (Fig. 10).[47] In fact, two closely-sequential phases of the action are shown: at the left Reuben looks down into the empty well (Genesis 37.29), and at the right he hurries away, obviously agitated, to confront his brothers (Genesis 37.30).[48] This second figure differs from ours insofar as he is leaping away, his arms are raised over his head, and his eyes are trained on the well. That our version may yet be Cotton Genesis related, however, is suggested by a variant interpretation of the same episode in

FIGURE 10. *Reuben's lamentation; detail of mosaic in San Marco, Venice.*

103

FIGURE 12. *Joseph is brought down to Egypt; British Library* cod. Roy 2B.VII, f.15r, *London.*

(upper-left) FIGURE 11. *Reuben's lamentation; Accad. dei Concordi* cod. 212. f.29r, *Rovigo.*

several medieval Joseph cycles which otherwise shows affinities with that tradition. The late fourteenth-century Padua Bible, for example, shows an iconographic scheme basically like that of San Marco except that, just as in our textiles, Reuben turns away from the well and rips the clothing from his chest (Fig. 11).[49] Indeed, this composition explains the otherwise incongruous circumstance that our Reuben is looking *away* from the well; he is not turning toward the preceding scene of the sale but rather toward his brothers (Genesis 37.30), who for lack of space have been deleted by the textile weavers (as they were in the four preceding scenes).

Scene 8, Joseph is Brought Down to Egypt: That Joseph and an Ishmaelite should be seated together on the same animal is highly unusual; it is paralleled neither in the Vienna Genesis, the Octateuchs, Paris 510, or in the Cotton Genesis,[50] where in each instance Joseph is seated and the Ishmaelites walk. This iconography does appear, however, among the spandrel carvings in the Salisbury chapter house and in the slightly-later and closely-related Queen Mary's Psalter (Fig. 12).[51] Although the cycle which may be constructed from these two monuments bears the imprint of legends found in a thirteenth-century metrical paraphrase of the Joseph story, its core may be shown to derive from the Cotton Genesis tradition.[52]

Scene 9, Joseph is Sold to Potiphar· Although there is no trace of this scene in the Vienna Genesis or in its iconographically-related Middle Byzantine ivories, it is well-attested in the other three Joseph traditions. Insofar as Potiphar is seated, our textiles conform to the Octateuch version,[53] to the exclusion of both the Paris 510[54] and the Cotton Genesis-San Marco[55] versions which show him standing. In the Octateuchs, however, Potiphar and the Ishmaelites are simply conversing at a distance, whereas in our textiles money is apparently being passed over Joseph's head. The single closest parallel for the textile's version of this episode is provided

FIGURE 13. *Joseph is sold to Potiphar; Kärntner Landesarchiv* cod. 6/19, f.53v, *Klagenfurt.*

104

358

by the twelfth-century Millstatt Genesis (Fig. 13),[56] an Austrian manuscript whose links to the Cotton recension have been documented by several scholars.[57]

The foregoing series of comparison has shown first, that surviving evidence is indeed sufficient to establish clear iconographic distinctions among the four known Joseph traditions for most of the nine scenes found on our Coptic textiles, and second, that our textiles' specific interpretation of those narrative events consistently parallels that characteristic of the Cotton Genesis recension, usually to the *exclusion* of the other versions. Not only does this prove what we had suspected, that Coptic weavers appropriated iconography developed in other, more favorable media, it provides important new confirmation for Kurt Weitzmann's hypothesis that the Cotton Genesis recension was Egyptian in origin[58] – our textiles are, after all, among the very earliest witnesses to that tradition with a known provenance. Yet, almost as important as our cycle's general affinities to the Cotton Genesis tradition are its specific departures from the Cotton manuscript itself, for in showing distinctive conflations[59] and variant iconographic interpretations[60] which otherwise are attested only in much later, western cycles, it provides invaluable new insights into the variety and complexity of that tradition relatively near its point of origin, and enhances the iconographic "credibility" of what otherwise may have seemed remote witnesses.[61] Clearly, much fundamental work remains to be done before the intricate genealogy of the Cotton Genesis iconographic tradition can be established, even in basic outline. What is already evident, however, is that Coptic Joseph textiles, despite their crude execution and mass distribution, will have an important role to play.[62]

NOTES

1. D. Thompson, *Coptic Textiles in the Brooklyn Museum*, Wilbour Monographs, 2, Brooklyn, 1971, 1ff.

2. G. Egger, "Koptische Wirkerei mit figuralen Darstellungen," *Christentum am Nil*, Recklinghausen, 1964, 243f.; and for the sculpture, H. Torp, *"Leda christiana:* The Problem of the Interpretation of Coptic Sculpture with Mythological Motifs," *Acta ad archaeologiam et artium historiam pertinentia, Institutum Romanum Norvegiae*, 4 (1969): 101.

3. Joseph's unusual popularity bears witness to his extraordinary status among Egyptian Christians, as well as Jews and Moslems, who saw in him a national hero and, from the time of Philo Judaeus (*On Joseph*) recognized in him a model of personal conduct. It should come as no surprise, moreover, that the wearer of "the coat of many colors" should himself appear frequently on ornately-decorated garments.

4. For an intact tunic of this sort, see O. von Falke, *Kunstgeschichte der Seidenweberei*, 1st ed., Berlin, 1913, 1, fig. 26.

The following is a preliminary list of plied-warp Joseph textiles. It draws on entry 84 of Deborah Thompson's forthcoming *Catalogue of the Byzantine and Early Mediaeval Antiquities in the Dumbarton Oaks Collection: 4, Late Antique and Mediaeval Textiles*. I would like to thank Dr. Thompson for generously sharing this information with me.

Athens, Museum of Decorative Arts nos. 749, 739. A. Apostolaki, Τὰ Κοπτικὰ ὑφάσματα τοῦ ἐν Ἀθήναις Μουσείου Κοσμητικῶν Τεχνῶν, Athens, 1932 (749: roundel; 739: roundel, reduced cycle);

Berlin, Staatliche Museen nos. 9109, 9110. O. Wolff and W.F. Volbach, *Spätantike und koptische Stoffe aus ägyptischen Grabfunden*, Berlin, 1926 (9109: roundel; 9110: clavi, highly-reduced cycle);

Brussels, Musées Royaux d'Art et d'Histoire nos. 311, 313, 1. Errera, *Collection d'anciennes étoffes égyptiennes*, Brussels, 1916 (both roundels, reduced cycles);

Japan, Kanegafuchi Spinning Company Collection. K. Akashi, *Coptic Textiles from Burying Grounds in Egypt in the Collection of Kanegafuchi Spinning Company*, Kyoto, 1955, 3: pls. 121, 134a (roundel, reduced cycle; central medallion with dream);

Leningrad, Hermitage nos. 11176a, 11176b. *Koptische Kunst: Christentum am Nil*, Villa Hügel, Essen, 1963, no. 360; and *Iskusstv vizantii v sobraniiakh SSR*, Moscow, Pushkin State Museum of Fine Arts, 1977, 1, no. 364 (both roundels). This list will be substantially enlarged in a forthcoming article on Joseph textiles by A. Kakovkin of the Hermitage.

Liberec, Nordböhmisches Museum no. 1846. L. Kybalová, *Die alten Weber am Nil: Koptische Stoffe, ein Beitrag zur ästhetischtechnologischen Problematic*, Prague, 1967, no. 83 (clavi, highly-reduced cycle);

London, British Museum no. 17.175. F. Kitzinger, "The Story of Joseph on a Coptic Tapestry," *Journal of the Warburg Institute*, 1 (1937): 266ff. (armband, reduced cycle);

London, Victoria and Albert Museum no. 271.1886. A.F. Kendrick, *Catalogue of Textiles from Burying-Grounds in Egypt: 3. Coptic Period*, Victoria and Albert Museum, Department of Textiles, London, 1922, no. 623 (linen tunic with four roundels);

Moscow, Pushkin Museum nos. 5167, 5173, 5174, 5179. R. Shurinova, *Koptskie tkani.*, Moscow, 1967, nos. 182-185 (5167: armband, reduced cycle; 5173: roundel, reduced cycle; 5174: roundel; 5179: roundel, reduced cycle);

Munich, Bernheimer Collection. Egger, "Koptische Wirkerei," 255 note 12;

New York, Metropolitan Museum of Art no. 63.178.2. *Age of Spirituality: Late Antique and Early Christian Art, 3rd to 7th Century*, Metropolitan Museum of Art, New York, 1977-1978, no. 412 (roundel);

New York, Tiffany Collection no. 56. *Antique Textiles Including Examples of Greek and Coptic Tapestries of the Early Christian Era*, Tiffany Studios, New York, n.d., no. 56 (roundel, reduced cycle);

Paris, Louvre nos. X4276, X4590, X4208. P. du Bourguet, *Musée National du Louvre, catalogue des étoffes coptes: I*, Paris, 1964, G326, G327. G335;

Prague, Kunstgewerbemuseum no. 1242. Kybalová, *Die alten Weber am Nil*, no. 93 (roundel);

Trier, Städtisches Museum no. 17. Von Falke, *Kunstgeschichte*, 20, fig. 24 (roundel);

Turin, Museo Egiziano. Kitzinger, "The Story of Joseph," 268, note 2 (roundel);

Vienna, Österreichisches Museum für Angewandte Kunst no. T691. *Koptische Kunst* (1963), no. 361 (armband, reduced cycle);

Washington, D.C., Dumbarton Oaks no. 53.2.114. Thompson, *Catalogue. . .*, no. 84 (roundel, reduced cycle).

5. 26.5 x 28 cm. See note 6 and, for an excellent color illustration, Kybalová, *Die alten Weber am Nil*, no. 92.

6. *Ca.* 26.7 cm.

7. No. 17; 29.5 x 28.0 cm. For a color illustration, *Koptische Kunst*, 359 (pl. X).

8. The two phases of the action are clearly distinguished, for example, by the Middle Byzantine illustrated Octateuchs. The copy in Istanbul (Topkapi Seraglio Lib. cod. 8) shows at the left of the first miniature on folio 124r Joseph receiving his instructions, while folio 58r of Vatican Library 747 shows Joseph walking "out of the vale of Hebron" (Genesis 37.14). For the Istanbul manuscript, see T. Ouspensky, *L'Octateuch de la bibliothèque du Sérail à Constantinople*, Bulletin de l'Institut Archéologique Russe à Constantinople, 12, Sofia, 1907, pl. XVI. That in the Vatican Library is unpublished.

9. L. Kybalová (*Die alten Weber am Nil, 141*), has suggested that this is the episode of Joseph being shown the way to Dothan by the stranger (Genesis 37. 15-17). This is unlikely, however, since the unidentified figure (who *looks* like the brothers in the subsequent scenes) raises his hand to greet Joseph, not to point out his pathway. Contrast that episode as it appears in the first Joseph mosaic cupola at San Marco (S. Bettini, *Mosaici antichi di San Marco a Venezia*, Bergamo, 1944, pl. LXXX).

10. Joseph's high position and extended arm suggest that he is being drawn up from the well and not lowered into it. Compare the two phases as portrayed at San Marco (*Ibid.*, pl. LXXX).

11. "The Study of Byzantine Book Illumination, Past, Present and Future," *The Place of Book Illumination in Byzantine Art*, Princeton, 1975, 22ff. The Middle Byzantine illustrated Octateuchs, for example, allot almost exactly the same number of pictorial episodes to Genesis 37.

11a. "The Story of Joseph," 26ff.

12. See especially, K. Weitzmann, "Die Illustration der Septuaginta," *Münchner Jahrbuch der bildenden Kunst*, 3-4 (1952-1953): 96ff. (*Studies in Classical and Byzantine Manuscript Illumination*, ed. H.L. Kessler, Chicago/London, 1971, 45ff.); and, for the fourth pictorial recension, "The Study. . .," 17. For the systematic distinction of these four traditions through the early episodes of the Joseph story, see G. Vikan, "Illustrated Manuscripts of

Pseudo-Ephraem's *Life of Joseph* and the *Romance of Joseph and Aseneth*," unpub. diss., Princeton, 1976, 46ff.

13. London, Brit. Lib. cod. Cotton Otho. B.IV. The Cotton codex, which is generally assigned to Alexandria and dated to the fifth or sixth century, was severely burned in 1731. On the approximately 150 remaining fragments, traces appear of several dozen Joseph episodes. Because the Genesis mosaics in the narthex of San Marco in Venice are so extremely close in iconography to what may be decifered on the scorched manuscript fragments, they are customarily used in their place for comparative studies. See K. Weitzmann, "Observations on the Cotton Genesis Fragments," *Late Classical and Mediaeval Studies in Honor of Albert Mathias Friend, Jr.*, Princeton, 1955, 55ff.; and *idem*, "The Mosaics of San Marco and the Cotton Genesis," *Atti del XVIII congresso internazionale di storia dell'arte (Venice, 1955)*, Venice, 1956, 152f.

For line-drawing reconstructions of the Cotton Genesis fragments see S. Tsjui, "Un essai d'identification des sujets des miniatures fragmentaries de la Genèse du Cotton," (in Japanese) *Bijutsu-shi (Journal of Japan Art History Society)*, 66-67 (1967): nos. 91ff.; and for the San Marco Joseph mosaics, see Bettini, *Mosaici antichi*, pls. LXXX-LXXXVII.

14. Vienna, Nat. Lib. cod. theol. gr. 31. This fragmentary purple manuscript, which is usually dated to the sixth century and assigned to Syria-Palestine, includes about forty Joseph episodes. See H. Gerstinger, *Die Wiener Genesis*, Vienna, 1931, pls. 27ff. For a discussion of its pictorial recension, see Weitzmann, "Die Illustration. . .," 101f.; and *idem*, "Zur Frage des Einflusses judischen Bilderquellen auf die Illustration des Alten Testamentes," *Mullus: Festschrift Theodor Klauser*, Münster, 1964, 407f. (*Studies*, 84f).

15. There are four Octateuchs with Joseph scenes: Vatican Lib. cod. gr. 747; Vatican Lib. cod. gr. 746; Istanbul, Topkapi Seraglio Lib. cod. 8; and Smyrna, Evangelical School cod. A.1 (burned in 1922). The first is datable on style to the eleventh century and the other three to the twelfth: they include about seventy Joseph scenes. For illustrations, see Ouspensky, *L'Octateuch*, and D. Hesseling, *Miniatures de l'Octateuque grec de Smyrne*, Leiden, 1909. For a discussion of their pictorial recension, see K. Weitzmann, *The Joshua Roll*, Studies in Manuscript Illumination, 3, Princeton, 1948, esp. 30ff; "Die Illustration. . .," 102ff, and "The Octateuch of the Seraglio and the History of its Pictorial Recension," *Actes du X. congrès d'études byzantine (Istanbul, 1955)*, Istanbul, 1957, 183ff.

16. Paris, Bibl. Nat. cod. gr. 510. There are thirteen Joseph episodes on folio 69v of this late ninth-century manuscript. See H. Omont, *Fac-similés des miniatures des plus anciens: Manuscrits grecs de la Bibliothèque Nationale du VIe au XIe siècle*, Paris, 1902, pl. XXVI; and, for its pictorial recension, Weitzmann, "The Study . . .," 17.

17. Bettini, *Mosaici antichi*, pl. LXXX. In this instance, the relevant miniatures in the Cotton Genesis (on folios 115, 112, and 72) are too extensively damaged to allow specific comparison. See Tsjui, "Essai d'identification," nos. 91-93.

18. None of our textiles, however, shows the arc of heaven so prominent in the mosaics.

19. Fol. 15r: Gerstinger, *Die Wiener Genesis*, pl. 29.

20. Vatican 746, fol. 115v; Seraglio 8, fol. 123v; Smyrna A.1, fol. 49v. See Ouspensky, *L'Octateuch*, pl. XVI; and Hesseling, *Miniatures*, pl. 120.

21. Fol. 69v: Omont, *Fac-similés*, pl. XXVI.

22. Vatican 747, fol. 58r; Vatican 746, fol. 116r; Seraglio 8, fol. 124r;

106

Smyrna A.1, fol. 50r. See Ouspensky, *L'Octateuch*, pl. XVI; and Hesseling, *Miniatures*, pl. 120.

23. Fol. 15v: Gerstinger, *Die Wiener Genesis*, pl. 30.

24. Fol. 69v: Omont, *Fac-similés*, pl. XXVI.

25. Fol. 72v. The preceding miniature (fol. 72r) seems to show Joseph standing before the enthroned figure of Jacob. However, the presence of a blue arc of heaven and a crescent moon at the upper left of the composition suggests that it is the episode of Joseph relating his second dream to his father and brothers. See Tsjui, "Essai d'identification," no. 93.

26. Fol. 73r. This is my own copy drawing made in June 1977 (contrast Tsjui, no. 94). I would like to thank D.H. Turner for generously putting the Cotton Genesis fragments at my disposal, and the American Council of Learned Societies for funding my research travel.

27. San Francisco, Greeley Collection, fol. 6v. See Vikan, "Illustrated Manuscripts," 52ff., 395ff.

28. Fol. 15v: Gerstinger, *Die Wiener Genesis*, pl. 30.

29. Vatican 747, fol. 58v; Vatican 746, fol. 116r; Seraglio 8, fol. 124r; Smyrna A.1, fol. 50r. See Ouspensky, *L'Octateuch*, pl. XVI; and Hesseling, *Miniatures*, pl. 120.

30. Fol. 69v: Omont, *Fac-similés*, pl. XXVI.

31. A. de Witt, *I mosaici del battistero di Firenze*, Florence, 1957, 4, pl. XXVII.

32. Bettini, *Mosaici antichi*, pl. LXXX. Two possible locations for this episode in the Cotton Genesis, the right half of folio 73r (our Fig. 5) and the upper half of folio 73v, are too extensively damaged to allow specific comparison. See Tsjui, "Essai d'identification," nos. 94, 95.

33. Vatican 747, fol. 58v; Vatican 746, fol. 116v; Seraglio 8, fol. 124r; Smyrna A.1, fol. 50v. See Ouspensky, *L'Octateuch*, pl. XVI; and Hesseling, *Miniatures*, pl. 121.

34. Fol. 69v: Omont, *Fac-similés*, pl. XXVI.

35. Unfortunately, the folio bearing this episode has been lost from the Vienna Genesis. It does, however, appear on a Middle Byzantine ivory plaque in Berlin (Staatliche Museen no. 569) which has been iconographically linked to the Vienna Genesis. See H. Graeven, "Typen der Wiener Genesis auf byzantinischen Elfenbeinreliefs," *Jahrbuch der kunsthistorischen Sammlungen der allerhöchsten Kaiserhauses*, 21 (1900): esp. 110f.; and A. Goldschmidt and K. Weitzmann, *Die byzantinischen Elfenbeinskulpturen: 1*, Berlin, 1930, no. 94. On the ivory, a nude Joseph is being drawn up by the arm from a low well. The Ishmaelite buyers are passing money for his purchase to a brother who lays his hand on Joseph's head. At the right of the plaque is the journey to Egypt.

36. Fol. 74r. See also Tsjui, "Essai d'identification," no. 96.

37. Bettini, *Mosaici antichi*, pl. LXXX.

38. C. Cecchelli, *La cattedra di Massimiano ed altri avorii romanoorientali*, Rome, 1944, pl. XVII. For the iconographic affinities of this Joseph cycle, whose dozen scenes include the placing into but not removal from the well, see Weitzmann, "Observations. . .", 128; and, more recently, F. Rupprecht-Schadewaldt, "Die Ikonographie der Josephssezenen auf der Maximianskathedra in Ravenna," unpub. diss., Heidelberg, 1969, 44ff., 109ff. The raised masonry well, which is a characteristic feature of Cotton recension monuments (Weitzmann, "Observations. . . ," 128), is not implied by the word λάκκος found in the Septuagint.

39. Vatican 747, fol. 58v; Vatican 746, fol. 116v; Seraglio 8, fol. 124r; Smyrna A.1, fol. 50v. See Ouspensky, *L'Octateuch*, pl. XVI; and Hesseling, *Miniatures*, pl. 121.

40. Fol. 69v; Omont, *Fac-similés*, pl. XXVI.

41. Cecchelli, *Cattedra*, pl. XVII.

42. R. Salvini, *Il chiostro di Monreale e la scultura romanica in Sicilia*, Palermo, 1962, "corpus," no. 18, south face. The eight (?) Joseph episodes on this capital are very closely related in iconography to the nearly twenty Joseph episodes on the thirteenth-century marble relief in the Cathedral of Santa Restituta, Naples (E. Bertaux, *L'Art dans l'Italie meridionale*, Paris, 1904, pl. XXXIV; and C.D. Sheppard, Jr., "Iconography of the Cloister of Monreale," *Art Bulletin* 31 (1949): 167). The single cycle which may be reconstituted from these two monuments shows many parallels to Cotton recension cycles.

43. According to the biblical narrative the staining of Joseph's cloak takes place only *after* he has been sold and taken away by the Ishmaelites (scene 8). This change in sequence is not, however, uncommon. For example, in the Octateuchs, Paris 510, and on the Maximianus cathedra the staining of the coat is directly coupled with the placing of Joseph into the well (see notes 39-41, above). Even Philo (*On Joseph* III.14) alters the biblical sequence.

44. For the relevant illustrations, see notes 35, 37, 39, and 40, above.

45. See, for example, Kitzinger, "The Story of Joseph," 266f., fig. 36a.

46. That Coptic weavers were motivated more by requirements of design than by narrative clarity is especially obvious in armband 5167 in the Pushkin Museum, where the departure for Shechem and the sale to the Ishmaelites scenes are arbitrarily split by the large central field of the textile. See also Kitzinger (*Ibid.*, 267), who remarks on the compositional identity of the two sale scenes on the armband in the British Museum.

47. Bettini, *Mosaici antichi*, pl. LXXX. The folio upon which this scene may have been found is missing from the Cotton Genesis (between fols. 74 and 75).

48. One brother appears at the far right of the composition. For a slightly different interpretation of this scene, see S. Tsuji, "La chaire de Maximien, la Genèse de Cotton et les mosaïques de Saint-Marc à Venise: A propos du cycle de Joseph," *Synthronon* 2 (1968): 44ff.

49. Rovigo, Accad. dei Concordi cod. 212, fol. 29r (another section of the manuscript is in the British Library, cod. add. 15277): G. Folena and G. Mellini, *Bibbia istoriata padovana della fine del trecento: Pentateuco-Giosuè-Ruth*, Venice, 1962, pl. 51. This cycle, which includes more than seventy Joseph episodes, shows numerous parallels to monuments of the Cotton Genesis tradition.

50. For the relevant illustrations, see notes 35, 37 (and Tsuji, "Essai d'identification," no. 97), 39 and 40.

51. London, Brit. Lib. cod. Roy 2B.VII, fol. 15r. See G. Warner, *Queen Mary's Psalter*, London, 1912, pl. 27. For the Salisbury sculpture, see P.Z. Blum, "The Middle English Romance 'Iacob and Iosep' and the Joseph Cycle of the Salisbury Chapter House," *Gesta* 7/1 (1969): fig. 3.

52. *Ibid.*, 18ff.

53. Vatican 747, fol. 59v; Vatican 746, fol. 120v; Seraglio 8, fol. 127r; Smyrna A.1, fol. 51v. See Ouspensky, *L'Octateuch*, pl. XVI; and Hesseling, *Miniatures*, pl. 124.

54. Fol. 69v: Omont, *Fac-similés*, pl. XXVI.

55. See, respectively, Tsuji, "Essai d'identification," no. 106; and Bettini, *Mosaici antichi*, pl. LXXXI.

56. Klagenfurt, Kärntner Landesarchiv cod. 6/19, fol. 53v. See A. Kracher, *Millstätter Genesis und Physiologus Handschrift*, Codices selecti, phototypice impressi, 10, Graz, 1967.

57. See Weitzmann, "Observations. . . ," 121ff.; H. Voss, *Studien zur*

107

illustrierten *Millstätter Genesis*, Munich, 1962, 62ff.; K. Koshi, "Bemerkungen über die Millstätter Genesis-zwei Josephsszenen im Hinblick auf die sogenannte (Cottongenesis-Rezension," *Kokuritsu-Seiyò-Bijutsukan-Nenpò (Bulletin of the National Museum of Western Art)* 6 (1972): 55ff.

58. Weitzmann, "Observations. . .", 130.

59. I.e., Scene 1, whose conflation parallels San Marco (Fig. 4) in contrast to the much more detailed treatment in the Cotton Genesis (Tsuji, "Essai d'identification," nos. 91-93); and Scene 2, whose conflation parallels the Post Byzantine Joseph apocryphon (Fig. 6) in contrast to the Cotton Genesis, which apparently provides a separate scene for the departure (Fig. 5, left side).

60. I.e., Scene 7, which parallels the Padua Bible (Fig. 11) and varies from the Cotton Genesis as it may be reconstructed by San Marco (Fig. 10); Scene 8, which parallels the Queen Mary's Psalter (Fig. 12) and varies from the Cotton Genesis (Tsuji, "Essai d'identification," no. 97); and Scene 9, which parallels the Millstatt Genesis (Fig. 13) and varies from the Cotton Genesis (*Ibid.*, no. 106).

61. Like the Post Byzantine apocryphon (Fig. 6), the Florence Baptistry mosaics (Fig. 7), the Monreale capital, the Padua Bible (Fig. 11), and the Queen Mary's Psalter (Fig. 12).

62. Although the vast majority of all surviving Coptic Joseph textiles belong to the nine-scene, Genesis 37 group analyzed above, a few isolated examples (also plied-warp roundels) recently discovered by Laila Abdel-Malek show a variant cycle of at least nine (?) scenes, some of which are from chapter 37 but others from much later in the narrative. Preliminary observations suggest that these scenes too may be linked to the Cotton Genesis tradition. Yet, what is especially interesting about this second cycle, which will be treated in detail in a dissertation by Ms. Abdel-Malek, is that some of its episodes include apocryphal elements, and thus raise basic questions about the Cotton tradition's relationship to the Septuagint. I would like to thank Ms. Abdel-Malek for generously sharing her discoveries with me in advance of their publication.

108

CONSTANTINE AND THE ORIGINS OF THE CHRISTIAN BASILICA

FEW archaeological problems have been longer and less conclusively debated than that of the origins of the Christian basilica. Ever since the great Renaissance architect, Alberti, noted the similarity of name and of architectural form between the Early Christian basilicas and the forum basilicas of Imperial Roman practice, students of classical architecture have been trying to establish the derivation of the Christian basilica from this, that, or the other type of pagan monument. The measure of their failure to secure general agreement is the very large and still increasing literature that has grown up around the problem.[1] There have, of course, been certain clear advances. Some of the older theories, such as that which derived the basilica from the Pompeian type of Roman house, need no longer be taken seriously; and there is a vastly greater body of reliable evidence available now than there was even a quarter of a century ago. Despite these advances, however, we are still very far from being able to give an agreed answer to the fundamental question, why it was that the fourth-century Church adopted the apsed basilical hall as the standard form of building for the celebration of the Eucharist, and so established an architectural and liturgical pattern that is still effective to the present day. The primary purpose of this article is to review the problem in the light of recent discoveries and of recent research, and to try to define, rather more precisely than is often done, the terms within which it can usefully be discussed.[2]

The basilica had at least five centuries of history behind it before it was adopted by the Christian church; and whatever may have been the relation of the Christian basilica to its pagan classical predecessors, it is obviously essential to any enquiry into the origins of the Christian basilica to know how the word was used, and what it implied architecturally in other fields, during the early centuries of the Christian era. The much-discussed question of the origin of the name 'basilica' and of the architectural form to which it came to be attached concerns us less directly. It will be enough, in the present context, to note briefly one or two of the more important advances that have been made in recent years in our knowledge of the early development of the classical basilica.

The literary and epigraphic evidence for the use of the term 'basilica' in classical antiquity has recently been summarised by Langlotz.[3] Apart from the fact that the

---

[1] For this literature, see the excellent and in many respects complementary summaries by E. Langlotz and F. Deichmann in *Reallexikon für Antike und Christentum*, ed. Th. Klauser, vol. i, 1950, 1225–59 (the article was written in 1943), and P. Lemerle in *Acad. R. de Belgique, Bull. de la Classe des Lettres et des Sciences Morales et Politiques*, 5, xxxiv, 1948, pp. 306–28. A. Stange, *Das frühchristliche Kirchengebäude als Bild des Himmels*, Cologne, 1950 (on which, see J. Kollwitz, *Byz. Zeitschr.* xlvii, 1954, pp. 169–71). For a summary of the papers on this subject read at a meeting of the Koldewey-Gesellschaft in 1953, see *Kunstchronik* vi, 1953, pp. 237 f. (in particular, the remarks by Th. Kempf, pp. 241–2).

[2] The writer's thanks are due to Professor Axel Boethius and to Mr. Hugh Last for many helpful suggestions made during the preparation of this article, and to Mr. G. U. S. Corbett for preparing the plans with which it is illustrated.

[3] *art. cit.*, 1225–6. See also G. Downey, *AJA* xli, 1937, pp. 194–211.

word is Greek and implies some sort of derivation from the Greek-speaking world, this evidence does not tell us much about the architectural connotations of the earliest phase. The feminine gender implies a missing feminine substantive; and the form of the adjective in -ikos is one that did not come into common use before the fourth century,[4] replacing the older form in -eios, as we find it for example in the name of the official seat of the Archon Basileus at Athens, the Stoa Basileios. It must, therefore, have been from the late classical or the Hellenistic world that the Romans borrowed the word, and, with it (presumably), the architectural form to which it was applied. But to what particular Hellenistic building or buildings it had belonged, we receive no hint. Later authors and inscriptions accept the word as a matter of course, just as we today accept the word 'palace' without any thought for its derivation from the Palatium, the Palatine Hill, on which the Roman Emperors had their first official residence. It is not until the seventh century A.D. that we get the explicit statement of Isidore of Seville (Etym. 15.4.11) that 'Basilica was formerly the name of the king's residence, which is how it got the name, for Basileus means king and Basilica the king's house'; and by that late date the possibility that learned conjecture had been at work is clearly too great for much reliance to be placed on his unsupported word.

The obvious explanation, that the word is borrowed from the Stoa Basileios and reflects the reputation of Athenian institutions in Rome, leaves unexplained the fundamental difference of architectural type between the Roman basilica and the Greek stoa; and it is at variance with what we know of the practical use of the basilicas of Republican Rome, which suggests that their original function was commercial rather than judicial.[5] An alternative theory is that recently put forward by Langlotz,[6] which would derive the name and (in certain of its aspects) the architectural type from the royal audience-halls of Hellenistic Egypt. Throne-rooms with longitudinal colonnades and clerestory lighting are a characteristic feature of Pharaonic palace architecture, e.g. the throne-room of Merenptah at Memphis; [7]and nothing would have been more in keeping with the policy of the Ptolemies than that they should have adopted a traditional setting for their own court ceremonial. Moreover, there is reason to believe that the essential constituents of the architectural type were current in other contexts in Hellenistic Egypt: the Diastolon of the Jews in Alexandria, built perhaps as early as the second century B.C. and destroyed in A.D. 117, seems to have been a five-aisled, colonnaded building with galleries;[8] and the persistence into Ptolemaic times of a tradition of clerestory lighting is securely attested by the name and form of the Roman Oecus Aegyptius, described by Vitruvius (VI. iii. 9) and exemplified in such surviving buildings as the House of the Mosaic Atrium at Herculaneum.[9] On the other hand, as Langlotz himself is careful to emphasise, the evidence is far from conclusive. There is no surviving contemporary account of a Ptolemaic palace, and none has ever been excavated. In the present state of our knowledge of Hellenistic archaeology, such a derivation,

---

[4] The new fashion is ridiculed by Aristophanes, Eq. 1378–81.

[5] E. Welin, Studien zur Topographie des Forum Romanum (Acta Inst. Rom. Regni Sueciae, ser. 8°, vi), 1953, pp. 111 f.

[6] 'Der architektonische Ursprung der christlichen Basilika,' Festschrift für Hans Jantzen, Berlin (Mann),

1951, pp. 30–6.

[7] AJA xxii, 1918, p. 75.

[8] H. Kohl and C. Watzinger, Antike Synagogen in Galilaea, 1916, p. 180.

[9] A. Maiuri, 'Oecus Aegyptius', in Studies Presented to David Moore Robinson, pp. 423–9, pls 25–6; and in Palladio, n.s. ii, 1952, p. 5, figs. 9–11.

therefore, however plausible, can neither be proved nor disproved, and it is idle to speculate whether the influence of this hypothetical Ptolemaic prototype reached Rome directly or through some Hellenistic intermediary.[10] It may perfectly well be that the immediate precursor of the Republican Roman basilica was some Hellenistic building or class of buildings of a more everyday character, to which the name *Basilike* had already somehow become attached, as in the analogous case of the Stoa Basileios. What is certain is that the word first appears in architectural Latin in the early second century B.C. as the name given to a type of large public hall, of which the Basilica Porcia, built by Cato in 184 B.C. on the south side of the Roman Forum, is the first recorded example. These halls seem in the first place to have been designed as covered extensions of the Forum area, from which they were often separated only by open colonnades; but already under the later Republic they had come to acquire a secondary and more official function, through the transfer to them of the seat of certain of the magistrates' courts, and provision for the work of these courts was an important factor in shaping their subsequent development. Whether or not the Basilica Porcia and its neighbour, the Basilica Aemilia, begun five years later, were the first buildings of their kind to be put up in Rome, may be discussed;[11] but we can hardly doubt that it was from them that the word passed into common Latin use to denote the particular class of building of which they are the recorded Roman archetype, and hence, by extension, to describe the architectural type that such buildings embodied.

For a knowledge of what these early basilicas were like, we are no longer dependent solely on the well-known passage of Vitruvius (V. i. 6–10), in which he describes the basilica that he had himself built, shortly after 27 B.C., at Colonia Julia Fanestris, the modern Fano (fig. 1, 5). This was a rectangular building, consisting of a lofty central hall, surrounded on all four sides by an internal portico and gallery, and lit by a clerestory; the main entrance was in the centre of one long side and, opposite it, an apsed rectangular projection, which contained the *tribunal*, the seat of the presiding magistrate, and which served at the same time as a shrine for the imperial cult (*aedes Augusti*). We now know that Vitruvius was following a familiar and long-established model. In Rome itself recent excavation has shown that the pre-imperial Basilica Aemilia was, like its successors, a rectangular hall with an internal ambulatory, set with one of the longer sides facing the Forum. Clearer, because more complete, is the evidence afforded by the American excavations at Cosa, in Southern Etruria, which have revealed a basilica of substantially Vitruvian type, dating from the middle of the second century B.C. (fig. 1, 4).[12] Cosa was an official military colony, with no architectural pretensions of its own, and we can hardly doubt that in the form of its basilica, as demonstrably in so much else, it followed the practice of contemporary Rome. When we recall that substantially the same type of basilica has been recorded also from two other republican

[10] The 'Hypostyle Hall' in Delos is commonly cited in this connection (G. Leroux, *Délos*, fasc. iia: *La Salle Hypostyle*, Paris, 1909; *Les origines de l'édifice hypostyle*, Paris, 1913); but, as Langlotz remarks, the architectural type has closer affinities with the oriental *apadana*.

[11] The discussion turns on the reference in Plautus, *Curculio*, 472: 'dites damnosos maritos sub basilica quaerito'. Plautus was already dead when the Basilica Porcia was begun, and this line is either a later insertion

or must refer to some earlier basilica. The adjective *basilicus* appears commonly in Plautus in the figurative sense of 'grand, costly'.

[12] *Memoirs of the American Academy in Rome* xx, 1951, pp. 71–3, fig. 66 (before excavation). For permission to reproduce the summary plan of this building since excavation, I am indebted to the American Academy and to its successive field-directors, Professor F. E. Brown and Mr. L. Richardson.

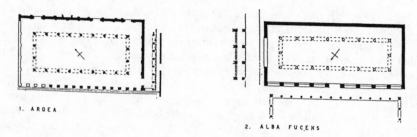

1. ARDEA

2. ALBA FUCENS

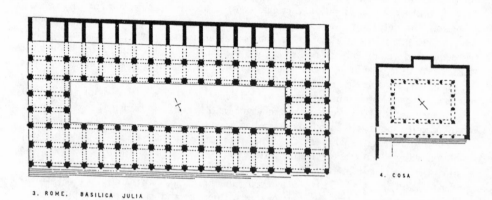

3. ROME. BASILICA JULIA

4. COSA

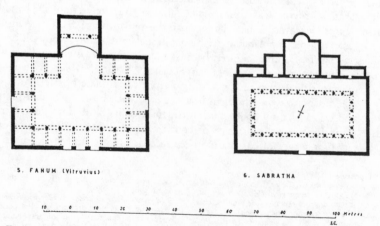

5. FANUM (Vitruvius)

6. SABRATHA

FIG. 1.—LATE REPUBLICAN AND EARLY IMPERIAL BASILICAS OF CENTRAL ITALIAN 'BROAD' TYPE.

sites, Ardea (fig. 1, 1)[13] and Alba Fucens (fig. 1, 2),[14] it becomes very clear that what one may conveniently call the Vitruvian type of basilica was widely diffused in Late Republican Italy.[15]

It was not, however, the only type current in Republican Italy. The basilica at Pompeii, built perhaps *c.* 100 B.C., follows what seems to be normal Italian practice in employing a centralised ambulatory rather than longitudinal colonnades (fig. 2, 1). But

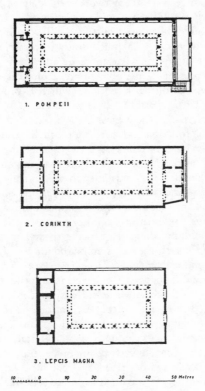

1. POMPEII

2. CORINTH

3. LEPCIS MAGNA

10 0 10 20 30 40 50 Metres

FIG. 2.—LATE REPUBLICAN AND EARLY IMPERIAL BASILICAS OF POMPEIAN TYPE.

it is one of the short sides that faces the Forum; and it is the longer axis that receives the full weight of architectural emphasis. In view of Pompeii's geographical position and South Italian contacts, it is tempting to suggest that in this the Pompeian basilica may resemble more closely the hypothetical Hellenistic archetype, and that the Vitruvian

[13] First half of the first century B.C.; there is no trace of a separate tribunal. Erik Wikén, *Bollettino dell'Associazione Internazionale degli Studi Mediterranei* v, 1934, pp. 7–21.

[14] Late Republican; there is no trace of a separate tribunal, unless this stood within the south aisle, above the *tabernae* that are incorporated in the podium near the middle of the rear wall; J. Mertens, *Memorie della*

Accademia Nazionale dei Lincei, s. 8, v, pp. 171–94, fig. 23.

[15] Cf. also the Basilica Julia (fig. 1, 3) and the early Imperial basilica at Sabratha (fig. 1, 6). The possible distinction between a primitive, completely centralised type (as at Ardea, and still substantially surviving in the Basilica Julia) and a more complex type, with a clearly established shorter axis (Cosa, Vitruvius's basilica at Fano) need not be further discussed in the present context.

basilica may represent a characteristically Roman adaptation of this same type. It is obvious, for example, that to the architect of the basilicas at Cosa and at Ardea, with their open, colonnaded fronts, ready access from the forum was an all-important consideration; and for this the 'broad' Vitruvian basilica was obviously better suited than its 'long' Pompeian counterpart. Like the whole question of Hellenistic origins, however, this must await the results of further research. For the present, all that we can say for certain is that there were these two clearly defined types of basilica already represented in Italy by the end of the second century B.C.

With the subsequent development of the basilica during the Empire we cannot here concern ourselves in detail. So much fresh information has come to light in recent years that, before attempting any more detailed reassessment, one would have first to assemble and to present a large body of archaeological evidence. One can, however, venture one or two useful generalisations, which have a bearing on the problem of the origin of the Christian basilica. It is quite clear, for example, that the word *basilica*, whatever its original connotations, came in time to be applied to buildings covering a wide range of function and an almost equally wide variety of architectural types. Domestic basilicas are recorded as early as the late first century B.C., when Vitruvius employs the term to describe a room that might form part of a wealthy private house (VI. 5. 2); and in later antiquity there are many such references, of which it will here be sufficient to mention two, the three *basilicae centenariae* (i.e. one hundred feet long) in the Villa of the Gordians on the Via Praenestina, and the basilica with an annexed pool on Sidonius Apollinarius's country estate in the Auvergne.[16] There were basilicas attached to public buildings, e.g. to the theatres at Nicaea, in Bithynia, and at Iguvium, in Umbria,[17] or to the baths at Narbonne,[18] the exact function of which we do not know. The *basilicae argentaria* (or *vascolaria*), *vestilia* and *floscellaria*, listed in the fourth-century Regionary Catalogue of Rome and its appendix, must have been covered bazaars, serving the needs of the metalworkers, clothiers, and flower-sellers respectively.[19] At Djemila in Algeria (the ancient Cuicul) excavation has revealed the actual remains of a fourth-century *basilica vestiaria*;[20] and the basilicas that are recorded as having been added to an existing market at Corfinium, in central Italy, were presumably covered market-halls of a similar, though perhaps more general, character.[21] A specialised military version of the basilica is described by Vegetius, and is attested epigraphically as early as the second century; it was used as an exercise-hall in bad weather, and we note without surprise that three of the five inscriptions referring to such basilicas come from Britain.[22] We do not know the precise purpose of the basilica that was built as an annex to a temple of Aesculapius at Civitas Vazitana Sarra in Tunisia, nor of the pair of basilicas adjoining a temple dedicated to two local Celtic divinities at Périgueux.[23] There is, however, at least one well-attested case of the use of the word to describe a hall used for cult purposes, and that is the *Basilica Hilariana*, an underground hall

[16] SHA, *vit. Gord.* 32. 3; Sidonius, *Epist.* ii. 2. 8.
[17] Pliny, *Epist.* x. 39; *CIL* xi, 5820 (Augustan).
[18] *CIL* xii, 4342 (mid-second century).
[19] *Libellus de regionibus urbis Romae*, ed. Nordh (*Acta Inst. Rom. Regni Sueciae*, ser. III, 8°), Lund, 1949, pp. 84, 100; cf. *CIL* vi, 9209.
[20] *Bull. Arch.* 1913, pp. 159–60; *CIL* viii, 20156 (A.D. 364–7).

[21] *CIL* ix, 3162 (undated).
[22] Vegetius (ed. Lang, 1885) ii, 23; *CIL* vii, 965 (Netherby, A.D. 222) and 445 (Lanchester, *temp.* Gordian, cf. 287); *CIL* iii, 6025 (Syene, c. A.D. 140); *CIL* xiii, 6672 (Mainz, A.D. 196).
[23] *CIL* viii, 12006 (A.D. 212); xiii 950–4 (early Imperial).

attached to the College of the Dendrophori (devotees of the mysteries of Magna Mater) on the Caelian Hill in Rome.[24]

All of these uses of the word *basilica* are attested either in the works of contemporary writers or in inscriptions; and there seems no reason to doubt that the factor which they had in common was a more or less close resemblance to, or derivation from, the architectural type embodied in the official judiciary basilicas, modelled on those of the capital, that were to be found in any Roman town of any civic pretensions. Such, at any rate, is the clear inference to be drawn from the passages in Vitruvius that refer to the domestic basilica (see above, pp. 70, 74); and a survey of the epigraphic evidence shows that it is to public, judiciary buildings of this sort that the overwhelming majority of the surviving inscriptions refer. At first, as we have seen, these buildings were strictly 'basilical', i.e. they had internal colonnades and clerestory lighting; and this seems to have remained the accepted type for such great public halls as the Basilica Ulpia in Rome or the Basilica Severiana at Lepcis Magna, right down to the end of the third century. Already, however, under the early Empire we begin to find buildings that were called *basilica* by virtue of their function rather than of their architectural form. Such (to cite three representative examples) were the public basilicas at Veleia, in the Appennine foothills near Parma (first century), at Timgad (Trajanic), and at Doclea in Dalmatia (first half of the second century),[25] all of which were single-naved halls occupying the whole of one side of the forum. These were basilicas without internal colonnades; and we may suspect (although there is very little direct evidence either way) that by no means all of those that had colonnades also had clerestories. We are less well informed about the various other classes of basilica referred to in the preceding paragraph; but what little we do know suggests a similar diversity of architectural type. The *Basilica Argentaria* in Rome is plausibly identified with an open colonnaded structure of Trajanic date, at the south-west corner of the Forum of Caesar,[26] whereas the fourth-century *Basilica Vestiaria* at Djemila[27] was a simple rectangular hall, with a door in the middle of one short side and, opposite it, a projecting apse. About the surviving cult-buildings that are usually known as basilicas—e.g. the well-known Neo-Pythagorean hypogeum at the Porta Maggiore;[28] the so-called 'Basilica Crepereia,' a basilical hypogeum associated with the cult of Faunus, which was found and destroyed in 1613 in Rome, in the via Panisperna;[29] and the small basilical building found in the precinct of the temple of the *Matronae Vacallinehae* at Pesch in the Rhineland[30]—there is an element of doubt, since there is no direct evidence that this was the word used to describe them in antiquity. What is certain is that, except for the omission (for obvious reasons) of a clerestory in the two underground examples, they follow closely the traditional basilical type, and the name would seem to be a reasonable inference from the title of the functionally analogous *Basilica Hilariana* (see above, p. 74).

It remains to mention the audience-halls of the imperial palaces in Rome and, under the later Empire, in the provinces. Plutarch (*Popl.* 15) refers by name to the

[24] *CIL* vi, 30973. See *Bull. Comm.* 1890, p. 20 and *Not. d. Scavi* 1869, pp. 348–9; unfortunately only the antechamber was excavated. To judge from the associated sculpture, it may have been as early as the late second century.
[25] Veleia: S. Aurigemma, *Velleia* (Rome, 1940), p. 34; R. Schultze, *Basilika* (Berlin, 1928), p. 49, fig. 36. Tim-

gad: Schultze, *op. cit.* pl. VII. Doclea: *ibid.* fig. 33.
[26] G. Lugli, *Roma Antica: il centro monumentale*, Roma, 1946, p. 251.   [27] See above, p. 74, n. 20.
[28] *Monumenti antichi dei Lincei* xxxi, 1926, cols. 601–860.
[29] *Bull. Comm.* xlvi, 1920, p. 73; cf. *CIL* vi, 1937.
[30] Schultze, *op. cit.* pp. 61–3, fig. 44.

basilica of Domitian's palace on the Palatine; but otherwise, as units within a larger whole, they play little part in the contemporary record. But on the analogy of the many other derivative uses of the word to describe the same architectural type, it is reasonable to suppose that they were known as basilicas, and under the early Empire, at any rate, they seem regularly to have been longitudinally colonnaded halls, with clerestory lighting and an apse at one end of the long axis. Such are the basilicas in Domitian's palace on the Palatine and in Hadrian's villa at Tivoli.[31] The function of the apsed basilical hall in Diocletian's Palace at Spalato[32] is variously interpreted; but the Magnaura, Constantine's throne-room in the imperial palace at Constantinople, seems to have been just such a colonnaded hall, set at the far end of an atrium-like forecourt.[33] Constantine's surviving throne-room at Trier[34] was an aisleless, apsed hall, which might well have served as a model fifty years later for the cloth-hall at Djemila.

Whether these palace basilicas were the simple outgrowth of the Emperor's judicial functions (influenced perhaps by the private basilicas of late Republican and early Imperial domestic architecture) or whether in some degree they represent a fresh borrowing from the same Hellenistic models as may have inspired the great Republican basilicas two and a half centuries earlier, it is impossible to say; nor is the question important for our present enquiry. It is quite clear that, whether or not the palace basilica derived in any way from a hypothetical Ptolemaic *basilike*, under the later Empire, with the increasing elaboration of court ceremonial, it came to acquire a function that would have seemed strangely familiar to a courtier of the divine Pharaoh. This is a point that may well be relevant to the problem of the origin of the Christian basilica.

To conclude this rapid survey of the development of the pre-Christian basilica, we may note that, in general terms, it was the 'broad' type that was current in the West, the 'long' type in the East. There were important exceptions. The basilica at Pompeii, for example, occupies a somewhat equivocal position, in that it combines a longitudinal arrangement of entrance and tribunal with a typically Italian centralised ambulatory;[35] and we may suspect that Italian (and probably South Italian) buildings of this type served as the model for such buildings as the basilica beside the Lechaeum Road at Corinth (which was a deliberate centre of Romanisation in Greece) or the Basilica Vetus at Lepcis Magna,[36] both of which reproduce essentially the Pompeian type (fig. 2, 2 and 3). But the normal judiciary basilica, both in Italy and in the Western provinces, was a 'broad' building, set with its long axis parallel to one side of the forum and laid out symmetrically about the shorter axis. In the Eastern provinces the judiciary basilica never seems to have been completely at home.[37] Its functions were already

[31] G. Giovannoni in *Saggi sull'Architettura Etrusca e Romana*, Roma, 1940, pp. 85–94 (the concrete vault is disputed); H. Winnefeld, *Die Villa des Hadrian*, Berlin, 1895, fig. 24.
[32] G. Niemann, *Der Palast Diokletians in Spalato*, Vienna, 1910, Abb. 129; only the vaulted substructures are preserved, but it is clear that these reflect the plan of the hall that once stood upon them. It is to be distinguished from the vestibule and plain rectangular hall opening off the 'Peristyle' or ceremonial atrium (the function of which is discussed by E. Dyggve, *Ravennatum Palatium Sacrum*, Copenhagen, 1941).
[33] Destroyed in 532. For a reconstructed plan, based on the contemporary sources, see E. Dyggve, *op. cit.*, p.

54, fig. 45; he suggests that Theodoric's throne room at Ravenna followed the same model.
[34] W. v. Massow, *Die Basilika in Trier*, Simmern (Hunsrück), 1948.
[35] See V. Müller, *AJA* xli, 1937, pp. 250–2.
[36] *Corinth*, i, 1932, pp. 193–211; *Fasti Archaeologici* iv (1949), 4021, fig. 88.
[37] The examples cited by Downey (*art. cit.* (n. 3) pp. 194–211) suggest the possible survival throughout the classical period of a class of buildings that were known as *basilikai*, but were partly open to the sky. Such buildings would presumably have been derived from late Hellenistic models.

substantially covered by the Stoa, except as a centre for the Imperial cult; and that, under local conditions, was better served by putting up a separate building. Wherever it is found, therefore, the judiciary basilica may probably be regarded as a more or less direct product of Romanisation. Nevertheless, where it did take root, its Hellenistic ancestry enabled it to do so vigorously and without violence to local architectural traditions; and it would be a mistake to regard the basilica in the East as a slavish copy of the Western type. The 'broad' basilica, an architectural type that reflects a long-established Italian predilection for centralised forms (cf. the atrium), is barely, if at all, represented in the East. Instead, we have a 'long' type, with longitudinal colonnades running without a break from entrance to *tribunal*, often seeming to sacrifice architectural logic in order to do so. The Caesareum at Cyrene, which was closely associated with the newly established Imperial cult, is an instructive early example of the success with which the new Roman wine could be poured into the old Hellenistic bottles.[38] Another striking and well-documented example is the Hadrianic basilica and forum at Kremna in Pisidia.[39] One has only to compare it with the loose agglomeration of porticoes that constitutes the agora of the neighbouring town of Termessos [40] to appreciate the Roman element in this otherwise strongly conservative, provincial Asiatic architecture.[41]

By the beginning of the fourth century, then, the Roman basilica had already five centuries of development behind it. In Rome and Central Italy the basilical tradition had been established by the great public halls of early-second-century Rome, with a possible collateral branch of the same family in South Italy, represented by the well-known basilica at Pompeii; and with a few possible but unproven exceptions, such as the domestic basilica and, later, the palatine throne-room, all subsequent basilicas in the West appear to derive from this source, either through the application of the name *basilica* to buildings that fulfilled the functions of the earlier basilicas but had not their architectural form, or through the use of the familiar architectural type in new and unfamiliar contexts. But it is probably true to say that to the ordinary Roman of A.D. 300 the colonnaded forum-basilica still represented the norm of ordinary usage and the logical justification for these wider uses of the word. In the Eastern provinces the position is complicated by the survival of other Hellenistic building types, functionally comparable but architecturally distinct, which may have included *basilikai* of a distinctively East Roman type. Nevertheless, although the Roman basilica was, in consequence, never so common in the East as it was in the West, it was successfully introduced; and since the architectural idiom was familiar and could be readily adapted to local conditions, by the end of the third century it may fairly claim to have become a familiar part of the architectural *koiné* of the Empire.

The problem that confronted the Christians after the conversion of Constantine was nothing less than the creation of a new monumental architecture to serve the requirements

---

[38] *JRS* xxxviii, 1948, p. 62, fig. 7. This building, which was restored by Hadrian after the Jewish Revolt, awaits detailed study; in its present state it represents a curious compromise between 'broad' and 'long' planning. The same features characterise the second-century basilica recently excavated at Smyrna (Izmir).

[39] K. Lanckoronski, *Städte Pamphyliens und Pisidiens*, ii, Vienna, 1892, pp. 164–5; for a better plan see Langlotz, *art. cit.* (n. 1), fig. 28, 10.

[40] Lanckoronski, *op. cit.* ii, pp. 21 f.

[41] Other accessibly published examples of judiciary basilicas from the Eastern provinces are those at Aspendos in Pamphylia (Lanckoronsky, *op. cit.* i, pp. 96–8, fig. 76), at Apamea in Syria (H. C. Butler, *American Archaeological Expedition to Syria, 1899–1900*, ii: *Architecture and other Arts*, New York, 1905, p. 55, fig. 22) and, probably, at Palmyra (*C. R. Acad. des Inscr.* 1940, pp. 237–49; the interior is not yet excavated, but it can hardly be other than a basilica, and the three doors indicate a 'long' plan. I owe this reference to Mr. R. G. Goodchild.)

of what, from a banned or barely tolerated cult, suddenly, in the course of a very few years, found itself an official state religion. Quite apart from its unhappy associations (a motive that can be overstressed : the Church early showed itself ready to adopt and turn to its own use those elements of pagan art or ritual that it found serviceable), the traditional pagan temple was architecturally quite unsuited to the needs of Christian worship. Pagan funerary architecture might afford models for its monumental martyr-shrines and baptisteries; but for its eucharistic celebrations, and for those other liturgical occasions that involved the presence of the Christian community in large numbers, it needed a new form of cult-edifice. The answer that it produced was the Early Christian basilica.

In discussing the sources from which the Early Christian basilica was derived, it is more than usually necessary to define one's terms with care, since it is clear that quite early in the post-Constantinian period the word *basilica* came to be used in a far looser sense that one is nowadays accustomed to give it. In present-day usage the Early Christian basilica may be defined as a more or less monumental hall with two (occasionally four) longitudinal colonnades, clerestory lighting, and, at the far end of the central nave, an apse. This was a norm that admitted of a great many variations of detail. There were basilicas with no apse (e.g. the first churches at Aquileia and at Parenzo)[42] or with two apses (e.g. at Orléansville);[43] there were basilicas with transepts between the nave and the apse (as frequently in Greece); there were basilicas without clerestories (e.g. the early churches of Southern Syria, whose form was dictated by local materials and building traditions);[44] and there were small churches everywhere—it is better not to call them basilicas, although they were often known as such, and although in a great many cases they can be shown to be the poor relations of their richer basilical neighbours —in which the nave is a simple hall without any internal subdivisions. Despite these variations, however, the basic type is remarkably consistent, and is what we mean today when we talk of 'the Early Christian basilica'.

It comes as something of a surprise, therefore, to find that a circular building, such as San Vitale at Ravenna, could be referred to in its foundation-inscription as a basilica,[45] or that as early as the end of the fourth century a pilgrim to the Holy Land could refer to the circular structure over the Holy Sepulchre as *basilica Anastasis*, and to the basilical church to the east of it as *ecclesia maior*.[46] Constantine himself, in a letter written to Bishop Macarios of Jerusalem, had referred to the latter building as βασιλική,[47] and *basilica* is what the Bordeaux Pilgrim calls it, a few years later.[48] Eusebius, Constantine's

---

[42] C. Cecchelli in *La Basilica di Aquileia*, Bologna, 1933, pp. 109–253; P. Verzone, *L'Architettura religiosa dell'alto Medioevo nell'Italia settentrionale*, Torino, 1942, pp. 31–4, with previous bibliography. B. Molajoli, *La Basilica Eufrasiana di Parenzo*, Padova, 1943, p. 25, fig. 28 (the mid-fifth-century 'pre-Eufrasian' basilica); its fourth-century predecessor, one of a pair of plain rectangular halls with neither apse nor internal colonnades, is referred to as *basilica* in the dedicatory inscription of its mosaic pavement (*ibid.*, p. 16, fig. 10).

[43] St. Gsell, *Monuments Antiques de l'Algérie*, ii, pp. 236–41.

[44] H. C. Butler, *op. cit.*, pp. 406 f.; J. Lassus, *Sanctuaires chrétiens de Syrie*, Paris, 1947, pp. 47 f.

[45] *CIL* xi, 1, 288 = *ILCV* 1795.

[46] *Peregrinatio Aetheriae*, ed. P. Geyer (*Corpus Script. Eccl. Lat.* xxxix), 48, 1 (p. 100), *et al.* For the interpre-

tation of the early texts relating to the Church of the Holy Sepulchre, see E. Wistrand, *Konstantins Kirche am heiligen Grab in Jerusalem nach den ältesten literarischen Zeugnissen* (*Acta Universitatis Gotoburgiensis*, 1952–1, Göteborg, 1952 (see further below, p. 8).

[47] *vit. Const.* iii, 29–32; e.g. (32) τὴν δὲ τῆς βασιλικῆς καμάραν πότερον λακυνάριαν ἢ δι' ἑτέρας τινὸς ἐργασίας γενέσθαι σοι δοκεῖ, παρὰ σοῦ γνῶναι βούλομαι. Both here and in Constantine's letter about the church at Mamre (*ibid.* iii, 53), βασιλική (rare elsewhere in Eusebius) probably represents 'basilica' in the original Latin draft of the letter (L. Voekl, *Riv. Arch. Crist.* xxix, 1953, pp. 58–60). The letter is important as indicating the Emperor's personal interest in, and control of, the detailed progress of the work.

[48] *Itinerarium Burdigalense*, ed. P. Geyer (*Corpus Script. Eccl. Lat.* xxxix), p. 23.

contemporary, is content with elegant periphrases, βασίλειος νεώς or βασίλειος οἶκος, and, although these may reasonably be held to imply the word *basilica*, his choice of language is of interest rather for the indication that it gives of the natural associations that the word had, at any rate in this context, for himself and for his contemporaries. Everything about this building was *basilikos*, as befitted the work of a *basileus*; and that this was no individual flight of literary fancy we can see a few years later from the parenthetical comment of the Bordeaux Pilgrim, *iusso Constantini imperatoris basilica facta est, id est dominicum*. The Christian basilica was born into a world that delighted in double meanings and symbolic allusions; and, with such connotations, it is not at all surprising that the word *basilica* should rapidly have come to lose any precise architectural significance it may have had. With the all-important exception that it records Constantine's own application of the word to one of the most important of his own foundations, the post-Constantinian literary record is not of much use to us in our present enquiry.

We have to turn instead to the archaeological remains, supplemented, whenever possible, by the writings of the pre-Constantinian Fathers. In dealing with this evidence, there are, broadly speaking, two possible lines of approach. Both are alike in assuming a certain continuity of development before and after Constantine; but whereas the first is concerned primarily with the analysis of what we know of the pre-Constantinian meeting-places of the Christian communities, the starting point for the second is the Early Christian basilica itself, which has then to be explained in terms of some aspect or aspects of the recent (and not necessarily Christian) past.

Of these two possible lines of approach, the first is methodologically the more attractive, since we can hardly doubt that, whenever possible, Constantine's establishment of the Church was rooted in existing Christian practice. It suffers, on the other hand, from the disadvantage that the archaeological evidence is very scanty, and that, in the absence of the remains of a substantial number of pre-Constantinian church-buildings, the literary evidence is hard to interpret with any precision. We know that from very early days, the Christian communities were accustomed to meet in private houses;[49] and the church of Dura Europos affords welcome evidence that, by the middle of the third century, the *domus ecclesiae* had evolved certain simple but recognisable forms to meet the practical and liturgical requirements of the Christian community.[50] Opening off the central courtyard, there is a large room for its meetings, a baptistery for the final initiation of the new members, and what may be a room in which to hold the *agape*; and upstairs there was the priest's lodging and, probably, rooms for the instruction of those awaiting baptism. One must not exaggerate the degree of architectural specialisation; the church at Dura remains essentially a house, indistinguishable from the outside (or indeed from the courtyard) from any of its neighbours. But that it also represents a tangible stage in the evolution of Christian church-architecture is clear from the fact that in large parts of Syria the normal church of the fourth century was patently developed from just this sort of house-church.[51] Indeed, it would be truer to say that it still was the house-church; as Lassus very rightly remarks of these fourth-century Syrian churches, it is not the basilica that constitutes the church, but the

[49] *Acts* i, 13; ix, 37–9; xx, 6–9.

[50] *The Excavations at Dura Europos*, v, 1934, pp. 238–88.

[51] J. Lassus, art. 'Syrie' in Cabrol-Leclercq-Marrou, *Dictionnaire d'archéologie chrétienne*, 1951, col. 1855 ff. (reassuming and revising his own *Sanctuaires chrétiens de Syrie*, Paris, 1947).

whole group of buildings of which the basilica is a part. Excellent early examples of this are the small church of Qirk Bizzé (Kirk Beza) in North Syria and the larger Julianos Church at Umm al-Jemal in the South, both dating from early in the fourth century and both, in detail, the product of local architectural traditions that go back well into the third century.[52]

What we can document from Syria, thanks to the large number of remains surviving undisturbed from late antiquity, we can, for the most part, only guess at elsewhere. It is only in Rome, where there is documentary evidence to show that a number of later churches arose on the site of buildings that had belonged to prominent members of the pre-Constantinian Christian community, that we can point with any certainty to the substantial remains of places of worship dating from before the Peace of the Church. An exceptionally well-preserved example (if it has been correctly identified) is the third-century house beside the church of San Martino ai Monti, which is commonly identified as the 'titulus Equitii'.[53] The function of the 'titulus' resembled that of the later parish church; and since this building shows no trace of any structural alteration during the fourth century, it would seem to afford welcome archaeological evidence of what is, a priori, a most likely state of affairs, namely that frequently, even in the capital, the old house-churches continued for a long time to serve the needs of the community before being replaced by more up-to-date church buildings. Unfortunately, the identification is not beyond question (see Appendix, p. 89); and even if this is the original titulus building, it is very unlikely that the central hall, a rectangular vaulted chamber divided into two aisles by a row of brick piers, was built as a church,[54] or indeed that, opening as it does directly off the street, it was itself ever used as the place of reunion of a proscribed cult. The same objection applies even more forcibly to the hall beneath San Clemente,[55] which is sometimes cited as a precursor of the Christian basilica, despite the fact that it lay wide open to a public street. As at Dura, the actual cult-rooms must surely have been withdrawn discreetly from the public gaze.

As a community grew, it might enlarge one of the rooms of an existing house, as it did at Dura; it might borrow and adapt an existing pagan structure, as the Christians of Antioch are said by the third-century author of the *Recognitiones* to have established their church in the private house of a wealthy citizen;[56] it must, on occasion, have had to erect a new building to serve as a church, and such a building would no doubt have included a substantial hall for the celebration of the eucharist. But neither in Rome nor elsewhere is there as yet any evidence to suggest that, prior to the Peace of the Church, the Christians had evolved, or even begun to evolve, a monumental architecture of their own; indeed, situated as they were in the middle of a world that was, on occasion, violently hostile, it seems far more likely that they had deliberately avoided doing so. Lactantius, an eye-witness, tells us that in 303 it was the work of a few hours to raze to the ground the church of the important Christian community of Nicomedia.[57]

---

[52] J. Lassus, art. 'Syrie' in Cabrol-Leclercq-Marrou, *Dictionnaire d'archéologie chrétienne*, 1951, figs. 11001 and 11020.

[53] R. Vielliard, *Les origines du titre de Saint-Martin aux Monts à Rome*, Rome, 1931.

[54] *Ibid.*, p. 26, fig. 4, and plan I.

[55] R. Krautheimer, *Corpus Basilicarum Christianarum Romae*, i, 1937, pp. 117–36. Cf. E. Junyent, 'La primitiva

basilica di S. Clemente,' *Riv. Arch. Crist.* v, 1928, pp. 231–78.

[56] Pseudo-Clement, *Recognitiones* x, 71 (Migne, *PG* i, in the version of Rufinus): 'ita ut ... Theophilus, qui erat cunctis potentibus in civitate sublimior, domus suae ingentem basilicam ecclesiae nomine consecraret.'

[57] *de mortibus persecutorum* (ed. Brandt and Laubmann, *Corpus Script. Eccl. Lat.* xxvii, 1893) 12, 5.

Archaeology may well have surprises in store; but, on the evidence at present available, we are probably justified in concluding that at the beginning of the fourth century the relatively unsubstantial house-church was still the only form of organised meeting-place known to the Christian world. That this primitive house-church made a notable contribution to the Christian architecture of the fourth century we cannot doubt; its influence is clearly visible both in the liturgical lay-out and fittings and in the buildings that surround the church proper. But, for the architectural origins of the Christian basilica we must look elsewhere.

It is to the evidence afforded by Constantine's own foundations that one naturally turns; and it is precisely in this field that recent research has made some of its most useful gains. The excavations of 1933–34 [58] established that Constantine's Church of the Nativity at Bethlehem consisted essentially of three separate elements united to form a single architectural complex: a spacious colonnaded forecourt ('atrium'); a basilical hall with five longitudinal naves; and at the east end of this hall, opening off the central nave, an octagonal structure sheltering the cave in which, by tradition, Christ was born (fig. 3, b). About its neighbour, the first Church of the Holy Sepulchre, archaeology can tell us less—little more, indeed, than the shape of the site, a long, narrow rectangle, rounded at the western end. But we are fortunate in possessing numerous contemporary accounts of what was, in its day, the most famous and influential building in Christendom; and the most recent study of these accounts, by the Swedish philologist Wistrand,[59] has confirmed and amplified, and in several important respects corrected, the proposals made by Dyggve shortly before and during the war.[60] As described by Dyggve, the Church of the Holy Sepulchre consisted of three main elements: to the east, a basilical hall; adjoining it to the west, on the same axis, an open colonnaded courtyard, rounded at the western end and enclosing, at the centre of the semicircle, the actual monument covering the Tomb; and, to the south of this courtyard, a baptistery and a colonnaded forecourt, or atrium. This picture requires correction in several important details; in particular, there does not seem to be any valid reason for displacing the atrium from the position which it is usually held to have occupied, to the east of the basilical hall, on the axis of the building; and, as Wistrand has now shown, it cannot have been very long after Constantine (certainly before Aetheria visited Jerusalem at the end of the fourth century) that the semicircular western end of the courtyard was transformed into the familiar circular structure that has dominated all subsequent accounts of, and speculation about, the site. But the most important and original of Dyggve's conclusions, that the building housing the sacred relic was at first an open courtyard, not a roofed structure, is convincing; and it would certainly have commanded wider and more immediate acceptance, if its author had not chosen to link it with a terminology that has won little support. In calling this monumental, perticoed courtyard 'basilica discoperta' and relating it to a number of other open, porticoed funerary buildings with apses (notably the shrine excavated by himself at Marusinac, near Salona) to which he applies the same term, he suggests a relationship to the normal roofed basilica that is attested neither by archaeology nor by philology. 'Basilica

[58] E. T. Richmond, *Q. Dep. Ant. Pal.* v, 1936, pp. 75–81; W. H. and J. H. Harvey, *Archaeologia* lxxxvii, 1938, pp. 7–17.

[59] See n. 46.

[60] *Bericht d. VI int. Kongr. für Archäologie, 1939*, Berlin, 1940, pp. 385 f.; *Gravkirken i Jerusalem*, Copenhagen, 1941 (résumé in French); *Actes du VIe Congr. int. d'études byz.*, 1948, ii, 1951, pp. 111–23.

G

discoperta' is not a technical term. It figures once only in the ancient literature, and then in a corrupt passage.[61] And although it may well be that open, apsed courtyards played a part in shaping the later development of the Christian basilica, particularly in connection with the cult of martyrs, just as the architectural type (as distinct from the name given to it by Dyggve) may have influenced the form of the courtyard enclosing the Holy Sepulchre, the influence of such buildings on the initial adoption of the roofed basilica as the standard eucharistic meeting-place of the early fourth-century Church has yet to be demonstrated. With these important reservations, we may accept Dyggve's account; and the first Church of the Holy Sepulchre falls into line beside the first Church of the Nativity as an axially composed group of three distinct buildings: an atrium-forecourt, a basilical hall, and a shrine housing the sacred relic (fig. 3, *a*).

The shrines enclosing the cave of the Nativity and the Holy Sepulchre and, by a simple extension of ideas, the larger complexes of which they were a part, both belong to the category of early Christian buildings known as 'martyria', that is to say they were built to house the relics of martyrs or the holy places associated with the life on earth of Christ or of his Old Testament forbears.[62] It comes as no surprise, therefore, to find that the same architectural scheme (atrium, basilical hall, martyrium) reappears in the most famous of the early western martyr-shrines, the great church that Constantine built over the traditional tomb of St. Peter in Rome (fig. 3, *c*). In St. Peter's the distinction between the basilical hall and the martyr-shrine is architecturally less marked than it is at Jerusalem and at Bethlehem; and the fact that, under the influence of St. Peter's, transepts came later to be a commonplace of western basilical architecture[63] has further softened the impact of this distinction on modern eyes. Nevertheless, as the recent excavations under St. Peter's have clearly shown, the original purpose of the transept was to frame and to display the tomb-shrine, which stood beneath a splendid canopy at the focal point of the whole architectural scheme, immediately in front of the apse.[64] The altar of the church probably stood elsewhere, possibly even (as commonly in the early churches of Italy and North Africa) in the body of the nave;[65] and there may well have been a screen or barrier dividing the nave from the transept on the line of the triumphal arch. It was not until two and a half centuries later, *c.* 600, that the altar was moved to its present position over the tomb, obliterating a distinction between the two halves of the building which, to Constantine's architects, must still have seemed perfectly clear.

With the subsequent development of the atrium and of the martyrium we are not here concerned.[66] What is important in the present context is that these three great

---

[61] *Itinera Hierosolymitana* (ed. P. Geyer, *Corpus Script. Eccl. Lat.* xxxix, 1898), p. 209. For the variant readings and for a criticism of the use of the term 'basilica discoperta', see A. M. Schneider, *Antiquity* xxiv, 1950, pp. 135–7.

[62] The fundamental study is that of A. Grabar, *Martyrium*, Paris, 1946. In early fourth-century usage the term could be applied either to the sacred relic (the 'witness' of the sacred truth) or to the building or group of buildings that housed it (Wistrand, *op. cit.*, p. 12, citing Eusebius).

[63] R. Krautheimer, 'The Carolingian Revival of Early Christian Architecture', *Art Bulletin* xxiv, 1942, pp. 1–38.

[64] B. M. Apollonj Ghetti, A. Ferrua, E. Josi, E.

Kirschbaum, *Esplorazioni sotto la Confessione di San Pietro in Vaticano*, 1951, i, pp. 161–72; J. B. Ward Perkins, *Journal of Roman Studies* xlii, 1952, pp. 21–4.

[65] *Italy*: see M. Mirabella Roberti, *Riv. Arch. Crist.* xxvi, 1950, pp. 181–94. *N. Africa*: J. B. Ward Perkins and R. G. Goodchild, *Archaeologia* xcv, 1953, pp. 1–82, and specially pp. 64–6. Later (certainly by the time of Gregory of Tours, and probably already in the fifth century) the altar of St. Peter's stood in the transept.

[66] In the West the rapid assimilation of the specialised martyrium-building to the ordinary basilical church (see Grabar, *op. cit.*) was an important factor in eliminating the distinction between churches such as St. Peter's and St. John Lateran (see below).

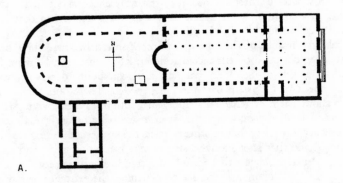

A.

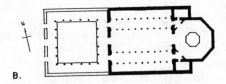

B.

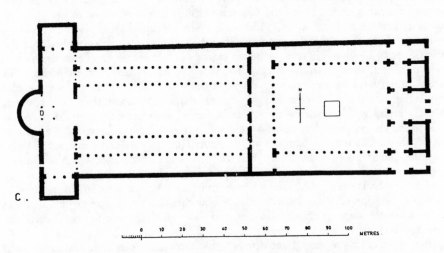

C.

Fig. 3—*a*. The Church of the Holy Sepulchre, Jerusalem (after Wistrand).
b. The Church of the Nativity, Bethlehem.
c. St. Peter's, Rome (the Details of the Atrium Are Hypothetical).

Constantinian sanctuaries, despite their manifest differences of detailed treatment, were clearly built to a common scheme; and that a constant element in that scheme was a longitudinally colonnaded basilical hall.

The full significance of the common element shared by these three buildings has, in the past, been obscured by the fact that another of Constantine's major foundations, the cathedral church of St. John Lateran, although built to serve a very different purpose, appeared to follow in part the same model. There does not seem to be any evidence to show that it ever had an atrium; but, both from the surviving remains of the old church and from the drawings that were made of it before the alterations of the sixteenth century, it is clear that in other respects the medieval building closely resembled old St. Peter's, and that it had a five-aisled nave, a narrow transept, and an apse. Since there is no evidence to suggest that St. John Lateran was built to serve any other purpose than that of episcopal church of the Bishop of Rome, the existence of a transept might well seem to invalidate the identification of the transept of St. Peter's as a martyrium, i.e. as an element functionally and architecturally distinct from the basilical nave; and since, further, it is now abundantly clear that transepts were not a normal part of the Early Christian basilica but an exceptional and intrusive feature, the Lateran transept might well seem to be a conclusive argument against regarding Constantine's own foundations as the models from which the lesser basilical churches of the Empire were derived.

The fact (if it were established) that Constantine's own great basilical foundations were not the models, but were themselves based on, or derived from the same source as, the simple basilical churches of normal fourth-century usage, would seem to compel one to regard the emergence of the early Christian basilica as the result of an evolutionary process rather than of conscious, individual choice. Such, indeed, is the reasoning implicit in many of the theories put forward in the past fifty years: it is implied that the Early Christian basilica is in some sense the logical product of a chain of past events and tendencies, each link of which is causally related to its neighbour; and although, in distinguishing between evolutionary development and individual choice, we are distinguishing between complementary aspects of a single process rather than between mutually exclusive alternatives—the whole history of architecture may be regarded as a history of the varying, and never wholly independent, balance between the creative individuality of artist and patron and the larger, impersonal forces that shaped and determined their work—it obviously makes a great deal of difference which of the two is at any particular moment the dominant partner. Archaeology, by its very methods, tends to emphasise the evolutionary, determinist aspect; and yet, everything that is known of the reign of Constantine tends to show that this was one of the moments in history when the element of individuality, and above all the personality of Constantine himself, was decisive.

It is therefore a very important new fact that excavations carried out between 1934 and 1938 under the floor of St. John Lateran have cast serious doubt on the Constantinian date of the transept.[67] These excavations have not yet examined that part of the

---

[67] The excavations were conducted by Professor Josi; the results are summarised by A. M. Colini in *Storia e Topografia del Celio nell'Antichità* (*Atti Pont. Acc. Rom. Arch.* 3: *Memorie* VII), pp. 344-59. The writer is indebted to Professor Josi for allowing him to examine the unpublished material and to test the point at issue; and to Mr. G. U. S. Corbett, who first suggested the significance of the new finds.

transept which projects beyond the north and south outer walls of the nave; and only when this has been done can the results be regarded as conclusive. What they have shown (fig. 4) is that the stylobates of the two inner colonnades are continuous right up to the shoulders of the original apse; whereas there is no continuous transverse foundation beneath the triumphal arch, at the junction of the present transept with the nave. In St. Peter's the converse is true: there was an enormous transverse foundation beneath the triumphal arch, whereas the stylobates of the nave colonnades break off when they reach the transept. The foundation plan of St. Peter's faithfully reflects the architectural logic of an independent transept; and the fact that the foundations of St. John Lateran convey no hint of such a transept is strong presumptive evidence that there was no such thing in the original plan. On this hypothesis, the transept would be an addition of the early Middle Ages, designed to bring St. John Lateran into line with St. Peter's, in an age when the original significance of the transept had been lost and the Vatican basilica had become the accepted model for Western European basilical architecture.[68] With the important reservation that further excavation is needed to establish the facts beyond dispute, it may fairly be said that the onus of proof now rests with those who maintain that the Lateran transept is an original feature; and Constantine's basilica, the episcopal church of Rome and his first great Christian building[69] in what was still the capital of his Empire, takes its place as a large but orthodox Early Christian basilica, with a five-aisled nave and a single western apse.

There is no reason to believe that the archaeological account is closed, or that there are no fresh surprises in store. Nevertheless, with so much new evidence to hand, it does seem legitimate to try to strike an interim balance, and to define the problem anew in terms of the evidence now available. We may summarise the present state of knowledge as follows:

1. There is nothing to show that the Christian Church before Constantine had evolved a monumental architecture that might have served as a model for the Constantinian and post-Constantinian basilica.

2. The church of St. John Lateran, the episcopal church of Rome and almost certainly the first substantial church to be built under the Emperor's patronage, seems (contrary to long-established belief) to have been built as a basilica of standard Early Christian type.

3. No less than three of Constantine's later foundations (the churches of the Holy Sepulchre, of the Nativity, and of St. Peter) are built to a common pattern, a central and consistent feature of which is the incorporation of a large basilical hall. Constantine himself refers to this feature as basilica; and the evidence recorded by his contemporary, Eusebius, leaves no doubt whatever of the Emperor's own direct and detailed concern with the form and progress of these great undertakings.

If we reject, as historically improbable, the idea of the spontaneous evolution of the Christian basilica from pagan models (an idea which is, moreover, very hard to reconcile

[68] See Krautheimer, art. cit. The most probable occasion would be the major restoration undertaken by Pope Sergius III (904-11).

[69] The date of its foundation is not recorded, but it is significant that its endowments were all in Italy, whereas those of the Lateran Baptistery included the Balkan districts (won by Constantine in 319), and those of St. Peter's the Eastern provinces (won in 324); see A. Piganiol, L'Empéreur Constantin, 1932, p. 113; H. v. Schoenebeck, Klio, Beih. xliii, 1939, pp. 88 ff.

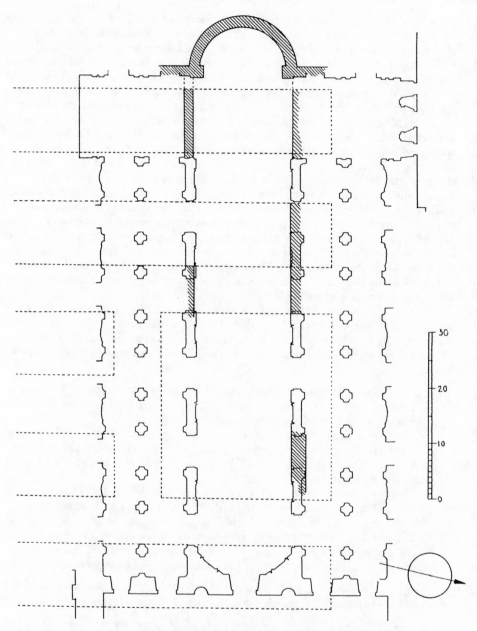

FIG. 4.—CHURCH OF ST. JOHN LATERAN.

The ascertained foundations of the Constantinian Church (*shaded*) in relation to the walls and piers of the present church (*outline*) and to the headquarters-building and barrack-blocks of the Severan Camp of the Equites Singulares (*dotted outline*).

with the rapidity with which the basilical church seems to have been accepted through-out the Empire), we are driven to conclude that its adoption as the standard form of Early Christian church was the direct consequence, whether by force of example or by actual administrative enactment, of its prior use in these great Imperial foundations; in particular, if we knew why Constantine and his advisers built the church of St. John Lateran as they did, we should have gone a long way towards solving the problem of the origins of the Christian Basilica.

That is a question to which it is not now, and may never be, possible to give a decisive answer; but formulated in these terms it does allow us to assess the probabilities more clearly, and to limit the field of enquiry to those elements that might reasonably be held to have attracted the attention of the Emperor and his advisers in their search for a type of building that should be suitable for the needs of the newly-enfranchised religion. It is possible, but in the writer's view improbable, that the architectural framework of the Early Christian basilica was an eclectic, artificial creation. Through all Constantine's activities as a reformer runs a strong thread of conservatism; his guiding purpose seems to have been, wherever possible, to breathe new life into old forms rather than to create new; and it would have been far more in keeping with his whole attitude, particularly in the early, experimental years of his reign, to have taken over and adapted an existing type of building. We may perhaps go further, and state that, in the absence of an existing Christian monumental architecture upon which to draw, the natural source of inspiration would have been the palatine architecture of the Imperial Court.[70] It is a commonplace of Early Christian archaeology that, both for its ceremonial and for the furnishings required for the performance of that ceremonial, the Church borrowed heavily from contemporary Imperial practice; and although some of the resemblances that we meet later may be the result of a gradual process of mutual assimilation, there are others (such as the Imperial canopy, which becomes the Christian *ciborium*)[71] that can be shown to go back certainly to the time of Constantine. It would have been natural, then, and in keeping with all that we know of the development of the outward forms of Christian worship at this time, if the architectural type embodied in the great new Imperial foundations had been derived from the ceremonial halls of contemporary Court life. It is important to remember that these audience-halls themselves played a conspicuous part in the contemporary ecclesiastical drama. At the Council of Nicaea, in 325, the ordinary sittings met in the town's largest church, but the final session was held in the great central hall of the Palace.[72] If only we knew something of the hall in the Lateran Palace in which Pope Miltiades held the Council of 313,[73] we might perhaps hold the key to the puzzle.

To suggest that the audience-halls of contemporary court ceremonial may have been

---

[70] So Langlotz, *art. cit.* (n. 4), pp. 34–6.

[71] See, recently, U. Monneret de Villard in *Archaeologia* xcv, 1953, pp. 102–3, discussing the canopy within the shrine of the Imperial cult (*temp.* Diocletian) in the legion-ary fortress at Luxor; cf. the Constantinian canopy over the central shrine in St. Peter's. For the relationship between the ceremonial of Church and Court, see A. Grabar, *L'Empéreur dans l'art byzantin*, Paris, 1936, *passim*; also A. Alföldi, *Röm. Mitt.* xlix, 1934, 1–118; l, 1935, 1–171.

[72] Eusebius, *vit. Const.* (ed. Heikel, 1902) iii. 10.

[73] Optatus (ed. Ziwsa, *Corpus Script. Eccl. Lat.* xxvi) i, 23: 'convenerunt in domum Faustae in Laterano.' A Basilica Julii '*in lateranis*' is mentioned in the appendix to the letters of Gregory the Great as the scene of the proclamation of the Emperor Phocas to the senate and clergy of Rome (ed. Migne, *Patr. Lat.* lxxvii, 1302), probably the same Basilica Julii as that in which the sup-porters of Boniface II (530–2) met to elect him in opposi-tion to the party of Dioscorus, which met in St. John Lateran (*Lib. Pont.* i, p. 281).

the immediate models for Constantine's great basilical churches is not to deny that other types of pagan basilica had an important influence on the subsequent development of the architectural type in Christian hands. It is very probable indeed that they did. Although, on this hypothesis, we must attribute the initial adoption of the basilical church in the provinces either to the example of the great Imperial foundations or to some more direct Imperial initiative, its widespread and immediate acceptance shows that the seed fell on ready ground. The wide currency of the pagan basilica meant that there were few awkward problems to be faced in adapting its Christian successor to local conditions and materials. It was, moreover, an architectural type that lent itself readily to modification; and it is to the phase immediately after its endorsement by the Church, rather than to that of its initial adoption, that we should ascribe such influences from existing Christian funerary usage as those on which Dyggve lays such emphasis. Pagan cult-buildings such as the 'Basilica Crepereia',[74] despite the familiar appearance of its mosaics on apse and triumphal arch, may have had little or no direct influence either on the initial adoption of the Early Christian basilica or on its subsequent development; but they are good evidence of what was felt to be suitable for a place of worship in a world of ideas that had much in common with the early stages of organised Christianity. The success of the Christian basilica is another aspect of the familiar truth that Christianity was born into a waiting world.

In conclusion we may note an aspect of the Early Christian basilica that was to be of immense importance for the later history of European architecture. One has only to glance at the public monuments erected in Rome during the last half-century of its life as the Imperial capital—the Aurelian Walls, the Baths of Diocletian and of Constantine, the Basilica of Maxentius, the 'Temple of Romulus' in the Forum—to realise how far the architecture of the capital had already progressed along the path that leads from classical antiquity to the Middle Ages.[75] The story is epitomised in the Basilica of Maxentius, where, for the first time, we find 'contemporary' concrete-vaulted architecture invading a domain that had hitherto been reserved for the conservative dignities of a dying classicism. What would have happened in the next fifty years, if Constantine had not transferred the capital elsewhere and left Rome to the contemplation of her vanished glories, is a fascinating subject for speculation. What did happen was that the only important buildings to be put up in Rome after 330 were churches; and by selecting the timber-roofed basilica to be the standard form of Christian meeting-place, Constantine ensured the triumphant survival in the West of a type of architecture that any progressive architect under the Tetrarchy would have pronounced a doomed survival from an outmoded past. 'Contemporary' architecture moved elsewhere, in the West to Milan and Ravenna, but above all eastwards, to Constantinople. It is one of the ironies of history that Rome, which for three centuries had been the home of all that was progressive in architecture, became overnight the stronghold of a vigorous but none the less authentic conservative tradition; whereas Greece and Anatolia, which under the Empire had clung obstinately to the traditions of their own classical past, through Constantinople now fell heir to the progressive traditions of Italy and became the centres of vital experiment. Just as Constantinople, through its churches, its public

[74] See p. 75, n. 29.
[75] J. B. Ward Perkins, 'The Italian Element in Late   Roman and Early Medieval Architecture', *Proc. Brit. Acad.* xxxiii, 1947, pp. 163–94.

buildings and its baths, shaped the future of monumental architecture in the Eastern Mediterranean, so it was the great Christian basilicas of Rome that established the pattern of western architecture for over a millennium to come.

J. B. WARD PERKINS

APPENDIX. THE IDENTIFICATION OF THE *TITULUS EQUITII*

The building usually identified as the *titulus Equitii* lies immediately to the west of the church of San Martino ai Monti, at a level considerably lower than that of the present church. It has been published and discussed by René Vieillard (*Les origines du titre de Saint-Martin aux Monts à Rome* (*Studi di Antichità Cristiana pubblicati per cura del Pontificio Istituto di Archeologia Cristiana*, iv) Rome, 1931), who concludes that it was the historical *titulus Equitii*, a house-church ceded to the Christian community by a certain Equitius early in the third century and, in view of the large central hall, very probably built expressly to serve this special purpose.

The essential passages in support of this identification are three:

(*a*) The list of signatories to the proceedings of the Church Council held in Rome in 499, three of whom describe themselves as 'presbyter tituli Aequitii' (J. D. Mansi, *Sacrorum Conciliorum nova et amplissima collectio*, Paris, 1901, viii, 436, 437).

(*b*) The surviving fragment of the Laurentian *Liber Pontificalis*, which can be dated between 514 and 519, i.e. to the period immediately following the events here described (*Liber Pontificalis*, ed. Duchesne, i, p. 46; cf. pp. xxx–xxxi):

'Hic (*sc.* Pope Symmachus, 498–514) beati Martini ecclesiam iuxta Sanctum Silvestrem Palatini inlustris viri pecuniis fabricans et exornans, eo ipso istante dedicavit.'

(*c*) The revised, mid-sixth-century edition of the *Liber Pontificalis*, which ascribes to Pope Silvester (314–35) the foundation of a church, which is referred to indiscriminately as *titulus Equitii* and *titulus Silvestri* (*ibid.*, i. p. 170):

'Hic (*sc.* Silvester) fecit in urbe Roma ecclesiam in praedium cuiusdam presbiteri sui, qui cognominabatur Equitius, quem titulum romanum constituit, iuxta termas Domitianas, qui usque in hodiernum diem appellatur titulus Equitii, ubi et haec dona constituit . . .'

a passage which is substantially repeated later (*ibid.*, p. 187):

'Hisdem temporibus constituit beatus Silvester in urbe Roma titulum suum in regione III iuxta thermas Domitianas qui cognominantur Traianas, titulum Silvestri, ubi donavit Constantinus Augustus . . . (list follows). Obtulit et omnia necessaria titulo Equiti.'

These two passages do not appear in either of the surviving summaries of the lost first edition.

From the first of these three documents it is certain that the *titulus Equitii* (or *Aequitii*) existed under that name in 499; and since the latest recorded foundation of a *titulus*-church is that of the *titulus Vestinae*, under Innocent I (401–17) (*Liber Pont.* i, p. 220), it is reasonable to suppose that it was already in existence at latest by the end of the fourth century.

From the second document we learn that Pope Symmachus founded a church of St. Martin *iuxta sanctum Silvestrem*. The present fabric of the church of San Martino ai Monti dates entirely from the reconstruction of the 'church of Saints Silvester and Martin' ('beati Silvestri et Martini ecclesiam'; *Liber Pont.* ii, p. 131) begun by Sergius II (844–7) and finished by Leo IV (847–55); but, although its predecessor may have occupied a slightly different site (Vieillard, *op. cit.* pp. 72–3), there does not seem to be any reason to question the identification of the adjoining third-century structures with the church of St. Silvester referred to in the Laurentian fragment. The courtyard of the early building was enclosed about this date, in what was evidently an attempt to provide something more closely resembling a symmetrical basilical plan, with a principal nave and two flanking aisles, and at the end of the nave a niche was cut in the classical masonry to house the mosaic portrait of a bishop, identified by Wilpert as Silvester himself and attributed to the early sixth century (*Die römischen Mosaiken und Malereien* iii, pl. 96; Vieillard, *op. cit.* fig. 22). That this building is in fact the building referred to in the early sixth century as the church of St. Silvester seems reasonably established.

The identification of this church of St. Silvester with the *titulus Equitii* rests on the passages cited from the *Liber Pontificalis*. If we may accept Duchesne's analysis of the text (i, p. 188, note 4; p. 200, note 119; cf. Vieillard, *Riv. Arch. Crist.* v, 1928, pp. 89–103), these two passages were inserted by the editor of the second edition: they show that by the middle of the sixth century the two names, of Equitius and of Silvester, were associated with the same building, and they reveal the efforts of the editor or of his sources to reconcile the contradiction implied by the double nomenclature; but, as evidence that the *titulus Equitii* was in fact founded by Silvester during the reign of Constantine, they carry little weight. Since, further, an examination of the surviving remains reveals no trace of early-fourth-century work, it is reasonable to conclude, with Vieillard, that the original *titulus*-foundation stood in the name of Equitius (probably the donor of the property), and that it was only later that his name came in some way to be associated with, and eventually superseded by, the better-known name of St. Silvester (we may compare the supersession of the name of the founder of the *titulus Pammachii* by those of Saints John and Paul), giving rise to the legend of a Constantinian foundation that we find recorded in the *Liber Pontificalis*.

That the *titulus Equitii* was founded before the Peace of the Church is not improbable, although it can be regarded as proved only if one accepts the view (Vieillard, *art. cit.*) that all references in the *Liber Pontificalis* to post-Constantinian foundations are mistaken, and that the number of the *tituli* was already closed by the time of Constantine. Vieillard's further contention, that the surviving buildings are those of the original *titulus Equitii* and that this was founded as early as the beginning of the third century (the approximate date of the buildings) is, on the other hand, open to serious question. It assumes that there was an absolute continuity of site, *i.e.* that the early-sixth-century chapel of St. Silvester occupies the precise site of the earlier *titulus*, of which it inherited the cult; and, however probable *a priori* this may seem to be, it is impossible, in the absence of any trace whatsoever of earlier Christian use, to exclude the possibility that the original *titulus* was in some adjoining building, or in some other part of the same group of buildings. Furthermore, even if these are the buildings of the original *titulus*, there is nothing whatever to show that they were built in the first place to serve as the place of reunion of a Christian community. The surviving remains in fact suggest something very different. They consist of a large central hall, measuring some 11 m. by 18 and divided by two piers into two aisles, running north and south, and each consisting of three cross-vaulted bays; at the south-west angle of the hall there is a vestibule, with three large doors opening off the street and others giving access directly into the hall and, in the angle between the hall and the vestibule, into a courtyard, which served to light the two northern bays of the hall; to the east of the hall a much-altered range of rooms opens off the eastern aisle; and doorways, now blocked, gave access to further rooms, lying to the north and east, and to a flight of stairs leading to an upper storey. Of the original decoration of the main hall there is no trace; but there is a substantial fragment of painted plaster still in position in the vault of the vestibule (Vieillard, *Les origines*, etc., figs. 10, 11; it belongs to an early modification of the original plan), and other fragments were copied in the seventeenth century (*ibid.* fig. 9; Wilpert, *op. cit.* p. 326, fig. 104). These are purely pagan in character; and it is very hard to reconcile either this decoration or the form of the hall, with its awkward central row of piers, and of the vestibule, wide open to the street, to the courtyard, and to the hall itself, with the requirements of an early-third-century Christian community. If these buildings are, indeed, what remains of the *titulus Equitii*, they were surely built originally to serve some other purpose (possibly as a covered market; this would explain the vaulted hall, the *taberna*-like rooms opening off it, and the ready access from the street), and it was not until later that they were converted to Christian use. They cannot be used as evidence for a specifically Christian architecture during the third century.

Postscript. The essential responsibility of Constantine for the adoption of the basilica into Christian use is one of the themes of an important article by Richard Krautheimer, which appears to have escaped the attention of others besides the present writer ('The Beginnings of Early Christian Architecture', *The Review of Religions* iii, 1938–9, pp. 127–48). In his article, Krautheimer rightly stresses that the basilica is one only of a number of monumental church-types represented in the fourth century, the element common to all of which seems to be that they are derived from the various types of assembly-hall current in pagan antiquity. Within this wider setting, while admitting the importance of the assimilation of the outward forms of the Christian cult to those of imperial ceremonial, Krautheimer is inclined to look rather to the public basilica, with its long-established associations with the imperial cult, than to the audience halls of palatine architecture.

MEMORIA, MARTYR'S TOMB AND
MARTYR'S CHURCH

THE text of the article which follows is substantially that of the address which the writer delivered at the opening session of the Seventh International Congress of Christian Archaeology, held at Trier in September 1965. Any value which such an address may possess lies very largely in its actuality, and I have therefore gratefully accepted the offer to publish it without the delays inevitable in assembling the formal Proceedings of the Congress. For the same reason I have prepared it for publication substantially as presented, eliminating only those passages that were of relevance purely to the workings of the Congress as such.

The title of this article is taken from the theme laid down for discussion at the opening session of the Congress. It is, of course, that treated in André Grabar's great work, *Martyrium — recherches sur le culte des reliques et l'art chrétien antique*; and since my remarks are bound to dwell mainly upon points of disagreement, I would like to preface them by paying proper tribute to what is unquestionably one of the most important and most influential books published in the last few decades within our field of studies. It is a work of rare imagination and of outstanding erudition. It was published in 1946 and a great deal of its contents have since passed into the common fund of knowledge and ideas. If there are some parts of it which we today are able to criticize, we owe this not only to the fresh information which has accumulated since that date but also in no small measure to the new perspectives which Grabar himself opened before us. *Martyrium* is, and will long continue to be, one of the fundamental publications in its field.

Grabar's thesis in its bare essentials is simple and may be briefly summarized. The cult of martyrs grew up within the funerary context of the cemeteries in which their mortal remains were buried, and it is this funerary context which dominates the architectural iconography of the martyria of the Constantinian and of the immediately post-Constantinian age. To understand these buildings we have to look to the mausolea of classical antiquity. Their subsequent development too was influenced by this factor, though in a more complex way. In the West the pattern of the martyrium church was established from the outset by Constantine's foundations in Rome. By building great basilical halls for the celebration of the mass directly over the burial-

[Journal of Theological Studies, N.S., Vol. XVII, Pt. 1, April 1966] places of the martyrs, and in particular by bringing the martyr-grave into direct relationship with the altar of the church above, Constantine's architects ensured that henceforward the development of church and martyr-shrine followed a single, integrated course. In the east the pattern was different. Here the martyrium remained physically distinct from the ordinary church, and it was normally a building of centralized plan, quite different from the basilical halls of normal liturgical usage; and although there was an increasing tendency for these centralized buildings to incorporate elements (such as, for example, an oriented chancel) which derive from the basilica, for a variety of reasons it was the martyrium which was the dominant architectural type. Furthermore, at any rate during the earlier stages of the post-Constantinian development, these centrally planned martyria continued to derive architecturally from the funerary architecture of classical antiquity. Their relationship to the great Constantinian foundations in the Holy Land is not so much one of lineal descent as of derivation from a common source.

Such in brief is Grabar's thesis. It is presented with a wealth of illustrative detail and a persuasiveness of argument to which no summary can do justice, but I hope and believe that I have fairly represented the essential outline of that part with which we are principally concerned today.[1] The only point upon which Grabar seems at times to speak with two voices is that of the relationship between the great Constantinian foundations and their successors, particularly in the east. On the one hand,[2] speaking of such fifth-century buildings as the Tomb of the Virgin at Jerusalem or the Church of the Theotokos on Mount Gerizim, he emphasizes that they are *not* copies of the Constantinian martyria: 'aucun d'eux ne copie directement les *martyria* constantiniens . . . il s'agit certes d'une famille de monuments apparentés, mais qui, sans dépendre les uns des autres, relèvent d'une même catégorie d'édifices antiques à plan central, dont ils reprennent les diverses variantes, en les adaptant à leur programmes propres.' On the next page, however, he continues:[3]

En Occident, Constantin laissa des églises qui consacrent le culte liturgique sur les reliques des saints; en Orient, il honora dans les *martyria*-églises semblables, mais dédiés au Christ, les emplacements sacrés des Théophanies. Sans pouvoir dire jusqu'à quel point cette distinction repose sur les directives personnelles de l'empereur, on peut affirmer qu'elle marque un moment décisif dans l'histoire de l'architecture. Car si des *martyria* de corps saints continuèrent à s'élever dans toute la

[1] For a convenient summary, by Grabar himself, see *Archaeology*, ii (1949), pp. 95 ff.   [2] *Martyrium*, i, p. 312.   [3] Ibid., p. 313.

chrétienté pendant plusieurs siècles, on verra . . . que les *martyria*-basiliques avec autel fixé sur le tombeau du saint définissent les principales caractéristiques de l'architecture ecclésiastique latine, tandis que les *martyria* à plan central dédiés au Christ en font autant pour l'Orient. Les fondations constantiniennes se dressent ainsi comme les chefs de file de monuments innombrables, en annonçant la séparation prochaine de l'architecture chrétienne des pays latins et des pays grecs.

I take this to mean that it was the Constantinian foundations which established the broad pattern of the subsequent development; but that outside the narrow circle of the great imperial foundations it was the classical mausolea which continued for a time to determine the actual architectural forms used.

I have quoted Grabar at length upon this last point because, as we shall see, it does seem to be one of the principal matters of possible disagreement. But we must for the moment defer the question of the great imperial foundations and their relation to the other martyr-shrines of the Christian world. Let us for the present be content to distinguish carefully between those martyr-shrines which can be shown to be earlier than the Edict of Milan of 313 and those which were later. If we do not do so, we run a serious risk of prejudging the very questions which we are here to examine.

We will begin then by looking at what is clearly the fundamental question, namely that of the architectural relationship between the early martyria and the mausolea of classical antiquity. Is there in fact a resemblance sufficient to indicate that the latter were, and continued right through the fourth century to be, the main effective source of inspiration for the builders of the Christian martyr-shrines?

I do not imagine that anyone will wish to question that classical funerary architecture was *one* of their sources. The martyrs were buried in the cemeteries, and the rites which grew up around their burial-places took shape within a setting of broadly conventional classical funerary architecture. Whatever may have been the detailed arrangements peculiar to the Christian cult of the honoured dead, all the evidence which we have suggests that these were very simple in character; there is no trace of a specifically Christian funerary architecture above ground before the time of Constantine. We may recognize certain features as well adapted to Christian requirements. To cite a single example, the courtyard in front of the little shrine of St. Peter on the Vatican obviously lent itself to the formal reunions of the members of the Christian community. But such features were a matter of selection, not of creation. We cannot point to a Christian funerary architecture as such before the Peace of the Church.

This circumstance did not change overnight any more than the house-churches of pre-Constantinian Rome were all replaced overnight by basilical churches on the new, post-Constantinian model. There must have been a long period of overlap, the exact duration of which would have varied greatly in particular cases, but which would certainly have been widespread enough to ensure a real measure of continuity with pre-Constantinian funerary practice. Again to cite a single specific example, we have the mausoleum of Marusinac at Salona.[1] This we learn from the *Passio* was built by a local matron, Asteria, to house the body of St. Anastasius of Aquileia, who was martyred in the Diocletianic persecution of 304. He was buried in a small chamber which was evidently built specially for the purpose beneath the apse, with a *fenestella* opening into the main tomb-chamber, where a square base marks the presumed site of the sarcophagi of Asteria and her husband. Except for the actual martyr-burial this was a typical Dalmatian family mausoleum, and it remained in use in this form until 395, when it was destroyed during a barbarian incursion. Only after this were the saint's remains transferred to an adjoining basilica, built specifically to house them.

(Let me, in passing, remark that the altar shown over the tomb in Dyggve's reconstruction[2] is purely conjectural. The excavators found neither the altar itself nor any emplacement for it. Similarly the excavations in St. Peter's have shown that, wherever the altar may have been (presumably in the nave and very possibly of a portable nature) it was certainly not over the grave of the Apostle. We are all familiar with the process whereby the hypothesis of yesterday becomes by constant repetition the accepted fact of tomorrow. The intimate relationship between altar and martyr-grave, so far from being an observed fact at this early date, is in reality one that still awaits demonstration.)

Marusinac is important as offering clear and specific evidence of a martyr-shrine established within a mausoleum of a well-known classical type which was built just before or very soon after the Peace of the Church,[3] and which remained in use throughout the fourth century. It was not the only one of its sort. An often-reproduced fifth-century woven fabric from Egypt shows a series of named martyr-shrines of

---

[1] *Martyrium*, i, pp. 94 ff. See Dyggve and Egger, *Forschungen in Salona*, iii (1939).

[2] Ibid., fig. 13; cf. Dyggve and Egger, op. cit., pp. 80 ff., Abb. 108–9.

[3] Dyggve and Egger, op. cit., pp. 106 ff. Anastasius was martyred probably in 304, certainly before 311, but there is nothing to show how soon after his death the mausoleum was begun. Since the arrangements for the martyr-cult are an integral part of the design, it cannot have been planned before his death, and there must have been an intermediate period of burial elsewhere.

precisely this architectural form, and at least one other surviving building of later fourth-century date, at Sopianae (Pecs) in Hungary,[1] is shown by its paintings and its *fenestella* to have been built in the first place as a martyrium. Grabar was wrong in regarding such two-story, rectangular mausolea as predominantly eastern,[2] but he was undoubtedly right in claiming this as a type of martyrium which derives directly from classical funerary architecture.

We may accept, then, that the architecture of some of the martyr-shrines of the fourth century does derive directly from classical funerary practice, for the simple reason that some of them were actual surviving classical mausolea, while others were built in a funerary architectural tradition which did not stop short overnight in 313. But it is one thing to show that some of them were so derived. It is something quite different to argue that this was the effective source of all martyrium architecture. It is this latter claim which we now have to examine in greater detail.

First of all let me mention two considerations of a general character which have a bearing on the whole problem. One of these is the fact that, to a degree that is unusual in classical architecture, the forms of funerary architecture seem to have been determined by the tastes and fancies of the individual. There were, of course, certain stereotyped forms of tomb, and one can distinguish certain broad regional or chrono-logical groups which represent the norms of taste and local practice in individual regions or provinces. But the variety of choice was very large indeed, and there are innumerable individual pieces which escape tidy classification. Think, for example, of the Pyramid of Cestius or the tomb of Eurysaces the Baker in Rome, or again of the towerlike tombs with pyramidal roofs of which one finds scattered examples in half the provinces of the Empire. There must be very few categories of later building for which one could not, with a little ingenuity, find parallels among the tombs and mausolea of the classical Roman world.

Another factor tending in the same direction was the steady break-down of the remarkably rigid demarcation of building-types which had been characteristic of so much of earlier classical architecture. Under the early Empire each aspect of daily life still had its own clearly defined architectural setting. You could not possibly mistake a temple for a market, or a law-court for a bathing establishment. By the third century these distinctions were rapidly disappearing. To cite a single notorious example, the last of the great official basilicas of the capital

---

[1] The altar shown in Dyggve's reconstruction of this tomb (Dyggve and Egger, op. cit., Abb. 128) is subject to the same criticism as that of the Marusinac restoration (p. 23, n. 1, above).

[2] *Martyrium*, i, pp. 96–97, and refs. ad loc.

was, architecturally speaking, a close and clearly deliberate adaptation of the vaulted frigidarium hall of one of the great Imperial bath-buildings; and as a corollary of this we find that by this date the term 'basilica' could be used of any large rectangular covered hall, irrespective of its specific shape or function.[1] The old formal conventions were breaking down rapidly, and by the time of Constantine it was becoming increasingly difficult to tell at a glance the sort of building with which one was dealing.

Such considerations would have little weight if, among the very large number of classical tombs and mausolea that has come down to us, there were numerous and obvious architectural precursors of the Early Christian martyr-shrines. But are there in fact such? Can one in fact establish a plausible architectural connexion between the two groups of buildings—between the mausolea of classical antiquity and the early Christian martyria?

In trying to answer this fundamental question it will be convenient to follow Grabar's classification of the early martyria into seven groups in accordance with the shapes of their plans: square martyria; rectangular martyria; simple apsidal structures; triconchoi; transverse or transeptal martyria (that is to say, those which are characterized by some sort of transverse hall or enclosure); circular or polygonal martyria; and finally a group of cruciform martyria, among which one has to distinguish further those of free-standing cruciform plan and those in which the cruciform element is inscribed within a building of some other external shape. In practice these categories do of course tend to overlap, but they constitute as good a classification as any other.

We have already discussed the mausoleum-martyria of elongated rectangular plan as characterized by the mausoleum at Marusinac. At least two other of Grabar's groups, the isolated apse and the square martyrium, may, I think, be accepted readily enough as being wholly or partly of funerary derivation.

The isolated apse or exedra[2] need not detain us long. It occurs sporadically in many pagan cemeteries; and not only is the apse a commonplace of later classical architectural iconography as a setting for whatever object—a statue, an altar, a throne—to which it was desired to do special honour, but it is also one of the best-attested types of early martyrium. Once again I need cite only the example of Salona, in the cemeteries of Marusinac and Manastirine.[3] Except as the potential

---

[1] See the writer's 'Constantine and the Origins of the Christian Basilica', *Papers of the British School at Rome*, xxii (1954), pp. 69–91.

[2] *Martyrium*, i, pp. 98–102.

[3] R. Egger, *Forschungen in Salona*, ii, p. 426; Dyggve and Egger, op. cit.

nucleus of later, more elaborate structures, the apsidal martyrium is not in itself a type of any great architectural significance; but such as it is, it may reasonably be accepted as having developed within the funerary context in which we first meet it.

As for the square mausoleum,[1] there were a great many forms in classical use and there is at least one of these forms which may reasonably be accepted as having influenced the builders of some of the Early Christian shrines. This is the simple, vaulted family mausoleum typical of the suburban cemeteries of Rome, beneath St. Peter's, for example, or beside the Via Latina. One finds tombs of very much this sort of shape in regions as diverse as Pannonia, and Dalmatia, Ephesus, and Roman Egypt, and one would expect them to have survived as martyria in precisely the same circumstances, and for precisely the same reasons, as the rectangular mausolea which we were discussing just now. Curiously enough, it is hard to point to any specifically Christian examples; but representations of small square martyr-shrines do appear in manuscripts and mosaics, and there are, of course, the well-known illustrations of the central shrine of the Holy Sepulchre, which show a somewhat elaborated version of the same general form. One would welcome more actual examples of fourth-century or early fifth-century date, but I see no reason to question Grabar's basic contention that the square mausoleum of pagan antiquity was carried over into Christian use as one of the building-types for the early martyria.

Whether we are justified in extending this idea to include the square *baldacchino*, or canopy,[2] I am far more doubtful. We find this feature used extensively in the mausolea of many parts of the Roman world, from Syria to Gaul and North Africa; and we also find it used in some early martyria, to which it was indeed well adapted, both sheltering the relic and displaying it freely to the view of the worshipper. The first shrine of St. John at Ephesus is usually restored along these lines (plausibly enough, although it is well to remember how scanty is the actual evidence); and we now have a fine Constantinian example in the openwork canopy over the central aedicula of St. Peter's. My only doubt is whether in such a context the canopy can be said to have any specifically funerary significance. As a symbol of the honour or venera-tion due to the person or object which it sheltered, it was already a commonplace both of religious usage and of court ceremonial; and in so far as the canopies of the pagan mausolea may have had a symbolic as opposed to a purely architectural significance, it was merely as a special instance of this wider idea. The same is surely true also of the

---

[1] *Martyrium*, i, pp. 77–87.
[2] Ibid., especially pp. 77 ff.

canopy-martyrium. It represents a generalized symbol of honour, not an architectural form inherited from funerary architecture as such.

Even with this reservation, however, we may still accept that there probably were fourth-century martyr-shrines which were square and which were either themselves Roman mausolea re-used or else were derived directly from pagan models. That makes three at any rate of Grabar's seven types of martyrium that were derived in whole or part from pagan funerary architecture. What about the other four?

About the first of these types, the transverse or transeptal hall, or (to use Grabar's phrase) the 'martyrium déployé en largeur',[1] I wonder very much whether the form so defined is distinctive enough to be significant. It is perfectly true that already before the Peace of the Church there were martyr-graves of which the enclosing precincts were wider than they were long. To the well-known and well-documented example of Manastirine at Salona we can now add that of the open courtyard, 'Campo P', which enclosed the *memoria* on the Vatican Hill. It is also true that at Manastirine this enclosure was later roofed, forming a transept within the basilica which represents the third and last stage of the shrine's architectural development; and true again that the Constantinian martyr-shrine of St. Peter stood in the centre of the great transverse hall which formed the transept of the basilica. Was there any meaningful continuity between the shape of 'Campo P' and that of the Constantinian transept? Possibly, possibly not. Who is to say? What is, on the other hand, perfectly clear both here and at Manastirine is that the shape of the primitive enclosure was determined in the first instance by the space available within a crowded suburban cemetery. It was an individual answer to an individual local situation, and this alone should make us very careful about drawing any conclusions of a general character. Moreover, the shape was eminently practical for its purpose, since it enabled a large number of people simultaneously to come into close contact with the object of their veneration, and it is therefore not at all surprising to find it repeated in the architecture of the Constantinian age. Personally I rather doubt whether the situation of Manastirine is more than a local accident and whether there was any meaningful relationship between the simple enclosures of the pre-Constantinian cemeteries and the transeptal halls of the later martyria. But I would hesitate to exclude the possibility.

I would, on the other hand, exclude absolutely from consideration a building to which Grabar makes frequent reference in this connexion, namely the *heroon*, or hero-shrine, at Kalydon in Aetolia;[2] and I would

---

[1] Ibid., pp. 120–41.
[2] Dyggve, Poulsen, and Rhomaios, *Das Heroon von Kalydon* (1934). Grabar

strongly question the propriety of referring to the Christian martyrium as if it were the direct successor of the Hellenistic *heroon* and, more generally, of treating the terms 'heroon' and 'mausoleum' as if they were for all practical purposes interchangeable.

To make such an equation is, in my belief, to invite confusion.[1] There are two aspects of the pagan *heroon* which distinguish it sharply from the ordinary funerary monument of the classical age. One (and this is surely the essential feature) is that it includes provision for public cult. The other is that commonly, though by no means invariably, it received special exemption from the provisions which forbade burial within the city limits. This later aspect *did* survive into the Roman period: very exceptionally in the west (the burial of Trajan in his Forum is the only example which springs to mind), more commonly in the east, where we have several well-attested examples dating from the second and third centuries A.D. in Asia Minor, at Miletus, for example, at Priene, and again at Ephesus, where we find the sarcophagus of the wealthy Celsus Polyaeanus laid in a vault beneath the library which he bequeathed to his native city.[2] The provision of public cult, on the other hand, appears to cease abruptly with the end of the Hellenistic age. With the important exception of the cult of the divinized emperor, the hero-cult plays no part in the Roman world, and it can have played no direct part either in shaping the outward forms of the Christian martyr-cult.

As for the further suggestion that the type of building represented at Kalydon was perpetuated in the temple-architecture of Roman Syria (for example, at Dura), and in this way came ultimately to influence the forms of the Christian martyrium,[3] the answer has been afforded in no uncertain terms by the recent excavations at Hatra.[4] The discovery of no less than a dozen small rectangular temples, each with a small cella or cult-recess in the middle of one long side, opposite the main entrance, proves unequivocally that this is a Mesopotamian form, owing little or nothing to Hellenistic influence.

A more promising line might be to consider the richly ornamented halls which are such a characteristic feature of the gymnasium–bath buildings of Roman Asia Minor. Here one is dealing with an archi-

is here following J. Roger in *Bull. Corr. Hell.* lxiii (1939), pp. 33–34, where the list of Roman period *heroa* appears to comprise any mausoleum of rectangular, temple-like form.

[1] I am indebted to Dr. Stefan Weinstock for helpful discussion of this point.
[2] *Forschungen in Ephesos*, v. i: *Die Bibliothek* (1955).
[3] *Martyrium*, i, p. 133.
[4] For a convenient summary of the results of these excavations, still largely unpublished, see H. Lenzen in *Arch. Anz.* 1955, pp. 334–75.

tectural tradition of indubitably Hellenistic derivation; there *is* a formal resemblance to the Kalydon *heroon*, and some of these 'Marmor-saalen' (for example, that of the second-century Baths of Vedius at Ephesus) are known to have been associated with the imperial cult. I offer the suggestion for what it is worth. However, I am here concerned far more with the negative point that, outside the field of the imperial cult, the Hellenistic *heroon* was dead and forgotten. Both the term and its implications can only confuse us in our search for the sources of the Christian martyrium.

When we turn to the fifth of Grabar's seven types, the *triconchos* or *cella trichora*,[1] we are dealing with a much more distinctive, clearly defined type of building. It was undoubtedly used for Christian martyria at an early date, and it is undoubtedly also a form of building that was already in use in classical times. The only question is whether at this earlier, pre-Christian stage we are justified in regarding it as a specifically funerary type.

To this question the answer must, I think, be No. The only surviving pagan tomb of this shape that I have been able to locate, is the well-known mausoleum of Claudia Antonia Sabina at Sardis;[2] to which we may add the evidence of a fourth-century Christian funerary inscription from Tolentino in north Italy, in which a certain Septimia Severina records that *sarcofagum et panteum cum tricoro disposuit et perfecit.*[3] When one reflects on the infinite variety of forms used in the tombs and mausolea of the Empire, this is very tenuous evidence for claiming the *triconchos* as a specifically funerary type—the more so in that there *is* a category of building, both pagan and Christian, in which it was used considerably and characteristically. I am referring, of course, to the triclinia and audience-halls of the palaces and wealthy villas, of which that at Piazza Armerina is only one recent example among many.[4]

Very much the same might be said of Grabar's sixth group, the martyria of circular or polygonal plan.[5] In this case there are good pre-Constantinian funerary precedents, namely the great imperial mausolea of the immediately preceding period. These, beginning with the tombs of Diocletian at Spalato and of Galerius at Thessaloniki, could I think very reasonably be regarded as the architectural precursors of the great rotunda of the Holy Sepulchre, of the octagonal Sanctuary of the Ascension on the Mount of Olives, of the octagon of the Church of the

---

[1] *Martyrium*, i, pp. 102–19.   [2] H. C. Butler, *Sardis*, i, pp. 170–4, fig. 189.
[3] *C.I.L.* ix. 5566.
[4] See the valuable article by Irving Lavin in *Art Bulletin*, xliv (1962), pp. 1–27, which includes a critical appendix on the late Roman residential triconches of Gaul, Spain, and North Africa.   [5] *Martyrium*, i, pp. 141–52.

Nativity, and of innumerable later martyria of similar and derivative plan—as well, of course, as of a long series of Constantinian and post-Constantinian mausolea in Rome and in north Italy. So far so good. But when one starts to look outside this very specialized and restricted field, it is a very different story. To find examples of circular or polygonal tombs in everyday use Grabar has to lean heavily on the evidence of the Renaissance antiquarians. But this is notoriously treacherous ground; indeed, I question whether the unsupported testimony of Montano, for example, is of any value at all except as an indication of the anti-quarian ideas current in his own day.[1] This is not to say that there were no circular or polygonal mausolea in ordinary, everyday use; but if so, they were exceptional. If the Early Christian martyria of this form derive at all from funerary prototypes, it is from the great imperial mausolea of the Tetrarchy.

That brings us to the last of our seven types, the martyrium in the shape of a cross.[2] Here there is an important distinction to be made, between the free-standing and the inscribed cross, that is to say between the cross which is visible as such from the outside and the cross which is contained in a building of some other shape, usually a square. The first of these types, the free-standing cross, is decidedly rare in pre-Christian architecture, whereas the inscribed cross is common in a wide variety of contexts. Two of these are of particular importance in connexion with the sources of Christian architecture. One is a group of pagan buildings in Syria which appears to foreshadow the cross-in-square plan of Christian usage, a group of which the so-called 'prae-torium' at Mismiyeh[3] may be taken as the type-example. The other is the very common and widespread form of mausoleum in which the entrance and three *arcosolia*, or sarcophagus-recesses, constitute a cruciform extension of the square central space.

As M. Lassus has well remarked,[4] both these inscribed types are functional in origin, the one as offering a convenient means of roofing a large centralized space, the other as providing access to several large burials within the limits of a small enclosed space. Very excep-tionally we find the internal cross allowed to project externally also already in pagan times (the destroyed 'Cappella del Crocifisso' at Cassino may have been an example of this); but the free-standing cross only really emerged as a significant building-type as a result of the

---

[1] For these ideas, see Erna Mandowsky and Charles Mitchell, *Pirro Ligorio's Roman Antiquities* (1963). There is no critical study of the drawings of Montano, upon the credibility of whose work so much of Grabar's demonstration ulti-mately rests.   [2] *Martyrium*, i, pp. 152–94.

[3] De Vogüé, *La Syrie Centrale* (1865–77), figs. 45–51, pl. 7.

[4] J. Lassus, *Sanctuaires Chrétiens de Syrie* (1947), pp. 116–17.

recognition by the architects of the fourth century of its symbolic appropriateness. For all practical purposes it was their creation.

In all of this Lassus is surely right. I have only one comment to add. Although the two types of building to which I have just referred represent what are perhaps the most consistent strains in the pre-Christian development of the cruciform plan, the cross was in fact already present in a far wider range of pagan buildings. To take a single example: the rudimentary cross-in-circle plan of a building such as the Pantheon or the Temple of Asklepios at Pergamon. The inscribed cross was a part of the general architectural heritage of late antiquity which was available to the architects of Christianity. In short, the cruciform element is present both in the pagan mausoleum and in the Christian martyrium; but it is present also in a far wider range of architecture, both before and after Constantine. The pattern is by no means so simple as we are asked to believe.

I cannot emphasize this last point too strongly. If I were asked to make a single general criticism of Grabar's thesis it would, I think, be just this, that in trying to establish a single architectural source for the early Christian martyria, he has been led to ignore this wider architectural perspective. The result is an over-simplification of an essentially complex picture, and such over-simplifications are almost bound to distort the evidence. Of the seven types of martyrium discussed, only three can be accepted without qualification as having been developed from the everyday funerary architecture of the pagan world. A fourth, the circular or polygonal martyrium, may reasonably be held to derive from a particular group of tombs, the imperial mausolea; and a fifth, the cruciform martyrium, is developed from an architectural form of which one of the common pre-Christian usages was funerary. The remaining two, the *triconchos* and the transverse or transeptal hall, have little or nothing to do with the architecture of the pagan mausolea. Pagan funerary architecture was *one* of the sources of the martyrium, but it was only one of several.

In passing I have ventured to suggest one of these other sources, namely the architecture of the imperial court, but I certainly do not want to press this suggestion at the expense of the wider conclusion that the sources of the martyrium, as of other branches of Christian architecture, were inevitably many and various. What we have to look for is not two successive phases of a single stream of architectural development, but a mingling of many streams to form something that was essentially new. The fact is that the emergence of an officially recognized, imperially sponsored Christianity had created a situation for which there were no neat, simple historical precedents, and this is just the sort of situation with which the archaeologist is not at all well equipped to deal. Archaeological method tends almost inevitably to emphasize rational, evolutionary solutions at the expense of the irrational element introduced by human behaviour and by human political situations. In dealing with the archaeology of historical times one cannot of course fail to be aware of the impact of events and personalities; but the attitudes of mind of the archaeologist are conditioned by the fact that so much of his work is concerned with the anonymous creations of people who have left no other record—and such attitudes have a natural bias towards orderly classifications and tidy schemes of evolutionary development.

This is at once a strength and a weakness—a strength because it enables us to detect and to describe the broad patterns which underlie the infinite variety of the individual, a weakness because there are certain situations in which it is the actions of the individual which are dominant and which alone can afford a key to the interpretation of the broader historical patterns. The age of Constantine was surely just such a moment. This was by any reckoning a turning-point in history; and however strongly one may believe that the broad sweep of events is dictated by forces outside the control of even the most powerful individual, one surely cannot deny that on such an occasion the element of human personality and of human choice can be a vital factor in determining the course of day-to-day events. If it is our business as archaeologists to ascertain the terms within which Constantine and his advisers were free to operate and by which their decisions were conditioned, it is also our business as historians to recognize that within these limits they were free to choose, and that one of our main tasks is to evaluate the motives and the results of their choice.

Take a single, very familiar example. It is surely failure to recognize this very circumstance which has stultified so much of the inquiry into the origin of the Christian basilica. Archaeologists have been so anxious to detect an orderly pattern and to show that the Christian basilica evolved from this, that, or the other type of pagan building, that they seem almost to have forgotten that this was a moment not so much of evolution as of revolution. Constantine and his advisers were faced with the need to provide a building suitable for an entirely new historical situation. No doubt their choice operated within clearly defined limits and was influenced at every turn by familiar architectural solutions. Nevertheless theirs was a deliberate act of choice; and unless we recognize that in this sense the Christian basilica was created by Constantine, we make nonsense of the whole historical situation.

Our answer to the question of the origins of the Christian martyrium must surely lie along similar lines. Not necessarily identical lines. The circumstances and requirements of the martyr-cult were altogether more varied than those involved in providing an ordinary place of worship; and, as we have seen, the architectural solutions adopted were correspondingly varied. Some of them do represent an evolutionary development from the buildings of the previous period. Such were the martyr's graves in mausolea like that of Marusinac, the forms of which did evolve imperceptibly into those of the simple country martyria which we see represented in contemporary illustrations, but which are often so hard to detect on the ground simply because they do fit so smoothly and neatly into the evolutionary series. At the other extreme we have the great imperial foundations like the Basilica of St. Peter, the Church of the Nativity and the Holy Sepulchre. Here the whole tendency of our inquiry is against the idea that Constantine was guided by any such *a priori* considerations as the idea that funerary architecture, and funerary architecture alone, provided the answers appropriate to this new situation. There were situations in which it would have been appropriate enough. What more natural than the idea of enclosing the Holy Sepulchre in a building modelled on the splendours of an imperial mausoleum? But what about the octagon of the Nativity or the Basilica Apostolorum beside the Via Appia?

We are in no way obliged to believe that there was a single, precisely formulated ideological programme. The whole field of late Imperial architecture lay wide open for exploitation, and in an eclectic age such as this was, Constantine and his advisers and agents would in any case have felt unusually free to choose whatever best suited their immediate purpose. It is no surprise to find a centralized, octagonal plan used also for the Great Church, or Domus Aurea, at Antioch, begun in 327 and dedicated in 341.[1] The fact that this was not a martyrium at all, but a palace church, should be sufficient to put us on our guard against attaching any strict programmatic meaning to the several architectural forms adopted. The extraordinary diversity of plan adopted everywhere by the Constantinian builders must have been due in no small degree to this same wide latitude of choice, and we may hazard the guess that the resulting choices were dictated as much by such practical considerations as the available building materials and skills as by any high-flown considerations of architectural ideology.

I have dwelt at length upon the earliest history of the martyrium, because it is here, I believe, that the currently accepted picture calls most urgently for modification and correction. About what followed I can be correspondingly brief. Moments of revolutionary change such

[1] G. Downey, *A History of Antioch in Syria* (1961), pp. 342–50.

as the reign of Constantine are in the nature of things short-lived, and they are regularly followed by periods of consolidation and development. The fourth century, which had begun as a period of revolutionary architectural innovation, closed with a canon of orthodox Christian architectural forms already beginning to take shape; and where Grabar is undoubtedly right is in his emphasis on the part played by the martyr-cult and by its architectural forms in the shaping of that canon. Where I disagree with him is in his insistence on the essentially evolutionary character of the development of the martyrium, an insistence which leads him to belittle the immediate impact of the great Constantinian foundations. The latter are seen by him merely as isolated special manifestations of the same evolutionary tendencies and as themselves having singularly little immediate influence upon the main evolutionary stream of development. Their importance, he believes, only came later.

This is a thesis which I find it quite impossible to follow. It is rather as if one were asked to believe that the architecture of eighteenth-century France pursued its way regardless of the building of Versailles. These were the great innovating monuments of their age; and given the revolutionary situation created by the official recognition of Christianity, I find it inconceivable that they should not have been from the outset a powerful source of inspiration and of imitation to contemporary architects. It is true that our knowledge of fourth-century architecture is still too imperfect for us to be able to follow the process in detail. But we can, I believe, catch many glimpses of it, and it is with one of these glimpses that I would like to conclude this paper.

We have seen that the cruciform martyrium was one of the earliest types of martyr-shrine to achieve widespread acceptance. Already in 381 we have an actual surviving example at Antioch, and just about this date we begin to get explicit references in the texts to the symbolical significance of the plan. From Cappadocia we have the familiar *ep.* 25 of Gregory of Nyssa, writing about 380, and describing a martyrium in his own city which took the form of an octagon with four projecting exedrae: σταυρός ἐστι . . . τὸ σχῆμα.[1] Or again from Milan in 382 we have the dedicatory verses of St. Ambrose:

> Forma crucis templum est, templum victoria Christi
> Sacra, triumphalis, signat imago locum.[2]

By this date the cruciform plan was not only widely distributed; it was also full of meaning.

There can be very little doubt that the effective fountain-head of this

---

[1] Migne, *P.G.* xlvi. 1093 ff.

[2] V. Forcella, *Iscrizioni Cristiane in Milano* (1897), no. 229.

symbolism was the great Church of the Holy Apostles in Constantinople. The early history of this building is very controversial, the controversy turning upon whether the relevant passages of the *Vita Constantini* are really the work of Eusebius of Caesarea (writing after Constantine's death in 337 and before his own death, not later than 340) or whether alternatively they are either spurious or at any rate substantially revised at some later date.[1] If they are authentic, then the church was the work of Constantine himself, built to house his own tomb. If not, it may have been built some years later by Constantius, as was later believed by many respectable authorities, including Procopius.

Now I have no intention of going into the details of this controversy, particularly since there does not seem to be any doubt about what in the present context may be regarded as the central fact, namely the translation to this church in 356 or 357 of the remains of SS. Andrew, Timothy, and Luke. Let us, for the purposes of discussion follow the account of events given recently by Krautheimer in the *Festschrift Theodor Klauser*.[2] Krautheimer accepts the Eusebian authorship and date of the *Vita* and holds that the first church of the Holy Apostles was indeed founded by Constantine (though not, of course, necessarily under that name); it was probably already, as it certainly was later, a cruciform building, and Constantine was buried at the geometrical centre of it, beside or beneath the altar and flanked by empty shrines ($\theta\hat{\eta}\kappa\alpha\iota$) bearing the names of the twelve apostles. The singularity of the building was that it combined the functions both of a mausoleum and of a church in regular liturgical use; and although within the climate of opinion prevailing in Constantine's own lifetime and immediately after his death this may not have seemed unduly startling, the close physical relationship between the altar and the imperial grave must increasingly have become an object of criticism, criticism which would have been brought to a head by the transfer to the church of the bodies of the Apostles in 356. This led to the decision to transfer the body of Constantine to a new, circular mausoleum, to be built alongside the church, very much after the pattern of Tor Pignattara and Santa Costanza in Rome; and with the completion of this new building and the rededication of the whole complex, perhaps in 370, it assumed the form in which it was familiar to later writers, that is to say a large, cruciform martyrium-church dedicated to the Holy Apostles and, adjoining it the circular dynastic mausoleum of Constantine, Constantius, and their successors.

[1] The case for a later date is well stated by Downey in *Dumbarton Oaks Papers*, vi (1951), pp. 53–80.

[2] *Mullus: Festschrift Theodor Klauser* (1964), pp. 224–9.

On the evidence available one obviously cannot hope for certainty, but personally I find Krautheimer's reconstruction of events as convincing as any other, not least because it catches so very neatly the hesitancies and uncertainties of this moment of unprecedented experiment and of headlong change. Many of our difficulties in interpreting the character and actions of Constantine arise from the fact that we know what happened next, whereas he did not. Once Christianity had had time to come to terms with its new position as a state religion and to evolve a formal body of public religious rites and observances, such a blatant expression of the notion of *Constantinos isapostolos* would have been impossible. And yet to Constantine himself, brought up in a tradition in which the emperor was the focus of formal religious observance and the sole repository of the traditions of the Hellenistic hero-cult, there would have been nothing incongruous in the idea of linking his own grave with the central cult observance of the new religion. This is just the sort of syncretistic idea which might be thrown up in such a moment of rapid transition.

When we turn to the buildings themselves we get just the same impression of a state of ideas still in rapid transition. The outstanding novelty of Constantine's building was its cruciform plan; and in the absence of convincing pagan precedents we can hardly doubt that it was deliberately chosen for its symbolic significance by Constantine himself. And yet the Eusebian account makes no mention whatsoever of the plan or of a symbolism which leaped to the eye of Gregory Nazianzen, Gregory of Nyssa, St. Ambrose, and their contemporaries forty years later. We can only conclude that such ideas were not yet part of the general currency of contemporary thought.

So far as the cruciform plan is concerned there is no hint as yet of the martyrium. That was to come in 356, when the building assumed its definitive form as a martyrium for the remains of the three Apostles, while the imperial mausoleum was translated to a separate but closely related building. Whether or not this was the first major translation of the remains of martyrs, it was certainly the first to be accomplished on such a scale and with all the weight of imperial authority behind it. With it the notion of the martyrium took definitive shape. Hitherto it had been linked essentially with one particular place, either the burial-place of a martyr or one of the 'places of witness' associated with the sacred events of Old Testament or New Testament history. Now the way was open for any church to participate in the sanctifying presence of a martyr's remains, and the long and fruitful processes of conflation and of natural interaction and assimilation between the ordinary church and the martyrium, processes which Grabar has described so well, were set in motion. And because the Church of the Holy Apostles was, as we know, a building which enjoyed great prestige and was widely copied at all periods, its cruciform plan, which had originated outside the milieu of the martyr-cult, became now one of the most powerful elements in shaping its onward development.[1]

The study of the material remains of Christian antiquity is one which does not stand still. Every day brings fresh discoveries and fresh ideas, and the more we learn, the more we see how much there is still to learn and how wide and fundamental are many of the gaps in our knowledge. It was still possible in 1946 for a scholar of the wide vision and courage of Grabar to attempt a synthesis of the whole field, and for a very long time to come we shall continue to be in his debt for that attempt. Today I doubt very much whether such a synthesis would be possible. What we can do is to modify the accepted theses wherever twenty years of fresh research have shown them to be untenable; we can define the gaps in our knowledge, as a first step to filling them; and above all we can re-examine the basic concepts of our discipline. Christian archaeology is no longer meaningful as the quasi-independent, almost self-enclosed branch of study which it was when the overwhelming majority of the sources lay in the churches and catacombs of Rome. Such a concept no longer makes sense geographically. It makes no better sense within the field of ideas. At the beginning of the third century Christianity was still a small, artistically and architecturally insignificant minority within a pagan classical world; by the end of the fourth century it was paganism that was a struggling minority, while Christianity with every passing year was acquiring a momentum and a coherence which permeate all its material remains. Between the two there stretches a period of compromise and of mutual assimilation, a period of often revolutionary experiment, which in the nature of things tends to elude the tidy classifications that we try to impress upon it.   J. B. WARD-PERKINS

[1] The impact of the church upon the architectural thinking of the second half of the fourth century may be accepted independently of its Constantinian or Constantian authorship.

Narration in Early Christendom

KURT WEITZMANN

PLATES 33-36

THE depiction of a story by pictorial means involves the problem of a relationship between literature on the one hand and the representational arts on the other. From the time script was invented and literature came into being down to the period from which we have the earliest extant codices with extensive picture cycles a slow, evolutionary process, in spite of deviations and regressions, can be observed with regard to this relationship. At the beginning it is rather vague and general and the artist did not always consult a literary source, but relied at times on an oral tradition whenever he wanted to represent a myth or an episode from history. As time went on, however, the relationship became more precise and more specific to the same degree that the literary sources were more often and more intensively consulted by an artist who set out to render a literary content with greater exactitude.

In the archaic and high classical periods of Greek art comparatively few, and in most cases only the most dramatic events were chosen and rendered in individual, self-contained compositions. Almost at the same time Greek artists began to line up a series of narrative representations, based either on a single hero's life or some kind of a literary unit, and taking the form of a row of metopes or of a frieze. This is the beginning of the method of the cyclic narrative which in the classical period was used on a rather limited scale, and in the Hellenistic period developed into a continuous narrative whereby the individual scenes are placed in front of a unifying landscape,

At the end of this long drawn-out process of binding the representational arts and literature still closer together, a new method was invented whereby a single episode was divided into several phases, so that the beholder might follow the various changes of action with the chief protagonist being repeated again and again. The result of this development is an enormous increase in the number of scenes and the formation of far more extensive picture cycles than had ever existed before. This innovation took place in the Early Hellenistic period, and the medium in which the vast expansion of narrative representations could unfold most vigorously, and to a degree not matched by any other medium, is the book which at that time was the papyrus roll. Thus the *art of storytelling in pictures* became inextricably linked with the history of book-illumination.[1]

There is evidence that within Greek civilization the illustration of the book started in Egypt, i.e. Alexandria. Here the Greeks must have seen illustrated Egyptian rolls and studied their manufac-

---

[1] For a more detailed discussion of the various methods of illustration cf. C. Robert, *Bild und Lied, Archaeologische Beiträge zur Geschichte der Griechischen Heldensage* (Philologische Untersuchungen hersg. von A. Kiessling und U. v. Wilamowitz-Moellendorf, Vol. V, Berlin 1881); Fr. Wickhoff,

Die Wiener Genesis (Vienna 1895); K. Weitzmann, *Illustrations in Roll and Codex, A Study of the Origin and Method of Text-Illustration* (Studies in Manuscript Illumination, No. 2, Princeton 1947) henceforth cited as *Roll and Codex*.

ture. But they learned from them not only the technical process, but even adapted iconographical motifs wherever they could as, e.g., demons in magical texts, figures of Egyptian gods for constellation figures in astronomical texts and the like.[2] Because of the perishable nature of papyrus and the very casual remains of papyrus rolls, the importance of this branch of Greek painting has only begun to be recognized by modern scholarship after a few very illuminating fragments of illustrated rolls have fairly recently come to light.

Perhaps the most important fragment is one found in Oxyrhynchus and now in Oxford (fig. 1) which belongs to the second or third century and is large enough to permit some general deductions with regard to illustrations of papyrus rolls in classical antiquity.[3] It consists of parts of three writing columns into which three sketchy drawings are intercalated. The content is a Herakles poem in ionic trimeter and our fragment is concerned only with the first deed, the adventure with the Nemean lion. The fight proper is depicted in the usual iconography where Herakles strangles the lion by pressing its head under his armpit. But what is new in the art of the narrative is the subdivision of this one episode into several consecutive phases. One preceding the fight proper depicts what seems to be the pursuit of the lion into a cleft, and the other, following it, shows Herakles with the lion's skin after his victory. It can be taken for granted that as the text went along other deeds were illustrated in the same manner by dividing them into several phases, always repeating the hero in the same brief, sketchy manner. The result of this new method, besides the increase in the number of scenes, is the quickening of the tempo from one action to the next.

From the formal point of view these miniatures in papyrus rolls have some shortcomings. The small figure scale and the rather sketchy technique forced the illustrator to disregard elaborate settings of landscape or architecture like those that had developed in Hellenistic and Roman fresco painting. Moreover he abandoned, to a large extent, carefully balanced compositions as seen in the works of the high classical period which induce the beholder to

tarry, and also continuous frieze compositions, since it was his endeavor to place each individual scene in the writing column at a varying level exactly where the text required it. On the other hand he developed new formal means in order to stress moving actions, usually from left to right in such a way that the beholder is induced to move from one scene to the next just as his eyes read consecutive lines of writing. It was already the ancient illustrator's aim to establish a sequence of phases as close together as possible so that the beholder may read a picture story without resorting to the text for understanding the essential features of a plot. Here we see a new principle in its nascent state which in our own days has developed into the motion picture.

Because of the survival of only a few fragments of illustrated papyrus rolls we are as yet in no position to assess accurately the extent to which classical texts were illustrated. Yet the indications are that it took place on a very large scale, not only in the poetical texts like the Herakles poem but also in prose texts, like that of a still unidentified romance in the Bibliothèque Nationale in Paris, suppl. gr. 1294 (fig. 2)[4] where one sees the remnants of three consecutive scenes, placed in the writing columns in exactly the same manner as in the Herakles papyrus. These lively and sketchily treated scenes in which vivid gestures are particularly emphasized have, again like those of the Herakles papyrus, no frame or colored background, and thus, in the best tradition of papyrus illustration, share the surface of the papyrus with the calligraphy. There is reason to believe that in classical antiquity papyrus illustration did not attract renowned painters—unlike miniature painting in the Middle Ages—and yet it would be misleading to judge the capacity of classical illustrators on the basis of only these two fragments which obviously were executed hastily and with limited skill.

The State Library in Munich owns a fragmentary papyrus drawing of about the fourth century A.D. pap. gr. 128 (fig. 3)[5] which is a rather accomplished brush drawing, representing the episode from the first book of the Iliad in which two heralds of Agamemnon, Talthybius and Eurybates,

---

[2] Roll and Codex 57ff.

[3] K. Weitzmann in The Oxyrhynchus Papyri, Vol. XXII (Oxford 1954), p. 85, no. 2331 and pl. XI.

[4] St. J. Gasiorowski, Malarstwo Minjaturowe Grecko-Rzymskie (Cracow 1928) p. 17, p. v and fig. 2; K. Weitzmann, Roll and Codex 51 (here the older bibliography) and fig. 40.

[5] A. Hartmann, "Eine Federzeichnung auf einem Münchener Papyrus," Festschrift für Georg Leidinger (Munich 1930) p. 103 and pl. XVII; K. Weitzmann, Roll and Codex, 54 and fig. 42; idem, "Observations on the Milan Iliad," Nederlands Kunsthistorisch Jaarboek V (1954) p. 246 and fig. 2.

take away Briseis from Achilles. This drawing provides the evidence that the Homeric poems were also illustrated in papyrus rolls, and quite ambitiously too, as befits the importance of a text which in classical antiquity was almost as widely read as the Bible in the Middle Ages. The mere conception of a set of 24 scrolls, each with a narrative cycle of scenes on the same scale as in the Herakles and the romance papyri almost staggers the imagination. Whereas in pre-Hellenistic art, scenes from the Iliad can be counted by the dozens now they must be numbered by the hundreds.

What are our earliest and most important examples of the new and expansive cyclic art that is reflected in the fragmentary papyrus rolls seen so far, all of which already belong to the Christian era? The first group of monuments one would have to discuss in this context are the so-called Megarian bowls, a group of Hellenistic terracotta cups which Carl Robert had introduced into the literature as *Homerische Becher*.[6] Two such bowls, whose hemispherical surface is unrolled in the drawings (figs. 4-5)[7] show two episodes of the 22nd book of the Odyssey each being subdivided in three phases: one deals with the unfaithful goatherd Melanthius who in the first scene is fettered by Eumaeus and Philoetius and in the second hanged by them, while

bowl depicts the final fate of the wooers, the stabbing of the seer Leiodes and the pardoning of the minstrel Phemius and the herald Medon (verses 310ff). In our opinion these bowls depend on illustrated papyrus rolls lost today, because, even after the transfer into the medium of terracotta reliefs, the basic quality of miniature painting—the element of transitory motion and the inducement to move quickly from one phase to the next—is still clearly preserved. The copyist even went so far—and this is very unusual in any medium except a manuscript proper—as to write as many verses of Homer's poem as he could on the ground of the cups. Actually the individual scenes are still placed within the limits of writing columns.

It is, therefore, quite an easy matter to make, on the basis of the Herakles and the romance papyri, a reconstruction drawing (Ill. A),[8] and to show how the three scenes of the Melanthius adventure were intercalated in the columns of a papyrus roll. On this scale a single book of the Odyssey, filling one scroll with about 30 writing columns, would require approximately an equal number of scenes. If we multiply 30 by 24 and do the same for the Iliad, we arrive at the staggering number of many hundreds of miniatures for a complete illustrated Homer of the Hellenistic period.

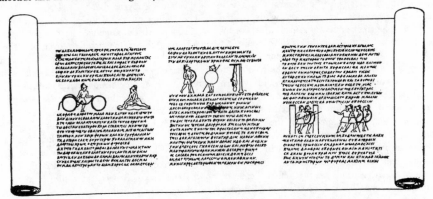

Ill. A. Reconstruction of an Odyssey Roll of the Hellenistic Period

in the third Athena incites Odysseus and Telemachus against the wooers (verses 161ff); the second

Moreover it must be realized that, besides Homer, other epic poems, especially those of the κύκλος

[6] C. Robert, *Homerische Becher* (50. Berliner Winckelmannsprogramm, Berlin 1890). F. Courby, *Les vases grecs à relief* (Paris 1922) Ch. XIX, 281ff. Both are inclined to date the earliest of them into the 3rd century B.C., while more recently a 2nd century date has been suggested for most of them and

even the early 1st century B.C. has been proposed for a late group. Cf. L. Byvanck-Quarles van Ufford, "Les Bols Homériques," *Bull. Antieke Beschaving* 29 (1954) 35ff.

[7] K. Weitzmann, *Roll and Codex*, 37ff and figs. 6-7.

[8] *ibid.* 77 and fig. A on p. 78.

ἐπικός, were likewise profusely illustrated, that dramas, especially those of Euripides, most popular in the Hellenistic and Roman period, were adorned with miniature cycles just as extensively, and that also many prose texts, romances like that of the Paris papyrus (fig. 2) had hundreds and hundreds of scenes. The evidence is based first of all on the Megarian bowls and, for the epic poems, on the so-called Iliac tablets, small reliefs in piombino that are packed with small sketchy scenes whose identification is aided by inscriptions including the titles of the books from which the miniatures were copied.[9] But besides these two major groups, narrative cycles that depend on illustrated books exist on certain sarcophagi, narrow friezes in fresco as they are found in a few instances in Pompeii, and still other media. A careful sifting of the Hellenistic-Roman monuments from this point of view must be the preliminary step towards collecting the material for a history of ancient book illumination.

The best reflections, e.g., of Euripidean picture cycles are once more to be found on the Megarian bowls of which a typical example exists in the Metropolitan Museum with five consecutive scenes from the "Iphigeneia at Aulis."[10] They illustrate very precisely the beginning of the drama, how Agamemnon sends to Clytaimnestra a messenger (fig. 6), who is intercepted by Menelaus, and how Menelaus reproaches Agamemnon while in the meantime Iphigeneia arrives at Aulis and Agamemnon is most unhappy about this turn of events. At least two more cups were needed, one of which actually exists, in order to illustrate the whole drama in this extensive cyclic fashion,[11] and even so we cannot be absolutely sure that the cycle of the three cups with approximately 15 scenes altogether is not abbreviated compared with the postulated manuscript model. By comparing such a sequence of dramatic, fast moving little scenes with the complex and centralized compositions of Apulian amphorae of the 4th century B.C. that reflect themes of Euripidean dramas,[12] it is self-evident that between these two groups of monuments must be placed

the origin of the new vastly extended picture cycles which stand out as the most decisive innovation in the long history of the narrative in representational art.

Another important change took place within the history of bookmaking when, at the end of the 1st century A.D. the parchment codex began to develop into its present-day form and to replace the papyrus roll, a process which deeply affected the system of book-illustration.[13] One of the earliest sets of illustrations that come from a parchment codex are the fifth century fragments of an Iliad in the Ambrosian Library in Milan, F. 205 inf.[14] They are remnants of a codex that in its original state comprised all 24 books of the Iliad in one volume, as compared with 24 separate papyrus rolls—an obviously great advantage since several hundred miniatures could now be collected in a single physical unit between two covers. One of the miniatures, e.g. fig. 7, depicts the leading away of Briseis by Agamemnon's heralds Talthybius and Eurybates, while the mourning, angry Achilles, surrounded by the Myrmidons, sits in his tent. The group at the right is so much like the one in the Munich drawing (fig. 3) that there can be no doubt that both belong to the same recension and that, therefore, the archetype of the Milan codex must have consisted of a set of illustrated papyrus rolls.

The leading away of Briseis is preceded by a miniature in which the same two heralds are demanding from Achilles the handing over of Briseis,[15] while in the following one (fig. 7) Thetis is seen comforting her angry son. Here we have once more a typical case of an *extended cyclic narrative* where one single episode is subdivided into several phases. Motion is handled with subtlety: none of the scenes is centered, the figures move from left to right, and while in the first and third scene where Achilles is approached he sits at the right in what one might call an "ascending rhythm," his place in the second scene where Briseis leaves him is at the left in a "descending rhythm."

In the codex the writing columns are isolated on

[9] O. Jahn, *Griechische Bilderchroniken* (Bonn 1873).

[10] K. Weitzmann, *Roll and Codex*, 44ff and figs. 9a-e.

[11] K. Weitzmann, "Euripides Scenes in Byzantine Art," *Hesperia* 18 (1949) 177ff and pls. 27-29.

[12] L. Séchan, *Études sur la tragédie grecque dans ses rapports avec la céramique* (Paris 1926) 231ff passim; K. Weitzmann, *Roll and Codex*, 16 and fig. 5.

[13] *ibid.* 69ff, 81ff. For the most up-to-date discussion of the origin of the codex cf. C. H. Roberts, "The Codex" *ProcBritAc*

40 (1955) 169ff.

[14] The most recent facsimile: A. Calderini, A. M. Ceriani and A. Mai, *Ilias Ambrosiana* (Bern 1953). A detailed and circumspect discussion of the miniatures and a complete bibliography up to date: R. Bianchi-Bandinelli, *Hellenistic-Byzantine Miniatures of the Iliad (Ilias Ambrosiana)* (Olten 1955). Cf. also *Roll and Codex*, 42ff, 54ff and passim.

[15] *Facs. op.cit.* pict. v.

individual pages and this, gradually, leads to a greater isolation of the individual miniatures. Now they begin to be framed where they had been frameless in the papyrus model, thus resembling panel painting. There can be little doubt that this change took place under the influence of actual panel painting and frescoes. Whereas in papyrus illustration the architectural and landscape elements had been confined to what iconographically was absolutely necessary, now we see a richer spatial setting fitted into a frame, such as the seashore with the ships in the miniature with the arrival of the heralds. The illustrators, working now in the more durable material of parchment and the refined technique of gouache grew more ambitious by belatedly introducing some earlier principles of narrative art, as we know them for instance from Pompeian frescoes, that centered on an isolated and at the same time more elaborate rendering of the most important moment of an episode. At this stage of the development book illumination becomes a much more complex art.

This broadening of artistic endeavors in book illumination coincides with the time in which Christian artists seized upon the illustrated book as one of the main vehicles for the narration of Biblical stories in extensive picture cycles. It cannot be emphasized strongly enough that in illustrating the Bible the Christians did not invent a new branch of art, but continued a then firmly established tradition of Hellenistic-Roman book production which, therefore, had first to be outlined and the method of its reconstruction to be explained in order to see the beginnings of Christian book illumination in the right perspective. Book art is a conservative art and the Christians adapted the main principles of narrative picture cycles as they had developed in Homer and Euripides rolls quite thoroughly, but raised it gradually to the higher level of a luxurious art whereby the text of the Bible was, at times, written in gold or silverscript on purple-stained parchment.

The best known representative of such an Early Christian luxury codex is the 6th Century Genesis fragment in Vienna, cod. theol. gr. 31.[16] Each of its 48 pages left to us is evenly divided between text and picture, an arrangement which resulted in the

shortening of the Bible text. On one of these pages (fig. 8) we see three scenes immediately following the sacrifice of Isaac which was on the preceding page, now lost. In the first the angel promises posterity to Abraham, in the second he returns to the waiting servants, and in the third Abraham receives news about his brother Nabor. These events in themselves are not of primary importance, and one would expect them to be included only as parts of a very extensive cycle in which scenes of lesser importance alternate with important ones for the sake of keeping the picture story moving—just as we have seen it in the Iliad illustrations.

The Vienna codex, when complete, must have contained between four and five hundred individual scenes of which an average of three are grouped together on one page. On the basis of this calculation two conclusions can be drawn: (1) that our earliest Bible manuscripts were illustrated just as profusely, or perhaps even more so, than the illustrated texts of classical antiquity; and (2) that these early Biblical cycles were so vast that on this scale neither a full Bible nor even a full Septuagint could ever be illustrated in their entirety.[17] Obviously the illustration of the Bible started out with individual or smaller groups of books within the Law, the historical, the poetical, and the prophetical groups. Of the Vienna manuscript we can be sure that it never contained more than just the Book of Genesis.

From the formal point of view the scenes still reflect the papyrus tradition in their close agreement with the underlying text, the limitation to what iconographically is absolutely necessary, the emphasis on vivid action and gestures and the lack of frame and background. Where landscape does occur in this instance in the lower right hand corner, it obviously is an intrusion, occupying an otherwise empty space since obviously only three scenes were available where the surface area easily could have accommodated four. In a sketch (Ill. B)[18] an attempt has been made to reconstruct the model of the Vienna Genesis according to the principles of papyrus illustration, by placing the scenes within the comparatively narrow writing columns —as we know them to have existed in early Bible manuscripts—of an unabbreviated Septuagint text.

16 Fr. Wickhoff, *Die Wiener Genesis* (Vienna 1895); H. Gerstinger, *Die Wiener Genesis* (Vienna 1931), here the older bibliography; K. Weitzmann, *Roll and Codex*, 89ff and passim.
17 K. Weitzmann, "Die Illustration der Septuaginta," *MJb*

3-4 (1952-53) 96ff.
18 K. Weitzmann, *Roll and Codex*, 90 and fig. D; idem *MJb* 102 and fig. A.

Ill. B. Reconstruction of the Model of the
Vienna Genesis

A second important Bible fragment, likewise of the 6th century, is a Genesis codex in London, the so-called Cotton Genesis, Cotton Otho B.VI, which, unfortunately, was burnt in 1731. But a sufficient number of charred and singed fragments have survived to permit a reconstruction of the codex which originally had about 330 miniatures.[19] On the one hand, its illustrations followed the papyrus tradition by placing the scenes within the writing columns, and on the other they introduced frames and background elements as was done similarly in the Milan Iliad. But in spite of these elaborations, the illustrators maintained in the best story telling tradition an extraordinarily dense sequence of phases of one and the same episode. The story of the Deluge, for example, shows the ark repeated five times, beginning with God's command to Noah to bring the animals and his family into the ark, followed by the execution of this command (fig. 9) and up to the scene in which Noah lets the dove out for the third time.[20]

In the 13th century, when the mosaicists of San Marco in Venice set out to decorate the narthex with a cycle of Old Testament scenes, they used the very Cotton Genesis as model,[21] and thus the mosaics become the primary source for the reconstruction of the fragmentary miniature cycle. Over

both sides of an arch, the episode of the Deluge is depicted by repeating the ark no less than eight times:[22] on the one side, one sees its construction and the bringing in of the fowl, the quadrupeds and the family; on the other side the flood proper, the sending forth of a raven and a dove, and finally the resting of the ark on Mount Ararat. Of some of these scenes no trace is left among the London fragments, and yet we have evidence that the Noah cycle of the Cotton Genesis before its damage by fire was still bigger than that of the mosaics and had as many as eleven scenes with the ark as the main feature.

The narthex of San Marco is by no means an isolated case where illustrated manuscripts served as models for Early Christian and mediaeval fresco painters and mosaicists and, therefore, monumental art will have to be investigated more systematically as to its possible dependence on narrative miniature cycles. But San Marco is unique in that the manuscript model is still in existence, and this permits us to establish a few general principles with regard to the relationship between miniature models and their copies in monumental art.

The main changes result from the necessity to use the surface area of the wall more economically, since the enlargement of the figure-scale could only be compensated by abbreviations of the miniature model. There are three ways of abbreviation most commonly used: first, the "omission" of entire scenes which we already discussed in connection with the Noah scenes.

The second is that of "condensation." In the miniature of Abraham speaking with the Lord, seen in a water color copy which was made from the miniature before it burned (fig. 10),[23] a huge hand of God is issuing from an enormous segment of the sky, while Abraham moves freely on a spacious strip of ground in a slightly swaying pose, in order to indicate the impact of the radiating divine power. In one of the narthex cupolae of San Marco (fig. 11) the corresponding figure of Abraham is squeezed between two neighbouring scenes and the shrunken segment of sky with a smaller hand of

[19] The latest writing on the Cotton Genesis: K. Weitzmann, "Observations on the Cotton Genesis Fragments," *Late Classical and Mediaeval Studies in honor of Albert Mathias Friend, Jr.* (Princeton 1955) 112ff. (Here the older bibliography).

[20] idem *MJb* 97 and figs. 1a-d.

[21] J. J. Tikkanen, "Die Genesismosaiken von S. Marco in Venedig und ihr Verhältnis zu den Miniaturen der Cottonbibel," *Acta Societatis Scientiarum Fennicae* 17 (Helsingfors 1889)

99ff; Weitzmann in *Friend Studies, op.cit.* 119ff.

[22] F. Ongania, *La Basilica di San Marco in Venezia* 1880-1893) pl. XVII; S. Bettini, *Mosaici antichi di San Marco a Venezia* (Bergamo 1944) pl. LVI-LVIII and LX-LXI.

[23] H. Omont, *Miniatures des plus anciens Manuscrits Grecs de la Bibliothèque Nationale du VIᵉ au XIVᵉ siècle*, 2nd ed. (Paris 1929) Introduction, 1ff and plate.

God is placed on top of the preceding scene as a space saving device.

The desire to save space leads to still a third principle, that of "conflation," so well known to textual critics. Another section of the same San Marco cupola (fig. 11 at the right) depicts the Journey of Abraham and Lot to Egypt. At the left a servant helps Sarah into the saddle, and at the right a group of soldiers marches ahead of Lot, while Abraham rides between them. It can be demonstrated that this composition is a conflation of two, originally separated, scenes, the left group with Sarah being still preserved on the recto side of a fragmentary page (fig. 12), while the Lot group is on its verso side (fig. 13).[24] In the conflated mosaic Abraham on horseback is placed in the center of a more complex scene which the monumental artist tried to turn into a balanced composition, whereby he aims at an effect comparable to the isolated pictures of the high classical period.

By lining up the Abraham scenes around the rim of the cupola the mosaicist achieved the effect of a continuous frieze—an effect which became only possible after the connection of the pictures with the text proper, where they stand in the writing columns at different levels, was dissolved. Basically this is the same process involved in the transfer of scenes from our reconstructed Iliad scroll (Ill. A) into the hemispheric surface of the Megarian bowls (figs. 4-5). At the same time the mosaicists retained from the manuscript tradition the iconographical preciseness and, in many instances, the dense sequence of phases within one episode. Thus we see in the complex mosaic decoration of San Marco an attempt to combine the principles of narrative art that come from miniature painting with those of the monumental tradition which tends to focus on more elaborate and comparatively more isolated scenes.

From the same point of view other monumental cycles in mosaic or fresco should be analyzed wherever an extended cycle of Biblical scenes suggests the use of illustrated manuscripts as models as, e.g., in the fifth century Old Testament scenes in Old St. Peter's and S. Paolo fuori le Mura, both being known only from later drawings,[25] or in the

frescoes of the Synagogue of Dura that date in the middle of the 3rd century.[26] The synagogue frescoes are particularly suitable for a study of their relationship to a postulated miniature model, since all three principles deduced from the San Marco mosaics, i.e. omission, condensation and conflation, show up again in this fresco cycle, which on account of its early date leads us considerably closer to the origin of Bible illustrations than any other cycle, manuscript or fresco.

In the comparatively small interior of the synagogue only a limited number of scenes from various books of the Old Testament could, of course, be accommodated, and the fresco painters made a careful selection of episodes of which they depicted normally two or three successive phases. Obviously omissions play a much greater role than in San Marco, where a far more extended wall space was reserved for scenes from the Book of Genesis alone. However, in a few cases—the clearest being the panel with the Vision of Ezekiel in the Valley of Dry Bones (fig. 14)—the Dura painter lined up a greater number of phases from one episode and at the same time in such a dense sequence that within this section apparently nothing was left out from the manuscript model. No less than six times is Ezekiel depicted in the Dura panel that illustrates but the first half of the 37th chapter, and the cinematographic element of moving quickly from one figure of the prophet to the next, changing the poses only slightly, is very effective indeed. At the same time the fresco painter condensed the scenes to such an extent, especially at the beginning, that one Ezekiel figure almost touches the next one. One may recall in this connection the miniature of the Cotton Genesis with the freely moving Abraham (fig. 10) and the corresponding San Marco mosaic with the spatially confined figure of Abraham (fig. 11) in order to visualize a similar process of condensation from the postulated miniature model into the Dura fresco.

Among the Dura frescoes we also find several cases of conflation of two scenes into one, like the one discussed in San Marco representing the Journey of Abraham, Sarah and Lot to Egypt (figs. 11-13). A striking example is the one that illustrates

24 Weitzmann in *Friend Studies, op.cit.* 121 and figs. 9-11.

25 J. Garber, *Wirkungen der frühchristlichen Gemäldezyklen der alten Peters- und Pauls-Basiliken in Rom* (Berlin-Vienna 1918).

26 An exhaustive study by Carl H. Kraeling is expected to appear soon. For the time being cf. his preliminary report *The Excavations at Dura Europos, Preliminary Report of the Sixth Season 1932-1933* (New Haven 1936) 337ff and pl. XLVII-LIII. Cf. also Comte Du Mesnil du Buisson, *Les Peintures de la Synagogue de Doura-Europos* (Rome 1939).

the episode of the ark of the covenant in the Temple of Dagon, the god of the Philistines (fig. 15). At the right the cult statue of Dagon is depicted twice, lying broken on the ground, since, according to the story (I.Reg.V-VI) it had miraculously fallen twice from the pedestal as a result of the presence of the ark, which the Philistines had forcibly taken and placed there. Thereafter the ark was returned to the Jews and carried away on an ox-cart, and this phase is depicted in the left half of the panel. The ark is represented only once in the center of a spatially unified composition while being simultaneously related to two consecutive phases of the same episode. In order to visualize the miniature model one would have to disentangle the fresco panel and to assume two miniatures, each with its own ark of the covenant. Actually, such miniatures do exist in the 11th century Greek Book of Kings in the Vatican Library, cod. gr. 333.[27] What the manuscripts were which served as models for the Dura painters is not easily determined. They could hardly have been the various books of the Hebrew Bible proper as we know them from the Septuagint translation, since in some fresco panels there occur legendary elements that cannot be explained by the Bible, but only by haggadic and similar legendary texts. So it seems perhaps more probable that texts of the latter kind were the illustrated ones.

The establishment of a relationship between the Dura frescoes and their miniature models is more than a mere hypothesis. We actually possess illustrated Biblical manuscripts that, although considerably later, belong pictorially to the same recension so that a common archetype must be assumed. This, in our opinion, can only have been a manuscript since in a manuscript only do we find the original state of extended narrative picture cycles before omissions, condensations and conflations took place. The central panel over the Thora niche contains, on its second layer of paint, two consecutive scenes from the end of the Book of Genesis, illustrating the impending death of Jacob. One represents the calling of his twelve sons and the other the blessing of Ephraim and Manasseh (fig. 16). The peculiarities of the latter scene are the half erect position of Jacob on the couch, the

pose of the two grandsons facing the spectator instead of Jacob, and Joseph's approach from the right with outstretched hands. All three features occur, very much alike, in the corresponding scene of a 12th century Greek Octateuch in the Seraglio in Istanbul.[28]

From this and similar examples from Genesis, Kings, and Prophets[29] far-reaching conclusions can be drawn: (1) that the Hellenized Jews before the middle of the third century—but how much earlier remains for the time being a matter of conjecture— had illustrated books which, to judge from the dense sequence of phases in the Ezekiel and a few other panels, must have existed with cycles just as extensive or perhaps even more so than the illustrated Homer and Euripides rolls of classical antiquity; (2) that these Jewish books were used by the Christians when they started to illustrate Holy Scripture with enormous cycles; and (3) that, once an extensive miniature cycle was created, it served as model not only for later miniaturists over a span of time of about a millennium, but for monumental painters as well.

Having thus demonstrated the profound influence of Greco-Jewish illustrations upon the Christian, there still remains to be discussed the problem of a direct dependence of Christian upon Greco-Roman book illustration. The Cotton Genesis, as we know from later copies in miniatures and the San Marco mosaics, contained the representation of the Creation of Adam in typical narrative fashion in three phases: (1) the "Shaping of Man" by the Creator seated on a throne; (2) "Man's Enlivement" through the touch of the head whereby the Creator bends over Adam's head from behind; and (3) his "Animation" by the induction of a winged Psyche as the symbol of the immortal soul which the Creator holds by the wings while facing Adam in a standing pose.[30] This detailed pictorial account of Adam's creation is not fully explained by the Biblical text, and therefore these three scenes could not have been invented for it. At the same time, one cannot consider it fortuitous that these three identical phases occur in ancient art in connection with the Creation of Man by Prometheus. Thus it seems quite self-evident that the Bible illustrator

---

[27] J. Lassus, "Les Miniatures byzantines du Livre des Rois," *Mélanges d'archéologie et d'histoire* 45 (1928) 38ff.

[28] T. Ouspensky, *L'Octateuque de la Bibliothèque du Serail à Constantinople* (Sofia 1907) p. 140, No. 163.

[29] The author is preparing a special study on the problem of

an iconographical relationship between the Dura frescoes and later Christian miniatures.

[30] Weitzmann, *Roll and Codex*, 176ff and figs. 177-182; idem *MJb* p. 115 and figs. 18-23.

must not only have known illustrations of the Prometheus myth, but used them with full awareness of their original meaning. The common archetype, most likely, was some kind of an illustrated mythological handbook like the *Bibliotheke* of Apollodorus.

These remarks can give only a few hints as to the nature and characteristics of Hellenistic-Roman, Jewish, and Early Christian book illustration, and to those principal features by which the illustrated books of these three cultural spheres are connected. From the wider point of view of the *art of the narrative in picture language*—to repeat this once more—book art stands at the end of a long evolutionary process which in archaic art started out with a rather vague relationship between picture and text, in the high classical period became more precise, and in the Hellenistic period reached a final solution in the manuscript where writing and picture were physically connected, and where the illustrator was placed in a position to check carefully each iconographic feature against the text, constantly before his eyes.

Another essential element in book art is its extreme conservatism. Once an archetype has been created, a process of constant and more or less faithful copying began, extending often over many centuries. This traditionalism is the prerequisite of a methodical study of what we call iconography. Moreover, this conservatism and traditionalism should not be explained as a lack of inventive capacity, but rather as an act of reverence towards a picture once a satisfactory artistic solution had been found for its composition. Miniature cycles originated in the Hellenistic period at the same time that Alexandrian scholars made the first ἔκδοσις of great works of literature, epic and dramatic, no longer permitting a minstrel or a chorodidaskalos to make changes at will. The codification of both text and picture cycle, at about the same time, must be considered as an expression of the same mentality which believed in the unchangeability of a truth once it had been clearly defined in word and picture. This attitude, of course, finds its clearest expression in connection with Holy Scripture.

One may well ask whether this way of treating text and pictures from the point of view of a fixed tradition averse to any alterations and so contrary to the thinking of the Greeks of the high classical period, is not the result of a reassertion of the Oriental mind in the Hellenistic civilization of Alexandria. This may well explain why in the long history of narrative art there is an apparent gulf between the *isolating, monoscenic method of narration* that was preferred in the high classical period, and the *expanded cyclic method of narration* in Hellenistic-Roman art, to which on the one hand forerunners exist in the so-called Phoenician silver bowls, while on the other, after its reappearance in Hellenistic art, it continued in Greco-Jewish book art, as reflected in the Dura frescoes, and culminated in Early Christian and medieval luxury codices like the Vienna and Cotton Genesis.

PRINCETON UNIVERSITY AND
THE INSTITUTE FOR ADVANCED STUDY

BOOK ILLUSTRATION OF THE 4TH CENTURY.
TRADITION AND INNOVATION

(Pl. CXXXI - CLII)

K. WEITZMANN

I. THE CHANGE FROM ROLL TO CODEX

The long history of the book, its writing and its illustration, witnessed three revolutionary innovations of decisive consequences. The first was the invention of the papyrus scroll by the Egyptians, a medium which permitted the writing of lengthy texts and the insertion of diagrammatic and even scenic illustrations, of which the Books of the Dead — the earliest illustrated one dating from the Middle Kingdom — are our most conspicuous extant testimonies. The second was the invention of the parchment codex with « many - folded skins » which came into being at the end of the first century A. D., as proved by the epigrams of Martial (1), and which, after a struggle of about two centuries, became the supreme ruler in the field of book production in the 4th century. The third was the invention of the printed book by Gutenberg in the 15th century when a new quantitative principle permitted the spread of written knowledge on an ever increasing scale.

It is the second revolutionary movement with which we are concerned. It affected the art of illustration even more than the art of writing: while it is true that in a codex the whole Aeneid could be written in a single volume, whereas 12 papyrus rolls were needed previously, the system of writing in vertical columns was not affected in principle. Yet for the illustrator, the clearly defined surface area of an individual parchment leaf provided entirely new

(1) MARTIAL, *Epigrams* XIV, 184, 186, 190. 192.

415

possibilities which, as we shall try to prove, permitted him to develop a modest handicraft into an ambitious art on which, for centuries to come, some of the best painters concentrated their artistic efforts (2). May it be said right at the beginning that the history of book illumination of the 4th century cannot be written on the basis of the few stray manuscripts left of this period, but that we can hope to reconstruct this history only by the archaeological method of inference whereby close copies of a later period must be introduced in order to fill the gaps of the lost originals. The Roman marbles that are copies of lost Greek originals are, as far as their methodological treatment is concerned, the best-known parallel. As a case of analogy, later manuscripts, which reveal themselves as copies of very early models, provide our main evidence — notwithstanding the possibility of errors and pitfalls which the employing of such a method entails.

The method of illustration in Greek papyri can best be demonstrated by astronomical texts with constellation pictures because in this branch of literature we possess not only the earliest extant example of an illustrated Greek papyrus roll, but also a very considerable number of mediaeval copies (3). To the second century B. C. belongs a papyrus roll of two meters in length, now in the Louvre (fig. 1) (4), which contains instructions about the spheres based on propositions of a certain Eudoxus and whose text columns are intercalated with constellation pictures — the scarab for the sun, Osiris for Orion, the Claws, the Scorpion and so on — which

---

(2) For the earliest phase of the illustrated book in the classical and Early Christian period see: G. THIELE, *De Antiquorum Libris Pietis Capita Quattuor* (Marburg 1897); TH. BIRT, *Die Buchrolle in der Kunst* (Leipzig 1907); ST. J. GASIOROWSKI, *Malarstwo Minjaturowe Grecko-Rzymskie* (Cracow 1928); E. BETHE, *Buch und Bild im Altertum (aus dem Nachlass hersg. von Ernst Kirsten)*, (Leipzig 1945); K. WEITZMANN, *Illustrations in Roll and Codex. A Study of the Origin and Method of Text illustration* (Princeton 1947) (hereafter cited: R. & C.); IDEM, *Greek Mythology in Byzantine Art* (Princeton 1951); IDEM, *Naration in Early Christendom: Am. J. Arch.* 61 (1957) 83 ff.; IDEM, *Ancient Book Illumination* (Cambridge 1959) (hereafter cited: A. B. I.).

(3) Cf. the very useful list of the illustrated astronomical manuscripts by. A. W. BYVANCK in the: *Mededelingen der Koninklijke Nederlandsche Akademie van Wetenshappen, Afd. Letterkunde,* N. R. XII No. 2 (1949) 199 ff.

(4) M. LETRONNE and. W. BRUNET DE PRESLE, *Notices et extraits des manuscrits de la Bibliothèque Impériale* 18,2 (1865) 25 f. Album pls. I-X; WEITZMANN, *R. & C.*, pp. 49 ff. and fig. 37; BYVANCK, l. c., pp. 205 ff. Nr. 1, (here fuller bibliography); WEITZMANN, *A. B. I.*, p. 6 and pl. I fig. 2.

are placed, frameless, wherever the text requires them. The text predominates and the pictures are subordinated. With a tenaciousness which is typical of conservative book art, this principle of illustration which we should like to term « Papyrus style » persists for centuries, even after new principles had developed in the meantime. A manuscript in Munich written in the year 818 in Salzburg (fig. 2) (5) shows exactly the same principle of illustration except that the simple diagrams with partly Egyptian symbols were replaced by images essentially based on Greek mythology, images which surely were not invented for the *Phaenomena* of Aratus — although this whole group of texts is known as *Aratea* — but most likely for the *Katasterismoi* ascribed to Eratosthenes of Cyrene (6). A typical example is the Constellation picture of Andromeda, fettered on two rocks which are rendered diagrammatically like stelae.

It was a revolutionary concept to separate text and picture and to enlarge each picture to the size of a whole folio as we see it in a manuscript in Leiden which was made in Reims in the second quarter of the 9th century (7). The seminude Andromeda (fig. 3) in a very articulated, relaxed pose (8) stems from a very good classical model which, indeed, seems to have been copied so faithfully that the style of the model still shines through in the Carolingian picture. Nordenfalk already (9) related the miniatures of the Leiden manuscript to those of the Filocalus calendar of the year 354, a manuscript to be discussed later in extenso. The stylistic evidence fits that of the text. The accompanying verses in the Leiden manuscript are taken from Festus Rufus Avienus, who wrote about the middle of the 4th century a versified *Aratea Phaenomena*.

Yet the artistic transformation from column picture to full page miniature is in this case not confined to an enlargement of the figure scale. Not only is a frame added, but this frame cuts

(5) WEITZMANN, *R. & C.*, p. 72.

(6) C. ROBERT, *Eratosthenis catasterismorum reliquiae* (Berlin 1878).

(7) G. THIELE, *Antike Himmelsbilder* (Berlin 1898) 77 ff. and figs. 18-57; BYVANCK, *l. c.*, p. 214 No. 37 (here fuller bibliogr.).

(8) THIELE, *op. cit.*, pp. 105 ff. and fig. 31. K. M. PHILLIPS, JR. PERSEUS and ANDROMEDA, *Am. Journ. Arch.* 72 (1968) 18 and fig. 51.

(9) C. NORDENFALK, *Der Kalender vom Jahre 354 und die lateinische Buchmalerei des IV. Jahrhunderts: Göteborgs Kungl Vetenskaps och Vitterhets Samhälles Handlinger*, Ser. A. 5,2 (1936) 28 ff.

through the rocks, thus giving the illusion that the rocky landscape
continues beyond the limitations of the picture frame. In other
words, the same rocks which in the Munich miniature are almost
diagrammatically designed for mere iconographical reasons, give
in the Leiden miniature the impression of a spatial landscape as
if seen through a window, and the blue ground adds to this illusion.

Here the miniaturist adapts principles, which were long before
developed in monumental painting. A fresco from Pompeii showing
the liberation of Andromeda by Perseus (fig. 4) (10) is laid out
according to the very same principle of pictorially cutting the rock
close to the left edge of the picture, thus stimulating the imagination of the beholder to conceive of a landscape continuing beyond
the lateral limits. In the Leiden Aratus this is a rather unique case
of a miniaturist being inspired by monumental painting for the
simple reason that no other Constellation picture required landscape
setting. It is obvious that in cases of scenic illustrations the opportunity of incorporating elements from monumental painting were much
greater and the addition of a landscape setting was one of the
effective means of raising miniature painting to a higher artistic
level.

Perhaps the best example to demonstrate the transition from
a simple papyrus illustration to an elaborate codex miniature is the
Milan Iliad. Although what is left of its originally much more
comprehensive picture cycle is as late as the 5th or perhaps 6th century. Bianchi Bandinelli, in a brillant analysis of the Milan Iliad,
has clearly demonstrated that there are different groups of miniatures which point to various models from earlier centuries (11). The
stylistically oldest group reaches back into the period of the papyrus
roll, being most convincingly represented by the miniature in which
Aphrodite, who is hurt, complains about it to Zeus (fig. 5). The lining
up of individual figures, void of background, reflects the very same
system of illustration as that of the second century Romance papyrus in Paris (fig. 6) (12), the only addition of the Iliad painter

(10) A. MAIURI, *Roman Painting* (Skira 1953) fig. on p. 79.

(11) R. BIANCHI BANDINELLI, *Hellenistic-Byzantine Miniatures of the Iliad* (Olten
1955) (here the older bibliography).

(12) GASIOROWSKI, *op. cit.*, pp. 17, V and fig. 2; WEITZMANN, *R. & C.*, p. 51 and
fig. 40; IDEM, *A. B. I.*, p. 100 and fig. 107.

being the frame, which is the first step to isolate a scene from the text and give it a panel-like appearance.

That the complex battle scenes in the Milan Iliad (fig. 7) were derived from monumental art needs hardly to be argued. Bianchi Bandinelli has attributed this double miniature to his group C, which reflects battle compositions that have their closest parallels in Roman art of the third century (13). Yet, this does not necessarily mean that at that time such compositions were already adapted for manuscripts. The answer to this problem of adaptation depends essentially on determining the time when the parchment codex was sufficiently popularized so that artists would take advantage of the new possibilities and this was hardly before the 4th century.

In one point we should like to elaborate on Bianchi Bandinelli's opinion of the genesis of the Milan Iliad cycle. According to him the different groups represent various manuscript traditions that were combined in the 6th century. If, however, the battle scenes of group C come from one manuscript and the conversation scenes of group A, reflecting the papyrus tradition, from another, then A would have been without battle scenes and C without conversation scenes which is not likely. We rather prefer the idea of a morphological growth of the picture cycle, whereby simple miniatures of group A at a certain state of development expanded both in size and compositional complexity under the impact of monumental painting. In other words we think that the single combat group in the center distinguished by a larger figure scale, is the one element that harks back to the papyrus tradition. The Megarian bowls, reflecting the early type of papyrus illustration (fig. 8) (14) provide the evidence for this type of concise narrative scene as demonstrated by a cup with three scenes from the *Little Iliad* (15) which easily fit into text columns as our reconstruction of a section of a papyrus roll tries to suggest. The illustrator of the Milan Iliad is, thus, not substituting one form of illustration for another, but grouping around the traditional nucleus additional figures, landscape and architectural background. It is along these lines that the illustrator

(13) BIANCHI BANDINELLI, *op. cit.*, pp. 62 ff. and 122 ff.

(14) WEITZMANN, *R. & C.*, pp. 18 ff., 77 ff. and figs. A-B.

(15) C. ROBERT, *Homerische Becher (50, Berliner Winckelmannsprogramm)* (Berlin 1890) 30 ff. No. E.; U. HAUSMANN, *Hellenistische Reliefbecher* (Stuttgart 1959) 54 No. 16.

seeks new solutions which are aimed at combining a narrative tradition with the embellishments of panel paintings.

In his most informative study of the substitution of the codex
for the roll, Colin Roberts (16) has clearly demonstrated by statistics
that in the second century A. D. less than 3% of the extant books
were codices, that not before the 4th century did the codex outnum-
ber, and then by far, the papyrus roll, and that « with the opening
of the 4th century the codex is near its triumph » (17). Moreover
he provided the evidence that the Christians took quicker advantage
of the new book form presumably because it was more economical.
At the same time we now have the evidence that very extensive
picture cycles of the Old Testament existed before the third century
since several panels of the frescoes of the synagogue of Dura —
the one with the Vision of Ezekiel in the Valley of the Dry Bones
is the most characteristic example — point to an established tradition of vast narrative cycles as they are typical of and must have
originated in manuscripts (18) that were made for the Hellenized
Jews of the Diaspora (19). Thus the illustration of the Old Testament reaches back into a period in which the papyrus scroll was
still supreme and, indeed, we still have evidence of biblical cycles
in the Papyrus style that have survived from the Middle Ages.

When at the turn of the 4th - 5th century Prudentius wrote
his *Psychomachia* and, presumably, at that time had miniatures
added to it, which were to influence mediaeval art for centuries,
the illustrator still used the papyrus style of inserting small concise
scenes in the writing column, as can be seen in the Paris manuscript
from the 9th - 10th century, which of all extant copies is the closest
to the Early Christian archetype (20) and this in spite of the fact

(16) C. H. ROBERTS, *The Codex: Proc. of the Brit. Academy* 40 (1955) 169 ff.

(17) IBIDEM, pp. 184 ff., 199.

(18) C. H. KRAELING, *The Excavations at Dura-Europos, Final Report* VIII, Part I:
The Synagogue (New Haven 1956) 398 ff. K. WEITZMANN, *Narration in Early Christendom: Am. J. Arch.* 61 (1957) 89 and pl. 36 figs. 14-15.

(19) The illustrated Graeco-Jewish books of the Old Testament which were available to the earliest Christian illustrators, must, indeed, have been widespread. Cf.
K. WEITZMANN, *Zur Frage des Einflusses jüdischer Bildquellen auf die Illustration des
Alten Testamentes: Mullus. Festschrift Theodor Klauser* (Münster 1964) 401 ff. (Here
also the older bibliography on this subject).

(20) R. STETTINER, *Die illustrierten Prudentiushandschriften* (Berlin 1895) 3 ff.,
167 ff. and pls. 1-12, 15-16.

that the archetype was in all likelihood already a codex. The very first miniature shows a frame all around, but this is an exception; in most instances the Carolingian copyist began with the framing and then abandoned it (21); even in the first miniature one will notice that the frame is an after-thought.

When the illustrator illustrated the Preface which contains a mystical application of the Abraham story as told in Genesis XIV, he could and did rely on an existing tradition of Old Testament-cycles. The very first miniature (fig. 9) shows the sacrifice of Isaac with the latter placed not upon the altar but in front of it and rendered in a movement as if he had tried to escape. We have demonstrated elsewhere that this very compositional scheme which we find also in Byzantine manuscripts, is based on a classical prototype which depicted the attempted, but not executed, sacrifice of the little Orestes boy by Telephus as told in the *Telephus* of Euripides (22). The illustrated Book of Genesis, which the first illustrator of the *Psychomachia* used, may then, with its papyrus style of illustration, hark back into a period when individual books of the Septuagint with very extensive cycles (23) were presumably still written on scrolls.

But, then, due to the new possibilities of the parchment leaf of the codex, the Bible illustration underwent, in the 4th century, the same kind of changes we have noticed in the *Milan Iliad*. The proof rests on the fragments of the so-called Quedlinburg Itala which can be dated into the very end of the 4th century (24). No longer are the scenes interspersed in the columns of the text, but four scenes are united in one full page miniature, though their framing still reveals that the original units would fit the two column text, would one try to reinstate them to their former system. Samuel and Saul from scenes that illustrate events from the 15th chapter of the first Book of Samuel (fig. 10), stand out as silhouettes against a neutral, grey-blue middle zone above which mountains and architecture are set up against a pink dawn or sunset, which gra-

---

(21) WEITZMANN, *R. & C.*, p. 98 and fig. 83.

(22) IBIDEM, pp. 174 ff. and figs. 173 and 175.

(23) For the origin of the Septuagint illustration cf. K. WEITZMANN, *Die Illustration der Septuaginta: Münchner Jahrbuch der bild. Kunst.* III. Ser. 3/4 (1952/53) 96 ff.

(24) H. DEGERING and A. BOECKLER, *Die Quedlinburg Italafragmente* (Berlin 1952).

dually changes into a cooler blue. We would assume this landscape, which is quite unrelated to the foreground, to have been added above the isocephalic figure composition by the very artist who combined the four scenes on one page and depicted for each pair of neighboring scenes a unifying, panoramic background (25). Boeckler, in his publication of the Quedlinburg Itala, argued that these miniatures were the first formulation of the subjects they depict and he saw a proof of this theory in the precepts for the painter written on the empty parchment before it was painted over. Such precepts, so Boeckler argues, were not necessary, had the artist had a model available. We know, of course, today from the frescoes of the Dura synagogue that extensive narrative cycles of the Books of Kings did exist before the middle of the third century. At the same time we believe that the precepts are sufficiently explained by the necessity to guide the painter, after the miniatures had lost their original close contact with the text and were grouped together on pages solely reserved for painting. Such a transfer has inherently the possibilities for many errors, the avoidance of which was the concern of this particular illustrator. In other words we believe that the illustrator of the Quedlinburg Itala did not invent a new biblical cycle but that he followed the same pattern as his colleague who illustrated the Milan Iliad when he converted an illustrated Books of Kings of the Papyrus style into a sumptuous luxury edition with panel-like miniatures that show the influence of monumental landscape painting.

II. THE FILOCALUS CALENDAR

One of the key monuments which gives us a varied insight into the process of transformation from roll to codex illustration is the Calender of Filocalus, well known through the writings by Strzygowski (26) and Nordenfalk (27), and especially the exhaustive

(25) The very same device of unifying panoramic londscapes or architectural prospects was used by the illustrator of the Milan Iliad when he placed two scenes side by side. Cr. WEITZMANN, *R. & C.*, p. 163 and fig. 159.

(26) J. STRZYGOWSKI, *Die Calenderbilder des Chronographen vom Jahre 354: Jahrb. des Arch. Inst I. Ergänzungsheft* (Belin 1888).

(27) Cf. note 9.

monograph by Henri Stern (28). Its importance for our investigation rests on the following points: 1) it is the only precisely dated manuscript of the 4th century; 2) though known today only from 17th century drawings based on an intermediary copy of the Carolingian period, these very faithful and reliable copies reveal that the original must have been an ambitious, luxury manuscript of high quality; 3) it is a polycyclic manuscript, in which various sets of pictures from different traditions were combined, each set having its own problem in the process of transformation; and 4) the miniatures represent in part secular iconography, in part imperial iconography and in addition they were made for a Christian by the name of Valentinus. Thus we are led into a realm, where various ideologies were fused and are not mutually exclusive.

A set of signs of the Zodiac in small medallions accompanying the text are still thoroughly in the papyrus tradition (29). In other words, in this case the illustrator did not make the step which is reflected in the constellation pictures of the Leiden Aratus, namely to enlarge them to the size of full-page illustrations.

The illustrator becomes aware of the possibilities of the format of the parchment leaf of the codex in another set of pictures where the representations of the months are depicted as personifications in full length (fig. 11). The older tradition is reflected in the Alexandrian World-chronicle in Moscow, which, though being still written on papyrus, is nevertheless a codex which harks back to an archetype not older than the year 392 A. D., the year of the destruction of the Serapeion in Alexandria with which the Chronicle ends. Here the months, represented as busts of which only a few traces are left (fig. 12) (30), are rendered in a form common in floor mosaics prior to the 4th century as witnessed by the Monnus mosaic in Trier from the middle of the third century (31).

(28) H. STERN, *Le Calendrier de 354. Étude de son texte et ses illustrations* (Paris 1953).

(29) STRZYGOWSKI, *op. cit.*, pl. XXIX, XXXI, XXXIII; STERN, *op. cit.*, pls. VII,$_2$, XI,$_2$, XII,$_2$.

(30) A. BAUER and J. STRZYGOWSKI, *Eine Alexandrinische Weltchronik:Denkschriften der K. Akademie d. Wissenschaften, Phil.-hist. Kl.*, 51, 2 (Vienna 1906) 144 ff. and pl. I Recto.

(31) F. HETTNER, *Antike Denkmäler* 1 (1889) pl. 47-49.

The illustrator of the Filocalus Calendar did not continue this tradition but rather turned to monumental art for inspiration.

It has generally been accepted that some floor mosaics from Rome reflect the same pictorial recension, and it has been made plausible by Stern that they themselves were not invented before the second quarter of the 4th century (32). A representation of the month of May of approximately the same date on a mosaic in the Antiquarium in Rome (fig. 13) (33) shows the same type of personification rather than an « Occupation with an agricultural task ». Space and illusionistic effect are indicated by two windows with balustrades and this very same motif we notice in the picture of March in the Filocalus Calendar, where a swallow is perched on a similar window balaustrade, a detail which indicates the dependence on the very same tradition of monumental painting on which the Roman mosaic also is based.

The model, if it had any frame at all, had most likely not more than a simple border like that of the mosaic. It was the book illustrator's idea to add a richer frame made up of architectural elements. But it also was in the tradition of book ornament to devaluate the structural elements as the artist does in the present case by increasing the number of conches of the pediment and placing two over its oblique sides. Here we get a clear insight into the process of adapting human figures from monumental art and amalgamating them into the decorative art of the book.

Likewise derived from monumental painting are the four city personifications of Rome (fig. 14), Alexandria (fig. 15), Constantinopolis and Treberis, i. e. Tier. The inclusion of Constantinople means of course that this set of the great capital cities of the Roman empire in this form could not be older than the second quarter of the 4th century. Certain elements, like the open windows in the Alexandria picture through which one can see boats sailing in the Mediterranean, are indicative of a survival of illusionistic effects rooted in the tradition of monumental painting. Here the miniaturist proves himself to be very much up to date in copying iconographical themes only recently created. Yet Calendars, Chronicles and other

(32) STERN, op. cit., pp. 289 ff.
(33) Ibidem, pl. XL, 2.

texts even before the invention of the codex required on occasion the illustration of cities. How were they depicted in the papyrus tradition?

Once more the Alexandrian World-chronicle gives us the answer. Where the illustrator was faced with the problem of finding a pictorial formula for the provinces of Asia Minor (34), he chose the same formula which traditionally had been used also for the representation of cities: a city wall flanked by towers and with a gate in the center (fig. 16). This was the formula used in ancient maps, as can be seen in the numerous copies of the *Geography* of Claudius Ptolomy (35). The illustrator of the Filocalus Calendar discarded this tradition, which was eminently suitable for the papyrus illustrator, who had always looked for the briefest, most concise and diagrammatic formula.

The precise model of the Filocalus pictures we, of course, no longer have, but there is a famous fresco, once in the Palazzo Barberini and now in the Terme Museum (fig. 17), with a goddess enthroned in a frontal position who holds, like the personification of Rome in the Calendar drawing, a Victory in one hand and a spear in the other (36). The type is sufficiently close to justify once more the assumption of a monumental painting as the inspiration for the Filocalus Calendar, and since the fresco can be dated around the turn from the third - 4th century (37) we must credit the miniaturist once more with having chosen as a model a type of the immediate past (38).

(34) BAUER - STRZYGOWSK, *op. cit.*, p. 147 and pl. II Verso.

(35) JOSEPH FISCHER, *Claudii Ptolemaei Geographiae codex Vat. Urbinas Graecus 82 (Codices e Vaticanis selecti XVIII)* (1932).

(36) J. WILPERT, *Die römischen Mosaiken und Malereien vom IV. bis XIII. Jahrh.* 1 (Freiburg 1916) 127 ff. and pl. 125; M. CAGIANO DE AZEVEDO, *La Dea Barberini: Riv. di Arch. e Storia dell'Arte*, N. S. III (1954) 109 ff. with color plate.

(37) A. RUMPF, *Stilphasen der spätantiken Kunst: Arbeitsgemeinschaft für Forschung des Landes Nordrhein-Westfalen. Geisteswissensch.* 44 (Köln 1957) 25 and pl. 20, 86.

(38) It also is very characteristic of the 4th century and its desire of raising book illumination to a higher level that the famous Tabula Peutingeriana in Vienna [H. J. HERMANN, *Die Frühmittel-alterlichen Handschriften des Abendlandes: Die illum. Hdss. der Nationalbibliothek Wien N. F.* 1 (Leipzig 1923) 5 ff.], which dates in the XIII. century but harks back to an archetype of the second half of the 4th century, has the older type of diagrammatic walled city replaced by the enthroned city personifications of very similar types as those of the Filocalus Calendar.

To the fresco copy of a goddess enthroned the miniature painter made additions: iconographically he introduced a putto pouring coins, thus symbolizing the money gift of the consul, the « sparsio », as seen similary on the consular diptychs (39), and for mere formal embellishment, he added curtains wh'ch take the place of a picture frame, a motif we shall discuss more thoroughly in connection with the next set of pictures. Here we see as an antithetic pair of full-page miniatures, the two Consuls of the year 354, Constantius II (fig. 18), the Augustus on the throne, distributing gold coins — the first mentioning of a sparsio like this is between 326 and 329 (40) — and Gallus Caesar (fig. 19), standing and holding in his extended hand a Victory who, on her part, offers a corona to the Augustus on the opposite page. In this way does the artist make a fine grada-tion of the order of rank and at the same time he depicts a motion that leads the eye from one picture into the other. This is artistically the most progressive step in exploiting the possibilities of the full-page miniature by going beyond the single page and perceiving the antithetic pair as an artistic unit. Once more we must raise the question as to whether also such imperial portraits, like the subjects of all other full-page miniatures of the Filocalus Calendar, had existed previously in roll illustration and, if so, what their form had been.

There is in the Vatican Library a collective volume of treatises on surveying, the so-called *Agrimensores*, written towards the middle of the 9th century at Fulda (41) after a model which in its totality cannot be older than 540 A. D. (42). Yet several of the individual treatises are considerably older, as e. g. the one entitled *De limiti-bus constituendis* by a certain Hyginus Gromaticus (43), who lived

(39) STERN, *op. cit.*, p. 132.

(40) *Ibidem*, 156 ff.

(41) H. ZIMMERMANN, *Die Fuldaer Buchmalerei in karolingischer und ottonischer Zeit: Kunstgesch. Jahrb, der K. K. Zentralkommission* 4 (1910) 90 ff. and pl. XII; A. GOLDSCHMIDT, *German Illumination* Vol. I. *Carolingian Period* (New York, s. d.) 19 and pl. 16.

(42) A. W. BYVANCK, *Een Antieke Miniatuur in het Handschrift Palatinus Latinus 1564 der Vaticaansche Bibliotheek: Mededeelingen van het Nederlandsch Historisch Instituut te Rome* 3 (1923) 123 and esp. p. 134.

(43) For the text of the Agrimensores in general cf. F. BLUME, K. LACHMANN und A. RUDORFF, *Die Schriften der Römischen Feldmesser* (Berlin 1848 and 1852); C. THU-LIN, *Die Handschriften des Corpus Agrimensorum Romanorum: Abhdlg. Preuss. Akad. Phil.-Hist. Kl.* (1911); *Idem, Corpus Agrimensorum Romanorum,* (Teubner ed. 1913).

in the time of Domitian or Trajan. Since this and other early treatises are prolifically illustrated we can be certain that their pictures
hark back to the papyrus period. Consequently the title miniature
with two portraits of emperors, unfortunately not inscribed (fig. 20),
also may very well go back to such an early date. The intrinsic
probability that, indeed, they reflect the papyrus tradition lies in
their form as medallion busts, of which the second one is left unfinish-
ed. The busts of the personifications of the months and now the
busts of the emperors suggest that, because of their abbreviated and
concise form, they were most suitable for the heading of or the
insertion into the narrow columns of writing of a papyrus roll which
imposed spatial limitations on the illustrator. For this very reason
the bust was also chosen, as we have tried to demonstrate elsewhere,
for the illustration of the 700 portraits in the *Hebdomades* of
Varro (44).

Returning to the imperial portraits in the Filocalus Calendar
we may assume, in analogy to the pictures of the Months and the
Personifications of the cities, that the illustrator, while copying the
human figure from monumental painting, made a contribution of
his own by framing them in a manner which reveals a certain ornamental complexity. The aedicula is structurally very clear and real
and obviously designed under the influence of some existing type of
architecture which, in our opinion, can be determined. The characteristic adornments of the aedicula are the conch in the pediment
and the parted curtains fastened to the columns. While both elements occur in various types of Roman architecture it can be made
plausible as we believe, that in book illumination it derives from
theater architecture and represented originally the Porta Regia.

Individually these two elements occur in aediculae which, as
part of a scenea frons (45), form the background in two Byzantine
Evangelist pictures of the 10th century. The first, from the Athos
monastery Philotheu (fig. 21) (46), depicts the Porta Regia, made

---

(44) WEITZMANN, *A. B. I.* pp. 116 ff.

(45) The relation of the background of certain Byzantine miniatures to tre architecture of the ancient theatre has been thoroughly discussed by A. M. FRIEND, *The
portraits of the Evangelists in Greek and Latin Manuscripts*, Part. II, *Art Studies* (1929)
4 ff. and esp. 9 ff.: Theatre Scenery and the Portraits of the Evangelists.

(46) E. WEITZMANN, *Die Byzantinische Buchmalerei des 9. und 10. Jahrh* (Berlin
1935), 46 and pl. LI, 302; *Idem., Geistige Grundlagen und Wesen der Makedonischen*

up of two heavy columns of colored marble (47) that carry a semi-circular architrave with a gable that includes a conch. This baldachin-like architecture is set against the colonnade of the scenae frons and rises above the proscenium wall, in front of which the Evangelist Mark is depicted enthroned in frontal position, just as, in the ancient theatre, statues of poets were placed in niches of the hyposcenium wall (48). The second picture, also representing the Evangelist Mark is from a 10th century Gospel book in Oxford (fig. 22) (49). Here the hyposcenium wall is much more explicit which, as if seen in perspective from below, cuts off the bases of the two columns of colored marble to which the parted curtains are fastened. But due to the lack of space the crowning gable with the conch is cut off (50). Both these Greek manuscripts belong to the so-called Macedonian Renaissance of the 10th century and obviously copy very early models from a period in which these theater backgrounds were not yet ornamentalized and still appear as an initial stage of transformation from monumental art — presumably fresco painting of architecture rather than existing architecture — into miniature painting. Most likely this happened in the first half of the 4th century (51), because almost immediately thereafter the aedicula was isolated from the rest of the scenae frons and used as a decoration for the Canon tables of Eusebius. This must have taken place shortly before the middle of the 4th century, i. e. the death of Eusebius in 338 or 339 (52). The architectural setting of the Greek Evangelists, the Canon tables with the conch in the gable and the parted curtains (53), the architectural frames of the

---

Renaissance. Arbeitsgemeinschaft für Forschung des Landes Nordrhein-Westfalen, Geisteswissenschaften 107 (Köln 1963) 26 and fig. 22.

(47) Cf. e. g. the theatre of Dugga in North Africa; M. BIEBER, *The history of the Greek and Roman Theater* (Princeton 1961²) 204 ff. and fig. 689 ff.

(48) FRIEND, *l. c.*, p. 28 and pl. XII, 39.

(49) WEITZMANN, *Byz. Buchm.*, p. 18 and pl. XXII, 120.

(50) *Idem, Geistige Grundl.*, p. 26 and color pl. 5.

(51) O third manuscript of the Macedonian Renaissance, the Gospel book in Stauronikita on Mount Athos, cod. 43, from the middle of the 10th century, will be discussed later on p.

(52) For the history of the Kanontables cf. the basic study by C. NORDENFALK, *Die spätantiken Kanontafeln* (Göteborg 1938).

(53) For a conch in a Canontable cf. the 10th century Gospel book in the Vatican, cod. Palat. grec. 220 [K. WEITZMANN, *Die Armenische Buchmalerei des 10. und beginnenden 11. Jahrh.* (Bamberg 1933) pl. V, 16], and for the curtains the 10th century

imperial portraits in the Filocalus Calendar are thus all derived from the same source.

In the light of this evidence one may well ponder whether the introduction of the scenae frons into miniature painting must not be accredited to Christian rather than pagan book illuminators of the 4th century. Yet we hesitate to draw such a conclusion from the meager evidence we have. The strong parallelism of the same architectural forms in secular and Christian book illumination speaks, in our opinion, rather in favor of imperial scriptoria which, in the first half and well until after the middle of the 4th century, produced secular and Christian luxury manuscripts side by side.

III. AUTHOR AND DEDICATION-PICTURES

While the Filocalus Calendar is perhaps the most diversified example we have through which the changes from roll to codex illustration can be demonstrated, it must at the same time be kept in mind that it represents a rather exceptional illustrated text. By far the majority of Early Christian and mediaeval miniature paintings can readily be divided into two groups: the frontispieces with the figures of either an author, or donor or a person to whom the manuscript is dedicated or the ruler in whose time it was executed — a category represented in the Filocalus by the two emperor portraits —, and the narrative cycles that are not represented in the Filocalus Calendar.

Our contention that portrait painting in papyrus rolls started out with busts, usually in medallion form finds its best support in the author portrait of Virgil. The « codex Vaticanus » (lat. 3225) (54) from either the end of the 4th (55) or the early 5th century (56) contains at the end of book VI of the Aeneid the offset of a lost

---

Abessinian Gospel book of Abba Garima [J. LEROY, *L'Evangeliaire Ethiopien du Couvent d'Abba Garima: Cahiers Archéologiques* 11 (1960) 131 ff.; WEITZMANN, *Geistige Grundl.*, p. 26 and fig. 21].

(54) *Fragmenta et Picturae Vergiliana Cod. Vat. lat. 3225: Codices e Vaticanis selecti* 1 (Rome 1930).

(55) Dated still in the 4th century by E. A. LOWE, *Codices Latini Antiquiores* 1 (Vatican City, Oxford 1934) 4 No. 11.

(56) J. DE WIT, *Die Miniaturen des Vergilius Vaticanus* (Amsterdam 1959) 153 ff.

medallion which can only have been a bust of Virgil that preceded
the text of book VII the beginning of which is now lost. If book
VII had such a portrait, then the other eleven books must have
had one too (57). But such a system of illustration is meaningful
only in the context of separate rolls, each containing one book,
whereas for a codex, containing all 12 books bound together (58),
one auther portrait at the beginning of the total *Aeneid* in a single
volume would normally have been sufficient.

The second Virgil in the Vatican, the so-called « Vergilius
Romanus » (lat. 3867) (59) which, though not much later than the
former (60), is executed in a rather provincial style, shows the same
phenomenon of repeating the author portrait, though not in front
of each book of the Aeneid, but of each *Eclogue*. Three of the
original six are preserved, consisting in this case not of medallion
portraits but of frontally seated author figures (fig. 23) who almost
seem to float on a surface area much too broad for them. They
were apparently conceived to fit narrower writing columns and this
suggests — although this has to remain a hypothesis — that also
the seated portrait, presumably frameless, existed in papyrus rolls (61),
though to what extent we do not know.

To fill the empty space the illustrator added a capsa for scrolls
and a lectern, but, significantly, no writing table, because the poet
is depicted meditating, holding the finished product, a roll, in his
hands, but not occupied with writing. These very same additions,
the capsa and the lectern, were made in an Evangelist portrait of

(57) WEITZMANN, *A. B. I.*, p. 116.

(58) Such a codex must have existed as early as the end of the first century A. D.,
as indicated by the epigram of Martial (XIV. CLXXXVI)

> Quam brevis inmensum cepit membrana Maronem
> ipsius vultus prima tabella gerit.

The « face » of the authour on the first page we assume, in analogy to the Vergilius
Vaticanus, to have been once more a medallion portrait.

(59) *Picturae Ornamenta-complura scripturae specimina codicis Vaticani 3867 qui
Codex Vergilii Romanus audit (Codices e Vaticanis selecti)* (Rome 1902).

(60) In an earlier study C. Nordenfalk (cf. note 9, *Der Kalender* 31 ff. proposed
a date as early as the 4th century, relating the miniatures to monuments of « Constantinian expressionism », but more recently [*Early Medieval Painting* (Skira 1957) p. 97]
he preferred a date in the first half of the 5th century, a date which is more in agreement with the palaeographical evidence (LOWE, *op. cit.*, Part I, p. 7 No. 19).

(61) WEITZMANN, *A. B. I.*, p. 121 and fig. 130.

St. John in a 10th century Gospel book at Stauronikita on Mount Athos, the most characteristic representative of the Macedonian renaissance (fig. 24) (62). John sits in front on the hyposcenium wall, which has been turned into an exedra, and he has not only a very statuaric appearance but is depicted in the pose of a meditating philosopher (63). Indeed, we have reason to believe that we have before us a faithful copy of a very early type of evangelist from the period when the transition was made from an ancient poet or philosopher into an Evangelist, who is not yet concerned with writing down his Gospel. The more or less simultaneous appearance of capsa and lectern in a pagan and a Christian miniature at about the time of the transition from a strip-like picture such as that of the Virgil miniature into a full page miniature with a very illusionistic background (64), points once more to an interrelated development of pagan and Christian book illumination. This parallelism I should like to demonstrate also in the following example.

The almost square format typical of the early codex gave the illustrator the chance to copy from monumental painting more complex compositions with other figures being added to that of the authour. One such instance is the group in which a man of letters is inspired by a muse. A 12th century *Aratus* manuscript in Madrid (fig. 25) (65), shows the seated poet and the muse Urania standing in front of him, both holding scrolls and pointing at the celestial globe between them. As has been recognized long ago (66), this composition is very similar to the Aratus-Urania group in the Monnus mosaic in Trier (fig. 26) which dates from the middle of the third cen-

---

(62) Friend, *Portraits, l. c., Part I, Art Studies* (1927) 134 and pl. VIII, 95-98; Weitzmann, *Byzn. Buchm.*, p. 23 and pl. XXX.

(63) One of the evangelists of the same manuscripts, St. Matthew, could actually be derived from an ancient statue of Epicurus (Weitzmann, *Geistige Grundlagen*, p. 30 and figs. 23-24).

(64) Because of the very illusionistic, painterly treatment of the landscape background in all four miniatures of this Gospel book we had been tempted (ibidem p. 30) to ascribe the archetype to the pre-Constantinian period, but in the light of our present study it hardly seems likely that any full page miniatures and especially such luxurious ones could have been made before Constantine. The illusionistic elements can, in our opinion, be sufficiently explained by the use of monumental paintings which either were of an earlier date or, if later, reflected models of an earlier date.

(65) Byvanck, *The Illustr. of the Aratea* (cf. note 3) p. 216 No. 44.

(66) E. Bethe, *Buch und Bild im Altertum* (Leipzig-Wien 1945) 84 ff and figs. 52-54.

tury (67), and thus we are led to believe that the illustrator of the
archetype of the Madrid codex, for which Thiele suggested a date
in the 4th - 5th centuries (68) copied a monumental painting. This,
of course, did not need to have been a mosaic, but was even more
likely a fresco. The effect of an open window in the upper left
corner we met in one of the representations of the Months in the
Filocalus Calendar and a similarly heavy curtain we noticed in its
pictures of the city personifications. In both instances we should
like to consider the curtains to be additions of the miniature painters. The archetype of the Aratus miniature must, thus, be assumed
to have been close in date to the Filocalus Calendar.

Almost a twin sister to the muse Urania is the personification
who inspires the Evangelist Mark in the well known Rossano Gospels (fig. 27) (69) and points at the scroll on his lap instead of the
celestial globe. But while the 12th century *Aratus* miniature can
be taken as a fairly faithful copy of a 4th century archetype, at
least in composition if not in stylistic details, the Rossano miniature
of the 6th century which likewise can be traced to an early archetype, has undergone considerable changes.

How in particular the two emperor-miniatures of the Filocalus
(fig. 18-19) had established a type of frontispiece that continued
though the Middle Ages though some significant changes and ad-
justments were made, may be demonstrated by a title miniature
to the *Bellum Judaicum* of Flavius Josephus in a manuscript in
Paris from the end of the 11th century executed in or around
Toulouse (fig. 28) (70). Here we also see two emperors in frontal
position: Vespasian at the right is turning to Titus at the left and
offering to his son the orb, apparently as an indication that he had
secured his son's succession. This offering of the orb should be
compared compositionally with the offering of the Nike by Gallus

---

(67) F. HETTNER (note 37) and K. SCHEFOLD, *Die Bildnisse der antiken Dichter,
Redner und Denker* (Basel 1943) 168 and 169 No. 5.

(68) THIELE, *Himmelsbilder, op. cit.*, p. 146.

(69) A. Muñoz, *Il codice purpureo di Rossano* (Rome 1907) p. 5 and pl. XV.

(70) *Les Manuscrits à peintures en France du VII⁺ au XII⁺ siècle, Exposition Bibl.
Nat.* (Paris 1954) 107 No. 313; *Byzance et la France Médiévale. Exposition Bibl. Nat.*
(Paris 1958) 63 No. 114 and pl. XXXI; J. PORCHER, *Medieval French Miniatures* (New
York 1959) 28 and pl. XIX.

Caesar. The basic difference is that in the Josephus miniature both emperors are seated on thrones, as it should be, since both are Augusti. Yet, Titus is artistically singled out as the more prominent one by holding a scepter, wearing an imperial mantle and, like Constantius II in the Filocalus, he is seated on what in the model must have been a folding chair with lion heads but was turned by the mediaeval copyist into a solid bench-like throne. Moroever, the emperors are no longer seated under a baldachin and we venture to suggest that the canopies had once existed in a more elaborate model but were omitted when the two emperor portraits originally facing each other on opposite pages as in the Filocalus, were condensed by the mediaeval illustrator into one full page miniature.

This condensation happened apparently at the time when the figure of Flavius Josephus was introduced on the opposite page, thus occupying the space that once had been taken by the second emperor. By depicting the author, offering his opus with veiled hands (fig. 29), the archetype, which originally, so we believe, had existed only of a pair of antithetic emperor portraits, was turned into a dedication scene. When this conceptual expansion happend remains still to be determined.

Quite a different solution of fusing the emperor and the author into a dedication scene can be seen in the antithetic pair of title miniatures in the late Carolingian Pseudo-Apuleius herbal in Kassel, cod. phys. fol. 10 (fig. 30) that was probably written in Fulda (71). Goldschmidt (72) had described the two figures as « two disputing authors ». However, the figure at the left wears a crown and is thus clearly marked as an emperor. An inscription *Constantinus Mag.* was read by Goldschmidt as *Magister*, although he admits that a physician of Salerno by that name cannot be the person depicted in the miniature, because he lived in the 11th century. One wonders whether it should not be read *Constantinus Magnus*, but since this inscription is later than the miniature, there is no way of

---

(71) Ch. Singer, *The Herbal in Antiquity: Journ. Hell. Stud.* 47 (1927) 43 ff. and figs. 29, 40, 45; Howald and *Sigerist, Corp. Medic. Lat.* 4 (Leipzig 1927) XIII. According to these authors the archetype of the Pseudo-Apuleius herbal was written before the 5th, but not before the 4th century and this date would seem to fit also the archetype of these dedication miniatures. — Bethe, *op. cit.*, p. 35 and fig. 11; p. 39.

(72) Goldschmidt, *Caroling. Illum.* p. 21 and pls. 19-20.

22

knowing whether the Carolingian illuminator had any such idea
about the identification of the emperor.

Even more problematical is the figure of Apuleius who explains
his book, which he holds open in his left hand, to the emperor,
while the latter listens and at the same time has the dedication copy
resting on his lap. It is irreconcilable with Roman court ceremonial
that a writer should be seated in the presence of the emperor, that
he should sit under a similar canopy and that he should wear a
similar type of chlamys. All these obvious incongruities can most
easily be understood as an act of conflation of a second emperor
portrait with that of an author, a conflation we should like to
ascribe to the Carolingian miniaturist. Yet the basic concept that
the figure at the right pays homage to the figure at the left is
maintained. A late-Roman miniature would no doubt have the
author depicted standing in front of the emperor enthroned like
Epictetus the philosopher standing in front of Hadrian enthroned,
as seen in the copy of the *Notitia Dignitatum* whose archetype leads
us into the 4th century (73) or like Oppian facing the enthroned
Caracalla in the *Cynegetica* of that author (74).

The importance of title miniatures like those of the Paris
Josephus and the Kassel Pseudo-Apuleius lies in the fact that each
one of them is a variant of a theme that was created in the 4th
century. At the same time one should be aware that the antithetic
pair of emperors is only one of many types of frontispieces whose
origin can be traced to the 4th century.

IV. NARRATIVE CYCLES

The one category of illustration not represented in the Filocalus
Calendar is the narrative cycle. On the evidence of extant fragments
of illustrated papyri, contemporary copies of miniatures in other
media like Terracotta bowls and copies in later manuscripts, in
which the system of papyrus illustration has survived, we know today

(73) H. OMONT, *Notitia Dignitatum Imperii Romani; Bibl. Nat. Ms. lat. 9661* (Paris
s. d.) pl. 14.
(74) K. WEITZMANN, *Greek Mythology in Byzantine Art* (Princeton 1951) 96 and
pl. XXIX, 100.

that the *Homeric poems* as well as the other poems of the « epic cycle », the dramas of Euripides and other dramatists, romances of every conceivable type and other prose texts were illustrated in papyrus rolls with extensive cycles (75). Moreover, we have, at the beginning, demonstrated in the case of the Milan *Iliad* how the individual pictures of these cycles were enriched as soon as they were taken over into the codex. The same process we assumed for the bible or at least for the Old Testament which, from the beginning, was illustrated with cycles so rich that they could have been conceived only for individual books of the Old Testament and not for its entirety (76). The fragments of the Quedlinburg Itala e. g. belong to a codex which surely never contained anything but the Books of Kings. We have today good reason to believe that the illustration of the Septuagint began with the Jews of the Diaspora and not only in one, but in many centers (77). Yet, to characterize the change from narrative papyrus to narrative codex illustration with only illustrated pagan and Christian texts would give an incomplete picture.

There existed a third artistic province, namely the imperial realm, which developed its own iconographical repertory and its own ceremonial style. In book illumination it found an outlet in World chronicles, Historiae Ecclesiasticae and other kinds of historical texts of a popular and episodical character. A papyrus leaf in Berlin No. 13296 from the 4th - 5th centuries has five very abbreviated colored pen drawings distributed over three writing columns (fig. 31) (78) while in the Alexandrian World chronicle in Moscow the pictures were removed from within the text column and placed in the inner and outer margins (fig. 32). What the leaves of both Papyrus codices have in common with the older papyrus roll trad-

(75) In his « Roll and Codex » (note 2) the author has laid out the method by which ancient book illumination can be reconstructed, and in his « Ancient Book illumination » (ibidem) a historical sketch was attempted with the aim of demonstrating what an extraordinary variety of texts with illustrations must have existed in classical antiquity prior to the invention of the codex.

(76) Cf. K. WEITZMANN, *Die Illustration der Septuaginta* (cf. note 23).

(77) K. WEITZMANN, *Zur Frage des Einflusses jüdischer Bilderquellen auf die Illustrationen des Alten Testamentes: Mullus. Festschrift Theodor Klauser* (Münster 1964) 401 ff. (here the older bibliography).

(78) H. LIETZMANN, *Ein Blatt aus einer antiken Weltchronik: Quantulacumque. Studies presented to Kirsopp Lake* (London 1937) 339 ff. and. pl.

tition is the most abbreviated nature of the illustration: in the Alexandrian Chronicle we see on the best preserved leaf (79) not scenes proper but just figures: at the left the emperor Theodosius with the young Honorius and underneath the patriarch Theophilus, at the right the feet of the emperor Valentinian and underneath the rival-emperor Eugenios while at the bottom the Serapeion is depicted, with whose destruction the Chronicle breaks off.

There is good reason to believe that as soon as luxury codices were produced a change took place from the almost pictographic type of illustration into a scenic one with variegated actions that were set into a spatial landscape with architecture wherever the situation called for it, — a change parallel to the one from single combat into multifigured battle scenes in the illustration of the Iliad. It is true that the only illustrated Byzantine chronicle we possess today, the *John Scylitzes* in Madrid with its more than 400 miniatures is not older than the 14th century (80), but there is evidence for the existence of illustrated Chronicles at a much earlier period. The 9th century codex of the homilies of Gregory of Nazianzus in Paris, cod. gr. 510 (81), e. g., contains a series of illustrations of historical events which were not invented for the homilies with which they are now connected, but for texts which explain the details of the pictures more thoroughly. The series of six scenes from the life of Julian the Apostate e. g. (fig. 33) begins with the emperor's visit to a demon in a cave and at the upper right there is sarcophagus, the tomb of Babylos, the martyr, which is not mentioned by Gregory, but in the *Historia Ecclesiastica* of Sozomenos, the 5th century Chronicler (82). Other scenes in Gregory can be explained by passages in Theodoret and Malalas and from this we conclude that all these Chronicles existed with extensive narrative cycles and most likely as early as the 5th century and in case of Malalas the 6th

(79) Strzygowski, *op. cit.*, p. 122 and pl. VI verso.

(80) G. Millet, *La collection chrétienne et byzantine des Hautes Études* (Paris 1903) 26 nos. B 369-375; p. 54 nos. C 869-1277; G. Schlumberger, *L'épopée byzantine à la fin du dixième siècle* 2 and 3 (Paris 1900 and 1905) passim. S. C. Estopañan, *Skylitzes Matritensis, I, Reproduciones y Miniaturas* (Barcelona-Madrid 1965).

(81) H. Omont, *Miniatures des plus anciens Manuscrits Grecs de la Bibl. Nat.* (1929)[2] 10 ff. and pl. XV-LX.

(82) K. Weitzmann, *Illustrations for the Chronicles of Sozomenos, Theodoret and Malalas: Byzantion* 16 (1942-43) 87 ff. and esp. 100 ff.

century. So far we have no evidence yet that any 4th century Chronicle existed with rich cycles of a similar nature. It is tempting to speculate that if Theodoret was illustrated then also the *Historia Ecclesiastica* of Eusebius, i. e. the very chronicle which was continued by Theodoret, might have existed with pictures. Nevertheless, that richly illustrated Chronicles must have existed alongside the simpler papyrus tradition in the 4th century can be inferred by the impact they had on other branches of illustrated texts.

In his painstaking analysis of the miniatures of the Vergilius Vaticanus, de Wit pointed out that most compositions were not invented for the text of the Aeneid but that the illustrator borrowed figure types as well as whole schemes from representations of a different context and adjusted them to the text of Virgil's poems. Aeneas himself is consistently depicted as a Roman emperor rather than a Trojan hero (83), and for scenes of an adlocution, a battle etc. de Wit introduced the triumphal columns of Trajan and Marcus Aurelius and other historical reliefs as the closest extant parallels. Perhaps the most striking example of such a borrowing can be seen in the miniature of the nightly council presided over by Ascanius, who sits on a faldistorium, presumably the « sella castrensis » (fig. 34) (84), which de Wit compared with scenes of Judgment and negotiations with foreign tribes on the Marcus Aurelius column.

Very similar observations were made by Boekler in connection with the miniatures of the Quedlinburg Itala (85). He too noticed that Saul was depicted as a Roman emporer (fig. 10), that adlocution, libation, battles etc. were rendered in compositional schemes that were borrowed from the iconography of Roman history and he pointed to the very same monuments as the most suitable parallels, namely the triumphal columns. Not that he or de Wit had suggested the columns were the immediate source, but they are our richest and most complex extant repertory of compositional schemes for the illustration of historical events. Furthemore it had not escaped Boeckler that the compositional schemes as well as the

(83) J. DE WIT, *Die Miniaturen des Vergilius Romanus* (Amsterdam 1959) 159 ff.

(84) *Ibidem*, pp. 146 ff. and pl. 27 No. 1.

(85) BOECKLER, *Itala* (cf. note 24) pp. 150 ff.

individual types were, indeed, the same as those used in the Vergilius Vaticanus.

Now it would seem highly unlikely that the illustrator of an epic poem or of a book from the Old Testament would walk around in Rome and sketch the same triumphal columns. We rather have to imagine a common source available in a scriptorium, particularly in the case of the Vergilius Vaticanus and the Itala which, as Boeckler made plausible (86), are stylistically so close to each other that the same scriptorium can be assumed, i. e. a scriptorium which produced illustrated pagan and Christian manuscripts side by side. What was this common source? In the light of our observations about illustrated World chronicles and related historical writings it seems to us more than likely that in this category of illustrated texts we have to look for the common source that was utilized by the illustrators of the Vergil and the Bible.

Nothing more than a mere sketch in its barest outlines could be attempted in a lecture, and it must be left for the future to write a more coherent and fuller documented history of book illumination in the 4th century. At the present it was our intention to focus on the following three aspects:

1) the juxtaposition of the codex illustration to the older papyrus illustration. Only after the latter had been studied more extensively within the last years and the evidence for its existence on a wide scale been established, was it possible to see the achievements of the 4th century codex illustration in their rigt perspective. Actually it was the time when amost every conceivable type of full-page miniature came into being and when narrative cycles became embellished so as to rival the effect of panel and fresco painting under whose influence they had come. No essential type of illustration has been added ever since and book illumination of the present day still profits from the inventions of the 4th century;

2) the emergence of the imperial iconography as the dominating realm. The fact that so little of early Chronicle illustration has survived obscures the historical rôle it had played, but its importance

(86) *Ibidem*, p. 169.

can still be sensed by the impact it had on all other branches of book illumination, pagan and Christian alike;

3) the lucky coincidence that the great technical innovation of the parchment codex came to fruition at a juncture in history when a climate prevailed in which pagan, Christian and imperial illustrations could be produced side by side in the same scriptoria and influence each other mutually. Already at the end of the 4th century a work like the Calendar of Filocalus could hardly have been produced any more for a Christian.

In view of the great splendor and luxuriousness of 4th century manuscripts like the Vergilius Vaticanus, the Quedlinburg Itala, the archetype of the Filocalus, and many others, it is safe to assume that the imperial court as patron must have played an essential rôle, athough we are in no position to claim for any of the extant codices an imperial commission.

When in the Middle Ages the two most conspicuous revival movements, the Carolingian Renaissance in the Latin West and the Macedonian Renaissance in the Greek East, looked for early models to copy, they found them essentially in books and to such an extent that one could almost speak of « book renaissances ». In both revival movements we find a similar close parallelism of pagan and Christian miniatures as we had found in the 4th century, and the explanation for this phenomenon may well be sought in the fact that their best products, like the Leiden Aratus, the Filocalus of the 9th century on which the later drawings are based, and the Kassel Ps.-Apuleius in the West and the various 10th century Gospel books in the East, all hark back to 4th century models, thus recreating similar conditions under which these models themselves were made, and in this way the achievements of the early codex illustration were kept alive and perpetuated as long as precious parchment codices were produced.

Acknowledgments

Armstrong, Gregory T. "Constantine's Churches: Symbol and Structure." *Journal of the Society of Architectural Historians* 33 (1974): 5–16. Reprinted with the permission of the Society of Arthitectural Historians. Courtesy of Yale University Art and Architecture Library.

Delbrueck, Richard. "Notes on the Wooden Doors of Santa Sabina." *Art Bulletin* 34 (1952): 139–45. Reprinted with the permission of the College Art Association of America. Courtesy of Yale University Sterling Memorial Library.

Dinkler, Erich. "Älteste Christliche Denkmäler." *Signum Crucis* (Tübingen: J.C.B. Mohr [Paul Siebeck], 1967): 134–78. Reprinted with the permission of J.C.B Mohr (Paul Siebeck). Courtesy of Yale University Divinity Library.

Finney, Paul Corby. "Did Gnostics Make Pictures?" *Numen* 41 (1980): 434–54. Reprinted with the permission of E.J. Brill. Courtesy of Yale University Cross Campus Library.

Kessler, Herbert L. "Scenes from the Acts of the Apostles on Some Early Christian Ivories." *Gesta* 18 (1979): 109–19. Reprinted with the permission of the International Center of Medieval Art. Courtesy of Yale University Art and Architecture Library.

Kitzinger, Ernst. "The Threshold of the Holy Shrine: Observations on Floor Mosaics at Antioch and Bethlehem." In Patrick Granfield and Josef A. Jungmann, eds., *Kyriakon: Festschrift Johannes Quasten* II (Münster in Westfalen, 1970): 639–47. Courtesy of Paul Corby Finney.

Kitzinger, Ernst. "The Cleveland Marbles." In *Atti del IX Congresso Internazionale di Archeologia Cristiana* (Vatican City, Pontificio

Istituto di Archeologia Cristiana, 1978): 653–75. Courtesy of Yale University Sterling Memorial Library.

Klauser, Theodor. "Studien zur Entstehungsgeschichte der christlichen Kunst IV." *Jahrbuch für Antike und Christentum* 4 (1961): 128–36. Reprinted with the permission of the author. Courtesy of Yale University Seeley G. Mudd Library.

Levi, Peter. "The Podgoritza Cup." *Heythrop Journal* 4 (1963): 55–60. Reprinted with the permission of Heythrop College. Courtesy of the *Heythrop Journal*.

Lietzmann, Hans. "The Tomb of the Apostles Ad Catacumbas." *Harvard Theological Review* 16 (1923): 147–62. Courtesy of Yale University Sterling Memorial Library.

McVey, Kathleen E. "The Domed Church as Microcosm: Literary Roots of an Architectural Symbol." *Dumbarton Oaks Papers* 37 (1984): 91–121. Reprinted with the permission of Dumbarton Oaks. Courtesy of Yale University Sterling Memorial Library.

Murray, Charles. "Art and the Early Church." *Journal of Theological Studies* n.s. 28 (1977): 303–45. Reprinted with the permission of Oxford University Press. Courtesy of Yale University Seeley G. Mudd Library.

Painter, K.S. "A Fourth-Century Christian Silver Treasure Found at Water Newton, England, in 1975." *Rivista di archeologia cristiana* 51 (1975): 333–45. Reprinted with the permission of Pontificio Istituto di Archeologia Cristiana. Courtesy of Yale University Sterling Memorial Library.

Quasten, Johannes. "The Painting of the Good Shepherd at Dura-Europos." *Mediaeval Studies* 9 (1947): 1–18. Reprinted from Mediaeval Studies, by permission of the publisher. Copyright 1947 by the Pontifical Institute of Mediaeval Studies, Toronto. Courtesy of *Mediaeval Studies*.

Reekmans, Louis. "La chronologie de la peinture paléochrétienne. Notes et réflexions." *Rivista di archeologia cristiana* 49 (1973): 271–91. Reprinted with the permission of Pontificio Istituto di Archeologia Cristiana. Courtesy of Yale University Sterling Memorial Library.

Reekmans, Louis. "Zur Problematik der römischen Katakomben-forschung." *Boreas* 7 (1984): 242–60. Reprinted with the permission of Westfälische Wilhelms-Universität. Courtesy of Yale University Sterling Memorial Library.

Toynbee, J.M.C. "A New Roman Mosaic Pavement Found in Dorset." *Journal of Roman Studies* 54 (1964): 7–14. Reprinted with the permission of the Society for the Promotion of Roman Studies. Courtesy of Yale University Sterling Memorial Library.

Vikan, Gary. "Joseph Iconography on Coptic Textiles." *Gesta* 18 (1979): 99–108. Reprinted with the permission of the International Center of Medieval Art. Courtesy of Yale University Art and Architecture Library.

Ward-Perkins, J.B. "Constantine and the Origins of the Christian Basilica." *British School at Rome, Papers* 22 (1954): 69–90. Reprinted with the permission of the British School at Rome. Courtesy of editor, Paul Corby Finney.

Ward-Perkins, J.B. "Memoria, Martyr's Tomb and Martyr's Church." *Journal of Theological Studies* n.s. 17 (1966): 20–37. Reprinted with the permission of Oxford University Press. Courtesy of Yale University Seeley G. Mudd Library.

Weitzmann, Kurt. "Narration in Early Christendom." *American Journal of Archaeology* 61 (1957): 83–91. Reprinted with the permission of the Archaeological Institute of America. Courtesy of Yale University Sterling Memorial Library.

Weitzmann, Kurt. "Book Illustration of the 4th Century. Tradition and Innovation." In *Akten des VII. Internationalen Kongresses für Christliche Archäologie* (Rome: Città del Vaticano, 1969): 257–81. Courtesy of Yale University Seeley G. Mudd Library.